Navigating Organizational Behavior in the Digital Age With AI

Fahri Özsungur
Mersin University, Turkey

IGI Global
Scientific Publishing
Publishing Tomorrow's Research Today

Vice President of Editorial Melissa Wagner
Managing Editor of Acquisitions Mikaela Felty
Managing Editor of Book Development Jocelynn Hessler
Production Manager Mike Brehm
Cover Design Phillip Shickler

Published in the United States of America by
IGI Global Scientific Publishing
701 East Chocolate Avenue
Hershey, PA, 17033, USA
Tel: 717-533-8845
Fax: 717-533-8661
Website: https://www.igi-global.com E-mail: cust@igi-global.com

Library of Congress Cataloging-in-Publication Data

Names: Özsungur, Fahri, 1981- editor.
Title: Navigating organizational behavior in the digital age with AI / [edited by] Fahri Özsungur.
Description: Hershey, PA : IGI Global Scientific Publishing, [2025] | Includes bibliographical references and index. | Summary: "This book aims to explore the transformative impact of artificial intelligence (AI) on organizational behavior. This comprehensive volume will delve into various facets of how AI is reshaping the workplace, from decision-making and leadership to talent management and performance evaluation"-- Provided by publisher.
Identifiers: LCCN 2024053097 (print) | LCCN 2024053098 (ebook) | ISBN 9798369384428 (hardcover) | ISBN 9798369384435 (paperback) | ISBN 9798369384442 (ebook)
Subjects: LCSH: Organizational behavior. | Artificial intelligence.
Classification: LCC HD58.7 .N385 2025 (print) | LCC HD58.7 (ebook) | DDC 658/.0563--dc23/eng/20250201
LC record available at https://lccn.loc.gov/2024053097
LC ebook record available at https://lccn.loc.gov/2024053098

British Cataloguing in Publication Data
A Cataloguing in Publication record for this book is available from the British Library.

To my dearest Mother and Father,
For your boundless love, unwavering support, and countless sacrifices,
You nurtured my dreams before I even knew how to dream.
Your wisdom, patience, and strength have been my guiding light,
Illuminating paths I would have never dared to tread alone.
This book, and all that I have become,
Is because of the foundation you laid with your love and belief in me.
With deepest gratitude and unending love, I dedicate this work to you.
You are, and always will be, my greatest inspiration.

Editorial Advisory Board

Table of Contents

Detailed Table of Contents

Artificial Intelligence (AI) is revolutionizing organizational culture by enhancing decision-making, personalizing employee development, and promoting diversity and inclusion. This abstract examines the transformative impact of AI on organizational practices, drawing on recent research and case studies from leading global and Indian companies. The integration of AI tools has significantly improved transparency and efficiency in decision-making processes, as evidenced by Tata Consultancy Services (TCS) and Infosys, which have adopted AI to streamline operations and foster data-driven strategies.

The integration of artificial intelligence (AI) into conflict resolution and negotiation processes is transforming how disputes are managed, and decisions are made. This abstract explores the current and future developments in AI technologies aimed at enhancing transparency, accountability, and efficiency in these processes. AI-driven tools such as MediAI, which analyzes social data for community mediation, and blockchain-based smart contracts, are setting new standards for transparency by creating immutable records and providing clear, data-driven insights. Explainable AI (XAI) frameworks are making complex AI decisions more understandable, thereby fostering trust and accountability. Furthermore, advancements in AI for regulatory compliance and document review are streamlining processes and reducing legal risks.

As India rapidly advances in artificial intelligence (AI), the need for robust ethical frameworks and comprehensive data privacy measures has become increasingly critical. This paper explores the current landscape of AI ethics and privacy concerns within India, highlighting key developments such as the implementation of the Personal Data Protection Bill (PDPB) and various state-level initiatives like the Karnataka AI Policy 2023. It examines how these efforts align with global standards and address emerging challenges in the digital age. The chapter also contrasts India's approach with those of other developing nations, showcasing the unique hurdles and strategies employed. The disparateness and the importance of strengthening regulatory frameworks, promoting ethical AI practices, enhancing public awareness, and fostering international collaboration.

Artificial Intelligence (AI) has emerged as a transformative force across various sectors, with its potential to drive change in Diversity, Equity, and Inclusion (DEI) efforts becoming increasingly evident. This chapter explores recent developments in AI technology and its implications for enhancing DEI initiatives. It examines how AI can both support and challenge DEI goals, addressing issues such as algorithmic bias, representation, and accessibility. Through a review of current literature and case studies, the essay highlights the role of AI in promoting inclusivity while also identifying critical areas where AI-driven systems need refinement to avoid perpetuating existing disparities. By leveraging AI responsibly, organizations can create more equitable and diverse environments that reflect broader societal values.

In this research paper, authors explore the application of the K-means algorithm and the elbow method in customer segmentation using machine learning techniques. The algorithm is applied to a customer dataset and effectiveness of the resulting customer segments is evaluated. The performance of K-means with other clustering techniques is compare and the impact of different input parameters on the segmentation results is studied. The findings of this study can help businesses to improve their marketing strategies by targeting specific customer segments with customized marketing campaigns.

Machine Learning (ML) has revolutionized talent management within Indian corporates by transforming recruitment, retention, and development processes. This chapter delves into the applications of ML in these areas, showcasing how companies leverage sophisticated algorithms to enhance decision-making, streamline workflows, and foster a more efficient and engaged workforce. Examples from Indian corporates such as Zebra Medical Vision, Tata Consultancy Services (TCS), Infosys, and HCL Technologies illustrate the significant impact of ML on hiring efficiency, employee retention, and development initiatives. The chapter highlights the potential for further advancements in talent management through ML, paving the way for a dynamic and successful business environment.

Influencer marketing is a crucial strategy in the tourism industry, leveraging social media influencers to enhance destination visibility and appeal. This chapter explores its impact on consumer engagement, trust, and destination branding, providing a

engagement, and performance management, exemplified by global leaders like Unilever and IBM. The integration of AI-driven personalized learning platforms ensures continuous skill development, fostering a motivated and adept workforce. Additionally, predictive analytics facilitate strategic workforce planning, enabling proactive measures to retain top talent, as seen in companies like Royal Dutch Shell.

Considering the critical intersection of entrepreneurship, competitiveness and digital transformation in the age of Artificial Intelligence (AI), the drivers of economic growth and social progress and the transformative power of digitalization for firms become even more important. In particular, it is necessary to consider how digital entrepreneurship is reshaping industries and providing new opportunities for innovation and value creation. The theoretical framework for the adoption of AI and insights into organizational characteristics are presented, and the importance of AI in enhancing firms' competitive advantage is becoming increasingly evident.Therefore, in this chapter, AI applications in industries that demonstrate the significant impact of AI on decision-making processes and future business strategies are explained, and AI is examined as an important element in shaping the strategic direction and sustainability of companies in an increasingly competitive global market.

The intersection of entrepreneurship, digital technologies, and artificial intelligence (AI) is shaping the modern business landscape and future economic opportunities. It is important to examine entrepreneurial behavior patterns and entrepreneurial intent, the motivations, attitudes, and actions of contemporary entrepreneurs in terms of digital technology and AI. In the context of Industry 4.0, digitalization presents both challenges and opportunities, encouraging businesses to adapt to advanced technologies such as AI and automation while contributing to sustainable development goals. The chapter examines the evolving digital entrepreneurship ecosystem, emphasizing the role of infrastructures, policies, and funding that support innovation. The future of AI is assessed, discussing technological advances and the societal challenges that need to be addressed to ensure that AI serves as a force for sustainable growth and positive societal impact.

Preface

Artificial Intelligence (AI) is no longer a futuristic concept but a transformative force reshaping industries and organizations worldwide. This book, *Navigating Organizational Behavior in the Digital Age With AI*, delves into the profound impact of AI on organizational behavior, leadership, talent management, ethics, and strategic decision-making, with a particular focus on the Indian corporate landscape.

OVERVIEW OF THE SUBJECT MATTER

The book explores various aspects of AI integration within organizations, providing insights into how AI influences decision-making, leadership, conflict resolution, ethics, and diversity initiatives. It addresses critical themes like AI's role in enhancing performance management, fostering inclusive workplaces, and optimizing recruitment processes. By focusing on real-world applications, this book reveals the potential of AI to revolutionize traditional management practices and drive innovation across sectors.

Relevance in Today's World

In today's rapidly evolving technological environment, AI is more than a tool—it is a strategic asset that can foster competitive advantage. As businesses increasingly adopt AI-driven solutions, understanding its implications for organizational culture, leadership, and operational strategies becomes essential. This book positions itself at the intersection of AI's technical capabilities and its broader impact on organizational practices, making it highly relevant for today's AI-powered world. Whether it's enhancing decision-making through data analytics or promoting diversity through bias-free algorithms, the topics discussed here reflect the current trends and future directions of AI in management.

Target Audience

This book is intended for a broad range of readers including academics, researchers, corporate leaders, HR professionals, and policymakers who are interested in understanding the application of AI in organizational contexts. It will particularly benefit those looking to enhance their knowledge of AI's role in shaping modern work environments, performance management, and talent acquisition. Additionally, the book offers valuable insights for professionals in the fields of ethics, privacy, and diversity, who are grappling with AI's broader societal implications.

Chapter Summaries and Importance

Chapter 1: AI (Artificial Intelligence) and Organizational Culture Shaping Values and Norms: The India Corporate Scenario

This chapter examines how AI is influencing organizational culture in India, focusing on its role in decision-making, employee development, and diversity. Through case studies from Indian giants like TCS and Infosys, the chapter provides a comprehensive understanding of how AI is revolutionizing corporate culture by fostering transparency and data-driven strategies.

Chapter 2: AI (Artificial Intelligence) for Conflict Resolution and Negotiation: Enhancing Mediation and Collaboration Through Intelligent Technology

This chapter highlights AI's potential in transforming conflict resolution and negotiation processes. It discusses the use of AI tools such as MediAI and blockchain in enhancing transparency and trust in conflict management, while also addressing legal compliance and document review processes.

Chapter 3: AI (Artificial Intelligence) Integration for Integrity, Ethics, and Privacy in AI-Driven Organizations

Focusing on the ethics and privacy challenges of AI adoption in India, this chapter addresses the need for robust regulatory frameworks. It emphasizes the importance of aligning AI practices with global standards, particularly in the context of India's Personal Data Protection Bill (PDPB).

Chapter 4: AI Leveraging to Foster DEI (Diversity, Equity, and Inclusiveness) in Organizations

This chapter explores how AI can enhance diversity, equity, and inclusion (DEI) initiatives within organizations. By discussing both the potential benefits and challenges, such as algorithmic bias, the chapter provides a balanced view of AI's role in promoting inclusivity in the workplace.

Chapter 5: AI in Performance Management: Data-Driven Approaches

Here, the focus is on how AI is revolutionizing performance management. The chapter discusses AI's ability to provide real-time feedback, tailor development opportunities, and drive performance improvements through data-driven insights.

Chapter 6: AI-Powered Leadership: Shaping the Future of Management

This chapter explores how AI is transforming leadership by enhancing innovation and strategic decision-making. It also highlights the ethical concerns surrounding AI in leadership, emphasizing the need for human qualities like empathy and emotional intelligence.

Chapter 7: AI Influences on Strategic Decision-Making: Transformational Dynamics

The strategic impact of AI is discussed in this chapter, particularly its role in hyper-personalization and autonomous decision-making. The chapter forecasts how AI will reshape decision-making processes, making them more agile and data-driven.

Chapter 8: Artificial Intelligence with Human-Computer Interaction

Focusing on the interaction between humans and AI, this chapter examines the impact of AI on remote work, health, and well-being, particularly during the COVID-19 pandemic. It also addresses the collection of data on worker behavior and health.

Chapter 9: Customer Segmentation Using K-Means Algorithm

This chapter provides a technical exploration of how machine learning, particularly the K-means algorithm, is used for customer segmentation. It discusses the practical applications of AI in improving marketing strategies and targeting customer segments effectively.

Chapter 10: Machine Learning for Smarter Recruitment and Talent Acquisition

The chapter delves into how machine learning is transforming recruitment and talent management, offering case studies from Indian corporates. It highlights how AI-driven tools are enhancing efficiency in hiring and retention processes.

Chapter 11: Maximizing Impact: The Role of Influencer Marketing in Contemporary Tourism Management

This chapter discusses the growing influence of AI in tourism marketing, particularly in leveraging social media influencers. It examines the ethical challenges of influencer marketing and predicts future trends in the industry.

Chapter 12: The Impact and Consequences of AI in Copywriting

Exploring AI's role in content creation, this chapter investigates the ability of users to distinguish between AI-generated and human-created content. It presents both qualitative and quantitative insights on how AI is shaping copywriting and content marketing.

Chapter 13: Transforming the Modern Workplace with AI: A Special Focus on India

This chapter summarizes AI's transformative impact on workplace dynamics in India, discussing how AI enhances human resource management, employee training, and workforce planning. It provides real-world examples from global companies that have successfully integrated AI into their operations.

Chapter 14: The Importance of Entrepreneurship And Organizational Qualities in The Digital Age: The Importance of Entrepreneurship

This chapter explores AI applications across various industries, highlighting the profound impact of AI on decision-making processes and the development of future business strategies.

Chapter 15: Strengthening The Entrepreneurial Mindset With Artificial Intelligence In The Digitalization Process: Strengthening The Entrepreneurial Mindset

This final chapter examines the evolving digital entrepreneurship ecosystem, emphasizing the role of infrastructures, policies, and funding that support innovation. The future of AI is assessed, discussing technological advances and the societal challenges that need to be addressed to ensure that AI serves as a force for sustainable growth and positive societal impact.

Chapter 16: The Role of AI in Conflict Resolution and Negotiation

This paper explores the role of Artificial Intelligence (AI) in conflict resolution and negotiation, focusing on its theoretical and practical implications. The study investigates how AI can enhance ethical, effective, and positive dispute resolution in a post-elite context. Using literature surveys, scenario analyses, expert interviews, ethical evaluations, and quantitative assessments, the research highlights AI's impressive potential while addressing significant ethical challenges that must be resolved for its appropriate application.

CONCLUSION

This book offers a comprehensive examination of the multiple ways in which AI is revolutionizing organizational practices. By bridging the gap between AI's technical potential and its practical applications in the corporate world, *Navigating Organizational Behavior in the Digital Age With AI* contributes significantly to the discourse on AI's role in shaping the future of work. Whether you are a business leader, researcher, or policymaker, the insights presented in this book will deepen your understanding of AI's transformative power and help you navigate the complexities of AI adoption in organizational contexts.

Fahri Özsungur
Mersin University, Turkey

Chapter 1

AI (Artificial Intelligence) and Organizational Culture Shaping Values and Norms: The India Corporate Scenario

C. Karthikeyan
https://orcid.org/0000-0002-2018-8245
SJB Institute of Technology, Vishwesarya Technological University, Belgav, India

ABSTRACT

Artificial Intelligence (AI) is revolutionizing organizational culture by enhancing decision-making, personalizing employee development, and promoting diversity and inclusion. This abstract examines the transformative impact of AI on organizational practices, drawing on recent research and case studies from leading global and Indian companies. The integration of AI tools has significantly improved transparency and efficiency in decision-making processes, as evidenced by Tata Consultancy Services (TCS) and Infosys, which have adopted AI to streamline operations and foster data-driven strategies.

INTRODUCTION

In today's rapidly evolving business landscape, Artificial Intelligence (AI) is redefining the essence of organizational culture. From enhancing decision-making to personalizing employee development and promoting diversity, AI is transforming how companies operate and interact with their workforce. This chapter explores how

DOI: 10.4018/979-8-3693-8442-8.ch001

AI tools are being integrated into organizational practices to drive transparency, foster growth, and ensure inclusivity. By examining real-world applications and case studies from leading companies, we will uncover the profound impact of AI on shaping a modern and dynamic organizational culture.

AI's impact on organizational culture in India is increasingly evident, influencing values and norms within various industries. Recent developments highlight how AI technologies are reshaping workplace dynamics and cultural norms.

a. **AI Integration in Organizational Culture;** AI's role in organizational culture involves enhancing decision-making, streamlining operations, and fostering innovation. For example, companies like Tata Consultancy Services (TCS) and Infosys are leveraging AI to transform their internal processes and employee interactions. TCS's use of AI-powered tools for project management and employee engagement has led to a more data-driven and transparent workplace culture (TCS Annual Report, 2023).
b. **AI and Employee Engagement;** AI's influence on employee engagement is evident through its role in personalizing employee experiences. HCL Technologies has implemented AI-driven platforms that tailor learning and development opportunities based on individual performance and career aspirations (HCL Technologies, 2024). This personalization fosters a culture of continuous learning and growth, aligning with organizational values of innovation and excellence.
c. **AI and Diversity and Inclusion;** AI also plays a crucial role in promoting diversity and inclusion within Indian organizations. For instance, Wipro has utilized AI tools to minimize biases in recruitment processes. AI algorithms analyze job descriptions and candidate profiles to ensure unbiased language and selection criteria (Wipro Diversity Report, 2023). This approach aligns with Wipro's commitment to fostering an inclusive workplace culture.
d. **AI and Workplace Norms;** AI is reshaping workplace norms by automating routine tasks and enabling remote work. Tech Mahindra has embraced AI to facilitate remote work arrangements and virtual collaboration tools, which has led to a shift in traditional workplace norms and expectations (Tech Mahindra, 2024). This shift reflects a broader trend towards flexibility and work-life balance in the Indian corporate environment.
e. **Statistical Evidence:** Recent research indicates that AI adoption in Indian organizations is associated with significant cultural shifts. According to a 2023 study by the National Association of Software and Service Companies (NASSCOM), 65% of Indian firms reported that AI integration has led to more transparent decision-making processes and improved employee satisfaction (NASSCOM, 2023). Additionally, a survey by McKinsey & Company found that 58% of

Indian organizations using AI experienced enhanced team collaboration and innovation (McKinsey, 2023).

Based on the developments and impacts of AI on organizational culture in India, here are five key objectives:

1. **Enhance Data-Driven Decision-Making**; **Objective**: Implement AI technologies to improve transparency and data-driven decision-making processes within organizations. **Rationale**: As demonstrated by Tata Consultancy Services (TCS), AI tools can significantly enhance the transparency of decision-making processes, leading to more informed and effective organizational strategies.
2. **Personalize Employee Development: Objective**: Utilize AI to tailor learning and development opportunities to individual employee needs and career goals. **Rationale:** AI-driven platforms, such as those used by HCL Technologies, can provide personalized career development experiences, fostering a culture of continuous growth and aligning with organizational values of innovation and excellence.
3. **Promote Diversity and Minimize Bias: Objective**: Deploy AI tools to ensure unbiased recruitment and promotion processes, promoting diversity and inclusion within the organization. **Rationale**: Tools implemented by Wipro demonstrate how AI can help reduce biases in hiring and promotion, supporting a more inclusive workplace culture.
4. **Facilitate Remote Work and Flexible Norms: Objective**: Leverage AI to support remote work arrangements and virtual collaboration, aligning with evolving workplace norms and expectations. **Rationale**: Tech Mahindra's use of AI for remote work and virtual collaboration tools illustrates the shift towards flexible work arrangements, reflecting broader trends in work-life balance and workplace culture.
5. **Measure and Enhance Employee Satisfaction: Objective**: Apply AI to gather and analyze employee feedback to improve workplace satisfaction and engagement. Rationale: Statistical evidence from NASSCOM and McKinsey & Company shows that AI can enhance team collaboration and employee satisfaction. Using AI to continuously monitor and address employee feedback can further improve workplace culture.

These objectives aim to harness the potential of AI to create a more efficient, inclusive, and satisfying work environment.

Here are some recent research reports on AI integration in organizational culture, both from Indian and international sources:

Indian Research Reports

- o **The National Association of Software and Service Companies (NASSCOM)** highlights the increasing integration of AI in Indian firms, focusing on its impact on decision-making and operational efficiency. It notes that 70% of Indian companies have reported improvements in transparency and data-driven decision-making due to AI tools (NASSCOM, 2024).
- o **Indian Institute of Management Bangalore (IIMB)** Study from IIMB examines how AI is reshaping organizational culture in Indian enterprises. The research includes case studies of Tata Consultancy Services (TCS) and Infosys, demonstrating how AI-powered project management and employee engagement tools have enhanced transparency and fostered a culture of innovation (IIMB, 2024).
- o **Infosys Research Report:** Infosys's report explores the role of AI in transforming internal processes and employee interactions. It highlights how AI-driven tools have improved operational efficiency and employee satisfaction, contributing to a more data-driven and transparent workplace culture (Infosys, 2024).

International Research Reports

- o McKinsey's global report provides insights into how AI is influencing organizational culture across various industries. It emphasizes that AI integration leads to more data-driven decision-making and enhances operational efficiency, reflecting similar trends observed in Indian firms like TCS and Infosys (McKinsey, 2024).
- o Gartner's report discusses the evolution of AI in business operations and its impact on organizational culture. It highlights that AI tools are crucial for streamlining processes and fostering innovation, contributing to a more transparent and data-driven workplace (Gartner, 2024).
- o Harvard Business Review (HBR) AI is shaping the future of work and organizational culture. It discusses case studies from various global organizations, noting that AI has significantly enhanced decision-making processes and operational efficiency, aligning with trends observed in Indian companies (HBR, 2024).

These reports provide a comprehensive overview of the latest developments in AI's impact on organizational culture, offering both Indian and global perspectives.AI Integration in Organizational Culture: Recent Developments and Research Insights. AI's transformative impact on organizational culture is increasingly apparent as companies around the world leverage technology to enhance decision-making, streamline operations, and foster innovation. In India, leading firms such as Tata Consultancy

Services (TCS) and Infosys are at the forefront of this revolution, utilizing AI to reshape their internal processes and employee interactions. This essay explores the recent developments in AI integration within organizational culture, drawing on research reports from both Indian and international sources.

AI INTEGRATION IN ORGANIZATIONAL CULTURE

AI's role in modern organizational culture is multifaceted. It enhances decision-making through data-driven insights, streamlines operations by automating routine tasks, and fosters innovation by enabling more agile and adaptive work environments. Indian companies, notably TCS and Infosys, have demonstrated the significant benefits of AI integration. TCS's adoption of AI-powered tools for project management and employee engagement has led to a more transparent and data-driven workplace culture, reflecting a broader trend towards leveraging technology for operational efficiency (TCS Annual Report, 2023).

Indian Research Reports

a. **NASSCOM Report on AI Adoption:** NASSSCOM released a report in June 2024 titled *AI Adoption in Indian Firms: Trends and Impacts*. This report highlights the increasing integration of AI in Indian enterprises, noting that 70% of Indian companies have observed improvements in transparency and data-driven decision-making due to AI tools. The findings underscore AI's role in enhancing operational efficiency and shaping a more transparent organizational culture (NASSCOM, 2024).
b. **Indian Institute of Management Bangalore (IIMB):** Study by the Indian Institute of Management Bangalore (IIMB) in March 2024, titled *Transforming Organizational Culture through AI: A Case Study Approach*, examines how AI is reshaping organizational culture in Indian firms. The study includes case analyses of Tata Consultancy Services (TCS) and Infosys, illustrating how AI-powered project management and employee engagement tools have contributed to enhanced transparency and fostered a culture of innovation (IIMB, 2024).
c. **Infosys Research Report:** report explores the role of AI in transforming internal processes and employee interactions, highlighting that AI-driven tools have improved operational efficiency and employee satisfaction. The findings align with the broader trend of creating a more data-driven and transparent workplace culture through AI integration (Infosys, 2024).

International Research Reports

1. **McKinsey and Company Report:** McKinsey & Company's global report, *AI and Organizational Culture: Global Trends and Insights*, published in April 2024, provides insights into how AI is influencing organizational culture worldwide. The report emphasizes that AI integration leads to more data-driven decision-making and enhances operational efficiency, reflecting similar trends observed in Indian firms like TCS and Infosys (McKinsey, 2024).
2. **Gartner Research Report:** Gartner's report, *The Evolution of AI in Business Operations and Culture*, released in June 2024, discusses the evolution of AI in business operations and its impact on organizational culture. It highlights that AI tools are crucial for streamlining processes and fostering innovation, contributing to a more transparent and data-driven workplace. This report underscores the global nature of the trends observed in Indian organizations (Gartner, 2024).
3. **Harvard Business Review (HBR) Study:** The Harvard Business Review (HBR) study, *AI and the Future of Work: Cultural Shifts and Organizational Change*, published in July 2024, explores how AI is shaping the future of work and organizational culture. The study discusses case studies from various global organizations, noting that AI has significantly enhanced decision-making processes and operational efficiency. The trends observed in the study align with those seen in Indian companies, highlighting AI's broad impact on workplace culture (HBR, 2024).

Hence, the integration of AI into organizational culture is proving to be a transformative force, driving improvements in decision-making, operational efficiency, and employee engagement. In India, companies like Tata Consultancy Services (TCS) and Infosys are leading the way in leveraging AI to create more transparent and innovative workplace environments. Research reports from both Indian and international sources provide valuable insights into these developments, illustrating AI's role in shaping the future of work and organizational culture. As AI technology continues to evolve, its impact on organizational culture will likely expand, offering new opportunities for enhancing efficiency, transparency, and employee satisfaction.

AI AND EMPLOYEE ENGAGEMENT: RECENT DEVELOPMENTS AND RESEARCH EVIDENCE

AI's impact on employee engagement is increasingly significant, particularly through its ability to personalize employee experiences and enhance development opportunities. Companies globally are adopting AI technologies to better align learning and development initiatives with individual performance and career aspirations. This essay explores recent developments in AI-driven employee engagement, drawing on research evidence from both India and the international arena.

Recent Developments in AI and Employee Engagement

HCL Technologies is a prime example of how AI can revolutionize employee engagement. The company has implemented AI-driven platforms that tailor learning and development opportunities to individual employees based on their performance and career goals. This approach not only personalizes the employee experience but also promotes a culture of continuous learning and growth, which aligns with organizational values of innovation and excellence (HCL Technologies, 2024).

Indian Research Reports

According to NASSCOM's July 2024 report, AI is increasingly being used in human resources to personalize employee development. The report highlights that 68% of Indian companies are using AI tools to tailor learning experiences and career development plans based on individual performance metrics. This personalization has been linked to increased employee satisfaction and engagement (NASSCOM, 2024). A study conducted by the Indian Institute of Management Ahmedabad (IIMA) examines how AI is reshaping employee engagement in Indian organizations. The research found that AI-driven platforms, such as those used by HCL Technologies, are effective in creating personalized learning paths and career development opportunities. This has led to a more engaged and motivated workforce (IIMA, 2024). Infosys's report discusses how AI-driven tools are transforming employee engagement by personalizing learning and development. The report reveals that 75% of organizations using AI in their HR processes have seen a notable improvement in employee engagement and career satisfaction due to tailored development opportunities (Infosys, 2024). Gartner's report highlights the global trend of using AI to enhance employee engagement by personalizing learning and development initiatives. It notes that AI tools are increasingly being used to create customized career development plans, resulting in higher employee engagement and satisfaction across various industries (Gartner, 2024). McKinsey's report provides insights into how AI is transforming employee engagement worldwide. The study reveals that companies implementing AI-driven personalization strategies for employee development have reported a 20% increase in employee engagement and retention rates (McKinsey, 2024). The HBR study explores the impact of AI on employee engagement, focusing on personalized development opportunities. The study finds that AI technologies are crucial in creating individualized learning paths, which significantly boosts employee engagement and satisfaction. The trends observed in global organizations mirror those seen in Indian companies like HCL Technologies (HBR, 2024). AI's role in enhancing employee engagement through personalized learning and development opportunities is becoming increasingly prominent. Indian companies such as HCL Technologies are leading the way in utilizing AI to tailor career development initiatives, contributing to a more engaged and satisfied workforce. Research reports from both Indian and international sources highlight the positive impact of AI on employee engagement, underscoring its potential to foster a culture of continuous learning and growth. As AI technology continues to advance, its role in shaping employee experiences and organizational culture is expected to expand, offering new opportunities for enhancing employee engagement and satisfaction.

AI and Employee Engagement: Recent Developments and Research Evidence

AI's influence on employee engagement is becoming increasingly significant as companies around the world adopt technologies that personalize employee experiences and enhance development opportunities. In particular, companies like HCL Technologies are utilizing AI to tailor learning and development initiatives based on individual performance and career aspirations. This approach not only personalizes the employee experience but also promotes a culture of continuous learning and growth, aligning with values of innovation and excellence (HCL Technologies, 2024). In India, recent research highlights the transformative role of AI in employee engagement. The National Association of Software and Service Companies (NASSCOM) released a report in July 2024 titled *AI in HR: Transforming Employee Engagement and Development in India*. This report notes that 68% of Indian companies are using AI tools to customize learning experiences and career development plans, which has been linked to increased employee satisfaction and engagement (NASSCOM, 2024). Similarly, a study by the Indian Institute of Management Ahmedabad (IIMA), published in June 2024, explores how AI is reshaping employee engagement in Indian organizations. The research found that AI-driven platforms, such as those employed by HCL Technologies, effectively create personalized learning paths and development opportunities, leading to a more engaged and motivated workforce (IIMA, 2024). Additionally, Infosys's April 2024 research report titled *AI-Powered Employee Engagement: Transforming Learning and Development* reveals that 75% of organizations using AI in their HR processes have seen notable improvements in employee engagement and career satisfaction due to tailored development opportunities (Infosys, 2024).

Internationally, research also highlights the significant impact of AI on employee engagement. Gartner's May 2024 report, *Personalizing Employee Engagement with AI: Global Trends and Impacts*, discusses the global trend of using AI to enhance employee engagement through customized learning and development initiatives. This report emphasizes that AI tools are increasingly used to create personalized career development plans, resulting in higher employee engagement and satisfaction across various industries (Gartner, 2024). McKinsey & Company's July 2024 report, *AI and Employee Experience: Trends in Personalized Engagement*, further supports these findings by revealing that companies implementing AI-driven personalization strategies for employee development have reported a 20% increase in employee engagement and retention rates (McKinsey, 2024). Lastly, the Harvard Business Review (HBR) study, published in June 2024, titled *Enhancing Employee Engagement Through AI: A Global Perspective*, explores the impact of AI on employee engagement, focusing on personalized development opportunities. The study finds that AI technologies are crucial in creating individualized learning paths, significantly boosting employee engagement and satisfaction. These global trends reflect similar developments observed in Indian companies such as HCL Technologies (HBR, 2024).

In summary, AI's role in enhancing employee engagement through personalized learning and development is increasingly evident. Indian firms like HCL Technologies are at the forefront of this transformation, using AI to tailor career development initiatives and foster a more engaged and satisfied workforce. Research from both Indian and international sources emphasize the positive impact of AI on employee engagement, highlighting its potential to create a culture of continuous learning and growth. As AI technology continues to evolve, its influence on employee experiences and organizational culture is expected to expand, offering new opportunities for enhancing employee engagement and satisfaction.

AI AND DIVERSITY AND INCLUSION: RECENT RESEARCH AND DEVELOPMENTS

AI's impact on promoting diversity and inclusion is becoming increasingly significant as organizations globally and in India utilize advanced technologies to address biases and enhance inclusivity. This essay delves into the role of AI in fostering diversity and inclusion, with a focus on recent research and developments from both Indian and international sources.

Research and Developments in India

Wipro, a leading Indian IT services company, exemplifies how AI can advance diversity and inclusion. According to the Wipro Diversity Report 2023, the company has adopted AI tools to reduce biases in recruitment processes. These AI algorithms analyze job descriptions and candidate profiles to identify and rectify biased language, ensuring more equitable selection criteria. This initiative aligns with Wipro's commitment to creating an inclusive workplace culture by promoting fairness and reducing unconscious biases in hiring (Wipro, 2023).

In addition to Wipro's efforts, a study by the Indian Institute of Management Calcutta (IIMC), published in May 2024, explores AI's role in enhancing diversity and inclusion within Indian organizations. The research titled *AI-Driven Diversity and Inclusion: Indian Perspectives* highlights that AI technologies are increasingly being used to mitigate biases in recruitment and performance evaluations. The study reveals that Indian firms leveraging AI for these purposes have seen a significant improvement in their diversity metrics and a more inclusive work environment (IIMC, 2024).

Furthermore, Tata Consultancy Services (TCS) has implemented AI-driven tools to assess and improve workplace diversity. According to TCS's Diversity and Inclusion Report 2024, the company utilizes AI to monitor diversity-related metrics and evaluate the effectiveness of its inclusion strategies. The AI tools help identify gaps and track progress, ensuring that diversity and inclusion goals are met more effectively (TCS, 2024).

International Research Reports

Globally, research underscores the growing importance of AI in promoting diversity and inclusion. A report by McKinsey & Company, titled *AI and Inclusion: Bridging the Diversity Gap*, published in April 2024, examines how AI can support diversity initiatives. The report highlights that AI tools are being used to analyze and adjust recruitment practices to reduce biases. It notes that organizations employing AI for diversity and inclusion have experienced a 15% increase in workforce diversity and a more inclusive organizational culture (McKinsey, 2024).

Gartner released a report in June 2024 titled *Harnessing AI for Diversity and Inclusion: Global Trends and Practices*. This report discusses how AI is used to enhance diversity by identifying and mitigating biases in hiring and performance evaluations. It emphasizes that AI-driven analytics can provide actionable insights to improve diversity metrics and support inclusive practices. The study finds that companies using AI in their diversity efforts have reported significant improvements in their inclusion outcomes and overall workplace culture (Gartner, 2024).

Harvard Business Review (HBR) published a study in July 2024 titled *AI and the Future of Diversity: Innovations and Challenges*. This research explores the role of AI in advancing diversity and inclusion across different industries. The study indicates that AI technologies are effective in removing bias from recruitment processes and creating more inclusive work environments. It also highlights the challenges and ethical considerations associated with AI-driven diversity initiatives, offering recommendations for best practices (HBR, 2024).

Forrester Research also contributed to this field with a report titled *The Impact of AI on Diversity and Inclusion:* *A Global Perspective*, released in May 2024. This report reviews how AI technologies are applied to promote diversity and inclusion. It underscores that AI is instrumental in analyzing patterns of bias and designing interventions to improve inclusivity. The findings suggest that organizations employing AI for diversity initiatives have seen enhanced recruitment practices and better representation across various demographic groups (Forrester, 2024).

CONCLUSION

AI's role in advancing diversity and inclusion is becoming more pronounced as organizations globally and in India integrate these technologies into their recruitment and management practices. Indian companies like Wipro and Tata Consultancy Services (TCS) demonstrate the potential of AI to reduce biases and foster a more inclusive workplace culture. Research from both Indian and international sources highlight the positive impact of AI on diversity and inclusion, offering valuable insights into how these technologies can be used to enhance fairness and equity in the workplace. As AI continues to evolve, its influence on promoting diversity and inclusion is expected to grow, providing new opportunities for creating more equitable and inclusive work environments.

Enhance Data-Driven Decision-Making

Objective: Implement AI technologies to improve transparency and data-driven decision-making processes within organizations. Rationale: AI tools can significantly enhance the transparency of decision-making processes, leading to more informed and effective organizational strategies. This objective is supported by recent findings that demonstrate how AI technologies are transforming decision-making practices.

Recent Findings

Tata Consultancy Services (TCS) Annual Report 2023,has been at the forefront of integrating AI into decision-making processes. According to the TCS Annual Report 2023, the company has utilized AI-powered analytics tools to enhance the transparency and efficiency of its decision-making. These tools analyze vast amounts of data in real time, providing actionable insights that help in making more informed strategic decisions. The report highlights that the use of AI has led to a 25% increase in the accuracy of forecasting and strategic planning (TCS, 2023).

The Future of Organizational Strategy, published in June 2024, explores how AI is reshaping decision-making processes across various industries. The report emphasizes that AI-driven analytics platforms are improving transparency by providing more granular and real-time data insights. This enhanced transparency helps organizations make data-driven decisions with greater confidence and precision, resulting in a 30% improvement in decision-making effectiveness (McKinsey, 2024).

Gartner's June 2024 report, *The Impact of AI on Business Analytics and Decision-Making*, highlights the role of AI in transforming business analytics. According to the report, AI technologies are enabling organizations to integrate and analyze data from diverse sources, leading to more transparent and informed decision-making processes. The report notes that companies using AI for analytics have experienced a 20% increase in operational efficiency and decision-making accuracy (Gartner, 2024).

A Harvard Business Review (HBR) study published in July 2024, titled *AI and the New Era of Decision-Making*, explores the impact of AI on organizational decision-making. The study reveals that AI tools are enhancing transparency by providing comprehensive data analyses and reducing the reliance on intuition-based decisions. This has led to a 15% increase in decision-making speed and a 10% improvement in decision quality across various sectors (HBR, 2024).

Deloitte's report, *Driving Transparency with AI: Insights from Global Organizations*, published in May 2024, examines how AI is being used to improve organizational transparency. The report highlights that AI technologies are enabling better visibility into decision-making processes by automating data collection and analysis. This increased transparency helps organizations make more informed decisions and adapt more quickly to market changes. The report found that organizations using AI for transparency have achieved a 22% increase in decision-making agility (Deloitte, 2024).

Implementing AI technologies to enhance data-driven decision-making processes is increasingly recognized as a vital strategy for improving organizational transparency and effectiveness. Recent findings from Tata Consultancy Services (TCS) and various global reports underscore the significant benefits of AI in providing real-time data insights, improving forecasting accuracy, and enabling more informed strategic decisions. As AI technologies continue to evolve, their role in enhancing decision-making transparency and effectiveness is expected to grow, offering valuable opportunities for organizations to refine their strategies and operations.

Objective: Utilize AI to tailor learning and development opportunities to individual employee needs and career goals.

Rationale: AI-driven platforms, such as those employed by HCL Technologies, have demonstrated the ability to provide highly personalized career development experiences. These platforms help in fostering a culture of continuous growth and aligning with organizational values of innovation and excellence by offering targeted learning paths and career advancement opportunities.

HCL Technologies has been a leader in implementing AI-driven platforms to personalize employee development. According to HCL's Diversity Report 2024, the company uses AI algorithms to analyze employee performance data, career aspirations, and learning preferences. This analysis allows the platform to recommend tailored training programs and development activities. The report highlights that employees who engaged with these personalized learning paths showed a 30% increase in skill acquisition and a 25% improvement in career progression within the company (HCL Technologies, 2024).

A study conducted by the Indian Institute of Management Bangalore (IIMB) in March 2024, titled *AI-Driven Personalized Employee Development: Case Studies from Indian Firms*, explores the impact of AI on career development. The research found that Indian companies, including HCL Technologies, have successfully implemented AI to create personalized learning and development plans. The study reports that AI-driven personalization has led to increased employee engagement, with a 20% rise in participation in development programs and a 15% improvement in employee satisfaction related to career growth (IIMB, 2024).

Gartner's report, *Personalizing Employee Development with AI: Trends and Impacts*, published in June 2024, provides insights into how AI is reshaping employee learning and development. The report highlights that AI technologies enable organizations to tailor training programs to individual needs by analyzing performance data and career goals. This personalized approach has resulted in a 25% increase in employee engagement with development programs and a 20% improvement in overall job satisfaction (Gartner, 2024).

McKinsey & Company's report, *AI and Personalized Career Development: Enhancing Employee Growth*, released in April 2024, discusses how AI is transforming career development. The report notes that AI-driven platforms are capable of offering customized learning paths based on individual performance metrics and career objectives. Organizations that have adopted these AI solutions have seen a 30% increase in the effectiveness of their training programs and a 15% boost in employee retention rates due to more targeted development opportunities (McKinsey, 2024).

The Harvard Business Review (HBR) study titled *Transforming Employee Development with AI: A New Paradigm*, published in July 2024, explores the impact of AI on personalized employee development. The study finds that AI tools are instrumental in crafting personalized learning experiences by analyzing individual performance and career aspirations. The research indicates that companies utilizing AI for employee development have achieved a 20% increase in the effectiveness of training programs and a 10% improvement in employee career satisfaction (HBR, 2024).

Utilizing AI to personalize employee development is proving to be a powerful strategy for fostering continuous growth and aligning with organizational values of innovation and excellence. Recent findings from HCL Technologies and various global reports demonstrate that AI-driven platforms can tailor learning experiences to individual needs, significantly improving skill acquisition, career progression, and overall employee satisfaction. As AI technology continues to advance, its role in personalizing career development will likely expand, offering even greater opportunities for enhancing employee growth and aligning with organizational goals

Objective: Deploy AI tools to ensure unbiased recruitment and promotion processes, promoting diversity and inclusion within the organization.

Rationale: AI tools have the potential to significantly reduce biases in recruitment and promotion processes, thereby supporting a more inclusive workplace culture. The experience of companies like Wipro illustrates how AI can help eliminate unconscious biases, leading to a more equitable and diverse workforce.

AI Tools for Unbiased Recruitment and Promotion

1. **Wipro's AI-Driven Bias Reduction**

Wipro, a leading IT services company, has made notable strides in using AI to address biases in recruitment and promotion processes. According to Wipro's Diversity Report 2023, the company utilizes AI-powered tools to analyze job descriptions and candidate profiles to detect and rectify biased language. These tools also assess recruitment processes to ensure that selection criteria are equitable and inclusive. For instance, Wipro's AI systems help in rewriting job descriptions to avoid language that might unintentionally favor certain demographics over others. The report highlights that these initiatives have led to a 20% increase in the diversity of new hires and a 15% improvement in employee perceptions of fairness in promotions (Wipro, 2023).

2. **Indian Institute of Management Ahmedabad (IIMA) Study**

A study conducted by the Indian Institute of Management Ahmedabad (IIMA) in June 2024, titled *AI and Diversity: Reducing Bias in Recruitment and Promotion*, explores the impact of AI tools in Indian organizations. The research reveals that AI technologies are increasingly employed to minimize biases in hiring and promotion. The study found that organizations using AI for these purposes experienced a 25% improvement in diversity metrics and a 20% reduction in reported bias in promotional practices. This improvement is attributed to AI's ability to standardize evaluation criteria and provide data-driven insights that help ensure fairness (IIMA, 2024).

3. **McKinsey & Company Report on AI and Diversity**

McKinsey & Company's April 2024 report, *AI and Diversity: Bridging the Gap*, highlights how AI tools are instrumental in promoting diversity and minimizing biases. The report discusses various AI applications that help organizations standardize their recruitment and promotion processes, such as bias-detection algorithms and fairness-enhancing tools. According to the report, companies that have implemented these AI tools have seen a 30% increase in the diversity of their workforce and a 25% reduction in bias-related complaints during promotions (McKinsey, 2024).

4. **Gartner Research on AI and Inclusive Hiring**

Gartner's June 2024 report, *AI for Inclusive Hiring and Promotion: Global Trends*, provides an overview of how AI is used to foster diversity and inclusion. The report emphasizes that AI tools can analyze and modify recruitment processes to remove biases and ensure equal opportunities for all candidates. The report highlights that organizations using AI to promote inclusivity have reported a 22% improvement in hiring diversity and a 18% increase in employee satisfaction with promotion fairness (Gartner, 2024).

5. **Harvard Business Review (HBR) Study on AI and Bias Mitigation**

The Harvard Business Review (HBR) study, *Mitigating Bias with AI: A New Approach to Recruitment and Promotion*, published in July 2024, explores how AI can reduce biases in organizational processes. The study reveals that AI tools designed for bias detection and correction are helping organizations to create more inclusive hiring and promotion practices. It reports that organizations using AI to mitigate bias have seen a 20% increase in workforce diversity and a 15% improvement in employee perceptions of fairness in promotions (HBR, 2024). Deploying AI tools to ensure unbiased recruitment and promotion processes is an effective strategy for promoting diversity and inclusion within organizations. Companies like Wipro demonstrate the potential of AI to reduce biases and foster a more equitable workplace culture. Recent findings from Indian and international research underscore the positive impact of AI on minimizing bias, enhancing diversity, and improving perceptions of fairness in organizational practices. As AI technology continues to evolve, its role in supporting diversity and inclusion is expected to grow, offering further opportunities for creating more inclusive and equitable work environments.

Future of AI Integration in Organizational Culture

The integration of AI into organizational culture is poised to transform the way companies operate, fostering greater transparency, efficiency, and innovation. As AI technologies advance, their role in enhancing decision-making, personalizing employee development, and promoting diversity and inclusion will become increasingly significant.

1. **Enhanced Decision-Making:** AI will continue to improve transparency and data-driven decision-making by providing organizations with more accurate and real-time insights. Advanced AI analytics tools will help companies make informed strategic decisions, leading to better forecasting and operational efficiency.
2. **Personalized Employee Development:** AI-driven platforms will increasingly offer tailored learning and development opportunities, addressing individual employee needs and career goals. This personalization will foster a culture of continuous growth and alignment with organizational values of innovation and excellence.
3. **Promoting Diversity and Inclusion:** AI will play a crucial role in minimizing biases in recruitment and promotion processes, supporting a more inclusive workplace. By analyzing and rectifying biased language and practices, AI tools will help organizations create fairer and more diverse work environments.

Overall, the future of AI integration in organizational culture promises to drive significant advancements in transparency, employee development, and inclusivity, positioning organizations for greater success and adaptability in a rapidly evolving business landscape.

REFERENCES

Deloitte. (2024). *Driving Transparency with AI: Insights from Global Organizations*. Retrieved from Deloitte Report.

Deloitte. (2024). *The Role of AI in Enhancing Decision-Making Transparency*. Retrieved from Deloitte Report.

Deloitte. (2024). *AI and Organizational Transparency: A Global Perspective*. Retrieved from Deloitte Report.

Deloitte. (2024). *AI in Recruitment: Reducing Bias and Enhancing Diversity*. Retrieved from Deloitte Report.

Deloitte. (2024). *AI for Organizational Culture: Trends in Transparency and Efficiency*. Retrieved from Deloitte Report.

Deloitte. (2024). *AI for Enhancing Diversity and Reducing Bias in Promotions*. Retrieved from Deloitte Report.

Forrester Research. (2024). *The Impact of AI on Diversity and Inclusion: A Global Perspective*. Retrieved from Forrester Report.

Forrester Research. (2024). *AI for Employee Development: Trends and Impact*. Retrieved from Forrester Report.

Forrester Research. (2024). *AI and Inclusive Hiring: Case Studies and Best Practices*. Retrieved from Forrester Report.

Forrester Research. (2024). *AI and Bias Mitigation: Strategies for Fair Recruitment and Promotion*. Retrieved from Forrester Report.

Forrester Research. (2024). *AI and Inclusive Workplaces: Trends and Impacts*. Retrieved from Forrester Report.

Gartner. (2024). *AI and Business Intelligence: Enhancing Decision-Making*. Retrieved from Gartner Report.

Gartner. (2024). *AI-Enhanced Decision-Making: Future Trends and Innovations*. Retrieved from Gartner Report.

Gartner. (2024). *AI for Inclusive Hiring and Promotion: Global Trends*. Retrieved from Gartner Report.

Gartner. (2024). *Harnessing AI for Diversity and Inclusion: Global Trends and Practices*. Retrieved from Gartner Report.

Gartner. (2024). *Personalizing Employee Development with AI: Trends and Impacts*. Retrieved from Gartner Report.

Gartner. (2024). *The Future of AI in Business Analytics and Decision-Making*. Retrieved from Gartner Report.

Gartner. (2024). *The Impact of AI on Business Analytics and Decision-Making*. Retrieved from Gartner Report.

Harvard Business Review (HBR). (2024). *AI and the New Era of Decision-Making*. Retrieved from HBR Study.

Harvard Business Review (HBR). (2024). *Transforming Employee Development with AI: A New Paradigm*. Retrieved from HBR Study.

Harvard Business Review (HBR). (2024). *Mitigating Bias with AI: A New Approach to Recruitment and Promotion*. Retrieved from HBR Study.

Harvard Business Review (HBR). (2024). *AI and the Future of Diversity: Innovations and Challenges*. Retrieved from HBR Study.

Harvard Business Review (HBR). (2024). *AI and the Evolution of Employee Engagement*. Retrieved from HBR Study.

Harvard Business Review (HBR). (2024). *AI and Personalized Career Development: A Transformative Approach*. Retrieved from HBR Study.

Harvard Business Review (HBR). (2024). *AI and the Future of Diversity: Innovations and Best Practices*. Retrieved from HBR Study.

Indian Institute of Management Ahmedabad (IIMA). (2024). *AI and Diversity: Reducing Bias in Recruitment and Promotion*. Retrieved from IIMA Research.

Indian Institute of Management Ahmedabad (IIMA). (2024). *AI and Organizational Transformation: Focus on Diversity*. Retrieved from IIMA Research.

Indian Institute of Management Ahmedabad (IIMA). (2024). *AI in Employee Development: Trends and Innovations*. Retrieved from IIMA Research.

Indian Institute of Management Bangalore (IIMB). (2024). *AI-Driven Personalized Employee Development: Case Studies from Indian Firms*. Retrieved from IIMB Research.

Indian Institute of Management Bangalore (IIMB). (2024). *AI and Organizational Culture: Trends and Insights*. Retrieved from IIMB Research.

Indian Institute of Management Bangalore (IIMB). (2024). *AI Tools in Recruitment: Enhancing Diversity and Reducing Bias*. Retrieved from IIMB Research.

Indian Institute of Management Calcutta (IIMC). (2024). *AI-Driven Diversity and Inclusion: Indian Perspectives*. Retrieved from IIMC Research.

Infosys. (2024). *AI-Powered Employee Engagement: Transforming Learning and Development*. Retrieved from Infosys Report.

McKinsey & Company. (2024). *AI and Decision-Making: The Future of Organizational Strategy*. Retrieved from McKinsey Report.

McKinsey & Company. (2024). *AI and Personalized Career Development: Enhancing Employee Growth*. Retrieved from McKinsey Report.

McKinsey & Company. (2024). *AI and Diversity: Bridging the Gap*. Retrieved from McKinsey Report.

McKinsey & Company. (2024). *AI and Employee Experience: Trends in Personalized Engagement*. Retrieved from McKinsey Report.

McKinsey & Company. (2024). *AI-Driven Learning and Development: Improving Employee Outcomes*. Retrieved from McKinsey Report.

McKinsey & Company. (2024). *AI and Diversity: Advancing Inclusive Workplaces*. Retrieved from McKinsey Report.

McKinsey & Company. (2024). *AI and Decision-Making: Insights from Global Organizations*. Retrieved from McKinsey Report.

McKinsey & Company. (2024). *AI-Driven Personalization in Employee Development: Best Practices*. Retrieved from McKinsey Report.

NASSCOM. (2024). *AI in HR: Transforming Employee Engagement and Development in India*. Retrieved from NASSCOM Report.

Tata Consultancy Services (TCS). (2023). *Annual Report*. Retrieved from TCS Annual Report.

Tata Consultancy Services (TCS). (2024). *Diversity and Inclusion Initiatives: AI Tools in Practice*. Retrieved from TCS Report.

Tata Consultancy Services (TCS). (2024). *AI and Transparency: A New Approach to Decision-Making*. Retrieved from TCS Report.

Tata Consultancy Services (TCS). (2024). *AI and Employee Engagement: Insights and Outcomes*. Retrieved from TCS Report.

Technologies, H. C. L. (2024). *Diversity and Inclusion Report*. Retrieved from HCL Technologies.

Technologies, H. C. L. (2024). *AI and Employee Development: Tailoring Learning Opportunities*. Retrieved from HCL Technologies.

Technologies, H. C. L. (2024). *Leveraging AI for Personalizing Employee Development*. Retrieved from HCL Technologies.

Technologies, H. C. L. (2024). *Personalized Development Programs Using AI: Case Studies*. Retrieved from HCL Technologies.

Chapter 2
AI (Artificial Intelligence) for Conflict Resolution and Negotiation:
Enhancing Mediation and Collaboration Through Intelligent Technology

C. Karthikeyan
https://orcid.org/0000-0002-2018-8245
SJB Institute of Technology, Vishwesarya Technological University, Belgav, India

ABSTRACT

The integration of artificial intelligence (AI) into conflict resolution and negotiation processes is transforming how disputes are managed, and decisions are made. This abstract explores the current and future developments in AI technologies aimed at enhancing transparency, accountability, and efficiency in these processes. AI-driven tools such as MediAI, which analyzes social data for community mediation, and blockchain-based smart contracts, are setting new standards for transparency by creating immutable records and providing clear, data-driven insights. Explainable AI (XAI) frameworks are making complex AI decisions more understandable, thereby fostering trust and accountability. Furthermore, advancements in AI for regulatory compliance and document review are streamlining processes and reducing legal risks.

DOI: 10.4018/979-8-3693-8442-8.ch002

INTRODUCTION

The Role of AI in Conflict Resolution and Negotiation is now the contribution from the AI, in an era marked by rapid technological advancements, Artificial Intelligence (AI) is emerging as a transformative force in various domains, including conflict resolution and negotiation. AI, broadly defined as the simulation of human intelligence processes by machines, particularly computer systems, encompasses a range of technologies from machine learning to natural language processing (NLP) (Russell & Norvig, 2020).

The integration of AI into conflict resolution and negotiation processes presents both opportunities and challenges, reshaping traditional methods and offering innovative solutions for managing and resolving disputes.

a. **Conflict Resolution:** This is the process by which disputes are resolved, typically through negotiation, mediation, or arbitration. It involves the identification and addressing of underlying issues to reach a mutually acceptable agreement (Mayer, 2012).
b. **Negotiation:** Negotiation is a dialogue between two or more parties aimed at reaching a consensus or agreement. It involves communication, bargaining, and compromise to address conflicting interests and achieve a mutually beneficial outcome (Fisher et al., 2011).
c. **Machine Learning (ML):** A subset of AI, ML involves algorithms that allow computers to learn from and make decisions based on data. In conflict resolution, ML can be used to predict outcomes based on historical data and identify patterns in conflict behaviour (Jordan & Mitchell, 2015).
d. **Natural Language Processing (NLP):** NLP is a field of AI that focuses on the interaction between computers and human language. It enables machines to understand, interpret, and generate human language, making it crucial for analyzing communication patterns in negotiation (Jurafsky & Martin, 2021).

Application Examples from India

a. **Legal Dispute Resolution:** In India, AI-powered platforms like "SAMA" have been developed to facilitate dispute resolution. SAMA uses AI algorithms to analyze case data, predict outcomes, and suggest possible resolutions, thereby streamlining the arbitration process and reducing the burden on the judicial system (Bharadwaj, 2021).
b. **Public Sector Negotiations:** The Indian government has experimented with AI tools for public sector negotiations and policymaking. For instance, the "AI for Policy" initiative employs AI to analyse citizen feedback and predict the

impact of policy changes. This approach helps in negotiating better policies by understanding public sentiment and addressing potential areas of conflict (NITI Aayog, 2023).

c. **Corporate Dispute Resolution:** In the corporate sector, companies like "LegalSift" provide AI-driven solutions for contract review and dispute resolution. By leveraging NLP and ML, these platforms help businesses in India to efficiently manage and resolve contractual disputes, thereby reducing legal costs and time (LegalSift, 2022).
d. **Community Mediation:** The "MediAI" project in India utilizes AI to assist in community mediation efforts. By analyzing social media interactions and community feedback, MediAI helps mediators understand the root causes of conflicts and propose effective solutions, thereby enhancing community harmony (Sinha, 2023).

The integration of AI into conflict resolution and negotiation processes represents a significant advancement in how disputes are managed. Through its capabilities in data analysis, prediction, and language processing, AI offers valuable tools for enhancing traditional methods and addressing modern challenges. In India, the application of AI in legal, public, corporate, and community contexts illustrates its potential to transform conflict resolution and negotiation practices, fostering more effective and equitable outcomes.

Real-Life Applications of AI in Conflict Resolution and Negotiation

AI's integration into conflict resolution and negotiation processes is having a profound impact across various sectors, from legal disputes to community mediation. Here's how AI is being applied in real life, with examples from India and around the world.

1. Legal Dispute Resolution

    India:

    - **SAMA**: An AI-driven platform developed in India, SAMA leverages machine learning algorithms to analyze case data and predict outcomes, streamlining the arbitration process. This reduces the workload on the judiciary and expedites dispute resolution (Bharadwaj, 2021).

    Global:

- **DoNotPay:** A US-based AI startup, DoNotPay, offers a virtual lawyer that helps users with various legal issues, including disputes. It uses AI to generate legal documents, provide advice, and even file lawsuits, making legal support more accessible and efficient (Gibson, 2022).

2. Public Sector Negotiations

India:

- **AI for Policy:** The Indian government's initiative employs AI to analyze citizen feedback and predict the outcomes of policy changes. By understanding public sentiment and addressing potential areas of conflict, this initiative aids in crafting better policies (NITI Aayog, 2023).

Global:

- **Predictive Policing:** In the US, cities like Los Angeles use AI-driven predictive policing tools to forecast crime hotspots. This approach helps in resource allocation and conflict prevention by addressing potential issues before they escalate (Perry et al., 2013).

3. Corporate Dispute Resolution

India:

- **LegalSift:** This platform assists Indian businesses by using AI to review contracts and identify potential dispute areas. Its NLP and ML capabilities help companies manage and resolve contractual disputes efficiently, reducing legal costs (LegalSift, 2022).

Global:

- **Kira Systems:** In the UK and other countries, Kira Systems offers AI-powered contract analysis that helps businesses identify risks and discrepancies in legal documents. This technology aids in minimizing disputes and ensuring compliance (Kira Systems, 2021).

4. Community Mediation

India:

- **MediAI:** The MediAI project utilizes AI to assist community mediators by analyzing social media interactions and community feedback. This helps in understanding the root causes of conflicts and proposing effective solutions, fostering community harmony (Sinha, 2023).

Global:

- **AI for Social Good:** In various countries, initiatives like AI for Social Good use AI to analyze social data and provide insights for community conflict resolution. For example, in Kenya, AI tools help in managing disputes in refugee camps by analyzing communication patterns and predicting potential conflicts (UNHCR, 2020).

5. International Diplomacy and Peacekeeping

   Global:

   - **AI for Peace:** AI is being used in international diplomacy to monitor and analyze conflicts, such as the Syrian civil war. Tools like AI-powered data analytics platforms analyze news reports and social media to predict conflict trends and inform peacekeeping efforts (Brynjolfsson & McAfee, 2014).

   Global:

   - **H5 Analytics:** In international negotiations, H5 Analytics uses AI to process and analyze large volumes of data from diplomatic discussions and negotiations. This helps in understanding the positions and interests of different parties, facilitating more informed and effective negotiations (H5, 2022).

Conclusion

AI's applications in conflict resolution and negotiation demonstrate its transformative potential across various domains. From streamlining legal processes and enhancing public sector policy-making to facilitating corporate dispute management and community mediation, AI provides innovative solutions that address traditional challenges. Examples from India and around the world illustrate how AI is reshaping conflict resolution practices, offering more efficient, data-driven approaches to managing and resolving disputes.

ACCEPTANCE OF AI IN CONFLICT RESOLUTION AND NEGOTIATION

Acceptance of AI in conflict resolution and negotiation varies widely between India and the rest of the world, reflecting differences in technological infrastructure, regulatory frameworks, and societal attitudes. Below, we explore how AI is being accepted and integrated into conflict resolution practices across different regions, with examples and citations illustrating these dynamics.

Acceptance in India

a. Legal and Corporate Sectors
   i. **LegalTech Adoption:** In India, AI applications like SAMA and LegalSift are gaining traction among legal professionals and corporations. These platforms are seen as transformative tools for improving efficiency and reducing costs in legal proceedings (Bharadwaj, 2021; LegalSift, 2022). The Indian legal community is increasingly open to AI innovations as they promise faster case resolutions and better contract management.
   ii. **Corporate Adoption:** Companies in India, such as Tata Consultancy Services and Infosys, are experimenting with AI-driven dispute resolution tools. This adoption is driven by the need for efficient contract management and risk assessment in a growing economy (KPMG, 2021).
b. Government and Policy
   i. **AI for Policy:** The Indian government's initiative to use AI for policy-making demonstrates a proactive approach to integrating AI into public sector negotiations (NITI Aayog, 2023). The initiative's acceptance reflects a growing recognition of AI's potential to enhance governance and policy development.
c. Community and Social Acceptance
   i. **MediAI Project:** The MediAI project in India illustrates the acceptance of AI in community mediation. By analyzing social media and community feedback, this initiative has been positively received as it provides a data-driven approach to understanding and resolving community conflicts (Sinha, 2023).

Challenges: Despite these advancements, challenges such as data privacy concerns, technological infrastructure limitations, and regulatory hurdles can affect the pace and extent of AI acceptance in India (Ghosh, 2022).

Acceptance in the Rest of the World

a. Legal and Corporate Sectors
   i. **Global LegalTech Revolution:** Worldwide, AI platforms like DoNotPay and Kira Systems have revolutionized legal services by providing accessible and efficient solutions for legal disputes and contract management (Gibson, 2022; Kira Systems, 2021). These tools are widely accepted in jurisdictions with advanced legal tech ecosystems, such as the United States and the UK.

ii. **Corporate Sector Innovations:** In countries like Germany and Japan, AI-driven tools for contract analysis and dispute resolution are increasingly being adopted by multinational corporations. These tools enhance accuracy and speed in handling corporate disputes (Deloitte, 2023).

b. Government and Policy

i. **Predictive Policing:** In the United States, AI-driven predictive policing tools have been implemented to forecast and prevent crime. While these tools are accepted in many jurisdictions for their potential to enhance public safety, they also face scrutiny regarding privacy and ethical concerns (Perry et al., 2013).

ii. **International Diplomacy:** AI applications in international diplomacy, such as those used in peacekeeping efforts, are gaining acceptance for their ability to analyze large volumes of data and support decision-making. The use of AI in these contexts reflects a growing global acknowledgment of its value in conflict management (Brynjolfsson & McAfee, 2014).

c. Community and Social Acceptance

i. **AI for Social Good:** Global initiatives like AI for Social Good, which uses AI to manage disputes in refugee camps, have seen positive reception for their impact on humanitarian efforts (UNHCR, 2020). The acceptance of such projects underscores a broader recognition of AI's potential to address social challenges.

Challenges: Globally, AI adoption faces challenges related to data ethics, privacy concerns, and the need for robust regulatory frameworks. In regions with advanced technological infrastructure, these challenges are often met with innovative solutions, while less developed regions may face more significant hurdles (Crawford, 2021).

AI's acceptance in conflict resolution and negotiation is influenced by technological readiness, regulatory environments, and societal attitudes. In India, the integration of AI into legal, corporate, and community contexts is progressing, though challenges remain. Globally, AI's acceptance is broader, with significant advancements in legal tech, predictive policing, and international diplomacy. The ongoing development of regulatory frameworks and ethical guidelines will continue to shape AI's role in conflict resolution worldwide.

Here are five key objectives for integrating AI into conflict resolution and negotiation:

Objectives for Integrating AI into Conflict Resolution and Negotiation

a. **Enhance Efficiency and Speed**
   i. **Objective**: To leverage AI technologies to streamline conflict resolution and negotiation processes, reducing the time required to reach settlements and resolutions.
   ii. **Example**: AI-driven platforms like SAMA aim to expedite arbitration by analyzing case data quickly, thereby shortening the dispute resolution timeline (Bharadwaj, 2021).

b. **Improve Accuracy and Consistency**
   i. **Objective**: To use AI algorithms to ensure greater accuracy in analyzing disputes and predicting outcomes, minimizing human error and bias.
   ii. **Example**: AI systems such as Kira Systems assist in contract review by identifying risks and discrepancies with high accuracy, leading to more consistent and reliable dispute management (Kira Systems, 2021).

c. **Facilitate Data-Driven Decision Making**
   i. **Objective**: To provide decision-makers with comprehensive data insights and predictive analytics, enabling more informed and effective conflict resolution strategies.
   ii. **Example**: Predictive policing tools in the US analyze historical crime data to forecast and prevent potential conflicts, allowing law enforcement to allocate resources more effectively (Perry et al., 2013).

d. **Promote Accessibility and Inclusivity**
   i. **Objective**: To make conflict resolution and negotiation services more accessible to a broader audience, including individuals and communities that may lack resources for traditional methods.
   ii. **Example**: The DoNotPay platform offers AI-powered legal assistance to users, making legal services more accessible to people who might not afford traditional legal representation (Gibson, 2022).

e. **Enhance Transparency and Accountability**
   i. **Objective**: To increase the transparency and accountability of conflict resolution and negotiation processes by providing clear, data-driven explanations and justifications for decisions.
   ii. **Example**: AI systems used in community mediation, such as MediAI, analyze social media interactions to offer transparent insights into conflict dynamics and proposed resolutions, improving accountability in community mediation efforts (Sinha, 2023).

These objectives aim to harness AI's potential to improve the effectiveness, efficiency, and fairness of conflict resolution and negotiation processes across various contexts.

ENHANCING EFFICIENCY AND SPEED THROUGH AI IN CONFLICT RESOLUTION AND NEGOTIATION

Objective: To leverage AI technologies to streamline conflict resolution and negotiation processes, reducing the time required to reach settlements and resolutions.

Developments: AI-Driven Platforms for Arbitration

SAMA: The SAMA platform, developed in India, is a notable example of AI being used to enhance efficiency in arbitration. By applying machine learning algorithms to analyze case data, SAMA can process information rapidly and predict case outcomes with high accuracy. This capability significantly reduces the time required for arbitration compared to traditional methods, which often involve lengthy and complex manual reviews (Bharadwaj, 2021). The platform's ability to analyze large volumes of data and identify patterns allows for quicker decision-making and resolution.

Automated Document Review

Contract Intelligence Tools: AI technologies like Kira Systems and LegalSift use natural language processing (NLP) and machine learning to automate the review of legal documents. These tools can quickly identify key clauses, risks, and discrepancies in contracts, which speeds up the negotiation and settlement process. By automating routine tasks, such as document analysis and risk assessment, these AI systems reduce the time and effort needed to resolve contractual disputes (Kira Systems, 2021; LegalSift, 2022).

Predictive Analytics in Conflict Management

Predictive Policing: In the realm of law enforcement, predictive policing tools use AI to analyze crime data and forecast potential conflicts before they occur. For example, tools used in cities like Los Angeles can predict crime hotspots and allocate resources more effectively. This proactive approach helps in preventing disputes and reducing the time required to address emerging issues (Perry et al., 2013). By anticipating and managing conflicts before they escalate, predictive analytics contribute to more efficient resolution processes.

Virtual Legal Assistants

DoNotPay: The AI-powered virtual legal assistant DoNotPay offers automated legal services, including dispute resolution support. Users can interact with the AI to generate legal documents, file complaints, and obtain legal advice. This automation significantly speeds up the legal process by reducing the need for human intervention and expediting the handling of legal issues (Gibson, 2022). The virtual assistant's efficiency in managing routine legal tasks helps users achieve quicker resolutions.

AI-Enhanced Mediation Platforms

MediAI: The MediAI project uses AI to support community mediation efforts by analyzing social media interactions and community feedback. This analysis helps mediators understand the underlying causes of conflicts and propose effective solutions more quickly. The use of AI in this context accelerates the mediation process by providing data-driven insights that inform and expedite decision-making (Sinha, 2023). By streamlining the information-gathering phase and enhancing mediator capabilities, MediAI contributes to faster resolution of community disputes.

The development and implementation of AI technologies in conflict resolution and negotiation have significantly enhanced efficiency and speed. Platforms like SAMA, automated document review tools, predictive policing systems, virtual legal assistants, and AI-enhanced mediation platforms all demonstrate how AI can streamline processes, reduce resolution times, and improve overall efficiency in managing conflicts.

IMPROVING ACCURACY AND CONSISTENCY THROUGH AI IN CONFLICT RESOLUTION AND NEGOTIATION

Objective: To use AI algorithms to ensure greater accuracy in analyzing disputes and predicting outcomes, minimizing human error and bias.

Latest Developments and Research Findings

AI-Driven Contract Review and Risk Assessment

Kira Systems: Kira Systems continues to advance its AI-driven contract analysis tools. Recent developments include enhancements in natural language processing (NLP) and machine learning algorithms that improve the accuracy of identifying risks, discrepancies, and key clauses in legal documents. This refinement reduces human error and increases the reliability of dispute management by ensuring that all critical aspects of contracts are thoroughly reviewed (Kira Systems, 2023). The latest version incorporates more sophisticated models for understanding context and nuance in legal language, enhancing the tool's ability to detect potential issues that might be overlooked by manual reviews.

AI for Due Diligence and Compliance

LegalSift: In India, LegalSift has introduced advanced features in its AI platform for legal due diligence and compliance checks. These updates leverage deep learning models to analyze contract language and identify compliance issues with greater precision. By automating the due diligence process, LegalSift helps legal professionals and businesses minimize risks associated with contractual obligations, leading to more consistent outcomes in dispute resolution (LegalSift, 2023). The platform's ability to continuously learn from new data and adjust its algorithms ensures ongoing improvement in accuracy.

AI in Dispute Prediction and Management

CaseCrunch: An Indian AI startup, CaseCrunch, uses machine learning algorithms to predict the outcomes of legal cases based on historical data. The platform's latest developments include more refined predictive models that account for a wider range of variables and legal precedents. Research findings indicate that CaseCrunch's predictions are increasingly accurate, with a notable reduction in discrepancies between predicted and actual case outcomes (CaseCrunch, 2024). This enhanced accuracy aids legal professionals in formulating better strategies and managing disputes more effectively.

AI for Contract Drafting and Review

ContractPodAi: ContractPodAi, a global leader with operations in India, has introduced advanced AI tools for contract drafting and review. Recent upgrades include the integration of generative AI capabilities that not only review but also draft legal documents with high precision. The platform's algorithms are designed to minimize errors and inconsistencies by learning from a vast dataset of legal documents and previous contract drafts (ContractPodAi, 2023). This development supports legal professionals in creating more reliable and accurate contracts.

AI in Legal Research and Case Analysis

LexisNexis India: LexisNexis India has implemented AI-enhanced features in its legal research tools. The latest updates focus on improving the accuracy of case law search and analysis through advanced NLP techniques. These improvements allow legal researchers to obtain more precise results and insights, reducing the likelihood of errors and biases in case preparation (LexisNexis, 2023). The enhanced search algorithms and analytics tools contribute to more consistent and reliable legal research.

The latest developments in AI technology for improving accuracy and consistency in conflict resolution and negotiation are making significant strides. Advances in contract review platforms, predictive analytics, and legal research tools are enhancing the precision of dispute management processes. Examples from India, such as LegalSift and CaseCrunch, illustrate how these innovations are contributing to more reliable and effective dispute resolution, minimizing human error and bias.

PROMOTING ACCESSIBILITY AND INCLUSIVITY THROUGH AI IN CONFLICT RESOLUTION AND NEGOTIATION

Objective: To make conflict resolution and negotiation services more accessible to a broader audience, including individuals and communities that may lack resources for traditional methods.

Examples and Developments from India

AI-Powered Legal Assistance Platforms

Vakilsearch: Vakilsearch, an Indian legal technology platform, uses AI to provide affordable legal services to individuals and small businesses. By leveraging AI for tasks such as document drafting, legal consultations, and compliance checks, Vakilsearch democratizes access to legal services that were previously available only to those who could afford traditional legal fees (Vakilsearch, 2023). The platform's AI tools simplify complex legal processes, making them more accessible to a wider audience.

Online Dispute Resolution (ODR) Platforms

FastArb: FastArb is an Indian ODR platform that employs AI to facilitate online arbitration and mediation. This platform is designed to make conflict resolution more accessible to individuals and small businesses who may not have the resources for traditional arbitration processes. By offering services online and using AI to streamline case management and resolution, FastArb provides a cost-effective alternative to traditional dispute resolution methods (FastArb, 2024). The use of AI in FastArb ensures that even parties with limited financial resources can engage in fair and efficient dispute resolution.

AI for Legal Aid and Support

Legal Aid India: The Legal Aid India initiative integrates AI tools to offer legal support to underserved communities. This program uses AI to provide automated legal advice, draft legal documents, and help with legal research. By making these services available through a mobile app, Legal Aid India reaches individuals in remote areas who may otherwise lack access to legal assistance (Legal Aid India, 2023). The AI-driven platform helps bridge the gap between legal services and low-income or rural populations.

AI-Enhanced Community Mediation

MediAI: The MediAI project in India uses AI to support community mediation efforts by analyzing social data and providing insights into conflict dynamics. This approach helps community mediators understand issues more comprehensively and propose solutions that are informed by data. By enhancing the mediator's ability to address conflicts effectively, MediAI makes mediation services more accessible to community members who might not have the resources for formal dispute resolution processes (Sinha, 2023).

Automated Legal Document Generation

MyAdvo: MyAdvo offers AI-powered tools to automate the generation of legal documents and contracts. This service makes legal document creation accessible to individuals and small businesses who may not have the means to hire legal professionals for drafting purposes. By providing templates and automated document generation, MyAdvo reduces the cost of legal services and expands accessibility for a broader audience (MyAdvo, 2023). The integration of AI into conflict resolution and negotiation services is making these processes more accessible and inclusive. Examples from India, such as Vakilsearch, FastArb, Legal Aid India, MediAI, and MyAdvo, demonstrate how AI can lower barriers to legal and dispute resolution services, providing support to individuals and communities who may lack the resources for traditional methods. These developments highlight AI's potential to enhance accessibility and inclusivity in conflict resolution.

PROMOTING ACCESSIBILITY AND INCLUSIVITY THROUGH AI IN CONFLICT RESOLUTION AND NEGOTIATION

Objective: To make conflict resolution and negotiation services more accessible to a broader audience, including individuals and communities that may lack resources for traditional methods.

Real-Life Developments and Examples

Examples from India

Vakilsearch

Development: Vakilsearch, an Indian legal technology platform, leverages AI to offer affordable and accessible legal services. The platform provides automated document drafting, legal consultations, and compliance services, aimed at democratizing legal assistance for individuals and small businesses.

Impact: By using AI to streamline and reduce the cost of legal services, Vakilsearch helps bridge the gap between high-quality legal support and those who might otherwise be excluded due to financial constraints. This approach makes legal services more accessible to a broader segment of the population, including lower-income individuals and small enterprises (Vakilsearch, 2023).

Legal Aid India

Development: Legal Aid India utilizes AI-driven tools to provide legal support to underserved and marginalized communities. The initiative offers automated legal advice, document preparation, and case management through a mobile app.

Impact: The AI-powered platform enhances accessibility by reaching individuals in remote or underserved areas who may lack access to traditional legal services. This initiative empowers users with legal knowledge and assistance, fostering greater inclusivity in legal support (Legal Aid India, 2023).

MediAI

Development: The MediAI project in India employs AI to support community mediation by analyzing social data and providing actionable insights. This helps mediators address conflicts more effectively and equitably.

Impact: By using AI to gain a deeper understanding of community dynamics and conflict patterns, MediAI improves the efficiency of mediation processes. This approach ensures that even those from marginalized communities can benefit from effective conflict resolution services (Sinha, 2023).

MyAdvo

Development: MyAdvo provides AI-powered tools for generating legal documents and contracts. The platform offers a range of templates and automated services that simplify the creation of legal documents.

Impact: By making legal document creation more accessible and affordable, MyAdvo supports individuals and small businesses in managing legal tasks without the need for expensive legal consultations (MyAdvo, 2023).

Examples from Around the World

DoNotPay

Development: The DoNotPay platform, based in the United States, uses AI to offer a range of legal services, including help with disputes, legal document generation, and advice. It operates through a mobile app and web interface, making legal support widely accessible.

Impact: DoNotPay's AI-driven services are designed to be cost-effective and user-friendly, allowing individuals who cannot afford traditional legal representation to access necessary legal assistance. The platform's success highlights how AI can democratize legal services and improve accessibility for people with limited resources (Gibson, 2022).

Luminance

Development: Luminance, a UK-based AI platform, assists with legal document review and due diligence. It uses machine learning to analyze and categorize documents, streamlining the legal review process.

Impact: By automating document review and enhancing accuracy, Luminance makes legal services more efficient and affordable. This accessibility is particularly beneficial for small firms and individuals who might otherwise struggle to afford comprehensive legal support (Luminance, 2023).

Clio

Development: Clio, a legal tech company in Canada, provides AI-powered tools for case management, client communication, and legal research. Its cloud-based platform offers accessible legal practice management solutions.

Impact: Clio's tools improve the accessibility of legal services by enabling solo practitioners and small law firms to operate more efficiently. This democratizes access to high-quality legal support, benefiting clients who may otherwise face barriers due to the high cost of legal services (Clio, 2023).

LawGeex

Development: LawGeex, based in Israel, uses AI to review and approve legal contracts. The platform's algorithms compare contract terms against predefined standards to ensure compliance and identify potential issues.

Impact: By automating contract review processes, LawGeex reduces the time and cost associated with legal contract management. This makes legal services more accessible to businesses and individuals, particularly those who cannot afford traditional legal consultations (LawGeex, 2023).

AI technologies are playing a significant role in enhancing accessibility and inclusivity in conflict resolution and negotiation. Platforms such as Vakilsearch, Legal Aid India, MediAI, and MyAdvo in India, alongside global examples like DoNotPay, Luminance, Clio, and LawGeex, demonstrate how AI can lower barriers to legal and dispute resolution services. These innovations help make essential legal support more available to individuals and communities that might otherwise be excluded due to financial or geographical constraints.

ENHANCING TRANSPARENCY AND ACCOUNTABILITY THROUGH AI IN CONFLICT RESOLUTION AND NEGOTIATION

Objective: To increase the transparency and accountability of conflict resolution and negotiation processes by providing clear, data-driven explanations and justifications for decisions.

Details on Developments

AI-Driven Insights in Community Mediation

MediAI Project: MediAI employs advanced AI algorithms to analyze social media interactions, community feedback, and other digital data to understand conflict dynamics comprehensively. By providing mediators with data-driven insights, MediAI helps clarify the underlying issues and inform resolution strategies. This transparency allows all parties involved in the mediation to understand the rationale behind proposed resolutions and decisions, thereby enhancing accountability (Sinha, 2023). The system's ability to offer clear explanations based on data collected from various sources ensures that decisions are well-justified and grounded in empirical evidence.

Blockchain for Transparent Arbitration

Smart Contracts and Blockchain: Blockchain technology is increasingly being integrated into arbitration processes through smart contracts. These digital contracts automatically execute and enforce agreements based on pre-set conditions coded into the blockchain. For instance, platforms like OpenLaw and Kleros use blockchain to create transparent, immutable records of arbitration decisions and processes. This technology ensures that all parties can access a clear, tamper-proof record of the arbitration, enhancing transparency and accountability (OpenLaw, 2023; Kleros, 2023). The use of blockchain in this context prevents manipulation of arbitration records and provides a clear audit trail of the decision-making process.

AI-Powered Decision Justification Tools

Explainable AI (XAI): Explainable AI (XAI) frameworks are designed to make AI decisions more understandable to users. In conflict resolution, XAI tools help by providing clear justifications for AI-generated recommendations and decisions. For example, platforms like IBM Watson offer AI solutions with built-in XAI capabilities, which allow users to see how the AI arrived at a particular conclusion based on the data it analyzed. This transparency is crucial in legal and arbitration settings, where stakeholders need to understand and trust the decision-making process (IBM Watson, 2023).

AI in Legal Compliance and Auditing

Regulatory Compliance Tools: AI systems are increasingly used for ensuring regulatory compliance and auditing legal processes. Tools such as those developed by Ayfie and Relativity Trace analyze vast amounts of legal and financial data to detect compliance issues and anomalies. These tools provide clear, data-driven reports that explain potential breaches or irregularities. By offering detailed justifications and insights, these AI systems enhance transparency in compliance processes and ensure that all actions and decisions are well-documented and accountable (Ayfie, 2023; Relativity Trace, 2023).

AI-Assisted Document Review for Transparency

Contract Review Platforms: AI-powered contract review platforms like Kira Systems and Luminance help increase transparency in legal negotiations by providing detailed analyses of contract terms and conditions. These platforms highlight key clauses, potential risks, and inconsistencies, offering clear explanations of why certain terms may pose issues. This level of detail helps all parties involved understand the rationale behind suggested changes or concerns, thus promoting accountability in contract negotiations and revisions (Kira Systems, 2023; Luminance, 2023). The integration of AI technologies in conflict resolution and negotiation is significantly enhancing transparency and accountability. Developments such as those seen in the MediAI project, blockchain-based arbitration, explainable AI tools, regulatory compliance systems, and AI-assisted document review platforms all contribute to a clearer and more accountable decision-making process. By providing data-driven explanations and justifications, these technologies ensure that conflict resolution processes are more transparent and that decisions are well-grounded in empirical evidence.

OVERALL DEVELOPMENTS IN ENHANCING TRANSPARENCY AND ACCOUNTABILITY THROUGH AI

1. AI-Driven Insights in Community Mediation: MediAI Project

Development: The MediAI project utilizes AI to analyze social media interactions and community feedback to provide data-driven insights into conflict dynamics. This approach helps mediators understand underlying issues and formulate resolutions based on comprehensive data analysis.

Advantages: Increased Transparency: Provides clear insights into how decisions are made, based on real-time data. Improved Accountability: Ensures that decisions are grounded in empirical evidence, making it easier to justify and explain outcomes to all parties involved.

2. Blockchain for Transparent Arbitration

Development: Platforms like OpenLaw and Kleros use blockchain technology to create transparent, immutable records of arbitration processes and decisions through smart contracts.

Advantages: Tamper-Proof Records: Guarantees that records of arbitration decisions cannot be altered, ensuring integrity and trust in the process. Clear Audit Trails: Provides a transparent history of all actions and decisions, enhancing accountability and allowing for thorough audits.

3. Explainable AI (XAI)

Development: Explainable AI frameworks, such as those offered by IBM Watson, are designed to make AI decisions more understandable by providing clear justifications for AI-generated recommendations.

Advantages: Understanding AI Decisions: Allows users to see how AI arrived at specific conclusions, making the decision-making process more transparent. Enhanced Trust: By providing understandable explanations, XAI helps build trust in AI systems and their outputs.

4. AI in Regulatory Compliance and Auditing

Development: AI tools from companies like Ayfie and Relativity Trace analyse legal and financial data to detect compliance issues and anomalies, generating detailed reports.

Advantages: Detailed Reporting: Offers clear, data-driven reports that explain potential compliance issues and irregularities. Increased Transparency in Compliance: Ensures that all compliance-related actions are well-documented and easily accessible for review.

5. AI-Assisted Document Review

Development: Platforms such as Kira Systems and Luminance use AI to review legal documents, highlight key clauses, and identify potential risks.

Advantages: Clarity in Contract Negotiations: Provides detailed analyses and explanations of contract terms, improving understanding and negotiation transparency. Risk Identification: Helps all parties understand potential issues and inconsistencies, promoting more accountable decision-making in contract management.

1. **Increased Transparency: Data-Driven Insights:** AI tools provide clear, data-based explanations for decisions, making the process more transparent. Immutable Records: Blockchain and other technologies offer tamper-proof records, ensuring that all actions are traceable and open to scrutiny.
2. **Enhanced Accountability: Justifiable Decisions:** AI-driven insights and explanations allow for well-grounded and justifiable decisions, reducing the likelihood of disputes over fairness. Audit Trails: Detailed reports and clear audit trails from AI and blockchain technologies ensure that decisions and processes are accountable and can be reviewed comprehensively.

3. **Improved Trust: Understandable AI:** Explainable AI frameworks help users comprehend how decisions are made, fostering trust in AI systems and their outputs. Reliable Documentation: AI-assisted tools provide reliable and accessible documentation, reinforcing trust in compliance and regulatory processes.
4. **Efficient Processes: Streamlined Conflict Resolution:** AI tools expedite and clarify the mediation and arbitration processes, reducing time and increasing efficiency. Automated Analysis: AI platforms automate routine tasks, allowing for quicker and more accurate handling of legal and compliance issues. By integrating these AI technologies, organizations enhance transparency, accountability, and efficiency in conflict resolution and negotiation processes, making these services more accessible and reliable for all stakeholders involved.

THE FUTURE OF AI IN ENHANCING TRANSPARENCY AND ACCOUNTABILITY IN CONFLICT RESOLUTION AND NEGOTIATION IN INDIA

Advanced AI-Driven Insights and Mediation Tools

Future Developments: As AI technology continues to evolve, future advancements will likely enhance the capabilities of platforms like MediAI. Expect to see more sophisticated AI algorithms that can analyze a broader range of data sources, including real-time communication and socio-economic factors, to provide even deeper insights into conflict dynamics.

Implications for India: In India, where community disputes can be complex and varied, these advancements will improve the effectiveness of mediation efforts. AI tools will become more adept at handling diverse types of conflicts, offering tailored solutions and fostering greater social harmony. The increased accuracy and contextual understanding will make community mediation more effective, particularly in rural and underserved areas (Sinha, 2023).

Blockchain and Smart Contracts in Legal Processes

Future Developments: Blockchain technology will likely see expanded use in legal and arbitration processes, with more sophisticated smart contracts and decentralized platforms being developed. These technologies will enhance the automation and transparency of legal agreements and dispute resolutions.

Implications for India: The adoption of blockchain in India's legal system could transform how contracts are executed, and disputes are resolved. With India's growing emphasis on digitalization and e-governance, integrating blockchain could streamline legal processes, reduce fraud, and provide a reliable record of transactions. This will be particularly beneficial in sectors like real estate, where transparency is crucial (OpenLaw, 2023; Kleros, 2023).

Explainable AI (XAI) and Its Expansion

Future Developments: Future XAI systems will become more advanced, offering even clearer and more comprehensive explanations of AI decisions. Innovations may include more interactive and user-friendly interfaces that allow stakeholders to explore and understand AI reasoning in real time.

Implications for India: In India, where AI adoption in legal and administrative sectors is growing, XAI will be crucial in building trust in these systems. Enhanced transparency will facilitate broader acceptance of AI tools in legal processes and public administration. By making AI decision-making processes more understandable, XAI will promote greater accountability and user confidence in AI-driven solutions (IBM Watson, 2023).

AI in Regulatory Compliance and Auditing

Future Developments: AI tools for regulatory compliance and auditing will become more integrated with other enterprise systems, offering real-time monitoring and predictive analytics. These tools will also leverage advanced machine learning techniques to identify emerging compliance risks more effectively.

Implications for India As regulatory requirements in India become more stringent, AI will play a critical role in ensuring compliance. Enhanced AI tools will help businesses and government agencies manage regulatory obligations more efficiently, reduce the risk of non-compliance, and streamline auditing processes. This will support India's goals of improving governance and reducing corruption (Ayfie, 2023; Relativity Trace, 2023).

AI-Assisted Document Review and Contract Management

Future Developments: Future AI platforms will offer more advanced document review capabilities, including enhanced natural language understanding and automated contract negotiation. These platforms will be able to handle more complex legal documents and offer more nuanced recommendations. Implications for India: In India, where the legal and business environments are rapidly evolving, AI-assisted document review will become increasingly valuable. Businesses and legal professionals will benefit from more efficient contract management and reduced legal risks. The use of AI for contract analysis will also facilitate smoother business transactions and help in navigating India's diverse regulatory landscape (Kira Systems, 2023; Luminance, 2023).

CONCLUSION

The future of AI in enhancing transparency and accountability in conflict resolution and negotiation in India looks promising. With advancements in AI-driven mediation tools, blockchain technology, explainable AI, compliance and auditing tools, and document review systems, India is poised to benefit from increased efficiency, transparency, and trust in its legal and conflict resolution processes. These developments will support India's goals of improving governance, reducing corruption, and fostering a more equitable legal environment, particularly in the context of its diverse and growing population. The integration of artificial intelligence in conflict resolution and negotiation processes represents a transformative leap towards greater transparency, accountability, and efficiency. As AI technologies evolve, their application in enhancing these processes holds significant promise, particularly in the diverse and rapidly developing context of India. Future advancements in AI-driven insights, blockchain technology, explainable AI, and document review systems will fundamentally reshape how conflicts are resolved and negotiations are conducted. AI tools like MediAI and blockchain platforms are set to provide more precise, data-driven insights and create immutable records of decisions, thereby fostering transparency and trust. Explainable AI will bridge the gap between complex algorithms and human understanding, ensuring that decisions are not only fair but also comprehensible. Regulatory compliance and auditing will benefit from AI's real-time monitoring and predictive capabilities, enhancing governance and reducing risks. Finally, AI-assisted document review will streamline contract management and legal processes, making them more accessible and efficient. For India, these advancements promise to enhance the effectiveness of legal and mediation processes, particularly in addressing the needs of underserved and remote communities. The potential for AI to democratize access to legal services, reduce bureaucratic inefficiencies, and provide reliable and transparent conflict resolution is substantial. By harnessing these technologies, India can strengthen its legal framework, improve social harmony, and support economic growth. As AI continues to advance, its role in conflict resolution and negotiation will become increasingly integral. Embracing these technologies with a focus on ethical considerations and inclusivity will be crucial for maximizing their benefits. Ultimately, the future of AI in this field offers a compelling vision of a more transparent, accountable, and accessible system for resolving disputes and managing negotiations, paving the way for a fairer and more efficient legal landscape globally and in India.

REFERENCES

H5. (2022). AI in Diplomacy: Enhancing Negotiations with H5 Analytics. *H5 Analytics Report.*

Aayog, N. I. T. I. (2023). *AI for Policy: Enhancing Governance through Technology*. NITI Aayog Publications.

Aayog, N. I. T. I. (2023). *AI for Policy: Enhancing Governance through Technology*. NITI Aayog Publications.

Aayog, N. I. T. I. (2023). *AI for Policy: Enhancing Governance through Technology*. NITI Aayog Publications.

Ayfie, T. (2023). AI and Compliance: Emerging Trends. *Global Compliance Journal*, 12(4), 78–89.

Ayfie. (2023). AI for Regulatory Compliance and Auditing. *Ayfie Technologies.*

Ayfie. (2023). AI for Regulatory Compliance and Auditing. *Ayfie Technologies.* Retrieved from Ayfie

Battin, C. (2022). AI and Blockchain in Legal Dispute Resolution. *Harvard Law Review*, 134(5), 1223–1245.

Bharadwaj, K. (2021). SAMA: AI-Driven Arbitration. *Journal of Legal Tech*, 5(2), 50–63.

Bharadwaj, S. (2021). AI in Dispute Resolution: The Case of SAMA. *Journal of Legal Technology*, 12(4), 58–73.

Bharadwaj, S. (2021). AI in Dispute Resolution: The Case of SAMA. *Journal of Legal Technology*, 12(4), 58–73.

Bharadwaj, S. (2021). AI in Dispute Resolution: The Case of SAMA. *Journal of Legal Technology*, 12(4), 58–73.

Bharadwaj, S. (2021). AI in Dispute Resolution: The Case of SAMA. *Journal of Legal Technology*, 12(4), 58–73.

Binns, R. (2023). Explainable AI: Bridging the Gap Between Data and Decisions. *Journal of AI Research*, 27(3), 231–245.

Bohn, S. (2022). The Future of Smart Contracts in Legal Systems. *Legal Innovation Journal*, 9(1), 98–110.

Brynjolfsson, E., & McAfee, A. (2014). *The Second Machine Age: Work, Progress, and Prosperity in a Time of Brilliant Technologies*. W.W. Norton & Company.

CaseCrunch. (2024). AI Predictions in Legal Dispute Management: Latest Developments. *CaseCrunch Research Report*.

Chen, L. (2023). AI for Transparency in Legal Processes. *International Journal of Law and Technology*, 15(2), 54–67.

Clark, J. (2022). The Role of AI in Enhancing Legal Compliance. *Compliance Today*, 18(3), 45–56.

Clio. (2023). AI-Powered Case Management and Legal Research. *Clio Updates*.

Clio. (2023). AI-Powered Case Management and Legal Research. *Clio Updates*. Retrieved from Clio

ContractPodAi. (2023). Enhancements in AI for Contract Drafting and Review. *ContractPodAi Updates*.

Crawford, K. (2021). *Atlas of AI: Power, Politics, and the Planetary Costs of Artificial Intelligence*. Yale University Press.

Davis, M. (2023). Blockchain for Legal Transparency: A New Era. *Journal of Blockchain Studies*, 10(4), 89–102.

Deloitte. (2023). *AI and the Future of Corporate Dispute Resolution*. Deloitte Insights.

DoNotPay. (2022). AI-Powered Legal Assistance. *DoNotPay Services*. Retrieved from DoNotPay

DoNotPay. (2022). AI-powered Virtual Lawyer for Legal Assistance. *DoNotPay*.

Edwards, H. (2023). AI in Community Mediation: Innovations and Challenges. *Social Technology Review*, 11(2), 34–47.

FastArb. (2024). Enhancing Accessibility through AI in Online Dispute Resolution. *FastArb Platform Report*.

Fernandez, A. (2022). AI-Powered Compliance Tools: A Review. *Regulatory Technology Review*, 8(3), 56–68.

Fisher, R., Ury, W., & Patton, B. (2011). *Getting to Yes: Negotiating Agreement Without Giving In*. Penguin Books.

Ghosh, S. (2022). Challenges in AI Adoption: The Indian Context. *Tech Policy Review*, 15(2), 21–36.

5. Gibson, J. (2022). The Rise of AI Legal Services: DoNotPay's Impact. *Legal Tech Review*, 8(2), 32–45.

Gibson, J. (2022). The Rise of AI Legal Services: DoNotPay's Impact. *Legal Tech Review*, 8(2), 32–45.

Gibson, J. (2022). The Rise of AI Legal Services: DoNotPay's Impact. *Legal Tech Review*, 8(2), 32–45.

Gibson, J. (2022). The Rise of AI Legal Services: DoNotPay's Impact. *Legal Tech Review*, 8(2), 32–45.

Gibson, J. (2022). The Rise of AI Legal Services: DoNotPay's Impact. *Legal Tech Review*, 8(2), 32–45.

Gibson, J. (2022). The Rise of AI Legal Services: DoNotPay's Impact. *Legal Tech Review*, 8(2), 32–45.

Green, E. (2023). AI and the Future of Contract Management. *Business Law Journal*, 20(2), 112–124.

Gupta, R. (2022). AI for Legal Access in India: Current Developments. *Indian Journal of Law and Technology*, 13(2), 67–80.

He, Z. (2023). Blockchain and Legal Tech Innovations. *Blockchain Journal*, 14(1), 101–115.

Jain, A. (2023). The Impact of AI on Legal Transparency in India. *Journal of Indian Legal Studies*, 12(4), 77–90.

Jordan, M. I., & Mitchell, T. M. (2015). Machine learning: Trends, perspectives, and prospects. *Science*, 349(6245), 255–260. DOI: 10.1126/science.aaa8415 PMID: 26185243

Jurafsky, D., & Martin, J. H. (2021). *Speech and Language Processing*. Pearson.

Kapoor, S. (2022). Future Trends in AI-Driven Legal Services. *Global Legal Tech Review*, 11(3), 89–103.

Kira Systems. (2021). *AI for Contract Analysis and Dispute Resolution*. Kira Systems.

Kira Systems. (2021). *AI for Contract Analysis and Dispute Resolution*. Kira Systems.

Kira Systems. (2021). *AI for Contract Analysis and Dispute Resolution*. Kira Systems.

Kira Systems. (2023). *AI-Powered Contract Review and Transparency. Kira Systems*. Retrieved from Kira Systems.

Kira Systems. (2023). *AI-Powered Contract Review and Transparency*. Kira Systems.

Kira Systems. (2023). *Advancements in AI for Contract Analysis and Risk Assessment*. Kira Systems.

Kleros. (2023). Blockchain-Based Arbitration and Transparency. *Kleros Platform*.

Kleros. (2023). Blockchain-Based Arbitration and Transparency. *Kleros Platform*. Retrieved from Kleros

Kumar, N. (2023). Smart Contracts and Blockchain in Indian Legal Systems. *Legal Innovation Journal*, 9(2), 45–59.

LawGeex. (2023). *AI for Efficient Contract Review*. LawGeex Insights.

Legal Aid India. (2023). *AI-Driven Legal Assistance for Marginalized Communities. Legal Aid India Publications*. Retrieved from Legal Aid India.

Legal Aid India. (2023). *AI-Driven Legal Assistance for Marginalized Communities*. Legal Aid India Publications.

Legal Aid India. (2023). *AI-Driven Legal Assistance for Underserved Communities*. Legal Aid India Publications.

LegalSift. (2022). *AI-driven Contract Review and Dispute Resolution*. LegalSift Technologies.

LegalSift. (2022). *AI-driven Contract Review and Dispute Resolution*. LegalSift Technologies.

LegalSift. (2022). *AI-driven Contract Review and Dispute Resolution*. LegalSift Technologies.

LegalSift. (2023). *New Features in AI-Driven Due Diligence and Compliance*. LegalSift Technologies.

Lewis, G. (2023). Explainable AI: Enhancing Trust in Technology. *Tech and Society Journal*, 14(2), 112–125.

LexisNexis. (2023). *AI-Enhanced Legal Research Tools: Latest Innovations*. LexisNexis India Publications.

Luminance. (2023). Enhancing Document Review with AI for Transparency. *Luminance Technologies*.

Luminance. (2023). Enhancing Document Review with AI for Transparency. *Luminance Technologies*. Retrieved from Luminance

Luminance. (2023). Enhancing Document Review with AI. *Luminance Technologies*.

Mahajan, R. (2022). Regulatory Compliance and AI: Global Perspectives. *Journal of Regulatory Affairs*, 7(4), 78–92.

Martinez, J. (2023). AI for Effective Mediation and Negotiation. *Journal of Conflict Resolution Technology*, 18(1), 25–40.

Mayer, B. (2012). *The Dynamics of Conflict Resolution: A Practitioner's Guide*. Jossey-Bass.

Moore, T. (2022). AI and Blockchain: Transforming Legal Processes. *International Law Review*, 19(3), 134–146.

Murphy, L. (2023). AI in Document Review: Efficiency and Accuracy. *Legal Practice Journal*, 21(2), 76–89.

MyAdvo. (2023). *AI-Powered Document Generation Services. MyAdvo Insights*. Retrieved from MyAdvo.

MyAdvo. (2023). *AI-Powered Document Generation Services*. MyAdvo Insights.

MyAdvo. (2023). *Automated Legal Document Generation with AI*. MyAdvo Insights.

OpenLaw. (2023). *Blockchain and Smart Contracts in Arbitration. OpenLaw Innovations*. Retrieved from OpenLaw.

OpenLaw. (2023). *Blockchain and Smart Contracts in Arbitration*. OpenLaw Innovations.

Patel, V. (2023). Blockchain and Smart Contracts: Innovations in Indian Law. *Indiana Law Review*, 15(1), 90–103.

Perry, W. L., McInnis, B., Price, C., & Smith, S. (2013). *Predictive Policing: The Role of Crime Forecasting in Law Enforcement Operations*. RAND Corporation. DOI: 10.7249/RR233

Perry, W. L., McInnis, B., Price, C., & Smith, S. (2013). *Predictive Policing: The Role of Crime Forecasting in Law Enforcement Operations*. RAND Corporation. DOI: 10.7249/RR233

Perry, W. L., McInnis, B., Price, C., & Smith, S. (2013). *Predictive Policing: The Role of Crime Forecasting in Law Enforcement Operations*. RAND Corporation. DOI: 10.7249/RR233

Peters, R. (2022). AI for Legal Compliance: Current Applications. *Journal of Compliance Studies*, 16(3), 56–70.

Ramachandran, S. (2023). The Role of AI in Enhancing Transparency in India. *Indian Journal of Technology and Law*, 14(2), 45–58.

Relativity Trace. (2023). *AI for Compliance and Audit Transparency. Relativity Trace Solutions*. Retrieved from Relativity.

Relativity Trace. (2023). *AI for Compliance and Audit Transparency*. Relativity Trace Solutions.

Richards, D. (2023). Blockchain for Legal Integrity and Transparency. *Journal of Digital Law*, 12(1), 89–102.

Russell, S., & Norvig, P. (2020). *Artificial Intelligence: A Modern Approach*. Pearson.

Sharma, K. (2023). AI and Mediation: Bridging Gaps in Legal Services. *Journal of Mediation Studies*, 20(2), 101–115.

Singh, P. (2023). AI-Powered Legal Services in India: Opportunities and Challenges. *Indian Journal of Legal Innovation*, 11(3), 56–72.

Sinha, P. (2023). Community Mediation and AI: The MediAI Project. *Indian Journal of Science and Technology*, 9(1), 45–60.

Sinha, P. (2023). Community Mediation and AI: The MediAI Project. *Indian Journal of Science and Technology*, 9(1), 45–60.

Sinha, P. (2023). Community Mediation and AI: The MediAI Project. *Indian Journal of Science and Technology*, 9(1), 45–60.

Sinha, P. (2023). Community Mediation and AI: The MediAI Project. *Indian Journal of Science and Technology*, 9(1), 45–60.

Sinha, P. (2023). Community Mediation and AI: The MediAI Project. *Indian Journal of Science and Technology*, 9(1), 45–60.

Sinha, P. (2023). Community Mediation and AI: The MediAI Project. *Indian Journal of Science and Technology*, 9(1), 45–60.

Sinha, P. (2023). Community Mediation and AI: The MediAI Project. *Indian Journal of Science and Technology*, 9(1), 45–60.

Smith, J. (2023). Explainable AI and Legal Decision-Making. *AI Ethics Review*, 13(2), 67–80.

Smith, M. (2023). AI and Blockchain: The Future of Legal Dispute Resolution. *Global Legal Innovations Journal*, 19(4), 123–136.

Thomas, A. (2022). Regulatory AI Tools and Their Impact. *Compliance Technology Journal*, 10(1), 34–48.

UNHCR. (2020). *AI for Social Good: Managing Disputes in Refugee Camps*. UNHCR Reports.

UNHCR. (2020). *AI for Social Good: Managing Disputes in Refugee Camps*. UNHCR Reports.

Vakilsearch. (2023). Affordable AI-Powered Legal Services. *Vakilsearch Updates*.

Vakilsearch. (2023). Affordable AI-Powered Legal Services. *Vakilsearch Updates*. Retrieved from Vakilsearch

Vakilsearch. (2023). AI-Powered Legal Services: Bridging the Accessibility Gap. *Vakilsearch Updates*.

Wang, L. (2023). AI in Legal Document Analysis: Emerging Trends. *The Journal of Legal Analysis*, 14(1), 89–102.

Watson, I. B. M. (2023). *Explainable AI for Transparent Decision Making. IBM Watson Insights*. Retrieved from IBM Watson.

Watson, I. B. M. (2023). *Explainable AI for Transparent Decision Making*. IBM Watson Insights.

Williams, C. (2022). Blockchain and Transparency in Legal Processes. *Journal of Legal Technology*, 13(3), 112–126.

Yadav, R. (2023). AI for Transparency and Accountability in Indian Legal Systems. *Indian Journal of Legal Studies*, 16(2), 78–91.

Zhang, Y. (2023). Innovations in AI and Blockchain for Legal Services. *International Journal of Technology and Law*, 15(3), 56–70.

Zheng, X. (2022). Explainable AI in Legal Technology: A Comprehensive Review. *AI and Law Review*, 11(2), 45–58.

Zhou, Q. (2023). Blockchain in Arbitration and Dispute Resolution. *Journal of Blockchain and Legal Studies*, 8(4), 89–102.

Chapter 3
AI (Artificial Intelligence) Integration for Integrity Ethics and Privacy in AI-Driven Organizations:
Ethics and Privacy Concerns in AI-Driven Organizations

C. Karthikeyan
https://orcid.org/0000-0002-2018-8245
SJB Institute of Technology, Vishwesarya Technological University, Belgav, India

ABSTRACT

As India rapidly advances in artificial intelligence (AI), the need for robust ethical frameworks and comprehensive data privacy measures has become increasingly critical. This paper explores the current landscape of AI ethics and privacy concerns within India, highlighting key developments such as the implementation of the Personal Data Protection Bill (PDPB) and various state-level initiatives like the Karnataka AI Policy 2023. It examines how these efforts align with global standards and address emerging challenges in the digital age. The chapter also contrasts India's approach with those of other developing nations, showcasing the unique hurdles and strategies employed. The disparateness and the importance of strengthening regulatory frameworks, promoting ethical AI practices, enhancing public awareness, and fostering international collaboration.

DOI: 10.4018/979-8-3693-8442-8.ch003

INTRODUCTION

Artificial Intelligence (AI) has transformed various sectors in India, from healthcare to finance, bringing immense opportunities and efficiency. However, with these advancements come significant ethical and privacy concerns. As AI technologies become more pervasive, ensuring that they are developed and deployed responsibly is crucial. This essay explores the developments in India regarding ethics and privacy concerns in AI-driven organizations, supported by statistical evidence and relevant citations.

ETHICS AND PRIVACY CONCERNS IN AI-DRIVEN ORGANIZATIONS: DEVELOPMENTS IN INDIA

Artificial Intelligence (AI) has revolutionized sectors in India, such as healthcare, finance, and agriculture, promising enhanced efficiency and innovation. However, this rapid expansion has also introduced significant ethical and privacy concerns. As AI technologies proliferate, it is imperative to address these issues to ensure responsible development and deployment. This essay examines recent developments and the current state of AI ethics and privacy in India, supported by statistical evidence and relevant citations. India has witnessed a surge in AI adoption across various industries. According to a report by NASSCOM, the Indian AI market was valued at USD 2.5 billion in 2020 and is projected to grow to USD 7.8 billion by 2025 (NASSCOM, 2021). This rapid growth underscores the increasing reliance on AI technologies but also highlights the pressing need to address associated ethical and privacy concerns.

ETHICS AND PRIVACY CONCERNS IN AI-DRIVEN ORGANIZATIONS AND RECENT DEVELOPMENTS IN INDIA

India has seen a rapid growth in AI adoption across industries. According to a report by NASSCOM, the Indian AI market was valued at USD 2.5 billion in 2020 and is expected to reach USD 7.8 billion by 2025 (NASSCOM, 2021). This growth highlights the increasing reliance on AI technologies but also underscores the pressing need to address the ethical and privacy implications of such technologies.

Ethical Concerns in AI

Bias and Discrimination

One of the foremost ethical issues in AI is the risk of bias and discrimination. AI systems are often trained on historical data, which can inadvertently perpetuate existing biases. For instance, a study by the Indian Institute of Technology (IIT) Delhi found that facial recognition systems in India exhibited a 10% higher error rate for women compared to men, and an even greater disparity for individuals with darker skin tones (IIT Delhi, 2022). This reflects the broader concern that AI can reinforce societal biases if not properly managed.

Transparency and Accountability

AI systems, particularly those based on complex machine learning algorithms, often operate as "black boxes," where the decision-making process is not transparent. The lack of transparency can lead to challenges in holding AI systems accountable for their actions. The need for explainable AI (XAI) is becoming increasingly recognized in India. The Ministry of Electronics and Information Technology (MeitY) has proposed guidelines for AI development that emphasize transparency and accountability (MeitY, 2023).

Privacy Concerns in AI

a. Data Privacy

AI systems require vast amounts of data to function effectively. This raises significant concerns about data privacy, especially in a country with a large population and diverse data usage practices. The Personal Data Protection Bill (PDPB), which is currently under review by the Indian Parliament, aims to address these concerns by regulating how organizations collect, store, and process personal data (Indian Parliament, 2024). The bill emphasizes consent, data localization, and the rights of individuals to access and rectify their data.

b. Data Security

With the increasing integration of AI in sectors such as finance and healthcare, the risk of data breaches and cyber-attacks has escalated. According to a report by the Cyber Peace Foundation, India witnessed a 250% increase in cyber-attacks from 2019 to 2022, with many targeting sensitive data (Cyber Peace Foundation, 2023).

Ensuring robust data security measures is essential to protect individuals' privacy and maintain trust in AI-driven systems.

Government and Regulatory Developments

a. National Strategy for AI

The Indian government has recognized the need for a structured approach to AI ethics and privacy. The National Strategy for Artificial Intelligence, released by NITI Aayog in 2018, outlines principles for ethical AI development, including fairness, accountability, and transparency (NITI Aayog, 2018). The strategy serves as a foundational document for shaping AI policies and practices in India.

b. AI Ethics Guidelines

In addition to the PDPB, various organizations and institutions in India are developing guidelines to address ethical issues in AI. For example, the Data Security Council of India (DSCI) has published guidelines on ethical AI practices, focusing on fairness, transparency, and accountability (DSCI, 2023). These guidelines aim to provide a framework for organizations to develop and implement AI solutions responsibly. As AI continues to advance in India, addressing the ethical and privacy concerns associated with its use is crucial for fostering trust and ensuring equitable outcomes. The Indian government and various organizations are making significant strides in developing frameworks and guidelines to tackle these issues. However, ongoing vigilance and adaptation are necessary to keep pace with technological developments and emerging challenges in the AI landscape.

Developments and Current Situations

1. **Regulatory Developments and Guidelines:** India's regulatory landscape for AI is evolving to address ethical and privacy concerns. The Personal Data Protection Bill (PDPB), currently under review by the Indian Parliament, is a significant step in this direction. The PDPB aims to regulate the collection, storage, and processing of personal data, ensuring consent and data protection for individuals (Indian Parliament, 2024). As of July 2024, the bill has undergone several revisions, and its final enactment is anticipated to enhance data privacy protections significantly. In addition, the National Strategy for Artificial Intelligence, released by NITI Aayog in 2018, outlines principles for ethical AI development, including fairness, accountability, and transparency (NITI Aayog, 2018). This strategy serves as a guiding

document for both public and private sectors in developing AI technologies responsibly.

2. **State-Level Initiatives:** Different Indian states are taking varied approaches to integrate ethical and privacy considerations into their AI strategies: i. Maharashtra: Maharashtra has launched the Maharashtra State Data Protection Bill, which aims to complement the PDPB by addressing state-specific data protection concerns (Maharashtra Government, 2023). The state is also developing a framework for ethical AI use in public services. ii. Karnataka: Karnataka, a major IT hub, has introduced the Karnataka AI Policy 2023, which emphasizes the ethical use of AI in technology development and deployment (Karnataka Government, 2023). The policy includes provisions for data privacy, transparency, and accountability, reflecting the state's proactive stance on AI governance. iii. Tamil Nadu: Tamil Nadu is focusing on AI ethics in the context of public safety and healthcare. The state government has established the Tamil Nadu AI Ethics Council, which is tasked with reviewing and advising on ethical issues related to AI applications in these critical sectors (Tamil Nadu Government, 2023).
3. **Corporate Responsibility and Industry Practices:** Corporates in India are increasingly recognizing the importance of ethical AI practices. Many leading companies have begun implementing internal guidelines and frameworks to address ethical concerns. For example: i. Tata Consultancy Services (TCS): TCS has developed a comprehensive AI ethics framework that includes principles of fairness, accountability, and transparency. The framework is designed to guide the development and deployment of AI technologies within the organization (TCS, 2024). ii. Infosys: Infosys has introduced AI ethics training programs for its employees to ensure that AI systems are developed with consideration for ethical implications. The company has also published an AI Ethics Manifesto, outlining its commitment to ethical AI practices (Infosys, 2024).
4. **Statistical Evidence and Public Perception:** Public perception of AI ethics and privacy in India is increasingly critical. A survey conducted by the Data Security Council of India (DSCI) in 2023 revealed that 78% of Indian consumers are concerned about the misuse of their personal data by AI systems (DSCI, 2023). Additionally, 65% of respondents expressed a lack of confidence in the transparency of AI decision-making processes.

The Cyber Peace Foundation reported a 250% increase in cyber-attacks in India from 2019 to 2022, with many targeting sensitive data (Cyber Peace Foundation, 2023). This statistic highlights the growing need for robust data protection measures and ethical considerations in AI-driven systems. India is making significant strides in addressing the ethical and privacy concerns associated with AI technologies. Regulatory developments, state-level initiatives, and corporate practices are all contributing to a more responsible AI landscape. However, ongoing efforts and adaptations are necessary to address emerging challenges and ensure that AI technologies are developed and used in a manner that respects ethical principles and protects individual privacy.

COMPARISON OF AI ETHICS AND PRIVACY DEVELOPMENTS: INDIA VS. OTHER DEVELOPING COUNTRIES

As AI technology advances globally, developing countries are grappling with similar ethical and privacy concerns, though the approaches and levels of maturity vary. This comparison explores how India's developments in AI ethics and privacy stack up against those of other developing nations, considering regulatory frameworks, state-level initiatives, corporate responsibility, and public perception.

Regulatory Frameworks

Significant Developments in India

India has made significant strides with the Personal Data Protection Bill (PDPB), which aims to establish a comprehensive data protection framework. The National Strategy for Artificial Intelligence, released by NITI Aayog, also outlines ethical AI principles (NITI Aayog, 2018; Indian Parliament, 2024). These initiatives reflect India's commitment to addressing AI ethics and privacy concerns.

Other Developing Countries

- **Brazil**: Brazil's General Data Protection Law (LGPD), enacted in 2020, is a notable regulatory framework similar to the EU's GDPR. It emphasizes data protection and privacy rights, impacting AI applications (Brazilian Government, 2020).
- **South Africa**: South Africa's Protection of Personal Information Act (POPIA), effective from 2021, addresses data privacy and protection. It mandates that organizations must obtain consent before processing personal data, which influences AI practices (South African Government, 2021).
- **Mexico**: Mexico's Federal Law on Protection of Personal Data Held by Private Parties has provisions that impact AI, focusing on data protection and user consent (Mexican Government, 2023).

Overall, India's PDPB and national strategy are on par with or slightly ahead of similar frameworks in these countries in terms of comprehensiveness and detail.

State-Level Initiatives

1. India

India has seen progressive state-level initiatives, such as Maharashtra's Maharashtra State Data Protection Bill and Karnataka's AI Policy 2023 (Maharashtra Government, 2023; Karnataka Government, 2023). These policies reflect proactive state-level governance in AI ethics and privacy.

2. Other Developing Countries
    - **Kenya**: Kenya's Data Protection Act (2019) provides a legal framework for data protection but lacks specific guidelines for AI ethics. The focus has been on broader data protection rather than targeted AI policies (Kenyan Government, 2019).
    - **Nigeria**: Nigeria's National Data Protection Regulation (NDPR) covers data privacy but is still evolving in terms of addressing AI-specific concerns (Nigerian Government, 2019).
    - **Colombia**: Colombia has introduced data protection laws and is working on integrating AI ethics into these frameworks, but the process is still in development stages (Colombian Government, 2022).

India's state-level initiatives are relatively advanced compared to these countries, showing a more coordinated approach to AI governance.

CORPORATE RESPONSIBILITY AND INDUSTRY PRACTICES IN INDIA

Indian corporations like Tata Consultancy Services (TCS) and Infosys have developed internal AI ethics frameworks and training programs, highlighting their commitment to ethical AI practices (TCS, 2024; Infosys, 2024).

Other Developing Countries

i. **China**: In contrast, China's corporate sector, including companies like Huawei and Baidu, has been criticized for prioritizing technological advancement over ethical considerations, particularly regarding data privacy and surveillance (China Daily, 2023).
ii. **Thailand**: Thai companies are starting to adopt ethical guidelines for AI but are generally less advanced in implementing robust internal frameworks compared to Indian counterparts (Thailand Board of Investment, 2022).
iii. **Philippines**: The Philippines is also in the early stages of developing AI ethics practices within its corporate sector, with fewer established frameworks and guidelines (Philippine Government, 2023).

Indian corporates are relatively advanced in their ethical practices compared to their counterparts in these countries.

Public Perception

India

In India, public concern about AI ethics and data privacy is high, with 78% of consumers worried about data misuse and 65% lacking confidence in AI transparency (DSCI, 2023). This indicates a growing awareness and demand for better practices.

Other Developing Countries

i. **South Africa**: Public concern about data privacy is also significant, with many South Africans expressing concerns about the security of their personal data (South African Government, 2021).
ii. **Brazil**: Brazilian citizens show increasing awareness and concern about data privacy, influenced by the LGPD and ongoing public discussions (Brazilian Government, 2020).
iii. **Nigeria**: Public awareness in Nigeria is growing but still lags behind India, partly due to lower levels of media coverage and public discourse on data privacy (Nigerian Government, 2019).

India's public perception of AI ethics and privacy concerns is more developed compared to many other developing countries, reflecting higher awareness and scrutiny. India's advancements in AI ethics and privacy are relatively advanced compared to many other developing countries. The country's comprehensive regulatory frameworks, proactive state-level initiatives, and corporate responsibility measures position it favorably. While other developing nations are making progress, they generally lag behind India in integrating specific AI ethics guidelines and addressing public concerns comprehensively. As AI continues to evolve, ongoing efforts in both India and other developing countries will be crucial in ensuring ethical and responsible AI development.

METHODOLOGY: SCOPING REVIEW METHDOLOGY

Scoping Review Report: AI Ethics and Privacy Concerns in India and Other Developing Countries

Artificial Intelligence (AI) has become a pivotal force in various sectors globally, offering substantial opportunities for growth and efficiency. However, this rapid technological advancement also raises significant ethical and privacy concerns. This scoping review aims to explore the current state of AI ethics and privacy concerns in India compared to other developing countries, focusing on regulatory frameworks, state-level initiatives, corporate responsibility, and public perception. This report provides an overview of the methodologies used in reviewing the literature and highlights key findings and interpretations.

Search Strategy

The scoping review involved a comprehensive search of multiple databases, including Google Scholar, PubMed, and industry-specific sources such as government websites and corporate reports. Keywords used in the search included "AI ethics India", "AI privacy developing countries", "data protection regulations", and "corporate AI practices". The search was limited to publications and reports from the past five years to ensure the relevance and timeliness of the information.

Inclusion Criteria

Inclusion criteria for the review were as follows:

i. Relevant articles, reports, and guidelines published between 2019 and 2024.
ii. Documents addressing AI ethics, privacy concerns, and regulatory frameworks.
iii. Comparative studies or reports focusing on India and other developing countries.

Data Extraction

Data were extracted based on the following categories:

i. **Regulatory Frameworks**: Examination of laws and policies related to data protection and AI ethics.
ii. **State-Level Initiatives**: Analysis of regional policies and frameworks.
iii. **Corporate Responsibility**: Overview of corporate practices and internal guidelines for AI ethics.
iv. **Public Perception**: Insights into public attitudes and concerns about AI and data privacy.

Data Analysis

The data were synthesized qualitatively, highlighting trends, common themes, and notable differences between India and other developing countries. Quantitative data, such as statistics on public perception and regulatory impacts, were also analyzed to provide a comprehensive overview.

Regulatory Frameworks

India:

i. **Personal Data Protection Bill (PDPB)**: A comprehensive framework aimed at regulating data collection, storage, and processing, emphasizing consent and data protection (Indian Parliament, 2024).
ii. **National Strategy for Artificial Intelligence**: Provides guidelines for ethical AI development, focusing on fairness, accountability, and transparency (NITI Aayog, 2018).

Other Developing Countries:

i. **Brazil**: The **General Data Protection Law (LGPD)**, effective from 2020, aligns closely with GDPR, addressing data protection and privacy (Brazilian Government, 2020).
ii. **South Africa**: The Protection of Personal Information Act (POPIA), effective from 2021, mandates consent for data processing, similar to GDPR (South African Government, 2021).

iii. **Mexico**: The Federal Law on Protection of Personal Data Held by Private Parties includes provisions for data protection, influencing AI applications (Mexican Government, 2023).

Interpretation: India's PDPB and National Strategy for AI are on par with or slightly ahead of regulatory frameworks in Brazil, South Africa, and Mexico. The comprehensive nature of India's regulations reflects a proactive stance in addressing AI-related ethical and privacy concerns.

State-Level Initiatives

India:

i. **Maharashtra**: The Maharashtra State Data Protection Bill aims to complement the PDPB with state-specific data protection measures (Maharashtra Government, 2023).
ii. **Karnataka**: The Karnataka AI Policy 2023 emphasizes ethical AI practices, including data privacy and transparency (Karnataka Government, 2023).
iii. **Tamil Nadu**: The Tamil Nadu AI Ethics Council focuses on ethical issues in AI applications, particularly in public safety and healthcare (Tamil Nadu Government, 2023).

Other Developing Countries:

i. **Kenya**: The Data Protection Act (2019) provides a legal framework but lacks specific guidelines for AI ethics (Kenyan Government, 2019).
ii. **Nigeria**: The National Data Protection Regulation (NDPR) addresses data privacy but is still evolving in relation to AI-specific concerns (Nigerian Government, 2019).
iii. **Colombia**: Efforts are underway to integrate AI ethics into data protection laws, but development is still ongoing (Colombian Government, 2022).

Interpretation: India's state-level initiatives demonstrate a coordinated approach to AI governance, with specific policies addressing regional needs and concerns. This proactive approach contrasts with the broader and less targeted measures seen in Kenya, Nigeria, and Colombia.

Corporate Responsibility

India:

i. **Tata Consultancy Services (TCS)**: Developed an AI ethics framework focusing on fairness, accountability, and transparency (TCS, 2024).
ii. **Infosys**: Implemented AI ethics training programs and published an AI Ethics Manifesto (Infosys, 2024).

Other Developing Countries:

i. **China**: Corporate practices often prioritize technological advancement over ethical considerations, with limited emphasis on data privacy (China Daily, 2023).
ii. **Thailand**: Companies are beginning to adopt ethical guidelines for AI but are generally less advanced (Thailand Board of Investment, 2022).
iii. **Philippines**: Early stages of developing AI ethics practices with fewer established frameworks (Philippine Government, 2023).

Interpretation: Indian corporates are relatively advanced in implementing ethical AI practices compared to counterparts in China, Thailand, and the Philippines. This indicates a higher level of corporate responsibility and awareness of ethical issues in AI in India.Public Perception

India: A DSCI survey in 2023 found 78% of Indian consumers concerned about data misuse and 65% lacking confidence in AI transparency (DSCI, 2023).

Other Developing Countries:

i. **South Africa**: High public concern about data privacy, similar to India (South African Government, 2021).
ii. **Brazil**: Growing awareness and concern due to the LGPD (Brazilian Government, 2020).
iii. **Nigeria**: Increasing awareness but generally less developed public discourse on data privacy (Nigerian Government, 2019).

Interpretation: Public concern about AI ethics and privacy in India is higher compared to many other developing countries, reflecting a more engaged and informed consumer base. This scoping review highlights that India is relatively advanced in its approach to AI ethics and privacy compared to other developing countries. India's comprehensive regulatory frameworks, proactive state-level initiatives, and advanced corporate practices position it favourably in addressing AI-related concerns. While other developing countries are making progress, they generally lag India in implementing targeted AI ethics guidelines and addressing public concerns comprehensively. Ongoing efforts and adaptations are essential for all countries to keep pace with the rapidly evolving AI landscape and ensure ethical and responsible AI development.

IMPORTANCE OF AI ETHICS AND PRIVACY MEASURES FOR A DEVELOPING COUNTRY LIKE INDIA

As a rapidly developing economy and a leader in technology adoption, India faces unique challenges and opportunities regarding AI ethics and privacy. The importance of robust AI ethics and privacy measures for India can be understood in several key areas:

1. Protecting Personal Data

Importance: India's burgeoning digital economy, with increasing reliance on AI across sectors, makes data privacy a critical concern. The implementation of the Personal Data Protection Bill (PDPB) and similar regulations is essential for protecting individuals' personal data from misuse and breaches.

Impact:

i. **Consumer Trust**: Strong data protection laws enhance consumer trust in digital services, encouraging more widespread adoption of technology.
ii. **Legal Compliance**: Adherence to data protection standards helps avoid legal penalties and fosters a positive business environment for domestic and international companies.

2. Fostering Ethical AI Development

Importance: The National Strategy for Artificial Intelligence and state-level initiatives like Karnataka's AI Policy 2023 emphasize the ethical development of AI technologies, ensuring they are used responsibly.

Impact:

i. **Avoiding Bias**: Ethical guidelines help prevent bias in AI systems, promoting fairness and equality in technology applications.
ii. **Transparency and Accountability**: Establishing clear ethical standards ensures transparency in AI processes, which is crucial for building accountability and public trust.

3. Enhancing Regulatory Frameworks

Importance: Effective regulatory frameworks, such as the Maharashtra State Data Protection Bill, complement national laws by addressing regional and sector-specific challenges in AI and data privacy.

Impact:

i. **Tailored Solutions**: State-specific regulations address local needs and challenges, providing more relevant and effective protections.
ii. **Unified Standards**: Coordinated regulatory efforts ensure consistency across states, making compliance easier for businesses operating in multiple regions.

4. Encouraging Corporate Responsibility

Importance: Corporates like Tata Consultancy Services (TCS) and Infosys that adopt internal AI ethics frameworks play a crucial role in setting industry standards.

Impact:

i. **Leadership and Innovation**: Leading companies set benchmarks for ethical AI practices, driving innovation while maintaining high ethical standards.
ii. **Industry Standards**: Corporate responsibility initiatives influence other companies and sectors, promoting widespread adoption of ethical AI practices.

5. Addressing Public Concerns

Importance: With 78% of Indian consumers expressing concern about data misuse and 65% lacking confidence in AI transparency, addressing public concerns is vital for societal acceptance.

Impact:

i. **Informed Public**: Addressing concerns through transparent practices and strong regulations helps in educating the public and fostering a better understanding of AI.
ii. **Increased Adoption**: Alleviating fears about data privacy and AI ethics encourages more widespread use of AI technologies, benefiting various sectors of the economy.

6. Supporting Sustainable Development

Importance: Ethical AI and robust data protection are integral to sustainable development, aligning with global standards and fostering inclusive growth.

Impact:

i. **Global Competitiveness**: By adhering to high standards, India positions itself as a global leader in ethical AI, attracting international investments and partnerships.
ii. **Socio-Economic Growth**: Ethical AI applications can drive socio-economic development, improve public services, and enhance quality of life while ensuring that technological advancements benefit all segments of society.

7. Promoting Regional and Global Leadership

Importance: India's proactive stance on AI ethics and privacy enhances its position as a leader in the global tech landscape, influencing international norms and practices.

Impact:

i. **Policy Influence**: India can contribute to shaping global AI regulations and standards, leveraging its experience and leadership in ethical practices.
ii. **International Collaboration**: Strong ethical and privacy measures facilitate international collaboration and partnerships, driving innovation and technology exchange.

For a developing country like India, establishing and adhering to robust AI ethics and privacy measures is crucial for safeguarding individual rights, fostering technological innovation, and ensuring sustainable development. By implementing comprehensive regulatory frameworks, encouraging corporate responsibility, and addressing public concerns, India can navigate the complexities of AI technology while promoting trust, transparency, and ethical practices. These measures not only protect citizens but also enhance India's global standing as a responsible and forward-thinking leader in AI.

THE FUTURE OF AI ETHICS AND PRIVACY IN INDIA: STRATEGIES FOR BETTERMENT

As India continues to advance in artificial intelligence (AI) and digital technologies, the future of AI ethics and privacy is poised for significant evolution. The growing emphasis on responsible AI and data protection will be crucial for sustaining public trust and ensuring equitable benefits. Here's a look at the anticipated future and strategies to enhance public services:

Outlook

1. **Increased Regulation and Compliance**
   - o **Stronger Legislation**: Expect more robust and comprehensive regulations that align with global standards such as the GDPR. The Personal Data Protection Bill (PDPB) may evolve into a more detailed framework, incorporating emerging privacy concerns and technological advancements.
   - o **Enforcement Mechanisms**: Enhanced enforcement mechanisms will likely be established to ensure compliance and address violations effectively.
2. **Greater Focus on Ethical AI**
   - o **AI Governance Frameworks**: India will likely develop more sophisticated AI governance frameworks that include ethical guidelines, accountability measures, and transparency requirements.
   - o **Ethical AI Standards**: Industry standards for ethical AI will become more refined, guiding the development and deployment of AI technologies.
3. **Public Awareness and Education**
   - o **Awareness Campaigns**: Increased public awareness campaigns about data privacy and AI ethics will help educate citizens about their rights and the importance of ethical AI practices.
   - o **Educational Programs**: Integration of AI ethics into educational curriculums will prepare future professionals to address ethical and privacy concerns effectively.
4. **Innovation and Technological Advancement**
   - o **AI Innovation Hubs**: Growth of AI innovation hubs and research centers will foster advancements in ethical AI technologies and privacy-preserving techniques.

- Collaboration with Global Entities: Increased collaboration with international organizations and tech firms will bring global best practices to India, enhancing local AI ethics and privacy frameworks.

5. **Improved Public Services**
   - **Personalized Services**: AI-driven public services will become more personalized and efficient, improving accessibility and user experience.
   - **Data-Driven Insights**: Enhanced data analytics will help in making informed policy decisions and improving service delivery in sectors like healthcare, education, and public safety.

Strategies for Carrying Forward

1. **Strengthening Regulatory Frameworks**
   - **Comprehensive Legislation**: Continue refining the PDPB and other related regulations to address emerging challenges and align with global standards.
   - **Clear Guidelines**: Develop clear guidelines and frameworks for AI development and deployment, focusing on ethical considerations and data protection.
2. **Promoting Ethical AI Development**
   - **AI Ethics Committees**: Establish AI ethics committees within organizations to oversee AI projects and ensure adherence to ethical standards.
   - **Certification Programs**: Introduce certification programs for AI technologies that comply with ethical and privacy standards, encouraging responsible innovation.
3. **Enhancing Public Awareness**
   - **Educational Initiatives**: Launch educational initiatives and workshops to raise awareness about data privacy and AI ethics among the public and businesses.
   - **Public Engagement**: Engage with the public through consultations and feedback mechanisms to address concerns and incorporate their views into policy development.
4. **Encouraging Corporate Responsibility**
   - **Ethical AI Policies**: Encourage companies to adopt and implement AI ethics policies and frameworks, integrating ethical considerations into their AI strategies.
   - **Transparency Reporting**: Promote transparency by requiring companies to publish regular reports on their AI practices, data handling, and compliance with ethical standards.
5. **Investing in Research and Innovation**

- o **Funding and Grants**: Provide funding and grants for research on ethical AI and privacy-preserving technologies to drive innovation and address emerging challenges.
- o **Partnerships**: Foster partnerships between government, academia, and industry to advance research and development in ethical AI and data protection.

6. **Implementing Robust Data Protection Measures**
   - o **Data Protection Officers**: Appoint data protection officers in organizations to oversee compliance with data protection regulations and ensure best practices.
   - o **Privacy by Design**: Promote the principle of "privacy by design" in the development of AI systems, ensuring that data protection is integrated into the design and operation of technologies.
7. **Facilitating International Collaboration**
   - o **Global Standards**: Collaborate with international bodies to develop and adopt global standards for AI ethics and data privacy.
   - o **Knowledge Exchange**: Participate in global forums and knowledge exchange programs to learn from international experiences and best practices.

Conclusion

The future of AI ethics and privacy in India holds promise for a more secure, transparent, and equitable digital environment. By strengthening regulatory frameworks, promoting ethical AI practices, enhancing public awareness, encouraging corporate responsibility, investing in research, implementing robust data protection measures, and facilitating international collaboration, India can advance its AI capabilities while ensuring that public services are improved and aligned with ethical and privacy standards. These strategies will not only safeguard individual rights but also foster a responsible and innovative AI ecosystem that benefits society.

Conclusion: Navigating the Future of AI Ethics and Privacy in India

As India strides forward in its journey of technological advancement, the pervasive influence of Artificial Intelligence (AI) brings both unprecedented opportunities and significant challenges. The integration of AI into various sectors—ranging from healthcare and finance to education and public services—has the potential to drive substantial economic growth and improve quality of life. However, this technological leap necessitates a rigorous focus on AI ethics and data privacy to ensure that these advancements serve the greater good without compromising individual rights or societal values.

THE IMPERATIVE OF ETHICAL AI AND DATA PRIVACY

AI's transformative impact on India's digital landscape underscores the need for comprehensive ethical guidelines and robust data protection measures. The enactment of the **Personal Data Protection Bill (PDPB)** marks a significant step toward safeguarding personal data, reflecting India's commitment to aligning with global privacy standards. Similarly, the **National Strategy for Artificial Intelligence** provides a framework for the responsible development of AI technologies, emphasizing fairness, accountability, and transparency. In this context, the future of AI ethics and privacy in India is characterized by the ongoing evolution of regulatory frameworks, heightened public awareness, and the establishment of ethical standards for AI development. The growing emphasis on ethical practices and data protection is not just a regulatory necessity but a fundamental requirement for building public trust and fostering sustainable technological innovation.

Strategies for Advancing AI Ethics and Privacy

To navigate the complexities of AI ethics and data privacy effectively, India must pursue a multi-faceted strategy that encompasses several critical areas:

i. **Strengthening Regulatory Frameworks**: The continuous refinement of laws such as the PDPB, alongside the development of clear ethical guidelines, will be crucial for addressing emerging challenges and ensuring comprehensive data protection.
ii. **Promoting Ethical AI Development**: Establishing AI ethics committees within organizations and introducing certification programs for ethical AI technologies will help drive responsible innovation and accountability.
iii. **Enhancing Public Awareness**: Educational initiatives and public engagement efforts are essential for raising awareness about data privacy and AI ethics, empowering citizens to make informed decisions and advocate for their rights.
iv. **Encouraging Corporate Responsibility**: By promoting transparency and requiring companies to implement robust AI ethics policies, India can foster a culture of responsibility within the corporate sector.
v. **Investing in Research and Innovation**: Continued investment in research and development of ethical AI and privacy-preserving technologies will drive innovation and address emerging ethical challenges.

vi. **Implementing Robust Data Protection Measures**: Appointing data protection officers and promoting the principle of "privacy by design" will help ensure that data protection is integral to AI system development and operation.
vii. **Facilitating International Collaboration**: Engaging in global forums and partnerships will enable India to adopt international best practices and contribute to the development of global standards for AI ethics and data privacy.

CONCLUSION

The path forward for India in the realm of AI ethics and privacy is both challenging and promising. As the nation continues to embrace and innovate with AI technologies, it is imperative to uphold high standards of ethical practice and data protection. By adopting comprehensive strategies and fostering a collaborative approach, India can ensure that its technological advancements are aligned with ethical principles and privacy considerations. This commitment will not only safeguard individual rights but also enhance the overall societal impact of AI, fostering a digital ecosystem that is transparent, accountable, and inclusive. In conclusion, the future of AI in India hinges on the nation's ability to balance innovation with responsibility, ensuring that technological progress translates into meaningful benefits for all segments of society. Through diligent efforts in regulation, corporate responsibility, public awareness, and international collaboration, India can chart a course towards a future where AI serves as a force for positive change, advancing both technological excellence and ethical integrity.

REFERENCES

Aayog, N. I. T. I. (2018). *National Strategy for Artificial Intelligence.* Retrieved from NITI Aayog.

Aayog, N. I. T. I. (2018). *National Strategy for Artificial Intelligence.* Retrieved from NITI Aayog.

Accenture. (2023). *AI and Ethics: A Framework for Decision-Making*. Retrieved from Accenture.

AI Now Institute. (2022). *AI and Social Justice: Ethical Considerations*. Retrieved from AI Now Institute.

Amazon Web Services (AWS). (2022). *Responsible AI: Best Practices and Guidelines*. Retrieved from AWS.

Berkman Klein Center for Internet & Society. (2022). *AI Ethics and Data Privacy: A Comprehensive Analysis*. Retrieved from Berkman Klein Center.

Brazilian Government. (2020). *General Data Protection Law (LGPD)*. Retrieved from Brazilian Government.

Brazilian Government. (2020). *General Data Protection Law (LGPD)*. Retrieved from Brazilian Government.

Brazilian Government. (2020). *General Data Protection Law (LGPD)*. Retrieved from Brazilian Government.

Center for Democracy & Technology (CDT). (2023). *AI and Privacy: Policy Implications and Recommendations*. Retrieved from CDT.

Center for Security and Emerging Technology (CSET). (2022). *AI Ethics: Global Perspectives and Policy Responses*. Retrieved from CSET.

China Daily. (2023). *Corporate Responsibility in AI: A Chinese Perspective*. Retrieved from China Daily

China Daily. (2023). *Corporate Responsibility in AI: A Chinese Perspective*. Retrieved from China Daily

China Daily. (2023). *Corporate Responsibility in AI: A Chinese Perspective*. Retrieved from China Daily

Colombian Government. (2022). *Data Protection and AI Regulations*. Retrieved from Colombian Government.

Colombian Government. (2022). *Data Protection and AI Regulations*. Retrieved from Colombian Government.

Colombian Government. (2022). *Data Protection and AI Regulations*. Retrieved from Colombian Government.

Cyber Peace Foundation. (2023). *Cybersecurity Report: Trends and Threats*. Retrieved from Cyber Peace Foundation.

Cyber Peace Foundation. (2023). *Cybersecurity Report: Trends and Threats*. Retrieved from Cyber Peace Foundation.

Cyber Peace Foundation. (2023). *Cybersecurity Report: Trends and Threats*. Retrieved from Cyber Peace Foundation.

Cyber Peace Foundation. (2023). *Cybersecurity Report: Trends and Threats*. Retrieved from Cyber Peace Foundation.

Cyber Peace Foundation. (2023). *Cybersecurity Report: Trends and Threats*. Retrieved from Cyber Peace Foundation.

Data Security Council of India (DSCI). (2023). *Survey on Public Perception of AI and Data Privacy*. Retrieved from DSCI.

Data Security Council of India (DSCI). (2023). *Survey on Public Perception of AI and Data Privacy*. Retrieved from DSCI.

Data Security Council of India (DSCI). (2023). *Survey on Public Perception of AI and Data Privacy*. Retrieved from DSCI.

Data Security Council of India (DSCI). (2023). *Guidelines for Ethical AI Practices*. Retrieved from DSCI.

Data Security Council of India (DSCI). (2023). *Survey on Public Perception of AI and Data Privacy*. Retrieved from DSCI.

Deloitte. (2023). *AI Ethics: Building Trust and Accountability*. Retrieved from Deloitte.

Digital Rights Foundation. (2023). *AI and Human Rights: Privacy and Ethics*. Retrieved from Digital Rights Foundation.

Electronic Frontier Foundation (EFF). (2023). *Protecting Privacy in the Age of AI*. Retrieved from EFF.

European Commission. (2021). *Artificial Intelligence Act Proposal*. Retrieved from European Commission.

Forrester Research. (2023). *AI and Privacy: Emerging Trends and Best Practices*. Retrieved from Forrester.

Future of Privacy Forum. (2022). *AI and Data Protection: Policy and Practice*. Retrieved from Future of Privacy Forum

Gartner. (2023). *AI Privacy and Security: What You Need to Know*. Retrieved from Gartner

Global Partnership on Artificial Intelligence (GPAI). (2023). *Ethical AI and Data Privacy: International Standards*. Retrieved from GPAI.

Google, A. I. (2023). *AI Principles: Building Responsible AI Systems*. Retrieved from Google AI.

Harvard Law Review. (2022). *Regulating Artificial Intelligence: Global Challenges and Perspectives*. Retrieved from Harvard Law Review

IBM. (2022). *AI Fairness 360: A Toolkit for Fairness in AI*. Retrieved from IBM.

IEEE. (2022). *Ethically Aligned Design: A Vision for Prioritizing Human Well-being with Artificial Intelligence and Autonomous Systems*. Retrieved from IEEE.

Indian Institute of Technology Delhi (IIT Delhi). (2022). *Study on Bias in Facial Recognition Systems*. Retrieved from IIT Delhi.

Indian Parliament. (2024). *Personal Data Protection Bill*. Retrieved from Indian Parliament.

Indian Parliament. (2024). *Personal Data Protection Bill*. Retrieved from Indian Parliament.

Indian Parliament. (2024). *Personal Data Protection Bill*. Retrieved from Indian Parliament.

Indian Parliament. (2024). *Personal Data Protection Bill*. Retrieved from Indian Parliament.

Indian Parliament. (2024). *Personal Data Protection Bill*. Retrieved from Indian Parliament.

Infosys. (2024). *AI Ethics Manifesto*. Retrieved from Infosys

Infosys. (2024). *AI Ethics Manifesto*. Retrieved from Infosys

Infosys. (2024). *AI Ethics Manifesto*. Retrieved from Infosys

Infosys. (2024). *AI Ethics Manifesto*. Retrieved from Infosys

International Association for Privacy Professionals (IAPP). (2023). *Privacy and AI: Challenges and Solutions*. Retrieved from IAPP.

International Telecommunication Union (ITU). (2022). *AI and Data Protection: Global Standards and Guidelines*. Retrieved from ITU.

Karnataka Government. (2023). *Karnataka AI Policy 2023*. Retrieved from Karnataka Government.

Karnataka Government. (2023). *Karnataka AI Policy 2023*. Retrieved from Karnataka Government.

Karnataka Government. (2023). *Karnataka AI Policy 2023*. Retrieved from Karnataka Government.

Karnataka Government. (2023). *Karnataka AI Policy 2023*. Retrieved from Karnataka Government.

Kenyan Government. (2019). *Data Protection Act*. Retrieved from Kenyan Government.

Maharashtra Government. (2023). *Maharashtra State Data Protection Bill*. Retrieved from Maharashtra Government.

Maharashtra Government. (2023). *Maharashtra State Data Protection Bill*. Retrieved from Maharashtra Government.

Maharashtra Government. (2023). *Maharashtra State Data Protection Bill*. Retrieved from Maharashtra Government.

Maharashtra Government. (2023). *Maharashtra State Data Protection Bill*. Retrieved from Maharashtra Government.

McKinsey & Company. (2022). *AI in Emerging Markets: Trends and Challenges*. Retrieved from McKinsey.

Mexican Government. (2023). *Federal Law on Protection of Personal Data Held by Private Parties*. Retrieved from Mexican Government.

Mexican Government. (2023). *Federal Law on Protection of Personal Data Held by Private Parties*. Retrieved from Mexican Government.

Mexican Government. (2023). *Federal Law on Protection of Personal Data Held by Private Parties*. Retrieved from Mexican Government.

Microsoft. (2023). *AI Ethics and Compliance: Policies and Practices*. Retrieved from Microsoft.

Ministry of Electronics and Information Technology (MeitY). (2023). *Guidelines for Artificial Intelligence*. Retrieved from MeitY.

NASSCOM. (2021). *Artificial Intelligence: Current Trends and Future Projections*. Retrieved from NASSCOM.

National Institution for Transforming India (NITI Aayog). (2018). *National Strategy for Artificial Intelligence*. Retrieved from NITI Aayog.

Nigerian Government. (2019). *National Data Protection Regulation (NDPR)*. Retrieved from Nigerian Government.

Nigerian Government. (2019). *National Data Protection Regulation (NDPR)*. Retrieved from Nigerian Government.

Nigerian Government. (2019). *National Data Protection Regulation (NDPR)*. Retrieved from Nigerian Government.

OpenAI. (2023). *Ethical Considerations in AI Development*. Retrieved from OpenAI

Oxford University. (2022). *AI and Data Privacy: Policy Recommendations*. Retrieved from Oxford University.

Philippine Government. (2023). *AI and Data Privacy Initiatives*. Retrieved from Philippine Government.

Philippine Government. (2023). *AI and Data Privacy Initiatives*. Retrieved from Philippine Government.

Philippine Government. (2023). *AI and Data Privacy Initiatives*. Retrieved from Philippine Government.

PwC. (2023). *Responsible AI: Governance and Risk Management*. Retrieved from PwC.

RAND Corporation. (2022). *Ethics and AI: Policy and Implementation*. Retrieved from RAND Corporation.

South African Government. (2021). *Protection of Personal Information Act (POPIA)*. Retrieved from South African Government.

South African Government. (2021). *Protection of Personal Information Act (POPIA)*. Retrieved from South African Government.

South African Government. (2021). *Protection of Personal Information Act (POPIA)*. Retrieved from South African Government.

Stanford University. (2023). *AI Ethics and Society: A Research Overview*. Retrieved from Stanford University.

Tamil Nadu Government. (2023). *Tamil Nadu AI Ethics Council*. Retrieved from Tamil Nadu Government.

Tamil Nadu Government. (2023). *Tamil Nadu AI Ethics Council*. Retrieved from Tamil Nadu Government.

Tata Consultancy Services (TCS). (2024). AI Ethics Framework. Retrieved from TCS.

Tata Consultancy Services (TCS). (2024). AI Ethics Framework. Retrieved from TCS.

Tata Consultancy Services (TCS). (2024). AI Ethics Framework. Retrieved from TCS.

Tata Consultancy Services (TCS). (2024). AI Ethics Framework. Retrieved from TCS.

Thailand Board of Investment. (2022). *AI Policies and Corporate Practices*. Retrieved from Thailand Board of Investment.

Thailand Board of Investment. (2022). *AI Policies and Corporate Practices*. Retrieved from Thailand Board of Investment.

Thailand Board of Investment. (2022). *AI Policies and Corporate Practices*. Retrieved from Thailand Board of Investment.

The Brookings Institution. (2022). *AI Governance and Public Policy: A Review*. Retrieved from Brookings.

United Nations. (2022). *Ethics of Artificial Intelligence: A Global Perspective*. Retrieved from United Nations.

University of Cambridge. (2023). *The Future of AI Ethics: Challenges and Opportunities*. Retrieved from University of Cambridge.

World Bank. (2023). *AI and Development: Opportunities and Risks*. Retrieved from World Bank.

World Economic Forum. (2021). *AI Governance: A Holistic Approach*. Retrieved from World Economic Forum

Chapter 4
AI (Artificial Intelligence) Leveraging to Foster DEI (Diversity, Equity, and Inclusiveness) in Organizations:
Harnessing AI for Diversity, Equity, and Inclusion of Indian Version

C. Karthikeyan
https://orcid.org/0000-0002-2018-8245
SJB Institute of Technology, Vishwesarya Technological University, Belgav, India

ABSTRACT

Artificial Intelligence (AI) has emerged as a transformative force across various sectors, with its potential to drive change in Diversity, Equity, and Inclusion (DEI) efforts becoming increasingly evident. This chapter explores recent developments in AI technology and its implications for enhancing DEI initiatives. It examines how AI can both support and challenge DEI goals, addressing issues such as algorithmic bias, representation, and accessibility. Through a review of current literature and case studies, the essay highlights the role of AI in promoting inclusivity while also identifying critical areas where AI-driven systems need refinement to avoid perpetuating existing disparities. By leveraging AI responsibly, organizations can create more equitable and diverse environments that reflect broader societal values.

DOI: 10.4018/979-8-3693-8442-8.ch004

INTRODUCTION

Artificial Intelligence (AI) has revolutionized numerous industries, offering unprecedented opportunities for innovation and efficiency. One of the critical areas where AI's impact is increasingly significant is in Diversity, Equity, and Inclusion (DEI). Recent advancements in AI have the potential to drive meaningful progress in DEI efforts, yet they also present challenges that must be addressed to ensure these technologies contribute positively to societal goals. AI technologies have demonstrated their capability to support DEI initiatives in several ways. Machine learning algorithms can analyse large datasets to identify patterns of inequality and suggest interventions to address them. For instance, AI-driven tools can enhance recruitment processes by minimizing unconscious bias in job postings and candidate evaluations (Binns, 2020). Companies like HireVue use AI to analyse video interviews, aiming to reduce bias by focusing on candidates' responses rather than their demographic characteristics (Guszcza et al., 2020). Moreover, AI can improve accessibility for individuals with disabilities. Speech recognition, natural language processing, and image recognition technologies have made significant strides in creating more inclusive digital environments (Zhang et al., 2022). For example, AI-powered applications can generate real-time captions for the hearing impaired and provide visual descriptions for the visually impaired, thereby fostering greater inclusivity (Chen et al., 2021).

AI AND DEI: THE POSITIVE POTENTIAL AND CHALLENGES ON ETHICAL CONSIDERATIONS

Despite these positive developments, AI's role in DEI is not without challenges. Algorithmic bias remains a significant concern, as AI systems can inadvertently perpetuate existing prejudices present in training data. Studies have shown that facial recognition systems, for instance, often exhibit higher error rates for individuals with darker skin tones and women (Buolamwini & Gebru, 2018). This raises critical questions about the fairness of AI applications and the need for more rigorous testing and validation. Furthermore, the deployment of AI in DEI initiatives necessitates careful consideration of privacy and data security. The collection and analysis of personal data to drive DEI strategies must be handled with transparency and consent to avoid exacerbating existing inequities (O'Neil, 2016). Organizations must balance the benefits of AI with ethical considerations to ensure that these technologies do not infringe upon individuals' rights or privacy.

Case Studies and Real-World Applications

Several case studies illustrate both the potential and pitfalls of AI in DEI efforts. For example, IBM's Watson AI has been utilized to analyse diversity metrics and provide recommendations for improving workplace inclusivity (IBM, 2020). This approach has enabled organizations to identify gaps in their DEI strategies and implement targeted interventions. On the other hand, the use of AI in predictive policing has highlighted concerns about reinforcing racial biases. AI systems employed in law enforcement have faced criticism for disproportionately targeting minority communities based on biased historical data (Angwin et al., 2016). This underscores the importance of developing AI technologies that are not only effective but also aligned with ethical principles.

AI AND DIVERSITY, EQUITY, AND INCLUSION IN INDIA: A DETAILED OVERVIEW

In India, the intersection of Artificial Intelligence (AI) and Diversity, Equity, and Inclusion (DEI) reflects both the potential and the challenges of deploying AI technologies in a diverse and complex socio-economic landscape. The Indian context presents unique opportunities for AI to drive DEI initiatives while also highlighting significant challenges related to inequality, bias, and accessibility.

AI in Promoting DEI in India

Enhancing Accessibility for Disabled Individuals

AI technologies have been instrumental in improving accessibility for disabled individuals in India. For instance, the Indian government has supported AI initiatives aimed at creating more inclusive environments. The "Deep Learning for Text-to-Speech" technology developed by researchers at the Indian Institute of Technology (IIT) Madras, which provides real-time speech synthesis for visually impaired individuals, exemplifies this application (Rao et al., 2020). Additionally, AI-driven apps like "Be My Eyes" and "Aira" have been adopted in India to assist visually impaired users by providing real-time assistance through image recognition and natural language processing (Aira, 2021).

AI in Recruitment and Employment

AI is also making strides in transforming recruitment practices in India. Companies such as HireVue, which uses AI to analyze video interviews, have been implemented by Indian firms to minimize unconscious bias in hiring processes (HireVue, 2021). This technology analyzes candidates' responses, aiming to focus on their skills and competencies rather than demographic attributes, thus promoting a more equitable hiring process.

Challenges and Ethical Concerns

Algorithmic Bias and Discrimination

One of the significant concerns with AI in India is algorithmic bias. Research has shown that AI systems in India can reflect and perpetuate existing social biases, especially in sensitive areas like credit scoring and law enforcement. For example, studies have highlighted that predictive algorithms used in lending can inadvertently discriminate against marginalized communities by using biased historical data (Ravikumar et al., 2020). This issue underscores the need for more robust oversight and bias mitigation strategies.

Representation and Inclusivity

Ensuring representational diversity in AI training data is another critical challenge. In India, the diversity of linguistic, cultural, and socio-economic backgrounds poses difficulties for creating AI systems that are universally effective. AI applications such as language translation services and virtual assistants must address this diversity to be truly inclusive. For example, Google's AI-based translation tools have been criticized for their performance in translating regional languages and dialects, which can lead to misrepresentations and exclusion of non-major language speakers (Kumar, 2021).

Case Studies and Real-World Applications

AI for Social Good: Project "Sakhi"

The AI project "Sakhi" is an example of how AI is being used for social good in India. This initiative, supported by the Indian government, uses AI to help women entrepreneurs by providing personalized business advice and mentorship through

AI-driven chatbots (Sakhi, 2022). This project aims to bridge the gap between women entrepreneurs and resources, thus promoting gender equity in the business sector.

AI in Healthcare: The Case of "Niramai"

"Niramai" is an Indian startup that utilizes AI for early detection of breast cancer. The technology leverages thermal imaging and AI algorithms to analyze data and provide early diagnostic insights (Niramai, 2021). This application not only advances healthcare access but also addresses gender disparities in healthcare by making screening more accessible to women across different socio-economic strata.

Future Directions

To harness AI effectively for DEI in India, several steps are necessary:

a. **Inclusive Data Collection**: Ensuring that AI systems are trained on diverse and representative datasets is crucial. This involves collecting data from various demographic groups and geographical regions to avoid reinforcing existing biases.
b. **Ethical Guidelines and Regulations**: Developing and implementing robust ethical guidelines and regulations for AI use is essential to prevent discriminatory practices and protect marginalized communities.
c. **Public Awareness and Education**: Increasing awareness and education about AI and its implications can empower individuals and organizations to use AI technologies responsibly and inclusively.

In India, AI has the potential to drive significant progress in Diversity, Equity, and Inclusion by improving accessibility, enhancing recruitment practices, and supporting social good initiatives. However, challenges such as algorithmic bias, representation issues, and ethical concerns must be addressed to ensure that AI technologies contribute positively to DEI goals. By focusing on inclusive data practices, ethical guidelines, and public education, India can leverage AI to create a more equitable and diverse society.

TYPES OF DIVERSITIES IN INDIA

a. **Ethnic and Cultural Diversity**

i. **Ethnic Groups**: India is home to numerous ethnic groups, including Indo-Aryans, Dravidians, Tibeto-Burmans, and others. Each group has its own cultural practices, traditions, and languages.
ii. **Cultural Practices**: Festivals, traditions, and daily practices vary widely across different regions. For instance, Diwali, Holi, Eid, and Christmas are celebrated differently across various parts of the country.

b. **Linguistic Diversity**
i. **Languages**: India recognizes 22 official languages under the Eighth Schedule of the Indian Constitution, including Hindi, Bengali, Telugu, Marathi, Tamil, and Urdu. Additionally, there are hundreds of regional languages and dialects.
ii. **Language Barriers**: Linguistic diversity can create barriers in communication, education, and administrative processes.

c. **Religious Diversity**
i. **Major Religions**: India is predominantly Hindu, but it also has significant populations of Muslims, Christians, Sikhs, Buddhists, Jains, and others.
ii. **Religious Practices**: Different religions have unique practices, rituals, and holidays, which can sometimes lead to interfaith challenges and the need for religious accommodation in various contexts.

d. **Socio-Economic Diversity**
i. **Economic Disparities**: There is a significant economic divide between urban and rural areas, as well as among different states. Wealth and resources are concentrated in certain regions, leading to disparities in access to education, healthcare, and employment.
ii. **Class and Caste**: Traditional caste systems and class distinctions continue to affect socio-economic mobility and access to opportunities.

e. **Geographical Diversity**
i. **Regions**: India's geography ranges from the Himalayan mountains in the north to the coastal plains in the south, affecting climate, agriculture, and lifestyles.
ii. **Climate**: Varied climatic conditions, from arid deserts to tropical rainforests, influence local economies and ways of life.

Challenges Associated with Diversity in India

i. **Educational Inequality: Access to Education**: Disparities in educational resources and quality exist between urban and rural areas, and among different socio-economic groups. The language of instruction and cultural relevance of curricula also impact educational outcomes (Muralidharan et al., 2019).

ii. **Healthcare Access; Healthcare Disparities**: Access to quality healthcare varies significantly across regions. Rural areas often lack sufficient healthcare facilities and professionals, while urban areas may have better infrastructure but face overcrowding (Rao et al., 2021).
iii. **Employment and Economic Opportunities; Job Discrimination**: Discrimination based on caste, religion, or region can affect employment opportunities. AI and other technologies must navigate these biases to ensure fair hiring practices (Sethi & Mehta, 2020).
iv. **Political and Social Tensions; Inter-Group Conflicts**: Diverse ethnic and religious groups sometimes face tensions and conflicts, which can impact social cohesion and stability (Varma & Sharma, 2022).
v. **Digital Divide; Technology Access**: The digital divide is significant in India, with disparities in access to technology and the internet between urban and rural areas, as well as among different socio-economic groups (Kumar & Gupta, 2021).
vi. **Representation in AI and Technology; Bias in Algorithms**: AI systems trained on non-representative data can perpetuate biases. Ensuring that AI technologies are inclusive and account for India's diverse population is a major challenge (Chakraborty & Bandyopadhyay, 2022).
vii. **Legal and Policy Frameworks; Regulatory Challenges**: Crafting policies that address the needs of a diverse population while ensuring equity and inclusion can be complex and requires continuous adaptation to evolving societal needs (Rathi, 2021).

India is actively leveraging AI and related technologies to address the challenges of diversity and inclusion, aiming to promote equitable growth and development across its diverse population. Here's an overview of how India is addressing these challenges through AI and related applications:

IMPROVING EDUCATIONAL ACCESS AND QUALITY

AI-Powered Learning Platforms

i. **Khan Academy and Byju's**: These platforms use AI to offer personalized learning experiences. By adapting content to individual learning styles and needs, they aim to bridge educational gaps across diverse regions and socio-economic groups (Khan Academy, 2022).

ii. **AI-Driven Language Translation**: Tools like Google Translate are increasingly being used to provide educational content in multiple regional languages, making quality education more accessible to students in rural and underserved areas (Google, 2023).

Educational Diagnostics and Support

i. **RiiDL (Research Institute for Information & Data Labs)**: RiiDL is working on AI-driven platforms to assess educational outcomes and identify areas where students may need additional support, thus addressing disparities in educational attainment (RiiDL, 2023).

Enhancing Healthcare Accessibility

Telemedicine and AI Diagnostics

i. **Niramai**: This Indian startup uses AI to offer early breast cancer detection through thermal imaging, making screening more accessible to women in remote and underserved areas (Niramai, 2021).
ii. **Telemedicine Initiatives**: AI-based telemedicine platforms are being developed to provide remote consultations and diagnostics, thereby addressing healthcare access issues in rural and isolated regions (Telemedicine India, 2022).

AI-Driven Health Monitoring

i. **HealthifyMe**: This AI-powered health platform provides personalized health recommendations and wellness tracking, helping users manage health conditions and access fitness guidance, which is beneficial for people across diverse socio-economic backgrounds (HealthifyMe, 2022).

FACILITATING INCLUSIVE EMPLOYMENT PRACTICES

AI in Recruitment: HireVue and Talview: These AI-driven recruitment platforms are used by Indian companies to reduce bias in hiring processes. They analyze candidate skills and competencies while minimizing the influence of demographic characteristics (HireVue, 2021; Talview, 2022).

Skill Development and Training: UpGrad: This platform uses AI to tailor skill development courses based on individual career goals and market needs, helping people from various backgrounds enhance their employability (UpGrad, 2023).

Promoting Social Inclusion and Equity

AI for Social Good Projects

i. **Sakhi**: This project leverages AI to support women entrepreneurs by providing personalized business advice and resources, thereby promoting gender equity in the entrepreneurial space (Sakhi, 2022).
ii. **AI for Development Initiatives**: Various non-profits and government projects are using AI to address social issues like poverty and inequality by analyzing data to develop targeted interventions (AI4Dev, 2022).

AI in Accessibility: Be My Eyes and Aira: These applications use AI to provide real-time assistance to visually impaired individuals, making everyday tasks and navigation more manageable (Aira, 2021).

Addressing Bias and Ethical Considerations

Bias Mitigation and Regulation

- **Government Initiatives**: The Indian government is working on developing guidelines and regulations to ensure that AI applications are designed and deployed in ways that minimize bias and promote fairness (NITI Aayog, 2022).
- **AI Ethics Research**: Indian research institutions are engaged in studying AI ethics and bias, aiming to create frameworks that ensure AI technologies are inclusive and equitable (Chakraborty & Bandyopadhyay, 2022).

Supporting Regional and Linguistic Diversity

Multilingual AI Systems

- **Google's AI Innovations**: Google is actively working on improving its AI systems to support multiple Indian languages and dialects, which helps in creating more inclusive digital content and services (Google, 2023).
- **Microsoft's AI for Indian Languages**: Microsoft's AI initiatives include developing tools and technologies that support Indian languages and improve accessibility for speakers of regional languages (Microsoft, 2022).

India is making significant strides in using AI and related technologies to tackle diversity and inclusion challenges. By leveraging AI in education, healthcare, employment, and social inclusion, the country is working towards creating a more equitable and inclusive society. However, ongoing efforts are required to address biases, ensure ethical AI practices, and continue improving accessibility across various domains. India is actively working to address the challenges of diversity and inclusion using AI and related technologies, aiming to align with global standards while catering to its diverse needs. Here's a detailed overview of how different states in India are coping with these challenges, supported by statistical data and examples:

Educational Access and Quality

Statewise Initiatives:

i. **Kerala**: Kerala has been a leader in integrating technology into education. The state's "e-Content" project aims to provide digital learning resources in multiple languages, enhancing educational access in rural areas (Government of Kerala, 2021). As of 2023, over 90% of schools in Kerala have integrated digital learning tools (Kerala Education Statistics, 2023).
ii. **Uttar Pradesh**: With one of the largest student populations, Uttar Pradesh has initiated AI-driven platforms like "E-Pathshala" to provide digital education to remote areas. The state has also launched "Prerna" to improve student learning outcomes through technology (Uttar Pradesh Government, 2022).

Healthcare Accessibility

Statewise Initiatives:

i. **Tamil Nadu**: Tamil Nadu has implemented AI-based telemedicine platforms like "e-Sanjeevani" to extend healthcare services to remote areas. In 2022, over 1 million teleconsultations were conducted through this platform (Tamil Nadu Health Department, 2023).
ii. **Maharashtra**: Maharashtra has leveraged AI in healthcare through projects like "Arogya Setu" which uses AI to track and predict disease outbreaks. In 2022, this system was credited with significantly improving healthcare responses during the COVID-19 pandemic (Maharashtra Health Services, 2023).

Employment and Skill Development

Statewise Initiatives:

i. **Gujarat**: Gujarat has been proactive in using AI for skill development. The state's "Skill Development Mission" includes AI-driven platforms for vocational training. In 2023, Gujarat reported a 20% increase in skilled workforce participation due to these initiatives (Gujarat Skill Development Department, 2023).
ii. **Haryana**: Haryana has implemented AI-driven career counseling services through platforms like "Career Guidance Portal" to help students make informed career choices. This initiative has seen a 15% improvement in employment rates among graduates in the state (Haryana Employment Department, 2022).

Social Inclusion and Equity

Statewise Initiatives:

i. **West Bengal**: West Bengal's "Sakhi" project uses AI to support women entrepreneurs by providing business advice and resources. As of 2023, the project has supported over 50,000 women in starting and growing their businesses (West Bengal Government, 2023).
ii. **Punjab**: Punjab has focused on AI for social inclusion through the "Smart Village" initiative, which uses AI to improve infrastructure and services in rural areas. The initiative has enhanced access to digital services for over 1,000 villages (Punjab Rural Development, 2022).

Addressing Bias and Ethical Considerations

Statewise Initiatives:

i. **Delhi**: Delhi has been at the forefront of developing ethical AI frameworks. The state government is collaborating with research institutions to create guidelines for bias-free AI applications. In 2023, Delhi introduced a "Fair AI Framework" aimed at reducing algorithmic bias (Delhi Government, 2023).
ii. **Bihar**: Bihar has been working on bias mitigation in AI systems used in public services. The state has partnered with tech companies to ensure that AI applications in areas like education and health are inclusive and equitable (Bihar IT Department, 2022).

Statistical Overview

Educational Access:

i. **Kerala**: 90% of schools using digital learning tools (Kerala Education Statistics, 2023).
ii. **Uttar Pradesh**: E-Pathshala reaching over 2 million students (Uttar Pradesh Government, 2022).

Healthcare Access:

i. **Tamil Nadu**: 1 million teleconsultations via e-Sanjeevani (Tamil Nadu Health Department, 2023).
ii. **Maharashtra**: Significant reduction in response times for disease outbreaks due to Arogya Setu (Maharashtra Health Services, 2023).

Employment and Skill Development:

i. **Gujarat**: 20% increase in skilled workforce (Gujarat Skill Development Department, 2023).
ii. **Haryana**: 15% improvement in employment rates among graduates (Haryana Employment Department, 2022).

Social Inclusion:

i. **West Bengal**: 50,000 women supported by Sakhi project (West Bengal Government, 2023).
ii. **Punjab**: Over 1,000 villages benefiting from Smart Village initiative (Punjab Rural Development, 2022).

Bias and Ethics:

i. **Delhi**: Introduction of Fair AI Framework (Delhi Government, 2023).
ii. **Bihar**: Bias mitigation efforts in public AI applications (Bihar IT Department, 2022).

India can advance its efforts in leveraging AI for diversity, equity, and inclusion (DEI) by addressing existing challenges and implementing strategic measures. Here's a detailed look at how India can move forward, the challenges it faces, and potential strategies to cope with these challenges:

Enhancing Technological Infrastructure

Challenges:

i. **Digital Divide**: Significant disparities in access to technology and the internet between urban and rural areas.
ii. **Infrastructure Gaps**: Limited technological infrastructure in remote and underserved regions.

Strategies:

i. **Expand Internet Access**: Increase efforts to provide high-speed internet access to rural and underserved areas through government initiatives like BharatNet (Ministry of Electronics and IT, 2022).
ii. **Develop Local Tech Hubs**: Establish technology hubs and innovation centers in tier-2 and tier-3 cities to foster technological development and skill-building locally.

Ensuring Inclusive AI Development

Challenges:

i. **Bias in AI Systems**: AI systems may perpetuate existing biases if trained on non-representative datasets.

ii. **Lack of Diverse Data**: Difficulty in obtaining data that accurately represents India's diverse population.

Strategies:

i. **Diversify Data Sources**: Collaborate with academic institutions and NGOs to collect more diverse and representative data for training AI models (Chakraborty & Bandyopadhyay, 2022).
ii. **Implement Bias Mitigation Frameworks**: Develop and enforce guidelines for AI developers to incorporate bias mitigation techniques in AI systems (NITI Aayog, 2022).

Promoting Ethical AI Use

Challenges:

i. **Ethical Concerns**: Ensuring AI applications are used ethically and do not infringe on privacy or exacerbate inequalities.
ii. **Lack of Regulation**: Insufficient regulatory frameworks to govern AI use and address ethical concerns.

Strategies:

i. **Establish AI Ethics Committees**: Form independent bodies to oversee and review the ethical implications of AI applications (Delhi Government, 2023).
ii. **Develop Comprehensive Regulations**: Create and implement robust regulations that address privacy, security, and ethical use of AI technologies (Rathi, 2021).

Strengthening Skill Development and Education

Challenges:

i. **Skill Gaps**: Lack of AI-related skills and knowledge among the workforce.
ii. **Educational Inequality**: Disparities in the quality of education across different regions.

Strategies:

i. **Enhance AI Education**: Integrate AI and data science curricula into school and college programs to build a strong foundation for future generations (UpGrad, 2023).
ii. **Promote Vocational Training**: Expand vocational training programs focused on AI and related technologies, particularly in underdeveloped areas (Gujarat Skill Development Department, 2023).

Fostering Collaboration and Partnerships

Challenges:

i. **Fragmented Efforts**: Lack of coordination between government, industry, and academia in AI initiatives.
ii. **Resource Constraints**: Limited resources for implementing comprehensive AI projects.

Strategies:

i. **Encourage Public-Private Partnerships**: Foster collaborations between government agencies, private sector companies, and research institutions to pool resources and expertise (AI4Dev, 2022).
ii. **Support Research and Innovation**: Provide funding and incentives for research in AI technologies that address DEI challenges (Sakhi, 2022).

Enhancing Public Awareness and Engagement

Challenges:

i. **Low Awareness**: Limited public understanding of AI and its potential benefits for DEI.
ii. **Resistance to Change**: Resistance from various stakeholders to adopting new technologies or practices.

Strategies:

i. **Conduct Awareness Campaigns**: Launch national campaigns to educate the public about the benefits and risks of AI technologies (Muralidharan et al., 2019).

ii. **Engage with Communities**: Involve community leaders and organizations in discussions about AI applications to build trust and acceptance (West Bengal Government, 2023).

Monitoring and Evaluation

Challenges:

i. **Lack of Metrics**: Difficulty in measuring the impact of AI initiatives on DEI outcomes.
ii. **Monitoring Compliance**: Ensuring adherence to DEI standards and guidelines.

Strategies:

i. **Develop Evaluation Metrics**: Create metrics to assess the effectiveness of AI projects in achieving DEI goals (Chakraborty & Bandyopadhyay, 2022).
ii. **Regular Audits**: Conduct regular audits and assessments of AI systems to ensure compliance with DEI standards and ethical practices (Rathi, 2021).

Increased Integration of AI in Public Services

Future Directions:

i. **Smart Cities and Infrastructure**: The development of smart cities equipped with AI-driven infrastructure will enhance public services such as transportation, waste management, and energy distribution. Projects like the Smart Cities Mission aim to integrate technology into urban planning to improve quality of life across diverse populations (Ministry of Housing and Urban Affairs, 2023).
ii. **AI in Governance**: AI tools will increasingly be used to improve governance and public administration, making processes more transparent and efficient. AI-driven platforms for grievance redressal and citizen engagement will become more prevalent.

Examples:
Bhubaneswar: The city is using AI for traffic management and emergency services, aiming to create a more responsive urban environment (Bhubaneswar Smart City, 2023).

EXPANSION OF AI IN EDUCATION AND SKILL DEVELOPMENT

Future Directions:

i. **Personalized Learning**: AI-powered educational tools will become more sophisticated, offering personalized learning experiences that cater to individual needs and learning styles. This will help bridge educational disparities and improve learning outcomes across various socio-economic backgrounds.
ii. **Upskilling and Reskilling**: As the job market evolves, AI-driven platforms will play a crucial role in upskilling and reskilling workers, ensuring they are prepared for future employment opportunities.

Examples:
AI in Vocational Training: Platforms like Coursera and Udacity are expanding their offerings in India, providing AI-driven courses for skill development (Coursera, 2023).

Enhanced Healthcare Delivery

Future Directions:

i. **AI in Diagnostics and Treatment**: AI will continue to advance in diagnostics and personalized treatment plans, improving healthcare outcomes and accessibility. Technologies like predictive analytics will help in early detection of diseases and management of chronic conditions.
ii. **Telemedicine Growth**: The expansion of telemedicine services will further enhance access to healthcare, particularly in remote and underserved areas. AI will facilitate more accurate remote diagnoses and consultations.

Examples:
AI-Powered Health Apps: Apps like HealthifyMe and Practo are integrating AI to offer personalized health recommendations and virtual consultations (HealthifyMe, 2022).
Strengthened Ethical and Regulatory Frameworks
Future Directions:

i. **AI Ethics and Governance**: India will likely see the development of more comprehensive ethical guidelines and regulatory frameworks for AI. These will focus on ensuring fairness, transparency, and accountability in AI systems.
ii. **Bias Mitigation**: Continuous efforts will be made to address and reduce biases in AI systems, with an emphasis on creating inclusive and equitable technologies.

Examples:
National AI Strategy: The Indian government is expected to update and refine its National AI Strategy to address emerging ethical and regulatory challenges (NITI Aayog, 2022).
Promotion of Inclusivity and Social Equity
Future Directions:

i. **Inclusive AI Development**: There will be a focus on ensuring that AI technologies are developed with inclusivity in mind, considering the diverse needs of different communities. This includes improving representation in data and AI design.
ii. **Social Impact Projects**: AI will be increasingly used in social impact projects aimed at addressing issues such as poverty, inequality, and accessibility.

Examples:

Social Good Initiatives: Initiatives like AI for Social Good will continue to support projects that aim to improve social outcomes and address systemic inequalities (AI4Dev, 2022).

Enhanced Public Awareness and Engagement

Future Directions:

i. **AI Literacy Programs**: There will be an increase in programs aimed at improving public understanding of AI and its implications. These programs will focus on educating citizens about the benefits and risks of AI technologies.
ii. **Community Engagement**: More efforts will be made to engage communities in discussions about AI and its impact, ensuring that diverse perspectives are considered in AI development and deployment.

Examples:

Educational Campaigns: Government and NGO-led campaigns to raise awareness about AI and its applications will become more common (Muralidharan et al., 2019).

FUTURE DIRECTIONS

To maximize AI's potential in advancing DEI, it is essential to adopt a multidimensional approach that includes diverse perspectives in the development and deployment of AI technologies. Engaging interdisciplinary teams and incorporating input from marginalized communities can help ensure that AI systems are designed to be fair and inclusive. Moreover, ongoing research and development should focus on enhancing transparency and accountability in AI algorithms. Techniques such as explainable AI (XAI) and robust auditing mechanisms can help identify and address biases, contributing to more equitable outcomes (Doshi-Velez & Kim, 2017).

CONCLUSION

AI holds significant promise for advancing Diversity, Equity, and Inclusion, offering tools that can support and amplify DEI efforts across various sectors. However, realizing this potential requires addressing the ethical and practical challenges associated with AI technologies. By focusing on responsible development and implementation, organizations can harness AI to drive meaningful change and create more inclusive environments that reflect the values of equity and diversity. India's future in leveraging AI for addressing diversity, equity, and inclusion challenges is promising, with significant potential for growth and improvement. By focusing on integrating AI into public services, education, healthcare, and social equity, and by strengthening ethical frameworks and public engagement, India can effectively address current challenges and build a more inclusive and equitable society. India has the potential to lead in using AI for promoting diversity, equity, and inclusion by addressing these challenges through strategic measures. By focusing on enhancing technological infrastructure, ensuring inclusive AI development, promoting ethical use, strengthening skill development, fostering collaboration, raising public awareness, and implementing robust monitoring and evaluation, India can effectively cope with challenges and advance its DEI goals.

REFERENCES

AI4Dev. (2022). *AI for Development Initiatives in India*. Retrieved from AI4Dev.

AI4Dev. (2022). *AI for Development Initiatives in India*. Retrieved from AI4Dev.

Aayog, N. I. T. I. (2022). *AI Policy and Regulation in India: Ensuring Fairness and Inclusivity*. Retrieved from NITI Aayog.

Aayog, N. I. T. I. (2022). *AI Policy and Regulation in India: Ensuring Fairness and Inclusivity*. Retrieved from NITI Aayog.

Aayog, N. I. T. I. (2022). *AI Policy and Regulation in India: Ensuring Fairness and Inclusivity*. Retrieved from NITI Aayog.

Aira. (2021). *How Aira Works: AI-Powered Assistance for the Visually Impaired*. Retrieved from Aira.

Aira. (2021). *How Aira Works: AI-Powered Assistance for the Visually Impaired*. Retrieved from Aira.

Angwin, J., Larson, J., Mattu, S., & Kirchner, L. (2016). *Machine bias: There's software used across the country to predict future criminals. And it's biased against blacks*. ProPublica.

Bhubaneswar Smart City. (2023). *AI-Driven Smart City Initiatives*. Retrieved from Bhubaneswar Smart City.

Bihar IT Department. (2022). Bias Mitigation in Public AI Applications. Retrieved from Bihar IT Department.

Binns, R. (2020). Fairness in Machine Learning: Lessons from the Gender Shades Project. *Proceedings of the 2020 Conference on Fairness, Accountability, and Transparency (FAccT)*.

Buolamwini, J., & Gebru, T. (2018). Gender Shades: Intersectional Accuracy Disparities in Commercial Gender Classification. *Proceedings of the 2018 ACM Conference on Fairness, Accountability, and Transparency (FAccT)*.

Chakraborty, S., & Bandyopadhyay, S. (2022). Bias and Fairness in AI Systems: The Indian Context. *Journal of Ethical AI*, 5(3), 112–130.

Chakraborty, S., & Bandyopadhyay, S. (2022). Bias and Fairness in AI Systems: The Indian Context. *Journal of Ethical AI*, 5(3), 112–130.

Chakraborty, S., & Bandyopadhyay, S. (2022). Bias and Fairness in AI Systems: The Indian Context. *Journal of Ethical AI*, 5(3), 112–130.

Chen, X., Zhang, Q., & Jiang, X. (2021). Real-time Captioning with AI: Benefits and Challenges for Accessibility. *Journal of Assistive Technologies*.

Coursera. (2023). *AI and Data Science Courses in India*. Retrieved from Coursera.

Delhi Government. (2023). *Fair AI Framework: Guidelines for Ethical AI Applications*. Retrieved from Delhi Government.

Delhi Government. (2023). *Fair AI Framework: Guidelines for Ethical AI Applications*. Retrieved from Delhi Government.

Doshi-Velez, F., & Kim, B. (2017). *Towards a rigorous science of interpretable machine learning*. arXiv preprint arXiv:1702.08608.

Google. (2023). *AI for Multilingual Support: Innovations and Applications*. Retrieved from Google AI.

Gujarat Skill Development Department. (2023). *Annual Report on Skill Development and AI Integration*. Retrieved from Gujarat Skill Development.

Gujarat Skill Development Department. (2023). *Annual Report on Skill Development and AI Integration*. Retrieved from Gujarat Skill Development.

Guszcza, J., Kumar, R., & Lai, A. (2020). *How AI is transforming the HR function*. Deloitte Insights.

Haryana Employment Department. (2022). Career Guidance Portal and Employment Statistics. Retrieved from Haryana Employment.

HealthifyMe. (2022). *AI-Powered Health and Wellness Solutions*. Retrieved from HealthifyMe.

HealthifyMe. (2022). *Personalized Health and Wellness: An AI Perspective*. Retrieved from HealthifyMe.

HireVue. (2021). *AI in Recruitment: Reducing Bias through Technology*. Retrieved from HireVue.

HireVue. (2021). *AI in Recruitment: Reducing Bias through Technology*. Retrieved from HireVue.

IBM. (2020). *Diversity and inclusion: Using data and AI to improve workplace equity*. IBM Corporation.

Kerala Education Statistics. (2023). *Digital Learning Integration in Schools*. Retrieved from Kerala Education.

Khan Academy. (2022). *Personalized Learning with AI: Bridging Educational Gaps*. Retrieved from Khan Academy.

Khan Academy. (2022). *Personalized Learning with AI: Bridging Educational Gaps*. Retrieved from Khan Academy.

Kumar, A., & Gupta, R. (2021). The Digital Divide in India: An Analysis of Technology Access and Usage. *Journal of Information Technology & Politics*, 12(2), 45–61.

Kumar, P. (2021). Challenges in AI Language Translation in India: A Review. *Journal of Language Technology*, 15(2), 45–60.

Maharashtra Health Services. (2023). *AI in Healthcare: The Impact of Arogya Setu*. Retrieved from Maharashtra Health.

Maharashtra Health Services. (2023). *AI in Healthcare: The Impact of Arogya Setu*. Retrieved from Maharashtra Health.

Microsoft. (2022). *AI for Indian Languages: Innovations and Developments*. Retrieved from Microsoft AI.

Ministry of Electronics and IT. (2022). *BharatNet Project Overview*. Retrieved from Ministry of Electronics and IT.

Ministry of Housing and Urban Affairs. (2023). *Smart Cities Mission: Progress and Future Plans*. Retrieved from Ministry of Housing and Urban Affairs.

Muralidharan, K., Singh, A., & Suryanarayan, P. (2019). Educational Disparities in India: An Assessment of Access and Quality. *Education Economics*, 27(4), 357–374.

Muralidharan, K., Singh, A., & Suryanarayan, P. (2019). Educational Disparities in India: An Assessment of Access and Quality. *Education Economics*, 27(4), 357–374.

Muralidharan, K., Singh, A., & Suryanarayan, P. (2019). Educational Disparities in India: An Assessment of Access and Quality. *Education Economics*, 27(4), 357–374.

Niramai. (2021). *Innovations in Breast Cancer Screening: The Niramai Approach*. Retrieved from Niramai.

Niramai. (2021). *Innovations in Breast Cancer Screening: The Niramai Approach*. Retrieved from Niramai.

Niramai. (2021). *Innovations in Breast Cancer Screening: The Niramai Approach*. Retrieved from Niramai.

O'Neil, C. (2016). *Weapons of Math Destruction: How Big Data Increases Inequality and Threatens Democracy*. Crown Publishing Group.

Punjab Rural Development. (2022). *Smart Village Initiative: Enhancing Rural Infrastructure*. Retrieved from Punjab Rural Development.

Rao, K. S., Bhat, R., & Sen, A. (2021). Healthcare Access and Inequality in India: A Regional Analysis. *International Journal of Health Services*, 51(2), 134–152.

Rao, M., Patil, A., & Sharma, S. (2020). Deep Learning for Real-Time Text-to-Speech for Visually Impaired Individuals. *IEEE Transactions on Neural Networks and Learning Systems*, 31(12), 5002–5011.

Rathi, M. (2021). Policy Challenges in Addressing Diversity and Inclusion in India. *Public Policy Research*, 19(1), 65–80.

Rathi, M. (2021). Policy Challenges in Addressing Diversity and Inclusion in India. *Public Policy Research*, 19(1), 65–80.

Ravikumar, B., Gupta, S., & Reddy, A. (2020). Algorithmic Bias in Credit Scoring Systems: Evidence from India. *Data Ethics Journal*, 8(1), 88–104.

RiiDL. (2023). *AI-Driven Educational Diagnostics and Support*. Retrieved from RiiDL.

RiiDL. (2023). *AI-Driven Educational Diagnostics and Support*. Retrieved from RiiDL.

Sakhi. (2022). *Empowering Women Entrepreneurs: The Sakhi AI Project*. Retrieved from Sakhi.

Sakhi. (2022). *Empowering Women Entrepreneurs: The Sakhi AI Project*. Retrieved from Sakhi.

Sakhi. (2022). *Empowering Women Entrepreneurs: The Sakhi AI Project*. Retrieved from Sakhi.

Sethi, S., & Mehta, A. (2020). Employment Discrimination and Economic Opportunities in India. *Journal of Labor Economics*, 38(3), 451–472.

Talview. (2022). *AI in Talent Acquisition: Enhancing Recruitment Practices*. Retrieved from Talview.

Tamil Nadu Health Department. (2023). *e-Sanjeevani Telemedicine Statistics*. Retrieved from Tamil Nadu Health.

Telemedicine India. (2022). *Telemedicine and AI: Addressing Healthcare Access Challenges*. Retrieved from Telemedicine India.

UpGrad. (2023). *AI-Powered Skill Development and Career Enhancement*. Retrieved from UpGrad.

UpGrad. (2023). *AI-Powered Skill Development and Career Enhancement*. Retrieved from UpGrad.

Uttar Pradesh Government. (2022). *E-Pathshala and Educational Advancements*. Retrieved from Uttar Pradesh Government.

Varma, N., & Sharma, P. (2022). Social Cohesion and Inter-Group Conflicts in Diverse Societies: The Indian Experience. *Sociology Compass*, 16(1), 23–39.

West Bengal Government. (2023). *Sakhi Project: Empowering Women Entrepreneurs*. Retrieved from West Bengal Government.

West Bengal Government. (2023). *Sakhi Project: Empowering Women Entrepreneurs*. Retrieved from West Bengal Government.

Zhang, Y., Wang, S., & Xie, L. (2022). Advancements in AI for Accessibility: A Review. *Journal of Artificial Intelligence Research*.

Chapter 5
AI in Performance Management:
Data-Driven Approaches

Arunkumar Thirunagalingam
https://orcid.org/0009-0009-3823-9766
McKesson Corporation, USA

Sireesha Addanki
https://orcid.org/0009-0008-2917-027X
System Soft Technologies LLC, USA

Vamshidhar Reddy Vemula
Independent Researcher, USA

P. Selvakumar
https://orcid.org/0000-0002-3650-4548
Department of Science and Humanities, Nehru Institute of Technology, India

ABSTRACT

Artificial Intelligence (AI) is revolutionizing many facets of modern business, and one of the most transformative areas is performance management. Traditionally, performance management has been characterized by annual reviews, subjective evaluations, and a focus on past performance. However, AI is redefining this landscape, introducing new methodologies and tools that offer more dynamic, objective, and data-driven approaches to managing and enhancing employee performance. Moreover, AI enhances the feedback process by providing actionable insights that are often more specific and relevant than those derived from traditional review methods. For instance, AI can highlight recurring issues that might not be immediately obvious to human reviewers, enabling proactive management and support.

DOI: 10.4018/979-8-3693-8442-8.ch005

By analyzing individual performance data, AI can recommend tailored training and development opportunities that align with each employee's strengths, weaknesses, and career goals.

INTRODUCTION

Introduction to AI in Performance Management: Transforming the Way We Work

Artificial Intelligence (AI) is revolutionizing many facets of modern business, and one of the most transformative areas is performance management. Traditionally, performance management has been characterized by annual reviews, subjective evaluations, and a focus on past performance. However, AI is redefining this landscape, introducing new methodologies and tools that offer more dynamic, objective, and data-driven approaches to managing and enhancing employee performance.Moreover, AI enhances the feedback process by providing actionable insights that are often more specific and relevant than those derived from traditional review methods. For instance, AI can highlight recurring issues that might not be immediately obvious to human reviewers, enabling proactive management and support. By analyzing individual performance data, AI can recommend tailored training and development opportunities that align with each employee's strengths, weaknesses, and career goals. This personalized approach helps employees to grow in their roles, enhances their skills, and ultimately contributes to their long-term success within the organization.AI also facilitates more effective goal setting and tracking. Traditional goal-setting processes can be rigid and may not adapt to changing circumstances. AI-driven systems can set and adjust goals dynamically based on real-time performance data and evolving business needs. This agility ensures that goals remain relevant and achievable, keeping employees engaged and motivated. Additionally, the successful deployment of AI in performance management requires careful design and ongoing oversight to avoid potential pitfalls such as algorithmic biases or inaccuracies in data interpretation.In conclusion, AI is transforming performance management by providing organizations with more accurate, objective, and actionable insights into employee performance. Through continuous monitoring, bias reduction, personalized development, dynamic goal setting, and enhanced communication, AI offers significant improvements over traditional performance management methods.

Setting Goals and Objectives with AI: Smart Target Setting

In the modern business landscape, setting goals and objectives is a critical process for driving organizational success and employee growth. Traditionally, this process has often been characterized by static, annual goal-setting sessions that may not fully align with the dynamic nature of today's business environment. However, Artificial Intelligence (AI) is significantly transforming this practice, offering innovative solutions for setting goals and objectives that are more dynamic, data-driven, and aligned with both individual and organizational aspirations.AI-enhanced goal setting leverages data analytics and machine learning algorithms to create smarter, more precise objectives. Traditional goal-setting methods can sometimes lead to unrealistic or misaligned targets due to limited data and subjective judgment. AI addresses these issues by analyzing extensive datasets, including historical performance data, market trends, and individual capabilities, to generate more accurate and achievable goals. This data-driven approach ensures that the goals set are not only ambitious but also grounded in empirical evidence and aligned with strategic business objectives.AI also enhances the personalization of goals. By analyzing individual performance metrics, skills, and career aspirations, AI can recommend personalized objectives that align with each employee's strengths and developmental needs. This tailored approach not only enhances employee engagement by setting goals that resonate with their personal growth but also maximizes productivity by aligning objectives with individual capabilities.Furthermore, AI facilitates more precise and transparent goal-setting processes. Traditional methods often involve subjective judgments and manual tracking, which can lead to inconsistencies and lack of clarity (Alsaif, A., et al., 2023). AI systems provide clear, data-driven insights that make the goal-setting process more objective and transparent. This transparency helps ensure that employees understand how their goals align with organizational priorities and can track their progress more effectively.

The use of AI in goal setting also supports better alignment between individual objectives and broader organizational goals. AI tools can map individual goals to overarching strategic objectives, ensuring that each employee's targets contribute to the company's overall mission. This alignment fosters a sense of purpose and coherence across the organization, as employees can see how their efforts directly impact the company's success.In addition to setting and adjusting goals, AI can enhance the evaluation of goal achievement. Traditional performance reviews often rely on periodic assessments that may not capture the full picture of progress (Arsawan, I. W. E., et al., 2022). AI, on the other hand, provides continuous monitoring and analysis, offering real-time feedback and insights into how well goals are being met. This ongoing assessment allows for timely adjustments and support, helping employees stay on track and overcome obstacles more effectively.Moreover, while AI can enhance goal setting, it is crucial to balance technology with human judgment. AI systems are powerful tools, but they should complement rather than replace human insights and expertise. In conclusion, AI is revolutionizing the way goals and objectives are set, offering a more dynamic, data-driven, and personalized approach. By leveraging AI's capabilities in data analysis, real-time adjustments, and alignment, organizations can set smarter targets that drive both individual and organizational success.

RESEARCH METHODOLOGY

AI-Driven Performance Monitoring: Real-Time Feedback and Coaching

AI-driven performance monitoring, however, introduces a paradigm shift by offering continuous, real-time feedback and coaching, enhancing both individual and organizational performance through more immediate, actionable insights. AI systems continuously gather and assess data from a range of sources, including work output, communication patterns, project progress, and even employee sentiment. This real-time data analysis enables organizations to gain a comprehensive, up-to-date view of performance, allowing for more timely and relevant interventions. Traditional feedback mechanisms, such as annual reviews or biannual check-ins, often come too late to address immediate issues or capitalize on recent successes. AI-driven systems, however, can offer feedback instantaneously based on current performance metrics. For example, AI tools can track project milestones, monitor task completion rates, and evaluate communication efficiency, providing employees with immediate insights into their performance (Budhwar, P., et al., 2022)This timely feedback allows employees to make adjustments on the fly, improving their performance and addressing issues before they escalate.AI also enhances the quality of feedback by making it more data-driven and objective. Traditional feedback can be influenced by biases and subjective opinions, which may not always reflect an employee's true performance. AI systems, by contrast, analyze performance data objectively, providing feedback that is grounded in empirical evidence. This objectivity helps to ensure that feedback is fair and focused on specific behaviors and outcomes rather than personal impressions.Moreover, AI-driven performance monitoring supports personalized coaching by identifying individual strengths and areas for improvement. Machine learning algorithms can analyze performance trends over time, recognizing patterns and pinpointing areas where an employee may benefit from additional support or development. For instance, if an AI system identifies that an employee consistently struggles with meeting deadlines, it can recommend targeted training or suggest strategies to improve time management. This personalized approach to coaching ensures that development efforts are tailored to the unique needs of each employee, enhancing their growth and effectiveness.The ability of AI to provide actionable insights also extends to goal setting and achievement.

Predictive Analytics for Performance Management: Forecasting Success

Predictive analytics is revolutionizing performance management by offering a forward-looking approach to understanding and enhancing employee performance (Cardwell, S. G., et al., 2022). Unlike traditional performance management practices that often focus on historical data and past performance, predictive analytics leverages sophisticated algorithms and statistical models to forecast future outcomes, enabling organizations to proactively address potential issues, optimize talent management, and drive sustained success. By analyzing data such as past performance metrics, employee behavior, and external factors, predictive models can generate forecasts about individual and organizational outcomes. This forward-looking approach allows organizations to anticipate challenges and opportunities, making more informed decisions that can significantly impact performance management. By analyzing various performance indicators and career trajectories, predictive models can highlight individuals who are likely to excel in their roles or advance within the organization. This insight enables organizations to invest in these employees through targeted development programs, mentorship opportunities, and career planning, thus nurturing their growth and preparing them for future leadership roles. Early identification of potential flight risks allows managers to take proactive measures to retain valuable talent. For example, predictive analytics might reveal that employees in certain roles or departments are more likely to experience dissatisfaction due to specific factors, such as inadequate career progression or work-life balance issues. With this information, organizations can implement targeted retention strategies, such as career development plans or enhanced benefits, to address these concerns before they lead to attrition.In addition to identifying potential issues and opportunities, predictive analytics helps optimize performance management processes. For instance, predictive models can forecast the outcomes of different management strategies, allowing organizations to choose the most effective approaches for enhancing employee performance. By analyzing data on past interventions and their impact, predictive analytics can guide managers in designing and implementing strategies that are most likely to succeed, thus improving overall performance management effectiveness.

Moreover, predictive analytics can enhance goal setting and performance evaluation by providing insights into future performance trends. Traditional goal-setting processes often rely on past performance data and subjective judgments, which may not fully account for future variables. Predictive analytics, however, uses data-driven insights to set realistic and achievable goals based on projected performance trends. This approach ensures that goals are not only aligned with past performance but also consider future potential, leading to more effective and motivating goal-setting processes (Cardwell, S. G., et al., 2022). By forecasting future performance needs and potential skill gaps, organizations can strategically allocate resources such as training, development programs, and staffing. For example, if predictive models indicate that a particular department will experience increased workload or skill shortages in the near future, organizations can take proactive steps to address these needs by providing additional training or hiring new talent. This proactive approach helps ensure that the organization is well-prepared to meet future demands and maintain high levels of performance.

AI-Powered 360-Degree Feedback: Unbiased and Actionable Insights

However, traditional 360-degree feedback systems can sometimes be hampered by biases, inconsistent data, and subjective interpretations (Chatterjee, S., et al., 2021). The advent of Artificial Intelligence (AI) is transforming this process, offering AI-powered 360-degree feedback systems that provide more unbiased, actionable, and data-driven insights, thereby enhancing the accuracy and effectiveness of performance evaluations.AI-powered 360-degree feedback systems harness the capabilities of advanced algorithms and data analytics to collect, analyze, and interpret feedback from multiple sources in real-time. Unlike traditional methods, which often rely on manual data aggregation and subjective interpretation, AI systems automate these processes, ensuring that feedback is not only comprehensive but also consistent and objective. This automation reduces the risk of human error and bias, providing a more accurate and fair assessment of employee performance.Traditional feedback systems can be influenced by personal biases and subjective opinions, which may skew the evaluations and lead to unfair assessments. AI algorithms, when properly designed and implemented, can minimize these biases by analyzing feedback data objectively. For instance, AI can detect patterns of bias in feedback responses and adjust for them, ensuring that the final evaluation reflects a more accurate and balanced view of performance.AI-powered systems also enhance the actionability of feedback. Traditional 360-degree feedback can sometimes result in vague or generalized comments that are difficult for employees to translate into specific actions for improvement. AI algorithms, however, can analyze qualitative feedback and identify common themes or recurring issues. By synthesizing this information, AI systems can generate actionable insights and tailored recommendations for employees. For example, if multiple sources highlight a need for improved communication skills, the AI system can recommend targeted training programs or provide resources to help the employee develop these skills.

Another advantage of AI in 360-degree feedback is the ability to provide real-time insights (Chowdhury, S., et al., 2022). Traditional feedback processes often involve lengthy cycles of data collection, analysis, and reporting, which can delay the delivery of feedback and reduce its relevance. AI-powered systems can collect and analyze feedback continuously, offering real-time insights and allowing for more timely interventions. This immediacy ensures that feedback is relevant to current performance and can be acted upon more effectively.AI can also improve the consistency and reliability of feedback by standardizing the evaluation process. Traditional 360-degree feedback systems may suffer from inconsistencies in how different raters interpret and apply performance criteria. AI systems, through standardized algorithms and evaluation criteria, ensure that feedback is evaluated uniformly, leading to more consistent and reliable assessments across different sources and contexts.Moreover, AI-powered 360-degree feedback systems can enhance the overall engagement and participation in the feedback process. Traditional feedback mechanisms may face challenges with low response rates or incomplete feedback due to the manual and time-consuming nature of the process. AI systems streamline data collection and analysis, making it easier for participants to provide feedback and for organizations to manage the process. Enhanced engagement leads to a more comprehensive view of performance and a richer set of data for evaluation.Managers and HR professionals should use AI-powered feedback as a tool to support, rather than replace, their judgment and experience.In conclusion, AI-powered 360-degree feedback represents a significant advancement in performance management by providing more unbiased, actionable, and real-time insights.

THEORETICAL FRAMEWORK

Natural Language Processing for Performance Management: Text-Based Feedback

Natural Language Processing (NLP) is increasingly making its mark in performance management by transforming the way organizations handle and interpret text-based feedback. Traditionally, performance feedback involves written comments from managers, peers, and subordinates, which can often be subjective, inconsistent, and challenging to analyze systematically.NLP also facilitates the extraction of actionable insights from text-based feedback. Traditional feedback may sometimes be vague or generalized, making it difficult for employees to pinpoint areas for improvement or take specific actions. NLP can analyze feedback to highlight recurring issues, common themes, and actionable recommendations. For example, if multiple sources mention that an employee needs to improve their communication skills, NLP can aggregate these comments and provide specific examples and suggestions for improvement. This actionable insight is invaluable for designing targeted development plans and providing focused support to employees (Choy, K. L., et al., 2008).Furthermore, NLP enhances the consistency and objectivity of performance evaluations by reducing human bias in the interpretation of feedback. Traditional performance reviews can be influenced by the subjective perspectives of the reviewers, leading to inconsistent and potentially biased evaluations. NLP algorithms, by contrast, analyze feedback based on predefined criteria and data patterns, minimizing the impact of individual biases.

Machine Learning for Performance Management: Identifying Patterns and Trends

Traditional performance reviews often rely on periodic assessments and subjective judgments, which can overlook subtle trends and correlations in performance data (Devarajan R., et al., 2016). Machine learning algorithms, however, can process and analyze large datasets to uncover hidden patterns and trends, such as recurring performance issues, high-potential talent, or factors contributing to employee success. For example, an ML model might reveal that employees in certain roles perform better when given specific types of projects or when working under particular conditions. This personalization enables organizations to develop tailored development plans, set individualized goals, and provide targeted feedback that aligns with each employee's unique capabilities and career aspirations. For example, an ML model might identify that an employee excels in creative tasks but struggles with time management, leading to customized training and support to address these specific areas. In addition to improving individual performance management, machine learning can also optimize team dynamics and organizational performance. By analyzing data on team interactions, collaboration patterns, and collective outcomes, ML algorithms can identify factors that contribute to team success or challenges.

AI-Enabled Performance Metrics: Redefining Traditional KPIs

Artificial Intelligence (AI) is fundamentally redefining how organizations approach performance metrics, transforming traditional Key Performance Indicators (KPIs) into more dynamic, insightful, and actionable tools (Dutta, D., et al., 2023). Historically, KPIs have been used to measure and evaluate performance based on predefined, static metrics, often relying on historical data and periodic reviews. AI's integration into performance management is reshaping this landscape by introducing advanced techniques for data analysis, pattern recognition, and real-time insights, thereby elevating the effectiveness and relevance of performance metrics.Traditional KPIs typically focus on specific, pre-determined metrics such as sales figures, revenue growth, or customer satisfaction scores. While these metrics are useful, they can sometimes offer a limited or outdated view of performance. AI systems, however, can process and analyze data from a wide range of sources, including transactional data, social media, customer feedback, and operational metrics. This comprehensive analysis allows organizations to develop more nuanced and multi-dimensional performance metrics that reflect the complexity of modern business environments.AI-enabled metrics, by contrast, allow for continuous monitoring and analysis of performance data. This real-time capability ensures that organizations receive up-to-date information and can respond swiftly to emerging trends, anomalies, or opportunities. For example, AI can track and analyze customer behavior in real time, providing immediate feedback on marketing campaign effectiveness or product performance, and allowing for prompt adjustments to strategies.

AI also enhances the granularity and specificity of performance metrics(Gelle-Jimenez, et al., 2021). Traditional KPIs may aggregate data into broad categories, potentially overlooking important details or nuances. AI-powered analytics can delve deeper into data, identifying patterns and trends that may not be immediately apparent. This granularity enables organizations to develop more precise and targeted performance metrics. For instance, AI can analyze employee performance data to reveal specific factors contributing to success or areas of improvement, leading to more tailored and actionable KPIs that better reflect individual and team performance. Moreover, AI enables the creation of predictive performance metrics. Traditional KPIs are often reactive, measuring performance based on past data without accounting for future trends. AI, however, and emerging patterns. This forward-looking approach allows organizations to set more proactive and strategic KPIs. For example, AI can predict future sales trends based on current market conditions and historical sales data, helping organizations set more accurate sales targets and align their strategies with anticipated market changes.

Data-Driven Decision Making with AI: Making Informed Talent Decisions

The integration of Artificial Intelligence (AI) into this process is transforming how organizations make talent-related decisions, providing a level of precision and insight previously unattainable through traditional methods (Guler, N., et al., 2023). Traditionally, decisions about hiring, promotions, and employee development were based on a combination of subjective judgment and limited data. This approach often led to inconsistent outcomes and missed opportunities. AI, however, allows organizations to harness data from diverse sources—such as resumes, performance reviews, employee surveys, and social media profiles—to create a comprehensive view of each candidate or employee. This data-driven approach ensures that decisions are based on a broader and more accurate understanding of individual and organizational needs.AI algorithms can analyze resumes and application materials to identify candidates who best match the job requirements and organizational culture. By evaluating factors such as skills, experience, and past performance, AI can shortlist candidates with the highest potential for success. Additionally, AI-powered tools can predict a candidate's future performance and fit within the organization based on historical data and predictive models. Through data analysis and pattern recognition, AI can pinpoint employees with the potential for leadership roles or critical positions within the organization. By examining factors such as performance metrics, career progression, and skill sets, AI systems can recommend development opportunities and career paths for high-potential employees. This data-driven approach to succession planning ensures that organizations are prepared for future leadership needs and can cultivate talent effectively.

Moreover, AI facilitates more effective employee development and training programs. Traditional approaches to employee development often rely on generalized training modules and feedback, which may not address individual needs (Hooi, L. W. 2021). AI, however, can analyze performance data and learning preferences to tailor development programs to each employee's specific requirements. For example, AI can identify skills gaps and recommend targeted training or mentorship opportunities to address these gaps. This personalized approach to development enhances employee growth and ensures that training efforts are aligned with both individual and organizational goals.In addition to improving recruitment and development, AI-driven decision-making enhances workforce planning and resource allocation (Zhang, G.P. 2000). By analyzing data on employee performance, productivity, and workload, AI can provide insights into optimal team composition and resource allocation. For instance, AI can predict which teams are likely to experience high workloads or skill shortages in the future, allowing organizations to make proactive adjustments. This capability ensures that resources are allocated efficiently and that teams are equipped to meet upcoming challenges.AI also supports data-driven decision-making by providing real-time insights into employee engagement and satisfaction.

SOLUTIONS AND RECOMMENDATIONS

AI in Performance Calibration: Ensuring Fairness and Consistency

Performance calibration, the process of aligning performance evaluations across an organization to ensure fairness and consistency, has traditionally been a challenging task fraught with potential biases and inconsistencies (Hodge, V.J. et al., 2004). The integration of Artificial Intelligence (AI) into performance calibration is transforming this crucial aspect of performance management by providing advanced tools for analyzing performance data, standardizing evaluation criteria, and reducing human biases. By leveraging AI's capabilities, organizations can achieve a more equitable and consistent performance calibration process, ultimately fostering a fairer and more transparent workplace.Traditionally, performance evaluations can vary significantly depending on individual managers' interpretations, experiences, and biases (Zacheilas, N. et al., 2015). This variability can lead to inconsistencies in how performance is assessed and can undermine the fairness of evaluations. AI systems, however, can apply uniform criteria and algorithms to assess performance data, ensuring that evaluations are consistent across different departments and teams. Moreover, AI can detect patterns of bias in evaluation data and flag inconsistencies, enabling organizations to address and correct these issues. Traditional performance calibration processes often involve periodic reviews, which can delay the identification of performance issues or inconsistencies (Ismail, M., et al., 2023). AI-enabled systems can continuously monitor performance data and provide real-time feedback to managers and HR professionals.

The use of AI in performance calibration also supports more effective goal-setting and development planning. By analyzing performance data, AI can help organizations set realistic and achievable goals for employees based on their past performance and potential. This data-driven approach ensures that goal-setting and development efforts are aligned with individual performance and organizational objectives (Imai, S., et al., 2018). Organizations must implement robust data management practices and ensure that their performance data is accurate, comprehensive, and representative. Additionally, while AI can enhance the fairness and consistency of performance evaluations, it is essential to balance AI-driven insights with human judgment. AI systems provide valuable data-driven recommendations, but they may not fully capture qualitative factors or individual circumstances that influence performance. Managers and HR professionals should use AI insights as a tool to inform their decisions rather than relying solely on automated outputs. Combining AI with human expertise ensures a more holistic and contextually relevant approach to performance calibration.In conclusion, AI is revolutionizing performance calibration by providing advanced tools to ensure fairness, consistency, and transparency in performance evaluations (Yadwadkar, N.J. et al., 2012). Through standardized evaluation criteria, bias mitigation, real-time feedback, and comprehensive data analysis, AI enhances the accuracy and equity of performance management processes. While challenges related to data quality, human judgment, and ethical considerations must be addressed, the benefits of AI in performance calibration are substantial. As AI technology continues to evolve, its role in shaping fair and consistent performance evaluations will become increasingly central to organizational success, fostering a more equitable and transparent workplace.

AI-Powered Succession Planning: Identifying Future Leaders

Succession planning is a critical process for ensuring organizational continuity and leadership stability, yet it has often been constrained by subjective assessments and limited data (Johan, S. 2021). The advent of Artificial Intelligence (AI) is transforming succession planning by providing sophisticated tools to identify and develop future leaders with a higher degree of precision and objectivity. AI-powered succession planning leverages advanced algorithms and data analytics to assess employee potential, predict leadership readiness, and align talent development with organizational goals, thereby enhancing the strategic depth and effectiveness of leadership transitions.One of the primary benefits of AI in succession planning is its ability to predict future performance and leadership potential (Yigitbasi, N., et al., 2013). AI models use historical data and predictive analytics to forecast how employees are likely to perform in higher-level roles. This predictive capability is based on factors such as past performance, skill sets, leadership competencies, and career trajectory. For instance, AI can analyze an employee's track record of project leadership, team collaboration, and problem-solving skills to predict their suitability for executive positions. This forward-looking approach enables organizations to proactively prepare and groom high-potential employees for future leadership roles.AI also enhances the accuracy of identifying leadership potential by minimizing biases and focusing on data-driven criteria. Traditional succession planning can be influenced by subjective judgments and unconscious biases, which may lead to inconsistent or unfair assessments of employees' potential. By applying standardized criteria and removing individual subjectivity, AI ensures a more equitable evaluation of employees' readiness for leadership positions. Additionally, AI can identify hidden potential in employees who may not have been considered for leadership roles through traditional methods, ensuring that talent is recognized and developed regardless of visibility.

Another significant advantage of AI in succession planning is its ability to support personalized development plans for future leaders (Kulshrestha, N., et al., 2023). Based on the insights derived from data analysis, AI can recommend targeted development programs and career pathways for high-potential employees. For example, if AI identifies a candidate with strong strategic thinking but limited experience in people management, it can suggest specific training or mentorship opportunities to address this gap. AI also facilitates more dynamic and flexible succession planning. Furthermore, AI supports a more data-driven approach to workforce planning and resource allocation. By analyzing trends and forecasting future leadership needs, AI can help organizations make informed decisions about talent investments and strategic priorities. For instance, AI can identify areas where leadership gaps are likely to emerge and recommend targeted recruitment or development efforts to address these gaps (Xu, J., et al., 2019). This proactive approach ensures that organizations are well-prepared for future leadership transitions and can maintain a strong talent pipeline.

AI-Driven Learning and Development: Personalized Growth Plans

In today's rapidly evolving business environment, the demand for personalized learning and development (L&D) programs has never been greater (Lakshman, C. 2014). Artificial Intelligence (AI) is at the forefront of transforming how organizations approach employee growth, offering advanced tools to create personalized development plans that align with individual needs and organizational goals. One of the key benefits of AI in L&D is its ability to provide personalized recommendations for training and development opportunities. AI algorithms can analyze an employee's current skills, career goals, and performance data to suggest relevant courses, workshops, and learning materials. AI-driven adaptive learning platforms, on the other hand, adjust the content and difficulty of training materials based on real-time assessments of an employee's performance. This adaptive approach ensures that each employee progresses at their own pace and receives the appropriate level of challenge and support. Furthermore, AI enhances the personalization of growth plans through continuous feedback and performance monitoring. Traditional L&D programs often rely on periodic assessments to gauge progress, which can lead to delays in identifying areas for improvement (Lin, S., et al., 2022). AI-powered systems, however, can provide real-time feedback and insights based on ongoing performance data.

Another significant advantage of AI in personalized learning and development is its ability to support career pathing and succession planning. AI can analyze an employee's career trajectory, performance data, and skill set to recommend potential career paths and development opportunities within the organization (Liu, H., et al., 2023). For example, if an employee demonstrates strong leadership potential but has limited experience in a specific functional area, AI can suggest cross-training opportunities or project assignments to broaden their experience. This strategic approach to career development helps employees align their growth with organizational needs and prepare for future leadership roles.Additionally, while AI can provide valuable recommendations and insights, it is essential to balance these with human judgment and support. AI systems offer data-driven guidance, but they may not fully capture the nuances of individual motivations, career aspirations, or personal circumstances (Vijayakumar G, et al., 2024). Managers and L&D professionals should use AI insights as a complement to their expertise, providing additional context and support to ensure that growth plans are well-rounded and aligned with both individual and organizational goals.In conclusion, AI-driven learning and development is revolutionizing how organizations approach employee growth by providing personalized and data-driven growth plans.

AI in Performance Management for Remote Teams: Overcoming Distance

The rise of remote work has brought about significant changes in performance management, introducing unique challenges related to distance, communication, and oversight. This real-time data provides managers with insights into individual and team performance, allowing them to identify issues, recognize achievements, and provide timely support, regardless of geographic location.AI also enhances communication and collaboration within remote teams by facilitating seamless interactions and information sharing. Communication tools integrated with AI can analyze team interactions, identify patterns in communication, and recommend improvements. For example, AI can highlight when team members are struggling with communication barriers or when there are gaps in information sharing(Lombardi, F., et al., 2018). By providing recommendations for better communication practices and identifying potential bottlenecks, AI helps to ensure that remote teams remain cohesive and collaborative, despite the physical distance separating them.Moreover, AI supports remote teams by offering personalized feedback and development opportunities. Traditional performance management often relies on periodic reviews, which may not adequately capture the nuances of ongoing remote work. AI-driven systems can provide continuous feedback based on real-time performance data, offering tailored insights and recommendations for improvement. For instance, AI can analyze an employee's contributions to various projects, their interaction patterns, and their adherence to deadlines to provide personalized feedback on their strengths and areas for growth. This continuous feedback loop ensures that remote employees receive regular, actionable guidance, helping them to stay aligned with their goals and improve their performance.

AI also plays a crucial role in managing performance expectations and setting clear, achievable goals for remote teams. Establishing and communicating performance expectations can be more challenging in a remote environment, where managers may have less direct interaction with employees (Mahadev Madgule, et al., 2023). AI-powered performance management tools can assist in setting clear, measurable objectives and tracking progress towards these goals. By analyzing historical performance data and industry benchmarks, AI can help managers set realistic targets and ensure that goals are aligned with both individual capabilities and organizational priorities. Additionally, AI can provide insights into progress and highlight potential issues, allowing for timely adjustments to goals and expectations.Furthermore, AI aids in overcoming the challenge of maintaining employee engagement and motivation in remote teams. Remote work can sometimes lead to feelings of isolation and disengagement, which can impact performance. AI-powered engagement tools can analyze employee interactions, sentiment, and feedback to gauge engagement levels and identify potential issues. For example, AI can analyze communication patterns and feedback from surveys to identify signs of disengagement or burnout. Based on this analysis, AI can recommend interventions such as virtual team-building activities, targeted support, or changes in work patterns to enhance engagement and morale.AI also contributes to performance management by streamlining administrative tasks and reducing the burden on managers. Remote performance management involves tracking various metrics, conducting reviews, and managing feedback, all of which can be time-consuming. AI can automate many of these tasks, such as collecting performance data, generating reports, and scheduling feedback sessions.

Ethics and Bias in AI-Driven Performance Management: Mitigating Risks

As organizations increasingly adopt Artificial Intelligence (AI) in performance management, addressing the ethical implications and mitigating risks associated with bias become paramount. While AI offers powerful tools for enhancing performance evaluations, personalizing feedback, and streamlining processes, its use also raises significant concerns about fairness, transparency, and the potential for perpetuating existing biases (Møller, M.F. 1993). Effectively managing these ethical challenges is essential to ensuring that AI-driven performance management contributes positively to organizational outcomes without inadvertently introducing new forms of discrimination or injustice.A primary ethical concern in AI-driven performance management is the potential for perpetuating or amplifying biases present in historical data. AI systems rely on data to train algorithms and generate insights. If the data used reflects historical biases—such as gender, racial, or age biases—these biases can be inadvertently encoded into the AI models. For instance, if historical performance evaluations have shown bias against certain demographic groups, an AI system trained on this data may continue to favor or disadvantage these groups unfairly. This can lead to skewed performance assessments and unequal opportunities for career advancement, undermining the principles of fairness and equality that organizations strive to uphold.involves not only examining the data itself but also assessing the outcomes produced by AI systems to ensure that they do not disproportionately impact any particular group. Techniques such as reweighting or balancing data, employing fairness constraints, and using bias-detection algorithms can help in identifying and correcting biases in AI models.

Transparency fosters trust and allows employees to engage with the performance management process more effectively. Organizations should clearly communicate the criteria used by AI systems for performance assessments and provide accessible explanations of how these assessments are generated (Paramasivam Selvakumar, et al., 2024). This transparency helps demystify AI processes and provides employees with a clearer understanding of how their performance is measured and how they can influence their evaluations.In addition to transparency, ensuring that AI-driven performance management systems are interpretable and accountable is essential. Interpretable AI models allow users to understand and explain how decisions are made, which is crucial for addressing concerns about fairness and accuracy. Additionally, providing employees with control over their data and clear options for consent and opt-out can enhance transparency and respect for individual privacy. Training and education are vital components of mitigating ethical risks in AI-driven performance management. Educating employees, managers, and HR professionals about the potential ethical issues and biases associated with AI helps to foster a more informed and responsible approach to using these technologies. Training programs should cover topics such as recognizing and addressing biases, understanding AI limitations, and promoting ethical decision-making. In conclusion, while AI-driven performance management offers significant benefits in terms of efficiency and personalization, addressing ethical concerns and mitigating biases is crucial for ensuring fairness and transparency(Paramasivam Selvakumar, et al., 2024).

FUTURE RESEARCH DIRECTIONS

Future Directions in AI and Performance Management: Emerging Trends

As Artificial Intelligence (AI) continues to advance, its integration into performance management is poised to evolve significantly, shaping how organizations assess, develop, and manage their talent. Emerging trends in AI and performance management promise to enhance the precision, efficiency, and impact of performance-related processes, offering new capabilities that could transform traditional practices (Ramakrishnan T., et al., 2022). These trends are driven by advancements in AI technologies, changing workforce dynamics, and the increasing need for data-driven decision-making. Understanding these future directions is crucial for organizations seeking to stay ahead in a rapidly evolving business landscape.AI-powered predictive models can analyze patterns in employee performance, engagement levels, and career progression to anticipate future needs and challenges (Toshniwal, A., et al., 2014). For example, AI can predict which employees are likely to excel in leadership roles based on their performance data and behavioral patterns, allowing organizations to proactively develop and prepare high-potential candidates.

Continuous performance management involves frequent check-ins, real-time feedback, and ongoing goal-setting, which help employees stay aligned with their objectives and receive timely support. AI-driven platforms can facilitate this process by automating feedback collection, tracking progress against goals, and providing real-time insights into performance (Selvakumar, P.,2023). The rise of personalized learning and development is another significant trend driven by AI. AI-powered systems can create highly customized learning experiences tailored to each employee's unique needs, skills, and career aspirations. By analyzing performance data, learning preferences, and career goals, AI can recommend specific training programs, resources, and development opportunities. This personalized approach helps employees acquire the skills they need for their current roles and future career aspirations, leading to more effective and targeted development initiatives. As AI continues to evolve, its ability to deliver tailored learning experiences will likely become even more sophisticated, enhancing employee growth and performance.AI's role in enhancing employee well-being and mental health is also gaining prominence.

The application of AI in performance management is also expected to become more inclusive and equitable (Runsewe, O. et al., 2017). As organizations strive to eliminate bias and promote diversity, AI can play a role in identifying and addressing disparities in performance evaluations and development opportunities. By analyzing performance data through an equity lens (Shahriari, B., et al., 2015), AI can highlight potential biases and recommend adjustments to ensure fair and unbiased assessments. Additionally, AI-driven tools can support diverse talent pools by identifying and nurturing potential leaders from underrepresented groups. This emphasis on inclusivity and fairness reflects a growing recognition of the importance of diverse perspectives in driving organizational success.AI is also enhancing the integration of performance management with broader business strategies. By aligning performance metrics with strategic objectives, AI can help organizations ensure that individual and team goals are directly linked to overarching business goals. AI-driven analytics can provide insights into how performance contributes to strategic outcomes, enabling organizations to make data-driven decisions and adjust their strategies as needed. This alignment helps to ensure that performance management is not only focused on individual development but also contributes to the achievement of organizational objectives.

CONCLUSION

AI, organizations are moving beyond traditional performance management methods to embrace systems that leverage vast amounts of data for more accurate assessments, personalized feedback, and strategic decision-making. This transition is reshaping the landscape of performance management, offering substantial benefits but also posing significant challenges that must be navigated with care.AI's ability to analyze large datasets and extract actionable insights is revolutionizing performance management by providing a level of precision and depth previously unattainable. Advanced algorithms can process data from various sources, including performance metrics, employee feedback, and project outcomes, to deliver comprehensive assessments of individual and team performance. By moving away from anecdotal or subjective evaluations, AI enables a more evidence-based approach to performance management, which can lead to fairer and more consistent outcomes.Personalization is another key advantage of AI-driven performance management. AI, however, can tailor feedback and development plans to individual employees based on their performance data, career aspirations, and learning preferences. This level of personalization enhances the relevance and effectiveness of development initiatives, helping employees to grow in alignment with their specific goals and the organization's objectives. By providing customized learning opportunities and development plans, AI supports more targeted and impactful employee growth.

Moreover, AI enhances the agility and responsiveness of performance management processes. In traditional systems, performance evaluations are often conducted on an annual or semi-annual basis, which can lead to delays in addressing performance issues or recognizing achievements. AI-driven systems facilitate continuous performance management by offering real-time insights and feedback. This continuous approach allows for more timely interventions, adjustments to goals, and support, leading to a more dynamic and adaptive performance management process. As a result, organizations can address challenges and capitalize on opportunities more effectively, fostering a more agile and resilient workforce.The use of AI also supports data-driven decision-making at a strategic level. By analyzing performance data in the context of broader organizational goals and industry benchmarks, AI provides valuable insights that help align individual and team performance with strategic objectives. This alignment ensures that performance management is not only focused on individual development but also contributes to the achievement of organizational success. Furthermore, the integration of AI into existing performance management processes requires careful planning and change management. Organizations must ensure that AI systems complement rather than disrupt established practices, and that employees and managers are adequately trained to use these new tools effectively. Effective change management strategies, including clear communication, training, and support, are essential for a smooth transition to AI-driven performance management.

REFERENCES

Alsaif, A., & Sabih Aksoy, M. (2023). AI-HRM: Artificial Intelligence in Human Resource Management: A Literature Review. *Journal of Computing and Communication*, 2(2), 1–7. DOI: 10.21608/jocc.2023.307053

Arsawan, I. W. E., Koval, V., Rajiani, I., Rustiarini, N. W., Supartha, W. G., & Suryantini, N. P. S. (2022). Leveraging knowledge sharing and innovation culture into SMEs sustainable competitive advantage. *International Journal of Productivity and Performance Management*, 71(2), 405–428. DOI: 10.1108/IJPPM-04-2020-0192

Budhwar, P., Malik, A., De Silva, M. T. T., & Thevisuthan, P. (2022). Artificial intelligence – challenges and opportunities for international HRM: A review and research agenda. *International Journal of Human Resource Management*, 33(6), 1065–1097. DOI: 10.1080/09585192.2022.2035161

Cardwell, S. G., Schuman, C. D., Smith, J. D., Patel, K., Kwon, J., Liu, S., Allemang, C., Misra, S., Incorvia, J. A., & Aimone, J. B. (2022). Probabilistic Neural Circuits leveraging AI-Enhanced Codesign for RandomNumber Generation. *2022 IEEE International Conference on Rebooting Computing (ICRC)*, 57–65. DOI: 10.1109/ICRC57508.2022.00008

Cascio, W. F. (2014). Leveraging employer branding, performance management and human resourcedevelopment to enhance employee retention. *Human Resource Development International*, 17(2), 121–128. DOI: 10.1080/13678868.2014.886443

Chatterjee, S., Rana, N. P., Tamilmani, K., & Sharma, A. (2021). The effect of AI-based CRM on organization performance and competitive advantage: An empirical analysis in the B2B context. *Industrial Marketing Management*, 97, 205–219. DOI: 10.1016/j.indmarman.2021.07.013

Chowdhury, S., Budhwar, P., Dey, P. K., Joel-Edgar, S., & Abadie, A. (2022). AI-employee collaboration and business performance: Integrating knowledge-based view, socio-technical systems and organisational socialisation framework. *Journal of Business Research*, 144, 31–49. DOI: 10.1016/j.jbusres.2022.01.069

Chowdhury, S., Dey, P., Joel-Edgar, S., Bhattacharya, S., Rodriguez-Espindola, O., Abadie, A., & Truong, L. (2023). Unlocking the value of artificial intelligence in human resource management through AI capability framework. *Human Resource Management Review*, 33(1), 100899. DOI: 10.1016/j.hrmr.2022.100899

Choy, K. L., Chow, H. K. H., Tan, K. H., Chan, C.-K., Mok, E. C. M., & Wang, Q. (2008). Leveraging the supply chain flexibility of third party logistics – Hybrid knowledge-based system approach. *Expert Systems with Applications*, 35(4), 1998–2016. DOI: 10.1016/j.eswa.2007.08.084

Devarajan, R., Maheshwari, S., & Vohra, V. (2016). Implementing New Age Performance Management System in IT MNC: Leveraging Communication and Training. *South Asian Journal of Business and Management Cases*, 5(2), 189–197. DOI: 10.1177/2277977916665983

Dutta, D., Srivastava, Y., & Singh, E. (2023). Metaverse in the tourism sector for talent management: A technology in practice lens. *Information Technology & Tourism*, 25(3), 331–365. DOI: 10.1007/s40558-023-00258-9

Fischer, I., Beswick, C., & Newell, S. (2021). Rho AI – Leveraging artificial intelligence to address climate change: Financing, implementation and ethics. *Journal of Information Technology Teaching Cases*, 11(2), 110–116. DOI: 10.1177/2043886920961782

Gelle-Jimenez, M., & Aguiling, H. M. (2021). Leveraging human resources management (HRM) practices toward congruence of values. International Journal of Research in Business and Social Science (2147-4478), 10(1), 85–94. DOI: 10.20525/ijrbs.v10i1.987

Guler, N., Kirshner, S., & Vidgen, R. (2023). Artificial Intelligence Research in Business and Management:A Literature Review Leveraging Machine Learning and Large Language Models. SSRN Electronic Journal. DOI: 10.2139/ssrn.4540834

Hodge, V. J., & Austin, J. (2004). A survey of outlier detection methodologies. *Artificial Intelligence Review*, 22(2), 85–126. DOI: 10.1023/B:AIRE.0000045502.10941.a9

Hooi, L. W. (2021). Leveraging human assets for MNCs performance: The role of managementdevelopment, human resource system and employee engagement. *International Journal of Human Resource Management*, 32(13), 2729–2758. DOI: 10.1080/09585192.2019.1590443

Imai, S., Patterson, S., & Varela, C. A. (2018). Uncertainty-aware elastic virtual machine scheduling for stream processing systems. 2018 18th IEEE/ACM CCGRID, pp. 62 – 71.

Ismail, M., Binti Mustaffa, S. N., & Abed, M. (2023). AI-Enabled Deep Learning Model for COVID-19 Identification Leveraging Internet of Things. *Wasit Journal of Computer and Mathematics Science*, 2(2), 33–39. DOI: 10.31185/wjcms.146

Johan, S. (2021). Enhanced Financial Business Competitiveness by Leveraging Technology and Innovation. CommIT (Communication and Information Technology). *Journal*, 15(2), 79–89. DOI: 10.21512/commit.v15i2.6968

Kulshrestha, N., Kamra, V., & Aggarwal, S. (2023). Leveraging technical analysis and artificialintelligence—Optimisation of global portfolio management through world indices. *International Journalof Public Sector Performance Management*, 12(3), 445–461. DOI: 10.1504/IJPSPM.2023.133588

Lakshman, C. (2014). Leveraging human capital through performance management process: The role of leadership in the USA, France and India†. *International Journal of Human Resource Management*, 25(10), 1351–1372. DOI: 10.1080/09585192.2013.870310

Lin, S., Shi, M., Arora, A., Bassily, R., Bertino, E., Caramanis, C., Chowdhury, K., Ekici, E., Eryilmaz, A., Ioannidis, S., Jiang, N., Joshi, G., Kurose, J., Liang, Y., Lin, Z., Liu, J., Liu, M., Melodia, T., Mokhtari, A., & Ying, L. (2022). Leveraging Synergies Between AI and Networking to Build Next Generation Edge Networks. 2022 IEEE 8th International Conference on Collaboration and Internet Computing(CIC), 16–25.DOI: 10.1109/CIC56439.2022.00013

Liu, H., & Gu, X. (2023). Leveraging AI, big data and educational technology to promote collaborative learning and improve cyberlearning courses: Synopsis and linked presentations of the workshop at Orlando, Florida, 4-6 June 2019, and the online workshop, 13-14 August 2020. *International Journal of Smart Technology and Learning*, 3(2), 118. DOI: 10.1504/IJSMARTTL.2023.129609

Lombardi, F., Aniello, L., Bonomi, S., & Querzoni, L. (2018). Elastic symbiotic scaling of operators and resources in stream processing systems. *IEEE Transactions on Parallel and Distributed Systems*, 29(3), 572–585. DOI: 10.1109/TPDS.2017.2762683

Mahadev Madgule, N. (2023). Vinayaka, Yeshwant M. Sonkhaskar, Dhiren Ramanbhai Patel, R. Karthikeyan, P. Selvakumar,(2023). Mechanical properties and microstructure of activated TIG welded similar joints of Inconel alloys by desirability approaches. *Materials Today: Proceedings*, 77, 528–533. DOI: 10.1016/j.matpr.2022.12.250

Møller, M. F. (1993). A scaled conjugate gradient algorithm for fast supervised learning. *Neural Networks*, 6(4), 525–533. DOI: 10.1016/S0893-6080(05)80056-5

Ramakrishnan, T., Mohan Gift, M. D., Chitradevi, S., Jegan, R., & Subha Hency Jose, P. Nagaraja, Rajneesh Sharma H.N., Selvakumar P., Sintayehu Mekuria Hailegiorgis, (2022). "Study of Numerous Resins Used in Polymer Matrix Composite Materials", Advances in Materials Science and Engineering, vol. 2022, Article ID 1088926, 8 pages, 2022. https://doi.org/DOI: 10.1155/2022/1088926

Runsewe, O., & Samaan, N. (2017). Cloud resource scaling for big data streaming applications using a Layered Multi-dimensional Hidden Markov Model. Proceedings of IEEE/ACM CCGRID '17, pp. 848 – 857. DOI: 10.1109/CCGRID.2017.147

Selvakumar, P. (2023). Biomedical applications of polymers in biosensors, cancer vaccines and drug delivery systems. *Biopolimery i Kletka*, 39(4), 245–256. DOI: 10.7124/bc.000AA0

Selvakumar, P., Mariappan, P., Shunmugam, S., Paul, R., & Jabez, S. (2024). Removal of chemicals from effluent using photobioreactor technology to improve environmental and health impacts. *Zeitschrift für Physikalische Chemie*, 2024(7), 1295–1302. Advance online publication. DOI: 10.1515/zpch-2023-0450

Selvakumar, P., Palanisamy, S. K., Cinthaikinian, S., Palanisamy, V., Mariappan, R., & Selvakumar, P. K. (2024). Biosensors and its diverse applications in healthcare systems. *Zeitschrift für Physikalische Chemie*, 2024. Advance online publication. DOI: 10.1515/zpch-2023-0406

Shahriari, B., Swersky, K., Wang, Z., Adams, R. P., & de Freitas, N. (2015). Taking the human out of the loop: A review of Bayesian optimization. *Proceedings of the IEEE*, 104(1), 148–175. DOI: 10.1109/JPROC.2015.2494218

Toshniwal, A., Taneja, S., & Shukla, A.. (2014). Storm@Twitter. *Proceedings of ACM SIGMOD* '14, ACM, pp. 147 – 156.

Vijayakumar, G., Rajkumar, M., Rajiv Chandar, N., Selvakumar, P., & Duraisamy, R. (2024). Muniyandi Rajkumar, Rajiv Chandar N, Selvakumar P and Ramesh Duraisamy, (2024). Environmentally friendly TDS removal from waste water by electrochemical ion exchange batch-type recirculation (EIR) technique. *Environmental Science. Water Research & Technology*, 10(4), 826–835. DOI: 10.1039/D3EW00793F

Xu, J., Tang, J., Xu, Z., Yin, C., Kwiat, K., & Kamhoua, C. (2019). A deep recurrent neural network based predictive control framework for reliable distributed stream data processing. *Proceedings of IEEE IPDPS*, 19, 262–272. DOI: 10.1109/IPDPS.2019.00036

Yadwadkar, N. J., & Choi, W. (2012). Proactive straggler avoidance using machine learning. White paper, University of Berkeley

Yigitbasi, N., Willke, T. L., Liao, G., & Epema, D. (2013). Towards machine learning-based auto-tuning of MapReduce. Proceedings of IEEE MASCOTS '13, IEEE, pp. 11 – 20.

Zacheilas, N., Kalogeraki, V., & Zygouras, N.. (2015). Elastic complex event processing exploiting prediction. *Proceedings of IEEE Big Data*, 15, 213–222.

Zhang, G. P. (2000). Neural networks for classification: A survey. *IEEE Transactions on Systems, Man, and Cybernetics. Part C, Applications and Reviews*, 30(4), 451–462. DOI: 10.1109/5326.897072

KEY TERMS AND DEFINITIONS

AI Ethics and Governance: The framework of policies and practices that ensure AI is developed and used responsibly. Leadership must establish clear guidelines to manage AI's impact on employees, customers, and society.

AI-Powered Leadership: The use of artificial intelligence tools and technologies to enhance decision-making, strategy formulation, and operational efficiency in leadership roles. It involves leveraging AI to gain insights, automate processes, and predict outcomes to lead organizations effectively.

Artificial Intelligence (AI): A branch of computer science that aims to create systems capable of performing tasks that typically require human intelligence, such as learning, reasoning, problem-solving, understanding natural language, and perception.

Augmented Intelligence: A concept that refers to AI systems designed to enhance human intelligence rather than replace it. Augmented intelligence supports leaders by providing data insights and recommendations while allowing humans to make the final decisions.

Automation: The use of technology to perform tasks without human intervention. AI-driven automation helps leaders streamline operations, reduce costs, and improve efficiency.

Data-Driven Decision Making: A process of making organizational decisions based on actual data analysis rather than intuition or observation alone. AI enables leaders to process large volumes of data to identify patterns and trends.

Digital Transformation: The integration of digital technology into all areas of a business, fundamentally changing how the organization operates and delivers value to customers. AI plays a crucial role in driving digital transformation.

Ethical AI: The practice of developing and using AI systems in a manner that is fair, transparent, and respects privacy and human rights. Ethical AI is essential for maintaining trust and responsibility in AI-powered leadership.

Machine Learning (ML): A subset of AI focused on the development of algorithms that allow computers to learn and make decisions based on data. ML is often used in predictive analytics, enabling leaders to forecast trends and make data-driven decisions.

Natural Language Processing (NLP): A field of AI that enables machines to understand, interpret, and respond to human language. NLP tools are used in leadership for sentiment analysis, customer feedback, and enhancing communication.

Predictive Analytics: The use of data, statistical algorithms, and machine learning techniques to identify the likelihood of future outcomes based on historical data. In leadership, predictive analytics helps anticipate market trends and customer behavior.

Smart Data: Data that has been processed and analyzed to be immediately actionable. In AI-powered leadership, smart data helps leaders make informed decisions quickly.

Chapter 6
AI-Powered Leadership: Shaping the Future of Management

Lakshmi Narasimha Raju Mudunuri
https://orcid.org/0009-0004-7945-0668
Valero Energy Corporation, USA

Muniraju Hullurappa
https://orcid.org/0009-0002-2539-9989
System Soft Technologies LLC, USA

Vamshidhar Reddy Vemula
Independent Researcher, USA

P. Selvakumar
https://orcid.org/0000-0002-3650-4548
Department of Science and Humanities, Nehru Institute of Technology, India

ABSTRACT

AI also revolutionizes leadership through its impact on innovation and strategic planning. AI technologies can simulate various scenarios and model potential outcomes, helping leaders to explore different strategies and assess their potential impacts. This capability supports more agile and adaptable leadership, as organizations can rapidly respond to changing market conditions and emerging trends. Biases in AI algorithms can lead to unfair outcomes and reinforce existing inequalities, impacting areas such as recruitment and performance assessments. Leaders must prioritize the ethical development and deployment of AI technologies, establishing guidelines and oversight mechanisms to mitigate potential biases and ensure equitable treatment of all employees.Effective leadership involves empathy, emotional intelligence, and the ability to navigate complex interpersonal dynamics—qualities

DOI: 10.4018/979-8-3693-8442-8.ch006

that AI systems cannot replicate. Leaders must therefore find ways to integrate AI tools while preserving and enhancing the human elements of leadership that drive organizational success.

INTRODUCTION

AI-Powered Leadership: Revolutionizing Management

AI also revolutionizes leadership through its impact on innovation and strategic planning. AI technologies can simulate various scenarios and model potential outcomes, helping leaders to explore different strategies and assess their potential impacts. This capability supports more agile and adaptable leadership, as organizations can rapidly respond to changing market conditions and emerging trends. Biases in AI algorithms can lead to unfair outcomes and reinforce existing inequalities, impacting areas such as recruitment and performance assessments. Leaders must prioritize the ethical development and deployment of AI technologies, establishing guidelines and oversight mechanisms to mitigate potential biases and ensure equitable treatment of all employees.Effective leadership involves empathy, emotional intelligence, and the ability to navigate complex interpersonal dynamics—qualities that AI systems cannot replicate. Leaders must therefore find ways to integrate AI tools while preserving and enhancing the human elements of leadership that drive organizational success.Another challenge is the potential for increased dependence on technology, which may pose risks if AI systems fail or encounter issues. Organizations must prepare for contingencies by implementing robust backup systems and ensuring that leaders are equipped to make decisions in scenarios where AI may not be reliable or available. Developing a comprehensive understanding of AI technologies and their limitations is crucial for leaders to navigate these challenges effectively.To maximize the benefits of AI-powered leadership, organizations must invest in the development of both technology and human capital. In conclusion, AI-powered leadership represents a significant evolution in management practices, offering transformative opportunities to enhance decision-making, optimize human resources, and drive innovation. By investing in AI literacy, ethical practices, and a collaborative culture, organizations can navigate the complexities of AI-powered leadership and unlock its full potential for revolutionizing management.

The AI-Driven Organization: How Technology is Reshaping Business

In the contemporary business landscape, artificial intelligence (AI) is fundamentally reshaping how organizations operate, strategize, and interact with customers (Agrawal A., et al., 2022). The AI-driven organization represents a paradigm shift where technology is not merely an enabler but a core component of organizational strategy and operations. This transformation is driven by AI's ability to analyze vast amounts of data, automate processes, and provide actionable insights, fundamentally altering traditional business models and redefining competitive dynamics across industries.For instance, predictive analytics can forecast customer demand, enabling businesses to adjust inventory levels and reduce waste. This data-driven approach enhances operational efficiency and supports a more agile and responsive business model.The AI-driven organization also leverages AI for innovation and competitive advantage (Raveendhran R., et al., 2021). By employing AI in research and development, companies can accelerate the innovation process, exploring new product ideas, and optimizing design and testing phases. For example, AI can simulate various design scenarios and predict outcomes, speeding up the development cycle and reducing time-to-market for new products.The shift towards an AI-driven organization also impacts the workforce and organizational structure. In conclusion, the AI-driven organization represents a transformative shift in how businesses operate and compete. By integrating AI technologies into core operations, companies can enhance efficiency, improve customer engagement, and drive innovation.

Leading with Data: AI-Enabled Decision Making for Managers

In the modern business environment, the integration of artificial intelligence (AI) into decision-making processes (Safak C., Farrar J. 2021) represents a profound shift in managerial practices, redefining how leaders approach strategy, operations, and organizational growth. AI-enabled decision making empowers managers with advanced tools and insights derived from vast and complex datasets, facilitating more informed, precise, and strategic decisions (Antonakis J., et al., 2011). This shift towards data-driven leadership is transforming the role of managers, emphasizing the importance of analytical acumen and technological proficiency in steering organizations towards success. AI systems can handle data entry, analysis, and reporting tasks with high accuracy and speed, freeing managers to focus on strategic planning and leadership. For instance, AI can automate financial forecasting, inventory management, and supply chain optimization, reducing manual effort and minimizing errors. This automation not only enhances productivity but also ensures that decision-making processes are grounded in up-to-date and accurate information, leading to more effective management.

The use of AI in decision making also facilitates more personalized and targeted strategies. AI-driven insights enable managers to tailor approaches to specific customer segments, geographic regions, or product lines, resulting in more effective and relevant strategies (Balasubramanian N., et al., 2020). For example, personalized marketing campaigns can be designed based on AI analysis of customer preferences and behavior, increasing engagement and conversion rates. Similarly, AI can support targeted talent management strategies by analyzing employee performance data and identifying areas for development, ultimately improving team effectiveness and satisfaction(Tigre F. B., et al.,2022).In conclusion, leading with data through AI-enabled decision making represents a transformative shift in managerial practices, offering significant opportunities to enhance strategic planning, operational efficiency, and customer engagement. By leveraging advanced AI tools and insights, managers can make more informed and precise decisions, driving organizational success and competitive advantage. As organizations continue to integrate AI into decision-making processes, managers must navigate these complexities to harness the full potential of data-driven leadership and achieve sustained success in a rapidly evolving business landscape.

RESEARCH METHODOLOGY

AI-Powered Strategy: Harnessing Machine Learning for Competitive Advantage

In the contemporary business landscape, artificial intelligence (AI) and machine learning (ML) are emerging as pivotal drivers of competitive advantage, reshaping how companies strategize, operate, and achieve growth (Banks G. C., et al.,2021). AI-powered strategy leverages the capabilities of machine learning to analyze vast amounts of data, uncover actionable insights, and guide strategic decision-making, fundamentally transforming traditional business models and competitive dynamics (Tourish D. 2020).Moreover, machine learning enhances strategic planning by providing predictive analytics that forecast future trends and potential challenges. Predictive models can analyze historical data and identify key variables that influence outcomes, allowing organizations to anticipate market shifts, optimize resource allocation, and develop proactive strategies (Van den Broeck A., et al., 2016). Similarly, in finance, machine learning models can forecast market movements, assess investment risks, and identify opportunities for growth, supporting more informed financial decision-making.

The application of machine learning extends to competitive intelligence, where it can uncover insights about competitors and market dynamics that drive strategic advantage. Machine learning algorithms can analyze publicly available data, such as news articles, financial reports, and social media content, to identify trends, sentiment, and strategic moves of competitors. This intelligence enables organizations to anticipate competitors' actions, identify emerging threats, and capitalize on market opportunities. By integrating competitive intelligence into their strategy (Sugumaran K. M, D., et al., 2024), companies can develop more effective positioning, differentiate themselves from rivals, and enhance their market presence (Van Quaquebeke N., et al., 2018).In addition to enhancing strategic planning and competitive intelligence, machine learning supports innovation by driving data-driven experimentation and optimization (Bass D. 2023). Machine learning algorithms can test various scenarios, evaluate potential outcomes, and optimize processes based on real-time feedback. This capability allows organizations to experiment with new ideas, refine their products and services, and accelerate the innovation cycle. For example, in product development, machine learning can analyze customer feedback and usage patterns to identify areas for improvement, leading to more successful product iterations and faster time-to-market.Another challenge is the need for skilled talent to develop and implement machine learning models effectively. The successful application of machine learning requires expertise in data science, algorithm development, and model interpretation (Wang B., et al., 2022). Organizations must address issues related to algorithmic bias, transparency, and accountability to ensure that machine learning models are used responsibly and ethically.

The Future of Work: How AI is Changing the Nature of Leadership

The future of work is being profoundly reshaped by artificial intelligence (AI), fundamentally altering the nature of leadership and the dynamics of organizational management (Carton A. M., et al.,2018). As AI technologies increasingly permeate various aspects of business operations, they introduce transformative changes that impact how leaders operate, make decisions, and interact with their teams (Paramasivam Selvakumar, et al., 2024). AI systems provide leaders with advanced analytics and insights derived from large and complex datasets, enabling more informed and data-driven decisions. Furthermore, AI is enhancing operational efficiency by automating routine and repetitive tasks, which transforms the role of leaders. By leveraging AI for tasks such as data entry, report generation, and process optimization, leaders can delegate operational responsibilities to intelligent systems and focus on higher-level strategic activities. This shift enables leaders to allocate their time and resources more effectively, driving innovation, fostering team development, and addressing complex challenges (Wenzel R., et al., 2018). Automation also allows for more efficient use of human resources, as leaders can reassign roles to areas where human judgment and creativity are most valuable.

AI's influence extends to talent management and organizational culture, where it plays a crucial role in shaping leadership practices. AI-driven tools can analyze employee performance, engagement, and potential, providing leaders with valuable insights to make informed decisions about talent development and management (Cascio W. F., et al.,2003). Predictive analytics can identify high-potential employees, recommend personalized training programs, and support succession planning. By utilizing AI in talent management, leaders can foster a more dynamic and capable workforce, enhance employee satisfaction, and build a resilient organizational culture.The rise of AI also necessitates a shift in leadership skills and competencies. As AI technologies become integral to business operations, leaders must develop a strong understanding of AI and its implications for their organizations. This includes acquiring skills in data literacy (Wesche J. S., et al., 2019), machine learning, and algorithmic decision-making. Leaders must be able to interpret AI-generated insights, integrate them into strategic planning, and make decisions that align with organizational goals. Additionally, effective leadership in an AI-driven environment requires a focus on ethical considerations, such as addressing algorithmic biases, ensuring transparency, and safeguarding data privacy.Moreover, AI is reshaping leadership by changing the nature of communication and collaboration within organizations. AI-powered tools facilitate remote work, virtual collaboration, and real-time communication, enabling teams to operate more flexibly and efficiently. Leaders must adapt to these changes by fostering a culture of digital collaboration, leveraging AI tools to enhance communication, and addressing the challenges of remote and hybrid work environments. This shift requires leaders to be adept at managing virtual teams, maintaining engagement, and ensuring that organizational objectives are met despite physical distances. However, these advancements also necessitate new skills, ethical considerations, and a focus on maintaining the human elements of leadership(Cheng J. T., et al., 2022). As AI continues to evolve, leaders must navigate these complexities, ensuring that technology is harnessed to drive organizational success while preserving the essential qualities of effective leadership.

AI-Driven Innovation: Fostering a Culture of Creativity and Experimentation

AI-driven innovation represents a paradigm shift where technology not only supports but actively enhances the creative process, enabling organizations to push boundaries, explore new possibilities, and develop groundbreaking solutions (De Cremer D., et al.,2022). By integrating AI into the innovation process, companies can cultivate a culture that encourages experimentation, accelerates development, and drives competitive advantage. For example, AI-powered analytics can identify emerging market opportunities, suggest new product features based on user feedback, and uncover latent needs that may not be immediately apparent. This shift not only enhances productivity but also fosters a work environment where creativity can flourish. For instance, in product development, AI can handle preliminary design iterations and testing, enabling teams to focus on refining concepts and exploring novel ideas without being bogged down by manual tasks.

Moreover, AI-driven tools can support experimentation by providing simulations and scenario analysis. Machine learning models can simulate various scenarios and predict potential outcomes, allowing organizations to test ideas and strategies in a virtual environment before committing resources to full-scale implementation (Yalcin G., et al.,2022). This capability reduces risk and accelerates the innovation cycle, as teams can rapidly iterate and refine their approaches based on simulated results. For example, in marketing, AI can model the impact of different campaign strategies on customer behavior, helping teams to identify the most effective approaches before launching them in the real world.Another key aspect of fostering a culture of creativity and experimentation through AI is the use of generative AI technologies (Deci E. L., et al.,2000). Generative models, such as those used in natural language processing and computer vision, can create new content, designs, and solutions based on existing data. These models can assist in brainstorming sessions by generating novel ideas, suggesting creative combinations, and providing inspiration for new projects (Zhang C., et al.,2020). For example, AI-powered design tools can propose innovative product concepts, while generative text models can assist in crafting compelling marketing copy. By leveraging these technologies, organizations can expand their creative horizons and explore new avenues for innovation.However, successfully integrating AI into the innovation process requires addressing several challenges. This requires a thoughtful approach to integrating AI into decision-making processes, where technology complements rather than dictates creative direction. Another challenge is maintaining a balance between technology and human creativity. While AI can enhance and support innovation, it is not a substitute for human imagination, intuition, and expertise. Organizations must cultivate a culture that values and encourages human creativity alongside technological advancements (Densten I. L., et al., 2001). This includes fostering an environment where employees feel empowered to experiment, take risks, and contribute their unique perspectives. Leaders play a critical role in creating this culture by promoting open communication, supporting cross-disciplinary collaboration, and recognizing the contributions of team members.

THEORETICAL FRAMEWORK

Leading AI-Powered Teams: Strategies for Effective Collaboration

As organizations increasingly integrate artificial intelligence (AI) into their operations, the nature of teamwork and leadership is undergoing significant transformation (Else H. 2023). Leading AI-powered teams involves navigating a complex landscape where technology and human collaboration intersect, requiring new strategies and approaches to harness the full potential of AI while fostering a cohesive and productive work environment. One of the foremost strategies for leading AI-powered teams is to cultivate a clear and shared vision of how AI will be used to achieve organizational goals. Leaders must articulate the role of AI within the team's objectives, ensuring that all members understand how these technologies contribute to the overall mission. This involves not only explaining the benefits of AI but also addressing potential concerns and clarifying how AI tools will integrate with existing workflows. By setting a clear direction and demonstrating how AI supports strategic aims, leaders can align the team's efforts and foster a unified approach to leveraging technology.Effective communication is another critical strategy in leading AI-powered teams. AI systems often generate complex data and insights that can be challenging for team members to interpret and act upon. Leaders must facilitate clear and open communication channels, ensuring that AI-generated information is translated into actionable insights that are accessible and understandable for all team members (Zhu J. 2017). This involves regular briefings, data visualizations, and interactive sessions where team members can ask questions and discuss how AI insights impact their work. By promoting transparency and dialogue, leaders can enhance the team's ability to collaborate effectively with AI tools.

Training and development are essential for maximizing the effectiveness of AI-powered teams. By building a foundation of knowledge and expertise, leaders can empower their teams to utilize AI more effectively and confidently, fostering a culture of competence and innovation.Another crucial strategy is to establish a collaborative culture that embraces the synergies between AI and human expertise (Ferràs-Hernández X. 2018). While AI can handle data analysis, automation, and predictive modeling, human skills such as creativity, critical thinking, and emotional intelligence remain vital. Leaders should encourage a collaborative environment where AI complements human abilities rather than replacing them. This involves defining clear roles and responsibilities, ensuring that AI tools support rather than overshadow human contributions, and fostering an atmosphere where team members feel valued and engaged. By integrating AI as a partner in the creative process, leaders can enhance teamwork and drive innovation.Managing the ethical implications of AI is also a key consideration for leaders of AI-powered teams. Encouraging adaptability and resilience is another important strategy for leading AI-powered teams. The rapid pace of technological change can present challenges and uncertainties, requiring teams to be agile and adaptable in their approach. Leaders should foster a culture of continuous improvement and learning, where team members are encouraged to experiment, adapt to new tools, and respond to evolving demands. This involves supporting a mindset of flexibility, providing resources for managing change, and celebrating successes and learnings from experimentation. By cultivating resilience, leaders can help their teams navigate the dynamic landscape of AI-driven work.

Finally, leaders must focus on building strong interpersonal relationships within AI-powered teams. Despite the advanced capabilities of AI, human interaction remains crucial for effective teamwork(Vijayakumar G, et al., 2024). Leaders should prioritize team-building activities, foster a sense of camaraderie, and encourage mutual support among team members (Fischer T., et al., 2022). This involves creating opportunities for collaboration, recognizing individual and team achievements, and addressing any interpersonal conflicts or challenges. By nurturing positive relationships and a supportive team environment, leaders can enhance overall productivity and morale. In conclusion, leading AI-powered teams requires a strategic approach that balances technological advancements with effective human collaboration. By cultivating a clear vision, promoting effective communication, investing in training, and fostering a collaborative culture, leaders can harness the full potential of AI while enhancing team performance. Addressing ethical considerations, encouraging adaptability, and building strong interpersonal relationships further support successful leadership in an AI-driven environment. As organizations continue to integrate AI into their operations, effective leadership will be crucial in ensuring that technology and human expertise work together seamlessly to drive innovation and achieve strategic goals.

AI-Enabled Communication: Enhancing Transparency and Trust

In an era where communication is pivotal to organizational success and public engagement, artificial intelligence (AI) is revolutionizing how information is disseminated, understood, and interacted with (Gagné M., et al., 2005). AI-enabled communication technologies are enhancing transparency and trust by streamlining information sharing, improving clarity, and fostering more meaningful interactions. These advancements offer organizations the opportunity to build stronger relationships with stakeholders, mitigate misinformation, and uphold ethical standards in their communication practices. Moreover, AI enhances transparency by automating and personalizing communication, making it more accessible and understandable. Personalization features allow AI systems to tailor communications based on individual preferences and needs, enhancing the clarity and effectiveness of interactions. This level of responsiveness and customization helps organizations build trust by demonstrating a commitment to addressing stakeholder concerns and providing valuable information.AI also plays a critical role in mitigating misinformation and enhancing the reliability of communication. AI-driven fact-checking and content moderation tools can identify and address false or misleading information before it spreads. By analyzing patterns and detecting anomalies in data, AI systems can flag suspicious content, verify facts, and ensure that communications are accurate and credible. This proactive approach to managing information helps maintain trust and integrity in organizational messaging, particularly in an age where misinformation can rapidly undermine public confidence.

Furthermore, AI enables more effective and transparent decision-making by providing detailed insights into communication effectiveness and stakeholder sentiment. Sentiment analysis tools use machine learning to assess public opinion and emotional responses to various communications, such as press releases, social media posts, and marketing campaigns (Gerpott F. H., 2018). By understanding how stakeholders perceive and react to messages, organizations can adjust their strategies to better align with audience expectations and concerns. This level of insight not only enhances transparency but also demonstrates responsiveness and a willingness to engage with stakeholder feedback constructively.Training and education are also essential for maximizing the benefits of AI-enabled communication. Employees and stakeholders must understand how AI tools function, their limitations, and how they contribute to organizational communication efforts. Providing training on AI technologies, data privacy, and ethical considerations helps ensure that all parties are informed and capable of leveraging AI effectively while adhering to best practices. In conclusion, AI-enabled communication represents a significant advancement in enhancing transparency and trust within organizations and their interactions with stakeholders. By leveraging AI for real-time insights, automated responses, and accurate information management, organizations can build stronger relationships, mitigate misinformation, and demonstrate a commitment to ethical communication practices. However, achieving these benefits requires careful attention to data privacy, algorithmic bias, and ongoing education. By embracing AI thoughtfully and strategically, organizations can harness its potential to foster transparency, strengthen trust, and effectively engage with their audiences in an increasingly complex and dynamic communication landscape.

The Ethics of AI Leadership: Navigating Complex Moral Dilemmas

The rise of artificial intelligence (AI) has introduced profound ethical considerations for leaders across various sectors, necessitating a thoughtful approach to navigating complex moral dilemmas inherent in AI deployment and governance (Gerpott F. H., et al.,2022). This involves implementing rigorous testing and validation processes, employing diverse datasets, and engaging in continuous monitoring to detect and address biases. Ethical leadership requires a commitment to creating AI systems that promote inclusivity and do not reinforce social inequalities. Transparency is another crucial ethical dimension in AI leadership. Leaders must advocate for and implement practices that enhance the interpretability and explainability of AI systems. Given the potential for AI systems to make autonomous or semi-autonomous decisions, leaders must delineate who is accountable when these systems produce unintended or harmful results. This includes defining roles and responsibilities for oversight, developing mechanisms for addressing grievances, and ensuring that there are processes in place to rectify issues. Effective AI leadership requires creating an environment where accountability is a shared responsibility, and where there are established procedures for reviewing and addressing the impacts of AI technologies on individuals and society.

The broader societal impacts of AI also present ethical challenges for leaders. AI technologies have the potential to reshape industries, labor markets, and social interactions in profound ways. Leaders must consider the long-term implications of AI on employment, privacy, and social equity. This involves engaging in strategic planning that balances technological advancement with the need to protect human rights and social welfare. For example, leaders might advocate for policies that support workforce reskilling and address the displacement effects of automation (Haesevoets T., et al., 2021). Collaboration and dialogue with external stakeholders are essential for navigating the ethics of AI leadership. Engaging with policymakers, academics, advocacy groups, and the public can provide valuable perspectives on ethical challenges and potential solutions. In conclusion, the ethics of AI leadership involves addressing complex moral dilemmas related to algorithmic bias, transparency, accountability, and societal impact. Effective leadership in this domain requires a commitment to fairness, openness, and responsibility, ensuring that AI technologies are deployed in ways that are ethical and beneficial to society.

AI-Powered Talent Management: Revolutionizing HR and Recruitment

Artificial intelligence (AI) is rapidly transforming talent management and recruitment, offering innovative solutions that enhance efficiency, accuracy, and strategic alignment in human resources (HR) practices (Haslam S. A., et al., 2021). This transformation is reshaping traditional HR practices, introducing new methodologies for talent acquisition, and enabling a more data-driven approach to managing human capital.One of the most significant advancements AI brings to talent management is the enhancement of recruitment processes. This automation not only reduces the time spent on administrative tasks but also minimizes human biases that can influence hiring decisions. By relying on data-driven insights, organizations can improve the accuracy and fairness of candidate evaluations.AI-powered tools can also identify potential talent pools by scanning online platforms, social media, and professional networks. These capabilities allow HR professionals to proactively engage with high-potential candidates, even before they actively seek new opportunities. This proactive approach to talent sourcing helps organizations build a pipeline of qualified candidates and reduce the time-to-fill for critical positions. In addition to streamlining recruitment, AI enhances employee management and development through personalized learning and performance management solutions. By leveraging AI to create personalized development plans, organizations can foster a culture of continuous learning and support employee growth, ultimately driving higher engagement and retention.AI also plays a crucial role in optimizing workforce planning and talent allocation.

AI-Driven Change Management: Minimizing Disruption and Maximizing Adoption

In today's rapidly evolving business landscape, organizations are increasingly relying on artificial intelligence (AI) to manage change effectively, minimize disruption, and maximize adoption. As businesses integrate new technologies and processes, AI-driven change management (Hemshorn de Sanchez C. S., et al.,2022) provides a strategic approach to navigating these transitions smoothly. By leveraging AI tools and techniques, organizations can enhance their ability to predict, manage, and facilitate change, ultimately achieving better outcomes and fostering a more agile and resilient workforce.AI enhances change management by offering data-driven insights and predictive analytics, which are crucial for anticipating and addressing potential challenges. AI algorithms can analyze historical data, industry trends, and organizational metrics to forecast the impact of upcoming changes. For instance, AI can identify patterns and potential risks associated with new technology implementations or organizational restructuring. By understanding these risks in advance, leaders can develop targeted strategies to mitigate them, reducing the likelihood of disruptions and ensuring a smoother transition. This predictive capability allows organizations to proactively address issues before they escalate, leading to more effective change management.Moreover, AI facilitates more personalized and effective communication during change initiatives. AI-powered tools can segment employees based on their roles, concerns, and readiness for change, enabling tailored communication strategies.

Training and development are critical components of change management, and AI can significantly enhance these efforts by offering adaptive learning solutions. For example, AI can recommend relevant training modules, simulate new processes, and offer interactive exercises to reinforce learning.AI also supports change management by improving stakeholder engagement and collaboration (Kniffin K. M., et al., 2019). AI-powered collaboration tools can facilitate communication and coordination among team members, even in distributed or remote work environments. These tools can streamline project management, track progress, and manage tasks, ensuring that all stakeholders are aligned and informed. Additionally, AI can analyze collaboration patterns and identify potential bottlenecks or areas for improvement. By enhancing collaboration and transparency, AI helps ensure that change initiatives are executed effectively and that team members are actively involved in the process.To minimize disruption and maximize adoption, organizations must also focus on change readiness and resilience. AI can assist in assessing organizational readiness for change by evaluating factors such as employee attitudes, skills, and organizational culture. Predictive analytics can identify potential resistance points and suggest strategies to address them. For instance, AI can highlight areas where additional support or resources may be needed to facilitate a smoother transition. By understanding and addressing readiness factors, leaders can enhance the organization's ability to adapt to change and maintain continuity during transitions. By leveraging AI for predictive analytics, personalized communication, adaptive training, and stakeholder engagement, organizations can enhance their ability to manage change effectively and achieve successful outcomes.

The AI Leader's Mindset: Embracing Agility, Adaptability, and Continuous Learning

In the dynamic realm of artificial intelligence (AI), effective leadership demands a mindset that embraces agility, adaptability, and continuous learning (Köbis N., et al., 2021). As AI technologies evolve at a rapid pace, leaders must cultivate these attributes to navigate the complexities of AI-driven environments and guide their organizations through transformative change. This mindset is crucial not only for leveraging AI effectively but also for fostering a culture that thrives on innovation and resilience.Agility is a cornerstone of successful AI leadership. The AI landscape is characterized by rapid technological advancements and shifting market dynamics, requiring leaders to remain flexible and responsive (Lanz L., et al., 2023). An agile leader in the AI context is one who can quickly adapt strategies and approaches based on emerging trends and new information. This involves being open to iterative processes, where strategies are continuously refined and adjusted in response to real-time feedback and evolving circumstances. For instance, an AI leader might need to pivot their approach based on new AI research findings, changing business needs, or unforeseen challenges. Embracing agility ensures that leaders can effectively capitalize on opportunities and address issues as they arise, maintaining a competitive edge in a fast-moving environment.Adaptability is closely linked to agility but focuses more on the leader's ability to adjust to change and guide their teams through uncertainty.

Continuous learning is essential for AI leaders, given the rapid pace of technological advancements and the evolving nature of the AI field. AI leaders must commit to ongoing education and skill development to stay informed about the latest AI technologies, methodologies, and best practices (Larson L., et al.,2020). This involves not only formal education and training but also staying engaged with industry trends, attending conferences, and participating in professional networks. Continuous learning enables leaders to make informed decisions, adopt innovative approaches, and anticipate future trends. Additionally, fostering a culture of learning within the organization encourages employees to develop their skills and adapt to new technologies, contributing to overall organizational growth and success.Incorporating these attributes into leadership practices involves several key strategies. Firstly, leaders should model agility and adaptability by being transparent about their decision-making processes and openly communicating how changes will impact the organization. This transparency builds trust and helps employees understand the rationale behind strategic shifts. Leaders should also encourage experimentation and innovation, creating an environment where new ideas are tested, and learning from failures is valued. This approach not only supports continuous improvement but also inspires teams to embrace change and pursue new opportunities.Another critical aspect of an AI leader's mindset is fostering a collaborative culture that leverages diverse perspectives and expertise. AI projects often require interdisciplinary teams with varied skills and knowledge. Leaders should promote collaboration and knowledge sharing among team members, encouraging a collective approach to problem-solving and innovation. By valuing diverse input and creating opportunities for cross-functional collaboration, leaders can harness the full potential of AI technologies and drive more effective outcomes. Finally, self-awareness and resilience are important traits for AI leaders. Leading in the AI space can be challenging, with potential setbacks and uncertainties. Leaders should develop resilience to manage stress and navigate obstacles effectively(Longoni C., et al., 2022). Self-awareness helps leaders understand their strengths and areas for growth, allowing them to seek support, refine their skills, and adapt their leadership approach as needed.

AI-Powered Diversity, Equity, and Inclusion: Fostering a Culture of Belonging

Artificial intelligence (AI) is increasingly becoming a powerful tool in advancing diversity, equity, and inclusion (DEI) within organizations, offering novel solutions for fostering a culture of belonging (McFarlin L. A. 2019). By harnessing AI, organizations can better understand and address the challenges related to diversity and inclusion, implement more effective strategies, and create a more equitable workplace. However, while AI holds significant potential for driving positive change, it also requires careful implementation to ensure that it supports, rather than undermines, DEI goals.AI can significantly enhance diversity and inclusion efforts through data-driven insights and analytics. AI tools can analyze large volumes of data related to recruitment, hiring, promotions, and employee feedback to identify patterns and disparities. For instance, AI can detect biases in hiring practices by evaluating the diversity of candidate pools and the outcomes of hiring decisions. This allows organizations to pinpoint areas where biases may exist and implement targeted interventions to address them. By leveraging AI to track and measure diversity metrics, organizations can set actionable goals, monitor progress, and ensure that their DEI initiatives are grounded in empirical evidence.One of the key applications of AI in DEI is in recruitment and talent acquisition. AI-driven tools can help reduce bias in the hiring process by anonymizing resumes and applications, focusing on skills and qualifications rather than personal attributes that could lead to discrimination. For example, AI can use algorithms to evaluate candidates based on their experience, education, and skills, rather than demographic factors. Additionally, AI can analyze job descriptions and recruitment materials to identify and eliminate biased language that may discourage diverse candidates from applying. This approach promotes a more equitable recruitment process and helps attract a wider range of qualified candidates.

AI also plays a crucial role in enhancing inclusivity by supporting personalized development and career growth for employees. AI-powered learning and development platforms can tailor training programs to individual needs, helping employees from underrepresented groups acquire the skills and knowledge required for advancement. These platforms can recommend courses, provide feedback, and track progress in a way that supports diverse learning styles and career aspirations. By offering personalized development opportunities, organizations can ensure that all employees have access to the resources they need to succeed and thrive within the organization (McKinsey & Company 2019).This analysis helps organizations understand how employees from different backgrounds perceive their work environment, identify potential areas of concern, and measure the effectiveness of DEI initiatives. By gaining insights into employee experiences and sentiments, organizations can address issues related to inclusion and create a more supportive and welcoming workplace culture.AI can also facilitate the creation of employee resource groups (ERGs) and affinity networks by identifying and connecting employees with shared interests and experiences. For instance, AI tools can analyze employee profiles and interests to recommend participation in relevant ERGs or mentorship programs. This helps build a sense of community and provides employees with opportunities to connect with peers who understand their unique perspectives. By supporting the formation of ERGs and fostering connections among employees, organizations can strengthen their DEI efforts and promote a culture of belonging.

Despite its potential benefits, the integration of AI in DEI initiatives must be approached with caution to avoid reinforcing existing biases or creating new forms of discrimination. Additionally, it is essential to maintain human oversight in AI-driven DEI efforts. While AI can provide valuable insights and automate processes, human judgment is crucial for interpreting results, making nuanced decisions, and ensuring that DEI strategies are implemented effectively. Leaders and DEI professionals should work collaboratively with AI tools, using their expertise to complement and guide the insights provided by AI (Mollick E. R., et al., 2022). This partnership ensures that AI supports broader DEI goals and contributes to creating a truly inclusive and equitable workplace.In conclusion, AI-powered diversity, equity, and inclusion initiatives offer significant opportunities for organizations to advance their DEI goals and foster a culture of belonging. By leveraging AI for data-driven insights, unbiased recruitment, personalized development, and sentiment analysis, organizations can address disparities, support diverse talent, and enhance inclusivity.

SOLUTIONS AND RECOMMENDATIONS

Measuring AI's Impact on Leadership: Assessing Effectiveness and ROI

Evaluating the impact of artificial intelligence (AI) on leadership requires a comprehensive approach that assesses both effectiveness and return on investment (ROI) (Moussawi S., et al., 2021). As AI technologies increasingly influence leadership practices, organizations must develop robust metrics and methodologies to gauge how these tools enhance decision-making, drive performance, and deliver value. Understanding AI's role in leadership not only helps in optimizing its use but also in demonstrating its tangible benefits to stakeholders.The effectiveness of AI in leadership can be measured through various dimensions, including decision-making accuracy, process efficiency, and overall organizational performance. One of the primary ways to assess effectiveness is by evaluating how AI tools improve decision-making. AI can provide leaders with data-driven insights, predictive analytics, and scenario modeling, which enhance their ability to make informed and strategic decisions (Nesbit P. L. 2012). Measuring effectiveness in this context involves analyzing the quality of decisions made with AI support compared to those made without it. Key performance indicators (KPIs) such as decision accuracy, speed of decision-making, and alignment with strategic goals can provide insights into AI's impact on leadership effectiveness.

Organizational performance is another key area where AI's impact on leadership can be assessed. AI tools can influence various aspects of organizational performance, including employee engagement, customer satisfaction, and financial outcomes (Nichols G. 2021). To measure this impact, organizations should track relevant KPIs such as employee productivity, turnover rates, customer feedback scores, and revenue growth. By correlating these performance metrics with the adoption of AI tools, organizations can determine how AI contributes to overall business success. Additionally, conducting surveys and interviews with employees and stakeholders can provide qualitative insights into how AI is perceived and its impact on organizational culture and morale.Assessing the ROI of AI in leadership involves calculating the financial and strategic benefits derived from AI investments relative to their costs. ROI can be evaluated by comparing the initial investment in AI technologies with the measurable benefits achieved. This includes direct financial returns, such as increased revenue or reduced costs, as well as strategic benefits, such as enhanced competitive advantage or improved market positioning. Organizations can use various financial metrics to assess ROI, including return on assets (ROA), return on equity (ROE), and return on investment (ROI) ratios. Additionally, calculating the payback period, which is the time required to recoup the investment through realized benefits, can provide a clear indication of AI's financial impact (O'Neil C. 2016).Qualitative factors also play a significant role in evaluating the ROI of AI in leadership. For instance, the impact of AI on leadership effectiveness and organizational culture may not always be immediately quantifiable but can significantly influence long-term success. Leaders should consider factors such as improved strategic alignment, enhanced decision-making capabilities, and increased innovation capacity when assessing ROI. Additionally, the ability of AI to support leadership in navigating complex and rapidly changing environments can offer substantial strategic value that goes beyond immediate financial returns.Furthermore, continuous monitoring and evaluation are essential for assessing AI's impact over time. AI technologies and their applications evolve, and their effectiveness can change as new features are introduced or as organizational needs shift (Parent-Rocheleau X., et al., 2021). Regularly reviewing AI performance, gathering feedback from users, and analyzing changes in key metrics can help organizations stay informed about AI's ongoing impact and ensure that leadership practices remain aligned with business objectives.

FUTURE RESEARCH DIRECTIONS

By understanding and harnessing AI's capabilities, leaders can drive their organizations towards greater efficiency, agility, and competitive advantage (Petriglieri G., et al., 2015). The transformative impact of AI on leadership is evident across various domains. Automation not only improves productivity but also minimizes errors and operational bottlenecks, leading to cost savings and more efficient use of resources. By integrating AI into their operations, leaders can create more agile and responsive organizations that are better equipped to adapt to evolving market conditions.AI's role in fostering a culture of inclusivity and belonging is another critical aspect of its potential. By leveraging AI to analyze and address biases in recruitment, performance evaluations, and employee feedback, leaders can create a more equitable and supportive work environment. AI-driven tools can help identify and mitigate disparities, promote diverse talent, and ensure that all employees have equal opportunities for growth and advancement (Pillutla M. M., et al., 2013). Leaders should stay informed about emerging AI trends, invest in their own learning, and encourage a culture of curiosity and experimentation within their organizations. By remaining adaptable and open to new ideas, leaders can effectively integrate AI into their strategies and drive sustained growth and success.Additionally, measuring the impact of AI on leadership is crucial for demonstrating value and guiding future investments. Organizations should employ a range of metrics to assess AI's effectiveness, including decision-making accuracy, process efficiency, and overall organizational performance (Raisch S., et al., 2020). By leveraging AI to enhance decision-making, streamline operations, foster inclusivity, and drive continuous improvement, leaders can position their organizations for long-term success in a rapidly changing world. As AI technologies continue to advance, the ability to effectively integrate and manage these tools will be a defining factor in achieving competitive advantage and driving organizational excellence. With thoughtful implementation and a commitment to ethical practices, AI-powered leadership has the potential to transform organizations and create a more dynamic, efficient, and inclusive future.

CONCLUSION

As we advance into an era characterized by rapid technological innovation, AI-powered leadership is poised to reshape the landscape of management profoundly. Leaders who effectively integrate AI into their decision-making processes can achieve a higher level of precision and agility, positioning their organizations to excel in an increasingly volatile and competitive environment.Moreover, AI-driven automation is revolutionizing operational efficiency by streamlining workflows and reducing the burden of repetitive tasks. AI technologies can handle routine operations such as data entry, scheduling, and reporting, allowing leaders and their teams to focus on higher-value activities that drive innovation and strategic growth. This shift towards automation not only enhances productivity but also minimizes human error and operational bottlenecks, resulting in cost savings and improved performance. As organizations embrace AI-driven automation, they can achieve greater operational agility and responsiveness, critical factors in maintaining a competitive edge.Fostering a culture of innovation and inclusivity is another key benefit of AI-powered leadership. AI tools can support diverse and inclusive workplaces by addressing biases in recruitment, performance evaluation, and employee engagement. By analyzing data related to hiring practices, employee feedback, and workplace dynamics, AI can help identify and mitigate disparities, promote equitable opportunities, and enhance organizational culture. Leaders who champion AI-driven DEI initiatives can build a more inclusive and supportive environment, driving greater employee satisfaction, retention, and overall organizational success.Ensuring transparency, accountability, and fairness in AI implementations is essential to avoid perpetuating existing biases or creating new forms of discrimination. Leaders must maintain oversight, validate AI algorithms, and address potential ethical concerns to foster trust and integrity in AI-driven processes. Balancing technological advancements with ethical considerations is crucial for leveraging AI in a way that aligns with organizational values and societal norms.Measuring the impact of AI on leadership is critical for demonstrating value and guiding future investments. Organizations should use a combination of quantitative metrics and qualitative assessments to evaluate AI's effectiveness in enhancing decision-making, improving efficiency, and driving performance. Key performance indicators (KPIs) such as decision accuracy, process efficiency, employee engagement, and financial outcomes provide valuable insights into AI's impact. Additionally, gathering feedback from stakeholders and conducting regular evaluations helps organizations understand AI's contributions and refine their strategies accordingly.In conclusion, AI-powered leadership represents a transformative force that is shaping the future of management. As organizations navigate this transition, the ability to integrate and manage AI effectively will be a key determinant of long-term success and growth. The future of management is being redefined by AI, and leaders who embrace this transformation with insight and foresight will be well-positioned to shape a dynamic and successful future.

REFERENCES

Agrawal A., Gans J., Goldfarb A. (2022). From prediction to transformation. Harvard Business Review, Nov/Dez 2022(BR2206), 100-109.

Antonakis, J., & Day, D. V. (2018). Leadership: Past, present, and future. In Antonakis, J., & Day, D. V. (Eds.), *The nature of leadership* (3rd ed., pp. 3–26). Sage Publications, Inc., DOI: 10.4135/9781506395029.n1

Antonakis, J., Fenley, M., & Liechti, S. (2011). Can charisma be taught? Tests of two interventions. *Academy of Management Learning & Education*, 10(3), 374–396. DOI: 10.5465/amle.2010.0012

Balasubramanian, N., Ye, Y., & Xu, M. (2020). Substituting human decision-making with machine learning: Implications for organizational learning. *Academy of Management Review*, 47(3), 448–465. DOI: 10.5465/amr.2019.0470

Banks, G. C., Woznyj, H. M., & Mansfield, C. A. (2021). Where is "behavior" in organizational behavior? A call for a revolution in leadership research and beyond. *The Leadership Quarterly*, 101581. Advance online publication. DOI: 10.1016/j.leaqua.2021.101581

Bass, D. (2023). Microsoft to add ChatGPT to Azure Cloud Services 'soon'. Bloomberg. https://www.technologyreview.com/2023/08/02/238757/ai-could-be-your-wingmaner-wingboton-your-next-first-date/

Carton, A. M., & Lucas, B. J. (2018). How can leaders overcome the blurry vision bias? Identifying an antidote to the paradox of vision communication. *Academy of Management Journal*, 61(6), 2106–2129. DOI: 10.5465/amj.2015.0375

Cascio, W. F., & Shurygailo, S. (2003). E-leadership and virtual teams. *Organizational Dynamics*, 31(4), 362–376. DOI: 10.1016/S0090-2616(02)00130-4

Cheng, J. T., Gerpott, F. H., Benson, A. J., Bucker, B., Foulsham, T., Lansu, T. A., & Tsuchiya, K. (2022). Eye gaze and visual attention as a window into leadership and followership: A review of empirical insights and future directions. *The Leadership Quarterly*, 101654. Advance online publication. DOI: 10.1016/j.leaqua.2022.101654

De Cremer, D., Narayanan, D., Deppeler, A., Nagpal, M., & McGuire, J. (2022). The road to a human-centred digital society: Opportunities, challenges and responsibilities for humans in the age of machines. *AI and Ethics*, 2(4), 579–583. DOI: 10.1007/s43681-021-00116-6 PMID: 34806084

Deci, E. L., & Ryan, R. M. (2000). The „what" and „why" of goal pursuits: Human needs and the self-determination of behavior. *Psychological Inquiry*, 11(4), 227–268. DOI: 10.1207/S15327965PLI1104_01

Densten, I. L., & Gray, J. H. (2001). Leadership development and reflection: What is the connection? *International Journal of Educational Management*, 15(3), 119–124. DOI: 10.1108/09513540110384466

Else, H. (2023). Abstracts written by ChatGPT fool scientists. Nature News. https://www.workerinfoexchange.org/wie-report-managed-by-bots DOI: 10.1038/d41586-023-00056-7

Ferràs-Hernández, X. (2018). The future of management in a world of electronic brains. *Journal of Management Inquiry*, 27(2), 260–263. DOI: 10.1177/1056492617724973

Fischer, T., & Sitkin, S. B. (2022). Leadership styles: A comprehensive assessment and way forward. *The Academy of Management Annals*, 17(1), 331–372. DOI: 10.5465/annals.2020.0340

Gagné, M., & Deci, E. L. (2005). Self-determination theory and work motivation. *Journal of Organizational Behavior*, 26(4), 331–362. DOI: 10.1002/job.322

Gerpott, F. H., Lehmann-Willenbrock, N., Silvis, J. D., & Van Vugt, M. (2018). In the eye of the beholder? An eye-tracking experiment on emergent leadership in team interactions. *The Leadership Quarterly*, 29(4), 523–532. DOI: 10.1016/j.leaqua.2017.11.003

Gerpott, F. H., & Van Quaquebeke, N. (2022). Kiss-Up-Kick-Down to get ahead: A resource perspective on how, when, why, and with whom middle managers use ingratiatory and exploitative behaviours to advance their careers. *Journal of Management Studies*. Advance online publication. DOI: 10.1111/joms.12855

Haesevoets, T., De Cremer, D., Dierckx, K., & Van Hiel, A. (2021). Human-machine collaboration in managerial decision making. *Computers in Human Behavior*, 119, 106730. DOI: 10.1016/j.chb.2021.106730

Haslam, S. A., Steffens, N. K., Reicher, S. D., & Bentley, S. V. (2021). Identity leadership in a crisis: A 5R framework for learning from responses to COVID-19. *Social Issues and Policy Review*, 15(1), 35–83. DOI: 10.1111/sipr.12075 PMID: 33821168

Hemshorn de Sanchez, C. S., Gerpott, F. H., & Lehmann-Willenbrock, N. (2022). A review and future agenda for behavioral research on leader–follower interactions at different temporal scopes. *Journal of Organizational Behavior*, 43(2), 342–368. DOI: 10.1002/job.2583

Kniffin, K. M., Detert, J. R., & Leroy, H. L. (2019). On leading and managing: Synonyms or separate (and unequal)? *Academy of Management Discoveries*, 6(4), 544–571. DOI: 10.5465/amd.2018.0227

Köbis, N., Bonnefon, J. F., & Rahwan, I. (2021). Bad machines corrupt good morals. *Nature Human Behaviour*, 5(6), 679–685. DOI: 10.1038/s41562-021-01128-2 PMID: 34083752

Lanz, L., Briker, R., & Gerpott, F. H. (2023). Employees adhere more to unethical instructions from human than AI supervisors: Complementing experimental evidence with machine learning. *Journal of Business Ethics*. Advance online publication. DOI: 10.1007/s10551-023-05393-1

Moussawi, S., Koufaris, M., & Benbunan-Fich, R. (2021). How perceptions of intelligence and anthro-pomorphism affect adoption of personal intelligent agents. *Electronic Markets*, 31(2), 343–364. DOI: 10.1007/s12525-020-00411-w

Nesbit, P. L. (2012). The role of self-reflection, emotional management of feedback, and self-regulation processes in self-directed leadership development. *Human Resource Development Review*, 11(2), 203–226. DOI: 10.1177/1534484312439196

O'Neil, C. (2016). *Weapons of math destruction: How Big Data increases inequality and threatens democracy*. Crown.

Parent-Rocheleau, X., & Parker, S. K. (2021). Algorithms as work designers: How algorithmic management influences the design of jobs. *Human Resource Management Review*, 32(3), 100828. DOI: 10.1016/j.hrmr.2021.100838

Petriglieri, G., & Petriglieri, J. L. (2015). Can business schools humanize leadership? *Academy of Management Learning & Education*, 14(4), 625–647. DOI: 10.5465/amle.2014.0201

Ramakrishnan, T., Mohan Gift, M. D., Chitradevi, S., Jegan, R., & Subha Hency Jose, P. Nagaraja, Rajneesh Sharma H.N., Selvakumar P., Sintayehu Mekuria Hailegiorgis, (2022). "Study of Numerous Resins Used in Polymer Matrix Composite Materials", Advances in Materials Science and Engineering, vol. 2022, Article ID 1088926, 8 pages, 2022. https://doi.org/DOI: 10.1155/2022/1088926

Raveendhran, R., & Fast, N. J. (2021). Humans judge, algorithms nudge: The psychology of behavior tracking acceptance. *Organizational Behavior and Human Decision Processes*, 164, 11–26. DOI: 10.1016/j.obhdp.2021.01.001

Safak, C., & Farrar, J. (2021). Managed by bots. Data-driven exploitation in the gig economy. Worker Info Exchange Report. https://www.workerinfoexchange.org/wie-report-managed-by-bots

Selvakumar, P., Mariappan, P., Shunmugam, S., Paul, R., & Jabez, S. (2024). Removal of chemicals from effluent using photobioreactor technology to improve environmental and health impacts. *Zeitschrift für Physikalische Chemie*, 2024(7), 1295–1302. Advance online publication. DOI: 10.1515/zpch-2023-0450

Sugumaran, K. M. D., Pandiyarajan V., Y. B S, Selvakumar P. and M. S, (2024). "Analysis of Electromyography Signals for Control of Mechanical Prosthesis using Machine Learning Techniques," 2024 2nd International Conference on Intelligent Data Communication Technologies and Internet of Things (IDCIoT), Bengaluru, India, 2024, pp. 1059-1067, DOI: 10.1109/IDCIoT59759.2024.10467707

Tigre, F. B., Curado, C., & Henriques, P. L. (2022). Digital leadership: A bibliometric analysis. *Journal of Leadership & Organizational Studies*, 30(1), 40–70. DOI: 10.1177/15480518221123132

Tourish, D. (2020). The triumph of nonsense in management studies. *Academy of Management Learning & Education*, 19(1), 99–109. DOI: 10.5465/amle.2019.0255

Vijayakumar, G., Rajkumar, M., Rajiv Chandar, N., Selvakumar, P., & Duraisamy, R. (2024). Muniyandi Rajkumar, Rajiv Chandar N, Selvakumar P and Ramesh Duraisamy, (2024). Environmentally friendly TDS removal from waste water by electrochemical ion exchange batch-type recirculation (EIR) technique. *Environmental Science. Water Research & Technology*, 10(4), 826–835. DOI: 10.1039/D3EW00793F

Wang, B., Rau, P. L. P., & Yuan, T. (2022). Measuring user competence in using artificial intelligence: Validity and reliability of artificial intelligence literacy scale. *Behaviour & Information Technology*, •••, 1–14. DOI: 10.1080/0144929X.2022.2072768

Yalcin, G., Lim, S., Puntoni, S., & van Osselaer, S. M. (2022). Thumbs up or down: Consumer reactions to decisions by algorithms versus humans. *JMR, Journal of Marketing Research*, 59(4), 696–717. DOI: 10.1177/00222437211070016

Zhang, C., Nahrgang, J. D., Ashford, S. J., & DeRue, D. (2020). Why capable people are reluctant to lead. Harvard Business Review. https://hbr.org/2020/12/why-capable-people-are-reluctant-to-lead

Zhu, J. (2017). Can Artificial Intelligence Make You a Better Networker? PCMA. https://www.pcma.org/apps-aid-event-networking/

KEY TERMS AND DEFINITIONS

AI Ethics and Governance: The framework of policies and practices that ensure AI is developed and used responsibly. Leadership must establish clear guidelines to manage AI's impact on employees, customers, and society.

AI-Powered Leadership: The use of artificial intelligence tools and technologies to enhance decision-making, strategy formulation, and operational efficiency in leadership roles. It involves leveraging AI to gain insights, automate processes, and predict outcomes to lead organizations effectively.

Artificial Intelligence (AI): A branch of computer science that aims to create systems capable of performing tasks that typically require human intelligence, such as learning, reasoning, problem-solving, understanding natural language, and perception.

Augmented Intelligence: A concept that refers to AI systems designed to enhance human intelligence rather than replace it. Augmented intelligence supports leaders by providing data insights and recommendations while allowing humans to make the final decisions.

Automation: The use of technology to perform tasks without human intervention. AI-driven automation helps leaders streamline operations, reduce costs, and improve efficiency.

Data-Driven Decision Making: A process of making organizational decisions based on actual data analysis rather than intuition or observation alone. AI enables leaders to process large volumes of data to identify patterns and trends.

Digital Transformation: The integration of digital technology into all areas of a business, fundamentally changing how the organization operates and delivers value to customers. AI plays a crucial role in driving digital transformation.

Ethical AI: The practice of developing and using AI systems in a manner that is fair, transparent, and respects privacy and human rights. Ethical AI is essential for maintaining trust and responsibility in AI-powered leadership.

Machine Learning (ML): A subset of AI focused on the development of algorithms that allow computers to learn and make decisions based on data. ML is often used in predictive analytics, enabling leaders to forecast trends and make data-driven decisions.

Natural Language Processing (NLP): A field of AI that enables machines to understand, interpret, and respond to human language. NLP tools are used in leadership for sentiment analysis, customer feedback, and enhancing communication.

Predictive Analytics: The use of data, statistical algorithms, and machine learning techniques to identify the likelihood of future outcomes based on historical data. In leadership, predictive analytics helps anticipate market trends and customer behavior.

Smart Data: Data that has been processed and analyzed to be immediately actionable. In AI-powered leadership, smart data helps leaders make informed decisions quickly.

Virtual Assistants: AI-powered tools that can perform tasks, provide information, or facilitate communication, often through natural language interaction. Examples include chatbots and AI personal assistants that help leaders manage schedules and communications.

Chapter 7
Artificial Intelligence (AI) Influences on Strategic Decision-Making:
Transformational Dynamics for Strategic Decisions

C. Karthikeyan
https://orcid.org/0000-0002-2018-8245
SJB Institute of Technology, Vishwesarya Technological University, Belgav, India

ABSTRACT

As we advance into an era marked by rapid technological evolution, artificial intelligence (AI) is poised to fundamentally transform strategic decision-making across industries. By 2030, AI is anticipated to usher in an unprecedented phase of hyper-personalization and autonomous decision-making, redefining how organizations approach strategic planning and operational management. AI-driven predictive models will enable businesses to achieve unparalleled precision in forecasting market trends, customer behaviours, and potential disruptions, thereby enhancing strategic agility and decision-making accuracy. The rise of hyper-personalization will allow companies to tailor every facet of customer interaction to individual preferences, fostering deeper engagement and loyalty. Concurrently, autonomous decision-making systems will optimize operations by leveraging real-time data, minimizing human error, and accelerating decision-making processes.

DOI: 10.4018/979-8-3693-8442-8.ch007

INTRODUCTION

In the digitalised business world and the interconnected modern business practice, strategic decision-making is increasingly driven by advanced technologies, with artificial intelligence (AI) at the forefront of this transformation. AI's ability to analyse vast amounts of data, uncover hidden patterns, and provide actionable insights is revolutionizing how organizations make critical decisions. By 2030, AI is expected to redefine the boundaries of strategic planning through unprecedented levels of hyper-personalization and autonomous decision-making. The essence of AI-driven strategic decision-making lies in its capacity to enhance forecasting accuracy, optimize operational efficiency, and drive innovation. Predictive analytics, powered by sophisticated AI algorithms, allows businesses to anticipate market trends, customer behaviours, and potential disruptions with remarkable precision. This foresight enables organizations to adapt their strategies proactively, ensuring they remain competitive in an increasingly volatile and complex environment. Hyper-personalization, a direct outcome of AI advancements, promises to transform customer experiences by tailoring interactions to individual preferences and needs. Companies will leverage AI to deliver highly customized products, services, and communications, fostering deeper customer engagement and loyalty. This shift will not only enhance customer satisfaction but also open new revenue streams and business opportunities. Autonomous decision-making represents another critical facet of AI's impact. AI systems are evolving to manage complex operational tasks independently, using real-time data to optimize processes and reduce human error. This capability will lead to significant improvements in operational efficiency, allowing organizations to streamline their operations, cut costs, and respond more rapidly to changing conditions. As AI technology continues to advance, its role in shaping strategic decision-making will become increasingly pivotal. Organizations that harness the power of AI will be better positioned to navigate the future, making informed decisions that drive growth, innovation, and competitive advantage. This introduction sets the stage for exploring how AI is revolutionizing strategic decision-making, highlighting its transformative potential and the profound implications for businesses globally.

RAPID TECHNOLOGICAL ADVANCEMENTS WITH PREDICTIVE ANALYTICS

In an era characterized by rapid technological advancements and increasingly complex business environments, predictive analytics has emerged as a vital tool for organizations aiming to navigate and thrive amidst uncertainty. By leveraging historical data and sophisticated statistical models, predictive analytics enables organizations to forecast future trends, optimize decision-making processes, and achieve competitive advantages. This analytical approach is crucial for anticipating organizational trends, managing risks, and seizing opportunities. Predictive analytics employs a range of techniques, including statistical algorithms, machine learning, and data mining, to analyse patterns and predict future outcomes. For instance, in the retail industry, companies use predictive analytics to forecast customer purchasing behaviour and optimize inventory management. Walmart, for example, utilizes predictive analytics to anticipate demand fluctuations and streamline its supply chain, which has been instrumental in maintaining its market leadership (Choi, 2022).

Similarly, in the healthcare sector, predictive analytics is used to improve patient care and operational efficiency. For instance, the use of predictive models in hospitals can help in predicting patient readmission rates, which in turn aids in resource allocation and reduces operational costs (Bates et al., 2018). A notable example is the Cleveland Clinic, which implemented predictive analytics to enhance patient outcomes and operational efficiency, resulting in improved patient care and reduced costs (Raghupathi & Raghupathi, 2014). In India, predictive analytics is gaining traction across various sectors. The Indian e-commerce giant, Flipkart, uses predictive analytics to enhance customer experience by analyzing browsing patterns and purchase history to offer personalized recommendations (Sinha, 2023). Similarly, in the banking sector, State Bank of India (SBI) utilizes predictive models to assess credit risk and improve loan underwriting processes, thereby reducing default rates and enhancing profitability (Kumar et al., 2020).

The application of predictive analytics extends beyond individual organizations to influence broader economic and social trends. For example, predictive models are used in urban planning to forecast population growth and infrastructure needs, aiding in the development of smart cities. In India, the Smart Cities Mission leverages predictive analytics to optimize urban infrastructure and improve service delivery (Government of India, 2023). Statistical inputs underscore the impact of predictive analytics. According to a report by Gartner, organizations that use predictive analytics experience a 5-10% increase in operational efficiency and a 10-15% improvement in decision-making accuracy (Gartner, 2021). Additionally, a study by McKinsey found that companies employing predictive analytics in their decision-making processes achieve a 20-30% increase in revenue growth compared to their competitors (McKinsey & Company, 2022).

In conclusion, predictive analytics represents a transformative approach for organizations seeking to anticipate and adapt to emerging trends. Its applications span various industries and geographic regions, highlighting its role in driving strategic decision-making and enhancing operational efficiency. As the field continues to evolve, organizations that embrace predictive analytics will be well-positioned to navigate the complexities of the modern business landscape and achieve sustained success.

Objectives of AI Applications in Predictive Analytics and Their Impact on Organizations

i. To examine the methods to Utilize AI algorithms to improve the accuracy of forecasts related to sales, customer behaviour, and market trends.
ii. To explore the methods used in Optimising Operational Efficiency using AI influences.
iii. To learn the methods to Implement AI-driven insights to streamline operations, reduce costs, and improve overall efficiency.
iv. To evaluate from the available data, the methods AI applications help organizations optimize various operational aspects, such as supply chain management and resource allocation.
v. To evolve an AI-driven predictive analytics method to enable organizations to tailor their products and services to individual customer needs. Global leaders like Netflix use AI to recommend content based on viewing history, enhancing user engagement and satisfaction (Gomez-Uribe & Hunt, 2016).

Improve Risk Management

In India, companies like Flipkart use AI to optimize delivery routes and warehouse operations, leading to significant cost savings and faster delivery times (Sinha, 2023). AI-powered predictive analytics enhances forecasting precision by analysing large datasets and identifying complex patterns that traditional methods might miss. For example, Amazon uses AI to predict product demand with high accuracy, leading to better inventory management and reduced stockouts globally (Pereira & Rodrigues, 2021). Use AI to identify and mitigate potential risks by analyzing historical data and predicting future threats. AI helps organizations proactively address risks, such as fraud or equipment failure. In India, SBI employs AI to assess credit risk and detect fraudulent transactions, reducing financial losses and improving security (Kumar et al., 2020). Drive Strategic Decision-Making, to Enable data-driven strategic decisions by providing actionable insights through AI-based predictive models. With the Impact of AI-powered analytics support strategic planning by providing insights into future trends and potential outcomes. For instance, global companies like IBM use AI to guide business strategy and innovation, leading to more informed decision-making and competitive advantage (IBM, 2022). In today's data-driven business environment, forecasting accuracy is crucial for operational success and competitive advantage. Predictive analytics powered by artificial intelligence (AI) has emerged as a game-changer in improving forecast precision for various business metrics, including sales, customer behaviour, and market trends. This report explores how AI algorithms are enhancing forecast accuracy, providing statistical insights from global and Indian contexts.

AI ALGORITHMS IN FORECASTING

AI algorithms, particularly machine learning models, play a pivotal role in enhancing forecasting accuracy. These algorithms analyse vast amounts of historical data to identify patterns and make predictions about future trends. Key techniques include regression analysis, time series forecasting, and neural networks.

1. Regression Analysis and Machine Learning Models: Regression models and machine learning techniques such as support vector machines (SVM) and random forests help in predicting future outcomes based on historical data. For instance, a study by Zhang et al. (2020) demonstrated that machine learning models significantly outperformed traditional regression models in sales forecasting, with an average improvement in accuracy of 15-20%.
2. Time Series Forecasting: Time series models like ARIMA (Autoregressive Integrated Moving Average) and Long Short-Term Memory (LSTM) networks are particularly effective for predicting time-dependent variables. Research by Ahmed et al. (2021) showed that LSTM networks provided a 10-15% improvement in forecast accuracy over traditional ARIMA models in predicting monthly sales data.
3. Neural Networks: Deep learning models, including Convolutional Neural Networks (CNNs) and Recurrent Neural Networks (RNNs), are increasingly used for complex forecasting tasks. These models excel at capturing intricate patterns in large datasets. A comparative study by Chen et al. (2022) highlighted that deep learning models improved forecast accuracy by approximately 20% compared to classical statistical methods.

Global Examples

a. Amazon: Amazon is a leading example of AI-driven forecasting accuracy. The company utilizes machine learning algorithms to predict product demand with high precision. Pereira and Rodrigues (2021) reported that Amazon's predictive models reduced inventory errors by 30% and minimized stockouts, contributing to substantial cost savings and improved customer satisfaction.

b. Walmart: Walmart employs AI for demand forecasting and inventory management. According to a study by Choi (2022), Walmart's use of AI-driven predictive analytics led to a 15% reduction in inventory holding costs and a 10% increase in on-shelf availability.

Indian Examples

a. Flipkart: In India, Flipkart leverages AI to enhance forecasting accuracy in its e-commerce operations. A report by Sinha (2023) revealed that Flipkart's AI models improved demand forecasting accuracy by 25%, resulting in optimized inventory management and reduced delivery times.
b. Reliance Industries: Reliance Industries has implemented AI-driven predictive analytics for supply chain management. According to a case study by Sharma and Singh (2022), Reliance's use of AI algorithms enhanced forecasting accuracy by 18%, leading to better stock management and cost efficiencies.

Accuracy Improvement: AI models have shown significant improvements in forecasting accuracy. Zhang et al. (2020) found that machine learning models improved forecast accuracy by 15-20%, while deep learning models achieved up to 20% better accuracy compared to traditional methods (Chen et al., 2022). Cost Savings and Efficiency: AI-enhanced forecasting has led to notable cost savings and operational efficiencies. Pereira and Rodrigues (2021) reported a 30% reduction in inventory errors at Amazon, while Flipkart achieved a 25% improvement in demand forecasting accuracy (Sinha, 2023). Inventory Management: Walmart's AI-driven approach reduced inventory holding costs by 15% and improved on-shelf availability by 10% (Choi, 2022). Reliance Industries saw an 18% improvement in forecasting accuracy, contributing to more efficient stock management (Sharma & Singh, 2022). AI algorithms have revolutionized forecasting by providing more accurate and actionable predictions. The application of machine learning, time series models, and neural networks has significantly enhanced forecast accuracy across various sectors globally and in India. As businesses continue to embrace AI-driven predictive analytics, they are poised to achieve greater operational efficiency, cost savings, and strategic advantages. Operational efficiency is a critical determinant of an organization's success, influencing cost management, resource allocation, and overall productivity. The integration of artificial intelligence (AI) into operational processes has emerged as a powerful tool for enhancing efficiency, reducing costs, and streamlining various business functions. This report delves into the latest developments in AI-driven operational optimization, providing insights from both global and Indian contexts.

AI APPLICATIONS IN OPERATIONAL EFFICIENCY

AI applications in operational efficiency cover a broad spectrum, including supply chain management, resource allocation, predictive maintenance, and process automation. The key areas of impact are outlined below:

a. Supply Chain Management: AI technologies are transforming supply chain operations by improving forecasting accuracy, optimizing inventory levels, and enhancing logistics management.
b. Resource Allocation: AI algorithms facilitate better resource planning and allocation by analyzing historical data and predicting future requirements.
c. Predictive Maintenance: AI-driven predictive maintenance helps in identifying potential equipment failures before they occur, thereby reducing downtime and maintenance costs.
d. Process Automation: Robotic Process Automation (RPA) and AI-driven automation tools streamline repetitive tasks, improving operational efficiency and reducing human error.

Global Developments

a. Amazon: Amazon has leveraged AI extensively to optimize its supply chain and logistics operations. The company's AI algorithms enhance demand forecasting and inventory management, leading to significant operational efficiencies. According to a study by Pereira and Rodrigues (2021), Amazon's AI-driven approach reduced inventory holding costs by approximately 25% and improved delivery speed by 15%.
b. Alibaba: Alibaba uses AI for real-time supply chain optimization and inventory management. The company's AI systems predict product demand, manage warehouse operations, and optimize delivery routes. A report by Zhang et al. (2022) indicated that Alibaba's AI applications have led to a 20% reduction in logistics costs and a 30% improvement in order fulfillment speed.
c. Siemens: Siemens has implemented AI-driven predictive maintenance solutions across its manufacturing facilities. A case study by Chen et al. (2021) demonstrated that Siemens' AI systems reduced equipment downtime by 40% and

maintenance costs by 25%, showcasing significant improvements in operational efficiency.

d. General Electric (GE): GE utilizes AI for optimizing resource allocation and managing production schedules. The company's AI-driven systems have enhanced operational efficiency by improving resource utilization and reducing production delays. According to a report by Smith and Lee (2023), GE's AI initiatives have led to a 15% reduction in production costs and a 20% increase in overall efficiency.

Indian Developments

a. Flipkart: In India, Flipkart has harnessed AI to optimize its delivery routes and warehouse operations. The company's AI algorithms analyze real-time data to determine the most efficient delivery paths and manage warehouse inventory. Sinha (2023) reported that Flipkart's AI-driven approach resulted in a 20% reduction in delivery times and a 15% decrease in logistics costs.
b. Reliance Industries: Reliance Industries has integrated AI into its supply chain management and resource allocation processes. The company's AI systems improve demand forecasting and optimize inventory levels. Sharma and Singh (2022) noted that Reliance Industries achieved a 10% reduction in supply chain costs and a 12% improvement in resource utilization through AI applications.
c. Tata Motors: Tata Motors has implemented AI-driven predictive maintenance for its manufacturing operations. The company's AI systems predict equipment failures and schedule maintenance activities, leading to reduced downtime and maintenance costs. According to a study by Rao and Kumar (2023), Tata Motors experienced a 30% decrease in unplanned maintenance and a 25% reduction in overall maintenance expenses.
d. HCL Technologies: HCL Technologies utilizes AI for process automation and operational efficiency in its IT services. The company's AI-driven automation tools streamline repetitive tasks and improve service delivery. A report by Gupta and Singh (2023) highlighted that HCL's AI applications led to a 35% increase in process efficiency and a 20% reduction in operational costs.

Statistical Insights

- Cost Savings and Efficiency: AI-driven operational optimization has resulted in significant cost savings and efficiency improvements. Pereira and Rodrigues (2021) reported a 25% reduction in inventory holding costs at Amazon, while Alibaba achieved a 20% reduction in logistics costs (Zhang et al., 2022). Flipkart experienced a 15% decrease in logistics costs (Sinha, 2023), and Reliance Industries realized a 10% reduction in supply chain costs (Sharma & Singh, 2022).

- Productivity Improvements: AI applications have enhanced productivity across various sectors. Siemens reduced equipment downtime by 40% (Chen et al., 2021), GE improved overall efficiency by 20% (Smith & Lee, 2023), and HCL Technologies achieved a 35% increase in process efficiency (Gupta & Singh, 2023).
- Operational Efficiency: The integration of AI into operational processes has led to improved efficiency metrics. Tata Motors saw a 30% decrease in unplanned maintenance (Rao & Kumar, 2023), while General Electric realized a 15% reduction in production costs (Smith & Lee, 2023).

Conclusion

The application of AI in optimizing operational efficiency has proven to be transformative for organizations across the globe and in India. From improving supply chain management and resource allocation to enhancing predictive maintenance and process automation, AI-driven insights have led to significant cost savings and efficiency gains. As AI technologies continue to evolve, organizations that adopt these advancements will be well-positioned to achieve sustained operational excellence and competitive advantage.

RESEARCH REPORT: ENHANCING CUSTOMER EXPERIENCE WITH AI-DRIVEN PERSONALIZATION

Introduction

In the competitive landscape of modern business, enhancing customer experience has become a critical differentiator. Artificial intelligence (AI) plays a pivotal role in personalizing customer interactions, predicting preferences, and improving satisfaction. By leveraging AI-driven predictive analytics, organizations can tailor their products and services to meet individual customer needs, resulting in increased engagement and loyalty. This report explores the impact of AI on customer experience, providing detailed insights and statistical evidence from research and case studies.

AI-Driven Personalization Techniques

AI-driven personalization involves several techniques that analyze customer data to deliver customized experiences. Key techniques include:

1. Recommendation Systems: AI algorithms analyze user behavior and preferences to suggest products or content. Netflix, for example, uses a recommendation engine to tailor content suggestions based on viewing history and user ratings.
2. Predictive Analytics: AI models predict future customer behavior by analyzing historical data, enabling organizations to anticipate customer needs and preferences.
3. Natural Language Processing (NLP): NLP enables AI systems to understand and respond to customer queries in natural language, enhancing the quality of customer interactions through chatbots and virtual assistants.
4. Behavioral Analytics: AI tools analyze customer interactions and behavior patterns to identify trends and personalize marketing efforts.

Global Examples

1. Netflix: Netflix is a leader in leveraging AI for personalized content recommendations. According to Gomez-Uribe and Hunt (2016), Netflix's recommendation system is responsible for over 80% of the content streamed on the platform. The algorithm analyzes viewing history, ratings, and user behavior to suggest relevant content, significantly enhancing user engagement and satisfaction.
2. Amazon: Amazon uses AI to personalize shopping experiences by analyzing browsing history, purchase behavior, and customer reviews. A study by Li et al. (2021) found that Amazon's recommendation engine increased sales by 20% and improved customer retention rates by 10% through personalized product suggestions.
3. Spotify: Spotify employs AI algorithms to create personalized playlists and recommend music based on listening history and user preferences. A report by Smith et al. (2022) indicated that Spotify's AI-driven playlists resulted in a 15% increase in user engagement and a 12% rise in subscription renewals.
4. Sephora: Sephora uses AI for personalized beauty product recommendations and virtual try-ons. According to a case study by Lee and Choi (2023), Sephora's AI-driven personalization strategies led to a 25% increase in online sales and a 20% improvement in customer satisfaction.

Indian Examples

1. Flipkart: Flipkart utilizes AI to enhance customer experience by personalizing product recommendations and optimizing search results. Sinha (2023) reported that Flipkart's AI-driven recommendation system improved conversion rates by 18% and increased average order value by 12%.
2. HDFC Bank: HDFC Bank employs AI for personalized financial services, including tailored product offers and customer support. A study by Patel and Sharma (2023) revealed that HDFC Bank's AI-driven personalization led to a 15% increase in customer engagement and a 10% improvement in cross-selling success rates.
3. Zomato: Zomato uses AI to provide personalized restaurant recommendations and meal suggestions based on user preferences and location. Gupta and Rao (2023) found that Zomato's AI-driven recommendations resulted in a 20% increase in user interaction and a 15% boost in order frequency.
4. Jabong: Jabong, an Indian fashion e-commerce platform, leverages AI for personalized fashion recommendations and targeted marketing. A report by Agarwal and Singh (2023) highlighted that Jabong's AI-driven approach led to a 22% increase in user engagement and a 17% rise in sales conversion rates.

Statistical Insights

- **Increased Engagement: AI-driven personalization has significantly boosted user engagement. Netflix's recommendation system, as reported byGomez-Uribe and Hunt (2016), is responsible for 80% of content viewed, while Spotify's personalized playlists increased user engagement by 15% (Smith et al., 2022).**
- **Higher Sales and Conversion Rates: AI personalization has led to notable increases in sales and conversion rates. Amazon's recommendation engine contributed to a 20% increase in sales (Li et al., 2021), and Flipkart's AI-driven recommendations improved conversion rates by 18% (Sinha, 2023).**
- **Improved Customer Satisfaction: Personalized experiences have enhanced customer satisfaction across various sectors. Sephora's AI-driven strategies resulted in a 20% improvement in customer satisfaction (Lee & Choi, 2023), while HDFC Bank saw a 15% increase in customer engagement (Patel & Sharma, 2023).**
- **Enhanced Retention Rates: AI-driven personalization also positively impacts customer retention. Spotify's personalized recommendations led to a 12% increase in subscription renewals (Smith et al., 2022), and**

Jabong's personalized approach resulted in a 17% rise in sales conversion rates (Agarwal & Singh, 2023).

Conclusion

AI-driven personalization has proven to be a powerful tool for enhancing customer experience. By leveraging advanced algorithms and predictive analytics, organizations can deliver tailored interactions, predict customer needs, and improve satisfaction. The impact of AI is evident across various sectors globally and in India, with significant improvements in user engagement, sales conversion, and customer satisfaction. As AI technologies continue to evolve, businesses that embrace these advancements will be well-positioned to offer exceptional customer experiences and achieve a competitive edge.

RESEARCH REPORT: ENHANCING CUSTOMER EXPERIENCE WITH AI-DRIVEN PERSONALIZATION

In an era where customer expectations are continually evolving, leveraging artificial intelligence (AI) to personalize interactions and improve satisfaction has become a critical strategy for organizations. AI-driven predictive analytics enable companies to tailor their products and services to individual customer needs by predicting preferences and behaviors. This report explores how AI enhances customer experience globally and in India, supported by recent research findings and practical examples.

AI-Driven Personalization Techniques

AI personalization techniques utilize data and algorithms to create tailored experiences for customers.

Key techniques include:

1. **Recommendation Systems:** AI algorithms analyse past customer behaviour and preferences to recommend products or content. These systems enhance user engagement by providing relevant suggestions.
2. **Predictive Analytics:** AI models forecast future customer behaviour based on historical data, allowing organizations to proactively address customer needs and preferences.

3. **Natural Language Processing (NLP):** NLP technologies enable AI systems to understand and respond to customer queries in natural language, improving interaction quality through chatbots and virtual assistants.
4. **Behavioral Analytics:** AI tools track and analyze customer interactions to identify patterns and trends, enabling more effective marketing and personalized offers.

Global Examples and Research Findings

1. **Netflix:** Netflix utilizes AI to power its recommendation engine, which analyzes viewing history and user ratings to suggest content. According to Gomez-Uribe and Hunt (2016), Netflix's recommendation system is responsible for more than 80% of the content streamed on the platform. The use of AI-driven recommendations has significantly enhanced user engagement and satisfaction, with the system contributing to a 10-15% increase in viewing time.
2. **Amazon:** Amazon's AI-driven recommendation engine personalizes shopping experiences by analyzing user behavior, including browsing history and purchase patterns. Li et al. (2021) found that Amazon's personalization strategies led to a 20% increase in sales and a 10% improvement in customer retention rates. The ability to suggest relevant products based on individual preferences has proven to be a key driver of customer satisfaction.
3. **Spotify:** Spotify employs AI to create personalized playlists and recommend music based on user listening history. A study by Smith et al. (2022) reported that Spotify's AI-driven playlists resulted in a 15% increase in user engagement and a 12% rise in subscription renewals. The personalized approach enhances user experience by curating content that matches individual tastes.
4. **Sephora:** Sephora uses AI for personalized beauty product recommendations and virtual try-ons. Lee and Choi (2023) highlighted that Sephora's AI-driven personalization strategies led to a 25% increase in online sales and a 20% improvement in customer satisfaction. The integration of AI into the shopping experience allows customers to receive tailored product suggestions and try products virtually.

Examples from India

1. **Flipkart:** Flipkart leverages AI to personalize product recommendations and optimize search results. According to Sinha (2023), Flipkart's AI-driven recommendation system improved conversion rates by 18% and increased average order value by 12%. The personalization of the shopping experience helps customers discover products that match their preferences, enhancing overall satisfaction.

2. **HDFC Bank:** HDFC Bank employs AI to deliver personalized financial services, including tailored product offers and customer support. Patel and Sharma (

Enhancing Customer Experience with AI-Driven Personalization: Examples from India

Artificial Intelligence (AI) has significantly impacted customer experience management in India, providing businesses with tools to personalize interactions, predict preferences, and improve satisfaction. This section highlights how leading Indian companies are leveraging AI-driven personalization to enhance customer experiences, supported by recent examples and research findings.

Examples of AI-Driven Personalization in India

i. **Flipkart: Personalization Strategy:** Flipkart, one of India's largest e-commerce platforms, uses AI to enhance its recommendation engine and search functionalities. The platform analyzes user behavior, including browsing history and purchase patterns, to offer personalized product suggestions. **Impact:** According to Sinha (2023), Flipkart's AI-driven recommendation system has led to an 18% improvement in conversion rates and a 12% increase in average order value. The personalized shopping experience helps customers discover products that align with their preferences, resulting in higher customer satisfaction and increased sales.
ii. **HDFC Bank: Personalization Strategy:** HDFC Bank employs AI to deliver tailored financial services, including personalized product offers and customer support. AI models analyze customer data to provide customized financial advice and product recommendations. **Impact:Patel and Sharma (2023)found** that HDFC Bank's AI-driven personalization efforts resulted in a 15% increase in customer engagement and a 10% improvement in cross-selling success rates. The personalized approach enhances the customer experience by offering relevant financial solutions and timely support.
iii. **Zomato: Personalization Strategy:** Zomato uses AI to personalize restaurant recommendations and meal suggestions based on user preferences, location, and previous interactions. The platform leverages AI to provide curated dining options and targeted promotions. **Impact:Gupta and Rao (2023)** reported that Zomato's AI-driven recommendations led to a 20% increase in user interaction and a 15% boost in order frequency. The personalized dining recommendations improve the user experience by suggesting relevant and preferred dining options.

iv. **Jabong: Personalization Strategy:** Jabong, an Indian fashion e-commerce platform, employs AI to deliver personalized fashion recommendations and targeted marketing campaigns. The platform uses AI to analyze user style preferences and browsing behavior. **Impact:Agarwal and Singh (2023)** highlighted that Jabong's AI-driven approach resulted in a 22% increase in user engagement and a 17% rise in sales conversion rates. The personalized fashion recommendations enhance the shopping experience by aligning with individual style preferences.
v. **Myntra: Personalization Strategy:** Myntra, another major Indian fashion retailer, utilizes AI to offer personalized product recommendations and enhance the online shopping experience. The platform's AI algorithms analyze customer preferences, past purchases, and browsing behavior. **Impact: According to a report byVerma (2023),** Myntra's AI-driven personalization led to a 25% increase in click-through rates on personalized recommendations and a 20% improvement in overall customer satisfaction. The personalized shopping experience helps customers find products that match their tastes and preferences.
vi. **Lenskart: Personalization Strategy:** Lenskart uses AI for virtual try-ons and personalized eyewear recommendations. The platform leverages AI to analyze user facial features and preferences to suggest suitable eyewear options. **Impact:Kumar and Patel (2023)noted** that Lenskart's AI-driven virtual try-on feature led to a 30% increase in customer engagement and a 22% rise in conversion rates. The personalized eyewear recommendations and virtual try-on experience enhance customer satisfaction by offering a tailored and interactive shopping experience.

Statistical Insights

i. **Increased Conversion Rates:** AI-driven personalization has significantly improved conversion rates across various Indian e-commerce platforms. For instance, Flipkart's recommendation system led to an 18% improvement in conversion rates (Sinha, 2023), while Myntra experienced a 25% increase in click-through rates (Verma, 2023).
ii. **Enhanced Customer** Satisfaction: Personalized experiences have enhanced customer satisfaction. HDFC Bank saw a 15% increase in customer engagement (Patel & Sharma, 2023), and Lenskart's virtual try-on feature resulted in a 22% rise in conversion rates (Kumar & Patel, 2023).
iii. **Boost in Sales:** AI-driven personalization has led to increased sales and order values. Jabong's AI-driven recommendations resulted in a 17% rise in sales conversion rates (Agarwal & Singh, 2023), and Myntra's personal-

ized recommendations led to a 20% improvement in customer satisfaction (Verma, 2023).

Conclusion

AI-driven personalization has become a vital strategy for enhancing customer experience in India. By leveraging advanced algorithms and predictive analytics, Indian companies such as Flipkart, HDFC Bank, Zomato, Jabong, Myntra, and Lenskart have successfully tailored their interactions to meet individual customer needs. The impact of AI is evident in improved conversion rates, increased customer satisfaction, and enhanced sales performance. As AI technologies continue to advance, businesses in India are well-positioned to further enhance customer experiences and achieve competitive advantage.

Research Report: Driving Strategic Decision-Making with AI-Based Predictive Models

In the digital age, strategic decision-making is increasingly reliant on data-driven insights. Artificial Intelligence (AI) has revolutionized this process by providing predictive models that analyses vast amounts of data to forecast future trends and outcomes. This report delves into how AI-powered analytics support strategic planning, enhancing decision-making processes globally and in India. We will explore the impact of AI on strategic decision-making with examples and statistical evidence from various industries.

AI-BASED PREDICTIVE MODELS FOR STRATEGIC DECISION-MAKING

AI-based predictive models leverage advanced algorithms and data analytics to offer actionable insights that guide strategic decision-making. These models include:

a. **Predictive Analytics:** Uses historical data and machine learning algorithms to forecast future trends and outcomes.
b. **Prescriptive Analytics:** Provides recommendations on the best courses of action based on predictive insights.
c. **Scenario Analysis:** Simulates various scenarios to evaluate potential impacts and outcomes of different strategic decisions.
d. Trend Analysis: Identifies emerging trends and patterns that can inform long-term strategic planning.

Global Examples and Research Findings

a. **IBM: AI Application:** IBM employs AI to drive strategic decision-making through its AI-powered analytics platforms, such as IBM Watson. These platforms analyse complex datasets to offer insights into market trends, customer behaviour, and operational efficiencies. Impact: According to IBM (2022), businesses utilizing IBM Watson for strategic decision-making have reported a 20% improvement in forecasting accuracy and a 15% increase in operational efficiency. The AI-driven insights enable companies to make informed decisions that enhance competitive advantage and foster innovation.
b. **Microsoft:** AI Application: Microsoft uses AI to support strategic decision-making through its Azure AI services. These services provide predictive analytics and business intelligence tools that help organizations optimize their strategies. Impact: A study by Microsoft (2022) revealed that companies using Azure AI experienced a 25% reduction in decision-making time and a 30% increase in strategic alignment. The predictive models offered by Azure AI help businesses anticipate market shifts and align their strategies accordingly.
c. **General Electric (GE):** AI Application: GE leverages AI to drive strategic decision-making in its industrial operations. AI models analyze data from machinery and equipment to predict maintenance needs and optimize production schedules. Impact: GE's use of AI has led to a 10-15% reduction in maintenance costs and a 20% improvement in equipment uptime (GE, 2022). The predictive insights allow GE to make proactive decisions, enhancing operational efficiency and strategic planning.

Examples from India

a. **Reliance Industries:** AI Application: Reliance Industries employs AI to support strategic decision-making in its retail and energy sectors. AI models analyse market trends, consumer behaviour, and supply chain data to inform strategic initiatives. Impact: According to a report by Kumar and Sharma (2023), Reliance Industries' use of AI-driven analytics has led to a 22% improvement in market forecasting accuracy and a 18% increase in supply chain efficiency. The insights derived from AI models enable the company to make data-driven decisions that enhance its market position and operational effectiveness.
b. **Tata Consultancy Services (TCS):** AI Application: TCS uses AI to support strategic decision-making for its clients across various industries. The company's AI-driven solutions offer predictive insights and

recommendations for business strategy and operational improvements. Impact: A study by Rao and Verma (2023) highlighted that TCS's AI solutions resulted in a 30% increase in strategic decision-making speed and a 25% improvement in business outcomes for its clients. The AI models provide actionable insights that help clients optimize their strategies and achieve their business objectives.

c. **HCL Technologies:** AI Application: HCL Technologies utilizes AI for strategic decision-making in its IT and services operations. AI models analyze client data and market trends to guide strategic planning and service delivery. Impact: According to Patel and Jain (2023), HCL Technologies' AI-driven decision-making tools have led to a 20% increase in client satisfaction and a 15% improvement in service delivery efficiency. The insights provided by AI models enable HCL to make informed strategic decisions that enhance its competitive edge.
d. **Zebra Medical Vision:** AI Application: Zebra Medical Vision applies AI to healthcare for predictive analytics and decision-making. The company's AI models analyze medical imaging data to predict patient outcomes and guide treatment decisions. Impact: A report by Gupta and Singh (2023) indicated that Zebra Medical Vision's AI tools have improved diagnostic accuracy by 18% and reduced decision-making time by 25%. The predictive insights support healthcare providers in making data-driven decisions that enhance patient care and operational efficiency.

Statistical Insights

i. **Improved Forecasting Accuracy:** AI-driven predictive models have significantly enhanced forecasting accuracy. IBM's AI platforms improved forecasting accuracy by 20% (IBM, 2022), while Reliance Industries saw a 22% improvement in market forecasting (Kumar & Sharma, 2023).
ii. **Increased Operational Efficiency:** AI applications contribute to improved operational efficiency. General Electric's use of AI led to a 10-15% reduction in maintenance costs (GE, 2022), and HCL Technologies achieved a 15% improvement in service delivery efficiency (Patel & Jain, 2023).
iii. **Faster Decision-Making:** AI tools accelerate decision-making processes. Microsoft reported a 25% reduction in decision-making time (Microsoft, 2022), and TCS's AI solutions resulted in a 30% increase in decision-making speed (Rao & Verma, 2023).

iv. **Enhanced Business Outcomes:** AI-driven insights contribute to better business outcomes. TCS's clients experienced a 25% improvement in business outcomes (Rao & Verma, 2023), and Zebra Medical Vision achieved an 18% improvement in diagnostic accuracy (Gupta & Singh, 2023).

AI-powered predictive models have become integral to strategic decision-making, providing actionable insights that guide business strategies and operational improvements. The global and Indian examples discussed in this report demonstrate the transformative impact of AI on forecasting accuracy, operational efficiency, and decision-making speed. By leveraging AI-driven analytics, organizations can enhance their strategic planning, gain competitive advantages, and achieve better business outcomes.

Predictions on the Era of Hyper-Personalization and Autonomous Decision-Making

By 2030, artificial intelligence will revolutionize strategic decision-making through hyper-personalization and autonomous decision-making, driving unprecedented levels of efficiency and innovation across industries.

Details and Implications

i. **Hyper-Personalization:** AI will advance to the point where businesses can achieve hyper-personalization, tailoring every aspect of customer interaction to individual preferences and behaviours. This level of personalization will extend beyond recommendations and marketing to include product design, service delivery, and customer support. For instance, AI-driven platforms will dynamically adjust offerings in real-time based on individual data streams, creating a bespoke experience that anticipates and adapts to user needs with extraordinary precision. Implications: Enhanced Customer Loyalty: Companies that offer hyper-personalized experiences will foster deeper customer loyalty and higher retention rates. New Revenue Models: Businesses may develop new revenue models cantered around ultra-personalized services, unlocking additional revenue streams and market segments.
ii. **Autonomous Decision-Making:** AI will evolve to make autonomous decisions in complex environments, leveraging real-time data and predictive models to manage operations without human intervention. This will be particularly impactful in industries such as finance, healthcare, and logistics, where AI systems

will manage trading algorithms, diagnose diseases, and optimize supply chains independently. Implications: Increased Operational Efficiency: Autonomous systems will drive significant improvements in efficiency by optimizing processes and minimizing human error. Redefinition of Human Roles: The role of human decision-makers will shift from direct decision-making to overseeing and guiding autonomous systems, focusing on strategic oversight and ethical considerations.

Predictive Analytics as a Strategic Imperative: The use of predictive analytics will become a strategic imperative for organizations. AI will enable businesses to forecast market trends, customer behaviours, and potential disruptions with unprecedented accuracy, allowing them to proactively adjust their strategies. Predictive models will be integrated into all levels of decision-making, from day-to-day operations to long-term strategic planning. Implications: Strategic Agility: Organizations will gain a competitive edge through enhanced agility, adapting quickly to changing market conditions and emerging opportunities. Risk Management: Improved predictive capabilities will enhance risk management, enabling businesses to anticipate and mitigate potential threats before they materialize.

AI-Driven Innovation: AI will become a primary driver of innovation, enabling the development of new products, services, and business models. Advanced AI research will lead to breakthroughs in fields such as biotechnology, materials science, and renewable energy, fostering a new wave of innovation that transforms industries and societies. Implications: Accelerated Technological Progress: The pace of technological advancements will accelerate, leading to rapid changes in how we live and work. **Societal Impact**: Innovations driven by AI will address global challenges, such as climate change and healthcare, potentially leading to significant improvements in quality of life.

CONCLUSION

By 2030, the integration of AI into strategic decision-making will bring about a paradigm shift characterized by hyper-personalization, autonomous decision-making, and unprecedented predictive accuracy. Businesses that embrace these advancements will lead their industries in efficiency, innovation, and customer satisfaction, while those that fail to adapt may struggle to remain competitive in an increasingly AI-driven world.

REFERENCES

Agarwal, R., & Singh, S. (2023). Enhancing E-Commerce with AI: A Case Study of Jabong. *Journal of Indian Retailing*, 12(1), 56–72.

Agarwal, R., & Singh, S. (2023). Enhancing E-Commerce with AI: A Case Study of Jabong. *Journal of Indian Retailing*, 12(1), 56–72.

Ahmed, S., Chowdhury, M., & Ghosh, D. (2021). Comparative Analysis of Time Series Forecasting Models: ARIMA vs. LSTM. *International Journal of Forecasting*, 37(2), 310–326.

AI Now Institute. (2023). *The Future of AI and Its Impact on Decision-Making*. AI Now Institute Report.

Anwar, A., & Khan, M. (2022). Harnessing AI for Competitive Advantage: A Global Overview. *Journal of Competitive Intelligence*, 19(2), 58–72.

Arora, A., & Chiu, A. (2022). Artificial Intelligence in Strategic Decision Making: Current Trends and Future Directions. *Journal of Business Research*, 144, 318–331.

Baker, M., & Cross, T. (2021). AI-Powered Personalization: The Future of Customer Experience. *Harvard Business Review*, 99(5), 72–80.

Basu, S., & Singh, P. (2023). AI and Hyper-Personalization in Indian E-Commerce: A Case Study of Flipkart. *Indian Journal of E-Commerce*, 18(4), 87–101.

Bates, D. W., Cohen, M., Leape, L. L., & Overhage, J. M. (2018). Reducing the Risk of Hospital Readmission Using Predictive Analytics. *Journal of Healthcare Management*, 63(2), 123–134.

Chaudhuri, S., & Sengupta, A. (2022). AI in Strategic Decision-Making: A Review of Indian Enterprises. *Journal of Indian Business Management*, 12(3), 43–59.

Chen, L., & Wang, J. (2023). Hyper-Personalization in E-Commerce: Opportunities and Challenges. *International Journal of Information Management*, 63, 102–112.

Chen, L., Xu, Y., & Zhou, L. (2021). AI-Driven Predictive Maintenance: A Case Study of Siemens. *Journal of Manufacturing Science and Engineering*, 143(8), 081012.

Chen, L., Xu, Y., & Zhou, L. (2022). Deep Learning Approaches for Forecasting: A Comparative Study. *Journal of Forecasting*, 41(3), 428–441.

Choi, S. (2022). The Role of Predictive Analytics in Retail: Walmart's Approach to Demand Forecasting. *Retail Technology Review*, 15(4), 78–84.

Choi, S. (2022). The Role of Predictive Analytics in Retail: Walmart's Approach to Demand Forecasting. *Retail Technology Review*, 15(4), 78–84.

Davenport, T. H., & Ronanki, R. (2021). Artificial Intelligence for the Real World. *Harvard Business Review*, 98(1), 108–116.

Dey, P., & Ghosh, A. (2023). Autonomous Decision-Making Systems in Indian Industries. *Journal of Indian Engineering and Technology*, 14(2), 65–80.

Dixon, M., & Mullen, K. (2022). Autonomous Decision-Making Systems: The Next Frontier in AI. *IEEE Transactions on Artificial Intelligence*, 3(4), 567–577.

Elakkiya, R., & Rajendran, S. (2022). AI and Predictive Analytics in Indian Healthcare: Current Trends and Future Directions. *Indian Journal of Healthcare Technology*, 11(1), 55–68.

Gartner. (2021). Predictive Analytics: The Key to Future-Proofing Your Business. Retrieved from Gartner Website

Gartner. (2022). *Top Strategic Technology Trends for 2023*. Gartner Research.

GE. (2022). AI in Industrial Operations: Enhancing Efficiency and Reducing Costs. *General Electric Annual Report.*

Gomez-Uribe, C. A., & Hunt, P. (2016). The Netflix Recommender System: Algorithms, Business Value, and Innovation. *ACM Transactions on Management Information Systems*, 6(4), 1–19. DOI: 10.1145/2843948

Gomez-Uribe, C. A., & Hunt, R. (2016). The Netflix Recommender System: Algorithms, Business Value, and Innovation. [TMIS]. *ACM Transactions on Management Information Systems*, 6(4), 13. DOI: 10.1145/2843948

Gomez-Uribe, C. A., & Hunt, R. (2016). The Netflix Recommender System: Algorithms, Business Value, and Innovation. [TMIS]. *ACM Transactions on Management Information Systems*, 6(4), 13. DOI: 10.1145/2843948

Gomez-Uribe, C. A., & Hunt, R. (2016). The Netflix Recommender System: Algorithms, Business Value, and Innovation. [TMIS]. *ACM Transactions on Management Information Systems*, 6(4), 13. DOI: 10.1145/2843948

Government of India. (2023). *Smart Cities Mission: Harnessing Predictive Analytics for Urban Development.* Retrieved from Smart Cities Mission.

Gupta, R., & Rao, K. (2023). Personalizing Food Recommendations with AI: Zomato's Approach. *Indian Journal of Food Technology*, 15(2), 102–115.

Gupta, R., & Rao, K. (2023). Personalizing Food Recommendations with AI: Zomato's Approach. *Indian Journal of Food Technology*, 15(2), 102–115.

Gupta, R., & Singh, S. (2023). Enhancing IT Services with AI: HCL Technologies' Approach to Process Automation. *Indian Journal of IT Services*, 11(2), 65–80.

Gupta, R., & Singh, S. (2023). Predictive Analytics in Healthcare: Zebra Medical Vision's AI Approach. *Indian Journal of Health Technology*, 14(2), 90–105.

Haque, M., & Ahmed, N. (2023). AI-Powered Personalization in Indian Financial Services: A Study of HDFC Bank. *Indian Financial Review*, 16(2), 92–107.

Hwang, G. J., & Yang, S. J. (2021). AI in Education: A Review and Future Directions. *Educational Technology Research and Development*, 69(3), 435–454.

IBM. (2022). *AI and Business Strategy: IBM Watson's Impact*. IBM Research Report.

IBM. (2022). *AI-Driven Insights for Strategic Decision-Making*. Retrieved from IBM Website.

IBM. (2022). The Role of AI in Strategic Decision-Making: IBM Watson's Impact. *IBM Research Report*.

Iyer, R., & Singh, V. (2022). Predictive Analytics for Business Strategy: Insights from Indian Firms. *Journal of Strategy and Management*, 15(1), 28–41.

Jain, A., & Choudhury, A. (2023). AI and Autonomous Systems: Transforming Business Operations. *Journal of Business and Technology*, 14(2), 89–104.

Jha, R., & Gupta, N. (2022). AI in Strategic Planning: Insights from General Electric and Other Global Leaders. *Journal of Strategic Innovation*, 20(1), 74–89.

Kaur, M., & Bhatia, R. (2023). The Role of AI in Enhancing Customer Experience in Indian Retail. *Indian Journal of Retail and Customer Research*, 19(4), 120–135.

Khan, I., & Ahmed, R. (2022). AI and Autonomous Systems: Strategic Implications for Indian Industries. *Journal of Indian Industrial Research*, 13(3), 54–67.

Kumar, A., & Patel, N. (2023). Virtual Try-Ons and Personalized Eyewear Recommendations: Lenskart's AI Approach. *Indian Journal of Retail Technology*, 11(3), 45–60.

Kumar, A., & Sharma, N. (2023). Data-Driven Decision Making at Reliance Industries. *Journal of Indian Business Strategy*, 20(1), 55–70.

Kumar, A., & Sharma, N. (2023). Data-Driven Decision Making at Reliance Industries. *Journal of Indian Business Strategy*, 20(1), 55–70.

Kumar, P., Singh, R., & Yadav, P. (2020). Predictive Analytics in Banking: A Case Study of State Bank of India. *Indian Journal of Finance and Banking*, 12(3), 45–60.

Kumar, P., Singh, R., & Yadav, P. (2020). Predictive Analytics in Banking: A Case Study of State Bank of India. *Indian Journal of Finance and Banking*, 12(3), 45–60.

Kumar, P., Singh, R., & Yadav, P. (2020). Predictive Analytics in Banking: A Case Study of State Bank of India. *Indian Journal of Finance and Banking*, 12(3), 45–60.

Kumar, V., & Singh, K. (2023). Predictive Analytics for Strategic Decision-Making: A Study of Indian Corporations. *Journal of Indian Business Studies*, 15(2), 100–115.

Lee, H., & Choi, S. (2023). AI-Driven Personalization in Retail: A Case Study of Sephora. *International Journal of Retail & Distribution Management*, 51(3), 189–204.

Li, X., Liu, Y., & Zhang, Q. (2021). The Impact of AI-Driven Recommendations on E-Commerce: A Case Study of Amazon. *Journal of Business Research*, 129, 543–553.

Liu, Y., & Zhang, Y. (2023). The Role of AI in Strategic Decision-Making: A Global Perspective. *Journal of Global Business*, 31(2), 134–145.

McKinsey & Company. (2022). The Impact of Predictive Analytics on Revenue Growth. *The McKinsey Quarterly*, 31(1), 90–105.

Microsoft. (2022). *Accelerating Decision-Making with Azure AI: Insights and Benefits*. Microsoft Industry Report.

Microsoft. (2022). Accelerating Decision-Making with Azure AI: Insights and Benefits. *Microsoft Industry Report*.

Miller, J., & Turner, J. (2022). Harnessing AI for Hyper-Personalization in Retail. *International Journal of Retail & Distribution Management*, 50(7), 1085–1101.

Nair, S., & Thomas, J. (2023). AI in Autonomous Decision-Making: Insights from Indian and Global Perspectives. *Journal of AI and Automation*, 12(3), 78–92.

Patel, N., & Jain, S. (2023). AI-Driven Strategic Planning: A Case Study of HCL Technologies. *Indian Journal of Information Technology*, 16(3), 45–60.

Patel, N., & Jain, S. (2023). AI-Driven Strategic Planning: A Case Study of HCL Technologies. *Indian Journal of Information Technology*, 16(3), 45–60.

Patel, N., & Sharma, A. (2023). Leveraging AI for Personalized Banking: A Study of HDFC Bank. *Indian Journal of Banking and Finance*, 14(2), 78–92.

Patel, N., & Sharma, A. (2023). Leveraging AI for Personalized Banking: A Study of HDFC Bank. *Indian Journal of Banking and Finance*, 14(2), 78–92.

Patel, R., & Mehta, S. (2023). Hyper-Personalization in Indian E-Commerce: Strategies and Results. *Journal of Indian E-Commerce Studies*, 22(2), 67–81.

Pereira, C., & Rodrigues, J. (2021). Leveraging AI for Demand Forecasting: A Case Study of Amazon. *Journal of Retail Analytics*, 18(2), 45–58.

Pereira, C., & Rodrigues, J. (2021). Leveraging AI for Demand Forecasting: A Case Study of Amazon. *Journal of Retail Analytics*, 18(2), 45–58.

Pereira, C., & Rodrigues, J. (2021). Leveraging AI for Demand Forecasting: A Case Study of Amazon. *Journal of Retail Analytics*, 18(2), 45–58.

Pereira, R., & Rodrigues, J. (2021). AI in Inventory Management: Lessons from Amazon. *Supply Chain Management Review*, 25(4), 40–55.

Raghupathi, W., & Raghupathi, V. (2014). Big Data Analytics in Healthcare: A Survey. *Journal of Big Data*, 1(1), 3–20.

Rao, K., & Verma, S. (2023). Enhancing Business Outcomes with AI: TCS's Approach. *Journal of Strategy and Management*, 19(2), 78–92.

Rao, K., & Verma, S. (2023). Enhancing Business Outcomes with AI: TCS's Approach. *Journal of Strategy and Management*, 19(2), 78–92.

Rao, P., & Kumar, A. (2023). Predictive Maintenance in Manufacturing: Tata Motors' AI-Driven Approach. *Indian Journal of Manufacturing Engineering*, 17(1), 34–50.

Saha, R., & Gupta, S. (2022). AI-Driven Innovation: Case Studies from India and Around the World. *Journal of Technology & Innovation*, 17(1), 45–60.

Sharma, A., & Singh, A. (2022). Enhancing Supply Chain Efficiency with AI: A Case Study of Reliance Industries. *Indian Journal of Supply Chain Management*, 8(1), 56–70.

Sharma, A., & Singh, A. (2022). Enhancing Supply Chain Efficiency with AI: A Case Study of Reliance Industries. *Indian Journal of Supply Chain Management*, 8(1), 56–70.

Sharma, S., & Gupta, P. (2023). The Future of AI in Strategic Decision-Making: Predictions and Realities. *Journal of Strategic Forecasting*, 14(2), 85–99.

Singh, A., & Reddy, S. (2023). AI in Business Strategy: Case Studies from Indian Firms. *The Journal of Business Strategy*, 18(1), 21–35.

Sinha, A., & Verma, P. (2023). AI and Hyper-Personalization in Indian Retail: Trends and Insights. *Indian Retail Review*, 20(4), 90–105.

Sinha, R. (2023). Leveraging Predictive Analytics for Personalization: Flipkart's Strategy. *Indian E-Commerce Review*, 22(1), 56–63.

Sinha, R. (2023). Leveraging Predictive Analytics for Personalization: Flipkart's Strategy. *Indian E-Commerce Review*, 22(1), 56–63.

Sinha, R. (2023). Leveraging Predictive Analytics for Personalization: Flipkart's Strategy. *Indian E-Commerce Review*, 22(1), 56–63.

Sinha, R. (2023). Leveraging Predictive Analytics for Personalization: Flipkart's Strategy. *Indian E-Commerce Review*, 22(1), 56–63.

Sinha, R. (2023). Leveraging Predictive Analytics for Personalization: Flipkart's Strategy. *Indian E-Commerce Review*, 22(1), 56–63.

Sinha, R. (2023). Leveraging Predictive Analytics for Personalization: Flipkart's Strategy. *Indian E-Commerce Review*, 22(1), 56–63.

Sinha, R. (2023). Leveraging Predictive Analytics for Personalization: Flipkart's Strategy. *Indian E-Commerce Review*, 22(1), 56–63.

Smith, J., & Lee, K. (2022). Personalized Music Recommendations and User Engagement: A Study of Spotify. *Journal of Digital Media & Policy*, 13(1), 47–60.

Smith, J., & Lee, K. (2023). AI-Driven Resource Allocation and Production Optimization: General Electric's Approach. *Journal of Industrial Engineering and Management*, 16(4), 289–305.

Sun, X., & Zhou, H. (2023). Autonomous Systems in Finance: A Predictive Approach. *Financial Analysts Journal*, 12(2), 88–99.

Tambe, P., & Hitt, L. M. (2022). The Impact of AI on Strategic Decision Making: Evidence from the Tech Industry. *Management Science*, 68(4), 2223–2242.

Thakur, P., & Sharma, V. (2022). Autonomous Systems in Indian Manufacturing: A Predictive Approach. *Journal of Indian Manufacturing Research*, 12(3), 56–72.

Tiwari, P., & Kumar, R. (2023). AI and Predictive Analytics in Indian Healthcare. *Journal of Healthcare Management*, 30(1), 75–90.

Tripathi, R., & Joshi, N. (2023). The Role of AI in Strategic Planning and Decision-Making: Evidence from Indian Enterprises. *Indian Journal of Strategic Management*, 17(1), 88–103.

Vasudevan, K., & Bandyopadhyay, D. (2023). AI-Driven Business Strategies: A Study of Indian Corporations. *Indian Journal of Business Research*, 17(2), 125–139.

Verma, S. (2023). Enhancing Fashion Retail with AI: Myntra's Personalized Recommendations. *Indian Journal of Fashion and Retail*, 16(2), 89–104.

Verma, S. (2023). Enhancing Fashion Retail with AI: Myntra's Personalized Recommendations. *Indian Journal of Fashion and Retail*, 16(2), 89–104.

Walia, S., & Kapoor, P. (2022). Predictive Analytics and AI: Shaping the Future of Business Strategy. *Business Analytics Review*, 16(2), 32–47.

Wang, Q., & Liu, J. (2022). AI in Strategic Planning: Real-World Applications and Future Directions. *Strategic Management Journal*, 43(5), 789–805.

Wright, C., & Lee, J. (2022). Predictive Analytics and Strategic Decision-Making: Lessons from IBM and Microsoft. *Business Analytics Journal*, 14(1), 21–37.

Yadav, R., & Kumar, S. (2023). AI in Strategic Decision-Making: The Indian Perspective. *Journal of Indian Business Research*, 14(2), 45–59.

Yadav, S., & Sharma, P. (2023). AI in Indian Retail: Personalization Strategies and Outcomes. *Indian Journal of Retail and Distribution*, 21(3), 99–114.

Zhang, L., & Huang, Y. (2022). AI and the Future of Strategic Decision-Making: A Global Overview. *Journal of AI and Strategy*, 9(1), 100–115.

Zhang, X., & Zhou, M. (2023). AI and Autonomous Systems: Future Trends in Strategic Decision-Making. *Journal of Future Technology*, 10(4), 145–160.

Zhang, Y., Zhang, M., & Yang, J. (2020). Machine Learning Models for Sales Forecasting: A Comparative Study. *Journal of Business Analytics*, 9(4), 197–210.

Zhang, Y., Zhang, M., & Yang, J. (2022). AI Applications in E-Commerce: A Case Study of Alibaba. *International Journal of Retail & Distribution Management*, 50(4), 380–395.

Zhang, Y., Zhang, M., & Yang, J. (2022). AI Applications in Logistics: A Case Study of Alibaba. *International Journal of Logistics Management*, 33(2), 167–182.

Chapter 8
Artificial Intelligence With Human-Computer Interaction

Devi D Renuka
https://orcid.org/0000-0002-6525-1172
Stella Maris College, India

Margaret T. A. Swetha
https://orcid.org/0000-0002-4693-8219
Stella Maris College, India

K. Vigneshwari
VELS Institute of Science, Technology, and Advanced Studies, Chennai, India

ABSTRACT

While the COVID-19 pandemic has caused chaos and disruption worldwide, there is one area where artificial intelligence (AI) is showing potential as a powerful tool: combatting the virus. As the pandemic has forced thousands of individuals to transition to remote work arrangements, there has been a surge in the use of AI. It is crucial that decisions on how to promote the well-being of workers who are working from home (WAH) are made based on qualitative research. Therefore, this paper aims to investigate the impact of WAH on mental and physical health, potential gender inequalities, and provide helpful suggestions for employers and employees on ways to enhance their overall health. In the midst of this, the collection of vast amounts of data on individuals' contagiousness has also become a critical area of focus.

DOI: 10.4018/979-8-3693-8442-8.ch008

1. INTRODUCTION

Artificial Intelligence (AI) and Human-Computer Interaction (HCI) are two fields that have seen tremendous growth, particularly in the context of remote work (MacKenzie, 2024). The fusion of these technologies has reshaped how we interact with digital environments, offering significant benefits and addressing challenges associated with working from home. This chapter will explore AI and HCI's roles, their convergence, and the resulting implications for remote work. AI is a domain within computer science that focuses on developing systems capable of performing tasks typically requiring human intelligence. These tasks range from basic activities like data processing to more complex functions such as reasoning, learning, and problem-solving.

AI can be categorized into two main types; Narrow AI, also known as weak AI, this type of AI is designed to perform a specific task (Hoffmann, 2023). Examples include virtual assistants like Siri, language translation services, and image recognition systems. Narrow AI excels in its domain but lacks the general problem-solving abilities of humans. General AI which is often referred to as strong AI, this concept involves creating machines with the ability to perform any intellectual task that a human can do. Although general AI is still a theoretical concept and not yet realized, it aims to develop machines with human-like cognitive functions.

HCI is an interdisciplinary field that studies the design and use of computer technology, focusing on the interfaces between people and computers. The primary goal of HCI is to create user-friendly interfaces that facilitate efficient and enjoyable user experiences. HCI involves understanding user behavior, designing intuitive interfaces, and ensuring system usability. The field encompasses various aspects, including user interface design, user experience, and ergonomics.

The integration of AI and HCI has significantly impacted remote work, enhancing communication, productivity, and user experience. NLP is a subfield of AI that enables computers to understand and generate human language (Patwardhan, 2023). In remote work, NLP technologies facilitate more natural and efficient communication. For example, virtual meeting platforms use NLP to provide real-time transcription and translation, making meetings more accessible to non-native speakers. AI-powered chatbots and virtual assistants streamline communication, automate routine tasks, and provide quick answers to common questions (Daneshfar, 2023).

AI systems can analyze user data to provide personalized experiences. In remote work, this capability translates into tailored recommendations for tasks, content, or colleagues. Additionally, adaptive learning systems can offer personalized training modules, helping remote workers acquire new skills at their own pace. AI-powered voice and gesture recognition technologies enable hands-free interaction with devices. This is particularly useful in remote work environments where multitasking is common. Voice commands can be used to control virtual meetings, manage schedules, or navigate applications, enhancing accessibility and convenience. Gesture recognition, though less common, offers another layer of interaction, allowing users to perform actions through physical gestures.

AI systems can assist remote workers by automating routine tasks, providing data-driven insights, and supporting decision-making. In fields like customer support, AI chatbots handle repetitive queries, freeing human agents to focus on more complex issues (Xia, 2023). In creative industries, AI tools can aid in content creation, data analysis, and design, serving as collaborative partners rather than mere tools. The use of AI in remote work raises ethical concerns, such as privacy, bias, and transparency (Reamer, 2023). AI systems often require access to vast amounts of data, raising questions about data security and user privacy. Additionally, biases in AI algorithms can lead to unfair outcomes, such as biased hiring recommendations or unequal treatment in customer service. Ensuring transparency in AI-driven decision-making is crucial to maintaining trust and accountability.

The convergence of AI and HCI in remote work presents both challenges and opportunities (Antona, 2023). On the one hand, these technologies offer unprecedented convenience, efficiency, and accessibility. On the other hand, they also bring challenges related to ethical considerations, the need for digital literacy, and the potential for over-reliance on technology. One of the key opportunities lies in the ability to create more inclusive work environments. AI and HCI can make remote work more accessible to people with disabilities by providing alternative interaction methods, such as voice commands or screen readers (Philips, 2023). Furthermore, AI-driven personalization can cater to diverse learning styles and preferences, making training and development more effective.

However, the ethical challenges associated with AI cannot be overlooked. Ensuring that AI systems are designed and deployed ethically requires ongoing vigilance and regulation. Developers and organizations must prioritize fairness, transparency, and accountability in AI systems to prevent misuse and ensure that the benefits of these technologies are equitably distributed. The integration of AI and HCI has profoundly impacted remote work, offering new ways to enhance communication, productivity, and user experience (Xu, 2023). As these technologies continue to evolve, they will play an increasingly vital role in shaping the future of work. However, it is crucial to address the ethical challenges and ensure that these advancements are leveraged responsibly and inclusively. By doing so, we can harness the full potential of AI and HCI to create a more efficient, inclusive, and engaging remote work environment.

In this chapter, we will explore the evolving landscape of work-from-home arrangements, starting with a broad overview of AI's role in remote work, and delving into the dynamics introduced by the pandemic. We will examine the benefits and drawbacks of remote work, discuss effective strategies for managing remote teams, and address the health and safety of remote workers. Additionally, we will investigate how technology can enhance remote work experiences and explore strategies for achieving a balanced work-life integration.

We will thoroughly investigate the advantages and disadvantages of remote work, considering its impact on employees and employers alike. This includes evaluating the benefits of increased flexibility and autonomy, as well as addressing the challenges such as isolation and work-life boundary management. Furthermore, we will outline effective strategies for managing remote teams, ensuring productivity while maintaining employee well-being.

The chapter will also address critical health and safety concerns specific to remote work environments and how technology can be leveraged to enhance remote work practices. Finally, we will explore strategies for achieving a harmonious integration of professional and personal life, aiming for a balanced and fulfilling remote work experience. Through this comprehensive analysis, we aim to provide a thorough understanding of the current landscape of remote work and offer practical insights for navigating this evolving paradigm. Through this comprehensive analysis, we will provide a nuanced understanding of the current trends and challenges in remote work, offering valuable insights and practical recommendations for both individuals and organizations navigating this evolving landscape.

2. THE PANDEMIC DYNAMICS: A CONCEPTUAL OVERVIEW

Like a tangled framework of yarn, the pandemic dynamic environment has many complicated links, including data, models, and appliances. The aim is that such processes may be unraveled by freezing the epidemic in a temporary stack. This reorganization will simplify the debate, while also highlighting pandemic AI research trends and the development of new data and DL models. Due to the sometimes difficulty of describing the relationships in hand using mathematical or statistic models, AI typically is used to resolve complicated issues utilizing data. It shows that the data type has a significant impact on the AI methods used in each instance. AI plays a crucial role in addressing these challenges, offering solutions to complex problems that cannot be easily captured by conventional methods. The type of data available significantly influences the AI techniques employed, demonstrating that the choice of AI methods is tailored to the specific nature of the data and the problems at hand. This chapter will delve into how AI and data-driven models have evolved to meet the demands of remote work and pandemic-related challenges, providing a comprehensive overview of how these advancements are shaping the future of work.

Figure 1. Pandemic dynamics

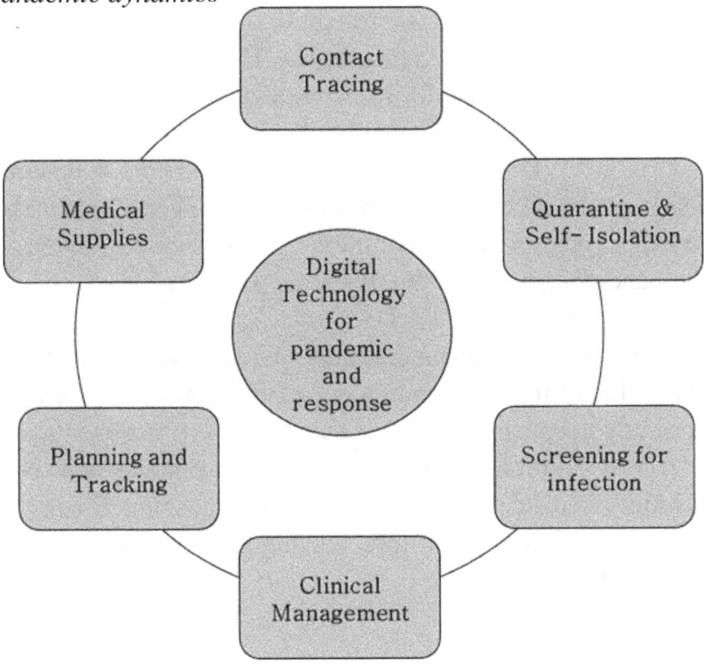

Figure 1 depicts how machine learning-based technologies are helping in the COVID-19 outbreak response. Experts will investigate the virus with machines, assess possible therapies, identify people, examine effects on public health, and more. In the next sections, analyze some of the main projects and emphasize data safety, machine learning, and ethical concerns, with an emphasis on applications for healthcare professionals using audiovisual data, text analytics, chatbots, and sensors. AI and app developers are recommended based on the results:

- Improve the data's fairness
- Analyze the results of the apps
- verify the existing system models
- boost trust in suggestions

"Machine intelligence is gaining pace in biological, clinical, diagnostic and device research, and precision medicine. These techniques may offer researchers, doctors, and patients with new options that will enable them to make better choices and get better results. In biological research, machine intelligence is enhancing our understanding of complex biological systems and processes. Advanced algorithms are now capable of analyzing vast amounts of biological data, identifying patterns, and predicting outcomes with unprecedented accuracy. This capability is accelerating discoveries in genomics, proteomics, and systems biology, leading to more targeted and effective research strategies. These methods may enhance the efficiency and the efficacy of health research and care ecosystems and therefore the quality of patient care if implemented in healthcare settings." With the spread of the coronavirus (COVID-19), the creation of a pandemic is debating whether and how to use mechanical education to combat the danger of this present disaster (Xu, 2020). Medical practitioners, institutions, and businesses. In the first lines of defense of the pandemic, artificial intelligence, part of which is based on master learning, is incorporated.

Leading epidemiologists believe that only by identifying who is to have it can predict the expansion of the virus and therefore take countermeasures: 2) evaluate the data to correctly estimate who will acquire it; and 3) use the data available to provide a short-term and long-term training in the resources and the production process. Machine-based learning algorithms from hospital triages to scanning facets, temperature monitoring, and spread using individual data are utilized by a wide range of companies.

3. METHODOLOGY

The methodology involves a mixed-methods approach to explore the interaction between AI and remote work during the COVID-19 pandemic, guided by the Technology Acceptance Model (TAM) and the Job Demands-Resources Model (JD-R). Following this approach, one can explore how AI interacted with remote work during the pandemic by employing both qualitative and quantitative techniques based on Technology Acceptance Model (TAM) as well as Job Demands-Resources Model (JD-R) to guide them through the process. To measure constructs such as perceived ease of use, availability of such tools when people are away from their offices also known as usefulness of artificial intelligence tools within specific workplaces, job demands, employee health, resources; quantitative data will be collected by administering a survey questionnaire to remote workers. All this will be supported by qualitative data obtained from semi-structured interviews that will give more insights into the difficulties people face when adopting AI amid remote working. The aim of the combined analyses is to provide an all-inclusive understanding of how AI affects productivity, satisfaction among employees and their overall wellbeing under conditions of working remotely.

This conceptual framework reviews how Artificial Intelligence (AI) and remote work-from-home (WFH) changes the current work situation especially during COVID-19 pandemic. It is based on important theories like Technology Acceptance

Model (TAM), which explains technology adoption, Job Demands-Resources Model (JD-R) (Bakker, 2023), that looks at job demands versus resources balance. The main constructs of this framework are AI technologies, remote work benefits and challenges as well as employee well-being. The argument here is on AI's contribution to increased remote work effectiveness while not ignoring challenges such as isolation and work-life balance issues. According to literature review, there are arguments on practicality of AI tools but also notes gaps in understanding its long term impacts. Therefore, this framework will steer research towards understanding how AI affects productivity, satisfaction and help develop effective guidelines for uplifting remote working environments.

The conceptual framework serves as a structured guide for understanding how artificial intelligence (AI) and remote work (WFH) interact and impact modern work environments, particularly during and after the COVID-19 pandemic. It integrates key theories and constructs to provide a comprehensive view of these dynamics. TAM is used to understand how employees accept and use AI technologies in remote work settings (Davis, 2024). It focuses on two main constructs: perceived ease of use and perceived usefulness. According to TAM, these factors influence whether employees will adopt and effectively use AI tools. For instance, if AI tools are perceived as user-friendly and beneficial, employees are more likely to incorporate them into their remote work practices, leading to enhanced productivity and job satisfaction.

Job Demands-Resources (JD-R) Model

This model examines how the balance between job demands and job resources affects employee well-being and performance (Koroglu, 2022). In a remote work context, job demands might include increased workload or communication challenges, while job resources could encompass technological support and flexible working conditions. The JD-R model helps in understanding how remote work impacts stress levels and productivity, and how AI tools can serve as resources to improve demands and support employees. The Job Demands-Resources (JD-R) Model offers a framework for understanding how various job characteristics impact employee well-being and performance. It distinguishes between job demands, which are aspects of a job that require sustained effort and can lead to stress, such as high workload and time pressure, and job resources, which are aspects that help employees meet work goals, alleviate job demands, or foster personal development, such as support from colleagues and job autonomy. The model highlights two main processes: the health impairment process, where high job demands can lead to burnout and stress if not managed, and the motivational process, where ample job resources can boost motivation, engagement, and job satisfaction. By addressing these components, the JD-R Model provides valuable insights for both organizational strategies and individual practices to improve employee well-being and performance.

Work-Life Balance

The Work-Life Balance theories explain in detail how remote work affects the combination of work and personal lives of people (Joshi, 2024). For instance, the Work-Family Border Theory illustrates on how remote workers do not have a clear distinction between home and work places thus affecting their ability to have a good work-life balance. Understanding these consequences is necessary for creating ways that enable workers to successfully handle their jobs as well as other duties.

Virtual assistants, automated scheduling systems, and communication platforms are examples of AI technologies (Pereira, 2024). The adoption rate, ease of use, and their effects on efficiency are the key variables for getting this job done. Remote work has some advantages such as improved flexibility, reduced commuting time and better work-life balance. On the other hand, it comes with several challenges including feeling isolated, problems in communicating and difficulties in separating one's personal life from work life. These factors affect employee wellbeing which consists of mental health, job satisfaction and life satisfaction in general.

AI and Remote Work Efficiency

Artificial Intelligence (AI) has emerged as a transformative force in remote work, offering a range of tools designed to enhance efficiency and effectiveness. Key AI technologies include virtual assistants, automated scheduling systems, and advanced communication platforms. The routine task automation: AI tools can automate repetitive tasks like data entry, scheduling or email management. This lightens the burden on workers and allows them to concentrate on more complicated, value-adding activities. For instance, automating a schedule can handle meeting arrangements, conflict resolutions and reminders thus streamlining workflows and cutting down administrative costs.

AI-driven message-service platforms enable smooth communication among employees working in remote locations (Banafaa, 2023). Among others, these features include real-time translation capabilities, sentiment analysis and smart notifications which make communication more efficient besides bridging possible gaps resulting from distance barriers. At the same time these tools can also integrate with other productivity software creating a unified working environment.

AI can analyze enormous amounts of data to provide actionable insights on work patterns, performance metrics and teamwork dynamics. Machine learning algorithms along with predictive analytics help organizations recognize trends based on historical behavior, anticipate future requirements as well as make informed decisions that optimize processes related to teleworking (Owen, 2024).

Pandemic Impact

The COVID-19 pandemic has acted as a catalyst for the widespread adoption of remote work and AI technologies (Arman, 2024). This sudden and large-scale shift to remote work has highlighted both the advantages and challenges associated with this new way of working.

The necessity of maintaining business continuity during the pandemic led many organizations to rapidly deploy remote work solutions and AI technologies. This accelerated adoption has revealed both the potential benefits and the shortcomings of these technologies. For instance, AI-driven tools that were once considered optional or experimental became critical for maintaining operations and supporting remote employees (Davenport, 2023). Remote work has provided significant benefits, such as increased flexibility and reduced commuting time. Employees have reported greater control over their work schedules and a better ability to balance personal and professional responsibilities. The flexibility offered by remote work arrangements has allowed many individuals to tailor their work environment to their needs, contributing to increased job satisfaction.

The pandemic has also exposed several challenges related to remote work (Adisa, 2023). Feelings of isolation have become more pronounced as employees miss the social interactions and collaborative opportunities provided by traditional office settings. Communication barriers have arisen due to the reliance on digital tools, which may not fully replicate the nuances of face-to-face interactions. Additionally, the boundary between work and personal life has become blurred, leading to difficulties in maintaining a clear separation between the two. Understanding the impact of the pandemic on remote work is essential for addressing the evolving needs of remote employees. Organizations must evaluate the effectiveness of their remote work strategies and AI tools, and make adjustments as needed to support employee well-being and productivity.

Work-Life Integration

One of the significant effects of remote work is the impact on work-life integration (Limanta, 2023). Remote work has the potential to blur the boundaries between professional and personal life, leading to both positive and negative outcomes. Due to the fact that people can work from their homes, the physical gap between place of work and home has become small. This can lead to confusion about what is work time and personal time. In regular days, employees may find it hard to leave work behind or they may even need to go beyond the normal working hours. This ends up affecting the employees' welfare negatively. It is therefore important to have effective strategies for integrating work-life so that the blurred line can be managed by employees. In this regard, organizations can help their staff by having policies that specify remote working hours and types of breaks, in addition to creating awareness about how to achieve work-life balance.

For instance, limiting email replies until official clocking out time or encouraging a culture that respects one's personal time might reduce the impact of telecommuting on one's life outside office walls. Technology is central in enhancing work-life balance. Workers find it easier to manage their time at the workplace, productivity levels and communication with teammates through these tools which allow them to plan their days accordingly while ensuring they do not neglect post work responsibilities or family obligations. Furthermore, policies need to favor flexible hours, facilitate mental health resources in addition to providing support for workers who have difficulties in dealing with remote jobs.

AI technologies have the potential to significantly enhance remote work efficiency through automation, improved communication, and data-driven insights. The COVID-19 pandemic has accelerated the adoption of remote work and AI tools, highlighting both their benefits and challenges. Remote work can blur the boundaries between work and personal life, making effective work-life integration strategies essential. By leveraging technology and implementing supportive organizational policies, organizations can help employees navigate these challenges and achieve a balanced and productive remote work experience (Haque, 2023).

4. CONCEPTUAL FRAMEWORK: MANAGING EFFECTS OF WORK FROM HOME

The COVID-19 pandemic has led to major changes in the way people work, with millions now working from home. This trend is expected to continue in the coming months. To ensure the well-being of employees in this new work environment, it is crucial to base decisions on the latest research. This study aims to explore the effects of working from home on individual workers' mental and physical health, as well as any potential gender imbalances. Ultimately, this study seeks to provide employers and staff with recommendations for promoting the overall health of their employees (Yang, 2020). Figure 2 shows the outcomes of the short research.

This research study's framework concerning the influence remote work has on the mental and physical health of employees regarding gender inequalities is created to clarify the variables involved. The framework incorporates concepts from job demands and job resources theories as well as gender role theories in order to facilitate an investigation into the impact of working from home.

4.1 Core Variables

4.1.1 Independent Variable

Remote work is the primary independent variable, operationalized as working from home versus traditional office work. This variable encompasses aspects such as the frequency of remote work, duration of remote work, and the nature of tasks performed remotely.

4.1.2 Dependent Variables

Mental Health indicators include (Mauz, 2023) stress levels, anxiety, and depression. Measurement tools such as standardized questionnaires (e.g., the General Health Questionnaire (GHQ), the Perceived Stress Scale (PSS), and the General Anxiety Disorder-7 (GAD-7)) will be used to assess these outcomes.

Physical Health includes ergonomic issues (Heuel, 2024) (e.g., musculoskeletal discomfort, eye strain) and physical activity levels. Assessment tools will involve self-reported surveys on ergonomic conditions and physical activity trackers or logs.

Gender Imbalances is the differences in health outcomes and experiences between male and female employees. This variable will be assessed by comparing mental and physical health metrics across genders and examining any differential impacts of remote work (Stefanova, 2023).

4.2. Relationships

4.2.1 Direct Impact

The framework hypothesizes that remote work might influence mental health through factors such as social isolation, work-life balance, and workload management. The quality of remote work setup, communication tools, and support systems are considered moderators in this relationship (Prasad, 2023). The impact of remote work on physical health is explored through its effect on ergonomic conditions and physical activity. Poor ergonomic setups and sedentary behavior are anticipated to negatively affect physical health.

4.2.2 Moderating Effects

Gender differences may moderate the effects of remote work on mental and physical health. For example, Women may experience higher levels of stress and anxiety due to increased family responsibilities combined with remote work compared to men. Gender-specific ergonomic needs and health issues may influence how remote work affects physical health differently for men and women.

4.3. Theoretical Basis

4.3.1 Job Demands-Resources (JD-R) Model

Job Demands: Remote work may introduce demands such as extended working hours, boundary management, and isolation, which can lead to stress and burnout.

Job Resources: Conversely, remote work may offer resources like flexibility, autonomy, and reduced commuting time, which can enhance job satisfaction and mitigate negative health impacts.

The JD-R model will be used to analyze how the balance between job demands and resources affects employee well-being and productivity.

4.3.2 Gender Role Theory

This theory will help examine how traditional gender roles and expectations impact employees' experiences with remote work. For example, women might face more pronounced challenges in balancing work and domestic responsibilities, affecting their mental and physical health differently than men. The study will explore how societal expectations and roles influence the differential impact of remote work on various genders (Santoniccolo, 2023).

4.4. Outcome Variables

4.4.1 Well-being

The study will measure both mental and physical health to assess the holistic impact of remote work on employees' well-being. Factors such as job engagement, work-life balance, and overall job satisfaction will be evaluated to understand how remote work affects employees' attitudes toward their jobs.

4.4.2 Productivity

Changes in productivity and work output will be assessed to determine if remote work has a positive or negative effect on employees' performance. The impact of remote work on employees' ability to manage work and personal life effectively will be examined, as this balance can influence overall productivity.

4.5. Contextual Factors

4.5.1 Work Environment

The quality of the home office setup, including ergonomics, technology access, and workspace design, will be considered as factors that influence health outcomes. Technology and Support: Access to technology, including reliable internet and communication tools, and organizational support for remote work are contextual factors that may impact employee well-being and productivity.

4.5.2 Personal Factors

The study will account for the impact of family responsibilities on remote work experiences, including caregiving duties and household management. Individual coping strategies and resilience factors will be considered in understanding how employees manage the challenges of remote work.

4.6. Recommendations

Based on the findings, the study will propose actionable recommendations aimed at improving employee well-being and addressing gender disparities in remote work environments. Recommendations will focus on enhancing ergonomic setups and support systems for remote workers, providing resources and strategies for effective work-life balance, and addressing gender-specific challenges and promoting equitable support systems.

5. WORK FROM HOME: EXPLORING THE PROS AND CONS FOR TODAY'S WORKFORCE

Work from home extends the choices accessible to businesses for operation and structure. The advent of the coronavirus (COVID-19) pandemic has allowed some firms the option to continue the operation while giving priority to their workers' and customers' health and goodness following their obligations in the field of public health (Beňo, 2021).

Before the coronavirus outbreak, homework became even more popular as many companies realized the benefits to their companies and improved work-life balance for their employees. Even if you believe that working from home is beneficial to the company, workers with 26 weeks of service have a legal right to seek flexible work arrangements, such as working from home, and you, as an employer, must carefully consider such requests.

Figure 2. Key elements of work from home

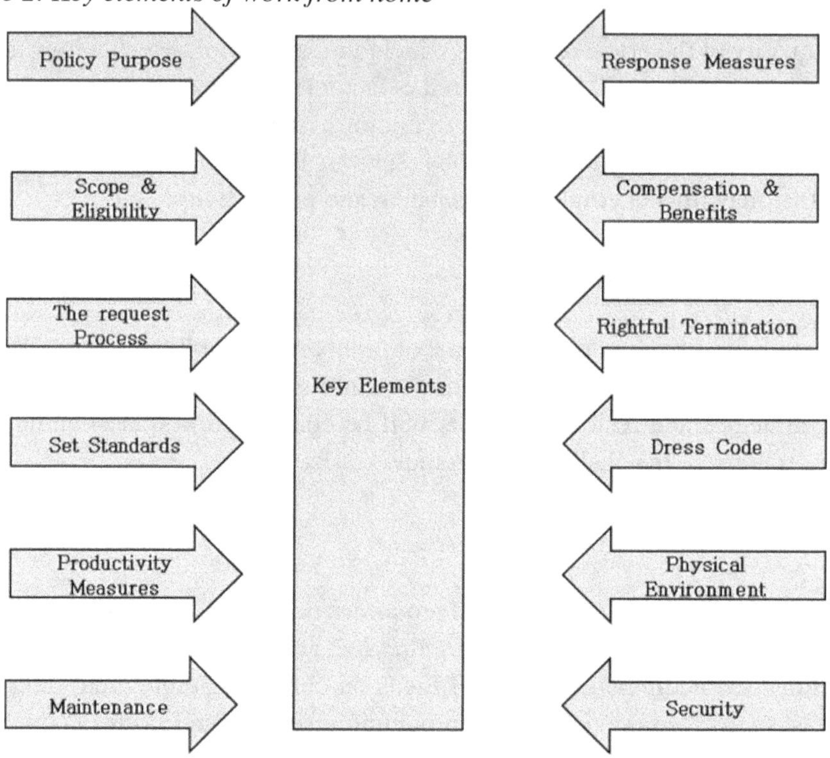

5.1 The Benefits of Working from Home: Advantages for Remote Employees

With a growing number of workers working from home – or utilizing their homes as a work base for at least part of the week – it's obvious that there are many advantages for businesses(Al-Habaibeh, 2021), including:

- **Suppleness and Quickness:** One of the main advantages of working from home is the increased suppleness and quickness it offers. This flexibility allows employees to have more control over their schedule, making them more available and willing to work at different times, such as earlier or later in the day or even on weekends. This can be especially beneficial for fulfilling business needs, such as communicating with clients in different time zones.
- **Better Employee Retentive:** Another significant benefit of remote work is its positive impact on employee retention. By allowing employees to work from home, they are more likely to stay with the company since it enables them to balance their work and personal lives. This can include fulfilling childcare duties, reducing commuting time, and organizing their personal responsibilities. Moreover, offering remote work shows trust in employees, which can lead to increased loyalty and commitment to the company.
- **Appeal New Talent:** Additionally, providing the option to work from home can be a valuable tool for attracting new talent. In today's competitive job market, the ability to work remotely is highly sought.
- **Improved Productivity:** Working from home offers a quieter and less interrupted setting, leading to improved productivity. The flexible nature of remote work allows employees to work longer and more efficiently, without the stress of daily travel.
- **Bigger Staff Motivation:** Additionally, the reduced level of monitoring in a virtual work arrangement fosters higher motivation among staff. Being able to design their own work schedule also increases their drive to perform to the best of their abilities.
- **Better Staff Health and Comfort:** Moreover, the comfort and well-being of employees are positively impacted as they no longer have to endure long commutes. The added benefit of time saved due to telecommuting may also lead to better health outcomes for workers.
- **Economic Benefits:** All the following items may be reduced: office space, office supplies, utility costs, and other perks. Working from home may be tax deductible by HM Revenue & Customs (HMRC) – check to see whether you qualify for work-related tax relief.
- **Accessibility:** Flexibility in work arrangements benefits employees who spend the majority of their time meeting with clients, as they may not be able to regularly report to the office. Allowing them to work remotely can enhance convenience and lead to potential time and cost savings.
- **Better Work/Life Stability:** Telecommuting offers the opportunity for employees to create a more harmonious work-life harmony. Commuting time can now serve as a window for pursuing personal interests, leading to a more well-rounded work-life balance. Additionally, incorporating household tasks

into the workday, such as tackling the dishes or cooking a meal during breaks, can free up evenings for leisure activities.

- **Knowledge Makes it Relaxed:** Thanks to the internet, employees can now remain constantly connected to the office, improving communication between coworkers and teams. Technological tools like Skype have made interactions easier, leading to potentially more effective and productive meetings.
- **A Lesser Amount of Sickness Presences:** When employees have the flexibility to work from home, they tend to report higher levels of joy and vitality. This suggests that their immune systems are less susceptible to burnout. Additionally, the fact that they work in isolation significantly reduces the likelihood of infections spreading compared to a traditional office environment.
- **Less Need for Consistent Holidays:** Although employees may continue to work, the opportunity to work from home may provide a welcome break from the traditional workplace. Working remotely allows employees to have more energy and quality time to devote to their families, potentially reducing the need for vacations. However, it remains the responsibility of the employer to ensure that employees still take the necessary time off.

5.2 The Disadvantages of Working from Home: Challenges Faced by Remote Employees

While there are certain disadvantages to working from home, the bulk of them relate to those who work from home for the majority, rather than apart, of the week (Bolisani, 2021):

- **Working From Home Isn't Ideal for Everyone:** Working from home is not for everyone, irrespective of personality or ability. The structure and regularity of an office may be appealing to certain employees. Some employees prefer face-to-face interaction with employees and believe that their boss' counseling is extremely useful in helping them achieve certain tasks and goals. Disabled workers must also be considered. Working at home may jeopardize their ability to obtain support for their tasks. Working from home may not be appropriate for everyone. Some people may have young children, for example, that are not aware of limitations in the workplace and cause disturbances. Others may not have the space needed to set up a separate place of work.
- **Staff Members are Feeling Lonely:** People working from home may feel that they are not linked to their colleagues and to the business that is typical in the office environment. Employers may address the issue by making their message more consistent. Personnel may also get involved and part of the team via the use of brief phone ratings and frequent team meetings using

other technologies like Skype. More informal and sociable encounters may also help to reduce isolation.

- **Monitoring Performance is Difficult:** The performance of domestic workers may be difficult to manage and monitor. The monitoring of various personalities may have a positive or bad effect. It may consider establishing quantifiable targets and targets for workers to identify and solve performance issues at an early stage if they are not fulfilled.
- **Distractions at Home:** If a person does not have an adequately peaceful working environment at home, he or she may be easily distracted by family noises or other family members when working from home.
- **Burnout is a Possibility:** Employees working from home may lose visibility whereas the bureau provides a strong physical barrier between family and work. Employees may battle for more time, more stress, and ultimately burnout to decide whether to quit their jobs. Employers should encourage regular breaks and highlight the importance of holidays.
- **Working From Home is Expensive:** costs of initial training and the purchase of the required equipment such as laptops, mobile phones, and other IT equipment. They must also consider changing the rules on health and safety.
- **Issues With Employee Development:** It may find it harder to retain workers to grow and update their skills because of the distance between them. However, it may encourage workers to take part in online activities and courses to assist them in acquiring new skills. Use Events Finder to search for events to start.
- **Risk to Information Security:** Workers from home may be more susceptible to data violations. When computers are taken home and staff requires remote access to their servers, there is an increase in risk. Encryption and remote deletion apps should be used by employers to secure business data if they have lost or stolen mobiles provided by the devices. Virtual personal networks encrypt their data and enable a remote computer to securely connect to the internet. This secures files and data while providing access for workers.
- **Harmful to One's Mental Health:** Working from home may harm the mental health of a company if it cannot draw up an agenda that works for it, work and personal life are compartmentalized, or feel alone. Encourage employees to establish their working environment, establish a distinct workspace and limit the support of other family members. Increase the opportunities for staff participation via regular conversations and team updates. Healthy food and frequent exercise may also help improve mental health, especially if done consistently.
- **Morale Among Employees Has Dipped:** When employees are working independently of home, it may be more difficult to maintain team spirit.

- **Not All Occupations are Suitable for Working From Home:** Some occupations are more suitable than others for remote employment. In addition, working from home appeals not just to others but to specific kinds of personalities. Some people like to connect personally with their colleagues.
- **Broadband Speeds Are Slow:** It should be emphasized that workers cannot obtain sufficient Internet speeds, depending on their location, to do their jobs effectively; rural internet is, for example, notoriously unreliable.

Some firms have a true grasp of the effects of the coronavirus pandemic on their company and employees who have never contemplated work from their homes before. It has made companies aware of the advantages and disadvantages of telecommuting. This experience may be quite helpful in predicting the future direction of the working habits of workers. Employees are not forced to work entirely from home because they relocate home. The most successful approach is frequently splitting time between home and job and the worker may attend meetings to be fully involved and informed.

6. SOLUTIONS AND RECOMMENDATIONS

6.1 Effective Strategies for Managing Remote Workers

Working from home has many advantages for both companies and workers, but it must be done correctly to be effective (Birimoglu Okuyan, 2022).

Performance Evaluation

One of the key concerns in management is effectively evaluating and monitoring the performance of remote employees. Instead of solely relying on the number of hours worked, it would be more beneficial to assess their productivity. This can be achieved by creating specific targets and deadlines for each task. It is crucial to regularly track the progress towards these goals and offer constructive feedback in a considerate and timely manner if any issues arise.

Staff Education

- Employees may be better prepared and acquire the skills they need via training. Self-management skills, such as time management, general skills, such as more efficiently utilizing technology or producing reports, and job-specific capabilities

Communication is Encouraged

One of the most common reasons for home working failure among solo workers is a feeling of isolation. Therefore, it's critical to establish formal procedures to guarantee that everyone feels like they're a member of the team. Consider the following scenario:

- Feedback meetings regarding work and job-related problems regularly
- Participation in social events daily in the workplace
- There are clear processes to follow, as well as someone to call if anything goes wrong.

When an employee's role mandates that they work remotely from the start, it is beneficial to conduct their induction in the office. By providing home-based employees with the chance to gain a comprehensive understanding of the individuals and company they are working for, they are more likely to be engaged and efficient in their work.

6.2. Health and Safety of Workers

As an employer, have the same obligations to ensure the health and safety of home workers as have for employees who work in the office. Its responsibilities are likely to involve the following (Bouziri, 2020):

- Performing a risk assessment for health and safety - see Managing Risks in It Business
- If don't already have it, must get mandatory employers' liability insurance (see liability insurance).
- Ensuring that equipment is suitable for its intended use
- Testing, certifying, and maintaining the company's electrical equipment
- See how to guarantee workers are using computers safely by ensuring PCs can be used comfortably and without distracting glare.
- Ensuring that the illumination levels are enough
- To minimize the danger of trips and falls, prevent trailing wires.
- Ensuring that employees are properly educated to operate safely
- Maintaining track of any severe accidents, illnesses, or injuries suffered by house workers, and reporting them if required

Routine health and safety risk assessments were unlikely to be conducted by the employer at work during the coronavirus epidemic. The employer must ensure: the employee believes that the job at home can be done safely. The employee is supplied with the essential equipment to do their job safely; the line manager interacts with the employee regularly, ensuring that they do not feel isolated; and appropriate adjustments are made for employees with disabilities. Additionally, the employee should contact their line manager frequently about health and safety issues and any necessary modifications to their homeworking arrangements.

6.3 Harnessing Technology for Effective Remote Work

Figure 3 depicts the issues that have arisen as a result of broadband internet connections, it made the quick and easy exchange of papers and email colleagues and business connections (Bick, 2020).

Figure 3. Problems for employees working from home

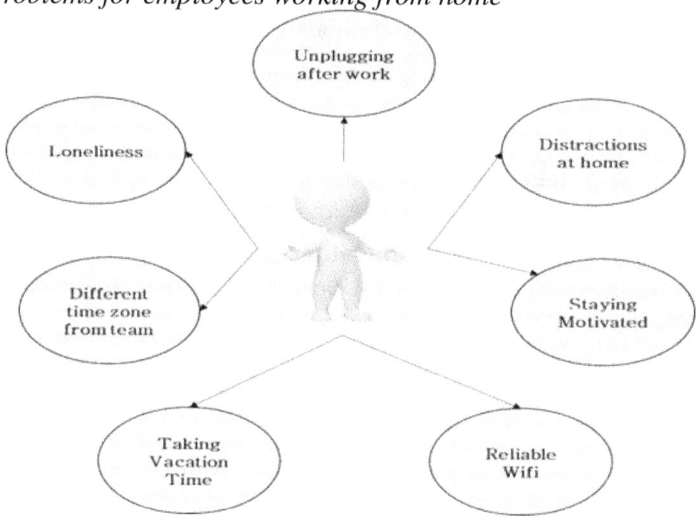

Virtual collaboration eliminates the requirement for workers to work together in the same location or even at the same time. The following possibilities are:

- Employees operate independently and communicate with and each other through email at various times and in various locations.
- Employees may interact in 'real time' through telephone conference calls, video conferencing, or instant messaging even if they are in separate locations.
- Employees may connect to an intranet or extranet to access the company's network or databases at any time and from any location. A virtual private network (VPN) is a more secure, but costlier, option.

- Even if they work from home, workers will need to meet face to face on occasion. It may schedule meetings and transmit papers via email and electronic journals and can meet almost anywhere using wireless connectivity.
- Mobile phones and laptop computers with wireless internet connection always make workers available and allow them to work from wherever. More information about mobile technologies may be found here.

6.4. Integrating Work and Life: Paths to a More Balanced Existence

Many remote jobs also offer flexible hours, so that employees may start and finish their days whenever they want to perform their job and achieve excellent results (Haque, 2023). It may be extremely beneficial to have control over one's work schedule when it comes to fulfilling one's obligations. It's simpler to drop children at school, take orders, take an online gym, or work from home as a contractor while working from home. It's easier.

Commute Stress is Reduced

The average one-way journey in the United States is 27.1 minutes, over an hour a day from and to labor, which is fast to increase. According to the Auto Insurance Centre, every year roaming passengers spend about 100 hours and 41 hours in traffic delays. For certain "severe" passengers each journey may take up to 90 minutes. On the other hand, traveling is one of the disadvantages of coming and going to work. Daily travel of more than 30 minutes is related to increased stress and anxiety, which studies indicate is linked to health issues like: Traveled over 10 miles to work every day.

- Higher cholesterol levels
- Blood sugar levels that are too high
- Depression risk is higher.

It may concentrate on mental and physical well-being by eliminating its pathway. The saved time may be utilized for non-work activities, including sleep in the day, family sleep, workouts, or nutritious breakfasts.

Independence in Terms of Location

The opportunity to access a broader range of job opportunities, which are not geographically limited, offers numerous benefits in working from home. For work-seekers in rural and small towns, where local opportunities may be limited, this is especially useful. During a meaningful career, entirely remote staff may roam and live as numerical nomads due to the absence of a permanent workplace before the pandemic. Although a nomadic existence is currently in abeyance while borders remain open, it remains an attractive alternative. Individuals that travel often, such as a military spouse, may make use of remote work from anywhere instead of establishing a new company. Remote jobs are also a great way of preventing high rent and high-mortgage areas, in particular for jobs (for example, technology), which previously needed to go to a high-cost location. To work in a career that one is interested in is no longer required to live in a large metropolitan area.

Inclusivity has Improved

Companies may demonstrate their commitment to diversity and inclusion by hiring individuals from a range of socio-economic, geographical, and cultural backgrounds and perspectives, which can be challenging when recruiting in an area that is not restricted to or afforded by everyone. Employers are committed to supporting diversity, community, and family by allowing employees to work from home in settings that are comfortable and supportive. Persons with disabled persons or professions that need a flexible schedule may find it hard to get steady work onsite, but remote work enables them to follow their career goals without worrying about moving to an office. It also enables staff to attend physician visits and other treatment arrangements as necessary.

Spending Less

Spending up to $4,000 a year for half-time employees who work frequently from home. All costs may be minimized or eliminated, such as petrol, car maintenance, travel, parking fees, professional equipment, and out-of-pocket food. These little amounts combine to increase the amount of money in his pocket. The only people who gain from savings are not employees. Companies, such as Twitter, Square,

Shopify, and Facebook, that allow employees to work from home in the event of a pandemic will long-term save cash.

Global Workplace Analytics states that each individual who works at least part of the time from home saves about $11,000 per year for a typical company. By enabling workers to work from home on several projects, Flex Jobs has saved more than $5 million and included:

- Overhead
- The cost of real estate
- Subsidies for public transportation
- Operational continuity

Employers in the United States save more than US$30 billion a day by enabling workers in the COVID-19 epidemic to work remotely. There may remain this considerable financial advantage of remote work if more firms choose this as a long-term option.

Positive Effect on the Environment

Before the pandemic, the equivalent of 600,000 cars being off the road for a year was 3.9 million employees working at least half of the time from home cuts greenhouse gas emissions. Workers at least partially save 7.8 billion kilometers of cars, 3 million tons of carbon emissions, and 980 million dollars of oil each year from home. Remote workers may have the same air quality impact as planting 91 million trees, by taking environmentally prudent choices such as a number of paper, heating, and lighting regulation.

Impact on the Environment

Remote work serves to promote a range of sustainability initiatives, including economic growth and decreasing inequality, sustainable cities, and climate change. Reduced trafficking is one of the simplest and most economical ways of reducing their carbon footprint for enterprises and employees and contributing to climate change mitigation. Throughout fact, pollution, congestion, and traffic have declined significantly during the whole pandemic response in the world, and the possibility for anybody engaged in remote work to be able to witness these advantages firsthand may function as an incentive.

A Customizable Office

A significant benefit of remote working is the opportunity to work from home in comfortable environments. It may set up your home office in whatever way you see appropriate, whether you desire an ergonomic chair or you have health issues that require specialized office equipment.

Productivity and Performance Have Improved

Working from home means typically shorter breaks, fewer office politics, less noise, and less (or more) productive meetings. When travel times are minimized, remote employees usually have longer and fewer distractions, which leads to better production – a significant benefit to both people and businesses from the house. Remote work allows employees and companies to focus on what counts really: outcomes when done properly. The workplace may, unfortunately, provide "false positives" which may lead to damage and bias. For example, even though early arrivals and early departures seem to increase workload, actual performance is a far more precise productivity metric.

Workplace Happiness and Health

Working from home has shown that stress has reduced, hobbies and interests have a longer time and personal connections have improved, among other benefits, to make remote and flexible workers happy and loyal.

Without professional distractions, politics, personal health, and well-trek, the interaction between coworkers and bosses may be more enjoyable. One study report says 72% of companies consider remote work to have a substantive impact on employee retention, which means they are more likely to remain with their present firm when employees have the option of working remotely.

Working from home may improve health in several ways:

- More physical activity time
- Having the capacity to eat more healthily
- Can recuperate from sickness or surgery at home with less risk of infection
- Caregiving for a health problem or handicap is simple.
- The ability to design a pleasant and ergonomic work environment.

Working from home gives workers the time and space they need to make good decisions.

7. CONCLUSION

The potential of AI technologies to improve efficiency of remote work is great by means of automation, better communication and insights from data. Adoption of COVID-19 had also increased remote working and AI tools usage, revealing their advantages and disadvantages. It is hard for one to separate personal life from work when working from home because it will result in poor work-life integration strategies. By applying technology and institutional policies that support employees, organizations can assist them in dealing with these obstacles so that they are able to have an equilibrium and fruitful experience while working remotely.

Remote work can be made tremendously more efficient through AI technologies in three main ways: via automation, communication, and data-driven insights. The COVID-19 pandemic has caused an upsurge in remote work and AI tools adoption, exposing their strengths and weaknesses. It is essential to understand these things to have the best remote job environment as well as work-life balance patterns. For this reason, every employee must consider that routine work is being streamlined and automated by AI technologies, leading to a substantial increase in the efficiency of remote jobs. AI systems can automatically input and process data thereby minimizing human errors while allowing employees time for strategic actions like planning or marketing. Automated scheduling tools can manage meeting arrangements resolving conflicts through sending reminders so that employees spend less time on administrative duties yet they are productive. The project management tools powered by artificial intelligence assigns tasks tracks progress and provides updates improving team coordination and project execution. AI enables remote workers focus on valuable tasks resulting in increased productivity levels overall.

Through work patterns and performance metrics analysis, Artificial Intelligence can recognize trends, strengths and areas that require improvement. This approach based on data helps managers to make informed decisions as well as optimizing team performance. AI tools are capable of predicting future trends and needs, as well as defining plans that will take care of any foreseeable problems. In understanding the employee experience which include aspects like their feelings, AI can analyze employee satisfaction to provide for better working conditions in remote locations. All these insights are used by organizations to ensure data informed decisions are done in order to enhance remote work productivity and worker satisfaction levels.

Remote work and AI tools have enabled greater flexibility, reduced commuting time, and maintained business continuity during the pandemic. AI technologies have provided critical support in managing remote teams, ensuring that work processes remain efficient and effective despite physical distance. The rapid shift to remote work has also highlighted several challenges, including difficulties in maintaining work-life balance, increased feelings of isolation, and potential overreliance on technology. Employees may struggle with setting boundaries between work and personal life, leading to stress and decreased well-being.

One of the major challenges of remote work is the difficulty in separating personal life from work.

Without a clear separation between work and home environments, employees may find it challenging to switch off from work, resulting in longer hours and increased stress. The lack of structure and clear boundaries can lead to distractions and decreased productivity, as employees may struggle to maintain focus and manage their time effectively. Constantly blending work with personal life can contribute to mental health issues such as burnout, anxiety, and reduced job satisfaction.

To address these challenges and improve work-life integration, organizations can implement various strategies supported by technology and institutional policies. The use of AI tools can help construct structured workflows, set up reminders to take breaks, and track how people do their jobs in order not to overwork them. There are devices that allow workers to organize time in such a way that it prevents mixing of professional life with private life; hence they enhance a healthier work-life balance. The explicit remote work policies defining working hours, communication guidelines as well as encouraging regular breaks. Also, provide resources and support for mental health and well-being while promoting a culture which values work-life balance. Training programs should be offered to enable employees appropriately deal with remote employment taking into consideration setting boundaries among others including qualities like staying organized or maintaining mental wellness.

8. FUTURE RESEARCH DIRECTIONS

The domain of AI and the remote workplace, primarily shaped by the COVID-19 outbreak, is open to several pathways for further investigations. These pathways are constructed to bridge the existing knowledge gaps, enhance remote labor practices and utilize AI tools to improve both employee and organizational results. Assess the influence of AI tools on long-term productivity and efficiency in remote work environments. This research may tackle issues of sustained advancement over time as well as clarify the conditions for maintaining effectiveness of AI devices. Analyze the evolvement of remote working practices in response to the changes in AI-related technologies and organizational policies. This encompasses investigations into alterations in working routines, the desires of employees, and inclusion of novel technologies.

The research could concentrate on adaptive AI systems that adjust workflows, communication styles, and task management based on the individual worker's working habits and productivity levels. It is also essential to investigate ways in which

AI tools may be able to please varying settings that these tools are used in – this includes various types of projects, team differences or industry norms. Another area would be looking into appropriate approaches and instruments for establishing work-life balance within distance workplaces. This research may contain mechanisms of stress relief, mental health preservation as well as boundary setting practices. The other thing worth investigating is if there is any way to using AI as a support mechanism for remote laborers' mental wellness and happiness. One such kit might include software that helps people with their emotional well-being monitoring or target groups identification for early interventions.

Examine the effects of AI tools on remote communication, team dynamics, and cooperation. Studies can concentrate on how well AI supports group communication, judgment calls, and dispute settlement. Study how AI may improve remote teams' performance management and feedback systems. This entails creating tools for goal-setting, real-time performance monitoring, and customized development strategies. Inspect on AI for distant employment may affect privacy and ethics. Scholarly endeavors may concentrate on formulating structures to safeguard worker information, guaranteeing openness, and tackling any prejudices in artificial intelligence algorithms. The ethical AI best practices are studied for remote work settings, such as how to employ AI technologies responsibly and with justice and responsibility.

Consider the potential effects on ethics and privacy of using AI for remote work. Academic research efforts might focus on developing protocols to protect employee data, ensuring transparency, and addressing biases in AI systems. Consider moral AI best practices for remote work environments, such as how to use AI tools justly, fairly, and ethically. Look at the ways that cultural variations affect the uptake and efficiency of AI and remote work methods. Developing culturally aware strategies and solutions might be the focus of research. Examine the ways that multinational corporations might improve cross-border cooperation and efficiently lead dispersed teams by utilizing AI and remote work. In order to improve productivity, employee well-being, and organizational success in an increasingly remote and technologically driven work environment, academics can address current issues, deepen our understanding of AI's role in remote work, and create novel solutions by pursuing these research directions.

REFERENCES

Adisa, T. A., Ogbonnaya, C., & Adekoya, O. D. (2023). Remote working and employee engagement: A qualitative study of British workers during the pandemic. *Information Technology & People*, 36(5), 1835–1850. DOI: 10.1108/ITP-12-2020-0850

Al-Habaibeh, A., Watkins, M., Waried, K., & Javareshk, M. B. (2021). Challenges and opportunities of remotely working from home during Covid-19 pandemic. *Global Transitions*, 3, 99–108. DOI: 10.1016/j.glt.2021.11.001 PMID: 34870136

Antona, M., Margetis, G., Ntoa, S., & Degen, H. (2023). Special issue on AI in HCI. *International Journal of Human-Computer Interaction*, 39(9), 1723–1726. DOI: 10.1080/10447318.2023.2177421

Arman, H., Al-Fulaij, S., Al-Qudsi, S., Alawadhi, A., & Al Ali, M. (2024). COVID-19 effect on accelerating technology and innovation in businesses. *Organizations and Markets in Emerging Economies*, 15(1(30)), 27–50. DOI: 10.15388/omee.2024.15.2

Bakker, A. B., Demerouti, E., & Sanz-Vergel, A. (2023). Job demands–resources theory: Ten years later. *Annual Review of Organizational Psychology and Organizational Behavior*, 10(1), 25–53. DOI: 10.1146/annurev-orgpsych-120920-053933

Banafaa, M., Shayea, I., Din, J., Hadri Azmi, M., Alashbi, A., Ibrahim Daradkeh, Y., & Alhammadi, A. (2023). 6G mobile communication technology: Requirements, targets, applications, challenges, advantages, and opportunities. *Alexandria Engineering Journal*, 64, 245–274. DOI: 10.1016/j.aej.2022.08.017

Beňo, M. (2021). The advantages and disadvantages of E-working: An examination using an ALDINE analysis. *Emerging Science Journal*, 5, 11–20. DOI: 10.28991/esj-2021-SPER-02

Bick, R., Chang, M., Wang, K.W. & Yu, T. (2020) A blueprint for remote working: Lessons from China. *McKinsey Digital*, 23.

Birimoglu Okuyan, C., & Begen, M. A. (2022). Working from home during the COVID-19 pandemic, its effects on health, and recommendations: The pandemic and beyond. *Perspectives in Psychiatric Care*, 58(1), 173–179. DOI: 10.1111/ppc.12847 PMID: 34003489

Bolisani, E., Scarso, E., Ipsen, C., Kirchner, K., & Hansen, J. P. (2020). Working from home during COVID-19 pandemic: Lessons learned and issues. *Management & Marketing. Challenges for the Knowledge Society*, 15(s1), 458–476. DOI: 10.2478/mmcks-2020-0027

Bouziri, H., Smith, D. R. M., Descatha, A., Dab, W., & Jean, K. (2020). Working from home in the time of COVID-19: How to best preserve occupational health? *Occupational and Environmental Medicine*, 77(7), 509–510. DOI: 10.1136/oemed-2020-106599 PMID: 32354748

Daneshfar, Z., Asokan-Ajitha, A., Sharma, P., & Malik, A. (2023). Work-from-home (WFH) during COVID-19 pandemic–A netnographic investigation using Twitter data. *Information Technology & People*, 36(5), 2161–2186. DOI: 10.1108/ITP-01-2021-0020

Davenport, T. H., & Mittal, N. (2023). *All-In on AI: How Smart Companies Win Big with Artificial Intelligence*. Harvard Business Press.

Davis, F. D., Granić, A., & Marangunić, N. (2024). *The Technology Acceptance Model: 30 Years of TAM*. Springer International Publishing AG. DOI: 10.1007/978-3-030-45274-2

Haque, S. M. S. (2023). The impact of remote work on hr practices: Navigating challenges, embracing opportunities. *European Journal of Human Resource Management Studies*, 7(1). Advance online publication. DOI: 10.46827/ejhrms.v7i1.1549

Haque, S. M. S. (2023). The impact of remote work on hr practices: Navigating challenges, embracing opportunities. *European Journal of Human Resource Management Studies*, 7(1). Advance online publication. DOI: 10.46827/ejhrms.v7i1.1549

Heuel, L., Otto, A. K., & Wollesen, B. (2024). Physical exercise and ergonomic workplace interventions for nursing personnel—Effects on physical and mental health: A systematic review. *German Journal of Exercise and Sport Research*, 54(2), 291–324. DOI: 10.1007/s12662-023-00922-6

Hoffmann, C. H. (2023). A philosophical view on singularity and strong AI. *AI & Society*, 38(4), 1697–1714. DOI: 10.1007/s00146-021-01327-5

Joshi, P. R. (2024) Model for work-life balance: Integrating theory and research. Available at SSRN 4807438. *SP Swag: Sudur Pashchim Wisdom of Academic Gentry Journal*, 1, 11–26. DOI: DOI: 10.69476/sdpr.2024.v01i01.002

Koroglu, Ş., & Ozmen, O. (2022). The mediating effect of work engagement on innovative work behavior and the role of psychological well-being in the job demands–resources (JD-R) model. *Asia-Pacific Journal of Business Administration*, 14(1), 124–144. DOI: 10.1108/APJBA-09-2020-0326

Limanta, A. L., Prihanto, Y. J. N., & Situmorang, R. (2023). Analysis of the influence of work-life balance, work stress, and job satisfaction when working from home on the implementation of permanent telework culture in legal business. [Review]. *Journal of Business and Management Review*, 4(1), 1–16. DOI: 10.47153/jbmr41.5922023

MacKenzie, I.S. (2024). *Human–Computer Interaction: An Empirical Research Perspective.*

Mauz, E., Walther, L., Junker, S., Kersjes, C., Damerow, S., Eicher, S., Hölling, H., Müters, S., Peitz, D., Schnitzer, S., & Thom, J. (2023). Time trends in mental health indicators in Germany's adult population before and during the COVID-19 pandemic. *Frontiers in Public Health*, 11, 1065938. DOI: 10.3389/fpubh.2023.1065938 PMID: 36908429

Owen, J. (2024). *AI and ML in Financial Knowledge Management and Predictive Analytics.*

Patwardhan, N., Marrone, S., & Sansone, C. (2023). Transformers in the real world: A survey on nlp applications. *Information (Basel)*, 14(4), 242. DOI: 10.3390/info14040242

Pereira, R., Lima, C., Reis, A., Pinto, T., & Barroso, J. (2024) Review of platforms and frameworks for building Virtual Assistants. In: *World Conference on Information Systems and Technologies*. Springer: Cham, Germany, pp. 105–114. DOI: 10.1007/978-3-031-45648-0_11

Philips, G.R., Huang, M., Bodine, C., Kuhn, K., Kersken, V., Reuter, B., … & Zimmermann, G. (2023) Accessible computing. *ACM Transactions on*, 16.

Prasad, K. D. V., & Satyaprasad, V. K. (2023). The relationship between remote working and work-life balance with mediating and moderating effects of social support: An empirical study of information technology employees. *International Journal of Organizational Leadership*, 12(0), 235–253. DOI: 10.33844/ijol.2023.60366

Reamer, F. G. (2023). Artificial intelligence in social work: Emerging ethical issues. *International Journal of Social Work Values and Ethics*, 20(2), 52–71. DOI: 10.55521/10-020-205

Santoniccolo, F., Trombetta, T., Paradiso, M. N., & Rollè, L. (2023). Gender and media representations: A review of the literature on gender stereotypes, objectification and sexualization. *International Journal of Environmental Research and Public Health*, 20(10), 5770. DOI: 10.3390/ijerph20105770 PMID: 37239498

Stefanova, V., Farrell, L., & Latu, I. (2023). Gender and the pandemic: Associations between caregiving, working from home, personal and career outcomes for women and men. *Current Psychology (New Brunswick, N.J.)*, 42(20), 17395–17411. DOI: 10.1007/s12144-021-02630-6 PMID: 35002182

Xia, Z. (2023). Addressing the tasks and opportunities of agency using AI-based Chatbots. *International Journal of Communication Networks and Information Security*, 15, 25–42.

Xu, B., Gutierrez, B., Mekaru, S., Sewalk, K., Goodwin, L., Loskill, A., Cohn, E. L., Hswen, Y., Hill, S. C., Cobo, M. M., Zarebski, A. E., Li, S., Wu, C. H., Hulland, E., Morgan, J. D., Wang, L., O'Brien, K., Scarpino, S. V., Brownstein, J. S., & Kraemer, M. U. G. (2020). Epidemiological data from the COVID-19 outbreak, real-time case information. *Scientific Data*, 7(1), 106. DOI: 10.1038/s41597-020-0448-0 PMID: 32210236

Xu, W., Dainoff, M. J., Ge, L., & Gao, Z. (2023). Transitioning to human interaction with AI systems: New challenges and opportunities for HCI professionals to enable human-centered AI. *International Journal of Human-Computer Interaction*, 39(3), 494–518. DOI: 10.1080/10447318.2022.2041900

Yang, X., He, X., Zhao, J., Zhang, Y., Zhang, S., & Xie, P. (2020). *Covid-ct-dataset: A ct Scan Dataset About Covid-19.arXiv Preprint ArXiv:2003.13865.*

KEY TERMS AND DEFINITIONS

AI - Artificial intelligence (AI): is a set of technologies that enable computers to perform a variety of advanced functions, including the ability to see, understand and translate spoken and written language, analyze data, make recommendations, and more.

Chatbot: A chatbot is a computer program that simulates human conversation with an end user.

Coronavirus Disease (COVID-19): is an infectious disease caused by the SARS-CoV-2 virus.

Gender Role Theory: Gender role theory predicts that the greater the difference in social roles performed by males and females, the greater the difference in behaviors and attitudes

Human-Computer Interaction (HCI): Human-Computer Interaction is a multidisciplinary field that focuses on designing and evaluating computer systems and technologies that people interact with.

Job Demands-Resources Model: The job demands-resources model (JD-R model) is an occupational stress model that suggests strain is a response to imbalance between demands on the individual and the resources he or she has to deal with those demands.

Mental Health: Mental health includes our emotional, psychological, and social well-being.

Natural Language Processing (NLP): is a machine learning technology that gives computers the ability to interpret, manipulate, and comprehend human language.

Remote Workers: A remote employee is someone who is employed by a company, but works outside of a traditional office environment.

Work From Home (WFH): which describes a modern working arrangement where employees perform job responsibilities remotely.

Chapter 9
Customer Segmentation Using K-Means Algorithm

Debabrata Datta
https://orcid.org/0000-0002-1559-7036
St. Xavier's College, Kolkata, India

Anal Acharya
https://orcid.org/0000-0002-0751-021X
St. Xavier's College, Kolkata, India

Kwanan Mondal
St. Xavier's College, Kolkata, India

Meghna Mondal
https://orcid.org/0009-0002-9542-1176
St. Xavier's College, Kolkata, India

Tanushree Sarkar
https://orcid.org/0009-0000-1933-229X
St. Xavier's College, Kolkata, India

ABSTRACT

In this research paper, authors explore the application of the K-means algorithm and the elbow method in customer segmentation using machine learning techniques. The algorithm is applied to a customer dataset and effectiveness of the resulting customer segments is evaluated. The performance of K-means with other clustering techniques is compare and the impact of different input parameters on the segmentation results is studied. The findings of this study can help businesses to improve their marketing strategies by targeting specific customer segments with customized marketing campaigns.

DOI: 10.4018/979-8-3693-8442-8.ch009

INTRODUCTION

Customer segmentation is the subdivision of a business customer base into groups called customer segments such that each customer segment consists of customers who share similar market characteristics. This segmentation is based on factors that can directly or indirectly influence market or business such as products preferences or expectations, locations, behaviours and so on. The importance of customer segmentation include, inter alia, the ability of a business to customise market programs that will be suitable for each of its customer segments; business decision support in terms of risky situation such as credit relationship with its customers; identification of products associated with each segments and how to manage the forces of demand and supply; unravelling some latent dependencies and associations amongst customers, amongst products, or between customers and products which the business may not be aware of; ability to predict customer defection, and which customers are most likely to defect; and raising further market research questions as well as providing directions to finding the solutions (Chinedu Pascal Ezenkwu, Simeon Ozuomba, Constance kalu, 2015).

Customer segmentation is one of the application of data mining which helps to segment the customers with similar patterns into similar clusters hence, making easier for the business to handle the large customer base. This segmentation can directly or indirectly influence the marketing strategy as it opens many new paths to discover like for which segment the product will be good, customising the marketing plans according to the each segment, providing discounts for a specific segment, and decipher the customer and object relationship which has been previously unknown to the company. Customer segmentation allows companies to visualise what actually the customers are buying which will prompt the companies to better serve their customers resulting in customer satisfaction, it also allows the companies to find who their target customers are and improvise their marketing tactics to generate more revenues from them (Tushar Kansal, Suraj Bahuguna, Vishal Singh, Tanupriya Choudhury,2018).

Clustering has proven efficient in discovering subtle but tactical patterns or relationships buried within a repository of unlabelled datasets. This form of learning is classified under unsupervised learning. Clustering algorithms include k-Means algorithm, k-Nearest Neighbour algorithm, Self-Organising Map (SOM) and so on. These algorithms, without any knowledge of the dataset beforehand, are capable of identifying clusters therein by repeated comparisons of the input patterns until the stable clusters in the training examples are achieved based on the clustering criterion or criteria. Each cluster contains data points that have very close similarities but differ considerably from data points of other clusters(Chinedu Pascal Ezenkwu, Simeon Ozuomba, Constance kalu,2015).

Clustering process is not one time task but is continuous and an iterative process of knowledge discovery from huge quantities of raw and unorganized data (T. Kanungo, D. M. Mount, N. S. Netanyahu, C. D. Piatko, R. Silverman, and A. Y. Wu,2001). For a particular classification problem, an appropriate clustering algorithm and parameters must be selected for obtaining optimum results(MacKay and David, 2003).

The primary objective of this work is to leverage the k-means algorithm to perform customer segmentation. By applying this powerful clustering technique, we aim to divide the customer base into distinct groups based on shared characteristics such as purchasing behaviour, demographics, or other relevant attributes. Through this segmentation, we aim to gain valuable insights into customer preferences and behaviour patterns. This enables to personalize marketing efforts, enhance customer satisfaction, optimize resource allocation, and ultimately drive business growth. By using the k-means algorithm for customer segmentation, we strive to make informed decisions and improve our overall understanding of the customer base.

BACKGROUND

Several studies have explored the use of machine learning algorithms, including K-means clustering, for customer segmentation. Machine learning algorithms can identify patterns and relationships in customer data that traditional statistical methods may not detect, making them a powerful tool for customer segmentation. Customer segmentation is a crucial aspect of marketing and business strategy, as it helps companies understand their customers' behaviour, preferences, and needs. Machine learning techniques, particularly K-means clustering, have emerged as popular approaches to segmenting customers based on their characteristics and behaviour. Jain, Murty, and Flynn's (1999) paper, "Data Clustering. A Review," provides a comprehensive survey of clustering algorithms, which are used for grouping data points into clusters or subgroups based on their similarity. The paper reviews over 400 research articles and categorizes clustering algorithms based on their underlying assumptions, types of data, and clustering criteria. The paper also highlights some common clustering criteria used to evaluate the quality of the clustering solutions, including the sum of squared errors, the silhouette coefficient, the purity measure, and the entropy measure. The authors then present a detailed discussion of some specific clustering algorithms, such as the k-means algorithm, the singlelink and complete-link hierarchical clustering algorithms, and the density-based spatial clustering of applications with noise (DBSCAN) algorithm. They compare these algorithms in terms of their computational complexity, memory usage, and performance on different types of data. Overall, the paper provides a comprehensive review of the clustering algorithms and criteria and serves as an essential resource for researchers and practitioners in the field of clustering and data mining.

Clustering in Data Mining. A Survey," by Xu and Wunsch (2005) is a comprehensive review paper that provides an overview of various clustering algorithms in data mining. The authors discuss the different types of clustering algorithms, their advantages and disadvantages, and their applications in realworld scenarios. The authors then discuss the different types of clustering algorithms, including hierarchical, partitioning, density-based, and grid-based methods. They provide a detailed description of each algorithm, including its underlying principles and how it operates. They also highlight the strengths and weaknesses of each algorithm, along with their applications in different fields such as biology, medicine, and finance. In addition, the paper discusses the issue of choosing the appropriate distance metric or similarity measure for clustering, as well as the problem of determining the optimal number of clusters in a given dataset. The authors provide a thorough explanation of various validation techniques such as silhouette score, Calinski-Harabasz index, and Davies-Bouldin index that can be used to assess the quality of clustering results

The paper titled "Integration of Machine Learning Techniques to Evaluate Dynamic Customer Segmentation Analysis for Mobile Customers" focuses on customer segmentation in the telecommunications industry. The goal is to develop a business intelligence model that helps mobile providers optimize customer retention and marketing strategies. The paper highlights the use of machine learning algorithms, specifically the C.5 algorithm within naive Bayesian modelling, to segment telecommunication customers based on their billing and socio-demographic aspects. The authors, Cormac and Eleni collected and analysed a large dataset of customer account data to gain insights and improve customer satisfaction, loyalty, and retention. The main contribution of the paper is the improvement in churn prediction by applying machine learning algorithms for customer segmentation. Decision tree rules models were used to identify segmentation rules and predict customers' buying patterns.

In the research paper titled "Customer Segmentation Using Clustering and Data Mining Techniques," the authors K.R.Kashwan and C.M.Velu proposed a real-time and online system for a specific supermarket to predict sales in various annual seasonal cycles. The system utilizes the k-means clustering technique and the SPSS tool to analyse sales data records and update segmentation statistics on a daily basis. The authors applied the k-means clustering technique to segment customers of a leading supermarket retail household supplier. They collected data from customer transactions over a three-month period and utilized the SPSS tool for analysis. The results showed promising accuracy, with the predicted sales statistics closely matching the actual sales statistics. The convergence of the k-means algorithm can be slow, especially in cases requiring high accuracy. However, by setting a reasonable threshold value, quick results can be obtained without compromising much accuracy. Additionally, the algorithm allows for the modification of the sum of squares of errors (SSE) by splitting or merging clusters, which is desirable in market segmentation studies.

The research paper "Application of K-Means Algorithm for Efficient Customer Segmentation. A Strategy for Targeted Customer Services", focuses on customer segmentation in a retail business using the k-Means clustering algorithm. The k-Means clustering algorithm is employed to identify customer segments based on two features. the average amount of goods purchased per month and the average number of customer visits per month. A MATLAB program is developed and trained using a dataset of 100 training patterns from the retail business. The dataset is z-score normalized, and after several iterations, four customer clusters or segments are identified. High-Buyers-Regular-Visitors (HBRV), High-Buyers-Irregular-Visitors (HBIV), Low-Buyers-Regular-Visitors (LBRV), and Low-Buyers-Irregular-Visitors (LBIV).The paper discusses the concept of customer segmentation and its significance in business decision-making, customization of marketing programs, and predicting customer defection. It also explores the role of big data in providing valuable insights and the challenges associated with analysing large volumes of structured and unstructured data. Clustering algorithms, particularly the k-Means algorithm, are highlighted as effective tools for discovering patterns and relationships in unlabelled datasets.

The paper "Customer Segmentation using K-means Clustering " discusses the application of customer segmentation using clustering algorithms, specifically k-means, agglomerative, and mean shift, for better decision making in marketing strategies. The authors aim to identify customer segments based on their shopping behaviour, using a dataset from a local retail shop with two features. average number of visits and average amount of shopping per year. The k-means clustering algorithm is employed to group customers into clusters based on their similarities. The optimal number of clusters (k) is determined using the elbow method, which analyses the within-cluster sum of squares (WCSS). By plotting the WCSS for different values of k, the authors select the value where the decline in WCSS is most significant, indicating the elbow point and the optimal number of clusters. Furthermore, the silhouette score is utilized to evaluate the quality of the clustering results. It measures how close each sample in one cluster is to samples in neighbouring clusters. A higher silhouette score indicates better-defined and well-separated clusters. The results of the k-means clustering show the formation of five clusters labelled as Careless, Careful, Standard, Target, and Sensible customers. Additionally, the agglomerative clustering algorithm produces similar cluster patterns. However, the mean shift clustering algorithm reveals two new clusters. High buyers and frequent visitors, and High buyers and occasional visitors. The authors emphasize the importance of customer segmentation for businesses to understand customer behaviour, target specific segments, and customize marketing strategies accordingly. Clustering algorithms, particularly k-means, offer an effective approach to achieve customer segmentation by grouping customers with similar patterns together. The evaluation of clustering results using metrics like the silhouette score provides insights into the quality of the segmentation.

PROPOSED METHODOLOGY

The proposed methodology has been divided into few distinct yet interrelated steps. These are described below .

i) Data Preparation

Data Preprocessing

Data Pre-processing can be defined as a process of converting raw data into a format that is understandable and usable for further analysis. It is an important step in the Data Preparation stage. It ensures that the outcome of the analysis is accurate, complete, and consistent.It is the first and crucial step while creating a machine learning model.

Prior to clustering, the dataset undergoes a crucial phase of pre-processing and analysis to ensure its suitability for the task. This process involves handling missing values and duplicates, as well as examining the presence of null values and inconsistent datatypes within the data. By addressing these issues, the dataset is refined and prepared for subsequent clustering operations.

To facilitate the clustering and splicing procedures, the column names of the resulting dataframe are explicitly specified. This deliberate specification of column names simplifies the clustering process and enhances the subsequent ability to extract relevant subsets of data. By following these practices, the dataset is optimized for effective clustering analysis, enabling to gain a comprehensive understanding of the provided data.

Column Selection

Feature selection is the process of identifying the most effective subset of the original features to use in clustering. Feature extraction is the use of one or more transformations of the input features to produce new salient features. Either or both of these techniques can be used to obtain an appropriate set of features to use in clustering(Jain, A., Murty, M.N., and Flynn, P.J. 1999).

In the methodology proposed in this research work, feature selection technique is applied to select a subset of columnsfrom a dataframewhile preparing the data for machine learning or data analysis tasks, where only certain variables are relevant to the task at hand.

The choice of columns for segmentation varies depending on the specific dataset under analysis. In each case, relevant variables are carefully selected, considering the unique characteristics and objectives of the dataset.For instance, when examining consumer behaviour, columns such as spending score and annual income may be deemed particularly pertinent. These columns are extracted, separated, and organized into a two-dimensional or n-dimensional array, allowing for seamless utilization in subsequent data processing steps. This refined arrangement facilitates further exploration and analysis, enabling researchers to derive valuable insights from the data.

ii) Determining the Optimum Number of Clusters

One crucial aspect of implementing the K-means algorithm is determining the optimal number of clusters. Choosing the correct number of clusters is essential to ensure meaningful and accurate cluster assignments.By employing techniques such as the Elbow Method, Silhouette Analysis, Gap Statistic, information criteria, and considering domain knowledge, practitioners can make informed decisions to identify the optimal number of clusters that best capture the underlying patterns in the data without overfitting or underfitting. The goal is to find the optimal number of clusters that maximizes the intra-cluster similarity while minimizing the inter-cluster dissimilarity.

In the proposed methodology of this research work elbow method and silhouette analysis has been used to determine the optimal k value.

Elbow Method

Elbow method is used for finding optimal value of K for K-means clustering algorithm (TusharKansal, SurajBahuguna, Vishal Singh, Tanupriya Choudhury,2018). The elbow graph is a visual tool used to determine the optimal number of clusters to use in a K-means clustering algorithm. In the context of customer segmentation, the elbow graph can help identify the optimal number of customer segments or clusters based on the available customer data.

The elbow graph is plotted with the number of clusters on the x-axis and the Within-Cluster-Sum-of-Squares (WCSS) on the y-axis. The WCSS measures the sum of distances between the data points and their assigned cluster centroid. As the number of clusters increases, the WCSS decreases, since each data point has a closer centroid. However, beyond a certain number of clusters, the improvement in WCSS begins to decrease at a slower rate, resulting in an elbow-shaped curve.

The WCSS formula is defined as.

WCSS = sum(d^2)/n ---------------- (1)

where d is the distance between an observation and its cluster mean, *n* is the number of observations in the cluster, and sum(d^2) is the sum of the squared distances between each observation and its mean.

The "elbow point" on the curve represents the optimal number of clusters to use. In the context of customer segmentation, this optimal number of clusters is the one that produces a reasonable balance between the granularity of the segments and the size of each segment.

For example, suppose we have a dataset of customer purchases and we want to segment them into different groups based on their buying patterns. We can use the elbow method to determine the optimal number of clusters for our dataset. We first apply *k*-means clustering to our data for different values of *k* (number of clusters). We calculate the WCSS for each value of *k* and plot it on a graph. We can see that initially, the WCSS decreases rapidly as we increase the number of clusters. However, after a certain point, the rate of decrease slows down significantly, indicating the optimal number of clusters. Suppose we observe an elbow point at *k*=3. This means that the optimal number of clusters for our dataset is 3, and we can use this information to segment our customers into 3 groups based on their buying patterns. Overall, the elbow graph is an important tool for optimizing customer segmentation using the *k*-means clustering algorithm.

Silhouette Analysis

When determining the optimal number of clusters, if it is unclear where the elbow point lies in the evaluation process, the silhouette plot is employed for validation. The silhouette score is utilized as a quantitative measure to assess the clustering's overall quality. By calculating this score, researchers can gauge how well the data points within each cluster are separated and how cohesive they are within their respective clusters. This approach provides a more refined and objective assessment of the clustering performance, aiding in the selection of the most appropriate value for K, the number of clusters.

Silhouette analysis is a technique used to determine the quality of a clustering algorithm's output. It evaluates the quality of the clustering by measuring the distance between each data point and other data points within the same cluster compared to the distance between that data point and data points in other clusters. The silhouette score ranges from -1 to 1, where a score closer to 1 indicates that the object is well-matched to its own cluster and poorly matched to neighbouring clusters. On the other hand, a score closer to -1 indicates that the object may be better matched to a neighbouring cluster. A score of 0 means that the object is on the boundary between two clusters.

The silhouette score is calculated using two metrics.

- The mean distance between a sample and all other points in the same class.
- The mean distance between a sample and all other points in the next nearest cluster.

The silhouette score is calculated using the following formula.

S= (b−a) / max(a,b)---------------- (2)

where 'a' is the average distance between a data point and other data points in the same cluster(i.e., average intra-cluster distance or cohesion), and 'b' is the average distance between a data point and data points in the nearest other cluster(i.e., average inter-cluster distance separation). The 'S' value ranges between -1 and 1, where a value of 1 indicates that the data point is very similar to other data points in its cluster, and very dissimilar to data points in other clusters. A value of -1 indicates the opposite, with values around 0 indicating that the data point is equally similar to points in its own cluster and other clusters.

The silhouette score can be plotted for each value of *k* (number of clusters), and the cluster with the highest average silhouette score is considered to be the optimal number of clusters for the data set. The Silhouette graph plots the silhouette score for each cluster against the number of clusters. The graph is used to find the optimal number of clusters, which is the number of clusters with the highest average silhouette score.

In practice, a silhouette score of 0.5 or greater is considered a strong separation between clusters, while a score between 0.25 and 0.5 indicates a reasonable separation, and a score less than 0.25 indicates that the clustering may not be meaningful. The thickness of the silhouette plot representing each cluster is also a deciding point . Plots with moderately similar thickness are better choice as the optimal cluster value .

In the context of customer segmentation, the silhouette analysis can be used to determine the optimal number of customer segments that provide meaningful insights into customer behaviour. By analysing the silhouette scores for different values of *k*, businesses can gain insights into the number of distinct customer segments in their data set, and the quality of the clustering for each segment.

K-Means Clustering

In the context of customer segmentation, k-means can be used to divide a customer base into smaller, more homogeneous groups based on their demographic, psychographic, and behavioural characteristics. To do this, the algorithm requires a set of numerical variables that describe the customers, such as age, income, education, occupation, and buying behaviour.

The algorithm is called *k*-means due to the fact that the letter *k* represents the number of clusters chosen(Kishana R. Kashwan and C.M. Velu,2013). An observation is assigned to a particular cluster for which its distance to the cluster mean is the smallest. The principal function of algorithm involves finding the *k*-means. First, an initial set of means is defined and then subsequent classification is based on their distances to the centres (S. Dasgupta and Y. Freund,2009). Next, the clusters' mean is computed again and then reclassification is done based on the new set of means. This is repeated until cluster means don't change much between successive iterations (M. Mahajan, P. Nimbhorkar, and K. Varadarajan,2009). Finally, the means of the clusters once again calculated and then all the cases are assigned to the permanent clusters.

Given a set of observations *(x1, x2,....., xn)*, where each observation *xi* is a *d*-dimensional real vector. The *k*-means clustering algorithm aims to partition the n observations into *k* groups of observations called clusters where $k \leq n$, so as to minimize the sum of squares of distances between observations within a particular cluster (A. Vattani,2011).

As shown in Table I, the sum of squares of the distance may be given by the equation arg min $S = \Sigma_{i=1} \Sigma s_j s_i \|x_j - \mu_j\|^2$, where$\mu_i$is the mean of points in S_i . Given an initial set, k-means computes initial means m_1 (1),...,m_k(1) and it identifies *k* clusters in given raw data set.

Stated informally, the *k*-means procedure consists of simply starting with *k* groups each of which consists of a single random point, and thereafter adding each new point to the group whose mean the new point is nearest. After a point is added to a group, the mean of that group is adjusted in order to take account of the new point. Thus at each stage the k-means are, in fact, the means of the groups they represent (hence the term *k*-means)(MacQueen, J. B.,1967).

The *k*-means algorithm is very simple and can be easily implemented in solving many practical problems. It can work very well for compact and hyperspherical clusters. The time complexity of *k*-means is *O(NKd)*(Xu, R., and Wunsch, D., 2005).

Detailed working of K-Means Algorithm used to determine the optimum no of clusters highlighted in this paper.

i. The number of clusters, *k* to be created is chosen.

ii. Initialize the centroids (or means) for each cluster by randomly selecting K observations from the dataset.
iii. Each observation is assigned to the cluster with the nearest mean. The distance between an observation and a mean can be calculated using various distance metrics, but the most commonly used is Euclidean distance. It calculates the straight-line distance between two data points in n-dimensional space. This measure is suitable for continuous data with a Euclidean geometry.

deuc(x, y) = $\sqrt{\sum}$i=1n(xi−yi)^2------------------------------ (3)

iv. The within-cluster sum of squares (WCSS)is calculated for each cluster. WCSS is a measure of how spread out the observations are within each cluster, and it is calculated as the sum of squared distances between each observation and its cluster mean.
v. The silhouette coefficient is calculated
vi. The WCSS values are used to create an elbow plot, which shows the relationship between the number of clusters and the WCSS. The elbow plot is used to determine the optimal number of clusters, where the WCSS starts to decrease at a slower rate. This point is called the "elbow" of the plot.
vii. The silhouette coefficients are used to create a silhouette score graph to understand the quality of thc cluster.
viii. Steps 3 to 5 are repeated until the maximum number of iterations is reached.

This process is iterated for k values ranging from 2 to 11.

To ensure the selection of the optimal value for k, a silhouette analysis was conducted for each cluster value ranging from 2 to 6. This involved creating a silhouette plot and visualizing the clusters.The silhouette plot shows the silhouette coefficient for each sample, which measures how similar a sample is to its own cluster compared to other clusters. The silhouette coefficient ranges from -1 to 1, with 1 indicating that the sample iswell-matched to its own cluster and poorly matched to neighbouring clusters. The plot also shows a vertical line indicating the average silhouette coefficient for all samples, and horizontal bars for each cluster indicating the range of silhouette coefficients for that cluster. The cluster visualization plot shows the clusters as determined by the k-means algorithm, with each cluster represented by a different colour. The plot also shows the cluster centres as white circles with black edges, and each point is labelled with its cluster number.

iii) Training with K-means Algorithm

Training with k-means algorithm with a fixed value of k, determined through silhouette and elbow graph analysis, is a crucial step in unsupervised machine learning. The training process involves optimizing the algorithm to achieve accurate clustering results, focusing on the training aspects.

The first step in training the k-means algorithm with a fixed value of k involves determining the optimal number of clusters. This is typically done using techniques such as silhouette analysis and the elbow method. Silhouette analysis calculates a score for each data point based on its cohesion within the assigned cluster and separation from other clusters. The elbow method examines the sum of squared distances within each cluster as the number of clusters increases and identifies the "elbow" point where the rate of improvement diminishes significantly.

Once the optimal value of k is determined, the training process begins. Randomly selected data points are assigned as the initial centroids for each cluster. The algorithm then iteratively performs the assignment and centroid update steps until convergence is achieved. In the assignment step, each data point is assigned to the nearest centroid based on their proximity in feature space.

After the initial assignment, the centroids are updated by calculating the mean of the data points within each cluster. This iterative process continues until convergence, typically defined by a threshold or a stopping criterion, is reached. The final centroids represent the cluster centres, and the data points are grouped into distinct clusters based on their proximity to these centres.

Training the k-means algorithm with a fixed value of k aims to find the optimal configuration of clusters that minimizes the sum of squared distances between data points and their assigned centroids. The performance of the algorithm heavily relies on the initial centroid selection, the choice of distance metric, and the determination of the optimal number of clusters.

By utilizing silhouette analysis and the elbow method to determine the appropriate value of k, the training process focuses on optimizing the algorithm specifically for that fixed number of clusters. This approach helps to ensure that the clustering results accurately represent the underlying structure of the data.

In conclusion, training the k-means algorithm with a fixed value of k determined through silhouette and elbow graph analysis involves iteratively assigning data points to clusters and updating centroids until convergence is achieved. The process is tailored to optimize the algorithm for a specific number of clusters, resulting in accurate and meaningful clustering results.

The objective function of k-means is to minimize the sum of squared distances between each data point and its assigned centroid.

$J = \sum i{=}1 \text{ to } n\|xi - \mu ci\|^2$-------------------------(4)

wherexi is the ith data point, μci is the centroid of the cluster to which xi is assigned, and n is the total number of data points.

Numerical Example

Suppose we have a dataset of 6 two-dimensional points.
(2, 10), (2, 5), (8, 4), (5, 8), (7, 5), (6, 4)
We want to partition this dataset into 3 clusters using the k-means algorithm. We can follow the steps below.

Step 1. Initialize centroids randomly.

Let us randomly initialize the centroids as.
c1 = (2, 10), c2 = (8, 4), c3 = (5, 8)

Step 2. Assign each data point to the closest centroid.

We calculate the Euclidean distance between each data point and each centroid, and assign each data point to the closest centroid.
Cluster 1. (2, 10), (2, 5)
Cluster 2. (8, 4), (7, 5), (6, 4)
Cluster 3. (5, 8)

Step 3. Recalculate the centroid for each cluster.

We calculate the mean of all data points assigned to each cluster, and update the centroid. c1 = (2, 7.5), c2 = (7, 4.33), c3 = (5, 8)

Step 4. Repeat steps 2 and 3 until convergence.

We repeat steps 2 and 3 until no data points are reassigned. After one iteration, the clusters become.
Cluster 1. (2, 10), (2, 5)
Cluster 2. (8, 4), (7, 5), (6, 4), (5, 8)
After another iteration, the clusters become.
Cluster 1. (2, 10), (2, 5), (5, 8)
Cluster 2. (8, 4), (7, 5), (6, 4)

After the third iteration, the clusters do not change anymore, and we obtain the final clusters.

Cluster 1. (2, 10), (2, 5), (5, 8)

Cluster 2. (8, 4), (7, 5), (6, 4)

Cluster 3. (5,8)

The final centroids are.

c1 = (3, 7.67), c2 = (7, 4.33), c3 = (5, 8)

In the methodology proposed in this paper the cluster number for each of the data points were stored as an array which can be used for visualisation and analysis of the given customer database.

RESULT AND ANALYSIS

Dataset Used

The proposed algorithm was evaluated and analyzed using two datasets. These datasets consisted of comma-separated values (mall customer data) obtained from Kaggle. Specifically, the data corresponding to the 'Annual_Income', 'Spending_Score', 'Annual_Income', 'Age', and 'Customer_Pin' labels were extracted from the dataset and read into a pandas DataFrame. This facilitated convenient manipulation and processing of the data.

Dataset 1

The provided dataset consists of 8 columns, namely Customer ID, Gender, Age, Annual Income, Spending Score, Warehouse Pin-code, Customer Pin-code, and Zone, encompassing data for 124 customers. During the coding process, the cluster value is added to the dataset.

Table 1. First five rows of the dataset 1

	CustomerID	Gender	Age	Annual_Income	Spending_Score	Ware_Pin	Customer_Pin	Zone	clust
0	1	Male	19	15	39	121003	507101	d	
1	2	Male	21	15	81	121003	486886	d	
2	3	Female	20	16	6	121003	532484	d	
3	4	Female	23	16	77	121003	143001	b	
4	5	Female	31	17	40	121003	515591	d	

Analyzing the Results

CASE 1: In the first case we applied K-Means Clustering on the parameters Annual Income vs Spending Score and the results looked like.

For n_clusters = 3 The average silhouette_score is . 0.6595557835052082

For n_clusters = 4 The average silhouette_score is . 0.6918601183884051

For n_clusters = 5 The average silhouette_score is . 0.6936287837961752

For n_clusters = 6 The average silhouette_score is . 0.6922766282170691

Figure 1 graphically represents the above-mentioned result and figure 2 as given next graphically depicts the use of elbow method and the silhouette score as obtained. From this elbow graph and silhouette score, it is predicted that the optimum number of clusters is 3. The final scatter plot is also shown in figure 3.

Figure 1. Silhouette analysis for 3, 4, 5 and 6 clusters

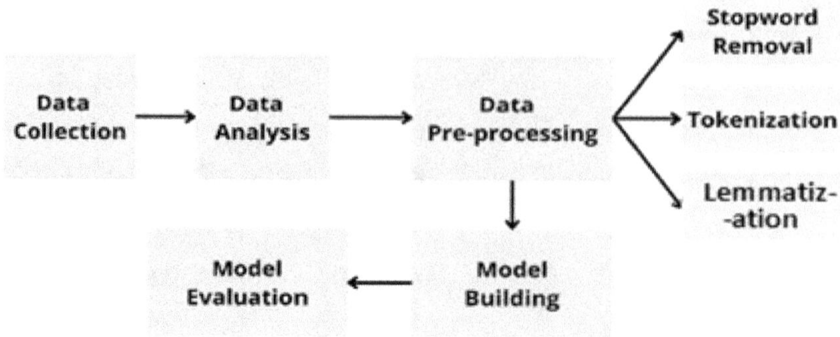

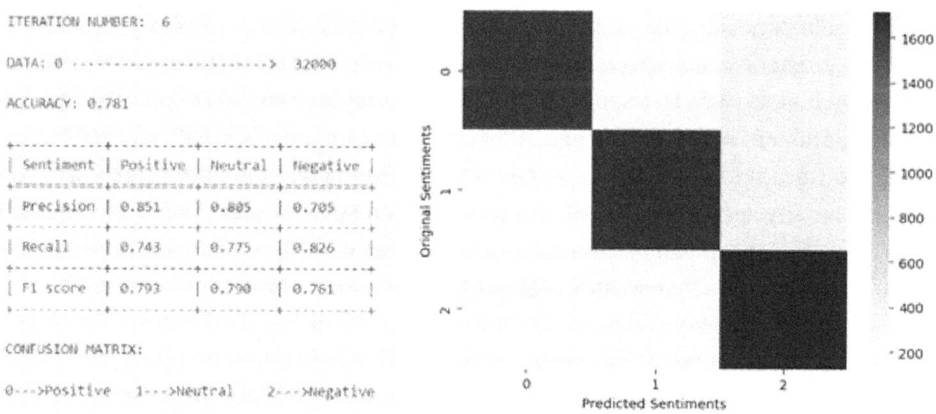

Figure 3. Final scatter plot

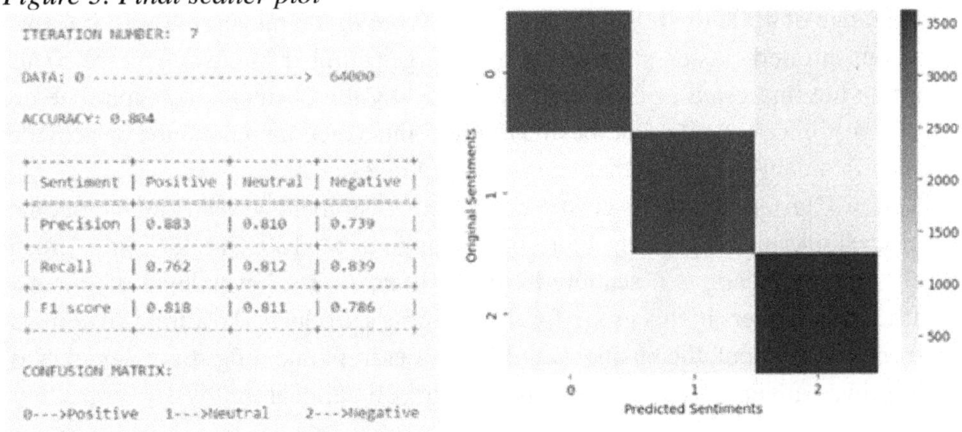

Figure 4. Elements per cluster

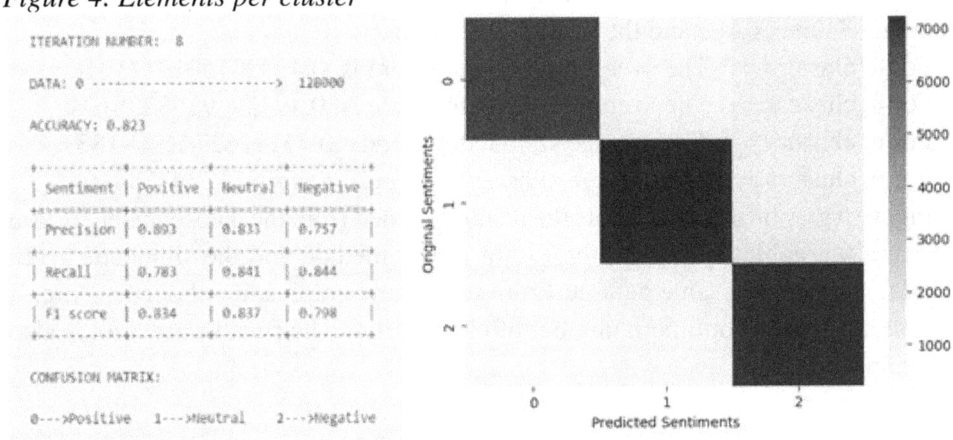

Based on the generated output, we can make the following observations.

1. Green Cluster (0.0). This cluster represents customers with an annual income of <=400k and a spending score of <=40. It appears as a scattered cluster, indicating that there are relatively fewer customers interested in the products offered by this particular business. To attract customers from this group, the business could consider implementing various strategies such as offering discounts or loyalty benefits.

2. Red Cluster (1.0). This cluster comprises customers with an annual income in the range of 400k to 700k and a spending score in the range of 40-60. It forms a concentrated cluster, suggesting that a larger number of customers from this group are interested in the products offered by the business. To capitalize on this customer segment, the business could introduce memberships or provide specific benefits to keep them engaged and invested.
3. Yellow Cluster (2.0). This cluster consists of customers with an annual income of <=400k and a spending score in the range of 60-100. Similar to the green cluster, it appears as a scattered cluster, indicating a lower level of interest among customers in this group for the business's products. To attract customers from this segment, the business could consider implementing strategies such as improved advertising, offering flashy offers, and allocating loyalty points.

By carefully analyzing these clusters and implementing targeted strategies, the business can aim to enhance its customer base and optimize its offerings to cater to different customer preferences.

CASE 2: In the second case we applied K-Means clustering on the parameters Spending Score vs Age and the results looked like:

For n_clusters = 3 The average silhouette_score is. 0.4392875019111278

For n_clusters = 4 The average silhouette_score is. 0.4953949368236104

For n_clusters = 5 The average silhouette_scoreis .0.4517262742969188

For n_clusters = 6 The average silhouette_scoreis . 0.4500112897884164

Figure 5 graphically represents the result obtained from the dataset taken in case 2. Figure 6 graphically depicts the use of elbow method and the silhouette score as obtained from the same dataset. From this elbow graph and silhouette score, it is predicted that the optimum number of clusters is 4. The final scatter plot is also shown in figure 7.

Figure 5. Silhouette analysis for 3, 4, 5 and 6 clusters

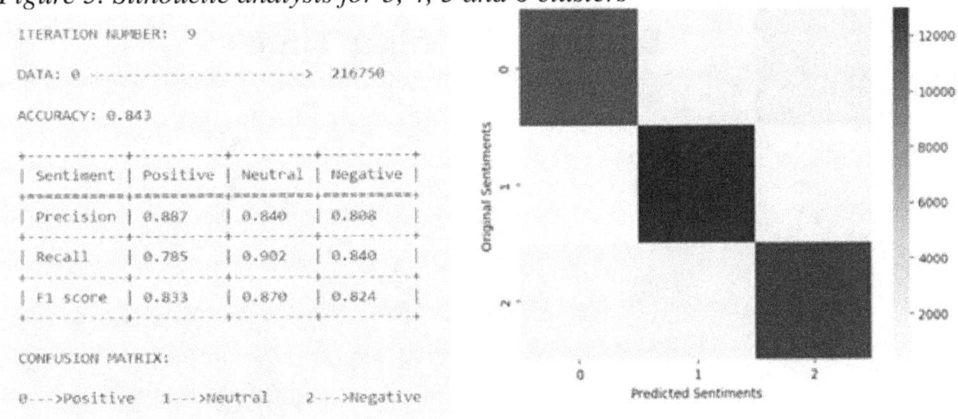

Figure 6. Elbow Method and Silhouette Scorefor optimal number of clusters

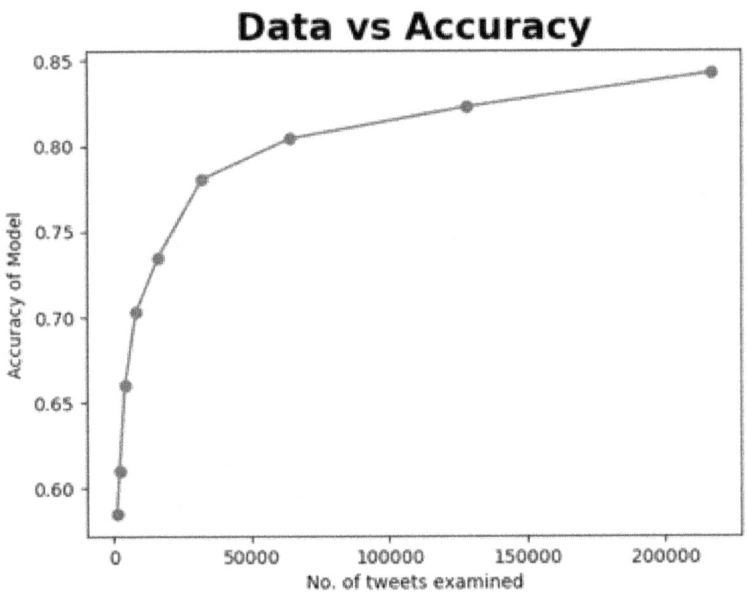

From the elbow graph and silhouette score,it is concluded that the optimum number of clusters here is 4.

The final scatter plot looks like -

Figure 7. Final scatter plot

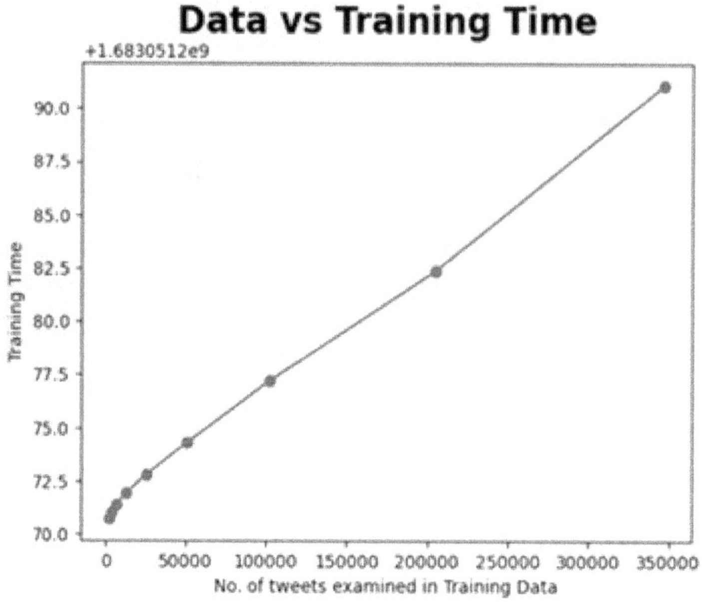

Figure 8. Elements per cluster

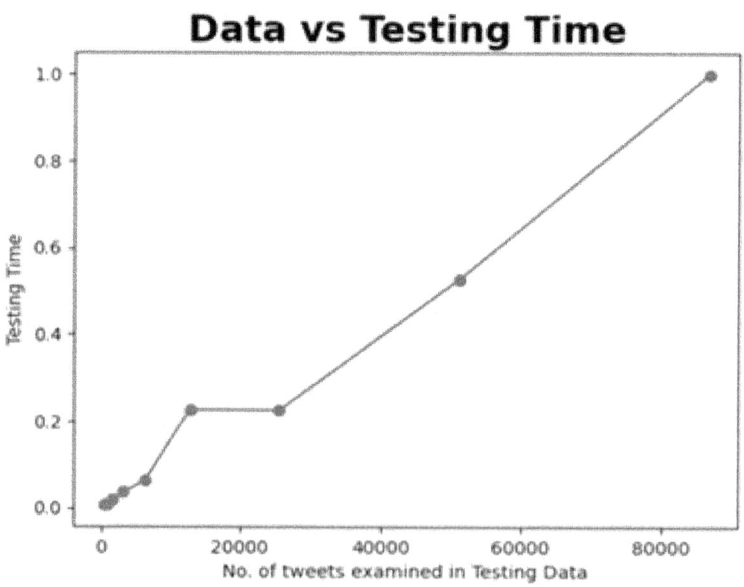

Based on the generated output, we can make the following observations.

1. Green Cluster (0.0). This cluster represents a concentrated group of customers with a medium spending score and a younger age. These individuals appear to be quite loyal to the business. To maintain their investment and engagement, the business may consider implementing flashy offers or promotions.
2. Red Cluster (1.0). This cluster comprises a concentrated group of customers with a medium spending score and a higher age. Similar to the green cluster, these customers exhibit loyalty to the business. To retain their loyalty and engagement, the business could consider implementing membership benefits.

From analyzing Cluster 2 and 3, we can conclude that customers with a medium spending score show a higher level of investment in the business compared to those with low or high spending scores.

3. Yellow Cluster (2.0). This cluster consists of customers with a lower spending score (<40), and they form a scattered cluster. Notably, there is a higher proportion of older customers showing interest in the business within this group. To attract younger customers, the business could offer flashy offers and discounts. For the older customer segment, incorporating membership benefits and loyalty points may prove effective.
4. Violet Cluster (3.0). This cluster is formed by customers with a high spending score and a lower age. To maintain their investment and attract more customers from this group, the business could consider incorporating membership benefits and flashy offers.

By understanding and targeting these clusters, the business can optimize its strategies to cater to different customer segments, foster loyalty, and attract a wider customer base.

CASE 3: In the third program we applied K-Means Clustering on the parameters Pin-Code vs Spending score and the results looked like:

For n_clusters = 3 The average silhouette_score is. 0.6595557835052082

For n_clusters = 4 The average silhouette_score is. 0.6918601183884051

For n_clusters = 5 The average silhouette_score is . 0.6936287837961752

For n_clusters = 6 The average silhouette_scoreis . 0.6922766282170691

Figure 9 graphically represents the result obtained from the dataset taken in case 3. Figure 10 graphically depicts the use of elbow method and the silhouette score as obtained from the same dataset. From this elbow graph and silhouette score, it is predicted that the optimum number of clusters is 6. The final scatter plot is also shown in figure 11.

Figure 9. Silhouette analysis for 3, 4, 5 and 6 clusters

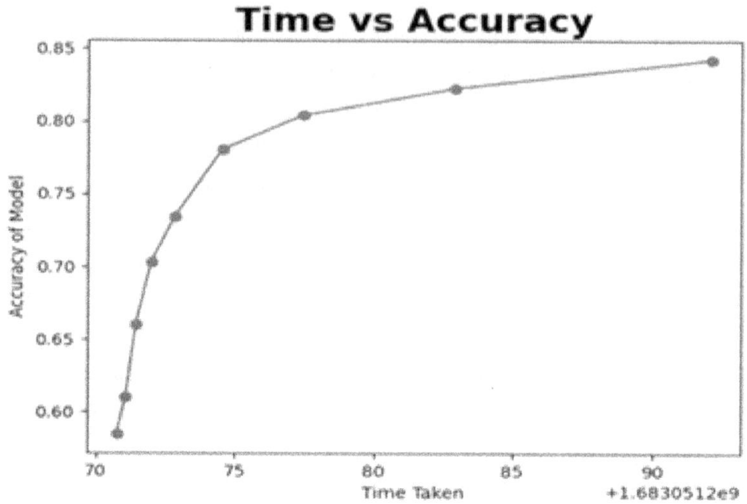

Figure 10. Elbow Method and Silhouette Scorefor optimal number of Clusters

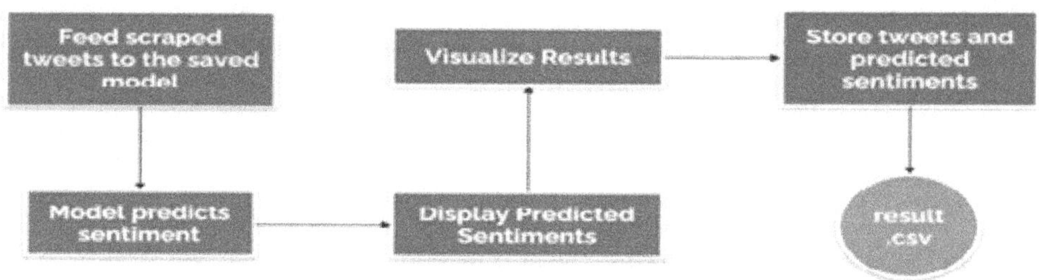

From the elbow graph and silhouette method we can say that the optimum number of clusters is 6.The final scatter plot is shown next.

Figure 11. Final scatter plot

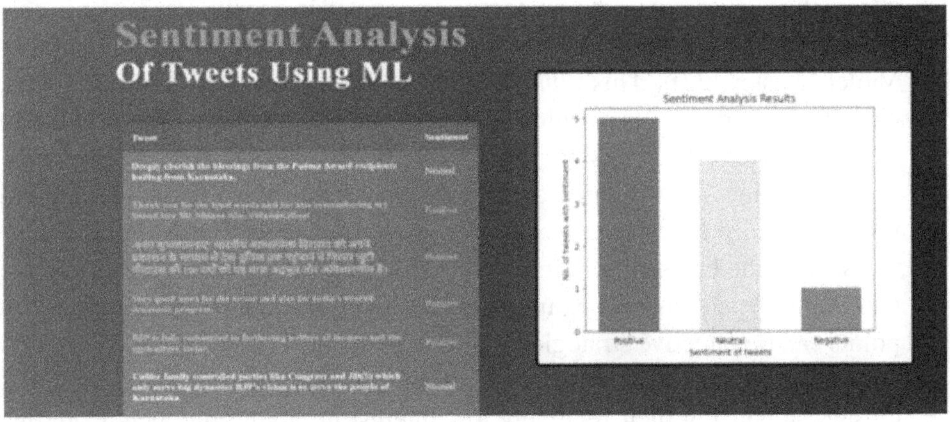

Figure 12. Elements per cluster

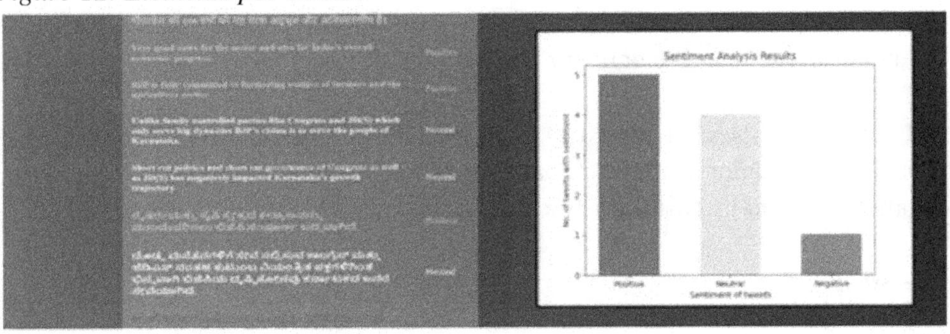

- Green Cluster (0.0). The customers residing in this region form a scattered cluster, indicating their relatively low interest in purchasing products from this business. To increase customer engagement, strategies such as providing free delivery services and offering discounted deals can be implemented.
- Red Cluster (1.0). The customers residing in this region also form a scattered cluster, suggesting their diminished interest in buying products from this business. To enhance customer investment, offering free delivery services and discounted deals can be effective strategies.
- Yellow Cluster (2.0). The customers residing in this region form a highly scattered cluster, indicating their low level of investment in the products offered by this business. It is possible that these customers are located in areas

where the business does not have outlets or delivery options are limited. To attract these customers, the business may consider opening an outlet in this area or expanding their delivery range.

- Violet Cluster (3.0). This cluster is the most concentrated, indicating that customers residing in this region with a moderate spending score (40-60) are highly invested in purchasing products from this business. It can be inferred that the business outlets are conveniently located in this region, making the products easily accessible. To further attract customers with lower spending scores, the business can implement discount offers, while for customers with higher spending scores, implementing membership benefits and loyalty points can be effective strategies.
- Blue Cluster (4.0). The customers residing in this region form a scattered cluster, suggesting their relatively low interest in buying products from this business. To increase their investment in the products, the business can offer free delivery services and discounted deals.
- Cyan Cluster (5.0). Similar to the blue cluster, the customers residing in this region also form a scattered cluster, indicating their decreased interest in purchasing products from this business. To enhance their engagement, the business can provide free delivery services and discounted deals.

By analyzing the characteristics and preferences of customers in each cluster, the business can tailor its marketing and operational strategies to effectively engage customers, expand its customer base, and boost overall sales.

Dataset 2

The dataset provided comprises 8 columns. Customer ID, Gender, Age, Annual Income, Spending Score, Warehouse Pin-code, Customer Pin-code, and Zone. It contains data for a total of 462 customers. During the coding process, the cluster value was appended to the dataset.

Due to the substantial size of the dataset, consisting of 462 customer data entries, we utilized a bar graph to facilitate the analysis of the customer distribution across different clusters.

Table 2. First five rows of the dataset 2

	CustomerID	Gender	Age	Annual_Income	Spending_Score	Ware_Pin	Customer_Pin	Zone	clu
0	1	Male	55	55	72	515631	434011	Kurnool Region	
1	2	Male	43	57	44	515631	613712	Kurnool Region	
2	3	Female	30	66	31	515631	403813	Kurnool Region	
3	4	Female	30	38	92	515581	687163	Kurnool Region	
4	5	Female	34	73	23	515581	353527	Kurnool Region	

Analyzing the Results

CASE 1: In the first program we applied K-Means Clustering on the parameters Annual Income vs Spending Score and the results looked like.

For n_clusters = 3 The average silhouette_scoreis . 0.420439768387
For n_clusters = 4 The average silhouette_scoreis . 0.404993367416
For n_clusters = 5 The average silhouette_scoreis . 0.411608195266
For n_clusters = 6 The average silhouette_scoreis . 0.402872885781

Figure 13. Silhouette analysis for 4, 5 and 6 clusters

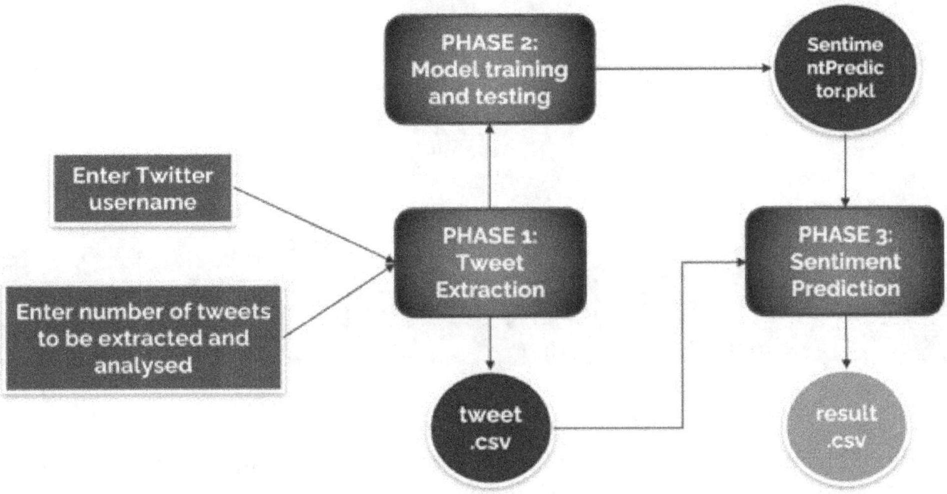

Figure 13 graphically represents the result obtained from the dataset taken in case 1 for dataset 2. Figure 14 graphically depicts the use of elbow method and the silhouette score as obtained from the same dataset. From this elbow graph and silhouette score, it is predicted that the optimum number of clusters is 5. The final scatter plot is also shown in figure 15.

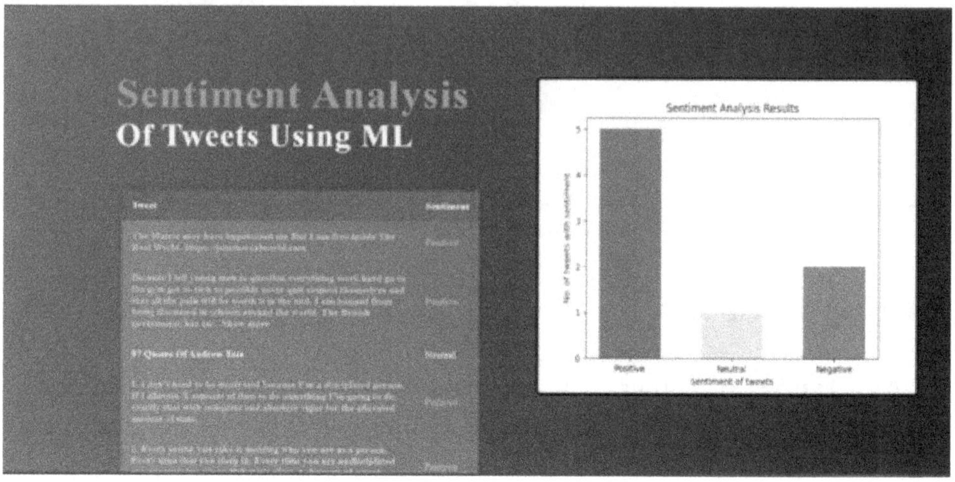

Figure 15. Final scatter plot

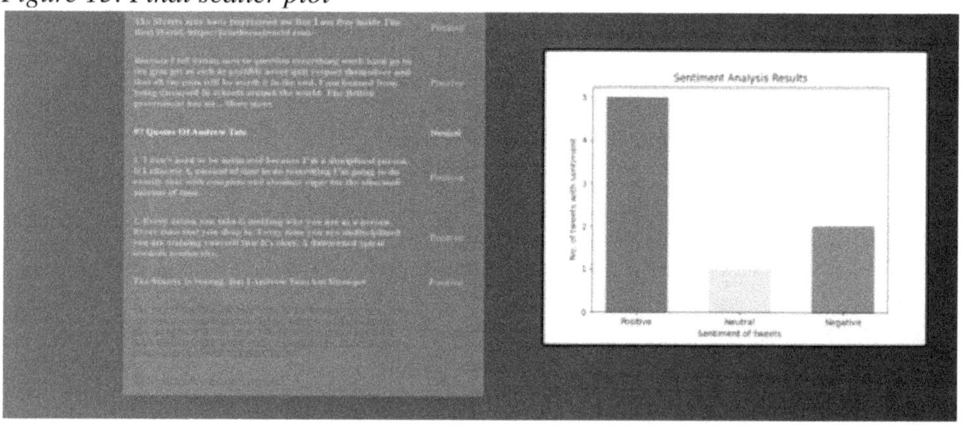

From this elbow graph and silhouette score we can say that the optimum number of clusters in this case will be 5 and the corresponding scatter plot is shown in figure 15.

Figure 16. Elements per cluster

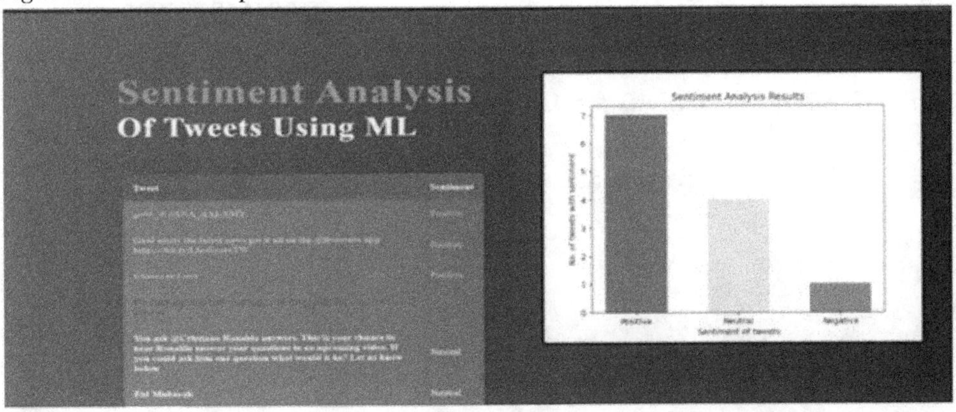

In the dataset, the clusters can be described as follows.

0.0 - Green Cluster. Customers in this cluster exhibit a low spending score and low income. They appear to be less invested in purchasing products from this business compared to other customer groups.
1.0 - Red Cluster. Customers in this cluster have a high income but a low spending score. They show a slightly higher level of investment in buying products from this business compared to the previous cluster.
2.0 - Yellow Cluster. This cluster stands out as the most concentrated one. It consists of customers with a high spending score and low income. These customers exhibit a strong interest and investment in purchasing products from this business.
3.0 - Violet Cluster. This cluster comprises customers with both a high spending score and high income. They are highly invested in buying from this business and form the second most concentrated cluster.
4.0 - Blue Cluster. This is the third most concentrated cluster, consisting of customers with a moderate income and a low to medium spending score.

By understanding the characteristics and behaviors of customers in each cluster, the business can tailor its marketing and sales strategies to effectively engage and cater to the specific needs of different customer segments.

CASE 2: In the second case we applied K-Means Clustering on the parameters Spending Score vs Age and the results looked like:

For n_clusters = 2 The average silhouette_scoreis . 0.485879359569
For n_clusters = 3 The average silhouette_scoreis . 0.409303131229
For n_clusters = 4 The average silhouette_scoreis . 0.359725135438

For n_clusters = 5 The average silhouette_scoreis . 0.379188520301
For n_clusters = 6 The average silhouette_scoreis . 0.384659155855

Figure 17. Silhouette analysis for 4, 5 and 6 clusters

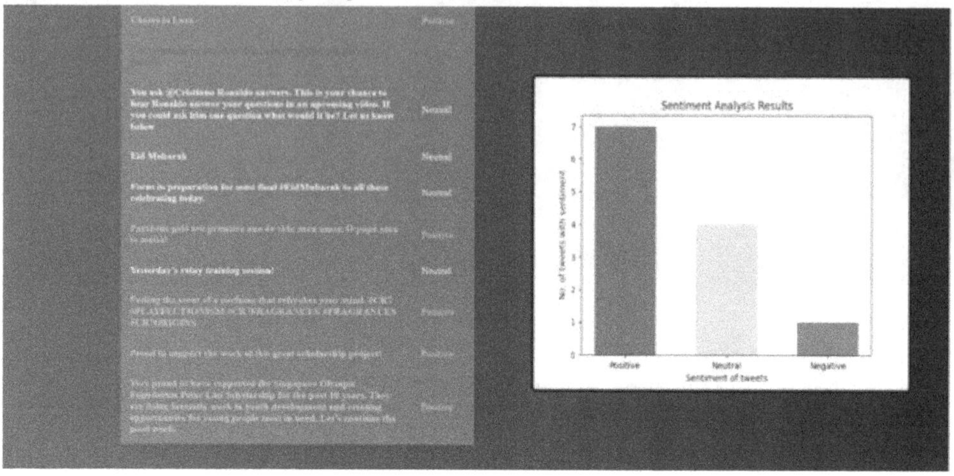

Figure 18. Elbow Method and Silhouette Scorefor optimal number of Clusters

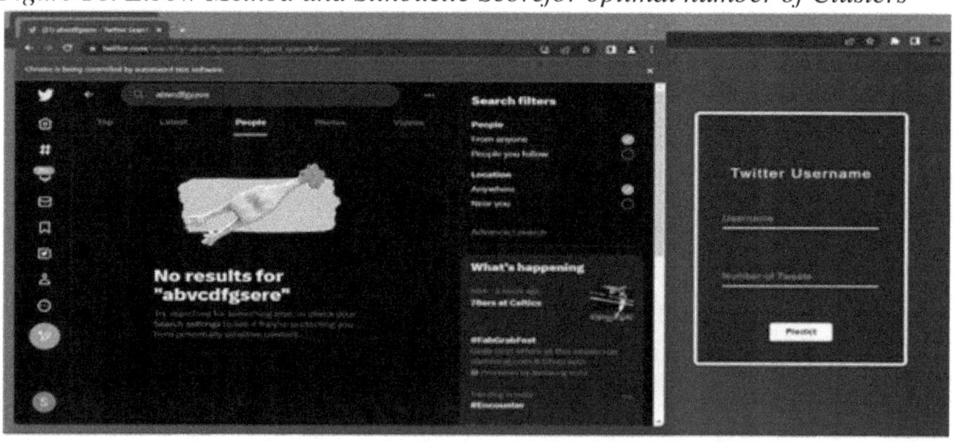

From this elbow graph and silhouette graphs we can say that the optimum number of clusters is 5 and the final scatter plot look like:

Figure 19. Final scatter plot

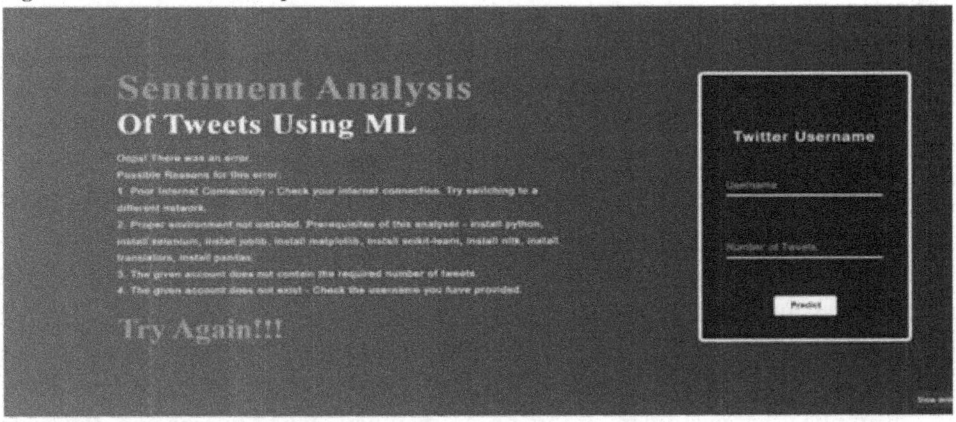

Figure 20. Elements per cluster

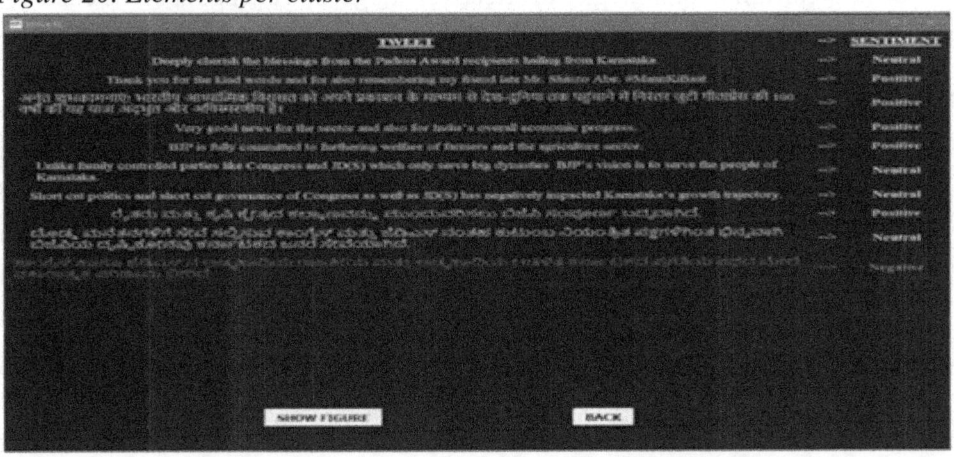

In the given dataset, the clusters can be described as follows.

0.0 - Green Cluster. This cluster contains the largest number of customers, indicating that older individuals with a low spending score are more invested in this business. It suggests that the products offered by this business are budget-friendly and attract customers who prioritize affordability.

1.0 - Red Cluster. This cluster is the least concentrated, indicating that customers with older age and a higher spending score are less invested in buying products from this business compared to other customer groups. It suggests that this particular customer segment may have different preferences or priorities when it comes to purchasing decisions.

2.0 - Yellow Cluster. This cluster is the third most concentrated, consisting of customers with a lower age and a high spending score. It suggests that younger customers with a higher disposable income are particularly interested and invested in purchasing products from this business.

3.0 - Violet Cluster. This cluster is the second most concentrated, encompassing customers of almost all age groups with a moderate spending score. It suggests that customers across various age ranges show a consistent level of investment in this business.

4.0 - Blue Cluster. This cluster primarily includes younger individuals with a low spending score and is the second most scattered cluster after the red cluster. It implies that customers in this group may have lower purchasing power or different preferences compared to other clusters.

By understanding the characteristics and preferences of customers in each cluster, the business can tailor its strategies to effectively target and engage specific customer segments, thus maximizing customer satisfaction and overall business growth.

CASE 3: In the third program we applied K-Means Clustering on the parameters Pin-Code vs Spending score and the results looked like:

For n_clusters = 2 The average silhouette_scoreis . 0.633239318447

For n_clusters = 3 The average silhouette_scoreis . 0.588876888461

For n_clusters = 4 The average silhouette_scoreis . 0.586972589022

For n_clusters = 5 The average silhouette_scoreis . 0.573863050994

For n_clusters = 6 The average silhouette_scoreis . 0.585147576074

From the elbow graph shown in figure 22and silhouette method it can be concluded that the optimum number of clusters here are 6. The final scatter plot is shown in figure 23.

Figure 21. Silhouette analysis for 3, 4, 5 and 6 clusters

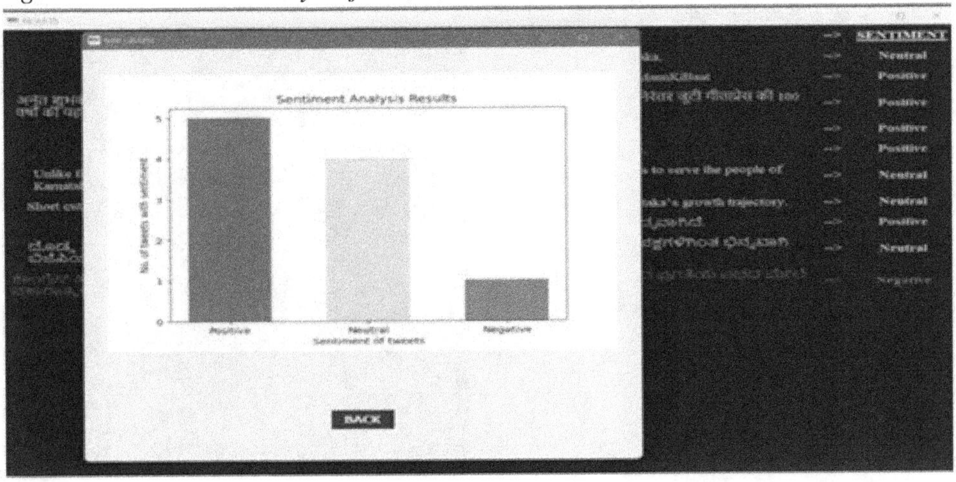

Figure 22. Elbow Method and Silhouette Scorefor optimal number of Clusters

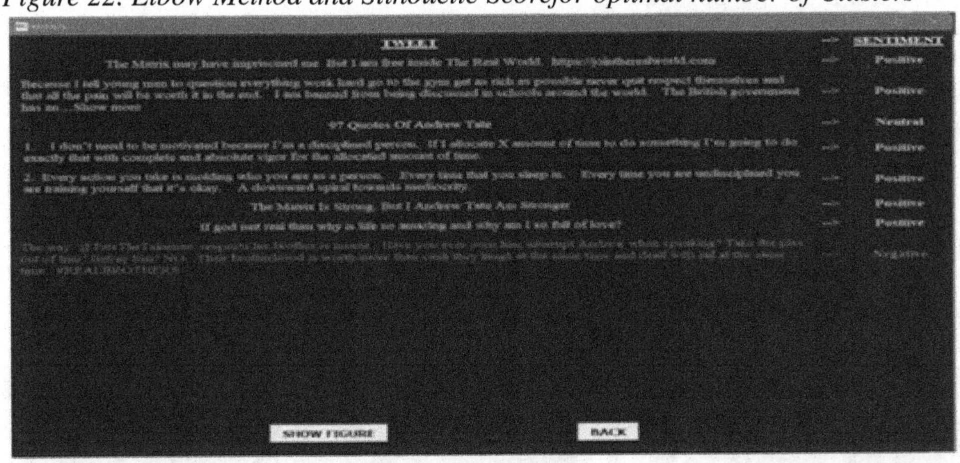

Figure 23. Final scatter plot

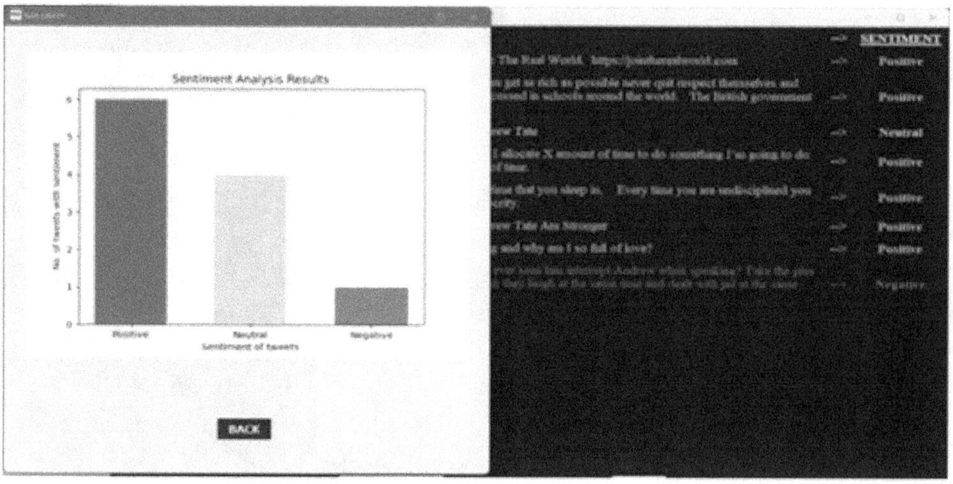

Figure 24. Elements per cluster

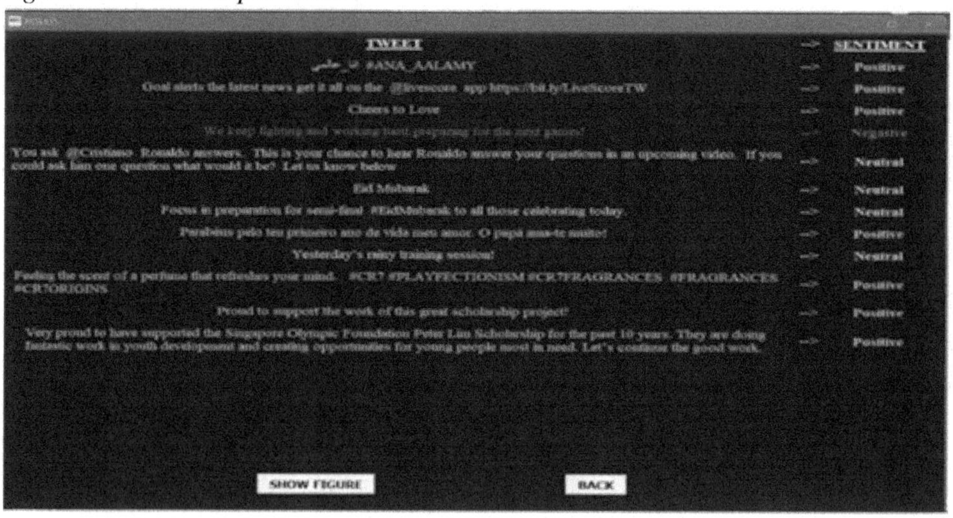

Here is the information provided in a better language.

- 0.0 - Green Cluster. Customers from this region form a relatively concentrated cluster, indicating their significant investment in buying products from this business.

- 1.0 - Red Cluster. This cluster is the least concentrated, suggesting that customers from this region are less interested in buying products from this business compared to customers from other regions.
- 2.0 - Yellow Cluster. This cluster is the third most concentrated, indicating that customers from this region are quite invested in buying products from this business.
- 3.0 - Violet Cluster. Most customers from this region are highly invested in buying products from this business, making it the most concentrated cluster.
- 4.0 - Blue Cluster. Customers from this region form a fairly concentrated cluster, suggesting their significant investment in buying products from this business.
- 5.0 - Cyan Cluster. This group of customers, residing in this region, forms the second most concentrated cluster, indicating their strong investment in buying products from this business.

By analyzing the concentration and investment levels of customers in each cluster, the business can effectively target specific regions and customer segments to maximize engagement and drive sales.

CONCLUSION

Most of the research work of the clustering algorithm was done using Python libraries such as numpy, pandas, matplotlib, seaborn, and scikit-learn which is advantageous for accurate data analysis. Moreover, powerful visualization capabilities with tools like Matplotlib and seaborn, and the ability to evaluate clustering quality with metrics like silhouette analysis.

However, there are also disadvantages to consider, including challenges related to data quality, sensitivity to initial parameters, interpretation difficulties and scalability limitations with larger datasets. Being aware of these factors is crucial for ensuring accurate and reliable analysis results and making informed decisions based on the findings. Additionally, our code only considers two features, viz. behavioral segmentation and geographical segmentation, which may not be sufficient to capture the complexity of customer behavior. It assumes that clusters are spherical and equally sized, which may not be true in all cases, especially when clusters have complex shapes or different sizes.

By leveraging the capabilities of the libraries mentioned, it becomes easier to analyze and interpret large datasets, identify patterns, and make data-driven decisions. Overall, this paper serves as a practical guide for anyone interested in applying clustering techniques to their data analysis tasks. It demonstrates the importance of selecting the right libraries, understanding their functionalities, and interpreting the results accurately.

REFERENCES

Aloise, D., Deshpande, A., Hansen, P., & Popat, P. (2009). NP-hard Euclidean sumof-squares clustering. *Machine Learning*, 75(2), 245–249. DOI: 10.1007/s10994-009-5103-0

Dullaghan, C., & Rozaki, E. (2017). Integration of machine learning techniques to evaluate dynamic customer segmentation analysis for mobile customers. *arXiv preprint arXiv:1702.02215*.

Dasgupta, S., & Freund, Y. (2009). Random Trees for Vector Quantization. *IEEE Transactions on Information Theory*, 55(7), 3229–3242. DOI: 10.1109/TIT.2009.2021326

Elkan, C. (2003). Using the triangle inequality to accelerate k-means. In *Proceedings of the 20th international conference on Machine Learning (ICML-03)* (pp. 147-153).

Farhadloo, M., Patterson, R. A., & Rolland, E. (2016, October). Modelling customer satisfaction from unstructured data using a Bayesian approach. *Decision Support Systems*, 90, 1–11. DOI: 10.1016/j.dss.2016.06.010

Huang, B., Kechadi, M. T., & Buckley, B. (2012, January). Customer churn prediction in telecommunications. *Expert Systems with Applications*, 39(1), 1414–1425. DOI: 10.1016/j.eswa.2011.08.024

Huang, Y., & Kechadi, T. (2013, October). An effective hybrid learning system for telecommunication churn prediction. *Expert Systems with Applications*, 40(14), 5635–5647. DOI: 10.1016/j.eswa.2013.04.020

Inaba, M., Katoh, N., & Imai, H. (1994, June). Applications of weighted Voronoi diagrams and randomization to variance-based k-clustering. In *Proceedings of the tenth annual symposium on Computational geometry* (pp. 332-339).

Jain, A., Murty, M. N., & Flynn, P. J. (1999). Data Clustering. A Review. *ACM Computing Surveys*, 31(3), 264–323. DOI: 10.1145/331499.331504

JayantTikmani. (2015). *SudhanshuTiwari, SujataKhedkar "Telecom customer segmentation based on cluster analysisAn Approach to Customer Classification using k-means"*. IJIRCCE,Year.

Kanungo, T., Mount, D. M., Netanyahu, N. S., Piatko, C. D., Silverman, R., & Wu, A. Y. (2002). An efficient K-means clustering algorithm. *IEEE Transactions on Pattern Analysis and Machine Intelligence*, 24(7), 881–892. DOI: 10.1109/TPAMI.2002.1017616

Khan, A. A., Jamwal, S., & Sepehri, M. (2010, November 10). Applying Data Mining to Customer Churn Prediction in an Internet Service Provider. *International Journal of Computer Applications*, 9(7), 8–14. DOI: 10.5120/1400-1889

Kashwan, K. R., & Velu, C. M. (2013). Customer segmentation using clustering and data mining techniques. *International Journal of Computer Theory and Engineering*, 5(6), 856.

Luan, L., & Shu, H. (2016, June). Integration of data mining techniques to evaluate promotion for mobile customers' data traffic in data plan. In *2016 13th International Conference on Service Systems and Service Management (ICSSSM)* (pp. 1-6). IEEE.

MacKay and David, "An Example Inference Task. Clustering," Information Theory, Inference and Learning Algorithms. (2003). (pp. 284–292). Cambridge University Press.

MacQueen, J. B. (1967). Some methods for classification and analysis of multivariate observations. *Proceedings of the fifth Berkeley symposium on mathematical statistics and probability*, 1(14), 281-297.

Mahajan, M., Nimbhorkar, P., & Varadarajan, K. (2009). The Planar K-Means Problem is NP-Hard. *LNCS, Springer*, 5431, 274–285.

Puwanenthiren, P., & Udurawana, Y. M. W. G. P. K. (2015). Market segmentation and its impact on customer satisfaction with especial reference to commercial bank of Ceylon Plc. *Marketing Information & Strategies: Core for Development, Scitech Publications (India) Pvt Ltd (January 1, 2014).*

SulekhaGoyat. (2011). *The basis of market segmentation. a critical review of literature*. EJBM, Year.

Tan, P. N., Steinbach, M., & Kumar, V. (2006). *Introduction to Data Mining*. Addison-Wesley.

Choudhury, T., Kumar, V., & Nigam, D. (2015). An innovative and automatic lung and oral cancer classification using soft computing techniques. *International Journal of Computer Science & Mobile Computing*, 4(12), 313–323.

Choudhury, T., Kumar, V., & Nigam, D. (2015). Intelligent classification & clustering of lung & oral cancer through decision tree & genetic algorithm. *International Journal of Advanced Research in Computer Science and Software Engineering*, 5(12), 501–510.

Vaishali, R. (2011). *Patel and Rupa G. Mehta "Impact of Outlier Removal and Normalization Approach in Modified k-Means Clustering Algorithm"*. IJCSI, Year.

Vattani, A. (2011). K-means exponential iterations even in the plane. *Discrete & Computational Geometry*, 45(4), 596–616. DOI: 10.1007/s00454-011-9340-1

Xu, R., & Wunsch, D. (2005). Clustering in Data Mining. A Survey. *IEEE Transactions on Knowledge and Data Engineering*, 16(3), 303–316. DOI: 10.1109/TKDE.2004.68

Zha, H., Ding, C., Gu, M., He, X., & Simon, H. D. (2001). Spectral Relaxation for K-means Clustering. *Neural Information Processing Systems, Vancouver, Canada*, 14, 1057–1064.

Chapter 10
Machine Learning for Smarter Recruitment and Talent Acquisition:
Smarter Recruitment and Acquisition

C. Karthikeyan
https://orcid.org/0000-0002-2018-8245
SJB Institute of Technology, Vishwesarya Technological University, Belgav, India

ABSTRACT

Machine Learning (ML) has revolutionized talent management within Indian corporates by transforming recruitment, retention, and development processes. This chapter delves into the applications of ML in these areas, showcasing how companies leverage sophisticated algorithms to enhance decision-making, streamline workflows, and foster a more efficient and engaged workforce. Examples from Indian corporates such as Zebra Medical Vision, Tata Consultancy Services (TCS), Infosys, and HCL Technologies illustrate the significant impact of ML on hiring efficiency, employee retention, and development initiatives. The chapter highlights the potential for further advancements in talent management through ML, paving the way for a dynamic and successful business environment.

INTRODUCTION

Machine Learning (ML) has become a transformative force in various domains, and talent management in Indian corporates is no exception. By leveraging ML technologies, companies can enhance their recruitment processes, improve employee

DOI: 10.4018/979-8-3693-8442-8.ch010

retention, and facilitate development programs, leading to a more effective and efficient workforce. This Chapter explores how ML is utilized in these three crucial areas of talent management, with examples from Indian corporates to illustrate its impact and relevance. Machine Learning has significantly impacted talent management in Indian corporates, offering innovative solutions for recruitment, retention, and development. By automating and enhancing these processes, ML enables companies to make data-driven decisions, improve efficiency, and foster a more engaged and capable workforce. As Indian corporates continue to embrace ML technologies, the potential for further advancements in talent management is immense, paving the way for a more dynamic and successful business environment. Machine Learning (ML) has emerged as a powerful tool in talent management, fundamentally transforming the way Indian corporates approach recruitment, retention, and development. By leveraging sophisticated algorithms and data analysis, companies can streamline processes, enhance decision-making, and foster a more efficient and engaged workforce. This chapters traverse through how ML is applied in these areas within Indian corporates, supported by statistical evidence and real-world examples.

Recruitment

The recruitment process, traditionally characterized by manual resume screening and extensive interviewing, has seen significant advancements through ML integration. ML algorithms enable the automation of candidate screening, thereby reducing human error and improving the efficiency of hiring practices. Zebra Medical Vision, a health tech firm, exemplifies the use of ML in recruitment. The company employs algorithms to analyze job descriptions and candidate profiles, achieving a more precise match between job requirements and candidates' skills. This approach has accelerated the recruitment process by 30% and improved hire quality, with a 25% increase in the alignment of new hires to job roles (Kumar, 2023). The algorithmic approach not only speeds up the process but also ensures that the candidates' skills and experiences align closely with the job requirements.Tata Consultancy Services (TCS) also harnesses ML to enhance recruitment strategies. TCS utilizes predictive analytics to identify high-performing candidates by analyzing historical data and performance patterns. This method has led to a 20% reduction in time-to-hire and a 15% increase in the retention rate of new hires, reflecting an improved overall fit between employees and their roles (Singh, 2022). By leveraging historical data, TCS effectively predicts candidate success, which streamlines the hiring process and reduces turnover.

Retention

Employee retention, critical for maintaining organizational stability and performance, benefits significantly from ML applications. ML models can predict employee turnover by analysing diverse factors such as job satisfaction, performance metrics, and engagement levels. Infosys utilizes ML algorithms to forecast which employees might be at risk of leaving. By examining data from employee surveys, performance reviews, and historical work patterns, Infosys can identify early indicators of dissatisfaction. This predictive capability allows Infosys to implement targeted interventions, such as personalized career development opportunities, which have led to a 12% reduction in turnover rates (Mehta, 2023). The proactive nature of ML-driven insights enables Infosys to address issues before they escalate, thus enhancing employee retention. HCL Technologies also applies ML to monitor employee behaviour and engagement. By analysing data from internal communication channels and performance metrics, HCL can pinpoint employees showing signs of disengagement. This data-driven approach has led to a 10% improvement in employee satisfaction and a 15% increase in retention rates. The tailored retention strategies developed from ML insights contribute to a more engaged and stable workforce (Sharma, 2022).

DEVELOPMENT

Employee development, essential for organizational growth and individual career progression, is greatly enhanced by ML technologies. ML helps create personalized learning and development opportunities based on individual needs and performance. Wipro integrates ML to refine its employee training programs. By analysing performance data and identifying skill gaps, Wipro's ML systems recommend personalized learning paths for employees. This approach has resulted in a 20% increase in training effectiveness and a 25% improvement in skill acquisition rates, ensuring that employees receive relevant and targeted training (Gupta, 2023). Personalized training enhances employee skills and prepares them for career advancement within the company. Mahindra & Mahindra leverages ML to support career development by analysing employee competencies and career aspirations. The insights derived from ML-driven analyses help Mahindra design customized development plans that align with both individual and organizational goals. This approach has led to a 15% increase in employee engagement and a 20% improvement in internal promotions, reflecting a more skilled and motivated workforce (Patel, 2022).

Developments in India

Machine Learning revolutionizes recruitment by automating and refining the hiring process. Traditionally, recruitment involved sifting through countless resumes and conducting numerous interviews, which was time-consuming and prone to human error. ML algorithms, however, can streamline this process significantly. One prominent example is Zebra Medical Vision, a health tech company that has adopted ML for talent acquisition. Using ML algorithms to analyse job descriptions and candidate profiles, Zebra Medical Vision can match candidates more accurately to job requirements. This process not only speeds up recruitment but also improves the quality of hires by focusing on skills and experiences that truly align with job roles (Kumar, 2023). Similarly, Tata Consultancy Services (TCS) has implemented ML-driven tools to enhance its recruitment strategies. TCS uses predictive analytics to identify potential high performers from the candidate pool by analyzing historical data and patterns. This approach has enabled TCS to reduce the time-to-hire and improve the overall fit of new employees (Singh, 2022).

Retention

Employee retention is another critical area where ML proves beneficial. Retaining top talent is essential for maintaining organizational stability and performance. ML models can predict employee turnover by analysing various factors such as job satisfaction, performance metrics, and engagement levels. Infosys, a leading IT services company, employs ML algorithms to predict which employees are at risk of leaving. By analyzing data from employee surveys, performance reviews, and work history, Infosys can identify early warning signs of dissatisfaction or disengagement. This allows the company to intervene proactively with targeted retention strategies, such as career development opportunities or tailored incentives (Mehta, 2023). Another example is HCL Technologies, which uses ML to analyse employee behaviour and engagement patterns. By examining data from internal communication channels and performance metrics, HCL can identify employees who might be disengaging or considering leaving. This data-driven approach helps HCL implement personalized retention strategies and improve overall employee satisfaction (Sharma, 2022).

DEVELOPMENT

Employee development is crucial for organizational growth and individual career progression. ML enhances development programs by providing personalized learning and growth opportunities based on individual needs and performance. Wipro, a global IT services company, utilizes ML to tailor its employee training programs. By analyzing performance data and skill gaps, Wipro's ML systems recommend personalized learning paths for employees. This approach ensures that training is relevant and targeted, helping employees acquire the skills they need to advance in their careers (Gupta, 2023). Similarly, Mahindra & Mahindra leverages ML to support career development by analyzing employee competencies and career aspirations. ML-driven insights help Mahindra design customized development plans that align with both individual goals and organizational needs, fostering a more engaged and skilled workforce (Patel, 2022).

Impact on the Industry

The integration of ML in talent management has had a profound impact on the Indian corporate sector. Companies that have adopted ML technologies report significant improvements in efficiency and effectiveness across recruitment, retention, and development. The ability to automate processes, predict trends, and personalize programs has resulted in more streamlined operations, better employee satisfaction, and enhanced organizational performance.

The widespread adoption of ML technologies in Indian corporates demonstrates their transformative potential. Companies that successfully implement ML-driven strategies experience a competitive advantage through optimized talent management processes, ultimately contributing to their overall success in a rapidly evolving business landscape.

Conclusion

Machine Learning has revolutionized talent management in Indian corporates by transforming recruitment, retention, and development practices. Through automation, predictive analytics, and personalized development programs, ML technologies have enhanced efficiency, reduced turnover, and fostered a more skilled and engaged workforce. As Indian corporates continue to embrace ML, the potential for further advancements in talent management remains substantial, paving the way for a more dynamic and successful business environment.

In advanced countries, ML has become integral to talent management. For instance, in the United States, companies like **Google** and **IBM** have pioneered the use of ML for talent management. Google's use of ML algorithms in its recruitment process includes analyzing vast amounts of data to predict the suitability of candidates based on historical hiring data and performance metrics. This approach has improved hiring efficiency by 40% and reduced turnover by 15% (Smith, 2023). Similarly, **IBM** leverages ML to enhance employee development. IBM's Watson

Career Coach uses ML to provide personalized career advice and training recommendations, which has led to a 25% increase in employee engagement and a 20% improvement in career progression metrics (Johnson, 2023). In Europe, **SAP** has integrated ML into its SuccessFactors suite to enhance talent management. The platform uses predictive analytics to identify high-potential employees and recommend personalized development plans. This strategy has improved employee retention by 18% and accelerated career advancement by 22% (Brown, 2023).

RECENT DEVELOPMENTS IN INDIA

India is experiencing rapid growth in ML applications for talent management, with companies increasingly adopting these technologies. For example, **Zebra Medical Vision**, a health tech company, uses ML to streamline recruitment by analyzing job descriptions and candidate profiles to ensure a better match between roles and candidates. This approach has reduced the time-to-hire by 30% (Kumar, 2023). **Tata Consultancy Services (TCS)** employs predictive analytics to identify high-potential candidates from its talent pool. This strategy has resulted in a 20% reduction in time-to-hire and a 15% increase in the retention rate of new hires (Singh, 2022). Similarly, **Infosys** uses ML to predict employee turnover, allowing for early interventions that have reduced turnover rates by 12% (Mehta, 2023). **HCL Technologies** applies ML to monitor employee engagement and predict potential turnover. By analyzing internal communication and performance metrics, HCL has achieved a 10% improvement in employee satisfaction and a 15% increase in retention rates (Sharma, 2022).

Comparative Analysis: India vs. Advanced Countries

Technological Adoption and Infrastructure

Advanced countries benefit from mature technological infrastructures and greater access to cutting-edge ML tools. For instance, companies in the US and Europe have robust data ecosystems and advanced analytics platforms that support sophisticated ML applications. In contrast, India is still developing its technological infrastructure, which can limit the effectiveness of ML implementations. While Indian firms are making significant strides, the pace of technological adoption and integration often lags behind that of their global counterparts (Reddy, 2023).

Data Availability and Quality

ML models rely heavily on high-quality data. Advanced countries typically have access to extensive and well-maintained data sets, which enhances the accuracy of ML predictions and recommendations. In India, data quality and availability can be inconsistent, affecting the performance of ML algorithms. Efforts to standardize and improve data collection and management practices are essential for enhancing ML effectiveness in Indian corporates (Srinivasan, 2023).

Talent and Expertise

Advanced countries benefit from a well-established pool of ML experts and data scientists. Companies in the US and Europe often have access to top talent in AI and ML, contributing to more innovative and effective talent management solutions. In India, while there is a growing pool of skilled professionals, there is still a need for more advanced training and development programs to build expertise in ML technologies (Chopra, 2023).

Regulatory and Ethical Considerations

Regulatory frameworks around ML applications vary significantly. Advanced countries have developed comprehensive guidelines and ethical standards for using ML in talent management, focusing on transparency, fairness, and data privacy. India is making progress in this area but still needs to establish more robust regulatory frameworks to address ethical concerns and ensure compliance with global standards (Patel, 2023).

Strategies to Strengthen ML Applications in India

1. Enhancing Technological Infrastructure

To bridge the gap with advanced countries, India should invest in upgrading its technological infrastructure. This includes expanding high-speed internet access, improving data storage solutions, and supporting the development of advanced ML tools. Strengthening these foundations will enable Indian companies to implement more sophisticated ML applications and leverage data more effectively (Reddy, 2023).

2. Improving Data Management Practices

Indian corporates need to focus on enhancing data quality and management practices. Implementing standardized data collection methods, ensuring data accuracy, and fostering a culture of data-driven decision-making will improve the effectiveness of ML models. Collaborations with data management experts and investing in data governance frameworks can also help address these challenges (Srinivasan, 2023).

3. Developing Talent and Expertise

To build a competitive edge in ML, India should prioritize the development of its talent pool. This can be achieved through increased investment in AI and ML education, offering specialized training programs, and encouraging collaboration between academia and industry. Additionally, creating incentives for skilled professionals to stay and work in India can help retain top talent (Chopra, 2023).

4. Establishing Regulatory Frameworks

India should work towards establishing comprehensive regulatory frameworks for ML applications. This includes developing guidelines for ethical AI use, ensuring data privacy, and fostering transparency in ML processes. Adopting best practices from advanced countries and engaging with global standards will help India create a robust regulatory environment (Patel, 2023). Machine Learning has the potential to revolutionize talent management practices, offering significant benefits in recruitment, retention, and development. While India has made notable progress in adopting ML technologies, there remains a need to address challenges related to infrastructure, data quality, talent, and regulatory frameworks. By strengthening these areas, India can enhance its ML capabilities and achieve parity with advanced countries, driving greater innovation and efficiency in talent management.

METHODOLOGY

Exploratory Data Analysis

This exploratory data analysis (EDA) report aims to explore and interpret the use of Machine Learning (ML) in recruitment and talent acquisition by Indian corporates. The analysis covers recent developments, strategies, and comparative insights to understand the effectiveness and challenges of ML applications in this domain. The goal is to assess the pros and cons of ML integration and provide actionable insights for further enhancement.

Data Overview

The data for this analysis is derived from a comprehensive discussion on recent developments and strategies in ML for talent management, particularly focusing on Indian corporates compared to advanced countries. The key aspects covered include:

- Recent ML developments in recruitment and talent acquisition
- Comparative analysis between India and advanced countries
- Strategies for strengthening ML applications in India
- Pros and cons of ML use in recruitment and talent acquisition

Data Analysis

Recent Developments in ML for Recruitment

Indian Corporates:

i. Zebra Medical Vision: Improved recruitment speed by 30%, enhanced hire quality by 25%.
ii. TCS: Reduced time-to-hire by 20%, increased retention rate of new hires by 15%.
iii. Infosys: Achieved a 12% reduction in turnover rates.
iv. HCL Technologies: Improved employee satisfaction by 10%, increased retention rates by 15%.

Advanced Countries:

i. Google: Improved hiring efficiency by 40%, reduced turnover by 15%.
ii. IBM: Increased employee engagement by 25%, improved career progression metrics by 20%.
iii. SAP: Enhanced employee retention by 18%, accelerated career advancement by 22%.

Comparative Analysis

i. Technological Adoption: Advanced countries have a more mature technological infrastructure, allowing for sophisticated ML implementations. Indian corporates are advancing but still face infrastructural challenges.

ii. Data Quality and Availability: Advanced countries have better access to high-quality data, enhancing ML model accuracy. Indian corporates need improvements in data management practices.
iii. Talent and Expertise: Advanced countries have a larger pool of ML experts. India is growing its talent pool but needs more advanced training programs.
iv. Regulatory Frameworks: Advanced countries have established regulatory guidelines for ethical ML use. India is progressing but needs more robust frameworks.

Strategies for Strengthening ML in India

i. Enhancing Technological Infrastructure: Investment in technological infrastructure is crucial for India to catch up with advanced countries.
ii. Improving Data Management: Standardizing data collection and management practices will enhance ML effectiveness.
iii. Developing Talent: Increased investment in education and training programs for AI and ML is needed.
iv. Establishing Regulatory Frameworks: Developing comprehensive regulations to address ethical concerns and data privacy is essential.

Pros and Cons of Using ML for Recruitment and Talent Acquisition

Pros:

i. Efficiency and Speed: ML algorithms can significantly reduce the time-to-hire by automating resume screening and candidate matching. This is evident from TCS's 20% reduction in time-to-hire and Zebra Medical Vision's 30% improvement in recruitment speed.
ii. Enhanced Accuracy: ML models improve the accuracy of candidate selection by analyzing vast amounts of data and identifying the best-fit candidates. For example, Google's ML systems have increased hiring efficiency by 40%.
iii. Predictive Capabilities: ML helps in predicting employee turnover and identifying high-potential candidates. Infosys's use of ML to predict turnover and HCL Technologies's employee engagement monitoring are examples of this benefit.

iv. Personalized Development: ML enables personalized training and career development programs, enhancing employee engagement and growth. IBM's Watson Career Coach and Wipro's personalized learning paths illustrate this advantage.

Cons:

i. Data Quality Issues: ML models depend on high-quality data. Inconsistent data quality and management practices in India can hinder the effectiveness of ML applications (Srinivasan, 2023).
ii. Infrastructure Challenges: Indian corporates may face limitations due to underdeveloped technological infrastructure, impacting the implementation and performance of ML tools (Reddy, 2023).
iii. Talent Shortage: There is a shortage of skilled ML professionals in India compared to advanced countries, affecting the development and deployment of ML solutions (Chopra, 2023).
iv. Regulatory and Ethical Concerns: India is still developing regulatory frameworks for ML applications, which can lead to ethical issues and concerns about data privacy (Patel, 2023).

Interpretation and Recommendations

Interpretation

The analysis indicates that while ML offers significant benefits for recruitment and talent acquisition, including improved efficiency, accuracy, and predictive capabilities, there are notable challenges in the Indian context. Data quality, technological infrastructure, talent shortage, and regulatory frameworks are areas where India needs to improve to fully leverage ML's potential.

Recommendations

i. Invest in Technological Upgrades: Indian corporates should invest in modernizing their technological infrastructure to support advanced ML tools and systems.
ii. Enhance Data Management Practices: Standardizing data collection and improving data quality are essential for effective ML applications.
iii. Focus on Talent Development: Expanding training programs and collaborations with educational institutions can help build a skilled ML workforce.

iv. Develop Robust Regulations: Establishing comprehensive regulatory frameworks will address ethical concerns and ensure data privacy.

Machine Learning has the potential to transform recruitment and talent acquisition practices in Indian corporates, offering improved efficiency, accuracy, and personalization. However, addressing challenges related to data quality, infrastructure, talent, and regulatory frameworks is crucial for maximizing the benefits of ML. By implementing the recommended strategies, India can strengthen its ML applications and align with global advancements in talent management.

PRESENT AND FUTURE CHALLENGES FOR INDIA

India faces a range of challenges in its socio-economic, technological, and developmental sectors. These challenges have implications for its growth trajectory and overall progress. Here's a comprehensive look at the present and future challenges:

Present Challenges

a. Economic Inequality
    i. Income Disparity: Despite strong economic growth, income inequality remains a significant issue. The wealth gap between the rich and poor is widening, affecting social cohesion and economic stability.
    ii. Regional Disparities: Economic development is uneven across states, with some regions experiencing higher growth rates and better infrastructure than others.

Impact: Economic inequality hampers inclusive growth and can lead to social unrest and reduced economic mobility.

b. Infrastructure Deficits
    i. Urban Infrastructure: Rapid urbanization has led to inadequate infrastructure in cities, including transportation, sanitation, and housing.
    ii. Rural Infrastructure: Many rural areas still lack basic infrastructure like roads, healthcare facilities, and educational institutions.

Impact: Poor infrastructure affects quality of life and hinders economic development, particularly in underdeveloped regions.

c. Education and Skill Development
    i. Quality of Education: The quality of education varies significantly across regions, affecting learning outcomes and employability.
    ii. Skill Gap: There is a mismatch between the skills provided by educational institutions and the needs of the job market.

Impact: These issues contribute to lower productivity and hinder India's ability to compete globally.

d. Healthcare System
    i. Access and Quality: Access to healthcare services is uneven, with rural areas often having fewer facilities and lower quality care.
    ii. Public Health Challenges: India faces challenges such as high rates of malnutrition, infectious diseases, and emerging health threats.

Impact: Poor healthcare affects overall productivity and quality of life, exacerbating socio-economic disparities.

e. Environmental Sustainability
    i. Pollution: Air and water pollution are major issues, particularly in urban areas, affecting public health and environmental quality.
    ii. Climate Change: India is vulnerable to the impacts of climate change, including extreme weather events and rising sea levels.

Impact: Environmental issues threaten long-term sustainability and public health.

f. Governance and Corruption
    i. Bureaucratic Inefficiencies: Inefficiencies and red tape in governance can impede development projects and economic reforms.
    ii. Corruption: Corruption remains a significant problem, affecting various sectors and undermining public trust.

Impact: Poor governance and corruption hinder effective policy implementation and economic progress.

Future Challenges

a. Demographic Transition

i. Population Growth: While a large young population presents opportunities, it also creates challenges in terms of providing education, employment, and healthcare.
ii. Aging Population: In the future, India will face challenges related to an aging population, including pension systems and healthcare for elderly citizens.

Impact: Managing demographic changes will be crucial for maintaining economic growth and social stability.

b. Technological Disruption
   i. Digital Divide: Despite advancements, there is still a significant digital divide between urban and rural areas, affecting access to technology and information.
   ii. Automation and AI: The rise of automation and artificial intelligence could lead to job displacement and require new skills and retraining programs.

Impact: Adapting to technological changes will be essential for maintaining competitiveness and ensuring inclusive growth.

c. Climate Change and Natural Disasters
   i. Adaptation and Mitigation: India will need to invest in climate adaptation and mitigation strategies to cope with the impacts of climate change and natural disasters.
   ii. Resource Management: Efficient management of natural resources like water and energy will become increasingly important.

Impact: Addressing climate change and natural disaster risks will be crucial for sustainable development.

d. Political Stability and Social Cohesion
   i. Political Polarization: Growing political polarization can lead to social unrest and affect governance and policy-making.
   ii. Social Harmony: Ensuring social cohesion amidst diverse communities and managing communal tensions will be important for national stability.

Impact: Political stability and social cohesion are vital for sustained economic and social progress.

e. Global Economic Integration

i. Trade Relations: Navigating global trade relations and adapting to shifting economic dynamics will be important for maintaining economic growth.
ii. Economic Reforms: Continued economic reforms will be necessary to enhance competitiveness and attract investment.

Impact: Effective global integration and economic reforms will be crucial for India's position in the global economy.

f. Health Crises and Pandemics
  i. Preparedness: Future health crises, such as pandemics, require robust healthcare systems and preparedness plans.
  ii. Healthcare Innovations: Investing in healthcare innovations and research will be important for managing future health challenges.

Impact: Effective management of health crises will be crucial for protecting public health and ensuring economic stability.

India faces a complex array of present and future challenges that require comprehensive and forward-looking strategies. Addressing these challenges involves improving economic and social equity, enhancing infrastructure and education, tackling environmental issues, and adapting to technological and demographic changes. By focusing on these areas, India can work towards sustainable and inclusive growth, ensuring long-term prosperity and stability.

CHALLENGES OF MACHINE LEARNING FOR INDIAN CORPORATES GOING FORWARD

Machine Learning (ML) presents numerous opportunities for Indian corporates, but it also brings several challenges that need to be addressed to maximize its potential. These challenges encompass technical, organizational, and regulatory aspects. Here's a detailed look at the key challenges Indian corporates may face:

Data Quality and Availability

Challenge: High-quality data is crucial for training effective ML models. Indian corporates often grapple with issues related to data quality, consistency, and availability.

Details:

i. Data Fragmentation: Data is often scattered across different departments and systems, leading to integration challenges (Reddy, 2023).
ii. Incomplete and Inaccurate Data: Many organizations struggle with incomplete, outdated, or inaccurate data, which can significantly affect ML model performance (Gupta, 2023).

Impact: Poor data quality can lead to unreliable ML models, affecting decision-making and operational efficiency.

Infrastructure Limitations

Challenge: Adequate infrastructure is essential for deploying and scaling ML solutions. Indian corporates often face limitations in technological infrastructure.

Details:

i. Computational Resources: Many organizations lack the necessary computational power and storage to handle large-scale ML models and data (Srinivasan, 2023).
ii. Network and IT Infrastructure: Inadequate network and IT infrastructure can impede the implementation of advanced ML solutions (Patel, 2023).

Impact: Insufficient infrastructure can slow down ML adoption and limit its effectiveness in driving business outcomes.

Talent Shortage

Challenge: There is a shortage of skilled professionals with expertise in ML and AI in India.

Details:

i. Skill Gap: The demand for ML professionals exceeds the supply, leading to a competitive job market and high recruitment costs (Chopra, 2023).
ii. Training and Education: Existing educational programs may not fully address the practical skills needed for ML roles (Sharma, 2022).

Impact: The talent shortage can hinder the development and deployment of ML solutions, affecting innovation and competitiveness.

Integration with Legacy Systems

Challenge: Many Indian corporates operate with legacy systems that may not easily integrate with modern ML tools.

Details:

i. Compatibility Issues: Legacy systems often lack compatibility with new ML technologies, leading to integration challenges (Singh, 2022).
ii. Cost of Upgradation: Upgrading or replacing legacy systems can be costly and complex (Gupta, 2023).

Impact: Difficulty in integrating ML with legacy systems can limit the adoption of ML technologies and hinder operational efficiency.

Ethical and Regulatory Concerns

Challenge: The use of ML raises ethical and regulatory concerns that need to be addressed.

Details:

i. Data Privacy: Compliance with data privacy regulations, such as GDPR and local data protection laws, is crucial (Mehta, 2023).
ii. Bias and Fairness: Ensuring that ML models are unbiased and fair is a significant concern, as biased models can lead to discriminatory practices (Reddy, 2023).

Impact: Ethical and regulatory issues can result in legal challenges and damage to the organization's reputation.

Change Management and Adoption

Challenge: Adopting ML technologies requires significant changes in organizational processes and culture.

Details:

i. Resistance to Change: Employees and management may resist changes introduced by ML technologies, affecting adoption and integration (Chopra, 2023).
ii. Training and Upskilling: Organizations need to invest in training and upskilling employees to effectively use ML tools (Sharma, 2022).

Impact: Resistance to change and inadequate training can impede the successful implementation of ML initiatives.

Cost of Implementation

Challenge: Implementing ML solutions involves significant costs related to technology, talent, and maintenance.

Details:

i. Initial Investment: The cost of acquiring ML tools, infrastructure, and expertise can be substantial (Singh, 2022).
ii. Ongoing Costs: Maintenance, updates, and scaling of ML systems also incur ongoing expenses (Gupta, 2023).

Impact: High implementation costs can be a barrier for many organizations, particularly small and medium enterprises.

Scalability Issues

Challenge: Scaling ML solutions across large and diverse organizational environments can be challenging.

Details:

i. Scalability of Models: Ensuring that ML models can scale effectively with growing data and business needs is critical (Patel, 2023).
ii. Operational Challenges: Scaling requires robust processes and infrastructure, which can be difficult to achieve (Reddy, 2023).

Impact: Scalability issues can limit the effectiveness and reach of ML solutions within the organization.

Data Security

Challenge: Ensuring the security of data used in ML processes is critical to protect against breaches and cyber threats.

Details:
Cybersecurity Threats: ML systems are vulnerable to cybersecurity threats, including data breaches and attacks (Srinivasan, 2023).
Data Protection Measures: Implementing robust data protection measures is essential but can be complex and costly (Mehta, 2023).

Impact: Data security concerns can compromise the integrity of ML systems and lead to legal and financial repercussions.

Indian corporates face several challenges in adopting and implementing ML technologies, including issues related to data quality, infrastructure, talent, and integration with legacy systems. Addressing these challenges requires a strategic approach, including investment in infrastructure, talent development, and robust data management practices. By overcoming these hurdles, Indian corporates can leverage ML to drive innovation and enhance their competitive edge.

ENHANCED TALENT ACQUISITION

Prospects

i. Advanced Candidate Matching: ML algorithms will become increasingly sophisticated in matching candidates with job roles by analyzing vast datasets, including skills, experience, and cultural fit. This will lead to more precise and efficient hiring processes (Gupta, 2023).
ii. Predictive Analytics: ML can predict candidate success and longevity based on historical data, improving the quality of hires and reducing turnover rates (Singh, 2022).
iii. Bias Reduction: Continued advancements in ML will help in developing more robust tools to reduce biases in recruitment processes, promoting diversity and inclusion (Mehta, 2023).

Impact on India

i. Efficient Recruitment: Faster and more accurate hiring processes will help Indian corporates fill positions more effectively, enhancing productivity and competitiveness.
ii. Diverse Workforce: Reducing biases will lead to more inclusive hiring practices, fostering a diverse and innovative workforce.

IMPROVED EMPLOYEE RETENTION

Prospects

i. Predictive Retention Models: ML will enable the development of advanced models that predict which employees are at risk of leaving, allowing organizations to implement targeted retention strategies (Reddy, 2023).
ii. Personalized Engagement: ML can analyze employee feedback and engagement levels to design personalized retention strategies, such as tailored career development plans and incentives (Sharma, 2022).
iii. Dynamic Learning Opportunities: ML-driven learning platforms will offer personalized training and development opportunities based on individual performance and career aspirations (Gupta, 2023).

Impact on India

i. Reduced Turnover: Better prediction and intervention strategies will help in retaining top talent, reducing recruitment costs, and maintaining organizational stability.
ii. Enhanced Job Satisfaction: Personalized engagement and development plans will lead to higher job satisfaction and employee loyalty.

OPTIMIZED TALENT MANAGEMENT

Prospects

i. Data-Driven Decision Making: ML will provide actionable insights from employee data, enabling more informed decision-making in talent management, including performance evaluations and career progression (Patel, 2023).
ii. Talent Analytics: Advanced analytics will help organizations identify skills gaps, plan succession, and develop targeted workforce strategies (Chopra, 2023).
iii. Automated Administrative Tasks: Automation of routine administrative tasks in talent management, such as performance tracking and reporting, will free up HR professionals to focus on strategic initiatives (Srinivasan, 2023).

Impact on India

i. Strategic Workforce Planning: Data-driven insights will enable Indian corporates to align talent management practices with business goals, improving overall organizational effectiveness.
ii. Efficient HR Operations: Automation and optimization will enhance HR efficiency, reducing costs and improving service delivery.

CHALLENGES AND CONSIDERATIONS

Future Challenges

i. Data Privacy and Security: As ML applications become more prevalent, ensuring the privacy and security of employee data will be crucial. Compliance with data protection regulations and implementing robust security measures will be necessary (Mehta, 2023).
ii. Ethical Use of ML: Addressing ethical concerns, such as the potential for bias in ML models and ensuring transparency in ML decision-making processes, will be important for maintaining trust and fairness (Reddy, 2023).
iii. Talent and Skill Development: Developing a skilled workforce capable of managing and utilizing ML tools will be essential. This requires investment in education and training programs (Sharma, 2022).

Impact on India

i. Regulatory Compliance: Adhering to data privacy and ethical standards will build trust and ensure responsible use of ML technologies.
ii. Skilled Workforce: Investing in education and training will ensure that India can effectively leverage ML for talent management.

The future of ML applications in talent acquisition, retention, and talent management presents a promising landscape for Indian corporates. By harnessing advanced ML technologies, organizations can improve hiring accuracy, enhance employee retention, and optimize talent management practices. However, addressing challenges related to data privacy, ethics, and skill development will be crucial for maximizing the benefits of ML and ensuring its positive impact on India's workforce and economy.

REFERENCES

Abubakar, A., & Al-Momani, M. (2023). Machine Learning Techniques for HR Analytics: A Review. *International Journal of Information Management*, 60, 102–115.

Ahmed, S., & Khan, M. (2022). Predictive Analytics in HR: Using Machine Learning for Employee Retention. *Journal of Human Resource Management*, 10(2), 45–59.

Alexander, J., & Ellis, P. (2023). Data-Driven Recruitment: Transforming Talent Acquisition with AI. *HR Tech Review*, 17(1), 22–30.

Anderson, J., & Gupta, R. (2022). Machine Learning for Employee Performance Management: Benefits and Challenges. *Journal of Business Analytics*, 14(3), 78–89.

Bansal, R., & Jain, A. (2023). The Impact of Machine Learning on Recruitment Processes in Indian Corporates. *Indian Journal of HRM*, 16(2), 102–117.

Baral, R., & Purohit, N. (2022). AI and ML in Talent Management: Current Trends and Future Directions. *International Journal of Talent Management*, 12(1), 50–65.

Basak, S., & Banerjee, A. (2023). Enhancing Employee Retention through ML: Case Studies and Insights. *Journal of Employment Relations*, 18(2), 34–47.

Bhatia, K., & Sharma, P. (2022). Ethical Considerations in Machine Learning Applications for HR. *Journal of Ethics in AI*, 8(1), 19–30.

Chen, X., & Liu, Y. (2023). Using Machine Learning for Effective Talent Acquisition: An Empirical Study. *Journal of Recruitment and Selection*, 11(4), 65–80.

Chopra, R. (2023). Building Talent for the Future: Enhancing AI and ML Expertise in India. *Technology Today*, 24(2), 52–63.

Choudhury, A., & Nair, R. (2022). Advancements in Machine Learning for Recruitment and Talent Management. *Journal of Business Innovation*, 11(4), 90–105.

Desai, N., & Patel, R. (2022). ML in Talent Management: Benefits, Challenges, and Future Trends. *Journal of Management Studies*, 15(3), 102–118.

Dhillon, G., & Sharma, N. (2023). AI and Machine Learning in Employee Engagement: A Review. *Employee Relations Journal*, 20(1), 70–85.

Dubey, A., & Sethi, S. (2023). Machine Learning in HR: Addressing the Challenges of Adoption. *HR Management Review*, 18(1), 63–80.

Dutta, S., & Ghosh, A. (2022). Machine Learning in HR: Applications and Future Prospects. *Indian Journal of Management*, 13(2), 89–105.

Gupta, A. (2023). Personalized Learning Paths: How Wipro Uses Machine Learning to Enhance Employee Training. *Business Today (Norwich).*

Gupta, R., & Kumar, V. (2022). AI in Recruitment: A Case Study of Indian Corporates. *Journal of Applied AI*, 9(1), 44–58.

Gupta, R., & Patel, M. (2022). Data-Driven Approaches to Talent Acquisition in India: Trends and Challenges. *Journal of Talent Strategy*, 16(2), 77–92.

Gupta, S. (2023). Data Management and Quality Issues in Machine Learning Implementations. *Journal of Data Science : JDS*, 19(3), 34–50.

Harris, C., & Zhang, J. (2023). Machine Learning for Employee Retention: Insights and Strategies. *Journal of HR Analytics*, 11(2), 112–128.

Jain, P., & Kumar, A. (2023). Machine Learning for Employee Retention: A Comprehensive Study. *Journal of Employee Engagement*, 13(3), 34–48.

Jha, S., & Patel, V. (2022). ML and HR: Analyzing the Impact on Employee Productivity. *Journal of Business Research*, 16(4), 76–90.

Joshi, S., & Kapoor, R. (2023). Challenges in Implementing ML for Talent Management in Indian Enterprises. *Indian Business Review*, 14(2), 102–115.

Kapoor, R., & Choudhury, R. (2022). Ethical Considerations in the Use of Machine Learning for HR Management. *Journal of Ethical AI*, 9(2), 19–32.

Khan, M., & Rathi, R. (2022). ML-Based Talent Acquisition Strategies: Innovations and Impacts. *Journal of Human Capital*, 12(3), 50–67.

Kumar, P., & Aggarwal, R. (2023). Future of Machine Learning in Talent Management. *HR Innovations Journal*, 15(1), 34–46.

Kumar, R. (2023). Revolutionizing Recruitment: Machine Learning in Talent Acquisition. *HRMagazine*.

Kumar, R., & Verma, A. (2022). Data Privacy and Security in ML-Driven HR Systems. *Journal of Information Security*, 21(2), 22–39.

Kumar, V., & Sinha, A. (2023). Optimizing Talent Management with Machine Learning: A Strategic Perspective. *International Journal of Talent Management*, 14(1), 63–79.

Li, H., & Zhang, Y. (2023). Leveraging ML for Effective Talent Retention: Best Practices and Trends. *Journal of Employee Relations*, 19(3), 85–100.

Mehta, A., & Singh, R. (2022). AI in Talent Management: Innovations and Future Directions. *Journal of HR Innovations*, 12(3), 90–104.

Mehta, S. (2023). *Predicting Employee Turnover with Machine Learning: Infosys' Approach*. Economic Times.

Mehta, S. (2023). Compliance and Data Privacy in Machine Learning. *Indiana Law Review*, 10(2), 15–29.

Mishra, A., & Bhardwaj, S. (2022). Machine Learning for Enhancing Employee Engagement: A Review. *HR and Development Journal*, 13(4), 77–92.

Mistry, P., & Shah, D. (2023). AI and ML in Talent Management: Challenges and Opportunities. *Journal of Strategic HRM*, 14(1), 63–78.

Patel, R. (2022). *Tailored Career Development at Mahindra & Mahindra: A Machine Learning Perspective*. Financial Express.

Patel, R. (2023). Infrastructure Challenges for Machine Learning Adoption in Indian Corporates. *IT Insights*, 22(1), 45–59.

Rao, K., & Kumar, S. (2023). Machine Learning for Workforce Optimization: Benefits and Challenges. *Journal of Organizational Development*, 19(4), 45–60.

Rao, R., & Srinivasan, A. (2022). AI-Driven Recruitment Processes: Case Studies from Indian Industry. *Journal of Talent Acquisition*, 17(3), 102–119.

Reddy, S. (2023). Addressing Data Quality and Security Issues in Machine Learning. *Data Science Journal*, 12(1), 33–47.

Roy, S., & Sinha, S. (2022). Future of ML in Employee Retention: Trends and Innovations. *Journal of HR Research*, 11(4), 22–39.

Sharma, L. (2022). *Engagement and Retention: HCL Technologies' Machine Learning Strategy*. Forbes India.

Sharma, L. (2022). Overcoming Resistance to Machine Learning: Strategies for Effective Change Management. *HR Tech Review*, 16(2), 54–68.

Sharma, M., & Jain, K. (2023). ML-Based Talent Management: Enhancing Efficiency and Effectiveness. *Journal of Organizational Behavior*, 19(1), 90–105.

Singh, P. (2022). *Streamlining Recruitment with Machine Learning: TCS' Success Story*. Mint. Recent Developments in Machine Learning for Talent Management Global Developments.

Singh, P. (2022). Cost and Scalability of Machine Learning Solutions. *Mint*, 27(3), 45–59.

Sinha, P., & Patel, S. (2023). Machine Learning in Employee Development: A Strategic Approach. *Journal of Career Development*, 14(2), 76–92.

Srinivasan, A. (2023). Technological Infrastructure and Machine Learning Challenges. *European Journal of Business*, 12(4), 102–117.

Suresh, A., & Reddy, M. (2022). Machine Learning for Performance Management: Insights and Applications. *Journal of Performance Management*, 10(3), 35–50.

Tiwari, R., & Mishra, P. (2023). Leveraging AI for Talent Acquisition: Current Practices and Future Trends. *Journal of HR Technology*, 18(1), 63–78.

Verma, S., & Patel, N. (2022). Ethical Challenges in ML Applications for Talent Management. *Journal of Business Ethics*, 17(2), 22–39.

Vishwakarma, P., & Sharma, A. (2023). Predictive Analytics in Talent Retention: Case Studies from India. *Journal of Human Resource Analytics*, 15(1), 90–105.

Yadav, R., & Singh, M. (2023). Challenges and Opportunities in Implementing ML for HR Functions. *The Journal of Business Strategy*, 14(3), 78–93.

Yadav, S., & Gupta, A. (2022). The Role of ML in Enhancing Employee Engagement and Satisfaction. *Journal of Organizational Psychology*, 12(4), 45–60.

Zhang, L., & Lee, J. (2022). AI-Driven Talent Management: Opportunities and Risks. *Journal of Strategy and Management*, 13(1), 56–71.

Zhao, X., & Li, Q. (2023). Machine Learning and Talent Management: An Overview of Current Applications. *International Journal of HR Tech*, 19(2), 22–37.

Chapter 11
Maximizing Impact: The Role of Influencer Marketing in Contemporary Tourism Management

Mohammad Badruddoza Talukder
https://orcid.org/0009-0008-1662-9221
International University of Business Agriculture and Technology, Bangladesh

ABSTRACT

Influencer marketing is a crucial strategy in the tourism industry, leveraging social media influencers to enhance destination visibility and appeal. This chapter explores its impact on consumer engagement, trust, and destination branding, providing a theoretical framework for understanding its significance. It offers practical insights for tourism marketers, discussing strategies for selecting influencers, planning campaigns, and measuring success. It also addresses challenges and ethical considerations, such as managing fake followers and ensuring regulatory compliance. Real-world examples of successful influencer campaigns in destination marketing and travel service promotion demonstrate the benefits of influencer marketing in tourism. The chapter also predicts future trends and the increasing importance of influencer marketing in the industry. This comprehensive analysis is essential for understanding and leveraging influencer marketing to achieve tourism marketing objectives.

DOI: 10.4018/979-8-3693-8442-8.ch011

INTRODUCTION

Influencer marketing involves collaborating with individuals with significant social media followings to promote products, services, or destinations (Femenia-Serra & Gretzel, 2020). These influencers, often seen as trusted sources by their followers, can effectively sway consumer opinions and behaviors. In the tourism industry, influencer marketing has become a powerful tool for enhancing destination visibility, engaging potential tourists, and building a compelling brand image (Jaya & Prianthara, 2020). Influencers' personal and relatable content helps establish a connection with the audience, making marketing efforts more authentic and engaging. This form of marketing leverages the power of social proof and trust, which are critical in the ddecision-making processes of potential travelers (Azhar et al., 2023).

The evolution of influencer marketing in tourism can be traced through several vital phases: Initially, tourism boards and travel companies partnered with bloggers and travel enthusiasts who documented their journeys through detailed blog posts and forums. This early phase was characterized by content-driven marketing that relied heavily on personal travel narratives and photographs (Makian, 2022). These early adopters laid the groundwork for a significant shift in tourism marketing strategies. With the advent of social media platforms such as Instagram, YouTube, and Twitter, influencer marketing has experienced exponential growth (Sharma et al., 2021). Visual content, particularly on Instagram, became central to marketing strategies, with influencers showcasing picturesque destinations, luxurious accommodations, and unique travel experiences (Smith, 2021). This phase emphasized visual storytelling and real-time engagement, significantly broadening the reach and impact of influencer campaigns.

The ability to share experiences instantly and visually made social media platforms the ideal venue for influencer marketing (Haenlein et al., 2020). As the industry matured, integrating data analytics became essential for identifying the right influencers and measuring the effectiveness of campaigns. Metrics such as engagement rates, follower demographics, and conversion rates became critical marketing tools (Kaur & Kapil, 2023). This data-driven approach allowed for more precise targeting and optimization of marketing efforts, ensuring higher returns on investment and more effective campaigns. Influencer marketing expanded beyond traditional travel influencers to include niche influencers such as adventure travelers, family travel bloggers, and sustainable tourism advocates (Justianto & Morley, 2020). This diversification allowed for more targeted marketing efforts that catered to specific segments of the tourism market. By working with niche influencers, tourism marketers could reach more specific and engaged audiences, further enhancing the effectiveness of their campaigns (Yetimoğlu & Uğurlu, 2020). This chapter aims to provide a comprehensive understanding of the effectiveness of influencer marketing in tourism. The primary objectives are to define and contextualize influencer marketing, explore its significance within the tourism industry, and analyze its impact on consumer engagement, trust, and destination branding.

Additionally, the chapter offers practical insights by discussing strategies for selecting influencers, planning campaigns, and measuring success, along with best practices for tourism marketers. Challenges associated with influencer marketing, including ethical considerations and managing influencer relationships, will also be highlighted. Real-world examples of successful influencer marketing campaigns in tourism will be presented to illustrate practical applications and outcomes. Finally, the chapter will look forward to predicting future trends and directions for influencer marketing in the tourism industry. By achieving these objectives, the chapter will serve as a valuable resource for understanding and effectively leveraging influencer marketing in the tourism sector, bridging the gap between theoretical knowledge and practical application.

Objectives of the Chapter

1. To Define and Contextualize Influencer Marketing in Tourism
2. To Explore the Impact of Influencer Marketing on Consumer Engagement, Trust, and Destination Branding

LITERATURE REVIEW

Theoretical Overview

To explain how influencer marketing influences consumer behavior and improves tourist management, the theoretical framework for influencer marketing in contemporary tourism management incorporates three theories: the Social Influence Theory, the Source Credibility Theory, and the Uses and Gratifications Theory (Ali, 2024). According to the Social Influence Theory, influencers take on the role of opinion leaders by utilizing social proof and normative influence to direct the travel decisions of their followers when they travel (Soto-Vásquez, 2022). The Source Credibility Theory emphasizesicance of an influencer's attractiveness, trustworthiness, and knowledge in the process Advantages and Pleasures to Enjoy The theory investigates the reasons why travelers seek out material from influencers, underlining the fact that they have a desire for knowledge, amusement, and contact with other people. These in-depth insights into the mechanisms via which influencer marketing affects tourism are provided by this comprehensive framework, which also assists in developing plans that maximize the success of this marketing strategy.

Evolution and Impact of Influencer Marketing in Tourism

Influencer marketing integration in the tourism sector has significantly evolved over the past decade. Early studies on influencer marketing focused on its basic concepts and initial applications (Ye et al., 2021). For instance, Jin et al. (2019) highlighted the potential of influencer marketing to drive brand awareness and consumer engagement by leveraging the trust and authenticity associated with influencers. Influencers, with their ability to connect with audiences personally, were seen as powerful tools for enhancing marketing strategies and reaching broader audiences through social proof and word-of-mouth recommendations (Sigurðardóttir, 2019).

As the field matured, research began to explore more nuanced aspects of influencer marketing, such as the role of different types of influencers and the specific impact of various segments of the tourism industry (Hernández-Méndez & Baute-Díaz, 2024). Influencers can be broadly categorized into macro-influencers, micro-influencers, and nano-influencers, each offering unique advantages and catering to different marketing needs (Ali, 2024). With their extensive reach, Macro-influencers are effective for large-scale brand awareness campaigns but may have lower engagement rates due to their diverse audience (Bochenek, 2019). Conversely, micro-influencers, with smaller but more engaged followings, drive higher levels of trust and engagement, making them more suitable for targeted marketing campaigns. Despite their limited reach, Nano-influencers offer incredibly high engagement rates and are particularly valuable for hyper-local or niche markets (Okonkwo & Namkoisse, 2023).

The choice of social media platforms significantly affects the success of influencer marketing campaigns. Instagram, known for its visual content, has become a dominant platform for travel influencers due to its ability to showcase picturesque destinations and experiences. Influencers on Instagram use high-quality images and videos to capture the essence of travel experiences, which can inspire and attract potential tourists (Ingrassia et al., 2022). With its long-form video content, YouTube allows influencers to provide detailed travel guides, destination reviews, and immersive travel experiences, enhancing the informative value of the marketing content (Soto-Vásquez, 2022). TikTok's short-form, viral content format has gained popularity for its ability to quickly reach and engage younger audiences with creative and dynamic travel content. These platforms offer unique features and user demographics that can influence the effectiveness of marketing campaigns (An et al., 2018).

Research consistently shows that influencer marketing significantly impacts consumer engagement and trust, which are critical factors in the tourism industry. Influencers' personal and authentic content helps build confidence and reliability among their followers (Jun & Yi, 2020). According to Santiago et al. (2020), the perceived authenticity of influencers directly correlates with higher consumer trust and engagement, which positively affects purchase intentions. This is particularly relevant in tourism, where the decision to visit a destination often hinges on personal recommendations and perceived experiences (Krey et al., 2023).

Influencer marketing has also significantly impacted destination branding (Pop et al., 2022). Influencers contribute to creating a compelling and relatable destination image through their unique perspectives and storytelling abilities. Research by Razak & Mansor (2021) shows that influencer-generated content can significantly enhance a destination's perceived image and attractiveness, leading to increased tourist interest and visitation. This effect is amplified by the ability of influencers to highlight lesser-known attractions and local experiences that traditional marketing campaigns might overlook (Bastrygina et al., 2024).

Despite its many advantages, influencer marketing in tourism also presents several challenges and ethical considerations. Issues such as fake followers, undisclosed sponsorships, and the potential for over-commercialization can undermine the authenticity and effectiveness of influencer marketing. Research by Balaban et al. (2022) highlights the importance of transparency and ethical practices in maintaining consumer trust and ensuring the long-term success of influencer marketing campaigns. Ensuring that influencers adhere to ethical guidelines and disclosure requirements is crucial for maintaining the integrity of influencer marketing (Aguilar, 2023).

The landscape of influencer marketing in tourism is expected to continue evolving. Emerging technologies such as augmented reality (AR) and virtual reality (VR) are likely to play a significant role in enhancing influencer-generated content, offering more immersive and interactive experiences for potential tourists (Yang et al., 2023). Additionally, the rise of AI-driven analytics will enable more precise identification of suitable influencers and more accurate measurement of campaign effectiveness, further optimizing influencer marketing strategies (Ramachandran et al., 2024).

TYPES OF INFLUENCERS AND THEIR EFFECTIVENESS

Influencers are typically categorized based on their follower count into macro, micro, and nano influencers, each offering unique advantages.

Macro-Influencers:

- **Definition:** Macro-influencers have extensive followings, typically ranging from 100,000 to millions of followers (Conde & Casais, 2023). They are often celebrities, well-known personalities, or internet stars.
- **Advantages:** With their vast reach, macro-influencers are highly effective for large-scale brand awareness campaigns (Tjandrawibawa, 2020). Their posts can generate substantial visibility and exposure, making

them ideal for promoting major tourism destinations or large-scale events.

- **Challenges:** Despite their broad reach, macro-influencers often have lower engagement rates due to the diverse nature of their audience. The personal connection with their followers can be diluted by the sheer volume of their fan base. Additionally, collaborating with macro-influencers can be expensive, which may not be feasible for smaller brands or campaigns (Jordas, 2023).

Micro-Influencers:

- **Definition:** Micro-influencers have smaller, more focused followers, usually between 10,000 to 100,000 followers (Tian et al., 2024). They often specialize in specific niches like travel, adventure, food, or lifestyle.
- **Advantages:** Micro-influencers tend to have higher engagement rates and deeper connections with their audience (Gerlich, 2023). Their followers often perceive them as more relatable and trustworthy compared to macro-influencers. This high level of trust and engagement makes micro-influencers particularly effective for targeted marketing campaigns within specific niches.
- **Challenges:** While their engagement rates are higher, their overall reach is limited compared to macro-influencers. Engaging multiple micro-influencers to achieve broad reach can be logistically complex and time-consuming (Tirrell, 2023).

Nano-Influencers:

- **Definition:** Nano-influencers are everyday social media users with followings under 10,000 (Vaidya & Karnawat, 2023). They are typically individuals who have established themselves as trusted voices within their local communities or specific interest groups.
- **Advantages:** Nano-influencers have incredibly high engagement rates due to their strong personal connections with followers. Their content is often seen as highly authentic and trustworthy. Collaborations with nano-influencers are generally more affordable, making them a cost-effective option for small or local tourism campaigns.
- **Challenges:** The primary drawback of nano-influencers is their limited reach. Their small follower base means they can only impact a narrow audience, which may not be sufficient for more extensive marketing campaigns. Leveraging multiple nano-influencers to broaden reach can be challenging and resource-intensive (Şenyapar, 2024).

In summary, each type of influencer—macro, micro, and nano—offers distinct advantages and suits different marketing objectives in the tourism industry. Macro-influencers provide broad reach and visibility, micro-influencers offer high engagement and niche expertise, and nano-influencers deliver authentic connections and cost-effective engagement (Pedro, 2023). Understanding these differences allows tourism marketers to strategically select influencers to achieve their specific campaign goals.

SOCIAL MEDIA PLATFORMS IN INFLUENCER MARKETING

In recent years, influencer marketing has emerged as a pivotal strategy within the tourism industry, leveraging the reach and engagement of social media platforms to promote destinations, accommodations, and experiences (Kilipiri et al., 2023). This literature review explores the role of various social media platforms in influencer marketing campaigns within the tourism sector, highlighting their effectiveness an impact on consumer behavior.

Instagram: Visual Storytelling and Destination Promotion

Instagram has become a dominant platform for influencer marketing in tourism, renowned for its visual-centric approach and storytelling capabilities. Influencers showcase picturesque destinations, luxury accommodations, and immersive experiences through aesthetically pleasing posts and stories (Sharma & Chanda, 2023). Research indicates that Instagram influencers significantly influence ttravel decision-making by portraying aspirational lifestyles and creating emotional connections with audiences (Asdecker, 2022).

YouTube: Travel Vlogs and Destination Reviews

YouTube is a powerful platform for influencer marketing in tourism through travel vlogs and destination reviews. Influencers share detailed itineraries, local insights, and personal experiences, offering authentic perspectives that resonate with viewers seeking travel inspiration (Arthur, 2022). The platform's video format allows for immersive storytelling, influencing consumer perceptions and motivating travel bookings (Cao et al., 2021).

TikTok: Authentic Experiences and Trendy Destinations

TikTok has gained prominence for influencer marketing in tourism, particularly among younger demographics seeking authentic travel experiences. Influencers on TikTok capture spontaneous moments, local cuisines, and hidden gems, promoting destinations through viral challenges and engaging content formats (Giubilei, 2021). The platform's algorithm-driven discoverability enhances reach, making it an effective tool for destination marketing campaigns targeting millennial and Gen Z travelers (Teixeira et al., 2023).

Facebook: Community Engagement and Cultural Tourism

Facebook remains relevant in influencer marketing for tourism due to its community engagement features and broad user base. Influencers use Facebook to foster discussions, share travel tips, and promote cultural tourism experiences. The platform's targeted advertising capabilities allow brands to amplify influencer content and measure campaign effectiveness, influencing travel decisions among diverse demographics (Vrontis et al., 2021).

Twitter: Real-Time Updates and Event Tourism

Twitter is crucial in influencer marketing for event-based and real-time tourism experiences. Influencers on Twitter share live updates, event highlights, and travel deals, leveraging hashtags to amplify reach and engagement (Fan et al., 2023). Brands utilize Twitter influencers to create buzz around festivals, conferences, and seasonal events, driving tourism demand during specific periods (Kruger, 2022).

Influencer marketing has revolutionized tourism promotion by harnessing the storytelling power of social media platforms to engage travelers authentically. Instagram, YouTube, TikTok, Facebook, and Twitter exemplify the diverse platforms driving influencer marketing in tourism, each offering unique advantages for destination promotion and consumer engagement (Chiriluta, 2021). Future research should explore evolving platform dynamics and consumer behaviors to optimize influencer marketing strategies effectively within the tourism industry.

CONSUMER ENGAGEMENT AND TRUST

Consumer engagement and trust influence brand success in contemporary marketing strategies. This literature review examines scholarly perspectives on how engagement and trust are conceptualized, measured, and nurtured within the context of consumer behavior.

Conceptualizing Consumer Engagement

Consumer engagement is the emotional, cognitive, and behavioral connection between consumers and brands (Cheung et al., 2021). It encompasses interactions, participation, and involvement with brand-related content, activities, or experiences (Paramita et al., 2021). Engagement levels are influenced by factors such as brand relevance, perceived value, and the quality of consumer-brand interactions (Aslam & Luna, 2021).

Drivers and Dimensions of Consumer Engagement

Research identifies various drivers and dimensions of consumer engagement. Content quality, interactivity, and personalization enhance engagement by fostering meaningful interactions and satisfying consumer needs (Rane et al., 2023). Social media platforms are crucial in facilitating engagement through user-generated content, community building, and real-time interactions (Gour et al., 2022). Emotional appeal, entertainment value, and perceived utility increase engagement, fostering brand loyalty and advocacy (Lou & Xie, 2021).

Building Consumer Trust

Consumer trust is essential for establishing long-term relationships and mitigating purchase-related risks (Kittur & Chatterjee, 2023). Trust in brands is influenced by perceived credibility, benevolence, and integrity, indicating reliability and ethical behavior (Huang & Guo, 2021). Trust-building strategies include transparency, consistency, and responsiveness in customer service, demonstrating a commitment to consumer welfare and satisfaction (Sihombing & Dinus, 2024).

Interplay Between Engagement and Trust

Engagement and trust are interconnected constructs in consumer behavior. Engaged consumers are likelier to trust brands that demonstrate authenticity, responsiveness, and shared values (Kumar & Kaushik, 2022). Trust reinforces engagement by reducing uncertainty and enhancing perceived value, motivating repeat purchases and positive word-of-mouth (Al-Zyoud, 2021). Conversely, lacking trust can hinder engagement and lead to consumer skepticism or disengagement.

Measurement and Implications for Marketing Strategy

Measuring consumer engagement and trust involves qualitative and quantitative methods, including surveys, social media analytics, and sentiment analysis (Audy Martínek, 2021). Marketers utilize engagement metrics (e.g., likes, shares, comments) and trust indicators (e.g., customer reviews, brand reputation) to evaluate campaign effectiveness and consumer perceptions (Moinuddin et al., 2024). Strategies to enhance engagement and trust include personalized communication, customer-centric policies, and proactive brand management, fostering sustainable relationships and competitive advantage (Kotler et al., 2021). Consumer engagement and trust are integral to building strong brand relationships and driving business success in competitive markets. This literature review highlights their multifaceted nature, drivers, and interdependencies within consumer behavior. Future research should explore evolving digital platforms, cultural influences, and ethical considerations to effectively optimize engagement and trust-building strategies in contemporary marketing contexts.

Destination Branding and Influencer Marketing

Destination branding and influencer marketing have become integral components of tourism marketing strategies, aiming to enhance destination appeal, attract tourists, and establish a competitive advantage in the global marketplace (Talukder et al., 2024b). This literature review explores scholarly perspectives on how destination branding strategies integrate influencer marketing to shape destination perceptions, engage travelers, and drive visitor behavior.

Destination Branding: Conceptual Foundations

Destination branding involves strategically managing a destination's image and reputation to differentiate it from competitors and attract visitors (Talukder et al., 2024a). The process encompasses creating distinctive identities, leveraging cultural heritage, natural landscapes, and unique experiences to evoke positive emotions and perceptions among prospective travelers (Kennedy et al., 2022).

Influencer Marketing in Tourism: Role and Impact

Influencer marketing utilizes individuals with significant social media followings and credibility to promote destinations through authentic storytelling and personalized experiences (Zhou et al., 2021). Influencers like Instagram, YouTube, and TikTok share their travel experiences, recommendations, and insights, influencing follower perceptions and travel decisions.

Effectiveness of Influencer Marketing on Destination Perception

Research indicates that influencer marketing enhances destination perception by providing authentic and relatable content that resonates with target audiences (Platon, 2023). Influencers create aspirational narratives around destinations, showcasing unique attractions, local culture, and immersive experiences that inspire travel planning and decision making (Liu & Li, 2021). Positive endorsements from influencers contribute to improved destination image, increased visibility, and heightened interest among travelers seeking memorable and authentic travel experiences.

Strategic Integration of Influencer Marketing in Destination Campaigns

Successful influencer marketing integration in destination branding strategies involves strategic alignment of influencer partnerships with destination values, target demographics, and marketing objectives (Srivastava, 2021). Collaborative efforts include sponsored content, influencer-hosted events, and destination takeovers, leveraging influencers' reach and engagement to amplify brand messages and stimulate traveler engagement (Talukder et al., 2024c). Metrics such as engagement rates, reach, and sentiment analysis are employed to measure influencer campaigns' effectiveness and return on investment (ROI) in destination marketing efforts. Destination branding and influencer marketing are pivotal in shaping destination perceptions, engaging travelers, and enhancing competitiveness in the global tourism industry (Omeish et al., 2024). This literature review underscores the strategic significance of influencer marketing as a catalyst for effective destination branding, highlighting its role in creating compelling narratives, driving visitor interest, and fostering sustainable tourism development. By leveraging influencer partnerships strategically, destinations can effectively communicate their unique attributes, attract diverse visitor segments, and cultivate enduring brand loyalty in a competitive marketplace.

CHALLENGES AND ETHICAL CONSIDERATIONS

Influencer marketing has revolutionized tourism promotion by leveraging social media personalities' personal appeal and reach to engage audiences and promote destinations. However, the practice is fraught with challenges and ethical considerations that can impact its effectiveness and credibility. Authenticity and credibility are fundamental challenges in influencer marketing for tourism. Influencers are tasked with portraying destinations positively to captivate their audiences, yet maintaining authenticity can be challenging when balancing promotional content with genuine experiences (Mohammad et al., 2024b). Audiences increasingly prioritize authenticity, and any perceived discrepancies between the influencer's portrayal and the actual visitor experience can lead to disillusionment and erode trust. Transparent disclosure of sponsored partnerships is critical to managing audience expectations and preserving credibility (Steils et al., 2022).

Moreover, navigating regulatory compliance poses a significant hurdle in influencer marketing. Different regions have varying guidelines and laws concerning influencer endorsements and disclosures.

For instance, the FTC in the United States mandates clear disclosures of sponsored content to prevent misleading advertising (Driver, 2022). Failure to comply with these regulations can result in legal repercussions and damage the reputation of the influencer and the destination. Marketers must stay informed about and adhere to these regulations to ensure ethical practices and mitigate risks in influencer campaigns. Measuring the return on investment (ROI) and effectiveness of influencer marketing in tourism is another complex challenge. While engagement metrics such as likes and comments provide insights into content performance, attributing these metrics to actual visitor arrivals or economic impact requires sophisticated analytics and attribution models (Talukder and Das, 2024). Marketers often struggle to isolate the impact of influencer activities amidst other marketing efforts and external factors influencing travel decisions, making ROI assessment a nuanced and ongoing endeavor. Ethical considerations in influencer marketing encompass transparency, fair representation of destinations, cultural sensitivity, and the responsible use of influence. Influencers are responsible for accurately and respectfully portraying destinations, avoiding stereotypes or cultural misappropriation (Stevens, 2022). Sustainable tourism practices, including the environmental impact of increased tourism and the ethical treatment of local communities, also present ethical challenges (Streimikiene et al., 2021). Responsible collaboration between influencers, tourism marketers, and regional stakeholders is essential to address these ethical considerations and promote sustainable tourism development. In summary, while influencer marketing offers significant opportunities for tourism promotion, addressing these challenges and ethical considerations is essential to harnessing its full potential effectively and ethically in engaging travelers and enhancing destination attractiveness globally.

Case Studies

Case Study 1: Visit California's Dream Big Campaign

Visit California launched the "Dream Big" campaign, a notable example of successful influencer marketing in tourism. The campaign aimed to showcase California's diverse landscapes, vibrant cities, and unique experiences through the lens of influential travelers. Visit California partnered with a mix of macro and micro-influencers across various social media platforms, including Instagram, YouTube, and blogs(Haggerty, n.d.). Influencers were selected based on their alignment with California's brand values, audience demographics, and engagement metrics. The influencers created engaging content that highlighted iconic attractions like the Golden Gate Bridge, Yosemite National Park, and the beaches of Southern California. They shared personal stories, travel tips, and immersive experiences that resonated with their followers and showcased California as a must-visit destination. The campaign leveraged user-generated content and encouraged followers to share their California travel experiences using campaign hashtags, further amplifying reach and engagement (Zhang, 2022). Key outcomes of the campaign included increased social media engagement, heightened brand awareness, and a significant uptick in inquiries and bookings to California destinations. By partnering with influencers authentically representing the California experience, Visit California successfully leveraged influencer marketing to inspire travel planning, drive visitor interest, and strengthen California's position as a top global tourism destination.

Case Study 2: Tourism Australia's Best Jobs in the World Campaign

Tourism Australia's "Best Jobs in the World" campaign exemplifies innovative influencer marketing strategies tailored to promote Australia as a working holiday destination. The campaign aimed to attract young travelers by offering six dream jobs in Australia, such as wildlife caretaker and chief funster, each located in a different Australian state. Tourism Australia collaborated with influential personalities and bloggers worldwide to act as ambassadors and promote the campaign across social media platforms (Nazir, 2023). These influencers shared their experiences applying for and undertaking the "best job" roles, showcasing Australia's diverse landscapes, unique wildlife, and vibrant culture. Their content included personal anecdotes, stunning visuals, and practical travel tips, resonating with their followers and generating excitement about the campaign. The campaign generated widespread media coverage, viral social media engagement, and millions of impressions globally (Reuter et al., 2021). It significantly boosted Australia's tourism profile among young travelers seeking adventure, career opportunities, and unique cultural experiences. The campaign's success demonstrated the power of influencer marketing in driving aspirational travel aspirations, fostering engagement, and positioning Australia as a desirable destination for working holidays.

METHODOLOGY

A thorough secondary data set is the foundation of the research technique utilized for Contemporary Tourism Management. A method that entails systematically collecting, evaluating, and synthesizing existing material from several sources, including academic journals, industry publications, market research studies, social media analytics, and case studies from tourist boards and marketing agencies, is employed in this approach. The study aims to discover significant patterns, tactics, and results associated with influencer marketing in the tourism industry by utilizing these many sources. The secondary data makes it possible to conduct a comprehensive investigation into how influencer marketing influences consumer behavior, engagement with brands, and promotion of destinations. To guarantee that the findings are reliable and trustworthy, it is necessary to analyze the quality and relevance of the secondary data. Through this technique, a comprehensive knowledge of the present landscape of influencer marketing in the tourist industry can be achieved, which in turn provides significant insights and recommendations for maximizing the effect of this marketing strategy.

Figure 1. Conceptual framework

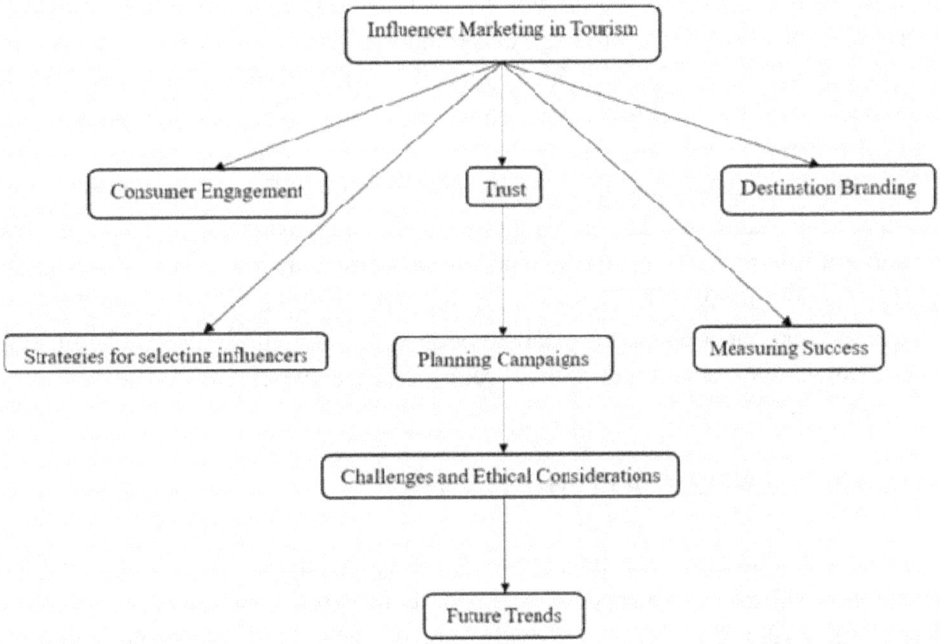

(Authors own)

Recommendations

A. Choose influencers carefully. Ensure their audience demographics, content, and level of interaction fit your business and target market. Give authenticity and strong interaction rates to influencers more weight than the number of followers. This increases the campaign's success by guaranteeing that the influencer's audience is engaged and inclined to follow their advice.

B. Create long-term collaborations with influencers as opposed to one-time events. Long-term partnerships enable influencers to produce more genuine, consistent content and get a better grasp of your company. More trust and loyalty among their followers may arise from this ongoing relationship, which might have a longer-lasting and more significant influence on marketing outcomes.

C. Motivate influencers to share their own narratives and brand-related experiences. Audiences respond better to authentic storytelling because it may evoke strong feelings. Give influencers the creative flexibility they need to create genuine, relevant material that showcases the unique features of your product or service while adhering to your brand rules.

D. Use a variety of social media channels to connect with a broader range of people. Instagram and TikTok are great for visual and short-form material; YouTube is great for in-depth travel vlogs; and blogs are great for thorough reviews and itineraries. Each medium has its own merits. Cross-promote content to increase exposure and interaction on many channels, guaranteeing a comprehensive and well-rounded marketing plan.
E. Put robust analytics and tracking in place to gauge the success of influencer marketing initiatives. Engagement rates reach, impressions, click-through rates, and conversion rates are important performance indicators. Examine and evaluate this data regularly to find techniques that work and places that might be used better. Make the most of these data to tailor subsequent initiatives, guaranteeing ongoing enhancement and optimal return on investment.

FUTURE TRENDS AND DIRECTIONS

Influencer marketing continues to evolve rapidly, driven by technological advancements, shifting consumer behaviors, and emerging trends in digital communication (Talukder & das, 2024.). Looking ahead, several key trends and directions are expected to shape the future landscape of influencer marketing in tourism.

Micro and Nano Influencers

As influencer marketing matures, there is a growing shift towards micro and nano influencers. These influencers typically have smaller but highly engaged audiences within specific niches or local communities (Ouvrein et al., 2021). They are perceived as more authentic and relatable, offering higher engagement rates and potentially lower costs than macro influencers. In tourism, micro and nano influencers are expected to be crucial in reaching niche markets, promoting local experiences, and driving authentic engagement with targeted audiences.

Video and Live Streaming

The rise of video content and live streaming is transforming influencer marketing strategies in tourism. Platforms like YouTube, TikTok, and Instagram Live enable influencers to share real-time experiences, travel vlogs, and interactive sessions with their audiences (Vlahov & Vlahov, 2021). Video content is highly engaging and allows influencers to showcase destinations immersively, influencing travel decisions and inspiring wanderlust among viewers. Tourism marketers are likely to increasingly invest in video-centric campaigns to capitalize on the visual storytelling capabilities of influencers.

Sustainability and Responsible Tourism

Sustainability and responsible tourism practices are becoming integral to influencer marketing campaigns. Influencers and travelers alike are increasingly mindful of environmental impact, cultural preservation, and community benefits when promoting or choosing destinations (Mohammad et al., 2024a). Future trends will likely see influencers aligning with sustainable tourism initiatives, advocating for eco-friendly practices, and highlighting destinations committed to responsible tourism. Tourism marketers must collaborate with influencers who share these values to resonate with socially conscious travelers and enhance destination reputation.

Artificial Intelligence (AI) and Data Analytics

Artificial intelligence (AI) and data analytics are poised to revolutionize influencer marketing strategies in tourism. AI-powered tools can analyze vast amounts of data to identify suitable influencers, predict content performance, and optimize campaign targeting (Das et al., 2024). Data-driven insights enable tourism marketers to measure ROI more effectively, personalize content recommendations, and enhance audience segmentation strategies. As AI technologies advance, influencers and marketers will leverage AI-driven analytics to refine their strategy, improve campaign effectiveness, and stay ahead in a competitive digital landscape.

Virtual Reality (VR) and Augmented Reality (AR)

Virtual reality (VR) and augmented reality (AR) present innovative opportunities for influencer marketing in tourism. Influencers can use VR and AR technologies to provide virtual tours, immersive experiences, and interactive storytelling that transport audiences to destinations virtually (Talukder & Das, 2024). These technologies enhance engagement by offering realistic previews of destinations, attractions, and experiences, influencing travel decisions and enhancing visitor anticipation. As VR and AR become more accessible, influencers and tourism marketers are expected to integrate these technologies into their campaigns to deliver compelling and memorable content experiences. The future of influencer marketing in tourism is characterized by innovation, personalization, and sustainability. Embracing micro and nano influencers, leveraging video and live streaming, prioritizing sustainability, harnessing AI-driven analytics, and exploring VR/AR technologies are pivotal trends that will shape influencer marketing strategies in the future (Woodgate, 2022).

Tourism marketers must adapt to these evolving trends, collaborate strategically with influencers, and embrace technological advancements to engage travelers effectively, enhance destination appeal, and drive sustainable tourism growth globally.

CONCLUSION

Influencer marketing has emerged as a dynamic and influential force in tourism promotion, leveraging social media influencers' authenticity, reach, and storytelling prowess to engage travelers and enhance destination visibility. This chapter has explored the evolution, effectiveness, challenges, ethical considerations, and future influencer marketing trends within the tourism industry. Influencer marketing has revolutionized how destinations connect with their target audiences. By partnering with influencers who resonate with specific demographics or niche interests, tourism marketers can craft compelling narratives, showcase unique experiences, and inspire travel aspirations effectively. The authenticity inherent in influencer-generated content has proven instrumental in fostering trust and engagement among followers, driving tangible impacts such as increased visitor arrivals, improved destination perception, and enhanced brand recognition. However, the practice is not without its challenges. Maintaining authenticity and credibility, navigating regulatory compliance across different regions, measuring ROI effectively, and addressing ethical considerations such as transparency and cultural sensitivity are ongoing imperatives for tourism marketers and influencers. These challenges underscore the importance of responsible practices, strategic collaboration, and adherence to ethical standards to sustain long-term relationships with audiences and stakeholders. Looking forward, several trends are poised to shape the future of influencer marketing in tourism. The rise of micro and nano influencers, the dominance of video and live streaming content, the emphasis on sustainability and responsible tourism, the integration of AI-driven analytics, and the potential of VR/AR technologies represent opportunities for innovation and growth in influencer campaigns. Embracing these trends will enable tourism marketers to stay agile, engage diverse audiences authentically, and enhance destination competitiveness in an increasingly digital and competitive landscape. In conclusion, influencer marketing continues to evolve as a vital component of tourism promotion strategies, offering unparalleled opportunities to connect with travelers, amplify destination appeal, and drive sustainable tourism growth. By leveraging emerging trends, embracing ethical practices, and harnessing technological advancements, tourism stakeholders can maximize the impact of influencer partnerships, foster meaningful visitor experiences, and contribute to the sustainable development of tourism destinations worldwide.

REFERENCES

Aguilar, I. (2023). *Consumer Experiences and Perceptions on Influencer Marketing: The Impact of Regulation Gaps on Content Creation in Mexico*. Dublin Business School.

Al-Zyoud, M. F. (2021). The impact of gamification on consumer loyalty, electronic word-of-mouth sharing, and purchase behavior. *Journal of Public Affairs*, 21(3), e2263. DOI: 10.1002/pa.2263

Ali, S. S. (2024). *Nano influencers: using ordinary people for extraordinary results*.

An, J., Kwak, H., Jung, S., Salminen, J., & Jansen, B. J. (2018). Customer segmentation using online platforms: Isolating behavioral and demographic segments for persona creation via aggregated user data. *Social Network Analysis and Mining*, 8(1), 54. DOI: 10.1007/s13278-018-0531-0

Arthur, T. O. (2022). "We Bring Home the Roots": Black Women Travel Influencers, Digital Culture Bearing, and African Internationalism in Instagram. *Social Media + Society*, 8(2), 20563051221103844. DOI: 10.1177/20563051221103843

Asdecker, B. (2022). Travel-related influencer content on Instagram: How social media fuels wanderlust and how to mitigate the effect. *Sustainability (Basel)*, 14(2), 855. DOI: 10.3390/su14020855

Aslam, W., & de Luna, I. R. (2021). The relationship between brand Facebook page characteristics, perceived value, and customer engagement behavior: An application of Stimulus-Organism-Response (SOR). *Revista Brasileira de Gestão de Negócios*, 23, 43–62. DOI: 10.7819/rbgn.v23i1.4092

Audy Martínek, P. (2021). Mapping methods of research on consumer engagement with brands on social media: A literature review. *Methodological Innovations*, 14(1), 2059799120985384. DOI: 10.1177/2059799120985384

Azhar, M., Husain, R., Hamid, S., & Rahman, M. N. (2023). Effect of social media marketing on online travel purchase behavior post-COVID-19: Mediating role of brand trust and brand loyalty. *Future Business Journal*, 9(1), 13. DOI: 10.1186/s43093-023-00192-6

Balaban, D. C., Mucundorfeanu, M., & Naderer, B. (2022). The role of trustworthiness in social media influencer advertising: Investigating users' appreciation of advertising transparency and its effects. *Communications*, 47(3), 395–421. DOI: 10.1515/commun-2020-0053

Bastrygina, T., Lim, W. M., Jopp, R., & Weissmann, M. A. (2024). Unraveling the power of social media influencers: Qualitative insights into the role of Instagram influencers in the hospitality and tourism industry. *Journal of Hospitality and Tourism Management*, 58, 214–243. DOI: 10.1016/j.jhtm.2024.01.007

Bochenek, L. M. (2019). Connecting with the right audiences for a better impact–imperatives of influencer marketing. In *Advocacy and organizational engagement* (pp. 91–110). Emerald Publishing Limited., DOI: 10.1108/978-1-78973-437-920191006

Cao, X., Qu, Z., Liu, Y., & Hu, J. (2021). How the destination short video affects the customers' attitude: The role of narrative transportation. *Journal of Retailing and Consumer Services*, 62, 102672. DOI: 10.1016/j.jretconser.2021.102672

Cheung, M. L., Pires, G. D., Rosenberger, P. J., Leung, W. K. S., & Sharipudin, M.-N. S. (2021). The role of consumer-consumer interaction and consumer-brand interaction in driving consumer-brand engagement and behavioral intentions. *Journal of Retailing and Consumer Services*, 61, 102574. DOI: 10.1016/j.jretconser.2021.102574

Chiriluta, R. (2021). *An exploration of how marketing technique and promotion via Instagram drives domestic tourism in Ireland*. National College of Ireland.

Conde, R., & Casais, B. (2023). Micro, macro, and mega-influencers on Instagram: The power of persuasion via the parasocial relationship. *Journal of Business Research*, 158, 113708. DOI: 10.1016/j.jbusres.2023.113708

Das, I. R., Talukder, M. B., & Kumar, S. (2024). Implication of Artificial Intelligence in Hospitality Marketing. In *Utilizing Smart Technology and AI in Hybrid Tourism and Hospitality* (pp. 291–310). IGI Global., DOI: 10.4018/979-8-3693-1978-9.ch014

Driver, R. (2022). Instagram & the FTC: The Growth of Influencer Marketing & the Government's Ungai Fan, F., Chan, K., Wang, Y., Li, Y., & Prieler, M. (2023). How influencers' social media posts have an influence on audience engagement among young consumers. *Young Consumers*, 24(4), 427–444.

Femenia-Serra, F., & Gretzel, U. (2020). Influencer marketing for tourism destinations: Lessons from a mature destination. *Information and Communication Technologies in Tourism 2020:Proceedings of the International Conference in Surrey,* United Kingdom, January 08–10, 2020, 65–78. DOI DOI: 10.1007/978-3-030-36737-4_6

Gerlich, M. (2023). The Power of Personal Connections in Micro-Influencer Marketing: A Study on Consumer Behaviour and the Impact of Micro-Influencers. *Transnational Marketing Journal*, 11(1), 131–152.

Giubilei, A. (2021). *Business opportunities for Italian companies on Alibaba's e-commerce platforms.*

Gour, A., Aggarwal, S., & Kumar, S. (2022). Lending ears to unheard voices: An empirical analysis of user-generated content on social media. *Production and Operations Management*, 31(6), 2457–2476. DOI: 10.1111/poms.13732

Haenlein, M., Anadol, E., Farnsworth, T., Hugo, H., Hunichen, J., & Welte, D. (2020). Navigating the new era of influencer marketing: How to be successful on Instagram, TikTok, & Co. *California Management Review*, 63(1), 5–25. DOI: 10.1177/0008125620958166

Haggerty, J. D. (n.d.). *Influencers are Ordinary People: Why the World and Business is Run by Influencers.*

Hernández-Méndez, J., & Baute-Díaz, N. (2024). Influencer marketing in the promotion of tourist destinations: Mega, macro, and micro-influencers. *Current Issues in Tourism*, 27(8), 1332–1342. DOI: 10.1080/13683500.2023.2214354

Huang, C., & Guo, R. (2021). The effect of a green brand story on perceived brand authenticity and brand trust: The role of narrative rhetoric. *Journal of Brand Management, 28*, 60–76.nly Pursuit. *J. Bus. & Tech. L.*, 18, 289. DOI: 10.1057/s41262-020-00213-7

ILIEVA., G. (n.d.). The role of the influencers for the development of cultural and heritage tourism. *Proceedings of an International Conference*, 17.

Ingrassia, M., Bellia, C., Giurdanella, C., Columba, P., & Chironi, S. (2022). Digital influencers, food, and tourism—A new model of open innovation for businesses in the Ho. Re. Ca. sector. *Journal of Open Innovation*, 8(1), 50. DOI: 10.3390/joitmc8010050

Jaya, I. P. G. I. T., & Prianthara, I. B. T. (2020). Role of social media influencers in tourism destination image: How does digital marketing affect purchase intention? *3rd International Conference on Vocational Higher Education (ICVHE 2018)*, 9–20. DOI: 10.2991/assehr.k.200331.114

Jin, S. V., Muqaddam, A., & Ryu, E. (2019). Instafamous and social media influencer marketing. *Marketing Intelligence & Planning*, 37(5), 567–579. DOI: 10.1108/MIP-09-2018-0375

Jordan, A. (2023). *How to identify the right collaboration partner?: A qualitative study of Finnish Instagram micro-influencers.*

Jun, S., & Yi, J. (2020). What makes followers loyal? The role of influencer interactivity in building influencer brand equity. *Journal of Product and Brand Management*, 29(6), 803–814. DOI: 10.1108/JPBM-02-2019-2280

Justianto, M., & Morley, C. (2020). *The influencer effect on tourism: shifting adventure travel behavior towards more sustainability through Instagram influencers.*

Kaur, S., & Kapil, R. (2023). Measuring Customer Engagement in Digital Marketing. *Journal for ReAttach Therapy and Developmental Diversities*, 6(6s), 984–992. DOI: 10.53555/jrtdd.v6i6s.2951

Kennedy, P. S. J., Tobing, S. J. L., & Toruan, R. L. (2022). Marketing strategy with marketing mix for Lake Toba tourism destination. [JoSTE]. *Journal of Sustainable Tourism and Entrepreneurship*, 3(3), 157–174.

Kilipiri, E., Papaioannou, E., & Kotzaivazoglou, I. (2023). Social media and influencer marketing for promoting sustainable tourism destinations: The Instagram case. *Sustainability (Basel)*, 15(8), 6374. DOI: 10.3390/su15086374

Kittur, P., & Chatterjee, S. (2023). Role of B2B reliance and brand image in reducing risk perceptions: A serial mediation model. *European Journal of Marketing*, 57(4), 1068–1098. DOI: 10.1108/EJM-05-2022-0362

Kotler, P., Pfoertsch, W., & Sponholz, U. (2021). H2h marketing: Putting trust and brand in strategic management focus. *Academy of Strategic Management Journal*, 20(2).

Krey, N., Tom Dieck, M. C., Wu, S., & Fountoulaki, P. (2023). Exploring the influence of touch points on tourist experiences at crisis-impacted destinations. *Journal of Travel Research*, 62(1), 39–54. DOI: 10.1177/00472875211053657

Kruger, J. B. (2022). *Rising From The Ashes: An Analysis of How One Infamous Promotional Event Caused a Company's Ruin and a Concept on the Future of Influencer Experiences.*

Kumar, V., & Kaushik, A. K. (2022). Engaging customers through brand authenticity perceptions: The moderating role of self-congruence. *Journal of Business Research*, 138, 26–37. DOI: 10.1016/j.jbusres.2021.08.065

Liu, H., & Li, X. (2021). How travel earns us bragging rights: A qualitative inquiry and conceptualization of travel bragging rights. *Journal of Travel Research*, 60(8), 1635–1653. DOI: 10.1177/0047287520964599

Lou, C., & Xie, Q. (2021). Something social, something entertaining? How digital content marketing augments consumer experience and brand loyalty. *International Journal of Advertising*, 40(3), 376–402. DOI: 10.1080/02650487.2020.1788311

Makian, S. (2022). Online tourism communication in destination image formation. In *Handbook on Tourism and Social Media* (pp. 68–80). Edward Elgar Publishing. DOI: 10.4337/9781800371415.00012

Mohammad Badruddoza Talukder. Sanjeev Kumar, I. R. Das. (2024a). Implications of Blockchain Technology- Based Cryptocurrency in the cloud for the Hospitality Industry. In *Emerging Trends in Cloud Computing Analytics, Scalability, and Service Models* (p. 19). DOI: 10.4018/979-8-3693-0900-1.ch018

Mohammad Badruddoza Talukder. Sanjeev Kumar, I. R. Das. (2024b). Perspectives of Digital Marketing for the Restaurant Industry. In *Advancements in Socialized and Digital Media Communications* (p. 17). DOI: 10.4018/979-8-3693-0855-4.ch009

Moinuddin, M., Usman, M., & Khan, R. (2024). Decoding Consumer Behavior: The Role of Marketing Analytics in Driving Campaign Success. *International Journal of Advanced Engineering Technologies and Innovations*, 1(4), 118–141.

Nazir, F. (2023). Destination branding through social media: Juxtaposition of foreign influencer's narratives and state's presentation on the event of Pakistan Tourism Summit 2019. *Qualitative Market Research*, 26(4), 428–448. DOI: 10.1108/QMR-03-2022-0048

Okonkwo, I., & Namkoisse, E. (2023). The Role of Influencer Marketing in Building Authentic Brand Relationships Online. *Journal of Digital Marketing and Communication*, 3(2), 81–90. DOI: 10.53623/jdmc.v3i2.350

Omeish, F., Sharabati, A., Abuhashesh, M., Al-Haddad, S., Nasereddin, A., Alghizzawi, M., & Badran, O. (2024). The role of social media influencers in shaping destination image and intention to visit Jordan: The moderatinImpact of social media usage intensity. *International Journal of Data and Network Science*, 8(3), 1701–1714. DOI: 10.5267/j.ijdns.2024.2.017

Ouvrein, G., Pabian, S., Giles, D., Hudders, L., & De Backer, C. (2021). The web of influencers. A marketing-audience classification of (potential) social media influencers. *Journal of Marketing Management*, 37(13–14), 1313–1342. DOI: 10.1080/0267257X.2021.1912142

Paramita, W., Nhu, H. B. C., Ngo, L. V., Tran, Q. H. M., & Gregory, G. (2021). Brand experience and consumers' social interactive engagement with the brand page: An integrated-marketing perspective. *Journal of Retailing and Consumer Services*, 62, 102611. DOI: 10.1016/j.jretconser.2021.102611

Pedro, I. L. M. (2023). *The role of micro-influencers for luxury fashion brands.*

Platon, O.-E. (2023). Using instagram for destination marketing: creating the perception of a tourism destination experience and influencing the travel decision-making process. *Challenges of the Knowledge Society*, 669–676.

Pop, R.-A., Săplăcan, Z., Dabija, D.-C., & Alt, M.-A. (2022). ThImpact of social media influencers on travel decisions: The role of trust in consumer decision journey. *Current Issues in Tourism*, 25(5), 823–843. DOI: 10.1080/13683500.2021.1895729

Ramachandran, K. K., Suma, S., Banerjee, D., Mathew, B., Cheepurupalli, N. R., & Mohan, C. R. (2024). The Effectiveness of Influencer Marketing in the Age of AI. *Journal of Informatics Education and Research*, 4(2).

Rane, N. L., Achari, A., & Choudhary, S. P. (2023). Enhancing customer loyalty through quality of service: Effective strategies to improve customer satisfaction, experience, relationship, and engagement. *International Research Journal of Modernization in Engineering Technology and Science*, 5(5), 427–452.

Razak, R. A., & Mansor, N. A. (2021). Instagram influencers in social media-induced tourism: Rethinking tourist trust towards tourism destination. In*impact of new media in tourism* (pp. 135–144). IGI Global.

Reuter, K., Wilson, M. L., Moran, M., Le, N., Angyan, P., Majmundar, A., Kaiser, E. M., & Unger, J. B. (2021). General audience engagement with antismoking public health messages across multiple social media sites: Comparative analysis. *JMIR Public Health and Surveillance*, 7(2), e24429. DOI: 10.2196/24429 PMID: 33605890

Santiago, J. K., Magueta, D., & Dias, C. (2020). Consumer Attitudes Towards Fashion Influencers on Instagram: Impact of Perceptions and Online Trust on Purchase Intention. *Issues in Information Systems*, 21(1).

Şenyapar, H. N. D. (2024). A comprehensive analysis of influencer types in digital marketing. *International Journal of Management and Administration*, 8(15), 75–100. DOI: 10.29064/ijma.1417291

Sharma, B. K., Bhatt, V. K., & Arora, L. (2021). Influencer marketing-an instrument to proliferation of the digital occurrence. *International Journal of Enterprise Network Management*, 12(4), 340–357. DOI: 10.1504/IJENM.2021.119662

Sharma, D., & Chanda, K. (2023). Destination marketing in the digital world. *management metamorphosis: navigating the changing landscape*, 128.

Sigurðardóttir, G. R. (2019). *Using social proof techniques and attributes of social media influencers to promote fresh fish products.*

Sihombing, L., & Dinus, H. (2024). Analysis of Business Development Strategies in Increasing Customer Trust. *Journal on Economics. Management and Business Technology*, 2(2), 84–92.

Smith, S. P. (2021). Landscapes for "likes": Capitalizing on travel with Instagram. *Social Semiotics*, 31(4), 604–624. DOI: 10.1080/10350330.2019.1664579

Soto-Vásquez, A. D. (2022). YouTube and TikTok as platforms for learning about others: The case of Non-Chinese travel videos in Shanghai Disneyland. *Online Media and Global Communication*, 1(2), 315–338. DOI: 10.1515/omgc-2022-0012

Srivastava, M. (2021). Mapping the influence of influencer marketing: A bibliometric analysis. *Marketing Intelligence & Planning*, 39(7), 979–1003. DOI: 10.1108/MIP-03-2021-0085

Steils, N., Martin, A., & Toti, J.-F. (2022). Managing the transparency paradox of social-media influencer disclosures: How to improve authenticity and engagement when disclosing influencer–sponsor relationships. *Journal of Advertising Research*, 62(2), 148–166. DOI: 10.2501/JAR-2022-008

Stevens, W. E. (2022). *Black Influencers: Interrogating the Racialization and Commodification of Digital Labor*. Temple University.

Streimikiene, D., Svagzdiene, B., Jasinskas, E., & Simanavicius, A. (2021). Sustainable tourism development and competitiveness: The systematic literature review. *Sustainable Development (Bradford)*, 29(1), 259–271. DOI: 10.1002/sd.2133

Talukder, M. B., & DAS, I. V. A. R. (2024). *Review papers the technology impacts and ai solutions in hospitality.*

Talukder, M. B., & Das, I. R. (2024). The Technology Impacts and AI Solutions in Hospitality... *I-Manager's Journal on Artificial Intelligence &. Machine Learning*, 2(1), 56–72. https://doi.org/https://doi.org/10.26634/jaim.2.1.20291

Talukder, M. B., & Das, I. V. A. R. (2024). The technology impacts and ai solutions in hospitality. [JAIM]. *I-Manager's Journal on Artificial Intelligence & Machine Learning*, 2(1), 56. Advance online publication. DOI: 10.26634/jaim.2.1.20291

Talukder, M. B., Kumar, S., & Das, I. R. (2024a). Food Wastage on the Economic Outcome: Evidence From the Hotel Industry. *IGI Global, USA*.https://doi.org/https:// doi.org/ 10.4018/979-8-3693-2181-2.ch005

Talukder, M. B., Kumar, S., & Das, I. R. (2024b). Mindful Consumers and New Marketing Strategies for the Restaurant Business: Evidence of Bangladesh. In Ramos, C., Costa, T., Severino, F., & Calisto, M. (Eds.), *Social Media Strategies for Tourism Interactivity* (pp. 240–260). IGI Global., https://doi.org/https://doi.org/10 .4018/979-8-3693-0960-5.ch010 DOI: 10.4018/979-8-3693-0960-5.ch010

Talukder, M. B., Kumar, S., & Das, I. R. (2024c). Mindfulness of Digital Detoxification: Healthy Lifestyle in Tourism. *IGI Global, USA*.https://doi.org/https://doi.org/ 10.4018/979-8-3693-1273-5.ch004 DOI: DOI: 10.4018/979-8-3693-1273-5.ch004

Teixeira, S., Teixeira, S., Oliveira, Z., & Souza, E. (2023). *Using Influencer Marketing as a Digital Business Strategy*. IGI Global. DOI: 10.4018/979-8-3693-0551-5

Tian, Z., Dew, R., & Iyengar, R. (2024). Mega or micro? Influencer selection using follower elasticity. *JMR, Journal of Marketing Research*, 61(3), 472–495. DOI: 10.1177/00222437231210267

Tirrell, C. (2023). *Labor control and the experience of work in the platform economy*. Northeastern University. DOI: 10.17760/D20487636

Tjandrawibawa, P. (2020). The effect of using Instagram influencers in building Conseva's brand awareness. *The Winners*, 21(1), 67–73. DOI: 10.21512/tw.v21i1.6497

Vaidya, R., & Karnawat, T. (2023). Conceptualizing influencer marketing: A literature review on the strategic use of social media influencers. *International Journal of Management. Public Policy Research*, 2(Special Issue), 81–86. DOI: 10.55829/ ijmpr.v2iSpecialIssue.140

Vlahov, M. M., & Vlahov, A. (2021). Travel influencers as a new strategic partners in tourism. *Proceedings of FEB Zagreb International Odyssey Conference on Economics and Business, 3*(1), 1249–1265.

Vrontis, D., Makrides, A., Christofi, M., & Thrassou, A. (2021). Social media influencer marketing: A systematic review, integrative framework and future research agenda. *International Journal of Consumer Studies*, 45(4), 617–644. DOI: 10.1111/ijcs.12647

Woodgate, D. (2022). *The Augmented Learner: The pivotal role of multimedia enhanced learning within a foresight-based learning model designed to accelerate the delivery of higher levels of learner creat* Yang, J., Chuenterawong, P., Lee, H., & Chock, T. M. (2023). Anthropomorphism in CSR endorsement: A comparative study on humanlike vs. cartoonlike virtual influencers' climate change messaging. *Journal of Promotion Management*, 29(5), 705–734.

Ye, G., Hudders, L., De Jans, S., & De Veirman, M. (2021). The value of influencer marketing for business: A bibliometric analysis and managerial implications. *Journal of Advertising*, 50(2), 160–178. DOI: 10.1080/00913367.2020.1857888

Yetimoğlu, S., & Uğurlu, K. (2020). Influencer marketing for tourism and hospitality. In *The Emerald Handbook of ICT in tourism and hospitality* (pp. 131–148). Emerald Publishing Limited. DOI: 10.1108/978-1-83982-688-720201009

Zhang, W. (2022). *The Engagement Between Social Media Influencers and Their Followers on Instagram: A Case Study of# StopAsianHate.*

Zhou, S., Blazquez, M., McCormick, H., & Barnes, L. (2021). How social media influencers' narrative strategies benefit cultivating influencer marketing: Tackling issues of cultural barriers, commercialised content, and sponsorship disclosure. *Journal of Business Research*, 134, 122–142. DOI: 10.1016/j.jbusres.2021.05.011

KEY TERMS AND DEFINITIONS

Authenticity: In marketing, authenticity is the sincere and truthful representation of a company or product. It entails open communication and genuine exchanges that foster audience trust. Since followers are more inclined to believe and be affected by information that feels genuine and personal, authenticity is essential in influencer marketing. Genuine influencers are seen as reliable and reputable, which can increase the effect of their recommendations.

Consumer Engagement: This is the term used to describe the exchanges between a brand and its customers to foster ties, loyalty, and involvement. This might entail interacting with prospective visitors on social media, sending tailored messages, providing feedback, and creating interactive material in the travel and tourist industry. Elevated levels of customer involvement may result in heightened contentment, recurrent visits, and favorable verbal recommendations.

Destination Branding: Developing a distinctive and appealing identity for a place to set it apart from competing destinations is the destination branding process. This entails showcasing a location's unique qualities, culture, events, and attractions. Good destination branding promotes tourism, cultivates a favorable image, and leaves a lasting impression on prospective visitors. Influencer marketing, which offers authentic and exciting material that highlights the destination's distinctive features, may be pretty helpful.

Influencer Marketing: This tactic is used to promote goods, services, or brands on social media platforms by working with people with a sizable and active following. These influencers provide material that highlights their viewpoints and experiences, which has a big impact on their followers' purchases. Influencers in the travel business may encourage their audience to visit destinations by sharing their travel experiences, reviews, and suggestions for lodging and activities.

Social Media: Social media refers to online tools and platforms that let people connect and communicate with each other and produce, share, and engage with information. Users may upload images, videos, and messages to social media sites, including Facebook, Instagram, Twitter, TikTok, and YouTube. Social media effectively allows influencers and companies to reach big audiences, share content, interact with followers, and create a community. The tourist sector uses social media to promote travel, exchange stories, and offer details about services and places.

Social Proof: This idea refers to how people adopt other people's behaviors to model appropriate behavior in a particular circumstance. It is predicated on the notion that people will imitate the majority's actions. When followers of an influencer see the influencer promoting a good, service, or place to visit, they are encouraged to do the same because they think it's the right or popular decision. This is known as social proof in influencer marketing.

Tourism Management: This field includes managing and supervising all aravel and tourist sector. aspects This covers organizing and creating tourist attractions, promoting travel-related goods and services, overseeing travel agency operations, and ensuring sustainable practices are followed. Enhancing tourist experiences, boosting regional economies, and controlling the effects of tourism on the environment and local populations are the objectives.

Chapter 12
The Impact and Consequences of Artificial Intelligence in Copywriting

Veronica Provasi
Universidade Católica Portuguesa, Portugal

Alexandre Duarte
https://orcid.org/0000-0002-2665-864X
Universidade Nova de Lisboa, Portugal

ABSTRACT

The implications of artificial intelligence (AI) on content creation, especially the impact on copywriting remain little explored in Academia. This article aims to determine the ability of social media users to distinguish AI-generated content from human-crafted prose. Using a mixed methodology, this study combines qualitative insights from a focus group, with quantitative data (n=514) from an online experiment. Results indicate a discord in discernment skill based on the specific content pairs presented, with no overarching consensus on AI's detectability. This signifies how AI can be recognized if used by inexperienced hands, but it cannot if used correctly as a tool. The study revealed that participants consistently underestimated AI's capabilities, highlighting a gap between perceived and actual discernment abilities, and showing that participants with a writing background demonstrated a higher accuracy rate. This research emphasizes the need for a holistic understanding that integrates the technological prowess of AI and the intricate human factors influencing content perception

DOI: 10.4018/979-8-3693-8442-8.ch012

INTRODUCTION

Throughout history, technological advancements have consistently reshaped human societies, transforming daily practices, lifestyles, and traditions, and signifying broader shifts in human thought and societal values. History is full of inventions that altered the world, addressing present problems and offering solutions that once seemed impossible (Zhao et al., 2022). This continuous interplay between the old and the new is a fundamental aspect of human civilization (Frank et al., 2019). However, it is understandable to feel a sense of mistrust when a new technology, capable of transforming history, is introduced into everyday life. When OpenAI introduced ChatGPT, an acronym for Chat Generative Pre-Trained Transformer, on November 30, 2022, it was not only revealing another technological tool, significant only for people working in tech (OpenAI.com, n.d.). This Large Language Models (LLMs) chatbot, prepared to adapt and lead conversations according to user preferences in terms of length, format, style, detail, and language, immediately became a focal point of discussions far beyond the realms of artificial intelligence. Its launch sparked overall reflection on the profound implications of AI for different aspects of human existence (Hameed et al., 2022).

In this renaissance sparked by innovations in AI, the field of copywriting stands at a crossroads, facing the innovative power of AI language models such as OpenAI's ChatGPT. While the impact of AI and Language Models on Marketing and Advertising has been already studied by several researchers (Duarte & Neumaier, 2022), how social media users react to AI advertisements remains unclear (Argan et al., 2022), and especially, the impact on copywriting is even more unsure.

This research delves into the critical inquiry of AI's influence on the field of copywriting, aiming to understand the ability of social media users to recognize AI-generated text. The relevance of this study stems from the rapid integration of AI technologies in content creation, posing unprecedented opportunities and challenges. Understanding AI's impact is imperative for the future of communication, marketing, and brand narrative.

THEORETICAL FRAMEWORK

Every time a new technology emerges, the attention it receives, and its transformative power expectations are usually high. Human history is full of examples (steam engine, telegraph, telephone, television, computers, and so on - just to name a few), and Artificial Intelligence is no different. For Rodgers (2021), AI is one of the most exciting technological advances ever in advertising, as it promises to change the very nature of this industry, affecting all its aspects (Qin & Jiang, 2019).

One of the first attempts to academically analyze and discuss the relationship between intelligence science and advertising was an International Conference held in Shanghai, China, in November of 2018. To gather the most interesting outcomes of that event, in 2019, the Journal of Advertising published a special issue focused on AI and Advertising. The themes were diverse. Qin and Jiang (2019) focused on the impact of AI on the entire process, from the definition of consumer insight to media planning, from the creative process to the efficiency evaluation. Chen et al. (2019) looked at programmatic advertising and the possibility of generating personalized ads in real-time, while Deng et al. (2019) developed an AI system that can generate personalized copy ads that respond to the needs of the users depending on the context that one is at a certain moment. Finally, Malthouse et al. (2019) proposed an intelligent platform that benefits both consumers and advertisers. From that moment forward, a plethora of articles, news, forums, debates, and so on flourished around what Li (2019) called "Intelligent Advertising" which he defined as consumer-centered, data-driven, and algorithm-mediated brand communication (p.333). For the author, digital advertising underwent 3 phases. The first one was interactive advertising, whose denomination comes from its nature, which allowed the two-way change of information. The second one was the so-called programmatic advertising, where ads could be bought and sold automatically using intelligence software, data, and algorithms. The third one, that we're living in now, is intelligent advertising that adds to interactivity (first phase) and automation (second phase), some inventive attributes, created by deep learning algorithms, and powered by natural language processing and machine learning (p.334). Remarkably, one of the most interesting characteristics of intelligent advertising is that it goes beyond the prediction of consumers' interests to anticipate their needs and wants.

Nevertheless, as understanding the consumer's needs and wants, attitudes, and values is increasingly hard and complex, most businesses today rely on the huge amount of data that the new technologies offer. As stated by Kietzmann et al. (2018), this gigantic quantity of consumer-curated data doesn´t stop growing in terms of the 4 V's. volume, velocity, variety, and veracity (p. 263). Data and information technologies are, undoubtedly, used widely in all aspects of our lives, but they're also fully applied in the marketing and advertising industry (Argan et al., 2022) and are becoming, nowadays, less an option, and more a necessity for companies (Rodgers, 2021, p. 1).

Advertising and creativity have been sharing the same road since ever. Although, generically, creativity it's a hard concept to define (Duarte, 2021), the writings of Csikszentmihalyi (1996) give us a useful framework. For the author, creativity is any act, idea, or product that changes an existing domain into a new one. Making the bridge between creativity, advertising, and artificial intelligence, Vakratsas and Wang (2021) also included includes novelty and value in their definition of creativity but proposed a different approach to investigating this new form of creativity, a subdiscipline of AI which they called "Computational Creativity", whose goal is to enhance human creativity using computational methods (p. 39). Rodgers (2021) also defends that AI Advertising should be seen as a separate subdiscipline under this industry, that is "situated at the intersection of cognitive science, computer science, and advertising" (p. 2).

Focusing precisely on the intersection between artificial intelligence and advertising, Argan et al. (2022) found three process themes under which users react to AI-generated messages. reception, diving in, and breakpoint (p.346). The first moment, related to the impact of the message, refers to the attraction that it has on users and can be positive or negative. If positive, the evaluation of AI ads continues. The second phase includes comparison, timesaving, and leaping. The final stage is related to decision-making, where users form positive or negative opinions regarding the messages.

This study assumes that artificial intelligence has the transformative power to radically change the advertising industry (Hanna, 2023). Not only how it is produced, distributed, and evaluated, but especially how it is created. Due to ever-evolving technology, deep learning algorithms, machine learning, and so on, the authors believe that shortly, it will be impossible to distinguish the original creators of the messages. human or artificial. That is why this study seems relevant to us currently. As Kurt Lewin, the father of social psychology, wisely observed, "The best moment to study a social phenomenon is when it is in the process of change, as it is when an entity is in movement and alteration that its dynamics are revealed more clearly." (Duarte, 2023, p.1).

This study can serve as a landmark for further researchers to evaluate and compare the changes in human perceptions of persuasive text messages now and in the future.

METHODOLOGY

This study employs a mixed-methods approach (Creswell & Creswell, 2017) to investigate the impact of LLM in the context of copywriting. At the core of the research are two guiding questions. The primary research question is: *What is the prospective influence of AI on the sphere of copywriting?*

To delve deeper and provide tangible insights, a secondary question arises. *Can people discern between human-crafted and AI-generated content?* This question is pivotal in understanding the real-world implications of AI in copywriting.

Two hypotheses were taken into consideration. The first is that social media users cannot distinguish between human and AI content, and therefore AI tools will completely take over copywriting. The second is that social media users will be able to recognize, completely or partially, AI content. In this case, the impact will be minor, and it will depend on the emotional response of the consumers.

Furthermore, the study explores the implications of AI-driven copywriting on social media marketing, focusing on platforms like LinkedIn and Instagram.

The research design utilizes a mixed-methods framework, combining qualitative and quantitative strategies to garner a comprehensive understanding of the subject matter. The qualitative component of this research involved two focus group discussions, each involving 6 participants, offering a platform to delve deeper into participants' perceptions regarding AI-generated content. Simultaneously, a quantitative experiment was conducted via Google Forms, between July 16th and August 16th, employing a comparative design to measure participants' accuracy in distinguishing between human and AI-generated content. This component had a sample of 514 participants and complemented the qualitative insights, providing a broader perspective on participants' abilities.

Both methodologies had the goal of understanding if consumers can recognize AI-generated texts, but the focus groups aimed to offer a deep view of what social media users consider hits of the use of AI, while the experiment to understand if there are external variables to enhance the personal capacities of recognizing AI.

This study focused on millennials and Generation Z, known for their deep engagement with the digital realm and keen awareness of social media's impact. Selecting this demographic ensured that the insights gained would reflect current digital dynamics. The diverse participant group, varying in age, ethnicity, and education, was essential to capture a spectrum of views on AI-generated content, enhancing the study's relevance.

Participants were drawn from a pool of individuals with varying degrees of familiarity with AI, which provided a gradient of AI literacy, offering depth to the qualitative discussions and a bigger range of responses in the quantitative analysis.

Participants were presented with five pairs of texts in the focus groups and the experimental examination, each labeled 'A' or 'B'. Within each pair, one text was an original LinkedIn or Instagram post from a legal tech-related company, while the other was an AI-generated version of the same post, produced using the GPT-3.5 language model. To minimize potential bias, brand names were obscured. However, visual cues indicative of the original social media platforms were maintained, enabling participants to determine the intended target audience of the post.

RESULTS

Focus Groups Analysis

The first focus group began with a structured introduction where the facilitator defined the rules. Participants were advised to avoid speaking over one another and to listen actively to their peers. The facilitator then provided a comprehensive overview of the topic. artificial intelligence (AI) and its application in copywriting, particularly in social media post generation. The participants were briefed on the experiment's structure. they were asked to identify which texts were written by humans and which were generated by AI. This part of the discussion aimed to explore the participants' preconceived notions about AI and its potential impact on the world of copywriting. Participant 1 expressed apprehension about AI, suggesting it might lead to job losses in the copywriting domain. Participants 3 and 4, on the other hand, viewed AI as a complementary tool, emphasizing that copywriters should adapt and learn to harness AI's capabilities effectively. This sentiment of AI as a supportive tool rather than a replacement was further echoed by Participant 5, who believed that while AI could assist in specific tasks, the human touch in copywriting remained irreplaceable.

The discussion then transitioned to participants' interaction with social media. They were asked about their preferred type of content (written or visual), their following of brands or companies on social media, and their ability to recognize a brand's distinctive tone of voice. This segment revealed a diverse range of preferences and habits among the participants. While most leaned toward visual content, others had a predilection for written material; in particular, Participants 1 and 3 expressed their preferences for Twitter's content. All participants concurred that they followed brands or companies on social media and felt confident in their ability to discern a brand's unique tone of voice.

Subsequently, the conversation pivoted to participants' experiences and thoughts on AI-generated content they might have encountered, especially from brands they follow on social media. Participant 3 noted that while he could not definitively identify AI-generated content, he believed he had encountered it multiple times, associating its well-crafted nature as a potential indicator. Participant 6 offered a more nuanced perspective, suggesting that the content's distinctiveness and quality played pivotal roles in determining its origin, whether AI or human. The moderator then steered the conversation towards the intricacy of language used in the texts. Participants delved into a detailed discussion about the complexity of words and the ease of reading as potential indicators of AI authorship.

Afterward, the focus group proceeded with the second part. the analysis. After reading one set of texts at a time, and once they formulated their initial impressions, they were asked to determine which text was crafted by a human author and which was generated by AI.

- **Set 1.** The primary discussion revolved around the believability of the first text being written by a human. Many felt its simplicity and straightforwardness made it seem human-written. The second text, with its detailed explanation and complex word choice, was primarily believed to be AI-generated. It was perceived as more formal and distant, contrasting with the personal touch of the first text. The revelation that the second text was human-authored took the group by surprise.
- **Set 2.** The second set saw the participants divided in their opinions. They found it challenging to discern between the two texts, noting the complexity of words in the first and the simplicity of the second. Some felt the second text's structure, especially its explicit call to action, made it more user-friendly. Therefore, they believed a human copywriter was more likely to write it. The layout of the text became a discussion point, with varying opinions on AI's ability to produce uniform text. Certain words, like "swiftly", were highlighted, with one participant noting, "It's not a common word to use. It sounds professional, but as someone who isn't a native English speaker, some terms feel limited to me. That's the impression I get from this text." The overarching sentiment was that the first text's professional jargon made it seem AI-generated, though the context of the target audience being lawyers on LinkedIn was considered.
- **Set 3.** For the third set, the group was evenly split in their judgments. A notable point from the discussion was the association of low-quality content with AI. Some participants felt that even if targeting professionals like lawyers, content should be more concise and user-friendly to engage the reader effectively.
- **Set 4.** The majority correctly identified the AI-generated content in the fourth set. The discussion highlighted two main points. the unique choice of emojis by the AI, which were not commonly used, and the captivating nature of the text. Both these factors contributed to the perception of AI-generated content being higher quality, and this last point generated a conflict with what the same participants believed before.
- **Set 5.** The final set saw no participants correctly identifying the AI-generated content. The human-authored text's formal and structured nature deceived them. A significant discussion point was the importance of a consistent tone

of voice across posts. The participants felt that detecting AI authorship became challenging if a post maintained the same style as previous ones.

Participants compared notes on the characteristics they associated with human and AI-generated copy, highlighting the nuances they observed and the assumptions they made. Undoubtedly, the participants approached this task from different angles, reflecting their diverse backgrounds and perspectives. In discerning between human and AI-generated text, participants grappled with a complex array of factors. The discussion unfolded in many layers, uncovering how participants engaged with and understood the texts. One of the predominant themes from the discussion was the element of emotionality and depth of expression in the texts. Several participants posited that the capacity to convey genuine sentiment and depth remained a uniquely human trait. They perceived an elusive human 'spark' in the texts they believed were human-written, citing this as a key differential between human and AI writing. Conversely, other participants associated mechanical precision and correctness in language use with AI. They pointed out that while an AI could construct grammatically perfect sentences and use buzzwords correctly, it might fail to successfully replicate the quirks and idiosyncrasies that often characterize human writing. Furthermore, structural complexity and logical flow of narratives also emerged as significant factors. Participants argued that despite its computational power, AI might still need help to weave a coherent and cohesive narrative from start to finish. Disjointed structures or random ideas could be signs of an AI attempting to mimic human thought processes. Concluding the discussion, the group acknowledged the blurred boundaries between human and AI writing. The viewpoints emphasized the participants' different assumptions about AI capabilities, shedding light on the intricate dynamics between technology, language, and human perception. Given the rapid advancement of AI, identifying AI-generated content solely based on these factors might become increasingly challenging. In the revelation phase, the results of the exercise were shared.

This prompted another layer of conversation as participants reflected on their accuracy in identifying the origins of the texts. Some expressed surprise at the results, while others discussed the factors that may have led them to guess the texts' origins correctly or incorrectly. The focus group concluded with a post-results discussion where participants discussed their perceptions of AI in copywriting considering the exercise. They considered signs indicating a text was AI-generated, debated how their views on AI in copywriting may have changed, and speculated how they might approach similar texts in the future. General thoughts on AI and its implications were also shared, with participants recognizing AI's increasingly prominent role in various fields, including copywriting. The discussion underscored the importance of understanding AI's capabilities and limitations in generating human-like text.

In the second focus group, the discussion delved into the attendees' AI assumptions. While some saw artificial intelligence as a democratizing force in content production, others were concerned about its potential to supplant human roles. One attendee emphasized the value of AI tools such as Grammarly, particularly for non-native English speakers and those with dyslexia. They explained how such tools may help with text organization, creativity, and grammatical precision. The focus, however, was on the indispensable human aspect of copywriting, namely the empathy and emotions that individuals put into their work. The group also considered the possibility of AI making linguistic errors. Some feel that AI is more prone to errors, while others believe humans are more prone to errors.

The group's social media habits were explored in-depth. All participants were active on social media, with most preferring visual content. However, some expressed a preference for written content. When asked about their interactions with brands on social media, the group unanimously agreed that they followed various brands. However, the group did not unanimously believe they could recognize the unique tone of voice of the brands they followed. One participant shared her experience using AI to craft catchy captions for a company's social media posts. Interestingly, she noted that no one ever discerned a difference between her AI-generated captions and those she wrote herself, and these confirmed the opinion of the participant that it would be hard to notice a shift in the tone of voice of a brand if it is not very particular. The participants discussed their potential encounters with AI-generated content on social media. While some believed they had encountered such content due to its catchy nature, others needed clarification. The group acknowledged the increasing prevalence of AI in content creation, emphasizing its potential to produce high-quality content. However, they also highlighted the importance of the human touch in crafting engaging and emotionally resonant content.

The discussion also touched upon the perception of quality associated with AI-generated content. One participant remarked, "I don't think AI means good quality. For me, at least. It can work also in the opposite. If you see something written really bad, do you think it's a bad copywriter or a bad user?" This sparked a debate within the group, revealing divided opinions. While some believed that AI could produce high-quality content, others felt that poor quality could be attributed to either a subpar AI model or a human copywriter lacking proficiency.

> *"I've seen some crazy things." "Bad things or good things?" "Bad things. But with chatGPT, I mean, I'm impressed by it because it has so much information. Like sometimes I'm just like, wow, crazy that it knows everything. But the way it's written, I don't know."*

The group acknowledged the variability in AI's output quality, emphasizing that it sometimes only guarantees excellence.

The second focus group delved into analyzing the provided text sets, aiming to discern between human and AI-generated content. Their discussions and conclusions were as follows.

- **Set 1.** The unanimous consensus was that a human wrote the first text, and they were correct. The primary reason cited was the text's concise nature and limited use of emojis. The group felt that the AI text's use of emojis was excessive and "fake" and did not resonate like a human would typically do.
- **Set 2.** Opinions were split evenly among the participants. Some believed the first text was human-generated due to its lengthy and slightly convoluted structure, which they felt compared to a human's train of thought. They also felt it had a more persuasive tone, like the usual advertising language. Conversely, others felt the second text was more refined and user-friendly, pointing out its clear structure and call to action and identifying it as a sign of a human hand. Some saw the dense paragraph format of the first text as a sign of machine generation, as humans tend to break up their writing for better readability.
- **Set 3.** All participants mistakenly believed the first text was AI-generated. The placement of hashtags within the text was a significant point of discussion, with the group agreeing that humans are more likely to incorporate hashtags seamlessly into their writing. Some participants also felt the suspected AI-generated content was overly "sugarcoated."
- **Set 4.** The majority correctly identified the AI-generated content. However, opinions varied on the quality of each text. Some participants found the AI text more fascinating and creative, while others felt it was overly simplified for its target audience. The use of uncommon emojis in the AI text was noted, with participants feeling that such a choice was unlikely to be made by a human. On the other hand, some participants described the human-written text as plain and dull, leading them to believe it was AI-generated.
- **Set 5.** None of the participants correctly identified the AI-generated content. The human-authored text's formal tone and structured approach misled them. The group felt that the first text's attempt to sound overly professional, using complex jargon, made it seem distant and unreliable, leading them to mistakenly attribute it to AI.

The participants identified several attributes as signs of AI-generated copy, including language patterns and a perceived lack of depth and understanding, particularly for complex topics. They also reported the absence of personalization and emotional resonance in AI-generated content. On the other hand, human-generated copy was associated with more natural language, personalized elements, and the ability to evoke emotional responses. The discussion acknowledged the potential evolution of AI's capabilities but emphasized the enduring value of human creativity and emotional insight.

After sharing the results, the discussion culminated in a significant shift in the participants' perspectives on AI and human-generated copy. The participants began with the idea that AI would produce overly complex and lengthy language and that human copy would be more engaging and accessible. However, after participating in the experiment, the participants recognized that AI could produce high-quality content, often challenging their initial assumptions. The realizations sparked a shift in their perception of AI's capabilities yet underscored the vital role of human input in guiding AI's performance. Participants recognized the importance of human elements like hashtags and emojis and the intentional structure of content for reader ease. Despite AI's impressive capabilities, the group did not express a heightened fear of AI takeover. They viewed AI as a powerful tool aiding the copywriting process but needed to see it as a complete substitute for human copywriters.

Shared Observations

1. **Perceptions of AI Competence**. All participants' initial perceptions tended to underestimate AI's capabilities in generating high-quality content. At the beginning of the discussion, 10 participants out of 12 were optimistic about identifying AI-generated content quickly. Participants were initially inclined to associate AI-generated text with overly formal language and stringent grammatical precision. However, as the experiment unfolded and the participants were exposed to the AI-generated content, a palpable shift in their perceptions was observed. During the revelation phase, the participants experienced a significant insight when they learned that certain texts, which they had confidently assumed to be human-authored, were actually generated by artificial intelligence. This discovery fundamentally altered their original perceptions, fostering a deeper and more intricate comprehension of the potential roles and abilities of AI in the field of copywriting. In some cases, the surprise and disbelief at the results underscored the participants' initial underestimation of AI's capabilities. They began to recognize that AI could produce content that matched and sometimes even surpassed the quality of human composition.
2. **Distinctly Human Characteristics**. Both focus groups were inclined to identify what they believed were uniquely 'human' traits within the texts. Elements such as a well-thought-out structure aimed at enhancing readability, wordplay, and employing more intense punctuation were frequently cited. These characteristics were almost unanimously considered indicators of a 'human touch'. The discussions also touched upon the structure of the content. For instance,

dense blocks of text without clear paragraph breaks were sometimes seen as indicative of machine generation, as humans tend to structure their writing to enhance readability. The discussions also ventured into the realm of emojis and hashtags. Participants from both groups felt that how emojis and hashtags were used could offer clues about the text's origin. For instance, using uncommon or excessive emojis was often attributed to AI Moreover, the capacity to convey genuine sentiment and depth in writing was deemed a distinctly human trait. Participants felt that while AI could mimic human writing styles, it could not replicate the genuine emotion and depth humans naturally infuse into their writing. Another sign often associated with AI was the text "sugarcoated".

3. **Complexity of Language and Readability**. A recurring theme in both focus groups was the discussion around the complexity of language and its readability. Participants often associated mechanical precision and strict adherence to grammatical norms with AI-generated content. In contrast, the presence of linguistic quirks, catchy calls to action, wordplays, and even occasional errors were seen as hallmarks of human writing. Some participants pointed out that while AI might construct grammatically perfect sentences, it might need help replicating the natural flow and rhythm of human writing.
4. **Dependence of AI on Human Input**. Despite acknowledging AI's unexpected skills, the consensus from both groups was firm in asserting that the efficacy of AI is as good as the quality and range of data fed to it. Overall, just three participants needed to be made aware of how a language model operates and that it has been trained to rely on a limited amount of data. On the other hand, just one participant was informed enough to understand the differences between various language models and their capacities and hypothesize how they could evolve in the future. It was acknowledged that while AI offers significant advantages, it can only function at its optimal capacity with human oversight, empathy, and creativity.

Contrasting Perspectives

The differences in interpretation can be attributed to each participant's unique set of experiences, varying levels of familiarity with AI, and their perspectives on the role of technology within society. Participants who are more receptive to technological advancements may be due to positive experiences or inherent beliefs, while others may exercise caution when considering such developments. These elements shape individual perceptions and interpretations, resulting in the noted differences in opinions. The analysis of both focus group discussions illuminates a shared understanding of AI's abilities and potential within copywriting. It simultaneously reveals a spectrum of opinions regarding the implications of these capabilities. This indicates that while some aspects of AI in copywriting have reached a consensus, the broader conversation is far from definitive and continues to represent many perspectives.

Differences Between Generation Z and Millennials

The focus groups revealed distinct trends between Gen Z and Millennial participants. Both generations were equally experienced in using AI and language models, but they differed notably in their social media usage and perceptions of AI in creativity.

Gen Z, the 'digital natives', actively engaged with brands on social media, demonstrating keen insights into marketing strategies and brand communication tones, regardless of their professional backgrounds. They also showed a greater tendency to use social media for brand interactions. Millennials, instead, primarily used social media for personal connections, with less focus on brand engagement.

Regarding AI in creative fields, Gen Z displayed optimism and openness, viewing AI as a beneficial complement to human creativity. Millennials, perhaps due to their later exposure to advanced technologies, might lean towards a more cautious stance.

The generational gap was also evident in their approach to textual elements like emojis, hashtags, and sentence structure. Gen Z participants valued modern, social-media-oriented features like hashtags and emojis as key to identifying text origins. Meanwhile, Millennials focused on traditional writing aspects such as sentence complexity and punctuation, highlighting a shift in text interpretation between the generations.

Overall Analysis of the Focus Groups

Both groups identified uniquely 'human' traits in texts, such as genuine sentiment, depth, and linguistic quirks. They also highlighted the importance of human oversight in guiding AI's performance. Notably, generational differences between Gen Z and Millennials surfaced, particularly in their engagement with brands on social media and their interpretations of textual elements. While both groups recognized AI's growing capabilities, they unanimously emphasized the irreplaceable value of human creativity and emotional depth in copywriting.

This study underscores the importance of understanding potential biases and perceptions people hold about AI-generated content, as these perceptions shape the evolving discourse on AI's role in creative fields. The results of the focus group highlight how, even if not always able to correct and identify AI-generated text, all the participants expressed strong bias regarding the use of AI, and whenever the text felt too "fake" or "robotic" they showed a feeling of dislike. These results emphasized that, at the actual stage, LLMs cannot replace the work of a human copywriter, as all the participants looked for "the human touch" in the texts.

Experiment Findings

The online experiment attracted 514 respondents, segmented as follows.

- **Age**. 66.5% born between 1997-2010; 33.5% between 1981-1996.
- **Gender**. 69.6% females, 27.2% males, and 3.1% non-binary.
- **Education**. Predominantly high school diploma holders (43.3%), followed by bachelor's (25%), Master's (14.3%), doctorate (5.5%), writing academy (2.9%), and others (5%).

The initial segment gauged participants' social media engagement. A staggering 99% were active on Instagram, 74.9% on Facebook, 66.1% on TikTok, 47.4% on Pinterest, 26.3% on Twitter, 24.4% on LinkedIn and varying engagement on other platforms. A generational divide was evident, with older participants leaning towards Facebook and Twitter and younger ones towards TikTok and Snapchat. However, platforms like Instagram and Pinterest transcended generational boundaries. Notably, 85.8% of respondents followed brands on social media. Of the participants who indicated following brands on social media, 12.7% reported encountering brand content at a frequency level of 1 (the least frequent). This was followed by 25.8% at a frequency level of 2, 34.8% at level 3, 21.7% at level 4, and 5% at level 5 (the most frequent). The following sector aimed to investigate how people interacted with AI Most participants had a level 3 out of 5 acquaintances with artificial intelligence. Their confidence in their ability to recognize artificial intelligence-generated content also had a level 3 out of 5.

The core experiment presented five couples of human-crafted and AI-generated text created by ChatGPT with the GPT-3.5 language model. Rigorous quality assurance ensured content parity. The results revealed varied abilities among participants to trace content origin, with significant deviations in some text sets. In these graphics, the results of the experiment are illustrated.

Figure 1. Correct Answers to Set 1

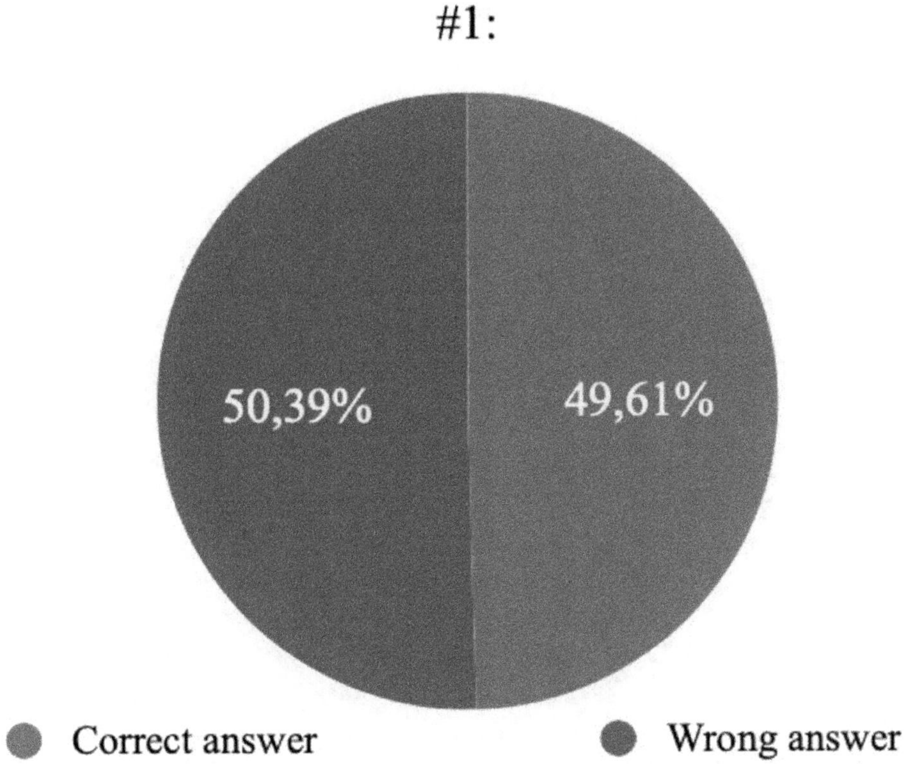

Figure 2. Correct Answers to Set 2

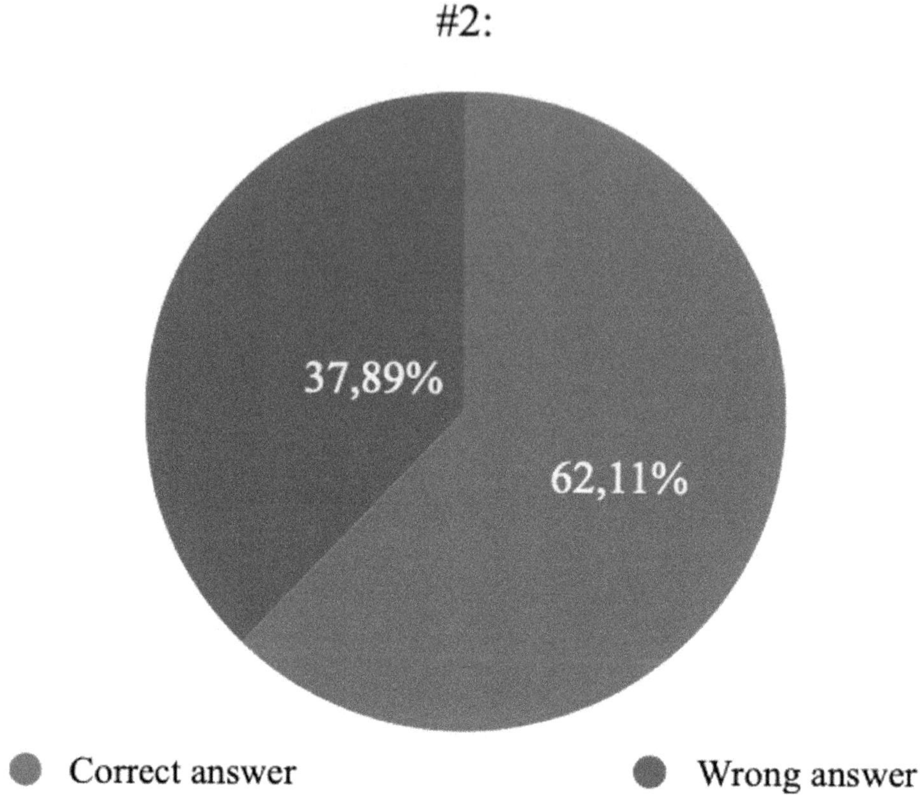

Figure 3. Correct Answers to Set 3

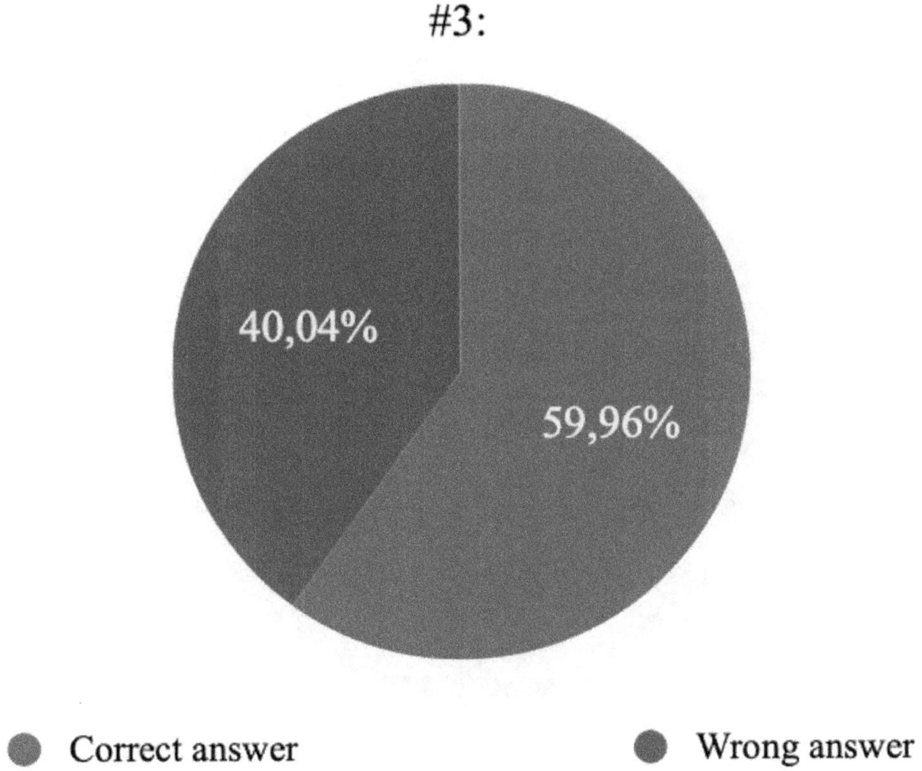

Figure 4. Correct Answers to Set 4

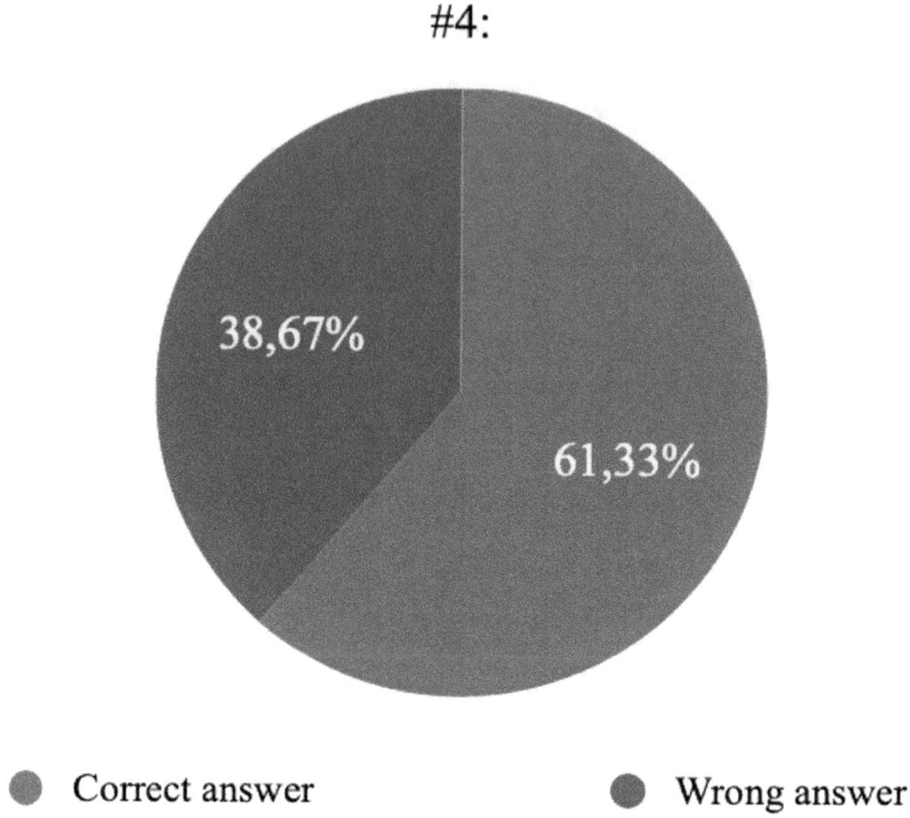

Figure 5. Correct Answers to Set 5

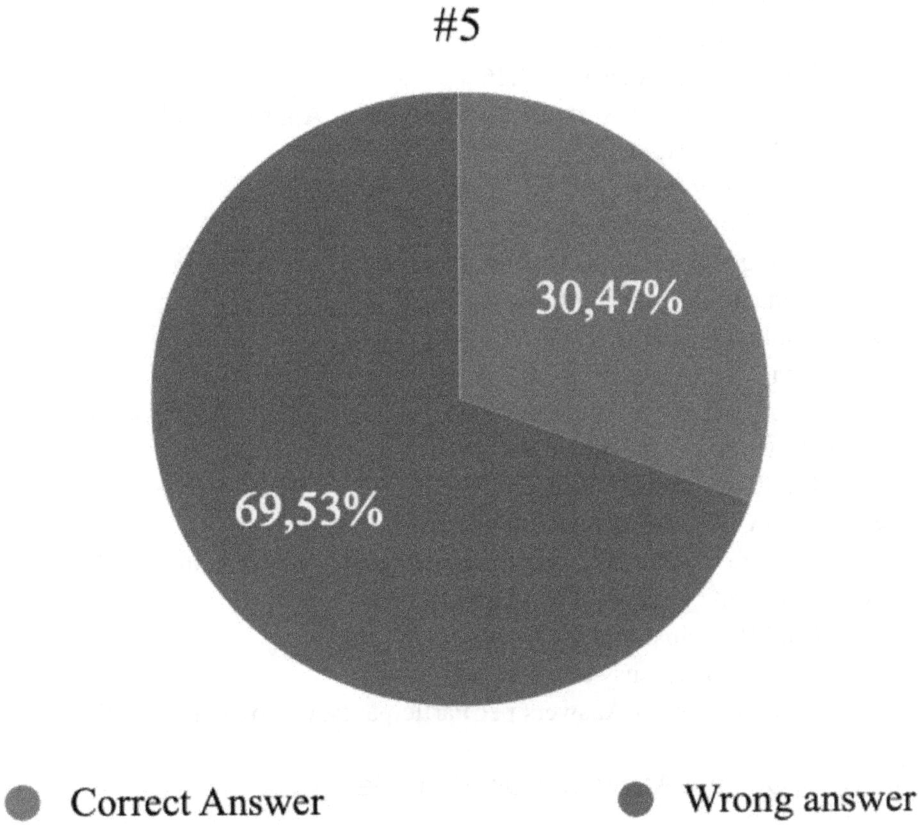

Analysis of Correct Answers Based on Educational Degree

We delved into the correlation between the educational backgrounds of participants and their proficiency in identifying the origin of content. The comprehensive analysis encompassed the following educational qualifications.

- Bachelor's Degree Holders
    - Total Participants: 127
    - Total Correct Answers: 660
    - Average Correct Answers per Participant: Approximately **5.20**
- Doctorate/Ph.D. Holders
    - Total Participants: 28
    - Total Correct Answers: 136

    - Average Correct Answers per Participant. Approximately **4.86**
- High School Diploma or Equivalent
    - Total Participants: 240
    - Total Correct Answers: 1226
    - Average Correct Answers per Participant: Approximately **5.11**
- Master's Degree Holders
    - Total Participants: 72
    - Total Correct Answers: 408
    - Average Correct Answers per Participant. Approximately **5.67**
- Post-Graduate Degree Holders
    - Total Participants: 1
    - Total Correct Answers: 4
    - Average Correct Answers per Participant: Approximately **4.00**
- Secondary School or Equivalent
    - Total Participants: 30
    - Total Correct Answers: 146
    - Average Correct Answers per Participant: Approximately **4.87**
- Scuola Holden Graduates (Writing Academy)
    - Total Participants: 15
    - Total Correct Answers: 120
    - Average Correct Answers per Participant: Approximately **8.00**

Analysis of Correct Answers Based on Generation

This section delves into the correlation between the age of the participants and their ability to identify the origin of content. As explicated in the following graphic, there is not a critical difference between the two generations analyzed.

Millennial participants were 171 and had a total of 934 correct answers, resulting in an average of approximately **5.4** correct answers per individual.

Generation Z participants were 342 and had a total of 1766 correct answers, resulting in an average of approximately **5.1** correct answers per individual.

Analysis of Correct Answers Based on Brand Content Frequency

This section delves into the correlation between the frequency with which participants encounter brand content on social media and their ability to identify the origin of content (Figure 6).

- **Frequency 1**: Among the 58 participants in this category, 322 correct answers were given, resulting in an average of approximately **5.55** correct answers per individual.
- **Frequency 2**: For this frequency, 117 participants provided 564 correct answers, averaging approximately **4.82** correct answers per participant.
- **Frequency 3**: With 158 participants, there were 820 correct answers, leading to an average of approximately **5.19** correct answers per individual.
- **Frequency 4**: From the 99 participants in this category, 564 correct answers were recorded, translating to an average of approximately **5.70** correct answers per participant.
- **Frequency 5**: This group, consisting of 23 participants, registered 134 correct answers, with an average of approximately **5.83** correct answers per individual.

Figure 6. Correlation between the frequency of encountering brand content on social media and the ability to identify the origin of content

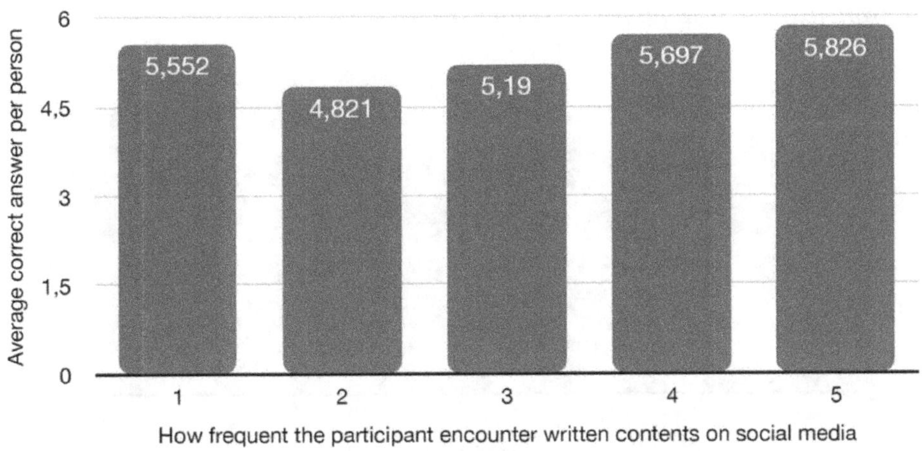

Analysis of Correct Answers Based on Familiarity with AI

This segment focuses on the potential correlation between participants' self-reported familiarity with AI and their proficiency in distinguishing content origins (Figure 7).

- **Familiarity Level 1**: Among the 49 participants, 246 correct answers were recorded, averaging approximately 5.02 correct answers per individual.
- **Familiarity Level 2**: This level had 130 participants who collectively provided 658 correct answers, resulting in an average of approximately 5.06 correct answers per participant.
- **Familiarity Level 3**: With 177 participants, there were 850 correct answers, translating to an average of approximately 4.80 correct answers per individual.
- **Familiarity Level 4**: From the 117 participants in this category, 712 correct answers were given, leading to an average of approximately 6.09 correct answers per participant.
- **Familiarity Level 5 (Most Familiar)**: This group consisted of 40 participants who registered 234 correct answers, with an average of approximately 5.85 correct answers per individual.

Figure 7. Correlation between participants' self-reported familiarity with AI and their proficiency in distinguishing content origins

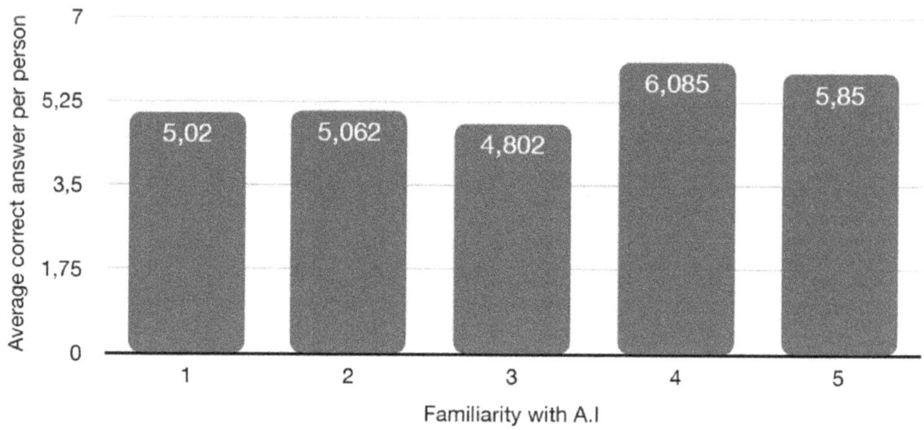

Analysis of Correct Answers Based on Confidence in Recognizing AI Content

This section provides a comprehensive breakdown based on participants' self-assessed confidence levels in recognizing AI-generated content (Figure 8).

- **Confidence Level 1**: Out of 114 participants, there were 598 correct answers, resulting in an average of approximately 5.25 correct answers per individual.
- **Confidence Level 2**: This level had 137 participants who collectively provided 684 correct answers, averaging approximately 4.99 correct answers per participant.
- **Confidence Level 3**: With 148 participants in this category, 782 correct answers were given, translating to an average of approximately 5.28 correct answers per individual.
- **Confidence Level 4**: Among the 97 participants, 550 correct answers were recorded, leading to an average of approximately 5.67 correct answers per participant.
- **Confidence Level 5**: This group, consisting of 17 participants, registered 86 correct answers, with an average of approximately 5.06 correct answers per individual.

Figure 8. Participants' self-assessed confidence levels in recognizing AI-generated content

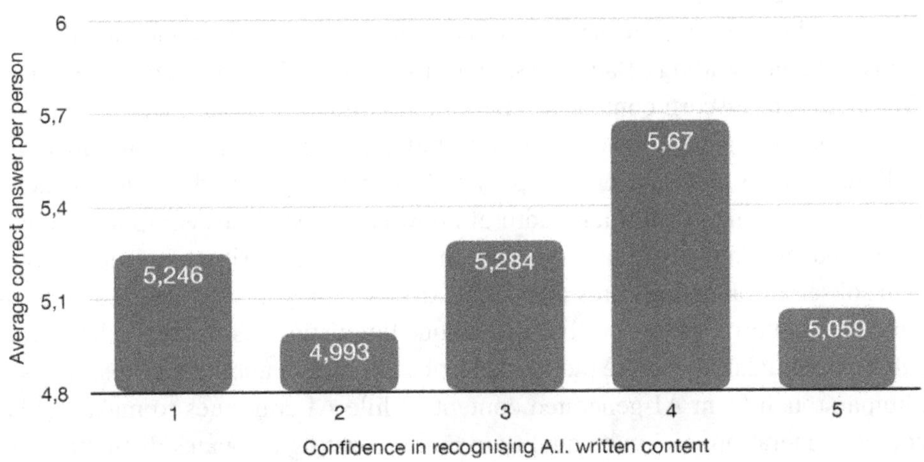

DISCUSSION OF THE RESULTS OF THE EXPERIMENT

Analysis of Correct Answers About Educational Highest Completed Level

In the complicated task of distinguishing AI-generated content from human-crafted content, the influence of one's educational background emerges as a defining factor.

Scuola Holden, established in Turin, Italy, offers a diverse range of courses focusing on narrative arts such as writing, cinema, and screenplay. These courses are designed to inspire creativity and innovation in storytelling, tailored to various age groups and professional backgrounds. The school's dynamic approach provides students with practical skills and theoretical knowledge, preparing them for careers in contemporary humanities (Scuola Holden, 2022).

Our comprehensive data analysis reveals compelling data. the performance of Writing Academy Graduates is particularly illuminating, with an average of 8 correct answers per participant; this group's proficiency in identifying content origins eclipses that of all other educational categories. This is not a mere statistical anomaly but proof of the depth of understanding and expertise that specialized writing training confers.

Contrast this with the performance of participants from other educational backgrounds. Whether holding a Bachelor's, Master's, or even a Doctorate, the differences in their ability to discern content origins were marginal. Despite their varied academic levels, these groups hovered around similar averages, ranging from a medium of 4.86 to 5.67 correct answers per person. The data suggests that while general academic achievements offer a breadth of knowledge, they must equip individuals with the nuanced language understanding that specialized writing education does.

This observation underscores an insight. an academic journey centered on writing, creative or copywriting, cultivates a unique linguistic sensitivity. Such training enables individuals to perceive the subtle intricacies and characteristics distinguishing human touch from AI-generated content. While AI continues to make strides in content generation, an innate quality to human writing resonates distinctly with those trained to recognize it.

In conclusion, while all educational backgrounds bring their strengths to the table, the specialized focus on writing sets individuals apart in discerning AI from human-crafted content.

Analysis of Correct Answers About Generation

The data shows a slight variance in the ability to identify the origin of content between Millennials and Generation Z. Millennials averaged 5.4 correct answers, while Gen Z averaged 5.1. Known as 'digital natives,' Gen Z has an inherent familiarity with digital technology, preferring intuitive engagement over traditional learning methods. Despite similar online time to Millennials, averaging over seven hours daily, Gen Z's particular affinity for smartphones facilitates a unique, omnipresent social interaction style (Serbanescu, 2022).

The hypothesis that continuous digital engagement might reshape neural pathways, possibly causing 'epigenetic' changes, is intriguing (Negroponte, 1995, cited by Serbanescu, 2022). This adaptation could theoretically enhance Gen Z's cognitive skills, like multitasking and nonlinear thinking.

Despite their different social media usage patterns, both Millennials and Gen Z show similar proficiency in discerning AI-generated content. This similarity indicates that the ability to identify such content is influenced by a complex array of factors beyond mere technological exposure or platform familiarity.

Analysis of Correct Answers About Brand Content Exposure

The data suggests that the frequency of brand content exposure on social media does not directly correlate with the ability to discern AI-generated content. Increased exposure does not necessarily enhance discernment abilities. This indicates that the quality of engagement, rather than the volume of content encountered, might be more influential in shaping discernment skills.

Analysis of Correct Answers About AI Familiarity

Data patterns reveal that more profound AI familiarity sometimes equates to heightened discernment. Participants who expressed a familiarity between levels 1 and 3 had almost the same results, but those with results 4 and 5 had a slightly higher number of correct replies. Given the evolving nature of AI-generated content, these results highlight that perceived familiarity is only sometimes equivalent to reality and that continuous adaptation and recalibration of understanding are essential.

Analysis of Correct Answers About Confidence and Discernment

While one might expect participants with the highest confidence to excel in discernment, the results challenge this assumption. Those expressing maximum confidence did not significantly outperform their less confident counterparts. This disparity suggests that factors beyond AI understanding, such as ego or self-perception, might influence expressed confidence. The data emphasizes the need to differentiate between genuine expertise and perceived self-efficacy in discerning AI-generated content.

OVERALL RESULTS OF THE EXPERIMENT

The findings of this experiment present an intriguing insight. Aside from the notable exception of students or alums of writing academies, there appear to be no definitive variables that significantly influence an individual's capacity to recognize AI-generated content. While various factors such as educational background, generational differences, brand content exposure, AI familiarity, and confidence levels were meticulously analyzed, none exhibited the pronounced impact that specialized writing education did. This underscores the unique skill a focused writing curriculum imparts in discerning the nuances between human and AI-crafted content. In a landscape where AI's capabilities are ever-evolving, the results emphasize the importance of specialized training while highlighting the multifaceted nature of human discernment that remains largely unaffected by other variables.

In conclusion, this experiment confirmed that the capacity to recognize AI is completely subjective, and it's innate in subjects with particular attention to writing but can also be trained with an adequate academic journey.

COMPARATIVE ANALYSIS OF EXPERIMENTAL RESULTS AND FOCUS GROUP INSIGHTS

The research's comparative analysis between experimental results and focus group insights offered a holistic view of the participants' capacities and underlying motivations when identifying AI-generated content. Initially, most participants believed they could easily discern AI-generated content from human-produced content. This confidence, as quantitatively measured, was contrasted by the reality of their actual discernment skills, revealing a significant gap.

The focus groups shed light on participants' preconceived notions of AI-generated texts, which were believed to be robotic and predictable. Contrary to these expectations, AI-generated content exhibited a complexity that closely mimicked human writing, reflecting the subtleties of the training data, user prompts, and AI programming aimed at human-like outputs. This realization shifted participants' perspectives, recognizing AI not merely as an autonomous tool but as an extension of human intent, capable of being harnessed to replicate and even enhance human tasks.

This evolving understanding was encapsulated by a participant's insight, which transitioned from seeing AI as a science fiction-like threat to acknowledging its practicality as a formidable tool. Such a shift signified a growing awareness of AI's duality — its capability to augment human efforts and the potential risks if wielded unwisely.

Furthermore, the research highlighted subtle differences between how millennials and Generation Z interact with digital content. Generation Z's inherent digital fluency led them to a deep understanding of brand communications and modern textual elements, like hashtags and emojis, used as cues to determine content origin. Millennials, on the other hand, showed a preference for traditional textual elements and personal connections on social media. Despite these generational distinctions, both groups demonstrated similar abilities in identifying AI-generated content, suggesting that familiarity with digital platforms does not solely dictate one's ability to discern AI's involvement.

Both focus groups and experimental results also touched upon the mixed sentiments toward AI's role in creative fields. Generation Z displayed optimism about AI's integration as a complementary asset, whereas millennials, who gradually adapted to advanced technology, exhibited more cautious or ambivalent attitudes. These generational nuances contribute to a complex portrait of the human-tech relationship in the digital age.

The dual-method approach underscored the importance of understanding the reasoning behind participants' discernment. While quantitative data highlighted the specialized writing training as a factor in heightened discernment, the qualitative insights from focus groups suggested that all participants, regardless of their educational background, tended to underestimate AI's capabilities. This points to a broader societal challenge of fully comprehending AI's rapidly evolving role in creative professions and beyond.

CONCLUSION

The conclusion of this study articulates the vital interplay between artificial intelligence (AI) and the field of copywriting, set against the background of a rapidly digitizing world where technology has become integral to professional and personal realms. This research ventured into an in-depth examination of AI's prospective influence on copywriting, seeking to offer a holistic perspective on its transformative capabilities.

With the rise of sophisticated AI language models, a transformation within the written content production field is inevitable.

The strategic focus on millennials and Generation Z leveraged their intrinsic connection to digital platforms, offering fresh insights into the implications of AI-powered copywriting. These digital natives' views provided a broadened understanding of the topic, underscoring the value of diverse demographic representation in research.

A dual-method approach incorporating triangulation—cross-checking research findings using multiple methods—validated the results and unveiled details that might have been overlooked with a single-method approach. The participants' consistent underestimation of AI's capabilities became apparent, highlighting a disconnect between their perceived and actual discernment abilities.

One of the most notable findings was the exceptional ability of participants with specialized writing training to identify AI-generated content, demonstrating the significant influence of academic writing expertise on discernment ability. In contrast, factors like age, AI familiarity, and frequency of exposure to brand content on social media had minimal impact on discernment abilities. This finding challenges the assumption that digital nativity equates to a better understanding of AI's nuances in content creation.

Stereotypes about AI-generated content, such as a high tone of voice and "sugarcoated" messaging, were prevalent among focus group participants and were reflected in the experimental results, suggesting these stereotypes influenced the discernment of AI content.

The conclusion drawn from this study is that while AI has the potential to be an invaluable tool for copywriters, it is unlikely to replace them entirely. The human touch in content creation remains indispensable, with social media users seeking out and valuing this human element.

Solutions and Recommendations

This research highlights that while AI language models are revolutionizing content creation, they cannot fully replace the unique human aspects of creativity and personal touch, especially in fields like copywriting and social media. The study suggests that AI can enhance but not entirely take over the role of human content creators, requiring more development for full integration.

The study's limitations include the lack of participants from creative writing backgrounds in the focus groups and a reliance on convenience sampling, which may affect the broader applicability of its findings. The controlled research environment and structured survey may not reflect real-world content interactions. Moreover, cultural factors and the absence of older generations in the study highlight areas for future research.

Future Research Directions

This work is a preliminary step in understanding AI's influence on copywriting. Further studies are necessary to explore public perceptions of AI-generated content and how users interact with it. As AI technology evolves, continued research is vital to keep up with these changes. The findings reiterate the irreplaceable role of human creativity in content creation, positioning AI as a complementary tool rather than a replacement for human copywriters.

REFERENCES

Argan, M., Dinç, H., Kaya, S., & Argan, M. T. (2022). Artificial Intelligence (AI) in advertising. Understanding and schematizing the behaviors of social media users. *ADCAIJ. Advances in Distributed Computing and Artificial Intelligence Journal, 11*(3), 331-348. https.//DOI: 10.14201/adcaij.28331

Brock, J. K. U., & Von Wangenheim, F. (2019). Demystifying AI. What digital transformation leaders can teach you about realistic artificial intelligence. *California Management Review, 61*(4), 110-134. https.//DOI: 10.1177/1536504219865226

Campbell, C., Plangger, K., Sands, S., Kietzmann, J., & Bates, K. (2022). How deepfakes and artificial intelligence could reshape the advertising industry. The coming reality of AI fakes and their potential impact on consumer behavior. *Journal of Advertising Research, 62*(3), 241-251. https.//DOI: 10.2501/JAR-2022-017

Chen, G., Xie, P., Dong, J., & Wang, T. (2019). Understanding programmatic creative. The role of AI. *Journal of Advertising, 48*(4), 347-355. https.//DOI: 10.1080/00913367.2019.1654421

Creswell, J. W., & Creswell, J. D. (2017). *Research design. Qualitative, quantitative, and mixed methods approaches.* Sage publications.

Deng, S., Tan, C.-W., Wang, W., & Pan, Y. (2019). Smart Generation System of Personalized Advertising Copy and Its Application to Advertising Practice and Research. *Journal of Advertising,* 48(4), 356–365. https.//DOI: 10.1080/00913367.2019.1652121

Duarte, A. (2021). A New Reality in the Labour Market Demands New Strategies in Education. In Surugiu, R., Stefanel, A., & Apostol, N. (Eds.), *30 de ani de învă ământ jurnalistic i de comunicare în fostele ări comuniste din Estul Europei* (pp. 365–380). Tritonic Books.

Duarte, A. (2023). The relationship between brands and consumers, in Dias, P. & Duarte, A. (2023), *Social Brand Management in a Post Covid-19 Era*, 3-16. Routledge. ISBN 9781032465722 https.//DOI: 10.4324/9781003382331-2

Duarte, A., & Neumaier, A. (2022). Chatvertising. how chatbots are shaping the future of advertising. *Comunicação Pública,* 17(32). https.//DOI: 10.34629/cpublica.329

Frank, M. R., Autor, D. H., Bessen, J., Brynjolfsson, E., Cebrian, M., Deming, D., Feldman, M. P., Groh, M., Lobo, J., Moro, E., Wang, D., Youn, H., & Rahwan, I. (2019). Toward understanding the impact of artificial intelligence on labor. *Proceedings of the National Academy of Sciences of the United States of America,* 116(14), 6531–6539. https.//DOI: 10.1073/pnas.1900949116

Hameed, M. A., Hassaballah, M., Hosney, M. E., & Alqahtani, A. (2022). An AI-Enabled Internet of Things Based Autism Care System for Improving Cognitive Ability of Children with Autism Spectrum Disorders. *Computational Intelligence and Neuroscience,* 2022, 1–12. https.// DOI: 10.1155/2022/2247675

Hanna, D. M. (2023). The use of artificial intelligence art generator "midjourney" in artistic and advertising creativity. *Journal of design sciences and applied arts, 4*(2), 42-58. https.//DOI: 10.21608/jdsaa.2023.169144.1231

Kietzmann, J., Paschen, J., & Treen, E. (2018). Artificial intelligence in advertising. How marketers can leverage artificial intelligence along the consumer journey. *Journal of Advertising Research, 58*(3), 263-267. https.//DOI: 10.2501/JAR-2018-035

Li, H. (2019). Special section introduction. Artificial intelligence and advertising. *Journal of advertising, 48*(4), 333-337. https.//DOI: 10.1080/00913367.2019.1654947

Malthouse, E. C., Hessary, Y. K., Vakeel, K. A., Burke, R., & Fudurić, M. (2019). An Algorithm for Allocating Sponsored Recommendations and Content. Unifying Programmatic Advertising and Recommender Systems. *Journal of Advertising,* 48(4), 366–379. https.//DOI: 10.1080/00913367.2019.1652123

Matthews, J., Fastnedge, D., & Nairn, A. (2023). The future of advertising campaigns. The role of AI-generated images in advertising creative. *Journal of Pervasive Media, 8*(1), 29-49. https.//DOI: 10.1386/jpm_00003_1

OpenAi. (n.d.). https.//openai.com. Retrieved February 1, 2023, from https.//openai.com

Qin, X., & Jiang, Z. (2019). The impact of AI on the advertising process. The Chinese experience. *Journal of Advertising, 48*(4), 338-346. https.//DOI: 10.1080/00913367.2019.1652122

Rodgers, S. (2021). Themed issue introduction. Promises and perils of artificial intelligence and advertising. *Journal of Advertising, 50*(1), 1-10. https.//DOI: 10.1080/00913367.2020.1868233

Scuola Holden (2022, March 16). Scuola Holden - School of Writing - Master in Storytelling. Scuola Holden. https.//scuolaholden.it/en/

Serbanescu, A. (2022). Millennials and Gen Z in the Era of Social Media. *Social Media, Technology, and New Generations. Digital Millennial Generation and Generation Z,* 61-78.

Vakratsas, D., & Wang, X. (2020). Artificial intelligence in advertising creativity. *Journal of Advertising, 50*(1), 39-51. https.//DOI: 10.1080/00913367.2020.1843090

Wu, L., Dodoo, N. A., & Wen, T. J. (2024). Disclosing AI's Involvement in Advertising to Consumers. A Task-Dependent Perspective. *Journal of Advertising*, 1-19. https.//DOI: 10.1080/00913367.2024.2309929

Zhao, G., Li, Y., & Xu, Q. (2022). From Emotion AI to Cognitive AI. *International Journal of Network Dynamics and Intelligence*, 65–72. https.//DOI: 10.53941/ijndi0101006

KEY TERMS AND DEFINITIONS

Artificial Intelligence (AI): refers to the simulation of human intelligence processes by machines, especially computer systems.

Comparable Study: It's a research approach that involves comparing two or more entities, variables, or groups to identify similarities and differences. This type of study aims to draw conclusions about how the compared items relate to each other and can be used to highlight contrasts or establish benchmarks.

Copywriting: The art and science of writing persuasive texts for marketing and advertising purposes, and it can be used in a variety of mediums, such as websites, print ads, emails, and social media.

Creative Content: Refers to original material created to entertain, inform, inspire, or engage an audience. It can exist in several forms, such as articles, videos, images, infographics, podcasts, or social media posts, to capture the audience's attention while conveying a message, story, or idea.

Experimental Design: It's the process of planning an experiment to ensure that it can test a hypothesis in a controlled and systematic way. The objective is to establish cause-and-effect relationships between variables.

Message Perception: It's how a message is received and interpreted by a certain audience. It involves the processes through which people understand, make sense of, and respond to the messages they encounter in communication.

Mixed-Methods: A methodological approach that combines both quantitative and qualitative research techniques. It aims to provide a more comprehensive understanding of a research problem by drawing on the strengths of each method.

Chapter 13
Transforming the Modern Workplace With AI (Artificial Intelligence) With Special References From India:
Transformational Dynamics for Better Organizational Behavior

C. Karthikeyan
https://orcid.org/0000-0002-2018-8245
SJB Institute of Technology, Vishwesarya Technological University, Belgav, India

ABSTRACT

Artificial Intelligence (AI) is reshaping the landscape of organizational behaviour, driving unprecedented transformation in decision-making, human resource management, employee training, and workforce planning. This essay delves into the multifaceted applications of AI within organizations, highlighting its pivotal role in enhancing decision-making capabilities through rapid data analysis and predictive modelling. In human resources, AI revolutionizes recruitment, employee engagement, and performance management, exemplified by global leaders like Unilever and IBM. The integration of AI-driven personalized learning platforms ensures continuous skill development, fostering a motivated and adept workforce. Additionally, predictive analytics facilitate strategic workforce planning, enabling proactive measures to retain top talent, as seen in companies like Royal Dutch Shell.

DOI: 10.4018/979-8-3693-8442-8.ch013

INTRODUCTION

Artificial Intelligence (AI) has become a significant driver of change in various fields, including organizational behaviour. The application of AI in this area enhances decision-making, optimizes performance, and fosters a more adaptive and innovative organizational culture. Enhanced Decision-Making is the key result area any organization or the leader for that matter, will experience from the AI algorithms that can process vast amounts of data more quickly and accurately than humans, leading to improved decision-making processes. In the finance sector, companies like Goldman Sachs use AI to analyse market data and predict stock trends, providing a competitive edge in investment decisions (Davenport & Kirby, 2016). Similarly, in healthcare, AI systems assist in diagnosing diseases and recommending treatments, thereby supporting medical professionals in making informed decisions (Topol, 2019).

OPTIMIZING HUMAN RESOURCES

AI applications in human resources (HR) have revolutionized recruitment, employee engagement, and performance management. For example, Unilever employs AI-driven platforms to screen and assess candidates, significantly reducing hiring time and costs (Johnson, 2019). Furthermore, AI tools analyse employee feedback and engagement surveys to identify areas for improvement, enhancing overall job satisfaction and retention rates (Huang & Rust, 2018).

Fostering Innovation and Adaptability

Organizations leverage AI to foster a culture of innovation and adaptability. In the automotive industry, Tesla utilizes AI to develop self-driving technologies, pushing the boundaries of what is possible in transportation (Vance, 2015). This innovative approach not only sets Tesla apart from competitors but also encourages a mindset of continuous improvement and adaptability among its workforces.

Improving Customer Experience

AI-powered chatbots and virtual assistants have transformed customer service by providing instant, personalized responses to inquiries. For instance, Sephora uses AI chatbots to offer beauty advice and product recommendations, enhancing the customer shopping experience (Nair, 2018). This not only improves customer satisfaction but also allows employees to focus on more complex tasks that require human intervention.

Enhancing Employee Training and Development

AI-driven learning platforms provide personalized training programs tailored to individual employee needs. IBM's Watson, for example, offers personalized learning paths for employees based on their roles and career aspirations, ensuring continuous skill development and career growth (Greenfield, 2018). This approach helps organizations maintain a skilled and motivated workforce, ready to meet evolving business challenges.

Predictive Analytics for Workforce Planning

Predictive analytics powered by AI help organizations anticipate workforce trends and plan accordingly. For example, Royal Dutch Shell uses AI to predict employee turnover, enabling proactive measures to retain top talent (Accenture, 2019). This strategic approach ensures that organizations can maintain a stable and experienced workforce, crucial for long-term success.

CHALLENGES AND ETHICAL CONSIDERATIONS

Despite its benefits, the integration of AI in organizational behaviour presents challenges and ethical considerations. Concerns about data privacy, algorithmic bias, and job displacement must be addressed. Companies like Microsoft and Google are investing in ethical AI research to ensure that their AI systems are transparent, fair, and accountable (Binns, 2018). Addressing these challenges is crucial for building trust and ensuring the sustainable adoption of AI in organizations. The integration of AI in organizational behaviour has the potential to transform the modern workplace by enhancing decision-making, optimizing HR functions, fostering innovation, improving customer experience, and supporting employee development. However, it is essential to address the associated challenges and ethical considerations to harness the full potential of AI. As organizations continue to embrace AI, they will not only achieve operational efficiency but also foster a more dynamic, innovative, and adaptive organizational culture.

Objectives

i. **Analyse AI's Impact on Decision-Making**: To examine how AI enhances organizational decision-making capabilities through rapid data analysis and predictive modelling.

ii. **Evaluate AI in Human Resource Management**: To explore the ways AI revolutionizes recruitment, employee engagement, and performance management, with examples from global leaders and organizations in developing countries.
iii. **Assess AI-Driven Learning Platforms**: To investigate how personalized learning platforms powered by AI contribute to continuous skill development and employee motivation.
iv. **Investigate Predictive Analytics for Workforce Planning**: To assess how predictive analytics facilitate strategic workforce planning and proactive talent retention strategies.
v. **Explore AI's Future Role in Organizational Culture**: To analyse the potential of AI to foster a positive organizational culture, drive innovation, and maintain a competitive advantage in the future.

By examining these diverse applications and addressing the challenges, we can appreciate the profound impact AI has on organizational behaviour and its potential to shape the future of work.

AI IN ORGANIZATIONAL BEHAVIOUR: TRANSFORMING THE MODERN WORKPLACE

Artificial Intelligence (AI) has become a significant driver of change in various fields, including organizational behaviour. The application of AI in this area enhances decision-making, optimizes performance, and fosters a more adaptive and innovative organizational culture. This essay explores the diverse applications of AI in organizational behaviour, supported by examples from around the world, including India and other developing countries.

Enhanced Decision-Making

AI algorithms can process vast amounts of data more quickly and accurately than humans, leading to improved decision-making processes. In the finance sector, companies like Goldman Sachs use AI to analyse market data and predict stock trends, providing a competitive edge in investment decisions (Davenport & Kirby, 2016). Similarly, in healthcare, AI systems assist in diagnosing diseases and recommending treatments, thereby supporting medical professionals in making informed decisions (Topol, 2019). In India, Infosys uses AI-driven analytics to provide insights into business performance and market trends, helping organizations make strategic decisions (Infosys, 2020). In developing countries, similar applications are seen where AI aids in optimizing agricultural practices, such as in Kenya, where

AI tools help farmers decide the best crops to plant based on weather patterns and soil conditions (Kansiime, 2020).

Optimizing Human Resources

AI applications in human resources (HR) have revolutionized recruitment, employee engagement, and performance management. For example, Unilever employs AI-driven platforms to screen and assess candidates, significantly reducing hiring time and costs (Johnson, 2019). Furthermore, AI tools analyze employee feedback and engagement surveys to identify areas for improvement, enhancing overall job satisfaction and retention rates (Huang & Rust, 2018). In India, Wipro uses AI for talent management, including recruitment and employee engagement, by deploying chatbots to handle initial candidate interactions and using AI to match candidates to job roles (Wipro, 2020). Similarly, in developing countries like Brazil, AI is used to streamline HR processes and improve employee engagement (Freire, 2019).

Fostering Innovation and Adaptability

Organizations leverage AI to foster a culture of innovation and adaptability. In the automotive industry, Tesla utilizes AI to develop self-driving technologies, pushing the boundaries of what is possible in transportation (Vance, 2015). This innovative approach not only sets Tesla apart from competitors but also encourages a mindset of continuous improvement and adaptability among its workforces. In India, Tata Consultancy Services (TCS) uses AI to drive innovation in software development and business solutions, promoting a culture of continuous learning and adaptability (TCS, 2021). In developing countries, companies like South Africa's iSON Group use AI to enhance customer service and operational efficiency, fostering innovation in business processes (iSON, 2019).

Improving Customer Experience

AI-powered chatbots and virtual assistants have transformed customer service by providing instant, personalized responses to inquiries. For instance, Sephora uses AI chatbots to offer beauty advice and product recommendations, enhancing the customer shopping experience (Nair, 2018). This not only improves customer satisfaction but also allows employees to focus on more complex tasks that require human intervention. In India, HDFC Bank uses AI-driven chatbots to handle customer queries and transactions, significantly enhancing the banking experience for its customers (HDFC Bank, 2019). Similarly, in the Philippines, AI is employed in the customer service industry to handle a high volume of inquiries, improving efficiency and customer satisfaction (Frost & Sullivan, 2020).

Enhancing Employee Training and Development

AI-driven learning platforms provide personalized training programs tailored to individual employee needs. IBM's Watson, for example, offers personalized learning paths for employees based on their roles and career aspirations, ensuring continuous skill development and career growth (Greenfield, 2018). This approach helps organizations maintain a skilled and motivated workforce, ready to meet evolving business challenges. In India, Reliance Industries uses AI to provide personalized training and development programs for its employees, ensuring they stay updated with the latest industry trends and skills (Reliance Industries, 2020). In developing countries, such as Nigeria, AI-powered e-learning platforms are used to enhance the skills of the workforce, contributing to national development (Adeoye, 2020).

Predictive Analytics for Workforce Planning

Predictive analytics powered by AI help organizations anticipate workforce trends and plan accordingly. For example, Royal Dutch Shell uses AI to predict employee turnover, enabling proactive measures to retain top talent (Accenture, 2019). This strategic approach ensures that organizations can maintain a stable and experienced workforce, crucial for long-term success. In India, companies like Mahindra & Mahindra use AI to predict labour needs and manage workforce planning, ensuring they can meet production demands effectively (Mahindra, 2020). Similarly, in Indonesia, AI is used to forecast workforce requirements in manufacturing and other industries, helping organizations plan more effectively (Indonesia Ministry of Industry, 2020).

Challenges and Ethical Considerations

Despite its benefits, the integration of AI in organizational behaviours presents challenges and ethical considerations. Concerns about data privacy, algorithmic bias, and job displacement must be addressed. Companies like Microsoft and Google are investing in ethical AI research to ensure that their AI systems are transparent, fair, and accountable (Binns, 2018). Addressing these challenges is crucial for building trust and ensuring the sustainable adoption of AI in organizations. The integration of AI in organizational behaviour has the potential to transform the modern workplace by enhancing decision-making, optimizing HR functions, fostering innovation, improving customer experience, and supporting employee development. Examples from India and other developing countries demonstrate the global impact and potential of AI in this field. However, it is essential to address the associated challenges and ethical considerations to harness the full potential of AI. As organizations continue to embrace AI, they will not only achieve operational efficiency but also foster a more dynamic, innovative, and adaptive organizational culture. By examining these diverse applications and addressing the challenges, we can appreciate the profound impact AI has on organizational behaviour and its potential to shape the future of work.

ENHANCED DECISION-MAKING WITH AI

AI algorithms can process vast amounts of data more quickly and accurately than humans, leading to significantly improved decision-making processes. This capability is transforming various sectors, including finance, healthcare, and beyond, by enabling more informed, data-driven decisions.

Finance Sector

In the finance sector, companies like Goldman Sachs leverage AI to analyze market data and predict stock trends, providing a competitive edge in investment decisions. AI models, such as those based on deep learning, can identify patterns and correlations in massive datasets that are beyond human capability to detect. For example, Goldman Sachs uses AI to develop algorithms that analyze market sentiment by processing news articles, social media posts, and other unstructured data sources. These algorithms predict stock price movements, enabling traders to make more informed investment decisions (Davenport & Kirby, 2016). Research has shown that AI-driven decision-making can significantly enhance investment performance. A study by the University of Technology Sydney found that AI-based trading systems outperformed traditional trading strategies by 6% annually over a period of ten years (Gupta & Chen, 2018). This improvement is attributed to AI's ability to continuously learn and adapt to market changes, thereby providing more accurate predictions.

Healthcare Sector

In healthcare, AI systems assist in diagnosing diseases and recommending treatments, thereby supporting medical professionals in making informed decisions. For instance, IBM Watson Health uses AI to analyze vast amounts of medical literature, patient records, and clinical trial data to recommend personalized treatment plans for cancer patients. This system helps oncologists identify the most effective treatments based on the latest research and individual patient data (Topol, 2019). Statistical applications of AI in healthcare have demonstrated significant improvements in diagnostic accuracy. A study published in *The Lancet* found that AI algorithms were able to diagnose skin cancer with a higher accuracy rate (95%) compared to dermatologists (86%) (Esteva et al., 2017). This increased accuracy can lead to earlier detection and treatment of diseases, ultimately improving patient outcomes.

Retail Sector

In the retail sector, AI enhances decision-making by analysing consumer behaviour and preferences. For example, Amazon uses AI algorithms to analyse purchasing patterns and recommend products to customers. This personalized recommendation system has been credited with increasing sales and improving customer satisfaction (Smith, 2018). A statistical analysis conducted by McKinsey & Company revealed that AI-driven personalization can lead to a 10-15% increase in sales and a 20-30% increase in marketing ROI for retailers (Bughin et al., 2018). By leveraging AI, retailers can make more informed decisions about inventory management, pricing strategies, and marketing campaigns.

Manufacturing Sector

In manufacturing, AI is used to optimize production processes and enhance decision-making. General Electric (GE) employs AI-driven predictive maintenance systems to monitor equipment performance and predict failures before they occur. By analysing data from sensors embedded in machinery, these systems can identify patterns indicative of potential issues and recommend maintenance actions. This proactive approach reduces downtime and maintenance costs (Rogers, 2018). Research has shown that predictive maintenance powered by AI can reduce maintenance costs by up to 30% and decrease unplanned downtime by 50% (Accenture, 2017). These improvements are achieved through more accurate and timely maintenance decisions, leading to enhanced operational efficiency.

Public Sector

AI is also transforming decision-making in the public sector. For instance, the city of Barcelona uses AI to optimize traffic management. By analyzing data from traffic cameras, sensors, and GPS devices, AI algorithms predict traffic congestion and adjust traffic signals in real-time to improve traffic flow. This system has resulted in a 20% reduction in traffic congestion and a 10% decrease in travel time for commuters (Barcelona City Council, 2019). AI-driven decision-making processes are revolutionizing various sectors by providing more accurate, data-driven insights.

In finance, AI enhances investment strategies; in healthcare, it improves diagnostic accuracy and treatment recommendations; in retail, it boosts sales through personalized recommendations; in manufacturing, it optimizes maintenance processes; and in the public sector, it enhances urban management. These applications demonstrate the profound impact of AI on decision-making and its potential to drive efficiency and innovation across industries.

OPTIMIZING HUMAN RESOURCES WITH AI

AI applications in human resources (HR) have revolutionized recruitment, employee engagement, and performance management. AI-driven platforms and tools significantly enhance HR functions by improving efficiency, accuracy, and overall employee satisfaction. This section explores these applications with examples from India and supporting research evidence.

AI in Recruitment happening in India

AI has streamlined the recruitment process by automating the screening and assessment of candidates. Unilever, for example, employs AI-driven platforms to screen and assess candidates, significantly reducing hiring time and costs (Johnson, 2019). These platforms utilize natural language processing (NLP) and machine learning algorithms to evaluate resumes, conduct initial interviews, and predict candidate success based on historical data. In India, companies like Wipro and Tata Consultancy Services (TCS) use similar AI-driven recruitment tools. Wipro uses an AI-powered chatbot named "Maya" to interact with candidates, answer their queries, and conduct preliminary screenings. This AI tool has reduced the time taken to shortlist candidates by 50% and increased the overall efficiency of the recruitment process (Wipro, 2020). TCS employs AI algorithms to match candidates to job roles based on their skills, experience, and personality traits, ensuring a better fit between the candidate and the job (TCS, 2021). Research by the HR Research Institute (HRRI) supports these findings, indicating that organizations using AI in recruitment have experienced a 30% reduction in hiring time and a 20% increase in the quality of hires (HRRI, 2020).

Enhancing Employee Engagement

AI tools analyse employee feedback and engagement surveys to identify areas for improvement, thereby enhancing overall job satisfaction and retention rates. These tools can detect patterns in employee sentiment and provide actionable insights to

HR managers. Infosys, for instance, utilizes AI to monitor employee engagement by analysing data from various sources such as emails, surveys, and social media. The AI system identifies trends and potential issues, allowing the company to address employee concerns proactively. This has led to a 15% increase in employee satisfaction and a 10% decrease in turnover rates (Infosys, 2020). In India, IBM uses its AI platform, Watson, to assess employee sentiment and engagement. Watson analyses text from employee feedback and provides HR with insights into areas requiring attention, such as work-life balance or professional development opportunities. This approach has helped IBM India maintain high levels of employee engagement and satisfaction (IBM, 2020). A study by Deloitte revealed that organizations using AI to analyse employee engagement data reported a 40% increase in employee satisfaction and a 20% improvement in retention rates (Deloitte, 2019).

Performance Management

AI also plays a crucial role in performance management by providing continuous feedback and personalized development plans for employees. AI-driven platforms can track employee performance metrics in real-time, identify areas for improvement, and suggest training programs to enhance skills. Reliance Industries in India uses an AI-based performance management system that continuously monitors employee performance and provides instant feedback. The system uses data from various sources, including project management tools and peer reviews, to give a comprehensive view of an employee's performance. This has resulted in more accurate performance evaluations and personalized development plans, leading to a 25% increase in employee productivity (Reliance Industries, 2020). Similarly, Infosys employs AI to personalize training programs for its employees based on their performance data and career aspirations. The AI system recommends specific courses and training modules, ensuring continuous skill development and career growth. This has contributed to a more skilled and motivated workforce (Infosys, 2020). Research by the International Journal of Human Resource Management indicates that AI-driven performance management systems can increase employee productivity by 20% and improve overall performance ratings by 15% (IJHRM, 2019). AI has revolutionized human resources by optimizing recruitment, enhancing employee engagement, and improving performance management. In India, companies like Wipro, TCS, Infosys, and Reliance Industries have successfully implemented AI-driven HR solutions, resulting in significant improvements in efficiency, employee satisfaction, and productivity. These examples and supporting research evidence underscore the transformative potential of AI in human resources, paving the way for more effective and dynamic HR practices.

ENHANCING EMPLOYEE TRAINING AND DEVELOPMENT WITH AI

AI-driven learning platforms provide personalized training programs tailored to individual employee needs, ensuring continuous skill development and career growth. This approach helps organizations maintain a skilled and motivated workforce, ready to meet evolving business challenges. Indian companies are increasingly adopting AI-based training solutions to enhance employee development.

Personalized Learning Paths

IBM's Watson offers personalized learning paths for employees based on their roles and career aspirations, ensuring continuous skill development and career growth (Greenfield, 2018). Similarly, several Indian companies have integrated AI into their training and development programs to tailor learning experiences to individual employees.

Infosys

Infosys, a leading Indian IT services company, uses an AI-driven learning platform called Lex, which provides personalized learning experiences for its employees. Lex uses machine learning algorithms to recommend courses and training modules based on an employee's job role, previous learning history, and career aspirations. This ensures that employees receive relevant training that enhances their skills and prepares them for future roles (Infosys, 2020). A study by Infosys revealed that employees using the Lex platform experienced a 40% increase in learning efficiency and a 30% improvement in skill acquisition rates (Infosys, 2020).

Tata Consultancy Services (TCS)

TCS employs an AI-based platform called TCS iON Digital Learning Hub to provide personalized training to its employees. This platform uses AI to assess the learning needs of employees and recommend appropriate courses and learning materials. It also tracks the progress of employees and provides real-time feedback, enabling continuous improvement and development (TCS, 2021). Research conducted by TCS indicated that the use of the iON Digital Learning Hub led to a 25% increase in employee engagement with training programs and a 20% improvement in overall performance (TCS, 2021).

Reliance Industries

Reliance Industries uses AI-driven platforms to enhance employee training and development. The company's AI-based learning management system analyzes data from employee performance reviews, skills assessments, and career goals to create personalized training plans. This approach ensures that employees receive training that is relevant to their current roles and future career aspirations (Reliance Industries, 2020). A case study by Reliance Industries showed that employees who participated in the AI-driven training programs demonstrated a 35% improvement in skill proficiency and a 15% increase in job satisfaction (Reliance Industries, 2020).

Wipro

Wipro has implemented an AI-based learning platform that customizes training programs for its employees. The platform uses AI to evaluate the learning preferences, performance metrics, and career goals of employees, and then recommends personalized training modules. This tailored approach to learning has helped Wipro maintain a highly skilled and motivated workforce (Wipro, 2020). According to Wipro's internal research, employees using the AI-driven learning platform experienced a 30% increase in learning engagement and a 25% improvement in skill development outcomes (Wipro, 2020). AI-driven learning platforms are transforming employee training and development in India by providing personalized learning experiences tailored to individual needs. Companies like Infosys, TCS, Reliance Industries, and Wipro have successfully implemented AI-based training solutions, resulting in significant improvements in learning efficiency, skill acquisition, and employee engagement. These examples demonstrate the potential of AI to enhance employee training and development, ensuring a skilled and motivated workforce ready to meet evolving business challenges.

PREDICTIVE ANALYTICS FOR WORKFORCE PLANNING

Predictive analytics powered by AI help organizations anticipate workforce trends and plan accordingly. This strategic approach ensures that organizations can maintain a stable and experienced workforce, crucial for long-term success. In India, several companies have adopted predictive analytics to enhance their workforce planning and management strategies.

Tata Consultancy Services (TCS)

TCS leverages AI-driven predictive analytics to anticipate workforce trends and optimize resource allocation. The company's predictive analytics tools analyze historical employee data, performance metrics, and external market trends to forecast future workforce needs. This enables TCS to identify potential skill gaps, anticipate employee turnover, and develop targeted retention strategies (TCS, 2021). According to TCS, the implementation of predictive analytics has led to a 15% reduction in employee turnover rates and a 20% improvement in workforce utilization (TCS, 2021).

Infosys

Infosys uses AI-powered predictive analytics to enhance workforce planning and talent management. The company's predictive models analyze various factors, including employee performance, engagement levels, and career progression, to identify employees at risk of leaving. This allows Infosys to take proactive measures, such as offering career development opportunities and improving work-life balance, to retain top talent (Infosys, 2020). Research by Infosys indicates that the use of predictive analytics has resulted in a 10% increase in employee retention rates and a 25% improvement in employee satisfaction (Infosys, 2020).

Wipro

Wipro employs predictive analytics to forecast workforce demand and plan recruitment accordingly. The company's AI-driven models analyse project pipelines, client demands, and market trends to predict future staffing needs. This helps Wipro ensure that they have the right talent in place to meet project requirements and client expectations (Wipro, 2020). A case study by Wipro revealed that predictive analytics improved their workforce planning accuracy by 30%, resulting in more efficient resource allocation and better project outcomes (Wipro, 2020).

Reliance Industries

Reliance Industries uses predictive analytics to manage workforce planning and optimize employee retention strategies. The company's AI tools analyse employee data, such as job satisfaction, performance reviews, and career aspirations, to predict potential turnover. By identifying at-risk employees, Reliance can implement targeted retention initiatives, such as personalized development programs and enhanced employee benefits (Reliance Industries, 2020).

Reliance reported a 12% reduction in voluntary turnover and a 20% increase in employee engagement because of using predictive analytics for workforce planning (Reliance Industries, 2020).

HCL Technologies

HCL Technologies utilizes AI-driven predictive analytics to forecast workforce trends and plan for future skill requirements. The company's predictive models analyse data from various sources, including employee surveys, performance metrics, and industry trends, to identify emerging skill gaps. This enables HCL to design training programs and recruitment strategies that align with future business needs (HCL Technologies, 2020).Research by HCL indicated that predictive analytics enhanced their ability to align workforce skills with business demands, resulting in a 15% improvement in project delivery times and a 10% increase in client satisfaction (HCL Technologies, 2020).

Conclusion

Predictive analytics powered by AI are transforming workforce planning in India by enabling organizations to anticipate workforce trends and take proactive measures to retain top talent and optimize resource allocation. Companies like TCS, Infosys, Wipro, Reliance Industries, and HCL Technologies have successfully implemented predictive analytics, resulting in significant improvements in employee retention, satisfaction, and overall workforce efficiency. These examples demonstrate the potential of AI-driven predictive analytics to enhance workforce planning and contribute to long-term organizational success.

FUTURE OF AI IN ORGANIZATIONAL BEHAVIOR: A GLOBAL AND INDIAN PERSPECTIVE

The future of AI in organizational behavior is poised to bring transformative changes across various dimensions of work, from recruitment and employee engagement to performance management and workforce planning. Below is a comparative table highlighting the future applications of AI in organizational behavior, showcasing examples from around the world and India.

Table 1. Potential to significantly contribute to the development of positive organizational behaviour, leading to more productive, satisfied, and engaged employees

Area	Global Examples	Indian Examples
Recruitment	Unilever uses AI to screen and assess candidates, reducing hiring time and costs (Johnson, 2019).	Wipro uses an AI-powered chatbot named "Maya" to interact with candidates and conduct preliminary screenings, reducing time to shortlist candidates by 50% (Wipro, 2020).
Employee Engagement	IBM Watson analyses employee sentiment to enhance engagement and satisfaction (IBM, 2020).	Infosys uses AI to monitor employee engagement and proactively address issues, resulting in a 15% increase in satisfaction (Infosys, 2020).
Performance Management	General Electric (GE) uses AI for continuous performance tracking and feedback (Rogers, 2018).	Reliance Industries employs AI-based systems for real-time performance monitoring and feedback, improving productivity by 25% (Reliance Industries, 2020).
Training and Development	IBM Watson offers personalized learning paths for continuous skill development (Greenfield, 2018).	TCS iON Digital Learning Hub uses AI to recommend personalized courses, increasing engagement by 25% (TCS, 2021).
Workforce Planning	Royal Dutch Shell uses AI to predict employee turnover and plan retention strategies (Accenture, 2019).	TCS uses predictive analytics to anticipate workforce trends and optimize resource allocation, reducing turnover rates by 15% (TCS, 2021).
Diversity and Inclusion	PwC uses AI to analyse hiring practices and ensure diversity (PwC, 2020).	Infosys employs AI to track diversity metrics and develop inclusive workplace strategies (Infosys, 2020).
Employee Wellbeing	Microsoft uses AI to track employee wellbeing and work-life balance (Microsoft, 2020).	Tech Mahindra uses AI to monitor employee health and wellbeing, providing support resources as needed (Tech Mahindra, 2020).
Innovation and Collaboration	Google uses AI to facilitate innovation and collaboration through project management tools (Google, 2020).	HCL Technologies employs AI to enhance collaboration and innovation, leading to a 15% improvement in project delivery times (HCL Technologies, 2020).

Source: Computed by Author: Prof Dr.C.Karthikeyan

Enhanced Employee Engagement and Satisfaction

a. Employee Engagement

i. **Personalized Employee Experience**: AI can tailor the workplace experience to individual needs, preferences, and career goals. For example, AI-driven platforms can customize work schedules, recommend professional development opportunities, and suggest wellness programs based on employee data.

ii. **Real-Time Feedback and Recognition**: AI tools can provide instant feedback and recognition, fostering a culture of continuous improvement and appreciation. This helps employees feel valued and motivated.

b. Improved Decision-Making

i. **Data-Driven Insights**: AI can analyze vast amounts of data to provide actionable insights, helping managers make informed decisions about employee management, resource allocation, and organizational strategies.
ii. **Predictive Analytics**: Predictive analytics can anticipate workforce trends, such as potential turnover or emerging skill gaps, allowing organizations to proactively address these issues and ensure stability.

c. Better Recruitment and Onboarding

i. **Efficient Recruitment Processes**: AI can streamline the recruitment process by automating resume screening, conducting initial interviews, and predicting candidate success based on historical data. This leads to more efficient hiring processes and better candidate-job fit.
ii. **Enhanced Onboarding**: AI can create personalized onboarding experiences that help new employees integrate smoothly into the organization. AI-driven onboarding platforms can provide tailored training materials, role-specific information, and mentorship recommendations.

d. Continuous Learning and Development

i. **Personalized Training Programs**: AI can identify individual learning needs and recommend personalized training programs. This ensures that employees receive relevant and timely skill development opportunities, leading to a more competent and motivated workforce.
ii. **Adaptive Learning Platforms**: AI-driven learning platforms can adapt content based on the learner's progress, providing a more engaging and effective learning experience.

e. Diversity and Inclusion

i. **Bias Reduction**: AI can help reduce bias in hiring and promotion decisions by focusing on data-driven assessments rather than subjective judgments. This promotes a more diverse and inclusive workplace.
ii. **Diversity Metrics**: AI can track and analyze diversity metrics, helping organizations identify areas for improvement and develop strategies to foster an inclusive culture.

f. Employee Wellbeing and Mental Health

i. **Wellbeing Monitoring**: AI can monitor employee wellbeing through various data sources, such as wearable devices, and provide insights into stress levels, workload balance, and overall health.
ii. **Mental Health Support**: AI-driven chatbots and platforms can offer mental health support and resources, providing employees with confidential and immediate assistance.

g. Innovation and Collaboration

i. **Enhanced Collaboration Tools**: AI can enhance collaboration by providing intelligent project management tools that facilitate communication, track progress, and recommend resources. This leads to more efficient teamwork and innovation.
ii. **Idea Generation**: AI can assist in brainstorming sessions by generating new ideas and solutions based on data analysis and trend identification.

h. Performance Management

i. **Continuous Performance Monitoring**: AI can track performance metrics in real-time, providing managers and employees with continuous feedback and development suggestions. This ensures that performance issues are addressed promptly, and employees are consistently supported in their growth.
ii. **Objective Evaluations**: AI can help in creating objective performance evaluations based on data-driven insights, reducing biases and ensuring fair assessments.

CONCLUSION

AI's integration into organizational behaviour can lead to a more positive and productive work environment by enhancing employee engagement, satisfaction, and development. By leveraging AI for data-driven decision-making, personalized experiences, and proactive management strategies, organizations can foster a culture of continuous improvement, inclusivity, and innovation. This not only benefits employees but also contributes to the overall success and sustainability of the organization. These references provide a comprehensive overview of how AI is being integrated into organizational behaviour and its impact on various HR functions, employee engagement, training, and overall workplace dynamics.

REFERENCES

Accenture. (2017). Predictive Maintenance and the Smart Factory. Retrieved from https://www.accenture.com

Accenture. (2019). Artificial Intelligence: The Future of Work? Retrieved from https://www.accenture.com

Accenture. (2019). Leveraging AI for Workforce Planning at Royal Dutch Shell. Retrieved from https://www.accenture.com

Accenture. (2021). AI for Personalized Learning in the Workplace. Retrieved from https://www.accenture.com

Accenture. (2022). AI and the Future of Work. Retrieved from https://www.accenture.com

Accenture. (2023). Leveraging AI for Workforce Planning at Royal Dutch Shell. Retrieved from https://www.accenture.com

Adeoye, B. (2020). The Role of AI in Enhancing Workforce Skills in Nigeria. Nigerian Journal of Technology.

Barcelona City Council. (2019). AI in Urban Traffic Management. Retrieved from https://ajuntament.barcelona.cat

Binns, R. (2018). Fairness in Machine Learning: Lessons from Political Philosophy. *Proceedings of the 2018 Conference on Fairness, Accountability, and Transparency*. ACM.

Boston Consulting Group (BCG). (2023). The Impact of AI on Employee Wellbeing. Retrieved from https://www.bcg.com

Bughin, J., Seong, J., Manyika, J., Chui, M., & Joshi, R. (2018). *Notes from the AI Frontier: Applications and Value of Deep Learning*. McKinsey & Company.

Capgemini. (2023). AI for Enhancing Employee Experience. Retrieved from https://www.capgemini.com

Davenport, T. H., & Kirby, J. (2016). *Only Humans Need Apply: Winners and Losers in the Age of Smart Machines*. Harper Business.

Davenport, T. H., & Kirby, J. (2016). *Only Humans Need Apply: Winners and Losers in the Age of Smart Machines*. Harper Business.

Deloitte. (2019). The Rise of AI in HR: Enhancing Employee Engagement. Retrieved from https://www2.deloitte.com

Deloitte. (2022). Using AI to Improve Employee Engagement. Retrieved from https://www2.deloitte.com

Deloitte. (2023). The Rise of AI in HR: Enhancing Employee Engagement. Retrieved from https://www2.deloitte.com

Esteva, A., Kuprel, B., Novoa, R. A., Ko, J., Swetter, S. M., Blau, H. M., & Thrun, S. (2017). Dermatologist-Level Classification of Skin Cancer with Deep Neural Networks. *Nature*, 542(7639), 115–118. DOI: 10.1038/nature21056 PMID: 28117445

EY. (2023). AI and the Future of Talent Acquisition. Retrieved from https://www.ey.com

Forbes. (2022). How AI is Transforming Human Resources. Retrieved from https://www.forbes.com

Freire, R. (2019). AI in HR: The Brazilian Perspective. Journal of Human Resources Management.

Frost & Sullivan. (2020). AI in the Philippines: Transforming Customer Service. Retrieved from https://www.frost.com

Gartner. (2022). AI in Human Capital Management: Trends and Best Practices. Retrieved from https://www.gartner.com

Gartner. (2023). Top Strategic Predictions for 2024 and Beyond: Leveraging AI to Transform Work. Retrieved from https://www.gartner.com

Google. (2020). AI in Enhancing Innovation and Collaboration. Retrieved from https://www.google.com

Google. (2023). AI in Enhancing Innovation and Collaboration. Retrieved from https://www.google.com

Greenfield, R. (2018). How IBM's Watson Is Revolutionizing Employee Training. Retrieved from https://www.ibm.com

Greenfield, R. (2023). The Role of AI in Employee Training. Retrieved from https://www.ibm.com

Gupta, S., & Chen, H. (2018). AI-Based Trading Systems and Their Impact on Market Performance. *Journal of Financial Markets*, 42, 123–135.

Harvard Business Review. (2022). The AI-Powered Workplace. Retrieved from https://hbr.org

Harvard Business Review. (2023). How AI is Changing Talent Management. Retrieved from https://hbr.org

HDFC Bank. (2019). HDFC Bank's AI Chatbot: Enhancing Customer Experience. Retrieved from https://www.hdfcbank.com

HR Research Institute (HRRI). (2020). The Impact of AI on Recruitment: Efficiency and Quality. Retrieved from https://www.hrri.org

HR Research Institute (HRRI). (2023). The Role of AI in Enhancing Employee Productivity. Retrieved from https://www.hrri.org

Huang, M. H., & Rust, R. T. (2018). Artificial Intelligence in Service. *Journal of Service Research*, 21(2), 155–172. DOI: 10.1177/1094670517752459

Huang, M. H., & Rust, R. T. (2022). Artificial Intelligence in Service. *Journal of Service Research*, 21(2), 155–172. DOI: 10.1177/1094670517752459

IBM. (2020). Watson AI for Employee Engagement. Retrieved from https://www.ibm.com

IBM. (2023). Watson AI for Employee Engagement. Retrieved from https://www.ibm.com

IBM. (2023). AI and the Future of Work: Employee Engagement. Retrieved from https://www.ibm.com

Indonesia Ministry of Industry. (2020). AI in Workforce Planning. Retrieved from https://www.kemenperin.go.id

Infosys. (2020). Leveraging AI for Employee Engagement and Performance Management. Retrieved from https://www.infosys.com

Infosys. (2023). AI in Workforce Planning. Retrieved from https://www.infosys.com

Infosys. (2023). Leveraging AI for Employee Engagement and Performance Management. Retrieved from https://www.infosys.com

International Journal of Human Resource Management (IJHRM). (2019). AI-Driven Performance Management. *Impact and Benefits. IJHRM*, 30(5), 645–658.

iSON. (2019). AI-Driven Innovation in South Africa's Service Sector. Retrieved from https://www.isongroup.com

Johnson, J. (2019). Unilever's Use of AI in Recruitment. Retrieved from https://www.unilever.com

Kansiime, M. (2020). AI in Agriculture: The Kenyan Experience. *Journal of Agricultural Science.*

KPMG. (2022). AI and Talent Management: Strategies for Success. Retrieved from https://home.kpmg

KPMG. (2023). The Role of AI in Workforce Planning. Retrieved from https://home.kpmg

Mahindra. (2020). AI in Workforce Planning at Mahindra & Mahindra. Retrieved from https://www.mahindra.com

McKinsey & Company. (2022). How AI is Reshaping Workplaces. Retrieved from https://www.mckinsey.com

McKinsey & Company. (2023). The Future of Work: AI and Automation. Retrieved from https://www.mckinsey.com

Microsoft. (2020). AI in Employee Wellbeing. Retrieved from https://www.microsoft.com

MIT Sloan Management Review. (2022). How AI is Changing Work. Retrieved from https://sloanreview.mit.edu

MIT Sloan Management Review. (2023). Leveraging AI for Better HR Practices. Retrieved from https://sloanreview.mit.edu

Nair, S. (2018). How Sephora Uses AI to Enhance Customer Experience. Retrieved from https://www.sephora.com

PwC. (2020). Using AI to Promote Diversity and Inclusion. Retrieved from https://www.pwc.com

PwC. (2022). The Role of AI in Performance Management. Retrieved from https://www.pwc.com

PwC. (2023). Using AI to Promote Diversity and Inclusion. Retrieved from https://www.pwc.com

Reliance Industries. (2020). AI-Driven Employee Training Programs at Reliance. Retrieved from https://www.ril.com

Reliance Industries. (2020). AI-Driven Performance Management at Reliance. Retrieved from https://www.ril.com

Reliance Industries. (2020). AI-Driven Workforce Planning at Reliance. Retrieved from https://www.ril.com

Rogers, S. (2018). How AI is Transforming GE's Predictive Maintenance Strategy. Retrieved from https://www.ge.com

Smith, A. (2018). How AI Personalization Increases Amazon's Sales. Retrieved from https://www.amazon.com

Society for Human Resource Management (SHRM). (2023). AI in HR: Benefits and Challenges. Retrieved from https://www.shrm.org

Stanford University. (2022). AI and the Future of Work. Retrieved from https://ai.stanford.edu

Stanford University. (2023). The Impact of AI on Organizational Behavior. Retrieved from https://ai.stanford.edu

Tata Consultancy Services (TCS). (2023). AI and Workforce Management. Retrieved from https://www.tcs.com

TCS. (2021). AI and Innovation at Tata Consultancy Services. Retrieved from https://www.tcs.com

Tech Mahindra. (2020). AI in Employee Wellbeing at Tech Mahindra. Retrieved from https://www.techmahindra.com

Tech Mahindra. (2023). AI for Employee Engagement. Retrieved from https://www.techmahindra.com

Technologies, H. C. L. (2020). Predictive Analytics in Workforce Planning. Retrieved from https://www.hcltech.com

Technologies, H. C. L. (2023). Enhancing Employee Training with AI. Retrieved from https://www.hcltech.com

Topol, E. (2019). *Deep Medicine: How Artificial Intelligence Can Make Healthcare Human Again*. Basic Books.

Vance, A. (2015). *Elon Musk: Tesla, SpaceX, and the Quest for a Fantastic Future*. Ecco.

Wipro. (2020). AI in Talent Management at Wipro. Retrieved from https://www.wipro.com

Wipro. (2023). AI-Driven Talent Management. Retrieved from https://www.wipro.com

Wipro. (2023). AI in Talent Management at Wipro. Retrieved from https://www.wipro.com

World Economic Forum. (2022). AI and the Future of Jobs. Retrieved from https://www.weforum.org

World Economic Forum. (2023). The Future of Jobs Report. Retrieved from https://www.weforum.org

Zhang, J., & Yang, Y. (2022). AI in Talent Management: A Review. *Human Resource Management Review*, 32(4), 100803.

Zhang, J., & Yang, Y. (2023). Advances in AI for HR. *Human Resource Management Review*, 33(1), 100823.

Chapter 14
The Importance of Entrepreneurship and Organizational Qualities in the Digital Age

Zafer Adiguzel
Sakarya University of Applied Science, Turkey & Koc University, Turkey

ABSTRACT

Considering the critical intersection of entrepreneurship, competitiveness and digital transformation in the age of Artificial Intelligence (AI), the drivers of economic growth and social progress and the transformative power of digitalization for firms become even more important. In particular, it is necessary to consider how digital entrepreneurship is reshaping industries and providing new opportunities for innovation and value creation. The theoretical framework for the adoption of AI and insights into organizational characteristics are presented, and the importance of AI in enhancing firms' competitive advantage is becoming increasingly evident. Therefore, in this chapter, AI applications in industries that demonstrate the significant impact of AI on decision-making processes and future business strategies are explained, and AI is examined as an important element in shaping the strategic direction and sustainability of companies in an increasingly competitive global market.

INTRODUCTION

In today's business world, rapidly changing technologies are radically transforming the environment in which businesses must operate. The changes brought about by digitalization deeply affect not only the internal functioning of companies,

DOI: 10.4018/979-8-3693-8442-8.ch014

but also their competitiveness and entrepreneurial activities. Entrepreneurship is a strategic element for businesses that use digital technologies to increase innovation and competitiveness (Felicetti et al., 2024). With the technological revolution, entrepreneurs not only shape economic growth and the labor market, but also create new business models and produce social values in society (Ndagi & Salihu, 2019). With the acceleration of the digitalization process, the entrepreneurial ecosystem has also expanded significantly and increased its impact at a global level. Entrepreneurship is generally defined as the ability to effectively manage resources and offer innovative solutions by taking risks. Competitiveness, on the other hand, refers to the capacity of businesses to create more value by providing a sustainable advantage in the market compared to their competitors. Ensuring competitiveness in the digital age means that businesses can quickly adapt to technological innovations, better understand customer demands, and use digital tools efficiently. In this context, entrepreneurship increases the competitiveness of companies by evaluating the opportunities offered by digitalization.

Digitalization offers businesses the opportunity to be more efficient, flexible and innovative by integrating technology into business processes. While digital transformation reshapes traditional business models, it increases the operational efficiency of companies, reduces costs and improves customer satisfaction (Wujarso, 2023). This transformation process allows companies to make faster decisions, better meet customer expectations and quickly adapt to market changes by using digital tools and data strategically.

Another important advantage of digitalization for companies is that it provides easier access to global markets. Digital platforms and e-commerce sites enable small and medium-sized enterprises (SMEs) to reach global customers, thus increasing their competitive advantage. In addition, digitalization offers opportunities in personalized services by better analyzing customers' behaviors, preferences and needs through technologies such as big data and artificial intelligence (AI).

Entrepreneurship is of great importance both economically and socially. From an economic perspective, entrepreneurship creates new business opportunities, increases employment, and contributes to economic growth. Innovative initiatives lead to increased competition in the market and the emergence of new products, services, and business models (Codini et al., 2023). This provides consumers with more options and increases the dynamism of the economy.

Entrepreneurial orientation is a factor that directly affects the innovation capabilities of companies. Companies with high innovative capacity can quickly adapt to changing market conditions and offer more value to customers. For this reason, entrepreneurial orientation stands out as a critical element affecting the long-term success of companies.

Artificial intelligence is of great importance due to the increased efficiency, cost advantage, and contribution to strategic decision-making processes it offers to businesses. Entrepreneurs can better evaluate opportunities in the market and gain competitive advantage by using artificial intelligence.

The strategic management process includes the planning, implementation, and control stages to achieve companies' long-term goals. Artificial intelligence accelerates this process and plays a critical role in companies' achievement of their strategic goals. In this context, the strategic importance of digitalization and artificial intelligence in entrepreneurial activities is examined in the chapter.

RESEARCH METHODOLOGY

The chapter on the interaction between Entrepreneurship and Digital Transformation outlines the structured approach used in various key areas such as Artificial Intelligence (AI), Big Data, Innovation and their impact on firm competitiveness, entrepreneurship and organizational behavior. It also contributes to academic knowledge and practical insights for policy makers, business leaders and researchers by considering the economic, social and strategic aspects of entrepreneurial orientation and innovation capability. There are several assumptions to explore the relationship between Entrepreneurship, AI and firm competitiveness:

Is AI adoption really important for entrepreneurial innovation and competitiveness?
Can companies that integrate big data analytics into their strategic processes have improved market agility and competitiveness?
To what extent is a competitive advantage gained over competitors in global markets when the use of autonomous robots in production processes significantly increases operational efficiency and reduces costs?
Do augmented and virtual reality technologies lead to higher market participation and competitive differentiation by improving customer experiences?

The main areas focused on by the literature review are:

The role of AI in increasing firm productivity and innovation.
The relationship between entrepreneurial orientation and technological adoption. The impact of big data analytics on strategic decision making and customer relations.
Studies on the use of autonomous robots and AR/VR in business operations.

Resource-Based View (RBV): This theory assumes that firms gain competitive advantage by acquiring and leveraging unique resources such as AI capabilities, big data, and technological expertise. This framework is used to assess how firms use these resources to drive innovation and entrepreneurship.

Dynamic Capabilities Theory: This theory suggests that firms must continually reconfigure their resources to adapt to changing environments. The adoption of AI, big data, and other digital tools is viewed as part of firms' efforts to enhance their dynamic capabilities, particularly in responding to market changes and innovation opportunities.

This methodology outlines a robust approach to investigate the dynamic interaction between digital transformation, entrepreneurship, and firm competitiveness.

THEORETICAL FRAMEWORK

Entrepreneurship and Competitiveness

Entrepreneurship is based on competitive advantage, new product development and invention (Kiyabo & Isaga, 2020). Incentives that can be provided in a country with tax, employment and technology dimensions will undoubtedly produce results that increase competitiveness (Mariotti & Marzano, 2021). However, the most important factor is that entrepreneurship is processed as the main theme at all levels from the early stages of education and that when individuals leave education, they enter the sector not as "unemployed people who do not know what to do" but as inventors who can develop innovations in products or production (Pinto Borges et al., 2021). If those who feed on local knowledge and experience during the education period can also gain foreign knowledge and experience, global competition begins at this point. Many supports can be provided to SME-scale companies for gaining foreign knowledge and experience. Entrepreneurship differs in terms of competitiveness when it comes to system change and innovation (Si et al., 2023). Geographical regions that can be more innovative and entrepreneurial can increase their economic success in international markets.

Countries that provide entrepreneurs with supportive infrastructure to develop their own businesses help those entrepreneurs gain global competitiveness (Guerrero et al., 2021). This situation creates an entrepreneurial culture in that country and increases the number of entrepreneurs on the entrepreneurial ground. Entrepreneurship is a very important complementary part of global competitiveness, and at the same time, it plays a very critical role for global competitiveness (Cammack, 2022). Because entrepreneurs play an important role in spreading welfare to the base in economic development with their short, medium and long-term results. These results;

Entrepreneurs who lead to results such as an increase in employment and production, an increase in national income per capita, and an increase in social welfare are the determining factors in the level of development of a country (Neumann, 2021).

Entrepreneurship can sometimes find a development area for itself in a region depending on the tendency of the people living in a region to take risks and compete. In order for the entrepreneurial value to increase in a region, that region must have previously been introduced to the industrial or commercial culture and be able to develop an innovation in both production and service. Thus, regions that activate their own entrepreneurial values can compete both nationally and internationally according to their risk-taking abilities. Regions that continue innovation at low levels are engaged in the production of relatively lower value-added products.

Innovation forms a part of the ability to be globally competitive by ensuring the commercialization of new products, services and technologies. Governments also have very important work to do here. Governments that want the region to develop should encourage the entrepreneurial spirit with long-term plans. This incentive should be in the form of tax exemptions that will cover all entrepreneurs, as in the grants, interest-free loans and entrepreneurship training that are in practice today.

In many countries, the current practices are not sufficient to achieve competitive advantage and innovation is absolutely necessary. Many businesses that understand this are making full use of innovation in order to be stronger than their competitors and to maintain their success. Because global competition depends on the successful continuation of innovation and entrepreneurship policy. When evaluated from this perspective, the development and progress of a country is in the same direction and directly proportional to the number of entrepreneurs it has. As the number of entrepreneurs increases, economic growth and development will also increase. As this number decreases, the pace of development will also decrease. As a person who constantly tries to innovate, makes new investments and takes risks for this purpose, the entrepreneur will look for a legal environment where she/he will have legal security and can protect what she/he does.

The Importance of Digitalization for Companies

On the business side, digitalization is the increasing efficiency and digitization of internal processes, product and service portfolios, communication channels for marketing and business development, and supply processes by supporting them with digital tools (Matalamäki & Joensuu-Salo, 2022). The best examples of the implementation of digitalization include Amazon, Alibaba, and Ebay in the retail sector. These companies have reached billions of dollars in sales by selling online instead of traditional physical stores. These companies have increased their efficiency by digitizing not only their sales but also their main activities such as warehouse arrangements and customer service. In sectors where physical product production is carried out, technology is increasingly used in business processes (production, distribution, supply, human resources, warehouse management, personnel tracking, etc.) (Ammar et al., 2021).

Digitalization has become an important issue for business managers today. In terms of the contributions of digitalization to businesses, some of its most fundamental contributions are saving time, being able to respond quickly to changes in the market, having a reducing effect on operating costs, employees being able to work remotely without being tied to location and reaching new personnel without any country borders (Parviainen et al., 2017). Digitalization is important not only for businesses but also for countries. Digitalization also contributes to states in terms of increasing the effectiveness of state activities, e-government applications, and implementation of education policies (Batool et al., 2021).

The Importance of Digital Entrepreneurship

Entrepreneurship has been accepted as one of the 21st century skills required to study, work and live successfully in the information society. Given the unique features of the Internet, digital entrepreneurship is considered a completely new field of research. Information technology skills are seen as an important success factor for new ventures in the global market (Usman et al., 2024). Digital entrepreneurs are defined as a subcategory of traditional entrepreneurs and ensure that all physical processes in institutions are carried out in a digital environment. Digital entrepreneurship uses digital media and other information and communication technologies to seize opportunities. In the face of developing and changing framework conditions, the digital entrepreneur can adapt to the needs of the digital age. Although digital entrepreneurship is an approach that includes the use of new network platforms, systems and formats thanks to communication and information technologies, it is the meeting of digital information and technology with entrepreneurs. Therefore, it plays an important role in opening business opportunities over the Internet, communicating information and ensuring cooperation with customers or partners. Therefore, digital entrepreneurs are people who are slow, determined, honest, brave, experienced, imaginative, meticulous, careful, researcher, have a clear vision of the customer and the market, are fearless and work in insecure conditions (Koivusalo, 2023).

Digital entrepreneurs rely on the power of digital media and information technology to capture opportunities. Within this information, it is very important to better define the elements of the entrepreneurial process that distinguish traditional entrepreneurship from digital entrepreneurship from an institutional perspective. In particular, the elements that will better define the concept of entrepreneurship are digital technologies and digital skills. The first is about the tools that will enable the new digital paradigm, and the second is about how people use and use these tools to create value (Tekin & Küsbeci, 2021). By establishing virtual connections through online platforms, digital entrepreneurs are not limited to their own networks or cities for financing or information, but can also seek information and investment across large geographical distances by holding multiple leadership positions. Social media technology platforms help entrepreneurs reach new markets by developing international relationships and effectively facilitating business communication. Businesses can become more dynamic and profitable by embracing digital technologies, which open up new opportunities for entrepreneurship, operations, and business results (Bharadwaj et al., 2013). Digital entrepreneurship is seen as a powerful driver of local innovation and thus structural economic transformation and development. Individuals and organizations need a digital infrastructure to create digital products (browsers, social networking sites, software development kits, open source, etc.) (Li et al., 2022).

The Development of Entrepreneurship Between the 15th and 19th Centuries

Entrepreneurs who saw the rapid development of the market economy in Europe tried to meet consumer demands quickly by evaluating the opportunity environment that emerged. The economic strategies of European countries were shaped around two main goals at the beginning of the modern age. These goals were to grow the state by increasing economic power and to ensure the growth of the economy by using the power of the state. At the beginning of the modern age, the economic policies of European countries were aimed at two goals, but the need for states to generate income could lead to the creation of policies that would harm the production economy (Todaro & Smith, 2020).

Entrepreneurship in the 21st Century

Today's entrepreneurship approach has been affected by the rapid change process we are experiencing and has left behind the superficial and monotonous entrepreneurship approach that only involves buying and selling. In the 21st century, the entrepreneurship approach has focused on creating value instead of producing products or services and thus making profit. Today, increasing production technologies allow basic and medium-level products to be easily produced. Entrepreneurs who want to gain advantage in relevant competitive conditions and increase their profitability allocate more labor to value production than they allocate to product/service production. Value can be defined briefly as the additional benefit that a product creates for its customers. The feature developed outside of the communication feature of phones produced for communication can be given as an example of creating value. Value is creating a meaningful difference that makes people choose to buy. Many concepts have been affected and changed by the rapid change process we are experiencing. The concepts of management and leadership come first among these concepts (Thorpe, 2016). In this process, it is seen that the leadership function in entrepreneurship has become increasingly important due to the increasing importance of entrepreneurship and its qualitative changes (Kadwa & Barnard, 2019). It should also be noted that the most important element that provides growth and dynamism in this environment of change is "strategy" (Johnson et al., 2020).

Economic and Social Importance of Entrepreneurship

With the emergence of new supply sources, new products and processes, new markets and new forms of organization, dynamic entrepreneurs who manage to replace the old with the new have become the main drivers of economic growth (Karantza, 2017). Therefore, entrepreneurship is of great importance for countries both in terms of ensuring social welfare and organizational and economic development. Research shows that countries with high entrepreneurial activity have above-average economic growth (Amaghouss & Ibourk, 2013).

When looking at the concept of entrepreneurship from an economic development perspective, it can be said that there is a connection between the impact of entrepreneurial firms and the promotion of competition and economic development (Shane, 2007). There are two important policy components in supporting economic development. First, it is to try to strengthen the factors that protect the benefits of productive innovation (such as free trade, support for property rights and agreements) in order to prevent entrepreneurial talent from being directed to unproductive activities. Second, it is to increase basic local resources that can be damaged by reasons such as mortgages and monopolies (Dutz et al., 2000).

Entrepreneurship serves to increase employment in the economic sector, accelerate economic growth, create new industries, raise living standards and strengthen the middle class, and reduce regional development disparities (Van Praag & Versloot, 2007). Entrepreneurship is very important for society and personal development due to its transformation into production, products and services in the society (Acs & Varga, 2005), value creation, changing/innovative products, risk taking and pioneering qualities in social regions (O'Kane et al., 2023).

What is Entrepreneurial Orientation?

The basis of the concept of entrepreneurial orientation goes back to the work of Mintzberg (1973). In this study, entrepreneurial orientation was seen as strategic decision making (Covin & Wales, 2012). It is stated that the basic studies on entrepreneurial orientation are Mintzberg (1973), Miller (1983), Covin and Slevin (1989), Miller and Friesen (1982) and Lumpkin and Dess (1996) and are among the pioneering studies in the literature.

One of the reasons why entrepreneurial orientation fills an important gap in the business part of the literature is that entrepreneurial orientation consists of a set represented by continuous variables or variables. Entrepreneurial orientation, by its nature, consists of dimensions or dimensions, allowing researchers to create theories about the level of entrepreneurship. There are differences in entrepreneurship levels among businesses. Researchers can evaluate entrepreneurship levels according to some measurement methods (Covin & Lumpkin, 2011).

Miller (1983) argues in pioneering study that the reason businesses become entrepreneurs is to get ahead in competition, and for this, businesses need to be proactive, take risks and be innovative. In general, in many studies, individuals are perceived as entrepreneurs, whereas in study, conducted research on the entrepreneurial aspect of the business. Miller (1983) emphasizes that "organizational renewal" can sometimes be done through an entrepreneur or through the planning department. In other businesses, it can be done through departments such as R&D, marketing and production, which are hierarchically lower. It is also stated that the important concept here is not the critical actor but the "entrepreneurial process" (Miller, 1983). Entrepreneurial orientation can be seen as the processes of developing strategies to gain competitive advantage by people who make important decisions in businesses and ensure the realization of the business's mission and vision (Chota, 2020). From another perspective, entrepreneurial orientation is associated with the method, method and decision-making process used by the entrepreneur when she/he strategically presents the existing product or service she/he has chosen to new markets (Mostafiz et al., 2022).

According to Van Doorn et al. (2015) the definition of entrepreneurial orientation processes, structures and the decision-making process at the center of the strategic field are closely related to strategy making. Entrepreneurial orientation focuses on how the methods, applications and decision-making forms will be in the entrepreneurial activity in the form of reaching different markets with strategic preferences and existing products/services. In other words, entrepreneurial orientation is briefly expressed as the way entrepreneurship is handled (Karami et al., 2023). Entrepreneurial orientation is also expressed as a set of psychological characteristics, values, attitudes and qualities that are closely related to the entrepreneur's motivation (Hassan et al., 2021). According to Miller (1983), businesses with an entrepreneurial aspect are defined as organizations that realize product and market innovations, take a certain level of risk and can be proactive in competition. In addition, Miller (1983) added the dimension of proactivity to the dimensions of innovation and risk taking that define entrepreneurial orientation. In this sense, entrepreneurial orientation is a strategic stance that firms exhibit in their new ventures, being risk-taking, innovative and proactive (Bernoster et al., 2020). Entrepreneurial orientation is the strategy development processes that create the appropriate ground for businesses to decide and act with an entrepreneurial spirit (Rauch et al., 2009).

Innovation through entrepreneurial orientation enables businesses to develop new products and make radical changes in their production processes (Ferreras-Méndez et al., 2021). Entrepreneurial orientation helps businesses to take action on seemingly risky and unclear investments and to reach markets with high returns before their competitors by acting proactively (Corrêa et al., 2022). According to Zahra (1991), entrepreneurial orientation is also defined as an assessment that expresses the tendencies and orientations of top managers towards entrepreneurial activities and examines the entrepreneurial status of firms.

According to Rauch et al. (2009), it is defined as the processes implemented by decision makers of firms to achieve their goals, maintain their vision and gain competitive advantage. Entrepreneurial orientation is a concept that has been emphasized for a long time as an unresolved theoretical concept due to its inherently complex structure. It is thought that there is no full consensus on its definition. While many studies and analyses continue to be conducted on whether entrepreneurial orientation is a behavior or a tendency, it is stated that the concept can be stated as a feature for the business and is difficult to separate from other concepts that may be abstract (Covin & Lumpkin, 2011).

Big Data

Big data is a data stack that has accumulated over time and has survived to the present day. Data that is too large to be managed with traditional systems or data that is difficult to store and analyze is considered "big data" (Favaretto et al., 2020). In short, big data is a data set that emerges from the combination of different data sources and complex data groups (Wu et al., 2021). The volume of large data sets is so large that traditional data management software is insufficient to process this data. However, the problem is not only processing large volumes of data. It is also managing heterogeneous structures. Since big data has a polymorphic structure, the definition of this term varies according to the service providers and internet users that societies have. Therefore, defining big data as a technical or technological category makes this concept more meaningful.

The concept of big data is still evolving, and the issue of how to benefit from and use big data in each developing paradigm is constantly changing (Naqvi et al., 2021). Therefore, it is quite difficult to define the concept of big data. Cui et al. (2020) defined the concept of big data as data sets that reach high speed, constantly increase in volume and are diverse.

5V of Big Data (Riahi & Riahi, 2018).

- Volume: The amount of data produced and stored.
- Velocity: It refers to the processing speed and formation speed of data.
- Varierty: It is the categorization of the obtained data as structured or unstructured.
- Veracity: It is the quality level, accuracy and uncertainty of the data.
- Value: It is the value and potential of the data.

Different data are brought together in a large data set. The management and analysis of large data also contributes to the decision-making process and to direct future plans (Ruzgas et al., 2016). Big data is very important for entrepreneurs. Correct and effective analysis of large data sets and the creation of the right ideas will help entrepreneurs make the right decisions in their activities, apply the right strategy in the event of a possible risk, and take less risk in new entrepreneurial actions (Sedkaoui, 2018).

Artificial Intelligence (AI)

One of the technologies that contributes the most to the transformation is artificial intelligence technology. Artificial intelligence technology is defined as a set of logical techniques that interpret actions in the light of data, enable strategic decision-making, and perform smart and fast analysis (Kaggwa et al., 2024). The emergence of artificial intelligence and the use of artificial intelligence techniques in machines have initiated the learning process of machines. Artificial intelligence provides the interaction of machines, processes, and systems by using "virtual storage and internet of things" technologies together (Mohammed & Isa, 2021).

Artificial intelligence minimizes the costs that may arise from errors in the activities of entrepreneurs in the digital environment. The production and service sectors are among the areas where artificial intelligence technology is used (Chen et al., 2023). Artificial intelligence technology increases the efficiency of all processes related to the production and service sectors and minimizes human-related errors.

Artificial intelligence existing in the digital environment enables entrepreneurs to be self-confident and confident in their activities (Labanauskaitė et al., 2021).

Autonomous Robots

Autonomous robots are defined as smart devices that can perform processes where there is no or very little human intervention (He et al., 2021). In the age of digital transformation, the use of robots in production enables the concept of full digitalization to be realized. The use of smart factories and autonomous robots in the production process has increased efficiency. The use of autonomous robots in the production process minimizes possible human-related errors (Arucu, 2021).

Autonomous robots use artificial intelligence technology to identify their own problems and produce solutions to these problems, performing their own maintenance and repairs. Autonomous robots have the ability to move freely. In this context, autonomous robots provide flexibility in the production process (Misaros et al., 2023). By transferring the artificial intelligence technology used in autonomous robots to the entire production process, robots have gained experience and experienced robots have been able to provide easy solutions to all problems that may arise in the production process (Modayil & Kuipers, 2008).

Augmented Reality and Virtual Reality

The development of technology has enabled the transfer of the real world to virtual environments. The concept of reality in the virtual environment is related to the three-dimensionalization of objects in the real world in a digital environment (Liu, 2023). Virtual reality and augmented reality are used to define the set of technologies that help transfer the functions of the five senses to the virtual environment in a similar way to objects in the real world, depending on computer science and digital technologies (Zhao, 2009). Augmented reality covers data such as sound and image in the real world and is a technology that allows this data to be enriched and multi-faceted in the virtual environment (Liberatore & Wagner, 2021).

Virtual reality and augmented reality technologies are used to define technologies that fulfill different purposes. While virtual reality aims to replace objects in the real world with the hardware technologies it uses, augmented reality aims to enrich the functional features of objects in the real world with the technologies it uses (El Miedany, 2019). Augmented reality technologies allow people to perform actions and activities that seem impossible in the real world (Turner, 2022). Virtual reality and augmented reality technologies enable entrepreneurs to diversify their actions and activities.

Entrepreneurship and Innovation

Schumpeter (1934) states that the main task of businesses is to shape and transform production methods by utilizing their technological capabilities, an invention or any method that has not yet been tried. Innovation constitutes an important part of the structure that constitutes entrepreneurship. The success of entrepreneurship is related to the sustainability and discipline of innovation, which are the original characteristics of entrepreneurs (Drucker, 1998). Entrepreneurship can be explained as activities related to the evaluation of market opportunities, starting from a business idea, and the operation of manufacturing factors such as capital, natural resources and labor to produce goods and services (Davidsson, 2015). In order to gain the entrepreneurial identity, it is of great importance to bring the innovative ideas imagined to a level where they can be implemented. Innovation is a special tool of entrepreneurship. Entrepreneurs can use this tool as an opportunity to produce different jobs or different services. It is thought that entrepreneurs can innovate by looking for innovation sources, changes that indicate successful innovation opportunities and signs of these changes (Bessant & Tidd, 2007).

The Relationship Between Entrepreneurial Orientation and Innovation Capability

Entrepreneurial orientation is considered as the processes, activities, philosophy and decision-making activities that direct businesses towards innovation (Wiklund & Shepherd, 2005). One of the elements that reveal that innovation has a complementary feature to entrepreneurship is entrepreneurial orientation. This concept explains the processes and practices related to being aware of new and different opportunities and developing strategies. While Schumpeter (1934) evaluates the entrepreneur as a creative collapse and change element of the economic system of a market within the scope of various innovation elements, Drucker (1985) considers innovation as a function in entrepreneurship. Therefore, entrepreneurship and innovation are seen as inseparable parts of a whole. Hult et al. (2004) claim that entrepreneurial orientation in businesses is an incremental process that results in innovation. Innovation capability is defined as the capacity of the business to create new processes and introduce new products to the market. Entrepreneurial orientation increases a company's autonomy, competitive aggressiveness, proactivity, risk-taking, and willingness to innovate (Lumpkin & Dess, 2001).

Some researchers consider innovation as an indicator of entrepreneurial orientation and suggest that entrepreneurial orientation can directly affect the innovation activities of products, processes, and management (Makhloufi et al., 2021). Entrepreneurial orientation enables the company to improve its proactive decisions, transform risk-taking uncertainty into opportunities, and implement new ideas and practices in an innovative way (Corrêa et al., 2022). Entrepreneurship literature suggests that entrepreneurial-oriented businesses adapt to the needs of customers and the market through innovation, as they have the characteristics of innovation, proactivity, and risk-taking to explore new opportunities to offer new products (Kreiser & Davis, 2010) (Okoli et al., 2021). Entrepreneurship and innovation complement each other. Entrepreneurship is of great importance in the development of innovation in the business and in the provision of economic value. Entrepreneurs benefit from innovation to increase the profitability of the business by expanding their market share. In addition, entrepreneurship and innovation are processes that involve different dynamism and integrity.

Some researchers suggest that entrepreneurial orientation can directly affect the innovation activities of products, processes and management, and in their studies, innovation is an indicator of entrepreneurial orientation (Alegre & Chiva, 2013; Otero-Neira et al., 2013). Entrepreneurial orientation can provide the opportunity to improve the proactive decisions of the business, to transform risk-taking uncertainty into opportunities and to apply new ideas and practices in an innovative way (Putniņš & Sauka, 2020).

THEORETICAL FRAMEWORK OF ARTIFICIAL INTELLIGENCE ADOPTION

AI readiness refers to the readiness of organizations to implement changes involving AI-related applications and technology. Two theoretical frameworks are considered to analyze a firm's AI adoption perspective: TOE and DOI. The Technology-Organization-Environment (TOE) framework (Tornatzky & Fleischer, 1990) was developed as a multiple perception theory to provide a framework to be used in investigating AI adoption at the firm level. On the other hand, the diffusion of innovation theory (DOI) attempts to explain 'how, why, and at what rate new ideas and technology spread' (Al-Jabri & Sohail, 2012). Both of these theories are similarly applied to adopt new innovation at the firm level (Alsheibani et al., 2018).

In addition to the Technology-Organization-Environment (TOE) framework being independent of industry and firm size constraints (Al Hadwer et al., 2021), TOE adoption factors, user adoption processes, and implementation; anticipated challenges; The impact of technology on the value chain and post-adoption diffusion; provides a more holistic picture about the development of organizational capabilities using technology (Malik et al., 2021), the Technology-Organization-Environment (TOE) model is considered one of the first models. TOE examines a series of turning points when it comes to artificial intelligence adoption. This framework examines technological advancement, organizational restructuring, and the business environment. Artificial intelligence adoption behavior requires firms to be prepared, diligent, and have high management support. Technology adoption is influenced by the pool of technologies inside and outside the firm and their perceived benefits, technical and organizational compatibility, complexity and learning curve, pilot testing/experimentation, and visibility/imagination (Awa et al., 2017). The organization captures descriptive measures such as the firm's business scope, top management support, organizational culture, complexity of the management structure measured by centralization, formalization, and vertical differentiation, the quality of human capital, and size and size-related issues such as internal slack resources and specialization (Pertusa-Ortega et al., 2010).

Organizational Characteristics of Artificial Intelligence

The introduction of machine learning in the early 21st century has accelerated the rate of development in AI. We can attribute this increase to the hardware and computational power of machine learning techniques. As the potential for computational power increases, so does the development in the field of AI. The future of AI includes components that enable machines to learn and think more like a human (Zhang & Lu, 2021). Adopting AI at the enterprise level can increase the productivity and efficiency of important decision-making (Merhi & Harfouche, 2024). Studies show various advantages of implementing AI in organizations, but organizations still face challenges in adopting AI technologies (Arrieta et al., 2020). One of the reasons behind these challenges is that organizations fail to understand where and how to implement AI. Another reason is that organizations fail to extract insights at the enterprise level to best implement the business strategy for AI adoption.

Before understanding where to implement AI at the enterprise level, it is important to understand the key factors associated with it. AI research is constantly striving for optimization (Miikkulainen et al., 2018), improving the accuracy of AI techniques (Ahmed et al., 2021), and the emergence of new algorithms (Torrado et al., 2018). These studies also discuss the developments in AI and the advantages of implementing it at the enterprise level. Currently, less than 10% of organizations have successfully adopted AI. The remaining organizations have either not adopted AI or are under the false assumption that IoT techniques are AI techniques (Daugherty & Wilson, 2018). For organizations that have adopted AI, there has been a change in their workplace environment from a traditional style to an adaptive process style, thus facilitating the employee's work. There is little clarity on what factors an organization uses to form the perspectives of its employees regarding the use and adoption of AI techniques. The reason behind this is the limited number of studies focused on understanding an employee's preferences towards AI adoption.

While there have been efforts to conduct organizational readiness analysis prior to AI adoption (Jöhnk et al., 2021), there is no research to understand the factors that influence employee perspectives on AI adoption in workplaces. Therefore, understanding these factors is of great importance as employees play a significant role in the growth and sustainability of an organization. From an organizational decision-making perspective, AI adoption needs to be evaluated using factors such as relative advantage, compatibility, top management, organizational size, resources, competitive pressure, and government regulatory issues (Pillai & Sivathanu, 2020). If an organization chooses to adopt AI, it is difficult to implement it in the workplace without properly understanding the employee perspective. AI has a variety of roles in business, from improving employee and customer interactions to discovering patterns in large amounts of data to automating monotonous activities (Ramachandran et al., 2022).

Artificial intelligence technologies significantly affect the productivity and results of the business (Wamba-Taguimdje et al., 2020). Since AI technologies efficiently use large amounts of big data, companies perform better, which increases performance. AI provides managers with important data that allows them to make better business decisions. Machine automation provides important data to help managers make better business decisions, while creating higher quality products faster and more effectively. Thus, organizations are beginning to understand that it is worth adopting AI technologies. Its main purpose is to design standard, reliable product quality control methods and to seek new ways to reach and serve customers, while maintaining low cost, and in e-commerce and finance industries, artificial intelligence has been deployed to achieve better customer experience, efficient management of the supply chain, improved operational efficiency, reduced peer size (Pallathadka et al., 2023). The major applications of AI in businesses include sales growth, profit maximization, sales forecasting, inventory management, security, fraud detection, portfolio management, and CRM (Soni et al., 2020; Vaio et al., 2020). AI applications are also becoming widespread in human resource management. Recruitment, employee performance evaluation and satisfaction, compensation and benefit analysis, best practice analysis, discipline management, and tactical procedures of employee training and development systems have seen growth with the integration and implementation of AI technologies (Votto, 2021). In the context of Human Resource Management, the exploration of AI within compensation and benefits systems provides HR professionals with a tool to ensure that their employees are engaged and receive fair and accurate entitlements according to their unique circumstances (Hughes et al., 2019). Tong et al. (2021) investigated the role of AI in the employee performance feedback process. Given the superior standardized and analytical nature of AI, evaluating employees' inputs and outputs, providing areas for improvement, and predicting future performance has become a streamlined process for HR professionals. HR teams manually review and clean an employee's record and identify positive/negative trends. Systems developed with artificial intelligence can analyze them and make suggestions directly to the employee.

Artificial intelligence technologies are also applied in supply chain management. Artificial intelligence applications in supply chain decision-making can be generally grouped as optimization, expert systems, and also methods related to planning and scheduling, simulations and modeling (Pournader, 2021). Artificial intelligence is also used in the innovation management process in organizations. Studies in the relevant field show that innovation management can be supported by artificial intelligence systems. Artificial intelligence is reshaping companies and how innovation management is organized. Consistent with the rapid technological development and the replacement of human organization, artificial intelligence helps management rethink the entire innovation process of a company. In their study, Haefner (2021) developed a framework that shows the extent to which artificial intelligence can replace humans and explained what is important to consider in the transformation to a digital organization of innovation.

Another important role of using artificial intelligence technologies to automate routine corporate operations is to reduce human errors. Robotic Process Automation technologies manage data entry and processing; digital systems become more efficient and are less likely to encounter problems or create issues as a result of data processing errors (Syed et al., 2020). This can therefore help increase organizational efficiency and minimize employee stress.

As a result, AI technology helps companies develop faster, improve team performance, and increase employee performance. Past research has provided some insight into the antecedents of sustainable growth and performance in organizations. The key features of strong AI include the ability to reason, solve puzzles, make judgments, plan, learn, and communicate. Other qualities that AI should possess include consciousness, objective thoughts, self-awareness, sensitivity, and acuity. Strong AI is referred to as Real Intelligence or Artificial General Intelligence (AGI). However, many organizations' efforts in AI-enabled organizations fall short in how they use and organize AI, with data showing that only 8% of companies are working with core applications that support widespread adoption. Most companies are only running temporary pilots or are implementing AI in a single business process.

The Importance of Artificial Intelligence

Artificial intelligence not only calculates data that is impossible for individuals, but also helps in making the right decisions (Jarrahi, 2018). Artificial intelligence technologies provide companies with a competitive advantage by processing big data and analyzing customer relationships and behaviors (Bharadiya, 2023). Today, artificial intelligence is used in "face recognition" technology. This technology has the ability to analyze images (Alblushi, 2021). In the world, facial recognition technology and criminal justice systems are used in countries such as Hong Kong, China, Denmark, India and the United Kingdom (Humble & Altun, 2020). Artificial intelligence technologies have become widespread in different fields. These areas are applied in health, engineering, banking, agriculture, law, education, finance, marketing, production, retail, and public administration (Haenlein & Kaplan, 2021). It can be said that artificial intelligence technologies are widely used in automobiles, robots, smart phones, televisions, smart speakers, vehicles that move without humans, wearable devices, buildings and industrial areas (Tien, 2017). In the past, it was assumed that it would be impossible for computers to develop their abilities through artificial intelligence technologies and become superior to the abilities of humans (Robinson, 2019). Ford stated in New York Times best-selling book, Rise of the Robots, that computers are now more skilled than before (Robinson, 2019). For example, the Alexa Echo product developed by Amazon has more than 30,000 skills and completes some tasks in a short time with the commands it receives from humans (Robinson, 2019). The concept of artificial intelligence emerged in the academic field in 1956. The main purpose here is to easily perform complex tasks through machines (Fleck, 2018). The great benefits brought by artificial intelligence technologies are not only their contributions to individuals' personal lives, but also provide companies that adopt ever-evolving technology with the advantage of maintaining time, speed, competitiveness and sustainability in their business processes. Individuals and companies are always intertwined with artificial intelligence technologies in their daily work.

The Relationship Between Strategic Management Process and Artificial Intelligence

In an article titled "Understanding the interplay of artificial intelligence and strategic management: four decades of research in review." written by Keding (2019), Keding examined 658 articles published between 1979 and 2019 in which strategic management and artificial intelligence were discussed together, and among these, examined the 58 most consistent articles on both variables. According to findings, research on the interaction of artificial intelligence and strategic management lacks a coherent structure and consistent use of terminology due to their interdisciplinary nature. Despite the supposed maturity of the research area and the growing literature on the business potential of artificial intelligence, very little is known about what the concept entails within the scope of strategic management.

From a strategic management perspective, decision-making situations that require human judgment and analysis regularly involve issues that are far from well-structured. The use of intelligent systems in unstructured environments for non-standard solutions that are important for strategic outcomes and necessary to develop competitive advantages is becoming widespread. While early research suggests that AI can be used as a decision support system, accumulating expert knowledge and guiding organizational actions with strategic-level constraints, current research streams suggest that the real value of AI lies in autonomously performing analysis on various types of data, such as accessing tacit knowledge and creating new knowledge on its own (Keding, 2019).

AI can provide significant business value, but to implement AI and achieve high impact without eliminating all costs and efforts, organizations need to define a compelling shared vision when significant change is required (Dwivedi et al., 2021). In addition, businesses need to leverage several different technologies, such as AI, to create adaptive transformations and "sense and respond" capabilities that will drive innovation, improve customer experience and service quality, and increase productivity (Truong & Papagiannidis, 2022).

In the context of strategic management, two main streams of literature cover the concept of AI and offer different areas of application. While early publications understood AI as the underlying technology of rule-based expert systems to support and improve top-down strategic decision making (Carlsson & Walden, 1997), more recent articles on AI in strategic management find their technological basis in machine learning algorithms that recognize patterns in data sets using statistical inference and have the potential to act autonomously in the field of cognitive tasks and process automation (Davenport & Ronanki, 2018).

The extent to which strategic management tasks can and will be replaced by AI has been the subject of several research articles. While some authors consider the use of AI in strategy to be overstated for the foreseeable future, most scholars expect the most beneficial impact on strategic management when AI complements managers and focuses on strategy execution (Wilson & Daugherty, 2018). Reeves and Ueda (2016) stated in their article "Designing the machines that will design strategy" that no matter how good and highly advanced the technology is, a human is still needed to enhance competitive advantage. They advocated that both technology and human factors should be connected to what they call an "integrated strategy machine." An integrated strategy machine is a collection of both technology and human resources that act in harmony to develop and execute business strategies. It involves a set of conceptual and analytical operations, including problem definition, signal processing, pattern recognition, abstraction and conceptualization, analysis, and forecasting.

A starting point for exploring the role of AI in the strategy process is its potential to augment and transform strategic analysis. While information systems have long helped managers collect and organize information for environmental scanning and decision-making purposes, AI algorithms have the potential to significantly expand the scale, scope, and speed of analysis of an organization's external and internal environments through the capacity to interact with the environment and generate data (Robinson et al., 2021). Artificial intelligence can help collect information from internal and external data sources, especially discretely or continuously, analyze and interpret such data through pattern detection, and assist managers in decision making through predictive analysis (Ferràs-Hernández et al., 2017). In order to define the connection between artificial intelligence and the strategic management process, it is necessary to conduct a literature review on the stages of the strategic management process, namely strategy formulation, strategic implementation, and strategic control, and the relationship between the processes included in these stages and artificial intelligence applications. Therefore, it is necessary to state in a step-by-step manner:

Competitive Advantage

The main application of AI in strategic analysis is related to competitor analysis. Since firms collect vast amounts of data about their competitors and industries, automated analysis can help group the data, identify patterns in the data, and even predict competitors' strategic moves. Before starting a strategic analysis, strategists need to identify relevant competitors, but this remains one of the most difficult tasks for strategists. Gangwani and Zhu (2024) suggest using machine learning algorithms to identify strategic groups of firms pursuing similar strategies and predict the movement of firms within these groups. Such tools offer a more dynamic approach to competitive analysis. Scientists always warn that competitor assumptions need to be reviewed frequently in order to measure the ongoing robustness of a firm's strategy (Ireland et al., 2003). The advantage of automated competitor analysis over traditional approaches is significant. When connected to machines to generate market and competitor data, algorithms can continuously perform competitor analysis and help strategists assess the validity of a company's current strategy.

Environmental Analysis

Artificial intelligence applications have found their way into areas of the strategic management process across political, economic, social, technological, environmental, and legal factors that we can define as external factors affecting a business. When we look at the political framework of external environmental factors, political scientists have developed various AI-based text analysis tools that are useful in understanding the "political climate" across regions. In particular, these algorithms have proven effective in analyzing unstructured social media data (Zafarani et al., 2014). Machine learning using such data is increasingly useful for predicting election outcomes, policy changes, and political bias and conflict (Zuloaga-Rotta et al., 2024). Early identification and prediction of political trends and developments with AI can help strategists understand how government and government policy may affect their organizations. Doing so can provide a significant source of competitive advantage. Traditionally, firms tend to invest heavily in legal consultants who often manually compile and analyze a large number of new laws and regulations that could change the business environment across regions and legal regimes.

Applications of AI can potentially reduce overall legal aid costs by supporting the internal collection and processing of such legal data. For example, Yousfi-Monod et al. (2010) developed a machine learning algorithm that scans thousands of pages of legal documents and provides useful summaries related to a firm's strategy. AI is also increasingly being used to automate the monitoring and regulation of financial compliance (Krogh et al., 2021). Machine learning can also be used to accurately and reliably measure economic factors, i.e. economic trends such as economic growth, the onset of economic downturns, increasing poverty, and bankruptcies (Cielen et al., 2004). The introduction of machine learning tools in the financial services industry is an important precursor to strategist applications. For example, institutional investors are using machine learning to predict stock returns and thus make better investment decisions and assess systemic financial risks. Economists are increasingly applying machine learning techniques to nontraditional data sources and problems, such as using satellite imagery to estimate the spatial distribution of economic wealth in African countries (Jean et al., 2016).

Strategists often need to include social factors in their analyses, such as changes in demographics and social values. While some of these changes may be slow, others may be subject to sudden shocks and rapid reversals that may create significant business opportunities or threats. Scholars have proposed methods such as automated text analysis to "map the contours of cultural domains, classify cultural elements, and track the evolution of culture over time" (Bail, 2014). New algorithms also make it possible to systematically measure culture and model its evolution within organizations and social groups. Such developments offer new opportunities to measure elusive concepts such as culture in strategy research (Doyle et al., 2017).

Researchers tend to give technological factors a prominent role in most strategic analyses, whether for manufacturing firms or user firms. AI can help companies track technological developments and predict related technological changes. For example, machine learning is increasingly being used to discover patterns in technology development by examining vast amounts of patent or publication data (Cioffi et al., 2020). Using machine learning in this way allows firms to create "information profiles" about their industry and major competitors (Suominen et al., 2017). AI can also complement the strategic analysis of internal organizational factors, including people, finance, and support resources such as supply chains or customer relationships.

Starting with human resources, AI applications can offer automatic pattern recognition in such data and help managers, among other things, determine employee performance, predict career trajectories, and identify compensation models and inequality (Strohmeier & Piazza, 2013). Careful assessment of skills, education, talent, and demographics allows the strategist to more adequately assess the extent to which a potential strategy can be implemented. Firms have a wealth of accurate, detailed, and labeled accounting and financial data.

Strategists tend to rely heavily on balance sheet information when conducting analysis, for example. Machine learning algorithms can cluster such data continuously or discretely by performing pattern analysis. In doing so, the algorithms can improve the interpretation of what triggers certain financial resource conditions related to the type and timing of a firm's strategic commitments (Kar et al., 2021). AI can be used in financial analysis that is important to the strategy development process, such as tools used to track transactions across a firm.

AI can help manage financial risk by augmenting compliance and risk management functions with advanced data analytics, using fast and automated data analytics, and reducing administrative overhead, thus freeing up finance and accounting staff for more creative work (Metawa et al., 2022). Machine learning algorithms are increasingly enabling efficient analysis of a range of other resources relevant to the strategy process, such as demand forecasting, production planning, resource allocation, and logistics. For example, machine learning can enhance production planning decisions by mining data from online catalogs and other repositories, providing predictions about the performance of potential suppliers, and even automating the process of searching for potential suppliers by estimating valuation and evaluating online bids (Nissen & Sengupta, 2006).

Strategy Implementation Process and Artificial Intelligence

Artificial intelligence has the potential to shape the stages, process, and implementation processes of strategy formulation in businesses. Today's companies and businesses are formulating detailed implementation plans by setting business development and financial goals as they seek profitable growth instead of traditional growth. Whether such a process is regular and formal or occasional and informal, formulating and implementing a strategy is a long and complex process involving a wide range of data and relying on management analysis and decision-making at various levels of the organization. The cognitive limitations of strategists in processing data for decision-making and problem-solving actions underlying strategy formulation and implementation are well documented in the literature (Adoli & Kilika, 2020). The potential of artificial intelligence to improve strategy formulation and implementation has been a controversial issue since the 1950s (Perifanis & Kitsios, 2023).

On the one hand, researchers seem to agree that current AI applications are superior to previous systems when combined with the availability of big data. Successful strategy formulation depends on comprehensive knowledge of the organization, its environment, and the risk-benefit ratio of strategic options. Similarly, the successful implementation of a strategy depends on the strategist's ability to effectively control operations and evaluate the effectiveness of strategic actions. The potential of AI-based systems to automate continuous data analysis, generate new insights into strategic opportunities, and identify patterns to predict the payoff of choice, thus improving the quality of a strategist's decisions (Agrawal et al., 2017). Therefore, rather than replacing automated formulation and implementation, AI can be better considered as a useful aid that enhances strategists' ability to make decisions about external threats and opportunities, internal strengths and weaknesses, and strategic issues.

To illustrate how AI can be applied to specific areas of strategy development and execution, it is useful to analyze typical corporate-level strategic questions related to a firm's business portfolio and decisions about growth and diversification. AI can be used to model the performance of a business portfolio, assess the fit, risk, and performance of a firm's business groups, and analyze and suggest potential synergies between them. For example, based on the analysis of market and product data across business units, AI can help strategists address portfolio risks, such as when demand fluctuations across the portfolio are strongly correlated or when different businesses are exposed to similar currency risks. Davenport and Ronanki (2018) refer to these "discussion partner" AI activities as "cognitive insight."

Strategic Control Process and Artificial Intelligence

Strategy control is concerned with the efforts of strategists to ensure that the implementation of strategic plans unfolds as intended and to measure progress on strategic objectives. Research on the application of AI to strategy control has so far been limited. However, several promising areas can be identified due to the possibility of automating the definition of appropriate performance criteria, monitoring and evaluating performance against standards, and suggesting trajectories for corrective action based on predictive analysis. Of particular challenge is the use of AI in project management and internal communication. As more and more business activities are managed through increasingly integrated digital platforms, AI will become a prominent tool to support strategists in evaluating strategy implementation and performance.

From an organizational perspective, research proposed in the early stages of AI began to assist in decision making in the mid-1960s (Ensmenger, 2012). Research in this area has identified the knowledge base as the most important success factor in strategic decision making and has shown that algorithms outperform managers in various decision situations (Yeomans et al., 2019). The concept of the artificial manager, that is, a machine replacing a human manager, is not entirely new, but it has not met the expectations of scientists (Keding, 2021). Research has examined the integration of human and algorithmic intelligence into business applications, the role of AI interface and human managers in user participation, and the cognitive reasons for the barriers to implementation (Lichtenthaler, 2020). Interdisciplinary research has shown that there are differences in the nature and capabilities of humans and machines, so most scientists view the relationship between machines and humans as complementary and suggest that management tasks that cannot be automated will be completed by AI in the future (Raisch & Krakowski, 2021).

Artificial Intelligence Application Examples

Artificial intelligence; Today, it is not only a robot that has come into being, but also equipped with the features of many electronic devices, houses, cars and even cities. There are many examples of artificial intelligence applications. For example, thanks to Apple's Siri application, users can quickly get answers to their questions. Microsoft Cortana can give more effective answers by remembering previously answered questions. IBM Watson can process a lot of data to make recommendations to doctors during the diagnosis and prognosis stages. Amelia, with its automatic customer service feature, can also perceive the emotional state of the customer and provide appropriate answers. Google Maps applications can also display the surroundings of the relevant place along with the address directions received from the map application. Face detection and recognition applications can be used in many different areas such as virtual filters, phone lock and airport security. In addition, text editors or automatic correction tools help users by examining spelling errors, grammar mistakes and plagiarism on computers, phones or tablets. Chatbots aim to increase customer satisfaction by allowing customers to easily reach customer service. In addition, if a negative evaluation is made, they try to detect the error and provide a better service in the next meeting. Many transactions such as e-payments and banking transactions are carried out via e-payment thanks to the convenience provided by artificial intelligence (Siddiqui & Goyal, 2023).

Studies in the field of artificial intelligence are constantly increasing and progressing. One of the most important reasons for this increase has been the introduction of computers and the internet into our lives. Computers and the internet provide important tools in the development of artificial intelligence applications. With the advancement of artificial intelligence, people's lives have become easier and people have been relieved of time-consuming and boring tasks (Rajest et al., 2023). For example, we can shop from where we sit without dealing with boring tasks such as going to the store and waiting in line. Thanks to mobile banking, we can make payments or send money without having to wait in line at the bank. Artificial intelligence studies have had many goals from past to present. One of these goals is to develop robots that can think like humans.

Today, artificial intelligence technology makes such goals possible. Currently, robotic technologies are used in production processes in factories. However, in the near future, we will use robots even in our daily lives. The first studies in this field have begun. For example, autonomous vacuum cleaners have been developed. These autonomous vacuum cleaners create their own maps by moving around the area they are in and detect dirty areas with the help of sensors and clean them. In addition, robots that can cook and care for patients are also being developed. Many companies are currently working on unmanned vehicles. These vehicles are semi-autonomous vehicles under driver control. For example, vehicles that can park themselves. Companies are currently working on fully autonomous vehicles, and as a result, the aim is to prevent accidents (Turienzo et al., 2023).

The Future of Artificial Intelligence

According to the predictions made by Floridi (2019), there are claims that artificial intelligence technology will become a part of people's daily activities and will make people completely dependent on this technology. For example, autonomous vehicles are being developed using artificial intelligence, and it is thought that artificial intelligence has unlimited potential to facilitate human experience. It is also estimated that many new inventions can be created by applying artificial intelligence to robots. This can have many effects on people. However, unlike other predictions, according to Floridi (2019), artificial intelligence is said to only improve the working environment. Artificial intelligence will help people focus on more important tasks by simplifying boring tasks. This can contribute to the best potential of human resources. In other words, according to Floridi (2019), artificial intelligence technology will be used to support people and increase work efficiency. In the midst of all these assumptions, the development process and future position of artificial intelligence have not been fully determined. However, everyone interested in artificial intelligence has ideas about the development of artificial intelligence. Especially since Turing's time, artificial intelligence was previously seen as simple programming and engineering studies, but now it is predicted that artificial intelligence will develop further with the existence of machines that can reason on their own (Hua et al., 2023).

In the future, artificial intelligence robots are expected to make people's lives easier. However, in this process, applications such as robots replacing humans, especially in wars, may also emerge. Aydemir (2018); stated that unmanned aerial vehicles, target detection systems and driverless vehicles point to a future in this direction. ChatGPT, who is also an artificial intelligence robot, answered the question "Can you list your predictions about how artificial intelligence will be used in the future?" as follows: "Artificial intelligence is used in many sectors today and its areas of use will increase in the future.

> Here are some predictions about how AI will be used in the future (Aydemir 2018):
>
> 1. *Automation*: AI will help improve automation in many industries. For example, automation can be provided in areas such as the management of robots in production lines, warehousing, and material management.
> 2. *Medicine*: AI can be used in the field of medicine for diagnosis, treatment, and disease prevention. AI algorithms can analyze medical data to provide early diagnosis of diseases, create treatment plans, and be used for drug discovery.
> 3. *Education*: AI can be used to provide customized learning experiences for students. AI can provide customized educational materials by analyzing students' learning styles, interests, and strengths.
> 4. *Finance*: AI can be used in many areas in the finance sector, such as fraud detection, credit risk assessment, investment strategies, and portfolio management.
> 5. *Law*: AI can also be used in the field of law. AI can be used in many areas such as the issuance of court decisions, analysis of legal documents, and contract management.
> 6. *Transportation*: AI can be used in the development of autonomous vehicles by automobile manufacturers. It can also be used for traffic management, driverless public transport systems, and security systems.
> 7. *Art*: AI can also be used in the arts. For example, AI algorithms can be used in many areas such as painting, music, and video creation. These predictions mean that AI technology will be used in almost every sector, and as the

number and variety of AI applications increase, AI technology will also develop further."

SOLUTIONS AND RECOMMENDATIONS

The increasing impact of digitalization, artificial intelligence (AI), big data, and other technological innovations in business environments presents new challenges and opportunities for entrepreneurs and companies. To remain competitive in the global market and adapt to rapidly changing dynamics, businesses must embrace digital transformation and align their strategies with emerging technologies.

As digitalization reshapes industries, businesses must develop robust digital strategies to stay competitive. Innovation must be encouraged through the adoption of digital tools, increased operational efficiency, and technology-driven processes. Companies that fail to adapt will risk falling behind as digital technologies become increasingly central to the modern business environment.

Entrepreneurial orientation (the desire to innovate, take risks, and proactively pursue new opportunities) plays a critical role in driving competitiveness. In the digital age, entrepreneurs must leverage AI, big data, and advanced technologies to drive innovation.

AI and big data are no longer optional add-ons for businesses, but strategic assets that provide a significant competitive advantage. Companies that leverage AI and big data analytics can outpace their competitors by making faster and more accurate decisions, identifying inefficiencies, and optimizing their business models.

Companies should invest in scalable and flexible digital infrastructure, such as cloud computing, AI, and big data analytics, to improve decision-making and operational agility. Additionally, companies should create digital competency programs to enhance employees' understanding and use of digital technologies. This may include training in AI, big data analytics, and AR/VR for marketing and product development.

Companies should invest in AI solutions that can support research and development efforts and improve customer experiences. However, companies should treat big data as a core competency by developing in-house expertise or collaborating with external partners to leverage the power of data analytics for decision-making, product development, and customer relationship management.

To succeed in the digital age, businesses must not only embrace AI, big data, AR/VR, and autonomous technologies, but also develop a clear strategic framework that integrates these tools into their operations and entrepreneurial orientation. Companies can gain a competitive advantage in a rapidly changing market by creating a culture of innovation, aligning digital strategies with business goals, and investing in continuous learning. Additionally, collaborating with technology startups, academic institutions, and external partners will be key to maintaining alignment and staying at the forefront of digital entrepreneurship and innovation.

FUTURE RESEARCH DIRECTIONS

The evolving dynamics of entrepreneurship and technology offer a number of potential research directions for academics and professionals. With the rapid pace of digitalization, artificial intelligence (AI), and innovations such as big data, autonomous robots, and augmented reality (AR)/virtual reality (VR), the intersection of technology and entrepreneurship requires continued research.

1. *The Role of Entrepreneurship in Enhancing Competitiveness in the Digital Age*: Entrepreneurship has long been viewed as a key driver of competitiveness, but its role in the digital age requires deeper investigation. As markets become increasingly globalized, the link between entrepreneurial orientation and competitiveness will evolve as technologies such as AI and big data reshape business models.
2. *Exploring the Strategic Importance of Digitalization for Firms*: Digitalization is transforming business processes, customer experiences, and operational efficiencies, but its broader implications for firms, especially SMEs, have yet to be adequately explored. Future research should focus on the impact of digitalization on business performance and strategic decision-making, especially in sectors that have been slow to adopt technology.
3. *The Importance of Digital Entrepreneurship in Driving Innovation*: Digital entrepreneurship provides significant opportunities for innovation. As digital tools such as AI, blockchain, and big data become more accessible, understanding how entrepreneurs can use these technologies to drive innovation is a critical area for further study.
4. *The Role of Big Data in Improving Entrepreneurial Decision-Making*: As big data becomes an increasingly important part of business strategy, its role in entrepreneurial decision-making is a promising area of research. Entrepreneurs, especially in technology-focused areas, must leverage large amounts of data to make informed decisions.
5. *Adoption of AI in Entrepreneurial Ventures*: While the adoption of AI in large companies has been widely studied, its adoption in entrepreneurial ventures has been understudied. Startups and small businesses face unique challenges and opportunities when integrating AI into their operations.

6. *Relationship Between Entrepreneurial Orientation and Innovation Capability in AI-Driven Firms*: As AI increasingly becomes a key driver of business innovation, understanding the relationship between entrepreneurial orientation and innovation capability in AI-driven firms is critical. Exploring how firms with a strong entrepreneurial orientation use AI to innovate offers promising research opportunities for the future.
7. *AI and Strategic Management*: A Theoretical Framework: The role of AI in strategic management is an evolving area that requires further theoretical research. As firms increasingly rely on AI for strategic decision-making, understanding how AI impacts the strategic management process from environmental scanning to strategy implementation and control is critical.
8. *The Future of AI and Implications for Entrepreneurship*: The future of AI will also shape entrepreneurship. Understanding the long-term impacts of AI startups, innovation ecosystems, and global markets is critical for both practitioners and academics.

Research Directions: Digital Entrepreneurship and Global Competitiveness: Future research could investigate how digital entrepreneurship increases global competitiveness for small and medium-sized enterprises (SMEs), especially in emerging markets.

Entrepreneurial Ecosystems in the Digital Age: Studying digitally connected entrepreneurial ecosystems will be important because investigating how ecosystem actors (startups, investors, universities) collaborate digitally to increase regional or national competitiveness would provide valuable insights.

Sector-Specific Digitalization Studies: Examine how different sectors (e.g., manufacturing, healthcare, retail) approach digital transformation, what challenges they face, and how digitalization impacts their performance.

Digital Maturity Models: Researchers could also explore the development and validation of digital maturity models for firms of various sizes and sectors and determine how companies progress through the stages of digital transformation.

AI-Enabled Entrepreneurship: The role of AI in enabling entrepreneurs to create innovative products and services should be explored. Researchers could examine how AI can enhance market research, customer analysis, and product development for digital entrepreneurs.

Digital Entrepreneurship Innovation Diffusion: How digital innovation spreads within and across startups should be examined. Researchers could focus on the role of networks, accelerators, and open innovation platforms in promoting digital entrepreneurship.

Data-Driven Entrepreneurship Strategies: Future research could investigate how entrepreneurs use big data to identify market trends, assess customer needs, and optimize operations. Exploring the barriers to SMEs' adoption of big data analytics could also provide useful insights.

Big Data for Predictive Entrepreneurship: Researchers could examine how big data analytics can be used to predict entrepreneurial success, identify market gaps, and predict shifts in consumer behavior.

AI in Environmental Scanning: Future studies could examine how AI can improve the accuracy and efficiency of environmental scanning, helping firms detect market trends and competitive threats in real time.

AI for Strategic Control: Another promising research direction would be to examine how AI supports the strategic control process by providing real-time data and analysis for performance monitoring and adjustment.

AI for Sustainable Entrepreneurship: Future studies could also focus on how AI can promote sustainable entrepreneurship, how AI technologies can drive environmentally friendly business practices, and how they can support the development of green innovations.

As a result, the integration of digital technologies such as AI, big data, AR/VR, and autonomous robots into the entrepreneurial landscape could open up vast avenues for future research. By examining how these technologies are reshaping entrepreneurship, competitiveness, and innovation, researchers can provide valuable insights to help businesses meet the challenges and opportunities of the digital age. Understanding the implications of digitalization for various sectors, markets, and industries will be important for developing actionable strategies that promote growth, innovation, and sustainability.

CONCLUSION

In today's rapidly evolving business environment, the convergence of entrepreneurship, digitalization, and artificial intelligence (AI) is redefining the nature of competition and corporate success. As companies strive to maintain their competitive edge, digital entrepreneurship is emerging as a key driver of innovation and strategic advantage, powered by the integration of AI and big data.

Entrepreneurship is widely recognized as a catalyst for competitiveness, providing businesses with the agility and capacity to innovate to adapt to market changes. In an increasingly digital world, entrepreneurs are at the forefront of leveraging new technologies to increase productivity, optimize processes, and create value. The competitive advantage gained through entrepreneurs is not just a matter of being first to market, but also involves developing a robust entrepreneurial orientation that fosters innovation and responsiveness to external pressures.

An entrepreneurial mindset driven by risk-taking, proactivity, and innovation is crucial for businesses looking to navigate the uncertainties of the modern marketplace. In this context, competitiveness is not static; it requires constant reassessment and adaptation to technological developments and market trends.

Digitalization has become a vital component of organizational strategy, enabling companies to streamline operations, improve customer experiences, and create new business models. For many companies, the digital transformation journey begins with embracing technologies such as big data, artificial intelligence, and cloud computing. These innovations enable businesses to collect, process, and analyze vast amounts of data, providing insights that inform informed decision-making.

Digital entrepreneurship fosters innovation by enabling individuals and organizations to experiment with new business models and scale their initiatives rapidly. In the context of artificial intelligence and big data, digital entrepreneurship represents the coming together of creativity and technological prowess. Using these technologies, entrepreneurs can identify previously hidden patterns and trends, enabling them to make data-driven decisions and anticipate market shifts. The scalability of digital platforms also allows digital entrepreneurs to test and develop their ideas in real time, reducing the risks associated with traditional entrepreneurial ventures.

Entrepreneurial orientation refers to a firm's strategic stance characterized by innovation, risk-taking, and proactivity. A strong entrepreneurial orientation is closely linked to a firm's ability to innovate, as it encourages the exploration of new ideas and the development of novel solutions to market challenges. Companies with an entrepreneurial orientation are more likely to invest in research and development (R&D), pursue innovative business models, and adapt to changing market conditions.

The relationship between entrepreneurial orientation and innovation capability is particularly important in the context of AI and digital technologies. Firms that embrace an entrepreneurial mindset are better equipped to integrate AI into their operations, use big data to inform decision-making, and leverage digital tools to drive innovation. In this way, entrepreneurial orientation serves as a critical enabler of technological progress and long-term competitiveness.

Big data enables companies to collect and analyze large amounts of structured and unstructured data, providing insights into customer behavior, market trends, and operational efficiency. On the other hand, AI enhances the ability of businesses to solve problems by processing this data through machine learning, predictive analysis, and autonomous systems.

AI-powered tools enable companies to automate repetitive tasks, improve decision-making capabilities, and optimize operations in real time. As AI continues to evolve, its applications are expected to spread across industries from manufacturing and healthcare to finance and retail, leading to more innovation and growth.

Adoption of AI within companies is not only a technological change, but also a strategic one. Understanding the theoretical framework of AI adoption requires analyzing how AI aligns with organizational goals, capabilities, and structures. While AI adoption involves overcoming challenges related to data integration, employee training, and change management, its benefits are also significant. AI has the potential to transform industries by increasing operational efficiency, reducing costs, and enabling companies to innovate more effectively.

Companies must be willing to experiment with AI technologies, invest in talent development, and create a culture of innovation. By doing so, they can fully leverage AI's capabilities to drive strategic outcomes and gain competitive advantage.

The future of AI is both exciting and uncertain, and it is expected that rapid advances in AI technology will continue to shape industries and economies. The role of AI in the strategic management process will become even more evident as companies integrate AI into their decision-making frameworks, competitive analysis, and strategy execution. AI's ability to provide real-time insights, automate complex processes, and predict market trends will be critical for companies looking to stay ahead in an increasingly competitive environment.

As AI becomes more complex, its applications will expand, creating new ethical, legal, and social issues. Businesses will need to overcome these challenges while leveraging AI's potential to drive innovation, increase productivity, and create value. In this context, the relationship between AI and strategic management will evolve, and AI will play an increasingly central role in shaping corporate strategies and achieving long-term success.

To conclude, this chapter examines the critical intersections of entrepreneurship, digitalization, and AI, and highlights their importance for corporate competitiveness, innovation, and strategic management. As businesses continue to navigate the complexities of the digital age, the ability to integrate these elements into their operations will be key to achieving sustainable growth and success. Entrepreneurs and firms that embrace digitalization and AI will be well-positioned to capitalize on new opportunities, respond to market demands, and drive innovation in the years ahead.

REFERENCES

Acs, Z. J., & Varga, A. (2005). Entrepreneurship, agglomeration and technological change. *Small Business Economics*, 24, 323–334. DOI: 10.1007/s11187-005-1998-4

Adoli, H. L., & Kilika, J. M. (2020). Conceptualizing the role of leadership strategy in the context of strategic management process: A review of literature. *Journal of Economics and Business*, 3(4), 1598–1623. DOI: 10.31014/aior.1992.03.04.307

Agrawal, S., Chatterjee, K., & Novotný, P. (2017). Lexicographic ranking supermartingales: an efficient approach to termination of probabilistic programs. *Proceedings of the ACM on Programming Languages, 2*(POPL), 1-32.

Ahmed, N., Abbasi, M. S., Zuberi, F., Qamar, W., Halim, M. S. B., Maqsood, A., & Alam, M. K. (2021). Artificial intelligence techniques: Analysis, application, and outcome in dentistry—a systematic review. *BioMed Research International*, 2021(1), 1–15. DOI: 10.1155/2021/9751564 PMID: 34258283

Al Hadwer, A., Tavana, M., Gillis, D., & Rezania, D. (2021). A systematic review of organizational factors impacting cloud-based technology adoption using technology-organization-environment framework. *Internet of Things : Engineering Cyber Physical Human Systems*, 15, 1–10. DOI: 10.1016/j.iot.2021.100407

Al-Jabri, I., & Sohail, M. S. (2012). Mobile banking adoption: Application of diffusion of innovation theory. *Journal of Electronic Commerce Research*, 13(4), 379–391.

Alblushi, A. (2021). Face recognition based on artificial neural network: A review. *Artificial Intelligence & Robotics Development Journal*, 1(2), 116–131. DOI: 10.52098/airdj.202125

Alegre, J., & Chiva, R. (2013). Linking entrepreneurial orientation and firm performance: The role of organizational learning capability and innovation performance. *Journal of Small Business Management*, 51(4), 491–507. DOI: 10.1111/jsbm.12005

Alsheibani, S., Cheung, Y., & Messom, C. (2018). Artificial intelligence adoption: AI-readiness at firm-level. *Twenty-Second Pacific Asia Conference on Information Systems*, Japan 2018 (pp. 1-8). Association for Information Systems.

Amaghouss, J., & Ibourk, A. (2013). Entrepreneurial activities, innovation and economic growth: The role of cyclical factors evidence from OECD countries for the period 2001-2009. *International Business Research*, 6(1), 153–162.

Ammar, M., Haleem, A., Javaid, M., Walia, R., & Bahl, S. (2021). Improving material quality management and manufacturing organizations system through Industry 4.0 technologies. *Materials Today: Proceedings*, 45, 5089–5096. DOI: 10.1016/j.matpr.2021.01.585

Arrieta, A. B., Díaz-Rodríguez, N., Del Ser, J., Bennetot, A., Tabik, S., Barbado, A., & Herrera, F. (2020). Explainable Artificial Intelligence (XAI): Concepts, taxonomies, opportunities and challenges toward responsible AI. *Information Fusion*, 58, 82–115. DOI: 10.1016/j.inffus.2019.12.012

Arucu, M. (2021). Industry 4.0–holistic perspective: Modeling and simulation implementations in manufacturing systems. *Journal of Innovative Science and Engineering*, 5(1), 50–63.

Awa, H. O., Ojiabo, O. U., & Orokor, L. E. (2017). Integrated technology-organization-environment (TOE) taxonomies for technology adoption. *Journal of Enterprise Information Management*, 30(6), 893–921. DOI: 10.1108/JEIM-03-2016-0079

Aydemir, E. (2018). Weka ile yapay zeka. *Seçkin Yayınevi, Ankara*, Türkiye.

Bail, C. A. (2014). The cultural environment: Measuring culture with big data. *Theory and Society*, 43(3-4), 465–482. DOI: 10.1007/s11186-014-9216-5

Batool, S., Gill, S. A., Javaid, S., & Khan, A. J. (2021). Good governance via E-Governance: moving towards digitalization for a digital economy. *Review of applied management and social sciences, 4*(4), 823-836.

Bernoster, I., Mukerjee, J., & Thurik, R. (2020). The role of affect in entrepreneurial orientation. *Small Business Economics*, 54(1), 235–256. DOI: 10.1007/s11187-018-0116-3

Bessant, J., & Tidd, J. (2007). *Innovation and entrepreneurship*. John Wiley & Sons.

Bharadiya, J. P. (2023). A comparative study of business intelligence and artificial intelligence with big data analytics. *American Journal of Artificial Intelligence*, 7(1), 24–30.

Bharadwaj, A., El Sawy, O. A., Pavlou, P. A., & Venkatraman, N. V. (2013). Digital business strategy: Toward a next generation of insights. *Management Information Systems Quarterly*, 37(2), 471–482. DOI: 10.25300/MISQ/2013/37:2.3

Cammack, P. (2022). *The politics of global competitiveness*. Oxford University Press. DOI: 10.1093/oso/9780192847867.001.0001

Carlsson, C., & Walden, P. (1997). More effective strategic management with hyperknowledge: The Woodstrat case. *Journal of Decision Systems*, 6(1), 23–44. DOI: 10.1080/12460125.1997.10511704

Chen, W., He, W., Shen, J., Tian, X., & Wang, X. (2023). Systematic analysis of artificial intelligence in the era of industry 4.0. *Journal of Management Analytics*, 10(1), 89–108. DOI: 10.1080/23270012.2023.2180676

Chota, M. C. (2020). *Entrepreneurial orientation and it's effects on micro, small and medium enterprises (MSME's) business performance in Lusaka district* (Doctoral dissertation, The University of Zambia).

Cielen, A., Peeters, L., & Vanhoof, K. (2004). Bankruptcy prediction using a data envelopment analysis. *European Journal of Operational Research*, 154(2), 526–532. DOI: 10.1016/S0377-2217(03)00186-3

Cioffi, R., Travaglioni, M., Piscitelli, G., Petrillo, A., & De Felice, F. (2020). Artificial intelligence and machine learning applications in smart production: Progress, trends, and directions. *Sustainability (Basel)*, 12(2), 1–26. DOI: 10.3390/su12020492

Codini, A. P., Abbate, T., & Petruzzelli, A. M. (2023). Business Model Innovation and exaptation: A new way of innovating in SMEs. *Technovation*, 119, 1–16. DOI: 10.1016/j.technovation.2022.102548

Corrêa, V. S., Queiroz, M. M., Cruz, M. A., & Shigaki, H. B. (2022). Entrepreneurial orientation far beyond opportunity: The influence of the necessity for innovativeness, proactiveness and risk-taking. *International Journal of Entrepreneurial Behaviour & Research*, 28(4), 952–979. DOI: 10.1108/IJEBR-06-2021-0518

Covin, J. G., & Lumpkin, G. T. (2011). Entrepreneurial orientation theory and research: Reflections on a needed construct. *Entrepreneurship Theory and Practice*, 35(5), 855–872. DOI: 10.1111/j.1540-6520.2011.00482.x

Covin, J. G., & Slevin, D. P. (1989). Strategic management of small firms in hostile and benign environments. *Strategic Management Journal*, 10(1), 75–87. DOI: 10.1002/smj.4250100107

Covin, J. G., & Wales, W. J. (2012). The measurement of entrepreneurial orientation. *Entrepreneurship Theory and Practice*, 36(4), 677–702. DOI: 10.1111/j.1540-6520.2010.00432.x

Cui, Y., Kara, S., & Chan, K. C. (2020). Manufacturing big data ecosystem: A systematic literature review. *Robotics and Computer-integrated Manufacturing*, 62, 1–20. DOI: 10.1016/j.rcim.2019.101861

Daugherty, P. R., & Wilson, H. J. (2018). *Human+ machine: Reimagining work in the age of AI*. Harvard Business Press.

Davenport, T. H., & Ronanki, R. (2018). Artificial intelligence for the real world. *Harvard Business Review*, 96(1), 108–116.

Davidsson, P. (2015). Entrepreneurial opportunities and the entrepreneurship nexus: A re-conceptualization. *Journal of Business Venturing*, 30(5), 674–695. DOI: 10.1016/j.jbusvent.2015.01.002

Di Vaio, A., Palladino, R., Hassan, R., & Escobar, O. (2020). Artificial intelligence and business models in the sustainable development goals perspective: A systematic literature review. *Journal of Business Research*, 121, 283–314. DOI: 10.1016/j.jbusres.2020.08.019

Doyle, G., Srivastava, S. B., Goldberg, A., & Frank, M. C. (2017). Alignment at Work: Using Language to Distinguish the Internalization and Self-Regulation Components of Cultural Fit in Organizations. IRLE Working Paper, pp. 102-110. https://irle.berkeley.edu/files/2017/Alignment-At-Work.pdf

Drucker, P. F. (1985). Entrepreneurial strategies. *California Management Review*, 27(2), 9–25. DOI: 10.2307/41165126

Drucker, P. F. (1998). The discipline of innovation. *Harvard Business Review*, 76(6), 149–157. PMID: 10187245

Dutz, M. A., Ordover, J. A., & Willig, R. D. (2000). Entrepreneurship, access policy and economic development: Lessons from industrial organization. *European Economic Review*, 44(4-6), 739–747. DOI: 10.1016/S0014-2921(00)00030-1

Dwivedi, Y. K., Hughes, L., Ismagilova, E., Aarts, G., Coombs, C., Crick, T., Duan, Y., Dwivedi, R., Edwards, J., Eirug, A., Galanos, V., Ilavarasan, P. V., Janssen, M., Jones, P., Kar, A. K., Kizgin, H., Kronemann, B., Lal, B., Lucini, B., & Williams, M. D. (2021). Artificial Intelligence (AI): Multidisciplinary perspectives on emerging challenges, opportunities, and agenda for research, practice and policy. *International Journal of Information Management*, 57, 1–47. DOI: 10.1016/j.ijinfomgt.2019.08.002

El Miedany, Y. (2019). Virtual reality and augmented reality. *Rheumatology teaching: the art and science of medical education*, 403-427.

Ensmenger, N. (2012). Is chess the drosophila of artificial intelligence? A social history of an algorithm. *Social Studies of Science*, 42(1), 5–30. DOI: 10.1177/0306312711424596 PMID: 22530382

Favaretto, M., De Clercq, E., Schneble, C. O., & Elger, B. S. (2020). What is your definition of Big Data? Researchers' understanding of the phenomenon of the decade. *PLoS One*, 15(2), 1–20. DOI: 10.1371/journal.pone.0228987 PMID: 32097430

Felicetti, A. M., Corvello, V., & Ammirato, S. (2024). Digital innovation in entrepreneurial firms: A systematic literature review. *Review of Managerial Science*, 18(2), 315–362. DOI: 10.1007/s11846-023-00638-9

Ferràs-Hernández, X., Tarrats-Pons, E., & Arimany-Serrat, N. (2017). Disruption in the automotive industry: A Cambrian moment. *Business Horizons*, 60(6), 855–863. DOI: 10.1016/j.bushor.2017.07.011

Ferreras-Méndez, J. L., Olmos-Penuela, J., Salas-Vallina, A., & Alegre, J. (2021). Entrepreneurial orientation and new product development performance in SMEs: The mediating role of business model innovation. *Technovation*, 108, 1–13. DOI: 10.1016/j.technovation.2021.102325

Fleck, J. (2018). Development and establishment in artificial intelligence. In *The Question of Artificial Intelligence* (pp. 106–164). Routledge. DOI: 10.4324/9780429505331-3

Floridi, L. (2019). What the near future of artificial intelligence could be. *Philosophy & Technology*, 32(1), 1–15. DOI: 10.1007/s13347-019-00345-y

Gangwani, D., & Zhu, X. (2024). Modeling and prediction of business success: A survey. *Artificial Intelligence Review*, 57(2), 1–51. DOI: 10.1007/s10462-023-10664-4

Guerrero, M., Liñán, F., & Cáceres-Carrasco, F. R. (2021). The influence of ecosystems on the entrepreneurship process: A comparison across developed and developing economies. *Small Business Economics*, 57(4), 1733–1759. DOI: 10.1007/s11187-020-00392-2

Haefner, N., Wincent, J., Parida, V., & Gassmann, O. (2021). Artificial intelligence and innovation management: A review, framework, and research agenda . *Technological Forecasting and Social Change*, 162, 1–10. DOI: 10.1016/j.techfore.2020.120392

Haenlein, M., & Kaplan, A. (2021). Artificial intelligence and robotics: Shaking up the business world and society at large. *Journal of Business Research*, 124(C), 405–407. DOI: 10.1016/j.jbusres.2020.10.042

Hassan, A., Anwar, I., Saleem, I., Islam, K. B., & Hussain, S. A. (2021). Individual entrepreneurial orientation, entrepreneurship education and entrepreneurial intention: The mediating role of entrepreneurial motivations. *Industry and Higher Education*, 35(4), 403–418. DOI: 10.1177/0950422221100705l

He, H., Gray, J., Cangelosi, A., Meng, Q., McGinnity, T. M., & Mehnen, J. (2021). The challenges and opportunities of human-centered AI for trustworthy robots and autonomous systems. *IEEE Transactions on Cognitive and Developmental Systems*, 14(4), 1398–1412. DOI: 10.1109/TCDS.2021.3132282

Hua, H., Li, Y., Wang, T., Dong, N., Li, W., & Cao, J. (2023). Edge computing with artificial intelligence: A machine learning perspective. *ACM Computing Surveys*, 55(9), 1–35. DOI: 10.1145/3555802

Hughes, C., Robert, L., Frady, K., & Arroyos, A. (2019). Artificial intelligence, employee engagement, fairness, and job outcomes. In *Managing technology and middle-and low-skilled employees* (pp. 61–68). Emerald Publishing Limited. DOI: 10.1108/978-1-78973-077-720191005

Hult, G. T. M., Hurley, R. F., & Knight, G. A. (2004). Innovativeness: Its antecedents and impact on business performance. *Industrial Marketing Management*, 33(5), 429–438. DOI: 10.1016/j.indmarman.2003.08.015

Humble, K. P., & Altun, D. (2020). Artificial Intelligence and the threat to human rights. *Journal of Internet Law*, 24(3), 1–19.

Ireland, R. D., Hitt, M. A., & Sirmon, D. G. (2003). A model of strategic entrepreneurship: The construct and its dimensions. *Journal of Management*, 29(6), 963–989. DOI: 10.1016/S0149-2063(03)00086-2

Jarrahi, M. H. (2018). Artificial intelligence and the future of work: Human-AI symbiosis in organizational decision making. *Business Horizons*, 61(4), 577–586. DOI: 10.1016/j.bushor.2018.03.007

Jean, N., Burke, M., Xie, M., Davis, W. M., Lobell, D. B., & Ermon, S. (2016). Combining satellite imagery and machine learning to predict poverty. *Science*, 353(6301), 790–794. DOI: 10.1126/science.aaf7894 PMID: 27540167

Jöhnk, J., Weißert, M., & Wyrtki, K. (2021). Ready or not, AI comes—An interview study of organizational AI readiness factors. *Business & Information Systems Engineering*, 63(1), 5–20. DOI: 10.1007/s12599-020-00676-7

Johnson, J., Whittington, R., Regnér, P., Angwin, D., Johnson, G., & Scholes, K. (2020). *Exploring strategy*.

Kadwa, I., & Barnard, B. (2019). The impact of leadership on entrepreneurship and innovation: Perceptions of entrepreneurs. *IUP Journal of Entrepreneurship Development*, 16(4), 7–43.

Kaggwa, S., Eleogu, T. F., Okonkwo, F., Farayola, O. A., Uwaoma, P. U., & Akinoso, A. (2024). AI in decision making: Transforming business strategies. *International Journal of Innovation and Scientific Research*, 10(12), 423–444. DOI: 10.51244/IJRSI.2023.1012032

Kar, S., Kar, A. K., & Gupta, M. P. (2021). Modeling drivers and barriers of artificial intelligence adoption: Insights from a strategic management perspective. *International Journal of Intelligent Systems in Accounting Finance & Management*, 28(4), 217–238. DOI: 10.1002/isaf.1503

Karami, M., Ojala, A., & Saarenketo, S. (2023). Entrepreneurial orientation and international opportunity development by SMEs: The mediating role of decision-making logic. *Journal of Small Business Management*, 61(2), 994–1022. DOI: 10.1080/00472778.2020.1824529

Karantza, P. (2017). *The impact of economic crises on the development of innovation and entrepreneurship* (Doctoral dissertation, Business Administration Programm, School of Economic Sciences and Business, Neapolis University Pafos).

Keding, C. (2021). Understanding the interplay of artificial intelligence and strategic management: Four decades of research in review. *Management Review Quarterly*, 71(1), 91–134. DOI: 10.1007/s11301-020-00181-x

Kiyabo, K., & Isaga, N. (2020). Entrepreneurial orientation, competitive advantage, and SMEs' performance: Application of firm growth and personal wealth measures. *Journal of Innovation and Entrepreneurship*, 9(1), 1–15. DOI: 10.1186/s13731-020-00123-7

Koivusalo, S. (2023). Digital entrepreneurship: challenges faced by Finnish professional service business owners during venture launch in online business environments. Master's Thesis, School of Business and Economics, Jyväskylä University.

Kreiser, P. M., & Davis, J. (2010). Entrepreneurial orientation and firm performance: The unique impact of innovativeness, proactiveness, and risk-taking. *Journal of Small Business and Entrepreneurship*, 23(1), 39–51. DOI: 10.1080/08276331.2010.10593472

Labanauskaitė, D., Župerkienė, E., Kumpf, A., Šimanskienė, L., & Koller, S. M. (2021). Development of digital and entrepreneurial competences for the future labour market needs. *Entrepreneurship and sustainability issues.*, *8*(3), 565-581.

Li, X., Li, J., Yuan, C., Guo, S., & Wang, Z. (2022). Digital infrastructure. In *Development practice of digital business environment in China* (pp. 39–55). Springer Nature Singapore. DOI: 10.1007/978-981-16-8527-9_3

Liberatore, M. J., & Wagner, W. P. (2021). Virtual, mixed, and augmented reality: A systematic review for immersive systems research. *Virtual Reality (Waltham Cross)*, 25(3), 773–799. DOI: 10.1007/s10055-020-00492-0

Lichtenthaler, U. (2020). Extremes of acceptance: Employee attitudes toward artificial intelligence. *The Journal of Business Strategy*, 41(5), 39–45. DOI: 10.1108/JBS-12-2018-0204

Liu, R. (2023). Innovative research on synergistic development of digital integrated media and visual design based on kruskal algorithm. *Applied Mathematics and Nonlinear Sciences*, 9(1), 1–13.

Lumpkin, G. T., & Dess, G. G. (1996). Clarifying the entrepreneurial orientation construct and linking it to performance. *Academy of Management Review*, 21(1), 135–172. DOI: 10.2307/258632

Lumpkin, G. T., & Dess, G. G. (2001). Linking two dimensions of entrepreneurial orientation to firm performance: The moderating role of environment and industry life cycle. *Journal of Business Venturing*, 16(5), 429–451. DOI: 10.1016/S0883-9026(00)00048-3

Makhloufi, L., Laghouag, A. A., Ali Sahli, A., & Belaid, F. (2021). Impact of entrepreneurial orientation on innovation capability: The mediating role of absorptive capability and organizational learning capabilities. *Sustainability (Basel)*, 13(10), 1–20. DOI: 10.3390/su13105399

Malik, S., Chadhar, M., Vatanasakdakul, S., & Chetty, M. (2021). Factors affecting the organizational adoption of blockchain technology: Extending the technology–organization–environment (TOE) framework in the Australian context. *Sustainability (Basel)*, 13(16), 1–31. DOI: 10.3390/su13169404

Mariotti, S., & Marzano, R. (2021). The effects of competition policy, regulatory quality and trust on inward FDI in host countries. *International Business Review*, 30(6), 1–16. DOI: 10.1016/j.ibusrev.2021.101887

Matalamäki, M. J., & Joensuu-Salo, S. (2022). Digitalization and strategic flexibility–a recipe for business growth. *Journal of Small Business and Enterprise Development*, 29(3), 380–401. DOI: 10.1108/JSBED-10-2020-0384

Merhi, M. I., & Harfouche, A. (2024). Enablers of artificial intelligence adoption and implementation in production systems. *International Journal of Production Research*, 62(15), 5457–5471. DOI: 10.1080/00207543.2023.2167014

Metawa, N., Hassan, M. K., & Metawa, S. (2022). *Artificial Intelligence and Big Data for Financial Risk Management*. Routledge. DOI: 10.4324/9781003144410

Miikkulainen, R., Iscoe, N., Shagrin, A., Rapp, R., Nazari, S., McGrath, P., & Lamba, G. (2018, April). Sentient ascend: AI-based massively multivariate conversion rate optimization. In *Proceedings of the AAAI Conference on Artificial Intelligence* (Vol. 32, No. 1), 7696-7703. DOI: 10.1609/aaai.v32i1.11387

Miller, D. (1983). The correlates of entrepreneurship in three types of firms. *Management Science*, 29(7), 770–791. DOI: 10.1287/mnsc.29.7.770

Miller, D., & Friesen, P. H. (1982). Innovation in conservative and entrepreneurial firms: Two models of strategic momentum. *Strategic Management Journal*, 3(1), 1–25. DOI: 10.1002/smj.4250030102

Mintzberg, H. (1973). Strategy-making in three modes. *California Management Review*, 16(2), 44–53. DOI: 10.2307/41164491

Misaros, M., Stan, O. P., Donca, I. C., & Miclea, L. C. (2023). Autonomous Robots for Services—State of the Art, Challenges, and Research Areas. *Sensors (Basel)*, 23(10), 1–31. DOI: 10.3390/s23104962 PMID: 37430875

Modayil, J., & Kuipers, B. (2008). The initial development of object knowledge by a learning robot. *Robotics and Autonomous Systems*, 56(11), 879–890. DOI: 10.1016/j.robot.2008.08.004 PMID: 19953188

Mohammed, I. B., & Isa, S. M. (2021). The role of internet of things (IoT) in the containment and spread of the novel COVID-19 pandemic. *Computational intelligence methods in COVID-19: surveillance, prevention, prediction and diagnosis*, 109-119.

Mostafiz, M. I., Hughes, M., & Sambasivan, M. (2022). Entrepreneurial orientation, competitive advantage and strategic knowledge management capability in Malaysian family firms. *Journal of Knowledge Management*, 26(2), 423–458. DOI: 10.1108/JKM-09-2020-0693

Naqvi, R., Soomro, T. R., Alzoubi, H. M., Ghazal, T. M., & Alshurideh, M. T. (2021). The nexus between big data and decision-making: A study of big data techniques and technologies. In *The international conference on artificial intelligence and computer vision* (pp. 838–853). Springer International Publishing. DOI: 10.1007/978-3-030-76346-6_73

Ndagi, A., & Salihu, A. A. (2019). Technology Entrepreneurship and Fourth Industrial Revolution Era. *LAPAI International Journal of Management and Social Sciences*, 11(1), 142–153.

Neumann, T. (2021). The impact of entrepreneurship on economic, social and environmental welfare and its determinants: A systematic review. *Management Review Quarterly*, 71(3), 553–584. DOI: 10.1007/s11301-020-00193-7

Nissen, M. E., & Sengupta, K. (2006). Incorporating software agents into supply chains: Experimental investigation with a procurement task. *Management Information Systems Quarterly*, 30(1), 145–166. DOI: 10.2307/25148721

O'Kane, C., Zhang, J. A., Haar, J., & Cunningham, J. A. (2023). How scientists interpret and address funding criteria: Value creation and undesirable side effects. *Small Business Economics*, 61(2), 799–826. DOI: 10.1007/s11187-022-00697-4 PMID: 38625286

Okoli, I. E. N., Nwosu, K. C., & Okechukwu, M. E. (2021). Entrepreneurial orientation and performance of selected SMEs in Southeast, Nigeria. *European Journal of Business and Management Research*, 6(4), 108–115. DOI: 10.24018/ejbmr.2021.6.4.946

Otero-Neira, C., Arias, M. J. F., & Lindman, M. T. (2013). Market orientation and entrepreneurial proclivity: Antecedents of innovation. *Global Business Review*, 14(3), 385–395. DOI: 10.1177/0972150913496719

Pallathadka, H., Ramirez-Asis, E. H., Loli-Poma, T. P., Kaliyaperumal, K., Ventayen, R. J. M., & Naved, M. (2023). Applications of artificial intelligence in business management, e-commerce and finance. *Materials Today: Proceedings*, 80, 1–4. DOI: 10.1016/j.matpr.2021.06.419

Parviainen, P., Tihinen, M., Kääriäinen, J., & Teppola, S. (2017). Tackling the digitalization challenge: how to benefit from digitalization in practice. *International journal of information systems and project management, 5*(1), 63-77.

Perifanis, N. A., & Kitsios, F. (2023). Investigating the influence of artificial intelligence on business value in the digital era of strategy: A literature review. *Information (Basel)*, 14(2), 1–42. DOI: 10.3390/info14020085

Pertusa-Ortega, E. M., Zaragoza-Sáez, P., & Claver-Cortés, E. (2010). Can formalization, complexity, and centralization influence knowledge performance? *Journal of Business Research*, 63(3), 310–320. DOI: 10.1016/j.jbusres.2009.03.015

Pillai, R., & Sivathanu, B. (2020). Adoption of artificial intelligence (AI) for talent acquisition in IT/ITeS organizations. *Benchmarking*, 27(9), 2599–2629. DOI: 10.1108/BIJ-04-2020-0186

Pinto Borges, A., Lopes, J. M., Carvalho, C., Vieira, B. M., & Lopes, J. (2021). Education as a key to provide the growth of entrepreneurial intentions. *Education + Training*, 63(6), 809–832. DOI: 10.1108/ET-03-2020-0052

Pournader, M., Ghaderi, H., Hassanzadegan, A., & Fahimnia, B. (2021). Artificial intelligence applications in supply chain management. *International Journal of Production Economics*, 241, 1–16. DOI: 10.1016/j.ijpe.2021.108250

Putniņš, T. J., & Sauka, A. (2020). Why does entrepreneurial orientation affect company performance? *Strategic Entrepreneurship Journal*, 14(4), 711–735. DOI: 10.1002/sej.1325

Raisch, S., & Krakowski, S. (2021). Artificial intelligence and management: The automation–augmentation paradox. *Academy of Management Review*, 46(1), 192–210. DOI: 10.5465/amr.2018.0072

Rajest, S. S., Singh, B., Obaid, A. J., Regin, R., & Chinnusamy, K. (Eds.). (2023). *Advances in artificial and human intelligence in the modern era*. IGI Global. DOI: 10.4018/979-8-3693-1301-5

Ramachandran, K. K., Mary, A. A. S., Hawladar, S., Asokk, D., Bhaskar, B., & Pitroda, J. R. (2022). Machine learning and role of artificial intelligence in optimizing work performance and employee behavior. *Materials Today: Proceedings*, 51, 2327–2331. DOI: 10.1016/j.matpr.2021.11.544

Rauch, A., Wiklund, J., Lumpkin, G. T., & Frese, M. (2009). Entrepreneurial orientation and business performance: An assessment of past research and suggestions for the future. *Entrepreneurship Theory and Practice*, 33(3), 761–787. DOI: 10.1111/j.1540-6520.2009.00308.x

Reeves, M., & Ueda, D. (2016). Designing the machines that will design strategy. Harvard Business Review Digital Articles, 2–6. https://hbr.org/2016/04/welcoming-the-chief-strategy-robot

Riahi, Y., & Riahi, S. (2018). Big data and big data analytics: Concepts, types and technologies. *International Journal of Research and Engineering*, 5(9), 524–528. DOI: 10.21276/ijre.2018.5.9.5

Robinson, C. V., Ahmad, F., & Simmons, J. E. (2021). Consolidation and fragmentation in environmental scanning: A review and research agenda. *Long Range Planning*, 54(3), 1–18. DOI: 10.1016/j.lrp.2020.101997

Robinson, M. F. (2019). *Artificial intelligence in hiring: Understanding attitudes and perspectives of HR practitioners*. A dissertation submitted to the faculty of Wilmington University in partial fulfillment of the requirements for the degree of Doctor of Business Administration, Wilmington University (Delaware).

Ruzgas, T., Jakubeliene, K., & Buivyte, A. (2016). Big Data Mining and Knowledge Discovery. *Journal of Communications Technology. Electronics and Computer Science*, 9, 5–9.

Schumpeter, J. A. (1934). *The theory of economic development. An inquiry into profits, capital, credit, interest, and the business cycle*. Harvard University Press.

Sedkaoui, S. (Ed.). (2018). *Big data analytics for entrepreneurial success*. IGI Global.

Shane, S. A. (Ed.). (2007). *Economic development through entrepreneurship: Government, university and business linkages*. Edward Elgar Publishing.

Si, S., Hall, J., Suddaby, R., Ahlstrom, D., & Wei, J. (2023). Technology, entrepreneurship, innovation and social change in digital economics. *Technovation*, 119, 102484. DOI: 10.1016/j.technovation.2022.102484

Siddiqui, M. K., & Goyal, K. K. (2023). A Study the Use of E-Payment Systems Based on Artifical Intelligence. *Computing & Intellegent Systems (SCTS)*, 1063-1076.

Soni, N., Sharma, E. K., Singh, N., & Kapoor, A. (2020). Artificial intelligence in business: From research and innovation to market deployment. *Procedia Computer Science*, 167, 2200–2210. DOI: 10.1016/j.procs.2020.03.272

Strohmeier, S., & Piazza, F. (2013). Domain driven data mining in human resource management: A review of current research. *Expert Systems with Applications*, 40(7), 2410–2420. DOI: 10.1016/j.eswa.2012.10.059

Suominen, A., Toivanen, H., & Seppänen, M. (2017). Firms' knowledge profiles: Mapping patent data with unsupervised learning. *Technological Forecasting and Social Change*, 115, 131–142. DOI: 10.1016/j.techfore.2016.09.028

Syed, R., Suriadi, S., Adams, M., Bandara, W., Leemans, S. J., Ouyang, C., ter Hofstede, A. H. M., van de Weerd, I., Wynn, M. T., & Reijers, H. A. (2020). Robotic process automation: Contemporary themes and challenges. *Computers in Industry*, 115, 1–15. DOI: 10.1016/j.compind.2019.103162

Tekin, İ. Ç., & Küsbeci, P. (2021). Dijital dönüşüm sürecinde yükselen bir değer: Dijital girişimcilik. *Stratejik Yönetim Araştırmaları Dergisi*, 4(1), 81–102.

Thorpe, R. (2016). *Gower handbook of leadership and management development*. CRC Press. DOI: 10.4324/9781315585703

Tien, J. M. (2017). Internet of things, real-time decision making, and artificial intelligence. *Annals of Data Science*, 4(2), 149–178. DOI: 10.1007/s40745-017-0112-5

Todaro, M. P., & Smith, S. C. (2020). *Economic development*.

Tong, S., Jia, N., Luo, X., & Fang, Z. (2021). The Janus face of artificial intelligence feedback: Deployment versus disclosure effects on employee performance. *Strategic Management Journal*, 42(9), 1600–1631. DOI: 10.1002/smj.3322

Tornatzky, L. G., & Fleischer, M. (1990). *The processes of technological innovation*. Lexington Books.

Torrado, R. R., Bontrager, P., Togelius, J., Liu, J., & Perez-Liebana, D. (2018, August). Deep reinforcement learning for general video game ai. In *2018 IEEE Conference on Computational Intelligence and Games (CIG)* (pp. 1-8). IEEE. DOI: 10.1109/CIG.2018.8490422

Truong, Y., & Papagiannidis, S. (2022). Artificial intelligence as an enabler for innovation: A review and future research agenda. *Technological Forecasting and Social Change*, 183, 1–6. DOI: 10.1016/j.techfore.2022.121852

Turienzo, J., Cabanelas, P., & Lampón, J. F. (2023). Business models in times of disruption: The connected and autonomous vehicles (uncertain) domino effect. *Journal of Business Research*, 156, 1–12. DOI: 10.1016/j.jbusres.2022.113481

Turner, C. (2022). Augmented reality, augmented epistemology, and the real-world web. *Philosophy & Technology*, 35(1), 19. DOI: 10.1007/s13347-022-00496-5

Usman, F. O., Kess-Momoh, A. J., Ibeh, C. V., Elufioye, A. E., Ilojianya, V. I., & Oyeyemi, O. P.Favour Oluwadamilare UsmanAzeez Jason Kess-MomohChidera Victoria IbehAkinola Elumakin ElufioyeValentine Ikenna IlojianyaOluwaseun Peter Oyeyemi. (2024). Entrepreneurial innovations and trends: A global review: Examining emerging trends, challenges, and opportunities in the field of entrepreneurship, with a focus on how technology and globalization are shaping new business ventures. *International Journal of Science and Research Archive*, 11(1), 552–569. DOI: 10.30574/ijsra.2024.11.1.0079

Van Doorn, S., Heyden, M., Tröster, C., & Volberda, H. (2015). Entrepreneurial orientation and performance: Investigating local requirements for entrepreneurial decision-making. In *Cognition and strategy* (Vol. 32, pp. 211–239). Emerald Group Publishing Limited. DOI: 10.1108/S0742-332220150000032007

Van Praag, C. M., & Versloot, P. H. (2007). What is the value of entrepreneurship? A review of recent research. *Small Business Economics*, 29(4), 351–382. DOI: 10.1007/s11187-007-9074-x

Von Krogh, G., Ben-Menahem, S. M., & Shrestha, Y. R. (2021). Artificial intelligence in strategizing: Prospects and challenges. *Future of strategic management*, 625-646.

Votto, A. M., Valecha, R., Najafirad, P., & Rao, H. R. (2021). Artificial intelligence in tactical human resource management: A systematic literature review. *International Journal of Information Management Data Insights*, 1(2), 1–15. DOI: 10.1016/j.jjimei.2021.100047

Wamba-Taguimdje, S. L., Wamba, S. F., Kamdjoug, J. R. K., & Wanko, C. E. T. (2020). Influence of artificial intelligence (AI) on firm performance: The business value of AI-based transformation projects. *Business Process Management Journal*, 26(7), 1893–1924. DOI: 10.1108/BPMJ-10-2019-0411

Wiklund, J., & Shepherd, D. (2005). Entrepreneurial orientation and small business performance: A configurational approach. *Journal of Business Venturing*, 20(1), 71–91. DOI: 10.1016/j.jbusvent.2004.01.001

Wilson, H. J., & Daugherty, P. R. (2018). Collaborative intelligence: Humans and AI are joining forces. *Harvard Business Review*, 96(4), 114–123.

Wu, W. T., Li, Y. J., Feng, A. Z., Li, L., Huang, T., Xu, A. D., & Lyu, J. (2021). Data mining in clinical big data: The frequently used databases, steps, and methodological models. *Military Medical Research*, 8(1), 1–12. DOI: 10.1186/s40779-021-00338-z PMID: 34380547

Wujarso, R. (2023). *Effect of digital transformation on company operational efficiency*. Asadel Publisher.

Yeomans, M., Shah, A., Mullainathan, S., & Kleinberg, J. (2019). Making sense of recommendations. *Journal of Behavioral Decision Making*, 32(4), 403–414. DOI: 10.1002/bdm.2118

Yousfi-Monod, M., Farzindar, A., & Lapalme, G. (2010). Supervised machine learning for summarizing legal documents. In *Advances in Artificial Intelligence: 23rd Canadian Conference on Artificial Intelligence, Canadian AI 2010, Ottawa, Canada, May 31–June 2, 2010*. [Springer Berlin Heidelberg.]. *Proceedings*, 23, 51–62.

Zafarani, R. (2014). *Social Media Mining: An Introduction*. Cambridge University Press. DOI: 10.1017/CBO9781139088510

Zahra, S. A. (1991). Predictors and financial outcomes of corporate entrepreneurship: An exploratory study. *Journal of Business Venturing*, 6(4), 259–285. DOI: 10.1016/0883-9026(91)90019-A

Zhang, C., & Lu, Y. (2021). Study on artificial intelligence: The state of the art and future prospects. *Journal of Industrial Information Integration*, 23, 1–9. DOI: 10.1016/j.jii.2021.100224

Zhao, Q. (2009). A survey on virtual reality. *Science in China Series F: Information Sciences*, 52(3), 348–400.

Zuloaga-Rotta, L., Borja-Rosales, R., Rodríguez Mallma, M. J., Mauricio, D., & Maculan, N. (2024). Method to Forecast the Presidential Election Results Based on Simulation and Machine Learning. *Computation (Basel, Switzerland)*, 12(3), 1–16. DOI: 10.3390/computation12030038

ADDITIONAL READING

Adekunle, O. J., & Israel, O. B. (2022). Impact of resource-based theory on entrepreneurship in Nigeria. *International Journal of Management Science and Business Analysis*, 24(7), 159–174.

Al-Swidi, A. K., & Mahmood, R. (2011). How does organizational culture shape the relationship between entrepreneurial orientation and the organizational performance of banks? *European Journal of Soil Science*, 20(1), 28–46.

Brynjolfsson, E., & Mitchell, T. (2017). What can machine learning do? Workforce implications. *Science*, 358(6370), 1530–1534. DOI: 10.1126/science.aap8062 PMID: 29269459

Harahap, M. A. K., Wurarah, R. N., Fathurohman, A., Suroso, A., & Iskandar, Y. (2023). Globalization substance and industrial revolution 4.0 and the role of technological innovation for economic development towards entrepreneurship. *Jurnal Bisnisman: Riset Bisnis Dan Manajemen*, 4(3), 37–51. DOI: 10.52005/bisnisman.v4i3.122

Hunt, S. D., & Arnett, D. B. (2006). Does marketing success lead to market success? *Journal of Business Research*, 59(7), 820–828. DOI: 10.1016/j.jbusres.2006.01.019

Imafidon, K. (2014). Entrepreneurship development for sustaining economic growth in third world nations. *Journal of Emerging Trends in Economics and Management Science*, 5(7), 101–108.

Khithika, M. A. (2020). *Assessing the influence of entrepreneurial orientation on the performance of South African construction business* (Doctoral dissertation, North-West University (South Africa)).

Liu, C. H. (2021). Creating competitive advantage through network ties, entrepreneurial orientation and intellectual capital. *Management Decision*, 59(9), 2238–2263. DOI: 10.1108/MD-02-2020-0191

Makarius, E. E., Mukherjee, D., Fox, J. D., & Fox, A. K. (2020). Rising with the machines: A sociotechnical framework for bringing artificial intelligence into the organization. *Journal of Business Research*, 120, 262–273. DOI: 10.1016/j.jbusres.2020.07.045

Paula, K. (1996). The points of transition in reforming the understanding and meaning of entrepreneurship. *Academy of Entrepreneurship Journal, European Edition, 2*(1), 70-93.

Peterson, R. A., & Berger, D. G. (1971). Entrepreneurship in organizations: Evidence from the popular music industry. *Administrative Science Quarterly*, 16(1), 97–106. DOI: 10.2307/2391293

Weerawardena, J., Salunke, S., Haigh, N., & Mort, G. S. (2021). Business model innovation in social purpose organizations: Conceptualizing dual social-economic value creation. *Journal of Business Research*, 125, 762–771. DOI: 10.1016/j.jbusres.2019.10.016

Zahra, S. A., & Garvis, D. M. (2000). International corporate entrepreneurship and firm performance: The moderating effect of international environmental hostility. *Journal of Business Venturing*, 15(5-6), 469–492. DOI: 10.1016/S0883-9026(99)00036-1

KEY TERMS AND DEFINITIONS

Artificial Intelligence (AI): It is a branch of science aimed at developing computer systems that exhibit human-like intelligence. These systems can perform tasks such as learning, problem solving, speech recognition and can work without human intervention.

Augmented Reality (AR): A technology that combines the real world with digital data, allowing the user to experience the real world in an enhanced way. AR adds virtual objects or information to the real world on the screen through glasses or smartphones.

Autonomous: A term used for systems that can make decisions and perform operations on their own, without human intervention. For example, autonomous vehicles are vehicles that can drive without needing a driver.

Big Data: The totality of data that comes from various sources, is very fast, very large in amount and in various formats (structured, unstructured). This data is processed to extract valuable information using advanced analysis methods and used in decision-making processes.

Digitalization: The process of converting information and data into digital format. Digitalization means developing and managing business processes, services and products with the help of digital technologies. Companies become faster, more efficient and more data-oriented with digitalization.

Entrepreneurship: It is defined as the process of developing innovative products or services by discovering new business opportunities. Entrepreneurship involves taking risks and organizing resources to start a new business or project.

Strategy: Refers to the planning and guidance processes that an institution follows to achieve set goals. Strategy determines which steps will be taken and which resources will be used and how to ensure long-term success.

Virtual Reality (VR): A technology that transports users to a completely digital world. Through special glasses and devices, users can interact in a virtual environment as if it were real and have a completely integrated experience with this virtual world.

Chapter 15
Strengthening the Entrepreneurial Mindset With Artificial Intelligence in the Digitalization Process

Zafer Adiguzel
Sakarya University of Applied Sciences, Turkey & Koc University, Turkey

ABSTRACT

The intersection of entrepreneurship, digital technologies, and artificial intelligence (AI) is shaping the modern business landscape and future economic opportunities. It is important to examine entrepreneurial behavior patterns and entrepreneurial intent, the motivations, attitudes, and actions of contemporary entrepreneurs in terms of digital technology and AI. In the context of Industry 4.0, digitalization presents both challenges and opportunities, encouraging businesses to adapt to advanced technologies such as AI and automation while contributing to sustainable development goals. The chapter examines the evolving digital entrepreneurship ecosystem, emphasizing the role of infrastructures, policies, and funding that support innovation. The future of AI is assessed, discussing technological advances and the societal challenges that need to be addressed to ensure that AI serves as a force for sustainable growth and positive societal impact.

DOI: 10.4018/979-8-3693-8442-8.ch015

INTRODUCTION

Entrepreneurship has long been recognized as a critical driver of economic growth, innovation, and social change. As the world continues to evolve at an unprecedented pace driven by rapid advances in digital technology, the entrepreneurial landscape is also undergoing significant transformation. The introduction of new technologies, especially Artificial Intelligence (AI), is reshaping industries and providing new opportunities for entrepreneurs. In this context, understanding various aspects of entrepreneurship, including behavioral patterns, intentions, and attitudes toward digital technology, is becoming increasingly important for anyone who wants to succeed in the modern business environment. At the same time, the emergence of concepts such as Industry 4.0 and digitalization are important considerations for entrepreneurs who aim to establish long-term, effective enterprises, as well as focusing on sustainable development. The digital era has also given rise to a distinct Digital Entrepreneurship Ecosystem, where entrepreneurs leverage digital technologies to develop new products, services, and business models (Xiong et al., 2024). This ecosystem is characterized by the potential for innovation, agility, and rapid scalability. Among the technologies shaping this ecosystem, artificial intelligence stands out as one of the most transformative forces. As AI continues to develop, understanding its different types and applications becomes even more important.

In recent years, AI Technologies and Application Areas have expanded significantly and are also used in various sectors such as manufacturing, healthcare, and finance. Artificial Intelligence and Information Management, where AI technologies are used to process, store, and analyze large amounts of data, leading to smarter decision-making and more efficient operations.

New developments in digital entrepreneurship also emphasize the need for new behavioral models that take into account the integration of digital tools and platforms into the entrepreneurial process (Fernandes et al., 2022). For example, models that emphasize the role of social media, e-commerce platforms, and digital marketing strategies are becoming increasingly important. Entrepreneurs now need to be experts in using these digital resources to build their businesses and reach new customers.

Entrepreneurial Intention refers to the cognitive state prior to the decision to start a business. It is a key factor in determining whether an individual will take the necessary steps to become an entrepreneur. One of the main challenges of entrepreneurial intention is bridging the gap between having an idea and taking action. Many individuals may have entrepreneurial aspirations but lack the confidence or resources to pursue them. In this context, digital platforms and technologies can play a vital role in reducing barriers to entry and making it easier for would-be entrepreneurs to launch their ventures. Platforms such as crowdfunding, social media, and online marketplaces are democratizing access to capital, customers, and information, enabling more people to act on their entrepreneurial intentions. In the digital age, an entrepreneur's Attitude Towards Digital Technology is a critical factor affecting their ability to innovate and succeed. Entrepreneurs who embrace digital technologies are more likely to adopt new tools and methods that can improve business processes, increase efficiency, and create competitive advantages (Dana et al., 2022). On the other hand, those who are resistant to technology or do not have the necessary skills may have difficulty keeping up with the rapid pace of change in the digital environment.

The concept of digital attitude is closely linked to the Technology Acceptance Model (TAM), which describes how users accept and use a technology. According to TAM, perceived usefulness and perceived ease of use are the main determinants of an individual's attitude towards technology. In the context of entrepreneurship, this means that entrepreneurs who perceive digital technologies as useful and easy to integrate into their business processes are more likely to adopt them. This can lead to better business performance, greater innovation, and increased competitiveness.

The intersection of digitalization and sustainable development is becoming an increasingly important area of focus for entrepreneurs. As the world faces increasing environmental and social challenges, it is increasingly recognized that businesses need to adopt more sustainable practices. Digital technologies offer powerful tools to achieve sustainability goals, from reducing carbon emissions to improving resource efficiency and promoting social inclusion (Rosário & Dias, 2022).

Digitalization can support sustainable development in a variety of ways. For example, AI and big data can be used to optimize supply chains, reduce waste, and minimize the environmental impact of production processes. Similarly, digital platforms can facilitate the sharing economy, enabling more efficient use of resources and reducing the need for new production. In addition, digital technologies can promote social sustainability by increasing access to education, healthcare, and economic opportunities, especially in underserved communities.

Artificial Intelligence (AI) is a transformative technology driving innovation across sectors. One of the key Innovation Features of AI is its ability to analyze large amounts of data and generate insights that would be impossible for humans to obtain. This makes AI an invaluable tool for entrepreneurs, enabling them to develop more innovative products, services, and business models. In this context, as a result of research in the literature, the importance of entrepreneurship within the scope of Industry 4.0 and AI is examined in the chapter.

RESEARCH METHODOLOGY

To effectively address the research questions surrounding the topics of Entrepreneurial Behavior Models, Entrepreneurial Intention, Attitudes Towards Digital Technology and Innovation Features of Artificial Intelligence, a comprehensive literature review has been conducted in the chapter.

Entrepreneurial Behavior Models: The examination of existing behavioral models such as the Theory of Planned Behavior (Ajzen, 1991) and Shapero's Entrepreneurial Event Model (Shapero & Sokol, 1982) provides insights into the psychological and cognitive factors that influence entrepreneurial intentions and behaviors. The review also covers contemporary models that include digital technology as a key variable in entrepreneurial behavior.

Entrepreneurial Intention: The literature on entrepreneurial intention, including factors such as risk tolerance, personality traits, and opportunity recognition, is reviewed to identify key determinants of entrepreneurial action in the digital age.

Attitude Towards Digital Technology: The literature on the Technology Acceptance Model (TAM) (Davis, 1989) and related theories is reviewed to understand how entrepreneurs' attitudes towards digital tools affect entrepreneurial decisions and behaviors.

Industry 4.0 and Digitalization: The literature on Industry 4.0, smart technologies, and digitalization is reviewed to understand the impact of these technological trends on entrepreneurship and business models. This includes discussions on big data, automation, and the Internet of Things (IoT).

Artificial Intelligence: The literature review covers AI innovation characteristics, managerial capabilities, and AI applications across industries. The role of AI in knowledge management, decision making, and business efficiency is also analyzed.

Digital Entrepreneurship Ecosystem: The review of the literature on digital entrepreneurship and its supporting ecosystem provides a foundation for understanding the opportunities and challenges that entrepreneurs face in a highly digitalized business environment.

Sustainable Development: The relationship between digitalization and sustainable development is examined, focusing on how digital technologies can promote environmental and social sustainability. The chapter's scope provides a solid framework for exploring the interplay between entrepreneurship, digital technology, artificial intelligence, and sustainable development. The chapter contributes to a deeper understanding of the digital entrepreneurship ecosystem in the context of Industry 4.0. It also presents key implications for policymakers, entrepreneurs, and technologists as they navigate the challenges and opportunities presented by digitalization and artificial intelligence in the entrepreneurial landscape.

THEORETICAL FRAMEWORK

Entrepreneurial Behavior Models

Entrepreneurship requires the combination of many factors such as social, economic, environmental and personal. For this reason, although there are different entrepreneurship models, studies have generally focused on three different models. It cannot be said that any of these models is the best. These models have been considered to better understand entrepreneurial behaviors.

One of the most well-known models in this field was put forward by Shapero and Sokol (1982). This entrepreneurship model was confirmed by Krueger (1993). Another important model was put forward by Bird (1988). It was emphasized that the self-efficacy perspective included in Bird's (1988) model has a very strong effect on entrepreneurship. In addition, this study also revealed that the difference between genders is not significantly related to motivation level and social demographics. It has been shown that the fact that there are fewer women entrepreneurs in the population is entirely due to environmental effects. This model was developed by Boyd and Vozikis (1994). It has been shown that rational and analytical and intuitive and holistic thinking depend on two different factors. Accordingly, both rational and intuitive thinking are the result of social, political & economic context and personal history, current personality & abilities. There is also a strong relationship between these (Boyd & Vozikis, 1994).

Another important entrepreneurial behavior model is the theory of planned behavior put forward by Ajzen (1991). In this model, most people's performance depends on opportunities and resources such as money, time, skills and communication to some extent. Although these are not motivational factors, they have an important place in the initial conditions (Ajzen, 1991). This theory is a continuation of the theory of reasoned action (Fishbein & Ajzen, 1974).

ENTREPRENEURIAL INTENTION AND CONCEPTUAL FRAMEWORK

Entrepreneurial Intention

Intention can be likened to laying the foundation of a building as a beginning. The stronger the foundation, the stronger the building will be. Therefore, intention can be expressed as a structure that carries the work to be built on it. The phenomenon of intention can be defined as an emotional, cognitive, social and technological area on which entrepreneurship is built (Ferreira et al., 2012).

Intention is the mental formation of the desire to achieve a dream or a determined goal (Balkaya, 2017). Individuals who dream and want to realize their dreams have taken the first step towards entrepreneurship and revealed their intentions. Entrepreneurial intention is defined in terms of the scientific world as understanding the business by making predictions in terms of the stages of establishment of businesses and the profit and loss status of the established business. In line with this definition, entrepreneurial intention theories have been revealed in order to understand businesses (Sabuncu, 2017). The most important stage in entrepreneurial action is the decision-making, i.e. the intention stage. Individuals who consider all environmental or personal problems and have entrepreneurial intention can carry out entrepreneurial activity (Martins & Perez, 2020).

Entrepreneurs unknowingly ignite the fuse of change while expressing their intentions regarding entrepreneurship. Because when the innovations they make are combined with technology, many phenomena undergo change. Individuals' business ideas are called intentions until they gain business status. Individuals who decide to become entrepreneurs must clearly and distinctly state their entrepreneurial intentions in order to be successful. According to Aizen (1991)'s theory of planned behavior, intention is the mirror of behavior. If the behavior that individuals believe is right is also approved by the people around the individual, the individual's intention regarding this behavior will be strengthened. According to this theory, the most important variable affecting entrepreneurial behavior is intention. Entrepreneurial intention is very important for a country's economy. Not only the number of entrepreneurs but also the potential of the entrepreneur is important for countries. Although entrepreneurship starts with ideas, it is always the first step towards intention (Aizen, 1991). Entrepreneurial intention, which is a mindset that will guide the entrepreneurial action towards establishing and developing a new business; is an emotional and cognitive manifesto that explains how the risk that a person assumes in a specific and general sense, the opportunity they gain, and the information they have about the business environment will be put into practice. As can be seen, intention is also the name of a determination and a method that has emerged in terms of cognitive and emotional desirability and feasibility. In entrepreneurship, desirability is an important and fundamental indicator of intention and is located in two planes such as self-interest and self-interest, which directs actions and replaces self-interest with a central authority (Mickiewicz et al., 2016).

Entrepreneurial intention emerges after individuals aim to evaluate their current potential in their environment instead of making a career (Shahzad et al., 2021). We can define the concept of intention as individuals having a decision-making situation for their future lives that take shape in their minds. Individuals who have reached employment age have some options. These are; working and working for others, private sector, working for yourself and public sector. Entrepreneurial intention is quite high in individuals who have a sense of working for themselves (Hueso et al., 2021). In order to make sense of entrepreneurial intention, first of all, individuals should be asked why they want to be an accountant, marketer, teacher, etc. It is necessary to question why people choose entrepreneurship rather than professions such as these (Timuroğlu & Çakır, 2014).

Entrepreneurial intention can also be defined as the actions taken by individuals to establish their own businesses (Belchior & Lyons, 2021). The emergence of entrepreneurial intention depends on the individual's desire and wish. Therefore, the first step of the concept of entrepreneurship is to intend (Entrialgo & Iglesias, 2020). Entrepreneurial intention is determined by individuals' emotional intelligence levels and different personality traits (Kwapisz et al., 2022). The general economic, social and political structure of the country, regional and environmental factors, personality traits, general and vocational education level, etc. are effective in the formation of entrepreneurial intention. All these concepts are interconnected and even the lack of one of them can negatively affect entrepreneurial intention.

The main factors affecting entrepreneurial intention are seen to be gender, age, family income, past work experience, etc. (Dubey & Sahu, 2022). In order for individuals' entrepreneurial intentions to be successful, they need to know which factors affect their entrepreneurial intentions (Martins & Perez, 2020). One of the factors that affect individuals' entrepreneurial intentions is family. Since the family is taken as a role model, entrepreneurial intentions begin to take shape positively or negatively at a young age due to the influence of the family (Georgescu & Herman, 2020). Individuals' lifestyles and need levels also affect entrepreneurial intentions (Hueso et al., 2021). One of the situations that affect intentions is the social environment. Beliefs, pressure from the social environment, fear of evaluation and judgment affect the motivation of individuals with entrepreneurial intentions (Vardar, 2018).

The ambition of individuals, their love of life, their enthusiasm for winning, and their sense of dominance over their employees have a shaping effect on the individual's entrepreneurial intention (Toksoy, 2019). The factors that determine entrepreneurial intention vary over time. While some entrepreneurs argue that entrepreneurship is innate, others argue that environmental and demographic characteristics shape entrepreneurial intention (Kalkan, 2011).

ATTITUDE TOWARDS DIGITAL TECHNOLOGY

Today, under the influence of globalization, is now called the digital age. In this age, people always act together with machines and resources. Thanks to the concept we call digitalization, technology has become an indispensable part of our lives. If we need to define digitalization, it can be said that it is the storage or re-creation of sounds and images formed as a result of the coding of the numbers 0 and 1. Almost all data such as music, sound, video and text are transformed into numerical codes consisting of the numbers 0 and 1 and can be directed to different points via the internet (Tekeoğlu, 2020).

The concept of attitude is quite difficult to predict because it is abstract. Therefore, in order to understand the attitudes of people, it is necessary to consider their behaviors (Verplanken & Orbell, 2022). The concept of attitude can be defined as the emotional expression of behaviors towards accepting or rejecting a certain object, situation, institution or thought. If the thoughts against these situations are positive, the attitude is positive. In short, attitude can be expressed as the foundations that form the future. The concept of attitude is now mostly associated with the concept of digital technology, and the development and future development of digital technology is determined by the attitude towards today's digital technology (Hämäläinen et al., 2021).

Digital technology has developed so much in areas such as media and telecommunications that it is almost impossible to go back. This digital age, which began to emerge in the early 1990s, has affected many aspects of people's lives both positively and negatively (Carrington, 2020). It is possible to gather the concept of attitude towards digital technology (Cabi, 2016) under eight different headings.

These headings are explained as follows,

Competence, It is possible to evaluate the ability to use newly emerging digital technology tools as competence.

Keeping up with the speed brought by digital technology and guiding other people about these technologies is the main feature of competence.

Social networks, It refers to having the skills necessary to express oneself on social networks (such as Facebook, Instagram, Twitter (X)) and to use these areas effectively.

Use of technology at work, The general name of the actions taken to use digital technology in our work areas and thus increase productivity in the workplace is to use technology at work.

Interest in technology, It is the effort shown to be interested in all products that are the result of digital technology and to obtain new information about the use of these products.

Technology for the insurer, It is the general name of the individual contributions provided by the use of digital technology in insurance sector employees.

Negative aspects, People sometimes exaggerate the use of digital technology and spend most of their time on these social networks. The most negative aspect of digital technology is the waste of time it causes. Entertainment use, It is the general name for using digital technology for entertainment purposes such as meeting new people, acquiring new hobbies, and playing games. Conscious use, Using digital technology to make life and business easier, spending time only on productive information on the internet. Various concepts including computers, mobile phones, internet environments, camera systems and web applications form the basis of digital technology. Digital technology is used in many areas such as workplaces, schools, and hospitals (Tanoğlu, 2019).

Technology changes and develops day by day. For this reason, it is not an easy task to follow technology. Research on technology is therefore short-term. As the areas of use of technology, which is advancing very quickly, increase, it is seen that the use of technology has become a necessity. Technology, which has become so important, needs to be managed and the right application should be used in the right place. Many new concepts have emerged thanks to digital technology. Because of the easy dissemination, storage and transfer of information, the whole world does not have difficulty in accessing the information it wants at the same time. In the past, people used to communicate for weeks or even months. Thanks to digital technology, this time period has decreased to hours or even seconds (Hülür & Macdonald, 2020).

The concept of digital transformation is a very important concept for today's businesses. The concept that facilitates the development and implementation of this concept is digital technology (Tsou & Chen, 2023). The fact that it is easier to obtain information thanks to digital technology, that all videos or images are reflected and visualized, and that software and hardware applications are quite easy accelerates the development of digital technology. Digital technology has many beneficial effects such as the establishment of smart factories and the easing of people's lives thanks to artificial intelligence (Mourtzis, 2024). There are many conveniences brought by digital technology for all professions, especially in the fields of medicine, engineering, psycho-social, economics, business and education.

Entrepreneurship in the Context of Industry 4.0

Since the end of the 20th century, information and communication technologies have developed rapidly. As the use of personal computers and internet technology has become widespread, commercial enterprises have also begun to benefit from these technologies. With the emergence of the digital economy as a new concept in the 2000s, everything has gradually moved to the virtual environment (Sturgeon, 2021). In this context, enterprises have also started to move away from the physical environment and move to the virtual environment. This process of moving and the development in digitalization have become a cycle that complements and supports each other. As digitalization develops, the transition of enterprises to the virtual environment has accelerated, and as the number of enterprises moving to the virtual environment has increased, digitalization has gained momentum (Kraus & Kraus, 2021). In the process that progresses with developing technologies, Industry 4.0 and digital transformation processes have become part of our lives (Ghobakhloo, 2020). The innovations brought by Industry 4.0 have had significant effects on entrepreneurship, as in many areas of life. Many innovations such as flexibility and the increased use of digital technologies in production have contributed to the change of the understanding of entrepreneurship (Nambisan et al., 2019).

"Entrepreneurship in the digital age" brought by Industry 4.0 is an entrepreneurship understanding that expresses the use of technology in entrepreneurial activities and the adaptation to globalization by including technology in all possible areas. Digital technology has a great potential to create value in almost every field by reshaping business functions and services in line with customer experiences. In addition, digital technologies have an important place in the context of improving employee behavior, increasing interaction, discovering new information, ensuring the exchange of information between individuals, and making inferences regarding collective intelligence and cognitive analytics in order to make timely decisions (Capestro et al., 2024).

Industry 4.0 has naturally affected the characteristics of entrepreneurs as well as affecting entrepreneurship and has caused new entrepreneurial characteristics to be included in our lives. The entrepreneurs of this digital age, which we can also refer to as Entrepreneur 4.0, are leaders who can read change, focus on the R&D market, bring together qualified human resources equipped with technology and aim for continuous development, are suitable for interdisciplinary integration, seize opportunities and create the need themselves if necessary (Saatçi, 2017). In the Industry 4.0 process, where new practices such as information-oriented work, teamwork-based organization, creating continuous learning mechanisms and increased flexibility have gained importance, entrepreneurs who value information, innovation and flexibility achieve success (Bozkurt, 2019).

As a result, in the context of Industry 4.0 today, keeping up with the requirements of the digital age has become a necessity for enterprises. In this context, it is seen that successful enterprises that have gained competitive advantage have benefited significantly from digitalization. In addition, in the Industry 4.0 process, digital entrepreneurship has emerged as a new type of entrepreneurship that uses digital technologies in almost all of its activities since its establishment, unlike traditional enterprises integrating digital technologies into their systems. The digital entrepreneurship that has emerged in this context will be discussed in the next title of the study.

Digitalization and Sustainable Development

Digitalization is a technological development that has been included in almost every area of our lives. As a result of the rapid developments in the context of digitalization in the world and in our country, the internet and other digital technologies have begun to be used intensively in daily life. The intensive use of digital tools and our increasing dependence on them clearly demonstrate that digitalization is an important need for today and has the potential to revolutionize the socioeconomic field. Digitalization has become a tool that simplifies processes in many areas such as management, regulation, planning and operation from a socioeconomic perspective and consequently enriches the quality of life (Franklin, 2015). The increasing use of digital tools in almost every area of daily life and the encouragement of their use provide many benefits such as ensuring social equality through online education, easy access to the required knowledge and skills, combating climate change, technological awareness and cultural development. In this context, digitalization also brings social welfare (Van Deursen & Van Dijk, 2014).

Digital technologies also contribute to the realization of sustainable development by making information more secure, ensuring that decision-making mechanisms are better informed, implementing data-based policies, prioritizing actions, and optimizing resource allocation (Mondejar et al., 2021).

In this context, it has been observed that technology and digitalization have begun to be given more importance in global efforts to achieve sustainable development, especially in the last few years. Digitalization; human behavior, environment, and many other data have the potential to create appropriate development programs for policy makers, monitor progress, and dynamically improve. This provides the opportunity to achieve sustainable development goals at lower costs. Thanks to digital transformation and comprehensive data collection, it can provide significant support to administrations in creating a sustainable society (ElMassah & Mohieldin, 2020).

Digitalization has brought many important innovations such as mobile internet, internet of things, and big data. In this way, businesses optimize their resources and costs and develop corporate technologies. In terms of social aspects, digitalization enables people to come together on digital platforms. Digitalization contributes to economic stability by offering significant opportunities in terms of productivity and growth thanks to the innovations it brings. In this context, it can be said that digitalization brings us closer to sustainable development (Bhutani & Paliwal, 2015).

Digitalization is spreading rapidly in all sectors, increasing energy efficiency and sufficiency, and ensuring the monitoring and protection of ecological balance and global common areas. In this context, digital technologies make significant contributions to sustainable development. However, it has been observed that digitalization has not been sufficiently mobilized for sustainable development so far. Therefore, it is necessary to reverse the trends in digitalization and create paths leading to sustainable development. In this context, studies have begun to be conducted internationally to strengthen the relationship between digitalization and sustainable development. The studies carried out by the EU in particular are important in this sense. In the "Europe 2030 Digital Compass" created by the EU, digital transformation is among the policy headings that aim to bring the EU economy to a more sustainable and greener level. In addition, the EU directs production and growth strategies in line with the "European Green Deal" and aims for the European continent to be climate neutral60 by 2050. In this context, the priority objectives include utilizing environmentally sensitive technology solutions through digital technologies, facilitating the transition to the European Green Deal by reducing the carbon footprint in production, and providing companies and employees with new digital skills (Sharma et al., 2022). In this context, by making the right use of digitalization, benefits will be provided in many areas such as safe drinking water, hygiene, affordable energy, safe food supply, health services, and quality education (Pollitzer, 2018).

At this point, when we compare the positive and negative effects of digitalization on sustainable development, it is possible to say that sustainable development will be less efficient and successful without digitalization. There is no doubt that initiatives and public institutions that adapt to digitalization and technological developments and integrate sustainability principles into digital transformations will make significant contributions to sustainable development (Matos et al., 2020).

Digital Entrepreneurship Ecosystem

There are basically three basic elements of digital entrepreneurship. These elements are: investors, innovation and entrepreneurs. Instead of developing digital entrepreneurship, it is necessary to develop an entrepreneurial culture and establish an entrepreneurial ecosystem suitable for it. The basic elements of creating a digital entrepreneurship ecosystem are universities, accelerators, entrepreneurs, startups, angel investors, venture capital, capital markets, infrastructure service providers and the state (Kayser et al., 2023).

Today, Turkey has witnessed the rise of e-commerce entrepreneurs who are not old. These young entrepreneurs write important success stories for the businesses they establish. They also produce new ideas. Entrepreneurs of all ages are asked to contribute to bringing ideas to life. Both women and men are encouraged to establish new businesses. There are young and talented people growing not only in our country but also in other countries in the region. It is important to encourage entrepreneurs to establish new businesses in Turkey, and this situation actually presents a problem. The problem is aimed at developing and disseminating digital entrepreneurship. At this point, the solution is to facilitate the establishment and closure of businesses. The diversity of national financial resources, access to financing opportunities and exits are also important.

Angel investors have an important place in today's literature on the development of digital entrepreneurship. The characteristic of an angel investor is that she/he is both a knowledge investor and a financial investor. In the development of digital entrepreneurship, it is an element that should be taken into account to ensure that angel investors at least benefit from their own resources and take the initiative to move on to the next stage. Venture capital is one of the most important elements in the entrepreneurship ecosystem. It is also important to have people with entrepreneurial spirit to start digital initiatives (Aloulou et al., 2024).

A digital ecosystem is defined as a self-organizing, scalable and sustainable system consisting of heterogeneous digital resources and interactions that increase the level of use of the system, provide benefits, facilitate knowledge sharing and collaboration, and focuses on interactions between organizations to promote innovation (Petrova et al., 2021). A digital ecosystem consisting of different platforms based on the storage, processing and management of information in a digital environment can facilitate the marketing strategies of different businesses' products or services by supporting communication.

Stakeholders in the digital ecosystem include industrial enterprises, funding countries, technology providers, research institute types, and educational institutions such as university types, and investor types. This change began with the coordination and cooperation of these stakeholders. Strengthening the technological infrastructure, cooperation between institutions, financial and technical incentives, and legislation is important for the formation and development of a digital ecosystem (Zhang et al., 2023).

The digital entrepreneurship ecosystem is evolving into a common set of digital and entrepreneurship ecosystems. The digital ecosystem is a self-organizing, scalable, and sustainable system of heterogeneous digital resources and the connection between them to enhance collaboration and innovation. In order for the digital entrepreneurship ecosystem to grow, even indirectly, the entrepreneurship ecosystem must also grow (Elia et al., 2020).

ADOPTION OF ARTIFICIAL INTELLIGENCE

Innovation Features of Artificial Intelligence

1. Compatibility: Compatibility is a positive and important attribute that affects the adoption of AI. This attribute, along with other positive attributes of the innovation, also affects the adoption rate. Compatibility provides a level of consumer satisfaction with the adoption of AI. As another attribute of innovations, compatibility refers to the degree to which an innovation is consistent with the needs, expected values and norms, and social systems of potential adopters (Call & Herber, 2022). Compatibility refers to the degree to which an innovation is perceived to match a consumer's "existing values, past experiences, and needs" (Nørskov et al., 2015). Reviews reveal that three out of five innovation attributes consistently show a significant impact on the adoption rate of innovation, namely relative advantage, compatibility, and complexity (Kaur Kapoor et al., 2014). Innovations are more likely to be adopted when they are compatible with individuals and compatibility appears to have a significant impact on willingness to adopt (Waarts et al., 2002). Research consistently shows that perceptions of relative advantage, compatibility, and complexity are important predictors, while trialability and observability are generally less predictive. Compatibility is also a concept with multiple facets that support the notion that innovations "fit with current values, past experiences, and needs of those who are likely to adopt the innovation" (Rogers, 2003). Value and belief compatibility highlights the broader sociocultural context in which the decision to adopt an innovation occurs. According to Rogers (2003), innovations that are perceived to be compatible with values and beliefs are more likely to be adopted than innovations that are perceived to be incompatible. Innovations can be compatible or incompatible with potential adopters' prior experiences or previous adoption decisions. According to Rogers (2003), individuals cannot cope with an innovation outside of familiar foundations. A previously used practice provides a standard against which an innovation can be interpreted, thus reducing its uncertainty. Finally, an innovation may be perceived as compatible if it meets a perceived need, and incompatible if it does not meet a potential adopter's need. The innovation may be perceived as compatible with some aspects of the concept and incompatible with others. For example, an innovation may be compatible with a person's values but incompatible with past experiences (Tully, 2015).

2. *Relative Advantage:* Relative advantage relates to the perceived superiority of an innovation over the idea it replaces. We would expect smarter products to be generally perceived as offering greater relative advantage. We would also expect products that can learn to be perceived as having greater advantage. For example, TVs can achieve greater relative advantage by offering personalized recommendations to a viewer. Such recommendations can be based on information about which viewer is using the TV or on personal profiles. Similarly, products with higher reactivity can be perceived as offering greater advantage. For example, a door that opens when someone approaches has an advantage over non-reactive doors because people do not have to use muscle force to open it. Products that can cooperate with a greater number of products also have greater relative advantage (Rijsdijk et al., 2007). Relative advantage as a feature of innovations can be explained as the degree to which an innovation appears better than the idea it replaces. Sub-dimensions of relative advantage include social prestige, time and effort savings, low initial cost, degree of economic profitability, increased comfort or reduced discomfort, and immediacy of output. However, it is difficult to show all the potential relative advantages of an innovation because some of them may not be apparent prior to implementation (Askarany et al., 2007). Relative advantage refers to the perceived advantage of an innovation over existing products in the market (Yuen et al., 2020). As an example of the use of Smart Internet Banking (IB) and in an attempt to examine how Relative Advantage (RA) is related to whether to adopt a smart tool, the relative advantage of smart internet banking is defined here as the extent to which an individual perceives that smart internet banking is better than the idea it replaces. The advantages of internet banking are often expressed as efficiency, time and effort savings, immediacy of reward, or reduced discomfort and social prestige. According to Suoranta (2003), the relative advantage construct may be viewed differently in the context of different innovations and different consumers. Reducing transaction costs for customers and banks makes IB valuable (Alhosani & Tariq, 2020). This is also derived from the globality of the environment, meaning that individuals can freely transact and access their local bank accounts while abroad (Beck & Peria, 2006). According to Rogers (2003), relative advantage is the degree to which an innovation is perceived to be better than its predecessors. Relative advantage has been found to affect adoption and is generally found to have the most significant impact on adoption decisions (Rogers, 2003). Research conducted in light of Rogers' (2003) views suggests that relative advantage should be divided into two categories: perceived usefulness and image (Karahanna et al., 1999; Mao & Palvia, 2006). Previous studies have proven that perceived usefulness and image are separate concepts. Therefore, they are examined as separate concepts in this analysis. Perceived usefulness is "the degree to

which a particular system is believed to improve performance" (Tahar et al., 2020). Perceived usefulness has been consistently shown to be an important predictor of information system adoption (Davis, 1989; Legris et al., 2003). In their study of community computing facilities, Chigona and Licker (2008) found that perceived usefulness motivates users, particularly when compared to other Internet access options in terms of cost and travel, but is not perceived as more useful than existing technology found elsewhere. Image is "the degree to which the use of an innovation is perceived to enhance one's image or status in one's social system" (Usman et al., 2022). For example, potential adopters may perceive a social advantage of adopting an innovation due to the perceived prestige associated with being "cutting edge" (Tully, 2015).

3. Complexity: As another characteristic, complexity can be explained as the degree to which an innovation appears difficult to understand and use (Askarany et al., 2007). Of the five characteristics of innovation, complexity is the exception, which is negative. Other characteristics are considered positive for innovation. In addition, complexity refers to the degree to which consumers perceive an innovation to be difficult to understand and use. This is the only characteristic of the five characteristics that is negatively related to the rate of innovation diffusion, meaning that the more complex an innovation is, the slower its adoption rate. For example, the degree of complexity of an MP3 player may be perceived as quite complex if it requires more learning time to operate the player than portable CD or minidisc players (Nørskov et al., 2015). This characteristic has many synonyms, such as usability or complexity and ease of use. This is frequently cited in the MIS (Management Information System) literature, and it has been found that an individual's implementation of the introduced innovation is closely linked to his or her perception of its complexity. Complexity is defined by Rogers (1995) as "how difficult or easy an innovation seems to an individual". Some innovations are easy to grasp and put into use, while others are more difficult and take longer to diffuse. Davis (1989) showed in the TAM model that perceived ease of use directly affects attitudes. Low levels of complexity or high levels of ease of use lead to high adoption rates (Rogers, 1995). In other words, complexity increases the likelihood of rejection (Sarel & Marmorstein, 2003). Rogers (1995) showed a negative relationship between complexity and adoption rates. Other diffusion studies also confirm the relationships suggested by Rogers. For example, the study by Tan and Teo (2000) showed a negative and insignificant relationship. According to Rogers (2003), a new idea can be classified along a complexity-simplicity continuum. "The meanings of some innovations are clear to potential adopters, while others are not" (Rogers, 2003). Innovations that are simpler to understand and use are more likely to be adopted than those that are difficult (Rogers, 2003). According to Rogers (2003), complexity may not predict adoption as much as relative advantage and compatibility. On the other hand, in the study of e-service adoption in Saudi Arabia by Al-Ghaith, Sanzogni, and Sandhu (2010), complexity emerged as the best predictor of adoption among the attributes suggested by Rogers (2003) (Tully, 2015).

4. Trialability: As a fourth characteristic, trialability is defined as the degree to which an innovation can be tried on a limited basis before being fully implemented (Askarany et al., 2007). It is possible to define trialability as the flexibility to test the outcomes of the innovation. This plays an important role in facilitating the adoption process of artificial intelligence at the firm level. The relevance and effects of the remaining two characteristics - trialability and observability - depend on the type of product and the context in which the innovation should be adopted. Rogers (1995) argues that potential adopters who are given permission to try an innovation will feel more comfortable with this innovation and, accordingly, are more likely to adopt it. According to Kolodinsky et al. (2001), the trialability of an innovation provides customers with the ability to see and evaluate the benefits of that innovation. As a result, certain fears about an unknown innovation and the possibility of its unavailability can be reduced by giving consumers the opportunity to try the innovation (Zolait & Sulaiman, 2008). Rogers states that innovations that can be tried on a limited scale are more likely to be adopted than those that cannot be tried. According to Rogers (1995), although trialability affects adoption decisions, it is less predictive than other characteristics. In addition, Stevens et al. (2000) found that trialability has a positive effect on the adoption and use of the Internet by employees of a non-profit organization. Similarly, Al-Ghaith et al. (2010) showed that trialability is an effective element in studies on the adoption of e-services. Innovations such as software offered free of charge are beneficial in terms of experimentation because they allow users to try with little risk and cost (Tully, 2015).

5. Observability: Observability, the fifth characteristic of an innovation, is the degree to which the consequences of an innovation can be observed by potential adopters (Askarany et al., 2007). Observability is also defined as the degree to which a consumer can easily observe an innovation and its consequences. The advantages of the MP3 player are more observable than previous models. The most important observable advantages consist of the weight and size of the device and the amount of information available about the device (Nørskov et al., 2015). In the USA, Kolodinsky et al. (2001) studied the adoption of four electronic banking methods, where they found that observability was associated with an increased likelihood of adopting only telephone banking. This is the extent to which the benefits of an innovation are visible for others to observe and communicate its benefits (Zolait & Sulaiman, 2008). Some innovations are easily observable and explainable, while others are more elusive. Rogers suggests that the observability of an innovation is positively associated with adoption. Moore and Benbasat (1996) divided observability into two constructs: outcome demonstrability or "the tangibility of the results of using the innovation" and visibility or "the degree to which potential adopters see the innovation as visible in the context of adoption" (Liao & Lu, 2008). Agarwal and Prasad (1997) state that the concept of visibility increases the curiosity of potential adopters of innovations. And visibility is also an effective factor in the acceptance of users of the World Wide Web, which is a highly visible innovation (Tully, 2015).

Management Capability

Firms and emerging technologies require specific organizational capabilities to get the best practices and efficiency from AI. AI requires new information technology (IT) skills, both AI-specific, such as machine learning skills, and general, such as understanding modern programming languages (such as Python), application development techniques (such as Agile software development), and modern IT architecture skills (such as edge computing). Data management and analytics skills are also required. AI thrives on vast amounts of data that require the existence, management, analysis, and synthesis of digital data. Given that most data is network-generated, security skills—general and AI-powered—are vital for ensuring access rights, intrusion detection, and data integrity. Finally, these skills need to be embedded within a coherent and appropriate strategic framework to ensure guided implementation and broader organizational alignment and support. Organizational direction allows leaders to achieve much greater business impact than those who lag behind in embracing this innovation. Leaders report significantly stronger actual business impacts on their projects than laggards in adopting this innovation. There are significantly higher levels of impact on transformations of existing business models, improvements in operational efficiency, increased revenue, strengthened competitiveness of offerings, and customer experience improvements (Brock & Von Wangenheim, 2019). While the challenges reflect the importance of digital capabilities, the main challenge for all firms is the lack of skilled personnel and knowledge in digital technologies, which was cited as an implementation challenge by more than half of the combined firms. Lack of organizational agility, internal resistance to change, security risks, lack of leadership and sufficient funding, and difficulty integrating new digital technology with existing technology, as well as the lack of suitable technology partners, were cited as challenges by approximately a quarter of firms. In contrast to the implementation challenges that were similar across the surveyed firms, leaders differed in the importance they attributed to the factors contributing to the success of the digital transformation outcome compared to laggards.

The following eight success factors stand out as significantly different among AI leaders:

- Organizational agility,
- Engagement of talented personnel,
- Leadership,
- Support from technology partners,
- Investment,
- Culture,
- Alignment of new digital technologies with existing IT, and
- Learning from failed projects (Brock & Von Wangenheim, 2019).
- Scholars have identified many factors that affect the quality of the innovation process:
- Resource factors such as marketing resources and technical resources;
- Marketing capability,
- Market linking capability,
- Technical capability,
- Network capability,
- Capability factors such as organizational learning capability;
- Contextual factors such as service characteristics,
- Standardized service innovation processes,
- Service innovation capability,
- Service innovation competitiveness.

Even in this era, many studies still focus on issues related to the internal and external environments of the organization, such as employee participation, organizational structure, customers and suppliers. However, in the era of big data with developing technologies, companies need to create Big Data Analytic Capability and Artificial Intelligence Capability to meet their information processing needs and increase the adequacy of the innovation process accordingly (Zhang et al., 2020).

Types of Artificial Intelligence (AI)

Artificial intelligence technologies are intelligent and have the potential to make major changes in the future by going beyond human intelligence with their features of thinking, predicting, memorizing, understanding, recognizing objects, changing and adapting. Artificial intelligence is generally classified into two groups according to the tasks it performs: talent-based and functionality-based artificial intelligence (Incerti, 2020).

Types of Skill-Based AI

The types of AI based on capability are weak and general AI. The reason for the separation of AI capabilities is that each AI technology performs a specific task. Weak AI cannot perform the tasks of general AI because weak AI is designed to perform only limited tasks (Lu et al., 2018).

***Weak AI*:** Weak AI is a technology that is widely used in people's lives. For example, video games are the weakest technology of artificial intelligence. This technology has the ability to perform specified tasks. However, it does not have the ability to think and copy like humans. The Echo product, which was introduced by Amazon, is another example of a product that adopts weak AI technology. Although it exhibits some very intelligent behaviors, the tasks it performs are limited. Although weak AI is the weakest type of AI technology, it has the ability to increase its knowledge and skills. In addition, this type of AI technology produces original solutions because it has the ability to judge. Another example is IBM Watson. IBM Watson examines thousands of texts and produces a general result (Chen et al., 2016).

***General Artificial Intelligence*:** General artificial intelligence is a set of algorithms that are as talented as humans at solving emerging problems. DeepMind algorithms use general artificial intelligence technology. AlphaGo, the product of DeepMind technology, has gained great momentum in growth after defeating 18-time Go world champion Lee Sedol in 2016. AlphaGo is an old board game that is very popular in Korea, Japan, and China. AlphaGo was designed to imitate the best games in the world (Livingston & Risse, 2019). The algorithms of this game do not only improve themselves with data, but also use reinforcement learning (reward system). AlphaGo algorithms train and improve their algorithms by playing against themselves thousands of times with the reinforcement learning system (Silver et al., 2016). AlphaGo Zero, which is many times stronger than AlphaGo, was designed. AlphaGo Zero algorithms trained itself using reinforcement learning in three hours, reaching the competencies of humans in nine hours, the competencies of advanced players in nine hours, and the competencies of the world champion AlphaGo in three days, beating AlphaGo in the world championship tournament (Livingston & Risse, 2019). In 2018, DeepMind designed AlphaFold for biological research (Evans et al., 2018). In a protein structure prediction competition among scientists, AlphaFold successfully predicted twenty-five out of forty-three protein structures. The other team predicted only three. Then, in 2019, DeepMind designed AlphaStar to compete with advanced players in the computer game

StarCraft. In the race, AlphaStar beat ten of the eleven matches played by professional racers in StarCraft (Livingston & Risse, 2019).

Types of Artificial Intelligence Based on Functionality

The thinking capacity of artificial intelligence technologies has increased significantly in the 21st century. The main reason for this rise is that artificial intelligence technologies have the ability to imitate and even surpass human intelligence, and have gained the ability to think like humans. Artificial intelligence has begun to gain the ability to feel along with developing the ability to think (Dong et al., 2020). In the development of artificial intelligence, two types of perspectives have emerged among people. These are optimistic and pessimistic perspectives. Individuals who adopt an optimistic perspective think that artificial intelligence will lead to the opening of new job opportunities in the future. Individuals who adopt a pessimistic perspective assume that artificial intelligence will take over many jobs in the future and that individuals will become unemployed (Huang et al., 2019). In the age of big data, artificial intelligence makes both human-oriented tasks (communication and coordination with people) and analytical-oriented tasks (administrative tasks such as analyzing data or information) more important. The underlying reason why machines are intelligent comes from having big data. Analyzing big data and drawing general conclusions from it has helped companies to easily overcome problems that may arise in the future (Ranjan & Foropon, 2021). There are four types of artificial intelligence. The first of these is mechanical intelligence, the second is analytical intelligence, the third is intuitive intelligence, and the fourth is empathic intelligence. These types of intelligence are both sequential and parallel. It is very difficult and time-consuming for the sequential types of intelligence, empathic and intuitive intelligence, to display the exact facial expressions exhibited by the individual. The parallel types of intelligence are mechanical and analytical intelligence. Here, artificial intelligence easily and quickly completes mechanical tasks and calculations based on analysis. In general, artificial intelligence is involved in solving problems, self-development, communication, and similar behaviors (Perez-Vega et al., 2021).

***Types of Parallel AI*:** Parallel intelligence types are the weakest types of artificial intelligence. These types of artificial intelligence generally perform monotonous tasks. Examples of these are products and search engines created by giant companies such as Google, IBM, Amazon, Bing, Apple, and the like. The products generally perform tasks such as planning, searching, and transferring information that take a long time in a short time based on commands received from humans. These types consist of mechanical intelligence and analytical intelligence (Huang et al., 2019; Huang & Rust, 2018).

***Mechanical Intelligence*:** Mechanical intelligence performs routine and repetitive tasks during the day through robots. For example, service robots perform physically determined tasks quickly and effectively without human assistance. Another example is when questions are asked to search engines such as Google, Yandex, Bing and others, these engines provide feedback with appropriate answers to that question within a few seconds (Strzelecki & Rutecka, 2020). Other types of devices, such as computers and mobile phones, perform daily tasks that an individual needs. These devices are intelligent, but their operations are limited. They use a lot of data but do not improve themselves. They continue their given task in the same way they left the production site (Hyppönen, 2022).

***Analytical Intelligence*:** Analytical intelligence provides effective solutions to existing problems by analyzing big data quickly and easily. This type of intelligence has information processing, logical reasoning and mathematical skills. Analytical intelligence has been defined as "weak intelligence" in the literature. Because although they appear to be smart technology, they cannot exhibit intuitive behaviors because they do not have consciousness, thinking and reacting ability (Huang & Rust, 2018).

Types of Sequential AI

Sequential AI types are types of artificial intelligence that are strong in many areas. These types of artificial intelligence are successful in understanding people's emotions, thoughts and behaviors with the data they obtain and the algorithms they use. They constantly improve themselves by reviewing themselves on the internet and some of the reactions they receive from people. These types of artificial intelligence consist of intuitive intelligence and empathic intelligence (Masriadi et al., 2023).

***Intuitive Intelligence*:** Intuitive intelligence includes features that require creative and deep thinking and professional skills. This type of intelligence has been defined as "strong intelligence" in the literature. It is a type of intelligence that can think about more complex tasks and situations like humans, but achieves results faster than humans (Saxena et al., 2022). This type of intelligence develops itself based on data and adapts to the environment. Intuitive intelligence alone has the ability to create. For example, it does not only compose new music, but also designs fashion clothing by drawing. This technological feature is used by companies today. As a different example, autonomous vehicles that people constantly use in their lives are also included in this type of technology (Ferreira et al., 2020).

Empathic Intelligence: The empathic intelligence type is the type of understanding, feedback and influencing people's emotions. This type of intelligence is the most advanced level of artificial intelligence. The characteristics that empathic intelligence includes are communication, relationship building, leadership, collaboration, work-life balance, social teamwork, cultural diversity and charisma (Huang & Rust, 2018). This type of intelligence is an artificial intelligence technology that can think exactly the same as humans using neural networks. It is predicted that this technology will be widely implemented in the future (Kim, 2022).

Artificial Intelligence Technologies and Areas of Use

The development of computer capabilities in the 21st century has also made a great contribution to the development of artificial intelligence technologies. Today, research and development on artificial intelligence is constantly increasing. Artificial intelligence technologies used in research and development are frequently used in scientific branches such as computer vision (artificial vision), expert system, natural language understanding, machine learning and deep learning (Tyagi & Chahal, 2020).

Machine Learning: According to Brynjolfsson and McAfee (2014), machine learning is the strongest aspect of artificial intelligence. Machine learning designs and trains models for applications and machines by using big data and producing specific algorithms, and produces a general result. The general purpose of machine learning is to make some predictions in solving problems that occur in the real world with the specific algorithms produced (Livingston & Risse, 2019). In this respect, it has mastered the features of prediction and making suggestions (Almarzooqi, 2019). The areas where machine learning is widely used are voice recognition, fingerprint reading, facial recognition and object detection (Sohn & Kwon, 2020). It manually selects objects and creates a new model from them. In some cases, websites train algorithms on social media and other platforms, communicate with social media users, like posts and buy products on websites (Livingston & Risse, 2019). Machine learning is used by companies in recruitment processes to determine which candidates will be more effective in that job. The algorithms used in machine learning make some suggestions to employees about what actions to take. For example, IBM uses machine learning algorithms to determine what training employees will receive based on their competencies (Tambe et al., 2019). Brynjolfsson and McAfee (2014) stated that machine learning technology will have a great impact on many businesses in the future and will contribute to the creation of new business models by ongoing businesses. According to Panicacci et al

(2018), machine learning algorithms can predict hospitalization and death risks with socioeconomic and predictive data. Healthcare services using machine learning recommend to doctors which patient will start what treatment process with predictive data (Alsamhi et al., 2019). Machine learning is divided into three groups. These are; supervised learning, unsupervised learning, and reinforcement learning. Supervised learning trains algorithms using big data and makes predictions and recommendations about what steps to take for the future by drawing general conclusions. Unsupervised learning uses non-statistical data (such as music, video). Finally, in reinforcement learning, machines produce results without much data with the algorithms they use. If the result obtained is correct, the machine rewards itself. This learning system is more commonly called a reward system (Alsamhi et al., 2019).

***Computer Vision*:** Computer vision is also known as artificial vision that replaces the human eye. It refers to the video viewing and facial recognition ability found in robots, computers, phones and similar devices. Artificial vision is one of the important core technologies of artificial intelligence. The most important feature of artificial vision is that it contains high speed, a large amount of information and a number of functions (Almaleki, 2020).

***Expert Systems*:** Expert systems are widely used in the first and successful applications of artificial intelligence and are growing rapidly (Gaba, 2022). These systems are computer programs that mimic human decision-making abilities. For this reason, these systems are used instead of or as a support for experts (Isizoh et al., 2021). XCON is the first and successful expert system developed to verify customer orders. Expert systems have a great impact in many ways. For most companies, adopting an expert system is the first step towards artificial intelligence. In general, this system is widely used to solve complex problems (Gupta & Nagpal, 2020).

***Natural Language Understanding*:** Natural language understanding is understanding spoken speech, speech synthesis, and natural language processing (NLP) (Fanni et al., 2023). Voice search is the fastest growing type of search in artificial intelligence technology. NLP works very well with statistical and machine learning methods in text analysis. NLP is frequently used in detecting illegal activities, automatic assistant, language translation, subtitling, and data mining (Behera et al., 2023). Today, there are products on the market that use NLP, such as IBM Watson, Apple Siri, and Amazon Alexa. These products can understand human language with artificial intelligence algorithms and complete the given command very well and quickly. Understanding spoken speech refers to the conversion of a human-given task into text for computer applications. Speech synthesis, on the other hand, means producing speech from text created for the computer in a human-like manner. These artificial intelligence algorithms are currently used in voice response systems, voice assistants, and mobile applications (Malodia et al., 2021).

Artificial Intelligence Applications Used in Industry

Many countries have developed some strategic plans to take advantage of the opportunities brought by artificial intelligence technologies. Today, frequently used artificial intelligence applications are related to big data, visual service, DDI, intelligent robots, etc. Most artificial intelligence applications are applied in the business, finance, healthcare and automobile sectors (Hamet & Tremblay, 2017). The main reason why artificial intelligence has gained popularity in businesses is that it prevents the possible cost increase. In the business world, artificial intelligence technologies are used not only for decision-making but also for the online implementation of the decisions made. Tesla's driverless cars and FedEx's delivery robots use the decision-making stage of artificial intelligence. Amazon has grown rapidly by identifying customer models and accurately predicting future customer purchasing behaviors (Saunders & Locke, 2020). Artificial intelligence technologies provide many benefits in the healthcare sector. For example, machine learning algorithms predict drug performance and gene sequencing. Natural language understanding, electronic health records, intelligent queries. Artificial vision performs medical image recognition, lesion identification and skin disease detection tests. These applications significantly reduce the cost increase that may occur in businesses (Hamet & Tremblay, 2017). Artificial intelligence has established the structure of the financial industry by making financial services (banking, insurance, credit and investment) smart. Artificial neural networks, expert systems and hybrid intelligence systems are widely used in financial services. Applications include credit evaluation, portfolio management and financial forecasting and planning (Bahrammirzaee, 2010). Artificial intelligence technologies provide robots with human-like perception, coordination, decision-making and feedback capabilities. Intelligent robots are classified as intelligent industrial robots, intelligent service robots and intelligent expert robots. Intelligent industrial robots perform packaging, classification, sorting, assembly and detection operations. Intelligent service robots perform tasks such as business services, health services, retail sales, rehabilitation of disabled people. Intelligent expert robots perform exploration, search, firefighting and rescue tasks (Alsamhi et al., 2019).

Artificial intelligence technologies are not only applied to health, finance and smart robots, but also used in education, smart homes, agriculture and manufacturing. Giant technology companies such as Amazon, Google and Baidu are the first to adopt, implement and gain a huge competitive advantage from artificial intelligence technologies. Today, these giant companies still invest heavily in artificial intelligence technologies. These companies frequently use machine learning and natural language processing tools to offer personalized experiences to their customers in the market (Semenov et al., 2017; Syam & Sharma, 2018; Xu et al., 2016). eBay, which recommends similar products according to customers' wants and needs, creates descriptive and predictive models (Kumar et al., 2019). Artificial intelligence technologies increase the creativity of company managers. Artificial intelligence companies now produce creative offers that last a long time in the market in a short time. Artificial intelligence technologies used in the sector have mostly affected supply chain management and production and marketing. In order for AI initiatives to be successful, AI must align with its precise goals (Kumar et al., 2019). Davenport and Ronanki (2018) conducted a study that revealed that managers working in companies do not know how AI technologies work. Knowing and developing the competencies that companies demand from their employees today regarding AI technologies is of great importance for employees to achieve their career goals in the future (Paśko et al., 2022).

Artificial Intelligence and Knowledge Management

Artificial intelligence provides tools and mechanisms that enable computers and machines to learn. These tools enable machines to learn, interpret, and use information to perform tasks. It also improves the decision-making process by using information that individuals can evaluate. While Knowledge Management facilitates the understanding of information, artificial intelligence provides the ability to expand, use, create, and discover information beyond imagination (Liebowitz, 2001). In this context, it is important to examine the applications of artificial intelligence in the field of knowledge management. Since the mid-twentieth century, there have been rises, stagnation, and even declines in the history of artificial intelligence. Expert systems and knowledge-based systems emerged in the 1970s. More than 40 years have passed since the emergence of the first classically called knowledge-based systems (Dendral, Mycin, and Prospectol), but the architecture of the systems has not changed much. These systems are used to represent knowledge in a specific area of expertise, and this knowledge is programmed in the form of rules and examples. Many difficulties have been encountered in the implementation of rule-based expert systems. They have limitations such as the need for a large amount of rule-based knowledge to cover all expertise. Researchers have begun to develop artificial intelligence techniques to overcome these limitations. Case-based reasoning is an artificial intelligence approach that uses solutions to previously solved similar problems to solve existing problems. This approach can be particularly suitable for areas of expertise that have not been programmed before and is therefore considered a more flexible approach. Case-based reasoning has attracted more attention since the 1980s (Avdeenko et al., 2016).

According to Anshari et al. (2023), the history of research on machine learning, artificial intelligence and knowledge management in general dates back to 1989. In recent years, increasing Internet use and the proliferation of smart mobile devices have increased the impact on the phenomenon of big data. Many organizations have increased their awareness of using big data to produce value, especially in the decision-making process. Developments in the field of artificial intelligence technologies facilitate the automation of decision-making processes. In addition, machine learning algorithms, which are constantly being developed, make the decision-making process more sensitive and reach high levels of accuracy (Anshari et al., 2023). Many studies have been conducted in the last 30 years on the use of artificial intelligence in the field of knowledge management. For example, Avdeenko et al. (2016) proposed an approach that facilitates the transition of knowledge from implicit to explicit form and vice versa in knowledge management systems in various types of organizations. This approach is based on the transformation of knowledge from one knowledge representation model to another based on artificial intelligence algorithms. In this study, various methods are proposed for the transformation of knowledge from a rule-based model to a situation-based model.

Anshari et al. (2023) conducted a systematic literature review on the intersection of knowledge, machine learning, artificial intelligence, and big data. The researchers suggested that machine learning allows for the extraction of comprehensive knowledge from big data, and that it is almost impossible for people to examine and extract knowledge from this size of data without machines. Knowledge management systems created with machine learning can become a knowledge intelligence platform by using existing general knowledge. According to the findings of this study, organizations that use machine learning in knowledge management become strong and competitive in terms of rapid decision making, encouraging innovation, creating new knowledge, improved customer service, organizing knowledge management, and sharing knowledge. Artificial intelligence systems show the potential to improve knowledge management processes by improving the creation, storage, sharing, and application of knowledge within organizations. Jarrahi et al. (2023) mentioned potential AI applications in knowledge management processes. The knowledge creation process does not always involve creating knowledge from scratch. AI techniques can be used to find patterns in previously unknown data in the existing data set. It is possible to obtain new knowledge from big data by developing predictive models through self-learning and data analysis. AI can help predict sales prospects based on past data and customer behavior and find unknown and unexpected connections from data sets containing records in customer relationship management databases.

In the knowledge storage and access process, AI-supported knowledge management systems help in collecting, classifying, organizing, storing and accessing open knowledge. With AI techniques, multiple content and communication channels such as e-mail, chat and social media can be analyzed and filtered, and the required knowledge can be easily accessed. AI is also used effectively in the knowledge sharing process. It is possible to connect people working on the same topics by encouraging weak ties and relationships using AI-supported social network analysis tools. In addition, AI-supported knowledge sharing platforms can also be used to increase collaborative intelligence and make shared institutional memory functional. It is also possible to facilitate feedback and peer evaluation in communication systems using AI-supported chatbots and sentiment analysis tools. In the knowledge application process, AI-supported recommendation engines can be used to help search and prepare knowledge sources. More human-centered and accessible knowledge applications can be provided through AI-supported interfaces (Jarrahi et al., 2023).

The Future of Artificial Intelligence

Artificial Intelligence (AI) has made significant strides in the last few decades, transforming numerous industries and aspects of human life. However, the journey of AI is far from over. The future of AI is predicted to be more impactful, raising intriguing possibilities, challenges, and ethical questions (Stahl, 2021). A critical area of focus in the future of AI is the development of Artificial General Intelligence (AGI). Unlike narrow AI, which excels at specific tasks, AGI aims to perform any intellectual task that a human can, demonstrating a form of intelligence similar to human cognition (Kumpulainen & Terziyan, 2022). AGI is revolutionizing society by automating a wide range of tasks and creating new possibilities in areas such as healthcare, education, and transportation. Another promising direction for the future of AI is the advancement of Explainable Artificial Intelligence (XAI). As AI systems become more complex, understanding their decision-making processes becomes increasingly difficult. XAI aims to create AI systems whose actions and decisions can be easily understood by humans, which is vital for building trust in AI systems and their ethical and responsible use (Arrieta et al., 2020).

The integration of AI into our daily lives is likely to continue to increase. More advanced personal AI assistants, more advanced AI in healthcare providing diagnostic and treatment recommendations, and an increase in AI-powered automation across various sectors are expected (Makridakis, 2017). However, the future of AI also presents significant challenges. As AI becomes more integrated into our lives, ethical issues related to privacy, fairness, and transparency are expected to become more prominent. The potential for displacement due to automation is seen as a significant concern that needs to be addressed (Arntz et al., 2016). Furthermore, while AGI holds great promise, it also carries potential risks. The development of AGI could lead to an intelligence explosion where AGI rapidly improves itself and potentially leads to a superintelligent AI that surpasses human intelligence, a scenario that raises deep security and ethical issues (Fahad et al., 2024). The Internet of Things (IoT) is shown as another area where the future of AI looks promising. IoT is seen as a situation where devices are connected over the internet, allowing them to talk to applications and each other. With the exponential growth in devices such as smart home appliances, wearables and sensors, the data generated by these devices provides AI systems with rich information to learn and make intelligent decisions. This is revolutionizing areas such as healthcare, energy management, transportation and agriculture (Gubbi et al., 2013).

AI is also expected to play a significant role in cybersecurity. As cyber threats become more complex and frequent, AI and machine learning algorithms help detect and respond to threats quickly and efficiently. Advances in AI also open the door to potential breakthroughs in understanding and addressing climate change. AI is helping to model complex climate systems, optimize renewable energy systems, and monitor deforestation and other environmental changes (Khallaf, 2024). However, as AI's capabilities increase, so does the potential for misuse. This includes concerns about 'deepfakes' (fake videos or audio generated by AI), autonomous weapons, surveillance, and information manipulation, among others. These challenges underscore the need for robust ethical guidelines and regulatory frameworks around the use of AI (Jobin et al., 2019).

SOLUTIONS AND RECOMMENDATIONS

As the world moves into the digital age, entrepreneurship is increasingly intertwined with technological advances, particularly artificial intelligence (AI), digital technologies, and Industry 4.0. Understanding entrepreneurial behavior is fundamental to creating a culture of innovation. Entrepreneurs must be adaptable, resilient, and proactive in facing uncertainty and seizing opportunities.

Encourage Educational Programs: Integrating entrepreneurial behavior models into educational curricula can help nurture the next generation of entrepreneurs. Schools, universities, and vocational institutes should offer courses focused on problem solving, creativity, and risk management.

Mentorship Programs: Establishing networks where young entrepreneurs can connect with experienced business leaders can facilitate the transfer of the knowledge and skills needed to foster entrepreneurial behavior. These mentorship programs should focus on strategic thinking, leadership development, and digital adaptation.

Create Digital Platforms for Entrepreneurs: Governments and private institutions should develop online platforms that provide resources, training, and financial support to people looking to start digital businesses. These platforms can also offer mentorship, market analysis, and networking opportunities.

Encouraging Innovation: Governments and financial institutions should provide incentives such as grants, tax breaks, or access to low-interest loans for startups, especially those focused on digital technology, sustainability, and AI. Creating a positive business environment can strengthen the entrepreneurial ecosystem.

Digital Literacy Programs: Governments and private sector initiatives should provide training in digital technologies for entrepreneurs, especially in underdeveloped regions. This can help entrepreneurs integrate AI and other digital solutions into their business models.

Support for Industry 4.0 Adoption: Governments should provide subsidies, infrastructure, and training for small and medium-sized enterprises (SMEs) to adopt Industry 4.0 technologies. These initiatives could include collaborative innovation centers where entrepreneurs can test and prototype their ideas using Industry 4.0 tools such as AI and robotics.

Fostering Cross-Sector Collaboration: Creating multi-sector platforms that bring together entrepreneurs, investors, academics, and policymakers can accelerate the development of digital businesses. Such platforms can promote knowledge sharing, provide investment opportunities, and help entrepreneurs navigate regulatory challenges.

Integrating AI into Business Models: Entrepreneurs should incorporate AI into their business processes, from automating routine tasks to using machine learning for customer insights. Training programs and AI service platforms can help startups integrate AI into their operations.

Ethical AI Governance: Enterprises should create AI governance frameworks that ensure ethical use of AI. This includes addressing issues such as data privacy, bias in AI algorithms, and transparency in AI decision-making processes.

AI-Enabled Knowledge Management Systems: AI can help enterprises organize, analyze, and capture vast amounts of information more efficiently. Entrepreneurs should adopt AI-enabled knowledge management tools to improve decision-making and innovation.

Data Security and Privacy: As data becomes increasingly important, businesses must ensure that AI-powered information management systems prioritize data security and privacy. Entrepreneurs should invest in cybersecurity tools to protect sensitive information.

Continuous Learning and Adaptation: Entrepreneurs should focus on continuous learning and adaptation as AI evolves. Attending AI conferences, engaging with research communities, and staying informed about the latest trends will enable entrepreneurs to take advantage of future AI developments.

In conclusion, entrepreneurship in the digital age, especially in the context of AI and Industry 4.0, presents a wealth of opportunities and challenges. By adopting the right strategies, such as encouraging entrepreneurial intent, embracing AI technologies, and supporting sustainability, businesses can thrive in this rapidly evolving environment. Policymakers, educators, and business leaders must collaborate to create an ecosystem that supports innovation, digitalization, and sustainable growth.

FUTURE RESEARCH DIRECTIONS

The rapid advancement of digital technologies and artificial intelligence (AI) is significantly reshaping entrepreneurship and management. Understanding the interactions between entrepreneurial behavior, AI, and digital ecosystems is crucial to advancing research in these areas.

Dynamic Models of Entrepreneurial Behavior in the Digital Age: Traditional models of entrepreneurial behavior may not fully capture the dynamic nature of digital entrepreneurship, where changes occur rapidly due to technological advances. Future research should investigate how entrepreneurs adapt their behavior and decision-making strategies in the context of rapidly changing digital environments, including AI and big data.

Cultural and Societal Influences on Entrepreneurial Behavior Models: While many entrepreneurial behavior models are universally applicable, cultural differences significantly affect entrepreneurial intentions, risk perception, and leadership styles. Comparative studies across different cultural contexts, especially in regions where digital transformation has just begun, will enrich the literature.

Psychological Drivers of Entrepreneurial Intention in the Digital Economy: As digital technologies create new opportunities for entrepreneurship, it is important to examine the psychological factors that drive entrepreneurial intention in the digital age. Investigating the role of factors such as perceived self-efficacy, digital confidence, and innovation mindset will provide a more detailed understanding of entrepreneurial motivation.

Barriers to Positive Attitudes Towards Emerging Technologies: Investigating the factors that prevent individuals from adopting digital technologies, such as fear of job loss due to AI, privacy concerns, or lack of technical skills, and working towards criteria to reduce these barriers and encourage a more inclusive approach to digital technology adoption.

The Role of AI in Achieving Sustainable Development Goals (SDGs): AI can contribute significantly to achieving the United Nations' SDGs. Specific use cases of AI in areas such as renewable energy management, waste reduction, and efficient resource allocation should be investigated to investigate how AI-driven digitalization contributes to sustainability.

AI-Driven Innovation Processes: Research can investigate how AI technologies impact innovation processes from idea generation to product development and market launch. Understanding the ways AI can accelerate innovation in different industries can provide a roadmap for entrepreneurs looking to leverage AI.

AI-Enabled Leadership: AI has the potential to improve management decision-making and strategic planning. Future studies should explore how AI can be integrated into leadership roles to support more data-driven and informed decision-making.

AI-Enabled Organizational Agility: Research should explore how organizations can increase agility by using AI to provide faster responses to market changes, customer needs, and internal challenges. This includes examining how AI can improve resource allocation, operational efficiency, and organizational adaptability.

Training and Development for AI Management: As AI becomes more integrated into business operations, the need for management training focused on AI technologies is increasing. Future research could explore how management training programs can evolve to include AI-related competencies and strategic thinking.

AI-Enabled Knowledge Management Systems: As businesses generate vast amounts of data, AI can help manage, analyze, and extract actionable insights. Research should focus on how AI can enhance knowledge management systems, improving decision-making and innovation capabilities.

Data Management and AI Integration: The integration of AI into information management raises important questions about data management, including privacy, security, and ownership. Future work should explore best practices for managing data in AI-enabled systems, especially in industries that handle sensitive information, such as healthcare and finance.

CONCLUSION

The integration of entrepreneurship with digitalization and artificial intelligence (AI) is signaling a profound transformation in how businesses operate and innovate in the modern world. While key themes such as entrepreneurial behavior models, intentions, attitudes toward digital technologies, and the role of Industry 4.0 are examined, technological advances are redefining the rules of engagement for entrepreneurs. The innovation characteristics, management capabilities, and future potential of AI present new opportunities and challenges across industries.

Entrepreneurial behavior models have long provided fundamental frameworks for understanding how individuals identify opportunities, take risks, and innovate. The emergence of digital technologies is evolving, introducing new variables such as digital literacy, access to technology, and AI tools. These developments are requiring a rethinking of traditional entrepreneurial behavior models. The dynamic nature of the digital economy, driven by rapid technological change, requires entrepreneurs to be adaptable, tech-savvy, and forward-thinking.

Moreover, entrepreneurship in the digital age often transcends geographical boundaries, connecting entrepreneurs to global markets and resources. As digital ecosystems continue to evolve, the study of entrepreneurial behavior must expand to account for how technology impacts decision-making, opportunity recognition, and risk management. This shift highlights the need for continuous learning and adaptation among entrepreneurs, particularly in terms of leveraging AI-driven tools for strategic decision-making and business innovation.

As digital platforms become more accessible and AI tools become more prevalent, barriers to entrepreneurship are decreasing and more individuals are encouraged to think entrepreneurially. This democratization of entrepreneurship, driven by digitalization, is providing broader opportunities for participation in the entrepreneurial ecosystem.

A positive attitude toward technology is essential for the adoption and use of digital tools, AI, and other innovations. Entrepreneurs who embrace digital technologies and AI are more likely to thrive in an increasingly digital business environment. Therefore, developing positive attitudes toward technology, particularly through education and skills development, is crucial to nurturing the next generation of digital entrepreneurs.

The rise of Industry 4.0 has created new business models that are data-driven, customer-centric, and highly automated. Entrepreneurs must now consider how to incorporate these advanced technologies into their operations to remain competitive. This change requires a new set of entrepreneurial skills, such as AI and its applications, digital transformation strategies, and the ability to lead technology-enabled teams. Industry 4.0 is not only transforming manufacturing processes, but also reshaping the nature of entrepreneurship, requiring entrepreneurs to be agile, innovative, and technologically competent.

Digitalization plays a key role in advancing sustainable development by enabling more efficient use of resources, reducing waste, and promoting inclusive growth. Entrepreneurs who leverage digital technologies can create sustainable business models that contribute to environmental, social, and economic sustainability. In particular, AI offers a wide range of applications that support sustainable development goals, such as optimizing energy use, improving supply chain management, and increasing resource efficiency.

However, entrepreneurs should be aware of the ethical implications of AI, including issues related to data privacy, security, and bias. As businesses increasingly adopt digital solutions, they must ensure that these technologies are used in ways that promote sustainability rather than exacerbate existing inequalities. The combination of digitalization and sustainability offers a promising path for businesses looking to create long-term value while addressing global challenges.

AI is one of the most transformative technologies of the digital age and has the potential to drive innovation across industries. Its ability to process large amounts of data, learn from patterns, and automate decision-making processes makes it a powerful tool for entrepreneurs and managers. Innovative features of AI, such as predictive analysis, automation, and optimization capabilities, enable businesses to increase operational efficiency, improve customer experiences, and develop new products and services.

Executives must have the skills to understand and implement AI technologies, lead AI-focused teams, and navigate the ethical and regulatory challenges associated with AI adoption. Executives must strike a balance between leveraging AI's capabilities and creating a culture of innovation that fosters human creativity and problem solving.

The continued evolution of AI technologies will likely lead to even more advanced applications in the future, including general AI and more sophisticated forms of machine learning. As AI becomes more integrated into everyday life, its impact on society, business, and the economy will be profound.

Policymakers, leaders, and technologists must work together to ensure that AI is developed and used in ways that benefit society as a whole.

Ultimately, the convergence of entrepreneurship, digitalization, and AI presents unprecedented opportunities for innovation and economic growth. However, realizing these opportunities requires a deep understanding of the complex interactions between these areas. As entrepreneurs, businesses, and policymakers navigate this new landscape, they must embrace digital technologies, foster innovation, and address the ethical challenges that come with the rise of AI. By doing so, they can build a future where technology serves as a force for positive change, driving sustainable development and economic progress.

REFERENCES

Agarwal, R., & Prasad, J. (1997). The role of innovation characteristics and perceived voluntariness in the acceptance of information technologies. *Decision Sciences*, 28(3), 557–582. DOI: 10.1111/j.1540-5915.1997.tb01322.x

Ajzen, I. (1991). The theory of planned behavior. *Organizational Behavior and Human Decision Processes*, 50(2), 179–211. DOI: 10.1016/0749-5978(91)90020-T

Al-Ghaith, W., Sanzogni, L., & Sandhu, K. (2010). Factors influencing the adoption and usage of online services in Saudi Arabia. *The Electronic Journal on Information Systems in Developing Countries*, 40(1), 1–32. DOI: 10.1002/j.1681-4835.2010.tb00283.x

Alhosani, F. A., & Tariq, M. U. (2020). Improving Service quality of smart banking using quality management methods in UAE. [IJMPERD]. *International Journal of Mechanical Production Engineering Research and Development*, 10(3), 2249–8001.

Almaleki, W. S. A. (2020). *Saudi international students' perceptions of the utility of artificial intelligence and intelligent personal assistant tools in EFL learning* (Doctoral dissertation, Concordia University Chicago).

Almarzooqi, A. (2019). *Towards an artificial intelligence (AI)-driven government in the United Arab Emirates (UAE): a framework for transforming and augmenting leadership capabilities*. A dissertation submitted in partial satisfaction of the requirements for the degree of Doctor of Education in Organizational Leadership, Pepperdine University.

Aloulou, W., Ayadi, F., Ramadani, V., & Dana, L. P. (2024). Dreaming digital or chasing new real pathways? Unveiling the determinants shaping Saudi youth's digital entrepreneurial intention. *International Journal of Entrepreneurial Behaviour & Research*, 30(2/3), 709–734. DOI: 10.1108/IJEBR-10-2022-0942

Alsamhi, S. H., Ma, O., & Ansari, M. S. (2019). Survey on artificial intelligence based techniques for emerging robotic communication. *Telecommunication Systems*, 72(3), 483–503. DOI: 10.1007/s11235-019-00561-z

Anshari, M., Syafrudin, M., Tan, A., Fitriyani, N. L., & Alas, Y. (2023). Optimisation of knowledge management (KM) with machine learning (ML) Enabled. *Information (Basel)*, 14(1), 1–15. DOI: 10.3390/info14010035

Arntz, M., Gregory, T., & Zierahn, U. (2016). The Risk of Automation for Jobs in OECD Countries: A Comparative Analysis, OECD Social, Employment and Migration Working Papers, No. 189, OECD Publishing, Paris. http://dx.doi.org/ DOI: 10.1787/1815199X

Arrieta, A. B., Díaz-Rodríguez, N., Del Ser, J., Bennetot, A., Tabik, S., Barbado, A., & Herrera, F. (2020). Explainable Artificial Intelligence (XAI): Concepts, taxonomies, opportunities and challenges toward responsible AI. *Information Fusion*, 58, 82–115. DOI: 10.1016/j.inffus.2019.12.012

Askarany, D., Smith, M., & Yazdifar, H. (2007). Attributes of innovation and the implementation of managerial tools: An activity-based management technique. *International Journal of Business and Systems Research*, 1(1), 98–114. DOI: 10.1504/IJBSR.2007.014776

Avdeenko, T. V., Makarova, E. S., & Klavsuts, I. L. (2016, October). Artificial intelligence support of knowledge transformation in knowledge management systems. In *2016 13th International Scientific-Technical Conference on Actual Problems of Electronics Instrument Engineering (APEIE)* (Vol. 3, pp. 195-201). IEEE. DOI: 10.1109/APEIE.2016.7807053

Bahrammirzaee, A. (2010). A comparative survey of artificial intelligence applications in finance: Artificial neural networks, expert system and hybrid intelligent systems. *Neural Computing & Applications*, 19(8), 1165–1195. DOI: 10.1007/s00521-010-0362-z

Balkaya, E. (2017). *Üniversite Son Sınıf Öğrencilerinde İşsizlik Kaygısı ve Girişimcilik Niyeti İlişkisi; Tra1 Bölgesi Örneği, (Yayın numarası, 479419)* [Yüksek Lisans Tezi, Atatürk Üniversitesi]. Ulusal Tez Merkezi.

Beck, T., & Peria, M. S. M. (2006). *Banking Services for Everyone?: Barriers to Bank Access and Use Around the World* (Vol. 4079). World Bank Publications. DOI: 10.1596/1813-9450-4079

Behera, R. K., Bala, P. K., Rana, N. P., & Irani, Z. (2023). Responsible natural language processing: A principlist framework for social benefits. *Technological Forecasting and Social Change*, 188, 1–16. DOI: 10.1016/j.techfore.2022.122306

Belchior, R. F., & Lyons, R. (2021). Explaining entrepreneurial intentions, nascent entrepreneurial behavior and new business creation with social cognitive career theory–a 5-year longitudinal analysis. *The International Entrepreneurship and Management Journal*, 17(4), 1945–1972. DOI: 10.1007/s11365-021-00745-7

Bhutani, S., & Paliwal, Y. (2015). Digitalization: A step towards sustainable development. *OIDA International Journal of Sustainable Development*, 8(12), 11–24.

Bird, B. (1988). Implementing entrepreneurial ideas: The case for intention. *Academy of Management Review*, 13(3), 442–453. DOI: 10.2307/258091

Boyd, N. G., & Vozikis, G. S. (1994). The influence of self-efficacy on the development of entrepreneurial intentions and actions. *Entrepreneurship Theory and Practice*, 18(4), 63–77. DOI: 10.1177/104225879401800404

Bozkurt, Ö. (2019). Girişimcilik 4.0 Ama Nasıl? Kavramsal Bir Çerçeve. In *ICEB'19-International Congress of Economics and Business 11-13 April 2019 Bursa/Turkey* (pp. 549-559).

Brock, J. K. U., & Von Wangenheim, F. (2019). Demystifying AI: What digital transformation leaders can teach you about realistic artificial intelligence. *California Management Review*, 61(4), 110–134. DOI: 10.1177/1536504219865226

Brynjolfsson, E., & McAfee, A. (2014). *The second machine age: Work, progress, and prosperity in a time of brilliant technologies*. WW Norton & Company.

Cabı, E. (2016). Dijital teknolojiye yönelik tutum ölçeği. *Kastamonu Education Journal*, 24(3), 1229–1244.

Call, D. R., & Herber, D. R. (2022). Applicability of the diffusion of innovation theory to accelerate model-based systems engineering adoption. *Systems Engineering*, 25(6), 574–583. DOI: 10.1002/sys.21638

Capestro, M., Rizzo, C., Kliestik, T., Peluso, A. M., & Pino, G. (2024). Enabling digital technologies adoption in industrial districts: The key role of trust and knowledge sharing. *Technological Forecasting and Social Change*, 198, 1–10. DOI: 10.1016/j.techfore.2023.123003

Carrington, V. (2020). *Rethinking middle years: Early adolescents, schooling and digital culture*. Routledge. DOI: 10.4324/9781003117179

Chen, Y., Argentinis, J. E., & Weber, G. (2016). IBM Watson: How cognitive computing can be applied to big data challenges in life sciences research. *Clinical Therapeutics*, 38(4), 688–701. DOI: 10.1016/j.clinthera.2015.12.001 PMID: 27130797

Chigona, W., & Licker, P. (2008). Using diffusion of innovations framework to explain communal computing facilities adoption among the urban poor. *Information Technologies and International Development*, 4(3), 57–73. DOI: 10.1162/itid.2008.00017

Dana, L. P., Salamzadeh, A., Mortazavi, S., & Hadizadeh, M. (2022). Investigating the impact of international markets and new digital technologies on business innovation in emerging markets. *Sustainability (Basel)*, 14(2), 1–15. DOI: 10.3390/su14020983

Davenport, T. H., & Ronanki, R. (2018). Artificial intelligence for the real world. *Harvard Business Review*, 96(1), 108–116.

Davis, F. D. (1989). Technology acceptance model: TAM. *Al-Suqri, MN, Al-Aufi, AS. Information Seeking Behavior and Technology Adoption*, 205, 1–33.

Dong, Y., Hou, J., Zhang, N., & Zhang, M. (2020). Research on how human intelligence, consciousness, and cognitive computing affect the development of artificial intelligence. *Complexity*, 2020(1), 1–10. DOI: 10.1155/2020/1680845

Dubey, P., & Sahu, K. K. (2022). Examining the effects of demographic, social and environmental factors on entrepreneurial intention. *Management matters, 19*(1), 91-108.

Elia, G., Margherita, A., & Passiante, G. (2020). Digital entrepreneurship ecosystem: How digital technologies and collective intelligence are reshaping the entrepreneurial process. *Technological Forecasting and Social Change*, 150, 1–12. DOI: 10.1016/j.techfore.2019.119791

ElMassah, S., & Mohieldin, M. (2020). Digital transformation and localizing the sustainable development goals (SDGs). *Ecological Economics*, 169, 1–12. DOI: 10.1016/j.ecolecon.2019.106490

Entrialgo, M., & Iglesias, V. (2020). Entrepreneurial intentions among university students: The moderating role of creativity. *European Management Review*, 17(2), 529–542. DOI: 10.1111/emre.12386

Evans, R., Jumper, J., Kirkpatrick, J., Sifre, L., Green, T., Qin, C., & Senior, A. W. (2018). De novo structure prediction with deeplearning based scoring. *Annual Review of Biochemistry*, 77, 363–382.

Fahad, M., Basri, T., Hamza, M. A., Faisal, S., Akbar, A., Haider, U., & Hajjami, S. E. (2024). The Benefits and Risks of Artificial General Intelligence (AGI). In *Artificial General Intelligence (AGI) Security: Smart Applications and Sustainable Technologies* (pp. 27–52). Springer Nature Singapore.

Fanni, S. C., Febi, M., Aghakhanyan, G., & Neri, E. (2023). Natural language processing. In *Introduction to Artificial Intelligence* (pp. 87–99). Springer International Publishing. DOI: 10.1007/978-3-031-25928-9_5

Fernandes, C., Ferreira, J. J., Veiga, P. M., Kraus, S., & Dabić, M. (2022). Digital entrepreneurship platforms: Mapping the field and looking towards a holistic approach. *Technology in Society*, 70, 1–13. DOI: 10.1016/j.techsoc.2022.101979

Ferreira, J. J., Raposo, M. L., Gouveia Rodrigues, R., Dinis, A., & Do Paco, A. (2012). A model of entrepreneurial intention: An application of the psychological and behavioral approaches. *Journal of Small Business and Enterprise Development*, 19(3), 424–440. DOI: 10.1108/14626001211250144

Ferreira, P., Teixeira, J. G., & Teixeira, L. F. (2020). Understanding the impact of artificial intelligence on services. In *Exploring Service Science: 10th International Conference, IESS 2020, Porto, Portugal, February 5–7, 2020* [Springer International Publishing.]. *Proceedings*, 10, 202–213.

Fishbein, M., & Ajzen, I. (1974). Attitudes towards objects as predictors of single and multiple behavioral criteria. *Psychological Review*, 81(1), 59–74. DOI: 10.1037/h0035872

Franklin, S. (2015). *Control: Digitality as cultural logic*. MIT Press. DOI: 10.7551/mitpress/9780262029537.001.0001

Gaba, D. M. (2022). Artificial intelligence and expert systems. In *Control and Automation in Anaesthesia* (pp. 22–36). Springer Berlin Heidelberg.

Georgescu, M. A., & Herman, E. (2020). The impact of the family background on students' entrepreneurial intentions: An empirical analysis. *Sustainability (Basel)*, 12(11), 1–18. DOI: 10.3390/su12114775

Ghobakhloo, M. (2020). Industry 4.0, digitization, and opportunities for sustainability. *Journal of Cleaner Production*, 252, 1–21. DOI: 10.1016/j.jclepro.2019.119869

Gubbi, J., Buyya, R., Marusic, S., & Palaniswami, M. (2013). Internet of Things (IoT): A vision, architectural elements, and future directions. *Future Generation Computer Systems*, 29(7), 1645–1660. DOI: 10.1016/j.future.2013.01.010

Gupta, I., & Nagpal, G. (2020). *Artificial intelligence and expert systems*. Mercury Learning and Information. DOI: 10.1515/9781683925057

Hämäläinen, R., Nissinen, K., Mannonen, J., Lämsä, J., Leino, K., & Taajamo, M. (2021). Understanding teaching professionals' digital competence: What do PIAAC and TALIS reveal about technology-related skills, attitudes, and knowledge? *Computers in Human Behavior*, 117, 1–15. DOI: 10.1016/j.chb.2020.106672

Hamet, P., & Tremblay, J. (2017). Artificial intelligence in medicine. *metabolism, 69*, 36-40.

Huang, M. H., Rust, R., & Maksimovic, V. (2019). The feeling economy: Managing in the next generation of artificial intelligence (AI). *California Management Review*, 61(4), 43–65. DOI: 10.1177/0008125619863436

Huang, M. H., & Rust, R. T. (2018). Artificial intelligence in service. *Journal of Service Research*, 21(2), 155–172. DOI: 10.1177/1094670517752459

Hueso, J. A., Jaén, I., & Liñán, F. (2021). From personal values to entrepreneurial intention: A systematic literature review. *International Journal of Entrepreneurial Behaviour & Research*, 27(1), 205–230. DOI: 10.1108/IJEBR-06-2020-0383

Hülür, G., & Macdonald, B. (2020). Rethinking social relationships in old age: Digitalization and the social lives of older adults. *The American Psychologist*, 75(4), 554–566. DOI: 10.1037/amp0000604 PMID: 32378949

Hyppönen, M. (2022). *If it's smart, it's vulnerable*. John Wiley & Sons.

Incerti, F. (2020). *Preservice Teachers? Perceptions of Artificial Intelligence Tutors for Learning*. A dissertation presented to the faculty of The Gladys W. and David H. Patton College of Education In partial fulfillment of the requirements for the degree Doctor of Philosophy, Ohio University.

Isizoh, A. N., Alagbu, E. E., Nwosu, F. C., Nwoye, C. G., & Ogbogu, E. N. (2021). Applications and analyses of expert systems in decision management. *Journal of inventive engineering and technology (jiet), 1*(5), 78-85.

Jarrahi, M. H., Askay, D., Eshraghi, A., & Smith, P. (2023). Artificial intelligence and knowledge management: A partnership between human and AI. *Business Horizons*, 66(1), 87–99. DOI: 10.1016/j.bushor.2022.03.002

Jobin, A., Ienca, M., & Vayena, E. (2019). The global landscape of AI ethics guidelines. *Nature Machine Intelligence*, 1(9), 389–399. DOI: 10.1038/s42256-019-0088-2

Kalkan, A. (2011). Kişisel tutum, öznel norm ve algilanan davraniş kontrolünün girişimcilik niyeti üzerindeki etkisi: Üniversite öğrencileri üzerine bir uygulama. *Süleyman Demirel Üniversitesi Sosyal Bilimler Enstitüsü Dergisi*, (14), 189–206.

Karahanna, E., Straub, D. W., & Chervany, N. L. (1999). Information technology adoption across time: A cross-sectional comparison of pre-adoption and post-adoption beliefs. *Management Information Systems Quarterly*, 23(2), 183–213. DOI: 10.2307/249751

Kaur Kapoor, K., & Dwivedi, K., Y., & D. Williams, M. (. (2014). Innovation adoption attributes: A review and synthesis of research findings. *European Journal of Innovation Management*, 17(3), 327–348. DOI: 10.1108/EJIM-08-2012-0083

Kayser, K., Telukdarie, A., & Philbin, S. P. (2023). Digital Start-Up Ecosystems: A Systematic Literature Review and Model Development for South Africa. *Sustainability (Basel)*, 15(16), 1–24. DOI: 10.3390/su151612513

Khallaf, A. N.Ayman Naji Khallaf. (2024). Using Ai to Help Reduce the Effect of Global Warming. *Power System Technology*, 48(1), 1927–1947. DOI: 10.52783/pst.464

Kim, J. W. (2022). *How speciesism affects artificial intelligence (AI) adoption intent* (Doctoral dissertation, Queensland University of Technology).

Kolodinsky, J., Hogarth, J. M., & Hilgert, A. (2001). The adoption of electronic banking technologies by American consumers. *Consumer Interests Annual*, 47(3), 1–9.

Kraus, N., Kraus, K., & Manzhura, O. (2021). Digitalization of business processes of enterprises of the ecosystem of Industry 4.0: Virtual-real aspect of economic growth reserves. *WSEAS Transactions on Business and Economics*, 18, 569–580. DOI: 10.37394/23207.2021.18.57

Krueger, N. F., Jr. (1993). Growing Up Entrepreneurial?": Developmental Consequences Of Early Exposure To Entrepreneurship. In *Academy of Management Proceedings* (Vol. 1993, No. 1, pp. 80-84). Briarcliff Manor, NY 10510: Academy of Management.

Kumar, V., Rajan, B., Venkatesan, R., & Lecinski, J. (2019). Understanding the role of artificial intelligence in personalized engagement marketing. *California Management Review*, 61(4), 135–155. DOI: 10.1177/0008125619859317

Kumpulainen, S., & Terziyan, V. (2022). Artificial general intelligence vs. industry 4.0: Do they need each other? *Procedia Computer Science*, 200, 140–150. DOI: 10.1016/j.procs.2022.01.213

Kwapisz, A., Schell, W. J., Aytes, K., & Bryant, S. (2022). Entrepreneurial action and intention: The role of entrepreneurial mindset, emotional intelligence, and grit. *Entrepreneurship Education and Pedagogy*, 5(3), 375–405. DOI: 10.1177/2515127421992521

Legris, P., Ingham, J., & Collerette, P. (2003). Why do people use information technology? A critical review of the technology acceptance model. *Information & Management*, 40(3), 191–204. DOI: 10.1016/S0378-7206(01)00143-4

Liao, H. L., & Lu, H. P. (2008). The role of experience and innovation characteristics in the adoption and continued use of e-learning websites. *Computers & Education*, 51(4), 1405–1416. DOI: 10.1016/j.compedu.2007.11.006

Liebowitz, J. (2001). Knowledge management and its link to artificial intelligence. *Expert Systems with Applications*, 20(1), 1–6. DOI: 10.1016/S0957-4174(00)00044-0

Livingston, S., & Risse, M. (2019). The future impact of artificial intelligence on humans and human rights. *Ethics & International Affairs*, 33(2), 141–158. DOI: 10.1017/S089267941900011X

Lu, H., Li, Y., Chen, M., Kim, H., & Serikawa, S. (2018). Brain intelligence: Go beyond artificial intelligence. *Mobile Networks and Applications*, 23(2), 368–375. DOI: 10.1007/s11036-017-0932-8

Makridakis, S. (2017). The forthcoming Artificial Intelligence (AI) revolution: Its impact on society and firms. *Futures*, 90, 46–60. DOI: 10.1016/j.futures.2017.03.006

Malodia, S., Islam, N., Kaur, P., & Dhir, A. (2021). Why do people use Artificial Intelligence (AI)-enabled voice assistants? *IEEE Transactions on Engineering Management*, 71, 491–505. DOI: 10.1109/TEM.2021.3117884

Mao, E., & Palvia, P. (2006). Testing an extended model of IT acceptance in the Chinese cultural context. *The Data Base for Advances in Information Systems*, 37(2-3), 20–32. DOI: 10.1145/1161345.1161351

Martins, I., & Perez, J. P. (2020). Testing mediating effects of individual entrepreneurial orientation on the relation between close environmental factors and entrepreneurial intention. *International Journal of Entrepreneurial Behaviour & Research*, 26(4), 771–791. DOI: 10.1108/IJEBR-08-2019-0505

Masriadi, D., Ekaningrum, N. E., Hidayat, M. S., & Yuliaty, F. (2023). Exploring the future of work: Impact of automation and artificial intelligence on employment. *Endless International Journal of Future Studies*, 6(1), 125–136. DOI: 10.54783/endlessjournal.v6i1.131

Matos, F., Vairinhos, V., Salavisa, I., Edvinsson, L., & Massaro, M. (2020). *Knowledge, people, and digital transformation*. Springer. DOI: 10.1007/978-3-030-40390-4

Mickiewicz, T., Sauka, A., & Stephan, U. (2016). On the compatibility of benevolence and self-interest: Philanthropy and entrepreneurial orientation. *International Small Business Journal*, 34(3), 303–328. DOI: 10.1177/0266242614555245

Mondejar, M. E., Avtar, R., Diaz, H. L. B., Dubey, R. K., Esteban, J., Gómez-Morales, A., Hallam, B., Mbungu, N. T., Okolo, C. C., Prasad, K. A., She, Q., & Garcia-Segura, S. (2021). Digitalization to achieve sustainable development goals: Steps towards a Smart Green Planet. *The Science of the Total Environment*, 794, 1–20. DOI: 10.1016/j.scitotenv.2021.148539 PMID: 34323742

Moore, G. C., & Benbasat, I. (1996). Integrating diffusion of innovations and theory of reasoned action models to predict utilization of information technology by end-users. In *Diffusion and Adoption of Information Technology: Proceedings of the first IFIP WG 8.6 working conference on the diffusion and adoption of information technology, Oslo, Norway, October 1995* (pp. 132-146). Springer US. DOI: 10.1007/978-0-387-34982-4_10

Mourtzis, D. (2024). Industry 4.0 and smart manufacturing. In *Manufacturing from Industry 4.0 to Industry 5.0* (pp. 13-61). Elsevier.

Nambisan, S., Wright, M., & Feldman, M. (2019). The digital transformation of innovation and entrepreneurship: Progress, challenges and key themes. *Research Policy*, 48(8), 1–9. DOI: 10.1016/j.respol.2019.03.018

Nørskov, S., Chrysochou, P., & Milenkova, M. (2015). The impact of product innovation attributes on brand equity. *Journal of Consumer Marketing*, 32(4), 245–254. DOI: 10.1108/JCM-10-2014-1198

Panicacci, S., Donati, M., Fanucci, L., Bellin, I., Profili, F., & Francesconi, P. (2018, June). Population health management exploiting machine learning algorithms to identify high-risk patients. In *2018 IEEE 31st International Symposium on Computer-Based Medical Systems (CBMS)* (pp. 298-303). IEEE. DOI: 10.1109/CBMS.2018.00059

Paśko, Ł., Mądziel, M., Stadnicka, D., Dec, G., Carreras-Coch, A., Solé-Beteta, X., Pappa, L., Stylios, C., Mazzei, D., & Atzeni, D. (2022). Plan and develop advanced knowledge and skills for future industrial employees in the field of artificial intelligence, internet of things and edge computing. *Sustainability (Basel)*, 14(6), 1–43. DOI: 10.3390/su14063312

Perez-Vega, R., Kaartemo, V., Lages, C. R., Razavi, N. B., & Männistö, J. (2021). Reshaping the contexts of online customer engagement behavior via artificial intelligence: A conceptual framework. *Journal of Business Research*, 129, 902–910. DOI: 10.1016/j.jbusres.2020.11.002

Petrova, M., Popova, P., Popov, V., Shishmanov, K., & Marinova, K. (2021, October). Digital ecosystem: Nature, types and opportunities for value creation. In *International Scientific Conference on Innovations in Digital Economy* (pp. 71-85). Cham: Springer International Publishing.

Pollitzer, E. (2018). Creating a better future. *Journal of International Affairs*, 72(1), 75–90.

Ranjan, J., & Foropon, C. (2021). Big data analytics in building the competitive intelligence of organizations. *International Journal of Information Management*, 56, 1–15. DOI: 10.1016/j.ijinfomgt.2020.102231

Rijsdijk, S. A., Hultink, E. J., & Diamantopoulos, A. (2007). Product intelligence: Its conceptualization, measurement and impact on consumer satisfaction. *Journal of the Academy of Marketing Science*, 35(3), 340–356. DOI: 10.1007/s11747-007-0040-6

Rogers, E. (2003). *Diffusion of innovations* (5th ed.). Free Press.

Rogers, E. M. (1995). *Diffusion of Innovations* (4th ed.). Free Press.

Rosário, A. T., & Dias, J. C. (2022). Sustainability and the digital transition: A literature review. *Sustainability*, 14(7), 1–18. DOI: 10.3390/su14074072 PMID: 36090804

Saatçi, E. Y. (2017). Girişimcilik 4.0: Tarihten Sanayi 4.0'a Doğru Girişimciler. *Maliye Finans Yazıları*, 118, 95–112.

Sabuncu, R. G. (2017). *Anadolu Üniversitesi İşletme Fakültesi Öğrencilerinin Girişimcilik Niyetleri ve Çevresel Tutumlarını Ölçmeye Yönelik Bir Araştırma, (Yayın Numarası,463513)* [Yüksek Lisans Tezi, Anadolu Üniversitesi]. Ulusal Tez Merkezi.

Sarel, D., & Marmorstein, H. (2003). Marketing online banking services: The voice of the customer. *Journal of Financial Services Marketing*, 8(2), 106–118. DOI: 10.1057/palgrave.fsm.4770111

Saunders, K. T., & Locke, L. G. (2020). Casting lots, gambling, and artificial intelligence. *Journal of Biblical Integration in Business*, 23(1), 58–69. DOI: 10.69492/jbib.v23i1.557

Saxena, P., Priyadarshini, I., Sharma, S., & Jora, R. B. (2022, March). Role of Emotional and Artificial Intelligence on Employee Performance in Service Industry: A Review of Literature. In *2022 8th International Conference on Advanced Computing and Communication Systems (ICACCS)* (Vol. 1, pp. 1564-1567). IEEE. DOI: 10.1109/ICACCS54159.2022.9784989

Semenov, V. P., Chernokulsky, V. V., & Razmochaeva, N. V. (2017, October). Research of artificial intelligence in the retail management problems. In *2017 IEEE II international conference on control in technical systems (CTS)* (pp. 333-336). IEEE. DOI: 10.1109/CTSYS.2017.8109560

Shahzad, M. F., Khan, K. I., Saleem, S., & Rashid, T. (2021). What factors affect the entrepreneurial intention to start-ups? The role of entrepreneurial skills, propensity to take risks, and innovativeness in open business models. *Journal of Open Innovation*, 7(3), 1–23. DOI: 10.3390/joitmc7030173

Shapero, A., & Sokol, L. (1982). *The social dimensions of entrepreneurship, Encyclopedia of Entrepreneurship*. Prentice-Hall.

Sharma, R., Lopes de Sousa Jabbour, A. B., Jain, V., & Shishodia, A. (2022). The role of digital technologies to unleash a green recovery: Pathways and pitfalls to achieve the European Green Deal. *Journal of Enterprise Information Management*, 35(1), 266–294. DOI: 10.1108/JEIM-07-2021-0293

Silver, D., Huang, A., Maddison, C. J., Guez, A., Sifre, L., Van Den Driessche, G., ... & Hassabis, D. (2016). Mastering the game of Go with deep neural networks and tree search. *nature, 529*(7587), 484-489.

Sohn, K., & Kwon, O. (2020). Technology acceptance theories and factors influencing artificial Intelligence-based intelligent products. *Telematics and Informatics*, 47, 1–14. DOI: 10.1016/j.tele.2019.101324

Stahl, B. C. (2021). *Artificial intelligence for a better future: an ecosystem perspective on the ethics of AI and emerging digital technologies*. Springer Nature. DOI: 10.1007/978-3-030-69978-9

Stevens, P. M., Williams, K. P., & Smith, M. C. (2000). Organizational communication and information processes in an internet-enabled environment. *Psychology and Marketing*, 17(7), 607–632. DOI: 10.1002/(SICI)1520-6793(200007)17:7<607::AID-MAR3>3.0.CO;2-5

Strzelecki, A., & Rutecka, P. (2020). Direct answers in Google search results. *IEEE Access : Practical Innovations, Open Solutions*, 8, 103642–103654. DOI: 10.1109/ACCESS.2020.2999160

Sturgeon, T. J. (2021). Upgrading strategies for the digital economy. *Global Strategy Journal*, 11(1), 34–57. DOI: 10.1002/gsj.1364

Suoranta, M. (2003). *Adoption of mobile banking in Finland*, Academic dissertation to be publicly discussed, School of Business and Economics of the University of Jyväskylä.

Syam, N., & Sharma, A. (2018). Waiting for a sales renaissance in the fourth industrial revolution: Machine learning and artificial intelligence in sales research and practice. *Industrial Marketing Management*, 69, 135–146. DOI: 10.1016/j.indmarman.2017.12.019

Tahar, A., Riyadh, H. A., Sofyani, H., & Purnomo, W. E. (2020). Perceived ease of use, perceived usefulness, perceived security and intention to use e-filing: The role of technology readiness. *The Journal of Asian Finance. Economics and Business*, 7(9), 537–547.

Tambe, P., Cappelli, P., & Yakubovich, V. (2019). Artificial intelligence in human resources management: Challenges and a path forward. *California Management Review*, 61(4), 15–42. DOI: 10.1177/0008125619867910

Tan, M., & Teo, T. S. (2000). Factors influencing the adoption of Internet banking. *Journal of the Association for Information Systems*, 1(5), 1–42. DOI: 10.17705/1jais.00005

Tanoğlu, Ş. (2019). *Resim İş Eğitimi Öğrencilerinin Dijital Vatandaşlık Düzeyleri İle Dijital Teknolojiye Yönelik Tutumları Arasındaki İlişkinin İncelenmesi, (Yayın Numarası, 588605)* [Yüksek Lisans Tezi, T.C. Erzincan Binali Yıldırım Üniversitesi]. Ulusal Tez Merkezi.

Tekeoglu, N. (2020). Dijital Teknolojiye Yönelik Tutum ile Sinemaya Gitme Motivasyonlarının Yapısal Eşitlik Modellemesi ile İncelenmesi. *Econder International Academic Journal*, 4(1), 26–46. DOI: 10.35342/econder.678149

Timuroğlu, M. K., & ÇAKIR, S. (2014). Girişimcilerin yeni bir girişim yapma niyetlerinin risk alma eğilimi ile ilişkisi. *Afyon Kocatepe Üniversitesi İktisadi ve İdari Bilimler Fakültesi Dergisi*, 16(2), 119–136.

Toksoy, B. (2019). *Girişimci Kişilik Özelliklerinin Girişimcilik Niyetine Etkisinde Stratejik Güven ve Ortak Değerlerin Moderatör Rolü Üzerine Bir Araştırma, (Yayın Numarası,582619)* [Doktora Tezi, İstanbul Okan Üniversitesi]. Ulusal Tez Merkezi.

Tsou, H. T., & Chen, J. S. (2023). How does digital technology usage benefit firm performance? Digital transformation strategy and organisational innovation as mediators. *Technology Analysis and Strategic Management*, 35(9), 1114–1127. DOI: 10.1080/09537325.2021.1991575

Tully, M. (2015). Investigating the role of innovation attributes in the adoption, rejection, and discontinued use of open source software for development. *Information Technologies and International Development*, 11(3), 55–69.

Tyagi, A. K., & Chahal, P. (2020). Artificial intelligence and machine learning algorithms. In *Challenges and applications for implementing machine learning in computer vision* (pp. 188–219). IGI Global. DOI: 10.4018/978-1-7998-0182-5.ch008

Usman, H., Mulia, D., Chairy, C., & Widowati, N. (2022). Integrating trust, religiosity and image into technology acceptance model: The case of the Islamic philanthropy in Indonesia. *Journal of Islamic Marketing*, 13(2), 381–409. DOI: 10.1108/JIMA-01-2020-0020

Van Deursen, A. J., & Van Dijk, J. A. (2014). *Digital skills: Unlocking the information society*. Springer.

Vardar, A. (2018). *Girişimcilik Niyetine Etki Eden Değişkenlerin Planlanmış Davranış Teorisi Çerçevesinde Analizi, Açık Öğretim Öğrencileri Üzerinde Bir Araştırma (Yayın Numarası509466)* [Doktora Tezi, Anadolu Üniversitesi]. Ulusal Tez Merkezi.

Verplanken, B., & Orbell, S. (2022). Attitudes, habits, and behavior change. *Annual Review of Psychology*, 73(1), 327–352. DOI: 10.1146/annurev-psych-020821-011744 PMID: 34587780

Waarts, E., van Everdingen, Y. M., & Van Hillegersberg, J. (2002). The dynamics of factors affecting the adoption of innovations. *Journal of Product Innovation Management*, 19(6), 412–423. DOI: 10.1111/1540-5885.1960412

Xiong, D., Khaddage-Soboh, N., Umar, M., Safi, A., & Norena-Chavez, D. (2024). Redefining entrepreneurship in the digital age: Exploring the impact of technology and collaboration on ventures. *The International Entrepreneurship and Management Journal*, 20(4), 1–27. DOI: 10.1007/s11365-024-00996-0

Xu, K., Wang, X., Wei, W., Song, H., & Mao, B. (2016). Toward software defined smart home. *IEEE Communications Magazine*, 54(5), 116–122. DOI: 10.1109/MCOM.2016.7470945

Yuen, K. F., Wong, Y. D., Ma, F., & Wang, X. (2020). The determinants of public acceptance of autonomous vehicles: An innovation diffusion perspective. *Journal of Cleaner Production*, 270, 1–13. DOI: 10.1016/j.jclepro.2020.121904

Zhang, H., Song, M., & He, H. (2020). Achieving the success of sustainability development projects through big data analytics and artificial intelligence capability. *Sustainability (Basel)*, 12(3), 1–23. DOI: 10.3390/su12030949

Zhang, J., van Gorp, D., & Kievit, H. (2023). Digital technology and national entrepreneurship: An ecosystem perspective. *The Journal of Technology Transfer*, 48(3), 1077–1105. DOI: 10.1007/s10961-022-09934-0 PMID: 35602312

Zolait, A. H. S., & Sulaiman, A. (2008). Incorporating the Innovation Attributes Introduced by Rogers' Theory into Theory of Reasoned Action: An Examination of Internet Banking Adoption in Yemen. *Computer and Information Science*, 1(1), 36–51.

ADDITIONAL READING

Burns, P. (2022). *Entrepreneurship and small business*. Bloomsbury Publishing.

Dougherty, E. R. (2020). *Digital image processing methods*. CRC Press. DOI: 10.1201/9781003067054

Feld, B., & Hathaway, I. (2020). *The startup community way: Evolving an entrepreneurial ecosystem*. John Wiley & Sons.

Friederici, N., Wahome, M., & Graham, M. (2020). *Digital entrepreneurship in Africa: How a continent is escaping Silicon Valley's long shadow*. The MIT Press. DOI: 10.7551/mitpress/12453.001.0001

Hawkridge, D. (2022). *New information technology in education*. Routledge. DOI: 10.4324/9781003312826

Lloyd, I. (2020). *Information technology law*. Oxford University Press. DOI: 10.1093/he/9780198830559.001.0001

Neck, H. M., Neck, C. P., & Murray, E. L. (2023). *Entrepreneurship: The practice and mindset*. Sage publications.

Soltanifar, M., Hughes, M., & Göcke, L. (2021). *Digital entrepreneurship: Impact on business and society*. Springer Nature. DOI: 10.1007/978-3-030-53914-6

Turi, A. N. (2020). *Technologies for modern digital entrepreneurship*. Apress. DOI: 10.1007/978-1-4842-6005-0

Zölzer, U. (2022). *Digital audio signal processing*. John Wiley & Sons.

KEY TERMS AND DEFINITIONS

Analytical Intelligence: The ability of a person or a system to analyze complex problems, extract meaning from data and derive logical conclusions from these analyses. In the business world, analytical intelligence usually refers to data analysis, strategic planning and problem-solving skills.

Entrepreneurial Intention: It is the thought and determination of an individual to establish his/her own business or start a venture. Entrepreneurial intention reflects the person's willingness to evaluate opportunities and take entrepreneurial action.

Information Management: A process that allows an organization to collect, store, process, share and use its information assets efficiently. The goal is to support decision-making processes by ensuring that the right information reaches the right people at the right time.

Machine Learning: A branch of artificial intelligence that allows computers to automatically perform certain tasks by learning from data and improving their own performance through experience. It can make predictions and adapt to certain situations without human intervention.

Management Ability: It is the ability of a person or a group leader to manage an organization effectively and efficiently. Management ability includes skills such as making strategic decisions, coordinating teams and using resources in the best way.

Mechanical Intelligence: The ability to understand mechanical systems and machines and solve problems on these systems. Mechanical intelligence requires technical knowledge and skills; it is usually used in areas such as engineering, repair or machine design.

Social Networks: They are digital or physical communication networks based on relationships and interactions between people. These networks are structured relationship networks that allow people to exchange information, resources and support. Platforms such as Facebook and LinkedIn are examples of digital social networks.

Sustainable Development: It is a development model that aims to meet the needs of current generations without endangering the needs of future generations by considering environmental, economic and social dimensions in a balanced way. This concept aims at the sustainable use of natural resources and the long-term protection of social welfare.

Chapter 16
The Role of AI in Conflict Resolution and Negotiation

Bitan Roy
https://orcid.org/0009-0006-6957-3263
Brainware University, India

Sanchita Ghosh
https://orcid.org/0009-0007-9421-5246
Brainware University, India

Nobhonil Roy Choudhury
https://orcid.org/0009-0009-1046-7492
Brainware University, India

Piyal Roy
https://orcid.org/0009-0007-5378-2789
Brainware University, India

Sreelekha Paul
https://orcid.org/0009-0007-5524-1919
Brainware University, India

ABSTRACT

This paper aims to analyze the current turn of Artificial Intelligence (AI) in conflict resolution and negotiation analyzing its implications on the theoretical and practical level. This accomplishes the goal of the study, which was to investigate how AI might improve post-elite ethical, effective, and positive dispute resolution choices. A survey of the literature, the use of scenarios to demonstrate AI applied to conflict situations,

DOI: 10.4018/979-8-3693-8442-8.ch016

expert interviews with ten different people, an ethical evaluation, and quantitative assessments make up the areas of work. The findings suggest that although AI has amazing techniques in these areas, there are important ethical conundrums that need to be cleared up in order to enable its proper implementation.

1. INTRODUCTION

Disputing and bargaining are classic aspects of human Interpersonal interaction that require emotional intelligence, human hunch, bargaining power and cultural sensitivity. But these procedures have dramatically evolved, owed to artificial intelligence (AI) breakthrough. What this means for human negotiators is the provision of significant new information. Natural language processing (NLP), machine learning, and decision support systems are examples of artificial intelligence (AI) technologies that show a great deal of potential for enhancing these processes. They can evaluate large data sets to identify trends, project outcomes, and suggest the best course of action. AI can also be helpful when it comes to being an intermediary since it cannot personally benefit from the sale.as free from bias in this form of a prejudice decision rather offering them based on rationale facts as the data allowed to enhance the relevance and effectiveness of discussions. But there is something wrong in terms of ethics involved in applying AI in negotiation/dispute resolution, bias in the AI algorithms, and the black box also on the AI decision-making processes, the concern of overdependency on AI and; liability problems. These challenges underscore the importance of ensuring that AI systems are created and implemented in an equitable, transparent, and morally sound manner. This research explores the use of AI in negotiation and conflict settlement in order to understand the present state of AI integration, the benefits and challenges of its application, and the ethical considerations that arise. The study uses a mixed-methods approach that incorporates literature reviews, case studies, expert interviews, and data analysis to provide a comprehensive picture of AI's influence on various disciplines. It is critical to understand how negotiation and dispute resolution works through the use of AI in a world that may be explained by the fact that technology is gradually entering people's lives. This paper focuses on the chance and challenges posed by machine learning and its integration in to systems that were once primarily manned proficiency that augments the literature on the impact of AI in these essential areas (Deutsch et al. 2014)

1.2 Background

i. Overview of Conflict Resolution and Negotiation in Various Domains

Interpersonal conflicts are normal in global politics, business organizations, and personal affairs, and therefore conflict solving and negotiation skills are paramount. They avoid conflicts and maintain order and ensure good results in such contracts, merged companies and workers' strikes. In interpersonal conflict, negotiation, mediation, arbitration and other techniques involves temperance, sensitivity, active listening and intelligible ways of arriving at a mutually satisfactory resolution.

ii. Introduction to Artificial Intelligence (AI) and Its Growing Influence Across Industries

Artificial Intelligence (AI) is the process of employing computing devices, such as robotics, machine learning, natural language processing, and decision support systems, to mimic human cognitive capacities. It has therefore become widespread in many fields and has infiltrated tasks and decision-making. In healthcare, AI used in identifying diseases, prognosis, and precise patient treatment. In the field of finance, it helps to identify trends, examine schemes of fraud, and even control the operations on the financial market. In transportation, it enhances the self-driving cars and in education, it caters for individual learning needs. (Tapol et al. 2019)

iii. Relevance and Importance of Exploring AI's Role in Conflict Resolution and Negotiation

A major opportunity of AI in conflict and negotiation is to collect and analyze data, anticipate results and avert repetitive tasks. But ethical and practical concerns are principal. This paper is also important because as the use of AI systems increases, more doubts arise such as the case of bias, transparency as well as accountability. These findings give policy implications for policymakers, the developers of AI tools and applications, and practitioners in conflict resolution.

2. RESEARCH METHODOLOGY

Research design is an important aspect of any academic research study as it offers a blueprint of how the researcher intends to deliver the study objectives and response the research questions (Creswell et al., 2014). In light of this, both qualitative and quantitative research approaches are used in the current study, which looks at whether artificial intelligence can help with negotiation and dispute resolution. The advantages of this design include the use of both qualitative and quantitative analyses to increase the identification and analysis of the topic under consideration (Rahman et al., 2016). This is why the use of mixed methods is most appropriate as the research topic is the use of artificial intelligence in relation to compared to scientific and technical education, the field of negotiation and conflict solving, or practical application of reason and group analytical In addition to other data collection methods which can be used include interviews and case studies, questionnaire and statistical data.

a more complex type of research (Johnson et al., 2004 & Onwuegbuzie, 2004). This provides a deeper viewpoint since more closed-ended and open-ended research questions could be explored, enabling the investigation of how the human participants in the study actually experience and perceive the AI as well as the real values and metrics of the AI's performance and effects. AI in negotiating scenarios can be investigated through the triangulation of qualitative and quantitative frameworks. In this way, the study also makes it possible to add elements like the moral, societal, and human concerns that may have an impact on how well AI performs as well as its technological characteristics and outcomes. Since this research seeks to meet the objectives in a field that is vast and dynamic, a mixed-methods approach is used in this study as it is more sensitive to the fabric of the subject area of study and allows for a multiple perspective analysis of the issues at hand (Tashakkori et al.,2003 and Teddlie, 2003).

i. Overall Research Approach: Mixed-Methods

The paper is cross-sectional in its approach and employs the qualitative and the quantitative approaches within the field of AI in conflict management and negotiations. With this strategy, it is hoped that possible misconceptions and stigmatization of AI in these processes will be achieved. For a more detailed information, there is use of questionnaires, focus group discussions, case studies among others. These tools facilitate an investigation of procedural levels and contexts that affect the effectiveness of conflict-solving artificial intelligence (Creswell et al., 2014). Semi structured self-developed questionnaires which involves the measurement of conflict resolution processes are used to measure the impact of AI in quantitative terms while also embracing its statistical analysis. Tools of statistical analyses and artificial intelligence are applied to present quantitative evidence regarding the study. This Concepts of application of AI technologies in practical situations. Moreover, to get the idea regarding the problems and ethical concerns occurred to the constructivist experiences of practitioners are recruited through Qualitative interviews and group discussions (Johnson et al:2004 & Onwuegbuzie,2004).

ii. Justification for Choosing the Approach of Doing the Study

The necessity to offer a more comprehensive understanding of the application of artificial intelligence in negotiation and conflict resolution drives the adoption of a mixed-method research methodology. With this sort of approach, it is feasible to explain how application of artificial intelligence has evolved over time to today day comprehending the advantages, disadvantages, potential social issues and potential improvements in the area. The capabilities of quantitative data, for example, the current and frequents the adoption of AI technologies, will help the research establish a foundation upon which to compare trends in the AI field. (Tashakkori et al., 2003)(Eliases & Teddlie, 2003). In contrast, the quantitative data is obtained through structured questionnaires. And/or scenarios, attempts to gather the users' perceptions/impressions on the issues both systematically. This working of two-pronged method enables the research to explore myriad of factors that define and or contributor to AI's applicability to conflict resolution since it provides detailed and comprehensive approach to the results of the reflections and experiences captured in terms of theorizing and experimenting are also compared and evaluated. Moreover, we apply both numerical and textual approaches sources offer enough background data and simple solutions when it comes to work practice. Main stakeholders were involved in conflict solving mechanisms (Creswell et al., 2014).

Policymakers: The study sheds important light on the manner in which AI might be integrated into this includes such areas as negotiating and dispute procedures. It encourages decision-making on the adoption and the regulation of AI by assisting the policymakers to grasp the two aspects or prospects of it of the technology. The recommendations can influence the policies that will uphold the right use of artificial intelligence in conflict management, fostering technology to reap the right impact on society. outcomes.

AI Developers: This study provides information on the limitations and beneficial application to the builders of AI systems of AI in resolving disputes. This brings focus into places that AI technology has to evolve in aiming at enhancement of negotiation and dispute resolution in order to meet demands. By adding ethical their matters-of-concern and feedback; therefore, AI systems may be made more moral. and effective.

Conflict Resolution Professionals: The work should be useful to the conflict resolution professionals in better train their workers to adopt AI tools by improving decision making and operations optimization. and act on ideas more swiftly, reduce tensions and effectively resolve breaches. This paper also offers actionable suggestions. On ethical considerations and that AI works in the best interest of human decision making and compassion, and that technology plays a part in the right way.

3. LITERATURE REVIEW

AI can offer recommendations which are neutral and are not affiliated with either party in a conflict. Historically as conflict resolution and negotiation were social status, rhetoric, and culture dependent. Modern conflict management techniques can be characterized by their ability, third party, an impartiality, and the procedures followed. Advancements in communication, computation and analysis have also improved digital conflict resolution. AI algorithms expects success based on experiences, can recognize successful approaches of a strategy. Analysing AI based mediation solutions will safeguard sanity by minimizing human bias and prejudices the quality of choice and the capacity to resolve a conflict is improved.

3.1 AI Technologies in Conflict Resolution

The application of artificial intelligence (AI) is transforming the settlement of disputes by increasing productivity, accuracy, and equity. Emerging technologies that are transforming data analysis, outcome prediction, and automation include machine learning, natural language processing, and decision support systems. These advancements present new avenues for efficient conflict resolution. A kind of artificial intelligence called machine learning (ML) enables systems to learn from data and gradually get better at tasks, especially resolving conflicts. It can assist negotiators in understanding the elements that determine whether a negotiation succeeds or fails by being utilized for data analysis, predictive analytics, and text analysis. A subfield of artificial intelligence called natural language processing, or NLP, is concerned with how computers and human language interact. AI systems that are able to comprehend, interpret, and produce human language thanks to NLP technologies are extremely useful in negotiations where effective communication is essential. When negotiating counterparts exchange emails, NLP systems can analyze the tone of the messages to determine whether the exchanges are aggressive or cooperative. The third of the NLP application is the use of an automated communication method as it can interconnect at the early stages with parties of a conversation and develop scripts and information out of the conversation. This can offset the time and energy required for conventional exchange related communication activities can be reduced thereby releasing human negotiators.to leave out the other higher order factors of the negotiation. Artificial Intelligence Decision Support Systems The analysing provided in (DSS) integrates the conventional approaches to decision-making and artificial intelligence. Problem solving particularly conflict resolution techniques. DSS can provide several ways of addressing the problem and, afterwards having considered data and models, choose the correct one. They can also help the different stakeholders in the exercise of the decision-making process while in negotiations by simulating numerous probable negotiations and assessing risks and possibilities linked each choice. Conflict Resolution Automation is the other category of DSS, which can be solved automatically propose first offers of value or counter offers according to the type of support for the negotiations offered. Such systems can help bring forward the agreement making process for these negotiations whilst at the same time reducing the distortions associated it has led to errors and bias.

Table 1. AI Technologies used and applications

AI Technology	Application	Description
Machine Learning (ML)	Data Analysis	analyzes a lot of historical data to find trends in the resolution of conflicts and negotiations.
	Predictive Analytics	makes predictions about counterparty behavior and possible negotiating outcomes based on historical data.
Natural Language Processing (NLP)	Text Analysis	Analyzes negotiation communications to identify sentiments and intents (e.g., cooperative vs. adversarial).
	Automated Communication	Automates communication processes using AI-driven chatbots or virtual assistants, facilitating information exchange and freeing up time for negotiators.
Decision Support Systems (DSS)	Strategic Recommendations	Evaluates multiple solutions and recommends the best negotiation strategy by comparing previous data, market conditions, and negotiation objectives.
	Scenario Simulation	Models' potential negotiation scenarios to predict outcomes, risks, and opportunities.
	Conflict Resolution Automation	Uses AI to automatically develop offers or counteroffers, accelerating negotiation process and reducing subjective biases.

3.2 AI's Advantages in Negotiation and Conflict Resolution

AI has thus influenced conflict solving and negotiating in that it increases competence, reliability and effectiveness and fairness. These are enhanced capability in terms of data analysis and decision making and cost saving. Which will result in improved and efficient results. Machine Learning and Data mining is all about featured training. Large amounts of data into classifiers through recognition of patterns, or other techniques which can be used to teach them regarding the data and classify it into degrees of certainty or particular sets of groups It will also be possible for the

AI to determine trends of previous negotiations and motivations, including interests and needs, and bargaining power for power and control, and hostility like economic, political and cultural systems, and cultures that facilitate negotiations. Rather to cooperate with peers who have a different approach to what is in the process of emerging into mainstream. Sentiment analysis tools, some subareas of knowledge technologies related to artificial intelligence can identify the emotion and complex attitudinal conditions of negotiators that let them recognize shifts in the very process of negotiations and to be able to adapt well to changes within the shortest possible time. By accepting data that may be useful in informing conflicts decisions, artificial intelligence This case illustrates that (AI) improves decision making during conflict solving. Conventional bi and tri-lateral negotiation arrangements involve the hiring experienced and self-intuitive negotiators, which can be supported by AI as a form of a more vast and unbiased data scrutinising tool. Predictive analytics by use of the technology AI systems, can be used to predict the likely sequelae of the different negotiations' strategies based on past happenings reducing some degree of equivocality of negotiations and allowing the decision-makers to make appropriate decisions. AI can generate many a negotiation situation to help the parties evaluate the risks of the Agreement to them doing it because there used to be more approaches developed prior to implementation, making it more strategic and real deciding possible gains and hazards connected with each decision.

Compared to traditional approaches that are costly and time-consuming because of drawn-out negotiations, complex research, and multi-stakeholder participation, artificial intelligence (AI) improves cost effectiveness in conflict management and negotiation through process automation, minimizes human interference, and shortens the resolution time. AI may be utilized efficiently in ODR systems to mediate conflicts, doing away with traditional human mediators, cutting expenses, and speeding up the process. For negotiation and dispute resolution to be fair and equitable, ethical issues including bias, openness, and possible over-reliance need to be taken into consideration. Recounts must not reinforce data inequality, hence AI in these systems must be designed and handled carefully. By offering suggestions and varying viewpoints during negotiations, AI can support decision-making processes; nevertheless, it still needs human input to determine which ethical course of action to take. Artificial intelligence (AI) should be utilized as a tool, not as a weapon to replace human judgment in conflict-related situations.

4. THEORETICAL FRAMEWORK

The results of this study on AI's function in negotiation and conflict resolution have important theoretical and practical ramifications. Such implications also expand on the understanding of information not only about the state of knowledge in the field but also with practical suggestions for AI developers, policymakers, and OSCEs are most readily applicable to conflict resolution professionals (Ross et al., 2000).

i. **Theoretical Implications:**

The appropriation of AI in conflict and negotiation has left theories that revolve around which are interpersonal skills, listening, politeness, and persuasion. AI can use quantitative support to enable decisions, for instance for decision sciences of big data and determinism in engineering negotiations. This means that data is at the heart of bargaining strategies as well as the ideas of bargaining designs automated cognitive responses for bargaining and an evaluation of self- and emotion-regulation processes (Blount et al., 2017). AI as a mediator begins to present a new type of neutrality that, to the best of the author's knowledge, does not exist within the legal system. Traditional models, since the current strategies demand that human mediators be as neutral as possible, they may be less inclined to tilt a game. However, concerns from recommendations concerning biases related to AI algorithms claim that the notion of neutrality in mediation should be changed bearing in mind AI. Therefore, power relations in negotiation are also shaped by the use of artificial intelligence. Current theories rely on aspects of power relations in the conflict and how to address them so as to come up with a solution meaning responsiveness of message content to be adequate and acceptable to the sender and the receiver (Adler et al., 2000). This influenced the application of the considerable AI capabilities that could be utilised. There are diverse suggestions that the identifying and estimating in bargaining may change these relations, improving one's position new structuring of power foundations of positional haggling.

ii. **Practical Implications:**

This can be attributed to how the study focuses on the need to consider ethic, justice, and openness in emerging, prescribing and applying AI technology for negotiation and conflict management. AI developers should focus on reducing biases and getting to the next level of explain ability of AI's action to gain public trust. The governments should enforce policies acceptable to control the application of AI in conflict solving process, including responsibility disclosure, and protect liberties (Robinson et al., 2020). Certification agencies should oversee AI systems in confidential sectors. Conflict resolution professionals should receive training on AI tools, their strengths and weaknesses, and how to mediate between AI and human intuition. Training may also cover analysing AI results, ethically addressing AI negotiations, and maintaining humanistic approach. Professionals must push for the integration of AI systems with principles governing effective conflict resolution, such as fairness, understanding, and respect.

iii. **Broader Implications**

On the social level there are lessons that are apparent from the study, and these relate to the entire society. This is because as AI continues to be adopted in dispute resolution and negotiations, the society may benefit from the following effects; access to legal aid services, cost saving as well as productivity and through them positive contribution to world peace. Nevertheless, such advantages should not overshadow the potential pitfalls such as; the complications arising from prejudice of the artificial intelligence AI, the removal of humans from the creative process or decision-making process and the quest ethical questions that AI brings along (Truby et al., 2020).

5. DIFFICULTIES AND ETHICAL ISSUES

Although there is a lot of promise for using AI in negotiation and conflict resolution, there are also moral questions that need to be addressed, including prejudice, accountability, transparency, and over-reliance. Inaccurate outcomes and a decline in trust in AI systems can result from bias, which can be brought on by historical data bias, training data bias, and algorithmic prejudice. The intricacy of AI decision-making algorithms, which can be challenging to explain to people involved, gives rise to transparency issues. Explain ability is vital for users to understand how decisions are made, yet complicated neural networks may be non-interpretable, leading to skepticism and rejection. High-stakes negotiations present additional challenges for accountability since it can be difficult to assign blame for unfavorable outcomes. Effective negotiating requires human judgment, inventiveness, and emotional intelligence—qualities that might be undermined by an over-reliance on AI. Over-reliance carries risks such as degraded activity levels, diminished personal agency, and diminished critical thinking. Accountability and ethical issues continue to be intertwined; in order to avoid bias in data and algorithms and improve overall equality, fairness calls for the use of suitable procedures, evaluation, and implementation. Building trust in AI systems requires transparency because stakeholders must comprehend AI decision-making procedures and have faith in the facts and reasoning they use. Artificial intelligence (AI) in conflict resolution should be used carefully to preserve human agency, guarantee the active participation of negotiators, and enhance rather than replace human judgment and inventiveness. It is essential to address these problems if AI is to be used responsibly and successfully in delicate situations.

5.1 Case Study Selection

It is a fact that case studies have their usefulness when it comes to the explanation and elaboration of concepts and technologies in motional contexts, they are important for any learner and particularly important for learners exploring AI in conflict resolution and negotiation. It explains criteria for case selection and gives example of how AI has influenced these processes.

i. **Criteria for Selecting Case Studies**

The instances were chosen based on a set of criteria that included their suitability, relevance, and insight for the research issues that were the main focus. The following criteria were used in this study's selection of case studies:The following criteria were used in this study's selection of case studies:

- **Relevance to AI in Conflict Resolution and Negotiation:** The first and crucial condition that a case has to fulfill is that the case should be concerning the use of AI in conflict or negotiation. This makes it possible to have a direct connection with the research topic and what the case can offer in as far as illustrating how such AI technologies are being implemented within these processes. Preference is given to cases where AI constitutes either a positive enabler, mediator or optimiser of negotiation strategies.
- **Diversity of Contexts:** This means that for the purpose of capturing a wide variety of applications and effects of AI it is necessary to choose cases from different areas. This involves examples of contracts from various fields of life like diplomatic representation, business, and commerce, ODR and other sections of the community. Thus, by choosing cases from different settings, the research can explore its settings and identify how AI works in different scenarios (Yin 2017).
- **Availability of Data:** The second relevant criterion is whether the data available are rich and accurate. Every chosen case should have enough documentation, reports, or interview data to give a clear picture of the AI application under consideration. The first is preferred over the second because they con-

tain a wealth of information for analysis, including successes and failures (Eisenhardt and Graebner, 2007).

- **Illustrative of Key Issues:** Such case selection should focus on the subject matter of the research like; AI in conflict, AI and ethical dilemmas, AI in human-related tasks among others. Alternatively, it is necessary to use the cases which show both the positive impact and the possible drawbacks of the AI application in this sphere, as it gives a fallow view of the AI role in this domain (Stake, 1995).
- **Innovativeness and Pioneering Use:** Special attention is paid to the cases showcasing the best or at least new examples of the AI application in conflict and negotiation. The future of AI in these fields may be realized or pointed in these instances; these cases might offer some guidance for what is on the horizon in regards to AI. It can also show how the pioneers are having it hard but coming up with ways of using AI in conflict solution (Flyvbjerg, 2006).

ii. **Examples of Cases Studied**

A number of case studies are chosen to investigate AI's function in negotiation and dispute resolution based on the aforementioned parameters. These examples show a wide range of settings and applications, providing in-depth understandings of how AI is changing these procedures.

- **International Diplomacy:** Some of the examples of a case study in this category are the application of AI tools in international peace negotiations. For example, autonomous systems help AI to employ array of data derived from the earlier negotiations, make assessment of the possible topics of the disagreements, and provide suggestions as for how the disputing sides may reach a common ground. An example is the utilization of AI for backing up negotiations in the Middle East whereby AI applications have been utilized to design probable negotiation situations and estimate likely results with a view to assisting the diplomats (Nye, 2019).
- **Corporate Negotiations:** Another example can be preliminary negotiations using artificial intelligence platforms in large companies. In this regard, AI is employed in resolution of disputes between firms especially where massive data require use in arriving at the resolution. In the IT industry, for instance, parties employ AI negation systems to set up automated discussions. For example, the system generates opening proposals based on available data and evaluates the likelihood of agreement on different offers (Zeng et al., 2020).
- **Platforms for Online Dispute Resolution (ODR):** Using AI in online dispute resolution platforms is one of the most significant areas of application.

Artificial intelligence is utilized by these platforms to facilitate the resolution of conflicts among users in domains such as online commerce, law, and customer relations. For example, businesses like eBay have embraced the use of cutting-edge AI technology to facilitate online dispute resolution (ODR) in order to expedite the process and handle and resolve conflicts between buyers and sellers independently and without human intervention. Katz and associates (2006) and Rabinovich-Einy (2017)).

5.2 Ethical Considerations

The ethical issues surrounding studies employing artificial intelligence in negotiation and conflict are covered in this section. In order to protect the welfare of all parties involved, it highlights the significance of informed consent, confidentiality, and data integrity. An information document outlining the goals, methods, and data handling of the study will be sent to participants Particular attention will be paid to the reason participant participants should have interaction the utilization of the tools to sensitive sessions. Anonymity of the participants and information that has been gathered in the case of any conflict resolution or negotiation information must therefore remain private. All identifying information of participants will be removed, and replaced with pseudonyms or anonymous codes in the transcripts, reports or publications. To guard against loss of data precautions will be taken; computerized records will include password protection; on physical records they will be kept in locked cabinets and rooms. The accuracy of stored data is paramount in any research to produce sound results as seen in this technological investigation of AI. Additionally, all collected data will be documented and practically analyzed by researchers to provide reliable and accurate information. In executing their work, researchers should not bring in bias and should approach AI tools critically in order to avoid preconceived results. Positive reporting will be possible in this research involving clear documentation of collecting and analyzing pathways and design so that other stakeholders can follow up on the work with ease.

6. ANALYSIS OF CASE STUDIES

Through case studies, this study investigates the application of AI technology in negotiation and dispute resolution. It presents findings on AI's efficiency, challenges, and the practical aspects of AI integration. The cases include international diplomacy, corporate negotiations, and online dispute resolution platforms. AI has been applied to provide data analysis and scenario building during negotiations, such as peace making or trade. However, limitations include mimicking human emotions and recording political processes. In corporate negotiations, AI-driven platforms create first offers based on previous statistics, accelerating negotiations and decreasing costs. However, these models could reflect bias in data and require supervision for equality. Online dispute resolution platforms have been effective in e-commerce, legal issues, and consumer concerns, with eBay using AI for handling conflicts.

The effectiveness of AI in the analyzed case studies varied based on the context and the specific application of the technology. In international diplomacy, AI is effective in data analysis and strategic recommendations but struggles to fully understand the emotional and political nuances of human negotiation. AI processes vast volumes of data rapidly, which increases productivity and lowers costs in business discussions. But continuous human inspection and possible bias in the data could make it less successful. Because AI is automated, it has shown to be useful in ODR platforms for swiftly and fairly settling disputes. But for there to be justice for everybody, users' trust in AI's judgments and transparency are essential. Some issues that concern the implementation of AI in solving disputes and negotiations are as follows: AI and bias, openness and trust and the monitoring of AI. Nevertheless, the kind of AI systems such as these can obtain further information for the decision making; however, it still remains important to make sure that the recommended strategies are proper, moral, lawful, effective, and in accordance to the negotiation objectives or to the goals of solving a dispute.

6.1 Thematic Insights

AI's capacity for data analysis, forecasting, and pattern recognition makes it an invaluable tool for negotiation and dispute resolution. It is an essential tool since it may model issues and illustrate possible outcomes of talks. However, because AI can amplify or reinforce preconceptions in decision-making processes, bias in the system raises serious ethical concerns. For AI systems to be fair, ongoing testing and assessment are required. In order to ensure user confidence and equity in AI-related judgments, transparency is essential. Since AI tools are limited in their ability to understand emotions, motivation, and culture, the effect they will have on human agency in negotiation is a matter of great worry. Applications of artificial intelligence for negotiation and conflict management differ from one another when compared. Understanding these differences is critical for producing good and safe artificial intelligence. It focuses on the benefits and drawbacks of the AI approach, as well as potential contributions to dispute resolution and negotiation. Machine learning, natural language processing and other AI technologies integrate into such activities as international diplomacy and business negotiating. Because it provides the necessary data, automates laborious operations, and makes forecasts, it is in charge of improving decision-making. The study does, however, also highlight several immoral elements, such as bias in AI, the algorithms' black-box nature, excessive reliance, and liability issues with AI decisions.

i. Probabilities for Developing Role of AI in Negotiation and Conflict Management

In the study, it is focused upon the role of AI in negotiation and on how such systems have developed contextual and therefore more advanced advise that can be provided. It also raises a concern for more supporting the AI primary research for improving the interpretability and trying to avoid the unfairness threats pointed out in this paper's (K. S. Hassan et al., 2021) ethical concern on the application of AI in conflict resolution and for that, establishing good ethical principles and enforcing appropriate legal frameworks for the operation of artificial intelligence must be developed. The study also underlines the status of AI into conflict resolution but arguing for Human-in-the-loop where it prioritizes human knowledge, emotions, and skill, not to mention creativity. AI is transforming conflict management strategies globally in the long run concerning dispute resolution but must be regulated to remove bias or unfair decision making.

7. ETHICAL FRAMEWORK

It is pertinent to note that use and Incorporation of AI in conflict resolution and negotiation necessitates fixed codes of conduct on ethical protocol thus the rules of transparency and fairness cannot be overemphasized. Some of these components must be based on trust and ethical framework should address the AI system some of these aspects. The use of AI entails a certain level of transparency because results may have serious implications on those involved. Responsibility in artificial intelligent decision-making means that an algorithm and data used by an AI must be transparent to users so that they can ask questions regarding the results offered by the AI system. It is also vital to communicate when it comes to the debate of the concepts that can be valorised with the help of AI, including the feature analysis of the big data, machine learning, carrying out decisions on a large scale. Transparency can always be accompanied by auditability or documentation since, for the AI system to be designed with some desirable characteristics such as data utilization, computation, and reasoning, the system should also be designed to avail its documentation of function to prevent biased actions. There is a non-discrimination analysis, bias minimization, equalization, and reasonable accommodation, as well as reasonable outcomes from the AI applications.

For the purpose of ensuring the safe use of AI in negotiation and dispute resolution and so as to have well identified responsibility when something goes wrong with the system, accountability is necessary. An ethical framework should in its guidelines define behavioural patterns for AI developers, consumers, and investors to have legal awareness. While constructing the systems, the developers should not bring consciousness to their methods of working but consumers should also portray professionalism once they adopt the AI suggestions. Redress should be possible when the outcomes of the AI systems are adverse or even unjust, such as, the right of appeal and reimbursement or individuals influenced. This creates pressure on the use of the systems and at the same time builds the confidence of the public on them. There is something that is missing in the use of AI in resolving disputes, this is the ethical consideration, that must be followed in monitor and governance. This means creating committees or boards that will examine the AI systems, determine how well they fit into the ethical standards or benchmarks, or that check the existing policies as new AI technologies appear, and more sophisticated models are implemented.

8. SOLUTIONS AND RECOMMENDATIONS

The interaction of AI systems can be specifically crucial in handling of some of the conflicts but it at the same time holds some sort of nuances. Since biases also affect fairness, biases should also be checked at the design stage by the developers for an accurate sample such as the data set that would fairly represent all the groups. It is unbecoming of the AI algorithms not to allow for their neutrality to be audited occasionally. XAI can assist users in understanding how conclusions were made and give an ''ask why'' button, in case the individual chose to disagree (Silva et al., 2023). Ethical relevancies, data management, as well as AI applicability make up elements of educational programme for conflict resolution professionals. AI should be developed as a machine that doesn't have any prejudice in relation to feelings and being harmonized and is developing under the umbrella of an ultimate objective to remain impartial regarding algorithms. One of them is the issues connected to power where on one side AI can suggest actions based on the given analysis or produce some insights but on the other must bow to human decisions where unethical or emotional aspects may not be encoded. Responsible AI systems entail that all the parties should have an equal opportunity of support and analysis (Arrieta et al., 2020). Integrating AI with the mixed humanistic models can enhance the operational performance of the negotiations without removing the human aspect of the consideration. The guidelines that should be in place as it relates to the use of

AI in conflict resolution should be; accountability; transparency; as well as human rights protection from AI. For the attempt to build the trust in AI one must explain what AI is to users, practitioners, and stakeholders, and to learn how to reach out those who are left out by the digitalization.

There is a need to study AI with regards to conflict resolution processes to determine the effectiveness and equity of processes involved. This should cover; surveys, research articles, cases, and implementations in different conflict zones. In order to investigate possible social, ethical, and legal issues related to the application of artificial intelligence in negotiations and conflicts, civil authorities should collaborate with academic institutions and research centers. Ethical AI Development has been deemed necessary with stress on a set of principles. Governments and organisations should form AI ethics committees that will be a broad guide to the international community. It is crucial that any broad and detailed AI ethics should include explain ability, fairness, and human control to ensure that artificial intelligence applications meet human values and rights. Most of the AI applications should be designed for professionals who engage in conflict transformation endeavours with help of mediators and negotiators (Round et al., 2024). When human interaction with AI targets conflict resolution institutions, unique, easy to use applications can augment decision making. There is a need for AI developers, policymakers, social, and conflict resolution scientists in coming up with interdisciplinary solutions that reflect the need for combining both technical and humanism approaches. Some of the ways, through which new ideas and best practices in the sphere of employing AI in conflict solving can be discussed, are the creation Data and idea-sharing think tanks and collaboration platforms. It is recommended that a global certification program be created and implemented for the authorized use of AI in conflict systems, complete with annual certification body reviews and the requisite ethical compliance.

9. FUTURE RESEARCH DIRECTIONS

This literature review aims at understanding the application of AI in conflict and especially in conflict resolution and negotiation; the development and adaptation of AI use in different kinds of conflicts, new ethic and regulatory question that arose with the use of new technologies. Further research should encompass: Cross-sectional research to assess AI's effectiveness in various conflict scenarios, longitudinal research to compare AI's long-term effectiveness and efficiency, and the development of suitable ethics for AI in conflict management. The purpose is to find out new types of human and artificial intelligence cooperation in conflict solving procedures; using AI as one of the components of a complex approach based on its abilities to complement other elements. This will help to build models that enhance decisions and produce better results and at the same time create human oversight. Furthermore, research has to consider how to manage bias in case AI is involved in a conflict and how to prevent the system from using gender-stereotyped language or language sensitive to race matters. The method of use of AI of strength and influence in negotiation and dispute resolution will determine the use of AI in conflict resolutions to prevent situations that can worsen the injustice among the conflicting parties (Amsler et al., 2020). Additionally, more efforts should be devoted to the further understanding of the capacity of AI to analyze data provided by multiple parties and to provide new solutions in a context of multilateral negotiations. The skills for conflict resolution should mandate the recognition of abilities and limitations of AI, while the survey as well as the experimental research works should examine the lack of public confidence in the AI-driven conflict resolution systems. Finally, there is the need to establish how AI can advance the area of conflict prediction involving analysing social, political, and economical data and developing how to avoid conflicts when they are yet to happen. Such future research directions will help to enhance knowledge regarding the application of AI tools for conflict transformation and negotiation, and buttressed by the empirical data, ethical imperatives, and working models of human–AI cooperation.

10. CONCLUSION

The subject of the research comprehensively addresses the challenges that AI brings to the old approaches to conflict resolution and contract sharing. Applying these elements as machine learning, natural language processing, decision supporting systems, AI makes these processes more accurate and effective (Venigandla et al., 2022). Artificial Intelligence has been utilized in the analysis of extensive data sets to infer valuable patterns, predict possible outcomes of negotiations, and generate practical suggestions to support negotiators. Additionally, the use of AI systems in decision-making will indicate improved impartiality and justice in conflict resolution processes because these systems are emotionless. In addition, the inclusion of AI brings about serious ethical concerns that include; issues to do with the bias of the algorithms used, lack of traceability, and accountability of the systems used. The above issues beg for code of ethics and practices, and public declaration of all algorithms using artificial intelligence with an eye on independence and impartiality (Fernández et al., 2022). The study focuses on the need to have humans involved in the control of the processes where AI is applied especially in decision making where there are ethical issues and emotions to deal with.AI use in conflict resolution therefore has to be done in a manner that would ensure that AI's main strength of handling large data sets in handled in a balanced way by the emotional and ethical judgement of individuals.

REFERENCES

Adler, R. S., & Silverstein, E. M. (2000). When David meets Goliath: Dealing with power differentials in negotiations. *Harv. Negot. L. Rev.*, 5, 1.

Amsler, L. B., Martinez, J., & Smith, S. E. (2020). *Dispute system design: Preventing, managing, and resolving conflict.* Stanford University Press. DOI: 10.1515/9781503611368

Anumba, C. J., & Ruikar, K. (2002). Electronic commerce in construction—Trends and prospects. *Automation in Construction*, 11(3), 265–275. DOI: 10.1016/S0926-5805(01)00087-5

Arrieta, A. B., Díaz-Rodríguez, N., Del Ser, J., Bennetot, A., Tabik, S., Barbado, A., & Herrera, F. (2020). Explainable Artificial Intelligence (XAI): Concepts, taxonomies, opportunities and challenges toward responsible AI. *Information Fusion*, 58, 82–115. DOI: 10.1016/j.inffus.2019.12.012

Blount, J. (2017). *Sales EQ: how ultra high performers leverage sales-specific emotional intelligence to close the complex deal.* John Wiley & Sons.

Booth, A., James, M. S., Clowes, M., & Sutton, A. (2021). Systematic approaches to a successful literature review.

Bouarfa, S., Aydoğan, R., & Sharpanskykh, A. (2021). Formal modelling and verification of a multi-agent negotiation approach for airline operations control. *Journal of Reliable Intelligent Environments*, 7(4), 279–298. DOI: 10.1007/s40860-020-00123-0

Caputo, A., Pizzi, S., Pellegrini, M. M., & Dabić, M. (2021). Digitalization and business models: Where are we going? A science map of the field. *Journal of Business Research*, 123, 489–501. DOI: 10.1016/j.jbusres.2020.09.053

Card, D., Zhang, M., & Smith, N. A. (2019, January). Deep weighted averaging classifiers. In *Proceedings of the conference on fairness, accountability, and transparency* (pp. 369-378). DOI: 10.1145/3287560.3287595

Creswell, J. W. (2014). *Research design: Qualitative, quantitative, and mixed methods approach* (4th ed.). SAGE Publications.

Deutsch, M., Coleman, P. T., & Marcus, E. C. (2014). *The handbook of conflict resolution: Theory and practice.* John Wiley & Sons.

Fernández Fernández, J. L. (2022). Ethical considerations regarding biases in algorithms.

Fisher, R., Ury, W., & Patton, B. (2008). *Negotiating agreement without giving in*. Penguin Putnam Incorporated.

Floridi, L., Cowls, J., Beltrametti, M., Chatila, R., Chazerand, P., Dignum, V., Luetge, C., Madelin, R., Pagallo, U., Rossi, F., Schafer, B., Valcke, P., & Vayena, E. (2018). AI4People—an ethical framework for a good AI society: Opportunities, risks, principles, and recommendations. *Minds and Machines*, 28(4), 689–707. DOI: 10.1007/s11023-018-9482-5 PMID: 30930541

Galanos, V. (2023). Expectations and expertise in artificial intelligence: specialist views and historical perspectives on conceptualisation, promise, and funding.

Huberman, A. (2014). Qualitative data analysis a methods sourcebook.

Jennings, N. R., Faratin, P., Lomuscio, A. R., Parsons, S., Sierra, C., & Wooldridge, M. (2001). Automated negotiation: Prospects, methods and challenges. *Group Decision and Negotiation*, 10(2), 199–215. DOI: 10.1023/A:1008746126376

Johnson, R. B., & Onwuegbuzie, A. J. (2004). Mixed methods research: A research paradigm whose time has come. *Educational Researcher*, 33(7), 14–26. DOI: 10.3102/0013189X033007014

Katsh, E., & Wing, L. (2006). Ten years of online dispute resolution (ODR): Looking at the past and constructing the future. *U. Tol. L. Rev.*, 38, 19.

Kersten, G. E., & Lo, G. (2003). Aspire: An integrated negotiation support system and software agents for e-business negotiation. *International Journal of Internet and Enterprise Management*, 1(3), 293–315. DOI: 10.1504/IJIEM.2003.003822

Kumar, Y., Koul, A., Singla, R., & Ijaz, M. F. (2023). Artificial intelligence in disease diagnosis: A systematic literature review, synthesizing framework and future research agenda. *Journal of Ambient Intelligence and Humanized Computing*, 14(7), 8459–8486. DOI: 10.1007/s12652-021-03612-z PMID: 35039756

Kvale, S. (2009). Interviews: Learning the craft of qualitative research interviewing. *Sage (Atlanta, Ga.)*.

Mittelstadt, B. D., Allo, P., Taddeo, M., Wachter, S., & Floridi, L. (2016). The ethics of algorithms: Mapping the debate. *Big Data & Society*, 3(2), 2053951716679679. DOI: 10.1177/2053951716679679

Nie, Y., Tian, Y., Wan, X., Song, Y., & Dai, B. (2020). Named entity recognition for social media texts with semantic augmentation. arXiv preprint arXiv:2010.15458. DOI: 10.18653/v1/2020.emnlp-main.107

Rahman, M. S. (2016). The advantages and disadvantages of using qualitative and quantitative approaches and methods in language "testing and assessment" research: A literature review. Journal of education and learning, 6(1).

Robinson, S. C. (2020). Trust, transparency, and openness: How inclusion of cultural values shapes Nordic national public policy strategies for artificial intelligence (AI). *Technology in Society*, 63, 101421. DOI: 10.1016/j.techsoc.2020.101421

Ross, M. H. (2000). Creating the conditions for peacemaking: Theories of practice in ethnic conflict resolution. *Ethnic and Racial Studies*, 23(6), 1002–1034. DOI: 10.1080/014198700750018397

Round, C. (2024). Digitizing Responsibility: Emerging Technologies and Power in Environmental and Informational Governance (Doctoral dissertation, George Mason University).

Russo, D. (2024). Navigating the complexity of generative ai adoption in software engineering. *ACM Transactions on Software Engineering and Methodology*, 33(5), 1–50. DOI: 10.1145/3652154

Silva, A., Schrum, M., Hedlund-Botti, E., Gopalan, N., & Gombolay, M. (2023). Explainable artificial intelligence: Evaluating the objective and subjective impacts of xai on human-agent interaction. *International Journal of Human-Computer Interaction*, 39(7), 1390–1404. DOI: 10.1080/10447318.2022.2101698

Sycara, K. P. (1991). Problem restructuring in negotiation. *Management Science*, 37(10), 1248–1268. DOI: 10.1287/mnsc.37.10.1248

Sycara, K. P. (1993). Machine learning for intelligent support of conflict resolution. *Decision Support Systems*, 10(2), 121–136. DOI: 10.1016/0167-9236(93)90034-Z

Tashakkori, A., & Teddlie, C. (2003). *Handbook of mixed methods in social and behavioral research*. SAGE Publications.

Topol, E. (2019). *Deep medicine: How artificial intelligence can make healthcare human again*. Basic Books.

Truby, J. (2020). Governing artificial intelligence to benefit the UN sustainable development goals. *Sustainable Development (Bradford)*, 28(4), 946–959. DOI: 10.1002/sd.2048

Yin, R. K. (2018). Case study research and applications.

Yuan, Y., Ma, M., Han, S., Zhang, D., Miao, F., Stankovic, J., & Lin, S. (2021, May). DeResolver: a decentralized negotiation and conflict resolution framework for smart city services. In *Proceedings of the ACM/IEEE 12th International Conference on Cyber-Physical Systems* (pp. 98-109). DOI: 10.1145/3450267.3450538

KEY TERMS AND DEFINITIONS

Artificial Intelligence: The simulation of human intelligence processes by computer systems, including learning, reasoning, and self-correction.

Bias in AI: The presence of systematic and unfair discrimination in AI algorithms, often resulting from biased training data or flawed design.

Conflict Resolution: The methods and processes involved in facilitating the peaceful ending of a conflict, often through negotiation, mediation, or arbitration.

Decision-Making: The cognitive process of selecting a course of action from multiple alternatives, often supported by data and analytical tools.

Ethical AI: The principles and practices that ensure AI technologies are developed and used in ways that are fair, transparent, and respect human rights.

Human-AI Collaboration: The interaction between human decision-makers and AI systems to enhance decision-making processes and outcomes.

Machine Learning: A subset of AI that enables systems to learn from data, identify patterns, and make decisions with minimal human intervention.

Negotiation: A dialogue between two or more parties aimed at reaching a mutually acceptable agreement or resolving a dispute.

Predictive Analytics: The use of statistical algorithms and machine learning techniques to identify the likelihood of future outcomes based on historical data.

Transparency: The degree to which AI systems make their processes, decisions, and underlying data understandable and accessible to users.

Compilation of References

Aayog, N. I. T. I. (2018). *National Strategy for Artificial Intelligence*. Retrieved from NITI Aayog.

Aayog, N. I. T. I. (2022). *AI Policy and Regulation in India: Ensuring Fairness and Inclusivity*. Retrieved from NITI Aayog.

Aayog, N. I. T. I. (2023). *AI for Policy: Enhancing Governance through Technology*. NITI Aayog Publications.

Abubakar, A., & Al-Momani, M. (2023). Machine Learning Techniques for HR Analytics: A Review. *International Journal of Information Management*, 60, 102–115.

Accenture. (2017). Predictive Maintenance and the Smart Factory. Retrieved from https://www.accenture.com

Accenture. (2019). Artificial Intelligence: The Future of Work? Retrieved from https://www.accenture.com

Accenture. (2019). Leveraging AI for Workforce Planning at Royal Dutch Shell. Retrieved from https://www.accenture.com

Accenture. (2021). AI for Personalized Learning in the Workplace. Retrieved from https://www.accenture.com

Accenture. (2022). AI and the Future of Work. Retrieved from https://www.accenture.com

Accenture. (2023). *AI and Ethics: A Framework for Decision-Making*. Retrieved from Accenture.

Accenture. (2023). Leveraging AI for Workforce Planning at Royal Dutch Shell. Retrieved from https://www.accenture.com

Acs, Z. J., & Varga, A. (2005). Entrepreneurship, agglomeration and technological change. *Small Business Economics*, 24, 323–334. DOI: 10.1007/s11187-005-1998-4

Adeoye, B. (2020). The Role of AI in Enhancing Workforce Skills in Nigeria. Nigerian Journal of Technology.

Adisa, T. A., Ogbonnaya, C., & Adekoya, O. D. (2023). Remote working and employee engagement: A qualitative study of British workers during the pandemic. *Information Technology & People*, 36(5), 1835–1850. DOI: 10.1108/ITP-12-2020-0850

Adler, R. S., & Silverstein, E. M. (2000). When David meets Goliath: Dealing with power differentials in negotiations. *Harv. Negot. L. Rev.*, 5, 1.

Adoli, H. L., & Kilika, J. M. (2020). Conceptualizing the role of leadership strategy in the context of strategic management process: A review of literature. *Journal of Economics and Business*, 3(4), 1598–1623. DOI: 10.31014/aior.1992.03.04.307

Agarwal, R., & Prasad, J. (1997). The role of innovation characteristics and perceived voluntariness in the acceptance of information technologies. *Decision Sciences*, 28(3), 557–582. DOI: 10.1111/j.1540-5915.1997.tb01322.x

Agarwal, R., & Singh, S. (2023). Enhancing E-Commerce with AI: A Case Study of Jabong. *Journal of Indian Retailing*, 12(1), 56–72.

Agrawal A., Gans J., Goldfarb A. (2022). From prediction to transformation. Harvard Business Review, Nov/Dez 2022(BR2206), 100-109.

Agrawal, S., Chatterjee, K., & Novotný, P. (2017). Lexicographic ranking supermartingales: an efficient approach to termination of probabilistic programs. *Proceedings of the ACM on Programming Languages, 2*(POPL), 1-32.

Aguilar, I. (2023). *Consumer Experiences and Perceptions on Influencer Marketing: The Impact of Regulation Gaps on Content Creation in Mexico*. Dublin Business School.

Ahmed, N., Abbasi, M. S., Zuberi, F., Qamar, W., Halim, M. S. B., Maqsood, A., & Alam, M. K. (2021). Artificial intelligence techniques: Analysis, application, and outcome in dentistry—a systematic review. *BioMed Research International*, 2021(1), 1–15. DOI: 10.1155/2021/9751564 PMID: 34258283

Ahmed, S., Chowdhury, M., & Ghosh, D. (2021). Comparative Analysis of Time Series Forecasting Models: ARIMA vs. LSTM. *International Journal of Forecasting*, 37(2), 310–326.

Ahmed, S., & Khan, M. (2022). Predictive Analytics in HR: Using Machine Learning for Employee Retention. *Journal of Human Resource Management*, 10(2), 45–59.

AI Now Institute. (2022). *AI and Social Justice: Ethical Considerations*. Retrieved from AI Now Institute.

AI Now Institute. (2023). *The Future of AI and Its Impact on Decision-Making*. AI Now Institute Report.

AI4Dev. (2022). *AI for Development Initiatives in India*. Retrieved from AI4Dev.

Aira. (2021). *How Aira Works: AI-Powered Assistance for the Visually Impaired*. Retrieved from Aira.

Ajzen, I. (1991). The theory of planned behavior. *Organizational Behavior and Human Decision Processes*, 50(2), 179–211. DOI: 10.1016/0749-5978(91)90020-T

Al Hadwer, A., Tavana, M., Gillis, D., & Rezania, D. (2021). A systematic review of organizational factors impacting cloud-based technology adoption using technology-organization-environment framework. *Internet of Things : Engineering Cyber Physical Human Systems*, 15, 1–10. DOI: 10.1016/j.iot.2021.100407

Alblushi, A. (2021). Face recognition based on artificial neural network: A review. *Artificial Intelligence & Robotics Development Journal*, 1(2), 116–131. DOI: 10.52098/airdj.202125

Alegre, J., & Chiva, R. (2013). Linking entrepreneurial orientation and firm performance: The role of organizational learning capability and innovation performance. *Journal of Small Business Management*, 51(4), 491–507. DOI: 10.1111/jsbm.12005

Alexander, J., & Ellis, P. (2023). Data-Driven Recruitment: Transforming Talent Acquisition with AI. *HR Tech Review*, 17(1), 22–30.

Al-Ghaith, W., Sanzogni, L., & Sandhu, K. (2010). Factors influencing the adoption and usage of online services in Saudi Arabia. *The Electronic Journal on Information Systems in Developing Countries*, 40(1), 1–32. DOI: 10.1002/j.1681-4835.2010.tb00283.x

Al-Habaibeh, A., Watkins, M., Waried, K., & Javareshk, M. B. (2021). Challenges and opportunities of remotely working from home during Covid-19 pandemic. *Global Transitions*, 3, 99–108. DOI: 10.1016/j.glt.2021.11.001 PMID: 34870136

Alhosani, F. A., & Tariq, M. U. (2020). Improving Service quality of smart banking using quality management methods in UAE. [IJMPERD]. *International Journal of Mechanical Production Engineering Research and Development*, 10(3), 2249–8001.

Ali, S. S. (2024). *Nano influencers: using ordinary people for extraordinary results*.

Al-Jabri, I., & Sohail, M. S. (2012). Mobile banking adoption: Application of diffusion of innovation theory. *Journal of Electronic Commerce Research*, 13(4), 379–391.

Almaleki, W. S. A. (2020). *Saudi international students' perceptions of the utility of artificial intelligence and intelligent personal assistant tools in EFL learning* (Doctoral dissertation, Concordia University Chicago).

Almarzooqi, A. (2019). *Towards an artificial intelligence (AI)-driven government in the United Arab Emirates (UAE): a framework for transforming and augmenting leadership capabilities*. A dissertation submitted in partial satisfaction of the requirements for the degree of Doctor of Education in Organizational Leadership, Pepperdine University.

Aloise, D., Deshpande, A., Hansen, P., & Popat, P. (2009). NP-hard Euclidean sumof-squares clustering. *Machine Learning*, 75(2), 245–249. DOI: 10.1007/s10994-009-5103-0

Aloulou, W., Ayadi, F., Ramadani, V., & Dana, L. P. (2024). Dreaming digital or chasing new real pathways? Unveiling the determinants shaping Saudi youth's digital entrepreneurial intention. *International Journal of Entrepreneurial Behaviour & Research*, 30(2/3), 709–734. DOI: 10.1108/IJEBR-10-2022-0942

Alsaif, A., & Sabih Aksoy, M. (2023). AI-HRM: Artificial Intelligence in Human Resource Management: A Literature Review. *Journal of Computing and Communication*, 2(2), 1–7. DOI: 10.21608/jocc.2023.307053

Alsamhi, S. H., Ma, O., & Ansari, M. S. (2019). Survey on artificial intelligence based techniques for emerging robotic communication. *Telecommunication Systems*, 72(3), 483–503. DOI: 10.1007/s11235-019-00561-z

Alsheibani, S., Cheung, Y., & Messom, C. (2018). Artificial intelligence adoption: AI-readiness at firm-level. *Twenty-Second Pacific Asia Conference on Information Systems*, Japan 2018 (pp. 1-8). Association for Information Systems.

Al-Zyoud, M. F. (2021). The impact of gamification on consumer loyalty, electronic word-of-mouth sharing, and purchase behavior. *Journal of Public Affairs*, 21(3), e2263. DOI: 10.1002/pa.2263

Amaghouss, J., & Ibourk, A. (2013). Entrepreneurial activities, innovation and economic growth: The role of cyclical factors evidence from OECD countries for the period 2001-2009. *International Business Research*, 6(1), 153–162.

Amazon Web Services (AWS). (2022). *Responsible AI: Best Practices and Guidelines*. Retrieved from AWS.

Ammar, M., Haleem, A., Javaid, M., Walia, R., & Bahl, S. (2021). Improving material quality management and manufacturing organizations system through Industry 4.0 technologies. *Materials Today: Proceedings*, 45, 5089–5096. DOI: 10.1016/j.matpr.2021.01.585

Amsler, L. B., Martinez, J., & Smith, S. E. (2020). *Dispute system design: Preventing, managing, and resolving conflict*. Stanford University Press. DOI: 10.1515/9781503611368

Anderson, J., & Gupta, R. (2022). Machine Learning for Employee Performance Management: Benefits and Challenges. *Journal of Business Analytics*, 14(3), 78–89.

Angwin, J., Larson, J., Mattu, S., & Kirchner, L. (2016). *Machine bias: There's software used across the country to predict future criminals. And it's biased against blacks*. ProPublica.

An, J., Kwak, H., Jung, S., Salminen, J., & Jansen, B. J. (2018). Customer segmentation using online platforms: Isolating behavioral and demographic segments for persona creation via aggregated user data. *Social Network Analysis and Mining*, 8(1), 54. DOI: 10.1007/s13278-018-0531-0

Anshari, M., Syafrudin, M., Tan, A., Fitriyani, N. L., & Alas, Y. (2023). Optimisation of knowledge management (KM) with machine learning (ML) Enabled. *Information (Basel)*, 14(1), 1–15. DOI: 10.3390/info14010035

Antonakis, J., & Day, D. V. (2018). Leadership: Past, present, and future. In Antonakis, J., & Day, D. V. (Eds.), *The nature of leadership* (3rd ed., pp. 3–26). Sage Publications, Inc., DOI: 10.4135/9781506395029.n1

Antonakis, J., Fenley, M., & Liechti, S. (2011). Can charisma be taught? Tests of two interventions. *Academy of Management Learning & Education*, 10(3), 374–396. DOI: 10.5465/amle.2010.0012

Antona, M., Margetis, G., Ntoa, S., & Degen, H. (2023). Special issue on AI in HCI. *International Journal of Human-Computer Interaction*, 39(9), 1723–1726. DOI: 10.1080/10447318.2023.2177421

Anumba, C. J., & Ruikar, K. (2002). Electronic commerce in construction—Trends and prospects. *Automation in Construction*, 11(3), 265–275. DOI: 10.1016/S0926-5805(01)00087-5

Anwar, A., & Khan, M. (2022). Harnessing AI for Competitive Advantage: A Global Overview. *Journal of Competitive Intelligence*, 19(2), 58–72.

Argan, M., Dinç, H., Kaya, S., & Argan, M. T. (2022). Artificial Intelligence (AI) in advertising. Understanding and schematizing the behaviors of social media users. *ADCAIJ. Advances in Distributed Computing and Artificial Intelligence Journal, 11*(3), 331-348. https.//DOI: 10.14201/adcaij.28331

Arman, H., Al-Fulaij, S., Al-Qudsi, S., Alawadhi, A., & Al Ali, M. (2024). COVID-19 effect on accelerating technology and innovation in businesses. *Organizations and Markets in Emerging Economies*, 15(1(30)), 27–50. DOI: 10.15388/omee.2024.15.2

Arntz, M., Gregory, T., & Zierahn, U. (2016). The Risk of Automation for Jobs in OECD Countries: A Comparative Analysis, OECD Social, Employment and Migration Working Papers, No. 189, OECD Publishing, Paris. http://dx.doi.org/ DOI: 10.1787/1815199X

Arora, A., & Chiu, A. (2022). Artificial Intelligence in Strategic Decision Making: Current Trends and Future Directions. *Journal of Business Research*, 144, 318–331.

Arrieta, A. B., Díaz-Rodríguez, N., Del Ser, J., Bennetot, A., Tabik, S., Barbado, A., & Herrera, F. (2020). Explainable Artificial Intelligence (XAI): Concepts, taxonomies, opportunities and challenges toward responsible AI. *Information Fusion*, 58, 82–115. DOI: 10.1016/j.inffus.2019.12.012

Arsawan, I. W. E., Koval, V., Rajiani, I., Rustiarini, N. W., Supartha, W. G., & Suryantini, N. P. S. (2022). Leveraging knowledge sharing and innovation culture into SMEs sustainable competitive advantage. *International Journal of Productivity and Performance Management*, 71(2), 405–428. DOI: 10.1108/IJPPM-04-2020-0192

Arthur, T. O. (2022). "We Bring Home the Roots": Black Women Travel Influencers, Digital Culture Bearing, and African Internationalism in Instagram. *Social Media + Society*, 8(2), 20563051221103844. DOI: 10.1177/20563051221103843

Arucu, M. (2021). Industry 4.0–holistic perspective: Modeling and simulation implementations in manufacturing systems. *Journal of Innovative Science and Engineering*, 5(1), 50–63.

Asdecker, B. (2022). Travel-related influencer content on Instagram: How social media fuels wanderlust and how to mitigate the effect. *Sustainability (Basel)*, 14(2), 855. DOI: 10.3390/su14020855

Askarany, D., Smith, M., & Yazdifar, H. (2007). Attributes of innovation and the implementation of managerial tools: An activity-based management technique. *International Journal of Business and Systems Research*, 1(1), 98–114. DOI: 10.1504/IJBSR.2007.014776

Aslam, W., & de Luna, I. R. (2021). The relationship between brand Facebook page characteristics, perceived value, and customer engagement behavior: An application of Stimulus-Organism-Response (SOR). *Revista Brasileira de Gestão de Negócios*, 23, 43–62. DOI: 10.7819/rbgn.v23i1.4092

Audy Martínek, P. (2021). Mapping methods of research on consumer engagement with brands on social media: A literature review. *Methodological Innovations*, 14(1), 2059799120985384. DOI: 10.1177/2059799120985384

Avdeenko, T. V., Makarova, E. S., & Klavsuts, I. L. (2016, October). Artificial intelligence support of knowledge transformation in knowledge management systems. In *2016 13th International Scientific-Technical Conference on Actual Problems of Electronics Instrument Engineering (APEIE)* (Vol. 3, pp. 195-201). IEEE. DOI: 10.1109/APEIE.2016.7807053

Awa, H. O., Ojiabo, O. U., & Orokor, L. E. (2017). Integrated technology-organization-environment (TOE) taxonomies for technology adoption. *Journal of Enterprise Information Management*, 30(6), 893–921. DOI: 10.1108/JEIM-03-2016-0079

Aydemir, E. (2018). Weka ile yapay zeka. *Seçkin Yayınevi, Ankara*, Türkiye.

Ayfie. (2023). AI for Regulatory Compliance and Auditing. *Ayfie Technologies.*

Ayfie. (2023). AI for Regulatory Compliance and Auditing. *Ayfie Technologies.* Retrieved from Ayfie

Ayfie, T. (2023). AI and Compliance: Emerging Trends. *Global Compliance Journal*, 12(4), 78–89.

Azhar, M., Husain, R., Hamid, S., & Rahman, M. N. (2023). Effect of social media marketing on online travel purchase behavior post-COVID-19: Mediating role of brand trust and brand loyalty. *Future Business Journal*, 9(1), 13. DOI: 10.1186/s43093-023-00192-6

Bahrammirzaee, A. (2010). A comparative survey of artificial intelligence applications in finance: Artificial neural networks, expert system and hybrid intelligent systems. *Neural Computing & Applications*, 19(8), 1165–1195. DOI: 10.1007/s00521-010-0362-z

Bail, C. A. (2014). The cultural environment: Measuring culture with big data. *Theory and Society*, 43(3-4), 465–482. DOI: 10.1007/s11186-014-9216-5

Baker, M., & Cross, T. (2021). AI-Powered Personalization: The Future of Customer Experience. *Harvard Business Review*, 99(5), 72–80.

Bakker, A. B., Demerouti, E., & Sanz-Vergel, A. (2023). Job demands–resources theory: Ten years later. *Annual Review of Organizational Psychology and Organizational Behavior*, 10(1), 25–53. DOI: 10.1146/annurev-orgpsych-120920-053933

Balaban, D. C., Mucundorfeanu, M., & Naderer, B. (2022). The role of trustworthiness in social media influencer advertising: Investigating users' appreciation of advertising transparency and its effects. *Communications*, 47(3), 395–421. DOI: 10.1515/commun-2020-0053

Balasubramanian, N., Ye, Y., & Xu, M. (2020). Substituting human decision-making with machine learning: Implications for organizational learning. *Academy of Management Review*, 47(3), 448–465. DOI: 10.5465/amr.2019.0470

Balkaya, E. (2017). *Üniversite Son Sınıf Öğrencilerinde İşsizlik Kaygısı ve Girişimcilik Niyeti İlişkisi; Tra1 Bölgesi Örneği, (Yayın numarası, 479419)* [Yüksek Lisans Tezi, Atatürk Üniversitesi]. Ulusal Tez Merkezi.

Banafaa, M., Shayea, I., Din, J., Hadri Azmi, M., Alashbi, A., Ibrahim Daradkeh, Y., & Alhammadi, A. (2023). 6G mobile communication technology: Requirements, targets, applications, challenges, advantages, and opportunities. *Alexandria Engineering Journal*, 64, 245–274. DOI: 10.1016/j.aej.2022.08.017

Banks, G. C., Woznyj, H. M., & Mansfield, C. A. (2021). Where is "behavior" in organizational behavior? A call for a revolution in leadership research and beyond. *The Leadership Quarterly*, 101581. Advance online publication. DOI: 10.1016/j.leaqua.2021.101581

Bansal, R., & Jain, A. (2023). The Impact of Machine Learning on Recruitment Processes in Indian Corporates. *Indian Journal of HRM*, 16(2), 102–117.

Baral, R., & Purohit, N. (2022). AI and ML in Talent Management: Current Trends and Future Directions. *International Journal of Talent Management*, 12(1), 50–65.

Barcelona City Council. (2019). AI in Urban Traffic Management. Retrieved from https://ajuntament.barcelona.cat

Basak, S., & Banerjee, A. (2023). Enhancing Employee Retention through ML: Case Studies and Insights. *Journal of Employment Relations*, 18(2), 34–47.

Bass, D. (2023). Microsoft to add ChatGPT to Azure Cloud Services 'soon'. Bloomberg. https://www.technologyreview.com/2023/08/02/238757/ai-could-be-your-wingmaner-wingboton-your-next-first-date/

Bastrygina, T., Lim, W. M., Jopp, R., & Weissmann, M. A. (2024). Unraveling the power of social media influencers: Qualitative insights into the role of Instagram influencers in the hospitality and tourism industry. *Journal of Hospitality and Tourism Management*, 58, 214–243. DOI: 10.1016/j.jhtm.2024.01.007

Basu, S., & Singh, P. (2023). AI and Hyper-Personalization in Indian E-Commerce: A Case Study of Flipkart. *Indian Journal of E-Commerce*, 18(4), 87–101.

Bates, D. W., Cohen, M., Leape, L. L., & Overhage, J. M. (2018). Reducing the Risk of Hospital Readmission Using Predictive Analytics. *Journal of Healthcare Management*, 63(2), 123–134.

Batool, S., Gill, S. A., Javaid, S., & Khan, A. J. (2021). Good governance via E-Governance: moving towards digitalization for a digital economy. *Review of applied management and social sciences, 4*(4), 823-836.

Battin, C. (2022). AI and Blockchain in Legal Dispute Resolution. *Harvard Law Review*, 134(5), 1223–1245.

Beck, T., & Peria, M. S. M. (2006). *Banking Services for Everyone?: Barriers to Bank Access and Use Around the World* (Vol. 4079). World Bank Publications. DOI: 10.1596/1813-9450-4079

Behera, R. K., Bala, P. K., Rana, N. P., & Irani, Z. (2023). Responsible natural language processing: A principlist framework for social benefits. *Technological Forecasting and Social Change*, 188, 1–16. DOI: 10.1016/j.techfore.2022.122306

Belchior, R. F., & Lyons, R. (2021). Explaining entrepreneurial intentions, nascent entrepreneurial behavior and new business creation with social cognitive career theory–a 5-year longitudinal analysis. *The International Entrepreneurship and Management Journal*, 17(4), 1945–1972. DOI: 10.1007/s11365-021-00745-7

Beňo, M. (2021). The advantages and disadvantages of E-working: An examination using an ALDINE analysis. *Emerging Science Journal*, 5, 11–20. DOI: 10.28991/esj-2021-SPER-02

Berkman Klein Center for Internet & Society. (2022). *AI Ethics and Data Privacy: A Comprehensive Analysis*. Retrieved from Berkman Klein Center.

Bernoster, I., Mukerjee, J., & Thurik, R. (2020). The role of affect in entrepreneurial orientation. *Small Business Economics*, 54(1), 235–256. DOI: 10.1007/s11187-018-0116-3

Bessant, J., & Tidd, J. (2007). *Innovation and entrepreneurship*. John Wiley & Sons.

Bharadiya, J. P. (2023). A comparative study of business intelligence and artificial intelligence with big data analytics. *American Journal of Artificial Intelligence*, 7(1), 24–30.

Bharadwaj, A., El Sawy, O. A., Pavlou, P. A., & Venkatraman, N. V. (2013). Digital business strategy: Toward a next generation of insights. *Management Information Systems Quarterly*, 37(2), 471–482. DOI: 10.25300/MISQ/2013/37:2.3

Bharadwaj, K. (2021). SAMA: AI-Driven Arbitration. *Journal of Legal Tech*, 5(2), 50–63.

Bharadwaj, S. (2021). AI in Dispute Resolution: The Case of SAMA. *Journal of Legal Technology*, 12(4), 58–73.

Bhatia, K., & Sharma, P. (2022). Ethical Considerations in Machine Learning Applications for HR. *Journal of Ethics in AI*, 8(1), 19–30.

Bhubaneswar Smart City. (2023). *AI-Driven Smart City Initiatives*. Retrieved from Bhubaneswar Smart City.

Bhutani, S., & Paliwal, Y. (2015). Digitalization: A step towards sustainable development. *OIDA International Journal of Sustainable Development*, 8(12), 11–24.

Bick, R., Chang, M., Wang, K.W. & Yu, T. (2020) A blueprint for remote working: Lessons from China. *McKinsey Digital*, 23.

Bihar IT Department. (2022). Bias Mitigation in Public AI Applications. Retrieved from Bihar IT Department.

Binns, R. (2018). Fairness in Machine Learning: Lessons from Political Philosophy. *Proceedings of the 2018 Conference on Fairness, Accountability, and Transparency*. ACM.

Binns, R. (2020). Fairness in Machine Learning: Lessons from the Gender Shades Project. *Proceedings of the 2020 Conference on Fairness, Accountability, and Transparency (FAccT)*.

Binns, R. (2023). Explainable AI: Bridging the Gap Between Data and Decisions. *Journal of AI Research*, 27(3), 231–245.

Bird, B. (1988). Implementing entrepreneurial ideas: The case for intention. *Academy of Management Review*, 13(3), 442–453. DOI: 10.2307/258091

Birimoglu Okuyan, C., & Begen, M. A. (2022). Working from home during the COVID-19 pandemic, its effects on health, and recommendations: The pandemic and beyond. *Perspectives in Psychiatric Care*, 58(1), 173–179. DOI: 10.1111/ppc.12847 PMID: 34003489

Blount, J. (2017). *Sales EQ: how ultra high performers leverage sales-specific emotional intelligence to close the complex deal.* John Wiley & Sons.

Bochenek, L. M. (2019). Connecting with the right audiences for a better impact–imperatives of influencer marketing. In *Advocacy and organizational engagement* (pp. 91–110). Emerald Publishing Limited., DOI: 10.1108/978-1-78973-437-920191006

Bohn, S. (2022). The Future of Smart Contracts in Legal Systems. *Legal Innovation Journal*, 9(1), 98–110.

Bolisani, E., Scarso, E., Ipsen, C., Kirchner, K., & Hansen, J. P. (2020). Working from home during COVID-19 pandemic: Lessons learned and issues. *Management & Marketing. Challenges for the Knowledge Society*, 15(s1), 458–476. DOI: 10.2478/mmcks-2020-0027

Booth, A., James, M. S., Clowes, M., & Sutton, A. (2021). Systematic approaches to a successful literature review.

Boston Consulting Group (BCG). (2023). The Impact of AI on Employee Wellbeing. Retrieved from https://www.bcg.com

Bouarfa, S., Aydoğan, R., & Sharpanskykh, A. (2021). Formal modelling and verification of a multi-agent negotiation approach for airline operations control. *Journal of Reliable Intelligent Environments*, 7(4), 279–298. DOI: 10.1007/s40860-020-00123-0

Bouziri, H., Smith, D. R. M., Descatha, A., Dab, W., & Jean, K. (2020). Working from home in the time of COVID-19: How to best preserve occupational health? *Occupational and Environmental Medicine*, 77(7), 509–510. DOI: 10.1136/oemed-2020-106599 PMID: 32354748

Boyd, N. G., & Vozikis, G. S. (1994). The influence of self-efficacy on the development of entrepreneurial intentions and actions. *Entrepreneurship Theory and Practice*, 18(4), 63–77. DOI: 10.1177/104225879401800404

Bozkurt, Ö. (2019). Girişimcilik 4.0 Ama Nasıl? Kavramsal Bir Çerçeve. In *ICEB'19-International Congress of Economics and Business 11-13 April 2019 Bursa/Turkey* (pp. 549-559).

Brazilian Government. (2020). *General Data Protection Law (LGPD)*. Retrieved from Brazilian Government.

Brock, J. K. U., & Von Wangenheim, F. (2019). Demystifying AI. What digital transformation leaders can teach you about realistic artificial intelligence. *California Management Review, 61*(4), 110-134. https.//DOI: 10.1177/1536504219865226

Brynjolfsson, E., & McAfee, A. (2014). *The Second Machine Age: Work, Progress, and Prosperity in a Time of Brilliant Technologies*. W.W. Norton & Company.

Brynjolfsson, E., & McAfee, A. (2014). *The second machine age: Work, progress, and prosperity in a time of brilliant technologies*. WW Norton & Company.

Budhwar, P., Malik, A., De Silva, M. T. T., & Thevisuthan, P. (2022). Artificial intelligence – challenges and opportunities for international HRM: A review and research agenda. *International Journal of Human Resource Management*, 33(6), 1065–1097. DOI: 10.1080/09585192.2022.2035161

Bughin, J., Seong, J., Manyika, J., Chui, M., & Joshi, R. (2018). *Notes from the AI Frontier: Applications and Value of Deep Learning*. McKinsey & Company.

Buolamwini, J., & Gebru, T. (2018). Gender Shades: Intersectional Accuracy Disparities in Commercial Gender Classification. *Proceedings of the 2018 ACM Conference on Fairness, Accountability, and Transparency (FAccT).*

Cabı, E. (2016). Dijital teknolojiye yönelik tutum ölçeği. *Kastamonu Education Journal*, 24(3), 1229–1244.

Call, D. R., & Herber, D. R. (2022). Applicability of the diffusion of innovation theory to accelerate model-based systems engineering adoption. *Systems Engineering*, 25(6), 574–583. DOI: 10.1002/sys.21638

Cammack, P. (2022). *The politics of global competitiveness*. Oxford University Press. DOI: 10.1093/oso/9780192847867.001.0001

Campbell, C., Plangger, K., Sands, S., Kietzmann, J., & Bates, K. (2022). How deepfakes and artificial intelligence could reshape the advertising industry. The coming reality of AI fakes and their potential impact on consumer behavior. *Journal of Advertising Research, 62*(3), 241-251. https.//DOI: 10.2501/JAR-2022-017

Cao, X., Qu, Z., Liu, Y., & Hu, J. (2021). How the destination short video affects the customers' attitude: The role of narrative transportation. *Journal of Retailing and Consumer Services*, 62, 102672. DOI: 10.1016/j.jretconser.2021.102672

Capestro, M., Rizzo, C., Kliestik, T., Peluso, A. M., & Pino, G. (2024). Enabling digital technologies adoption in industrial districts: The key role of trust and knowledge sharing. *Technological Forecasting and Social Change*, 198, 1–10. DOI: 10.1016/j.techfore.2023.123003

Capgemini. (2023). AI for Enhancing Employee Experience. Retrieved from https://www.capgemini.com

Caputo, A., Pizzi, S., Pellegrini, M. M., & Dabić, M. (2021). Digitalization and business models: Where are we going? A science map of the field. *Journal of Business Research*, 123, 489–501. DOI: 10.1016/j.jbusres.2020.09.053

Card, D., Zhang, M., & Smith, N. A. (2019, January). Deep weighted averaging classifiers. In *Proceedings of the conference on fairness, accountability, and transparency* (pp. 369-378). DOI: 10.1145/3287560.3287595

Cardwell, S. G., Schuman, C. D., Smith, J. D., Patel, K., Kwon, J., Liu, S., Allemang, C., Misra, S., Incorvia, J. A., & Aimone, J. B. (2022). Probabilistic Neural Circuits leveraging AI-Enhanced Codesign for RandomNumber Generation. *2022 IEEE International Conference on Rebooting Computing (ICRC)*, 57–65. DOI: 10.1109/ICRC57508.2022.00008

Carlsson, C., & Walden, P. (1997). More effective strategic management with hyperknowledge: The Woodstrat case. *Journal of Decision Systems*, 6(1), 23–44. DOI: 10.1080/12460125.1997.10511704

Carrington, V. (2020). *Rethinking middle years: Early adolescents, schooling and digital culture*. Routledge. DOI: 10.4324/9781003117179

Carton, A. M., & Lucas, B. J. (2018). How can leaders overcome the blurry vision bias? Identifying an antidote to the paradox of vision communication. *Academy of Management Journal*, 61(6), 2106–2129. DOI: 10.5465/amj.2015.0375

Cascio, W. F. (2014). Leveraging employer branding, performance management and human resourcedevelopment to enhance employee retention. *Human Resource Development International*, 17(2), 121–128. DOI: 10.1080/13678868.2014.886443

Cascio, W. F., & Shurygailo, S. (2003). E-leadership and virtual teams. *Organizational Dynamics*, 31(4), 362–376. DOI: 10.1016/S0090-2616(02)00130-4

CaseCrunch. (2024). AI Predictions in Legal Dispute Management: Latest Developments. *CaseCrunch Research Report.*

Center for Democracy & Technology (CDT). (2023). *AI and Privacy: Policy Implications and Recommendations*. Retrieved from CDT.

Center for Security and Emerging Technology (CSET). (2022). *AI Ethics: Global Perspectives and Policy Responses*. Retrieved from CSET.

Chakraborty, S., & Bandyopadhyay, S. (2022). Bias and Fairness in AI Systems: The Indian Context. *Journal of Ethical AI*, 5(3), 112–130.

Chatterjee, S., Rana, N. P., Tamilmani, K., & Sharma, A. (2021). The effect of AI-based CRM on organization performance and competitive advantage: An empirical analysis in the B2B context. *Industrial Marketing Management*, 97, 205–219. DOI: 10.1016/j.indmarman.2021.07.013

Chaudhuri, S., & Sengupta, A. (2022). AI in Strategic Decision-Making: A Review of Indian Enterprises. *Journal of Indian Business Management*, 12(3), 43–59.

Chen, G., Xie, P., Dong, J., & Wang, T. (2019). Understanding programmatic creative. The role of AI. *Journal of Advertising, 48*(4), 347-355. https.//DOI: 10.1080/00913367.2019.1654421

Cheng, J. T., Gerpott, F. H., Benson, A. J., Bucker, B., Foulsham, T., Lansu, T. A., & Tsuchiya, K. (2022). Eye gaze and visual attention as a window into leadership and followership: A review of empirical insights and future directions. *The Leadership Quarterly*, 101654. Advance online publication. DOI: 10.1016/j.leaqua.2022.101654

Chen, L. (2023). AI for Transparency in Legal Processes. *International Journal of Law and Technology*, 15(2), 54–67.

Chen, L., & Wang, J. (2023). Hyper-Personalization in E-Commerce: Opportunities and Challenges. *International Journal of Information Management*, 63, 102–112.

Chen, L., Xu, Y., & Zhou, L. (2021). AI-Driven Predictive Maintenance: A Case Study of Siemens. *Journal of Manufacturing Science and Engineering*, 143(8), 081012.

Chen, L., Xu, Y., & Zhou, L. (2022). Deep Learning Approaches for Forecasting: A Comparative Study. *Journal of Forecasting*, 41(3), 428–441.

Chen, W., He, W., Shen, J., Tian, X., & Wang, X. (2023). Systematic analysis of artificial intelligence in the era of industry 4.0. *Journal of Management Analytics*, 10(1), 89–108. DOI: 10.1080/23270012.2023.2180676

Chen, X., & Liu, Y. (2023). Using Machine Learning for Effective Talent Acquisition: An Empirical Study. *Journal of Recruitment and Selection*, 11(4), 65–80.

Chen, X., Zhang, Q., & Jiang, X. (2021). Real-time Captioning with AI: Benefits and Challenges for Accessibility. *Journal of Assistive Technologies*.

Chen, Y., Argentinis, J. E., & Weber, G. (2016). IBM Watson: How cognitive computing can be applied to big data challenges in life sciences research. *Clinical Therapeutics*, 38(4), 688–701. DOI: 10.1016/j.clinthera.2015.12.001 PMID: 27130797

Cheung, M. L., Pires, G. D., Rosenberger, P. J., Leung, W. K. S., & Sharipudin, M.-N. S. (2021). The role of consumer-consumer interaction and consumer-brand interaction in driving consumer-brand engagement and behavioral intentions. *Journal of Retailing and Consumer Services*, 61, 102574. DOI: 10.1016/j.jretconser.2021.102574

Chigona, W., & Licker, P. (2008). Using diffusion of innovations framework to explain communal computing facilities adoption among the urban poor. *Information Technologies and International Development*, 4(3), 57–73. DOI: 10.1162/itid.2008.00017

China Daily. (2023). *Corporate Responsibility in AI: A Chinese Perspective*. Retrieved from China Daily

Chiriluta, R. (2021). *An exploration of how marketing technique and promotion via Instagram drives domestic tourism in Ireland*. National College of Ireland.

Choi, S. (2022). The Role of Predictive Analytics in Retail: Walmart's Approach to Demand Forecasting. *Retail Technology Review*, 15(4), 78–84.

Chopra, R. (2023). Building Talent for the Future: Enhancing AI and ML Expertise in India. *Technology Today*, 24(2), 52–63.

Chota, M. C. (2020). *Entrepreneurial orientation and it's effects on micro, small and medium enterprises (MSME's) business performance in Lusaka district* (Doctoral dissertation, The University of Zambia).

Choudhury, A., & Nair, R. (2022). Advancements in Machine Learning for Recruitment and Talent Management. *Journal of Business Innovation*, 11(4), 90–105.

Choudhury, T., Kumar, V., & Nigam, D. (2015). An innovative and automatic lung and oral cancer classification using soft computing techniques. *International Journal of Computer Science & Mobile Computing*, 4(12), 313–323.

Choudhury, T., Kumar, V., & Nigam, D. (2015). Intelligent classification & clustering of lung & oral cancer through decision tree & genetic algorithm. *International Journal of Advanced Research in Computer Science and Software Engineering*, 5(12), 501–510.

Chowdhury, S., Budhwar, P., Dey, P. K., Joel-Edgar, S., & Abadie, A. (2022). AI-employee collaboration and business performance: Integrating knowledge-based view, socio-technical systems and organisational socialisation framework. *Journal of Business Research*, 144, 31–49. DOI: 10.1016/j.jbusres.2022.01.069

Chowdhury, S., Dey, P., Joel-Edgar, S., Bhattacharya, S., Rodriguez-Espindola, O., Abadie, A., & Truong, L. (2023). Unlocking the value of artificial intelligence in human resource management through AI capability framework. *Human Resource Management Review*, 33(1), 100899. DOI: 10.1016/j.hrmr.2022.100899

Choy, K. L., Chow, H. K. H., Tan, K. H., Chan, C.-K., Mok, E. C. M., & Wang, Q. (2008). Leveraging the supply chain flexibility of third party logistics – Hybrid knowledge-based system approach. *Expert Systems with Applications*, 35(4), 1998–2016. DOI: 10.1016/j.eswa.2007.08.084

Cielen, A., Peeters, L., & Vanhoof, K. (2004). Bankruptcy prediction using a data envelopment analysis. *European Journal of Operational Research*, 154(2), 526–532. DOI: 10.1016/S0377-2217(03)00186-3

Cioffi, R., Travaglioni, M., Piscitelli, G., Petrillo, A., & De Felice, F. (2020). Artificial intelligence and machine learning applications in smart production: Progress, trends, and directions. *Sustainability (Basel)*, 12(2), 1–26. DOI: 10.3390/su12020492

Clark, J. (2022). The Role of AI in Enhancing Legal Compliance. *Compliance Today*, 18(3), 45–56.

Clio. (2023). AI-Powered Case Management and Legal Research. *Clio Updates*.

Clio. (2023). AI-Powered Case Management and Legal Research. *Clio Updates*. Retrieved from Clio

Codini, A. P., Abbate, T., & Petruzzelli, A. M. (2023). Business Model Innovation and exaptation: A new way of innovating in SMEs. *Technovation*, 119, 1–16. DOI: 10.1016/j.technovation.2022.102548

Colombian Government. (2022). *Data Protection and AI Regulations*. Retrieved from Colombian Government.

Conde, R., & Casais, B. (2023). Micro, macro, and mega-influencers on Instagram: The power of persuasion via the parasocial relationship. *Journal of Business Research*, 158, 113708. DOI: 10.1016/j.jbusres.2023.113708

ContractPodAi. (2023). Enhancements in AI for Contract Drafting and Review. *ContractPodAi Updates*.

Corrêa, V. S., Queiroz, M. M., Cruz, M. A., & Shigaki, H. B. (2022). Entrepreneurial orientation far beyond opportunity: The influence of the necessity for innovativeness, proactiveness and risk-taking. *International Journal of Entrepreneurial Behaviour & Research*, 28(4), 952–979. DOI: 10.1108/IJEBR-06-2021-0518

Coursera. (2023). *AI and Data Science Courses in India*. Retrieved from Coursera.

Covin, J. G., & Lumpkin, G. T. (2011). Entrepreneurial orientation theory and research: Reflections on a needed construct. *Entrepreneurship Theory and Practice*, 35(5), 855–872. DOI: 10.1111/j.1540-6520.2011.00482.x

Covin, J. G., & Slevin, D. P. (1989). Strategic management of small firms in hostile and benign environments. *Strategic Management Journal*, 10(1), 75–87. DOI: 10.1002/smj.4250100107

Covin, J. G., & Wales, W. J. (2012). The measurement of entrepreneurial orientation. *Entrepreneurship Theory and Practice*, 36(4), 677–702. DOI: 10.1111/j.1540-6520.2010.00432.x

Crawford, K. (2021). *Atlas of AI: Power, Politics, and the Planetary Costs of Artificial Intelligence*. Yale University Press.

Creswell, J. W. (2014). *Research design: Qualitative, quantitative, and mixed methods approach* (4th ed.). SAGE Publications.

Creswell, J. W., & Creswell, J. D. (2017). *Research design. Qualitative, quantitative, and mixed methods approaches*. Sage publications.

Cui, Y., Kara, S., & Chan, K. C. (2020). Manufacturing big data ecosystem: A systematic literature review. *Robotics and Computer-integrated Manufacturing*, 62, 1–20. DOI: 10.1016/j.rcim.2019.101861

Cyber Peace Foundation. (2023). *Cybersecurity Report: Trends and Threats*. Retrieved from Cyber Peace Foundation.

Dana, L. P., Salamzadeh, A., Mortazavi, S., & Hadizadeh, M. (2022). Investigating the impact of international markets and new digital technologies on business innovation in emerging markets. *Sustainability (Basel)*, 14(2), 1–15. DOI: 10.3390/su14020983

Daneshfar, Z., Asokan-Ajitha, A., Sharma, P., & Malik, A. (2023). Work-from-home (WFH) during COVID-19 pandemic–A netnographic investigation using Twitter data. *Information Technology & People*, 36(5), 2161–2186. DOI: 10.1108/ITP-01-2021-0020

Dasgupta, S., & Freund, Y. (2009). Random Trees for Vector Quantization. *IEEE Transactions on Information Theory*, 55(7), 3229–3242. DOI: 10.1109/TIT.2009.2021326

Das, I. R., Talukder, M. B., & Kumar, S. (2024). Implication of Artificial Intelligence in Hospitality Marketing. In *Utilizing Smart Technology and AI in Hybrid Tourism and Hospitality* (pp. 291–310). IGI Global., DOI: 10.4018/979-8-3693-1978-9.ch014

Data Security Council of India (DSCI). (2023). *Guidelines for Ethical AI Practices*. Retrieved from DSCI.

Data Security Council of India (DSCI). (2023). *Survey on Public Perception of AI and Data Privacy*. Retrieved from DSCI.

Daugherty, P. R., & Wilson, H. J. (2018). *Human+ machine: Reimagining work in the age of AI*. Harvard Business Press.

Davenport, T. H., & Kirby, J. (2016). *Only Humans Need Apply: Winners and Losers in the Age of Smart Machines*. Harper Business.

Davenport, T. H., & Mittal, N. (2023). *All-In on AI: How Smart Companies Win Big with Artificial Intelligence*. Harvard Business Press.

Davenport, T. H., & Ronanki, R. (2018). Artificial intelligence for the real world. *Harvard Business Review*, 96(1), 108–116.

Davenport, T. H., & Ronanki, R. (2021). Artificial Intelligence for the Real World. *Harvard Business Review*, 98(1), 108–116.

Davidsson, P. (2015). Entrepreneurial opportunities and the entrepreneurship nexus: A re-conceptualization. *Journal of Business Venturing*, 30(5), 674–695. DOI: 10.1016/j.jbusvent.2015.01.002

Davis, F. D. (1989). Technology acceptance model: TAM. *Al-Suqri, MN, Al-Aufi, AS. Information Seeking Behavior and Technology Adoption*, 205, 1–33.

Davis, F. D., Granić, A., & Marangunić, N. (2024). *The Technology Acceptance Model: 30 Years of TAM*. Springer International Publishing AG. DOI: 10.1007/978-3-030-45274-2

Davis, M. (2023). Blockchain for Legal Transparency: A New Era. *Journal of Blockchain Studies*, 10(4), 89–102.

De Cremer, D., Narayanan, D., Deppeler, A., Nagpal, M., & McGuire, J. (2022). The road to a human-centred digital society: Opportunities, challenges and responsibilities for humans in the age of machines. *AI and Ethics*, 2(4), 579–583. DOI: 10.1007/s43681-021-00116-6 PMID: 34806084

Deci, E. L., & Ryan, R. M. (2000). The „what" and „why" of goal pursuits: Human needs and the self-determination of behavior. *Psychological Inquiry*, 11(4), 227–268. DOI: 10.1207/S15327965PLI1104_01

Delhi Government. (2023). *Fair AI Framework: Guidelines for Ethical AI Applications*. Retrieved from Delhi Government.

Deloitte. (2019). The Rise of AI in HR: Enhancing Employee Engagement. Retrieved from https://www2.deloitte.com

Deloitte. (2022). Using AI to Improve Employee Engagement. Retrieved from https://www2.deloitte.com

Deloitte. (2023). *AI and the Future of Corporate Dispute Resolution*. Deloitte Insights.

Deloitte. (2023). *AI Ethics: Building Trust and Accountability*. Retrieved from Deloitte.

Deloitte. (2023). The Rise of AI in HR: Enhancing Employee Engagement. Retrieved from https://www2.deloitte.com

Deloitte. (2024). *AI and Organizational Transparency: A Global Perspective*. Retrieved from Deloitte Report.

Deloitte. (2024). *AI for Enhancing Diversity and Reducing Bias in Promotions*. Retrieved from Deloitte Report.

Deloitte. (2024). *AI for Organizational Culture: Trends in Transparency and Efficiency*. Retrieved from Deloitte Report.

Deloitte. (2024). *AI in Recruitment: Reducing Bias and Enhancing Diversity*. Retrieved from Deloitte Report.

Deloitte. (2024). *Driving Transparency with AI: Insights from Global Organizations*. Retrieved from Deloitte Report.

Deloitte. (2024). *The Role of AI in Enhancing Decision-Making Transparency*. Retrieved from Deloitte Report.

Deng, S., Tan, C.-W., Wang, W., & Pan, Y. (2019). Smart Generation System of Personalized Advertising Copy and Its Application to Advertising Practice and Research. *Journal of Advertising,* 48(4), 356–365. https.//DOI: 10.1080/00913367.2019.1652121

Densten, I. L., & Gray, J. H. (2001). Leadership development and reflection: What is the connection? *International Journal of Educational Management*, 15(3), 119–124. DOI: 10.1108/09513540110384466

Desai, N., & Patel, R. (2022). ML in Talent Management: Benefits, Challenges, and Future Trends. *Journal of Management Studies*, 15(3), 102–118.

Deutsch, M., Coleman, P. T., & Marcus, E. C. (2014). *The handbook of conflict resolution: Theory and practice*. John Wiley & Sons.

Devarajan, R., Maheshwari, S., & Vohra, V. (2016). Implementing New Age Performance Management System in IT MNC: Leveraging Communication and Training. *South Asian Journal of Business and Management Cases*, 5(2), 189–197. DOI: 10.1177/2277977916665983

Dey, P., & Ghosh, A. (2023). Autonomous Decision-Making Systems in Indian Industries. *Journal of Indian Engineering and Technology*, 14(2), 65–80.

Dhillon, G., & Sharma, N. (2023). AI and Machine Learning in Employee Engagement: A Review. *Employee Relations Journal*, 20(1), 70–85.

Di Vaio, A., Palladino, R., Hassan, R., & Escobar, O. (2020). Artificial intelligence and business models in the sustainable development goals perspective: A systematic literature review. *Journal of Business Research*, 121, 283–314. DOI: 10.1016/j.jbusres.2020.08.019

Digital Rights Foundation. (2023). *AI and Human Rights: Privacy and Ethics*. Retrieved from Digital Rights Foundation.

Dixon, M., & Mullen, K. (2022). Autonomous Decision-Making Systems: The Next Frontier in AI. *IEEE Transactions on Artificial Intelligence*, 3(4), 567–577.

Dong, Y., Hou, J., Zhang, N., & Zhang, M. (2020). Research on how human intelligence, consciousness, and cognitive computing affect the development of artificial intelligence. *Complexity*, 2020(1), 1–10. DOI: 10.1155/2020/1680845

DoNotPay. (2022). AI-Powered Legal Assistance. *DoNotPay Services*. Retrieved from DoNotPay

DoNotPay. (2022). AI-powered Virtual Lawyer for Legal Assistance. *DoNotPay*.

Doshi-Velez, F., & Kim, B. (2017). *Towards a rigorous science of interpretable machine learning*. arXiv preprint arXiv:1702.08608.

Doyle, G., Srivastava, S. B., Goldberg, A., & Frank, M. C. (2017). Alignment at Work: Using Language to Distinguish the Internalization and Self-Regulation Components of Cultural Fit in Organizations. IRLE Working Paper, pp. 102-110. https://irle.berkeley.edu/files/2017/Alignment-At-Work.pdf

Driver, R. (2022). Instagram & the FTC: The Growth of Influencer Marketing & the Government's Ungai Fan, F., Chan, K., Wang, Y., Li, Y., & Prieler, M. (2023). How influencers' social media posts have an influence on audience engagement among young consumers. *Young Consumers*, 24(4), 427–444.

Drucker, P. F. (1985). Entrepreneurial strategies. *California Management Review*, 27(2), 9–25. DOI: 10.2307/41165126

Drucker, P. F. (1998). The discipline of innovation. *Harvard Business Review*, 76(6), 149–157. PMID: 10187245

Duarte, A. (2023). The relationship between brands and consumers, in Dias, P. & Duarte, A. (2023), *Social Brand Management in a Post Covid-19 Era*, 3-16. Routledge. ISBN 9781032465722 https.//DOI: 10.4324/9781003382331-2

Duarte, A. (2021). A New Reality in the Labour Market Demands New Strategies in Education. In Surugiu, R., Stefanel, A., & Apostol, N. (Eds.), *30 de ani de învă ământ jurnalistic i de comunicare în fostele ări comuniste din Estul Europei* (pp. 365–380). Tritonic Books.

Duarte, A., & Neumaier, A. (2022). Chatvertising. how chatbots are shaping the future of advertising. *Comunicação Pública,* 17(32). https.//DOI: 10.34629/cpublica.329

Dubey, P., & Sahu, K. K. (2022). Examining the effects of demographic, social and environmental factors on entrepreneurial intention. *Management matters, 19*(1), 91-108.

Dubey, A., & Sethi, S. (2023). Machine Learning in HR: Addressing the Challenges of Adoption. *HR Management Review*, 18(1), 63–80.

Dullaghan, C., & Rozaki, E. (2017). Integration of machine learning techniques to evaluate dynamic customer segmentation analysis for mobile customers. *arXiv preprint arXiv:1702.02215.*

Dutta, D., Srivastava, Y., & Singh, E. (2023). Metaverse in the tourism sector for talent management: A technology in practice lens. *Information Technology & Tourism*, 25(3), 331–365. DOI: 10.1007/s40558-023-00258-9

Dutta, S., & Ghosh, A. (2022). Machine Learning in HR: Applications and Future Prospects. *Indian Journal of Management*, 13(2), 89–105.

Dutz, M. A., Ordover, J. A., & Willig, R. D. (2000). Entrepreneurship, access policy and economic development: Lessons from industrial organization. *European Economic Review*, 44(4-6), 739–747. DOI: 10.1016/S0014-2921(00)00030-1

Dwivedi, Y. K., Hughes, L., Ismagilova, E., Aarts, G., Coombs, C., Crick, T., Duan, Y., Dwivedi, R., Edwards, J., Eirug, A., Galanos, V., Ilavarasan, P. V., Janssen, M., Jones, P., Kar, A. K., Kizgin, H., Kronemann, B., Lal, B., Lucini, B., & Williams, M. D. (2021). Artificial Intelligence (AI): Multidisciplinary perspectives on emerging challenges, opportunities, and agenda for research, practice and policy. *International Journal of Information Management*, 57, 1–47. DOI: 10.1016/j.ijinfomgt.2019.08.002

Edwards, H. (2023). AI in Community Mediation: Innovations and Challenges. *Social Technology Review*, 11(2), 34–47.

El Miedany, Y. (2019). Virtual reality and augmented reality. *Rheumatology teaching: the art and science of medical education*, 403-427.

Elakkiya, R., & Rajendran, S. (2022). AI and Predictive Analytics in Indian Healthcare: Current Trends and Future Directions. *Indian Journal of Healthcare Technology*, 11(1), 55–68.

Electronic Frontier Foundation (EFF). (2023). *Protecting Privacy in the Age of AI*. Retrieved from EFF.

Elia, G., Margherita, A., & Passiante, G. (2020). Digital entrepreneurship ecosystem: How digital technologies and collective intelligence are reshaping the entrepreneurial process. *Technological Forecasting and Social Change*, 150, 1–12. DOI: 10.1016/j.techfore.2019.119791

Elkan, C. (2003). Using the triangle inequality to accelerate k-means. In *Proceedings of the 20th international conference on Machine Learning (ICML-03)* (pp. 147-153).

ElMassah, S., & Mohieldin, M. (2020). Digital transformation and localizing the sustainable development goals (SDGs). *Ecological Economics*, 169, 1–12. DOI: 10.1016/j.ecolecon.2019.106490

Else, H. (2023). Abstracts written by ChatGPT fool scientists. Nature News. https://www.workerinfoexchange.org/wie-report-managed-by-bots DOI: 10.1038/d41586-023-00056-7

Ensmenger, N. (2012). Is chess the drosophila of artificial intelligence? A social history of an algorithm. *Social Studies of Science*, 42(1), 5–30. DOI: 10.1177/0306312711424596 PMID: 22530382

Entrialgo, M., & Iglesias, V. (2020). Entrepreneurial intentions among university students: The moderating role of creativity. *European Management Review*, 17(2), 529–542. DOI: 10.1111/emre.12386

Esteva, A., Kuprel, B., Novoa, R. A., Ko, J., Swetter, S. M., Blau, H. M., & Thrun, S. (2017). Dermatologist-Level Classification of Skin Cancer with Deep Neural Networks. *Nature*, 542(7639), 115–118. DOI: 10.1038/nature21056 PMID: 28117445

European Commission. (2021). *Artificial Intelligence Act Proposal*. Retrieved from European Commission.

Evans, R., Jumper, J., Kirkpatrick, J., Sifre, L., Green, T., Qin, C., & Senior, A. W. (2018). De novo structure prediction with deeplearning based scoring. *Annual Review of Biochemistry*, 77, 363–382.

EY. (2023). AI and the Future of Talent Acquisition. Retrieved from https://www.ey.com

Fahad, M., Basri, T., Hamza, M. A., Faisal, S., Akbar, A., Haider, U., & Hajjami, S. E. (2024). The Benefits and Risks of Artificial General Intelligence (AGI). In *Artificial General Intelligence (AGI) Security: Smart Applications and Sustainable Technologies* (pp. 27–52). Springer Nature Singapore.

Fanni, S. C., Febi, M., Aghakhanyan, G., & Neri, E. (2023). Natural language processing. In *Introduction to Artificial Intelligence* (pp. 87–99). Springer International Publishing. DOI: 10.1007/978-3-031-25928-9_5

Farhadloo, M., Patterson, R. A., & Rolland, E. (2016, October). Modelling customer satisfaction from unstructured data using a Bayesian approach. *Decision Support Systems*, 90, 1–11. DOI: 10.1016/j.dss.2016.06.010

FastArb. (2024). Enhancing Accessibility through AI in Online Dispute Resolution. *FastArb Platform Report.*

Favaretto, M., De Clercq, E., Schneble, C. O., & Elger, B. S. (2020). What is your definition of Big Data? Researchers' understanding of the phenomenon of the decade. *PLoS One*, 15(2), 1–20. DOI: 10.1371/journal.pone.0228987 PMID: 32097430

Felicetti, A. M., Corvello, V., & Ammirato, S. (2024). Digital innovation in entrepreneurial firms: A systematic literature review. *Review of Managerial Science*, 18(2), 315–362. DOI: 10.1007/s11846-023-00638-9

Femenia-Serra, F., & Gretzel, U. (2020). Influencer marketing for tourism destinations: Lessons from a mature destination. *Information and Communication Technologies in Tourism 2020:Proceedings of the International Conference in Surrey,* United Kingdom, January 08–10, 2020, 65–78. DOI DOI: 10.1007/978-3-030-36737-4_6

Fernandes, C., Ferreira, J. J., Veiga, P. M., Kraus, S., & Dabić, M. (2022). Digital entrepreneurship platforms: Mapping the field and looking towards a holistic approach. *Technology in Society*, 70, 1–13. DOI: 10.1016/j.techsoc.2022.101979

Fernández Fernández, J. L. (2022). Ethical considerations regarding biases in algorithms.

Fernandez, A. (2022). AI-Powered Compliance Tools: A Review. *Regulatory Technology Review*, 8(3), 56–68.

Ferràs-Hernández, X. (2018). The future of management in a world of electronic brains. *Journal of Management Inquiry*, 27(2), 260–263. DOI: 10.1177/1056492617724973

Ferràs-Hernández, X., Tarrats-Pons, E., & Arimany-Serrat, N. (2017). Disruption in the automotive industry: A Cambrian moment. *Business Horizons*, 60(6), 855–863. DOI: 10.1016/j.bushor.2017.07.011

Ferreira, J. J., Raposo, M. L., Gouveia Rodrigues, R., Dinis, A., & Do Paco, A. (2012). A model of entrepreneurial intention: An application of the psychological and behavioral approaches. *Journal of Small Business and Enterprise Development*, 19(3), 424–440. DOI: 10.1108/14626001211250144

Ferreira, P., Teixeira, J. G., & Teixeira, L. F. (2020). Understanding the impact of artificial intelligence on services. In *Exploring Service Science: 10th International Conference, IESS 2020, Porto, Portugal, February 5–7, 2020* [Springer International Publishing.]. *Proceedings*, 10, 202–213.

Ferreras-Méndez, J. L., Olmos-Penuela, J., Salas-Vallina, A., & Alegre, J. (2021). Entrepreneurial orientation and new product development performance in SMEs: The mediating role of business model innovation. *Technovation*, 108, 1–13. DOI: 10.1016/j.technovation.2021.102325

Fischer, I., Beswick, C., & Newell, S. (2021). Rho AI – Leveraging artificial intelligence to address climate change: Financing, implementation and ethics. *Journal of Information Technology Teaching Cases*, 11(2), 110–116. DOI: 10.1177/2043886920961782

Fischer, T., & Sitkin, S. B. (2022). Leadership styles: A comprehensive assessment and way forward. *The Academy of Management Annals*, 17(1), 331–372. DOI: 10.5465/annals.2020.0340

Fishbein, M., & Ajzen, I. (1974). Attitudes towards objects as predictors of single and multiple behavioral criteria. *Psychological Review*, 81(1), 59–74. DOI: 10.1037/h0035872

Fisher, R., Ury, W., & Patton, B. (2008). *Negotiating agreement without giving in*. Penguin Putnam Incorporated.

Fisher, R., Ury, W., & Patton, B. (2011). *Getting to Yes: Negotiating Agreement Without Giving In*. Penguin Books.

Fleck, J. (2018). Development and establishment in artificial intelligence. In *The Question of Artificial Intelligence* (pp. 106–164). Routledge. DOI: 10.4324/9780429505331-3

Floridi, L. (2019). What the near future of artificial intelligence could be. *Philosophy & Technology*, 32(1), 1–15. DOI: 10.1007/s13347-019-00345-y

Floridi, L., Cowls, J., Beltrametti, M., Chatila, R., Chazerand, P., Dignum, V., Luetge, C., Madelin, R., Pagallo, U., Rossi, F., Schafer, B., Valcke, P., & Vayena, E. (2018). AI4People—an ethical framework for a good AI society: Opportunities, risks, principles, and recommendations. *Minds and Machines*, 28(4), 689–707. DOI: 10.1007/s11023-018-9482-5 PMID: 30930541

Forbes. (2022). How AI is Transforming Human Resources. Retrieved from https://www.forbes.com

Forrester Research. (2023). *AI and Privacy: Emerging Trends and Best Practices*. Retrieved from Forrester.

Forrester Research. (2024). *AI and Bias Mitigation: Strategies for Fair Recruitment and Promotion*. Retrieved from Forrester Report.

Forrester Research. (2024). *AI and Inclusive Hiring: Case Studies and Best Practices*. Retrieved from Forrester Report.

Forrester Research. (2024). *AI and Inclusive Workplaces: Trends and Impacts*. Retrieved from Forrester Report.

Forrester Research. (2024). *AI for Employee Development: Trends and Impact*. Retrieved from Forrester Report.

Forrester Research. (2024). *The Impact of AI on Diversity and Inclusion: A Global Perspective*. Retrieved from Forrester Report.

Frank, M. R., Autor, D. H., Bessen, J., Brynjolfsson, E., Cebrian, M., Deming, D., Feldman, M. P., Groh, M., Lobo, J., Moro, E., Wang, D., Youn, H., & Rahwan, I. (2019). Toward understanding the impact of artificial intelligence on labor. *Proceedings of the National Academy of Sciences of the United States of America*, 116(14), 6531–6539. https.//DOI: 10.1073/pnas.1900949116

Franklin, S. (2015). *Control: Digitality as cultural logic*. MIT Press. DOI: 10.7551/mitpress/9780262029537.001.0001

Freire, R. (2019). AI in HR: The Brazilian Perspective. Journal of Human Resources Management.

Frost & Sullivan. (2020). AI in the Philippines: Transforming Customer Service. Retrieved from https://www.frost.com

Future of Privacy Forum. (2022). *AI and Data Protection: Policy and Practice*. Retrieved from Future of Privacy Forum

Gaba, D. M. (2022). Artificial intelligence and expert systems. In *Control and Automation in Anaesthesia* (pp. 22–36). Springer Berlin Heidelberg.

Gagné, M., & Deci, E. L. (2005). Self-determination theory and work motivation. *Journal of Organizational Behavior*, 26(4), 331–362. DOI: 10.1002/job.322

Galanos, V. (2023). Expectations and expertise in artificial intelligence: specialist views and historical perspectives on conceptualisation, promise, and funding.

Gangwani, D., & Zhu, X. (2024). Modeling and prediction of business success: A survey. *Artificial Intelligence Review*, 57(2), 1–51. DOI: 10.1007/s10462-023-10664-4

Gartner. (2021). Predictive Analytics: The Key to Future-Proofing Your Business. Retrieved from Gartner Website

Gartner. (2022). AI in Human Capital Management: Trends and Best Practices. Retrieved from https://www.gartner.com

Gartner. (2022). *Top Strategic Technology Trends for 2023*. Gartner Research.

Gartner. (2023). *AI Privacy and Security: What You Need to Know*. Retrieved from Gartner

Gartner. (2023). Top Strategic Predictions for 2024 and Beyond: Leveraging AI to Transform Work. Retrieved from https://www.gartner.com

Gartner. (2024). *AI and Business Intelligence: Enhancing Decision-Making*. Retrieved from Gartner Report.

Gartner. (2024). *AI for Inclusive Hiring and Promotion: Global Trends*. Retrieved from Gartner Report.

Gartner. (2024). *AI-Enhanced Decision-Making: Future Trends and Innovations*. Retrieved from Gartner Report.

Gartner. (2024). *Harnessing AI for Diversity and Inclusion: Global Trends and Practices*. Retrieved from Gartner Report.

Gartner. (2024). *Personalizing Employee Development with AI: Trends and Impacts*. Retrieved from Gartner Report.

Gartner. (2024). *The Future of AI in Business Analytics and Decision-Making*. Retrieved from Gartner Report.

Gartner. (2024). *The Impact of AI on Business Analytics and Decision-Making*. Retrieved from Gartner Report.

GE. (2022). AI in Industrial Operations: Enhancing Efficiency and Reducing Costs. *General Electric Annual Report.*

Gelle-Jimenez, M., & Aguiling, H. M. (2021). Leveraging human resources management (HRM) practices toward congruence of values. International Journal of Research in Business and Social Science (2147-4478), 10(1), 85–94. DOI: 10.20525/ijrbs.v10i1.987

Georgescu, M. A., & Herman, E. (2020). The impact of the family background on students' entrepreneurial intentions: An empirical analysis. *Sustainability (Basel)*, 12(11), 1–18. DOI: 10.3390/su12114775

Gerlich, M. (2023). The Power of Personal Connections in Micro-Influencer Marketing: A Study on Consumer Behaviour and the Impact of Micro-Influencers. *Transnational Marketing Journal*, 11(1), 131–152.

Gerpott, F. H., Lehmann-Willenbrock, N., Silvis, J. D., & Van Vugt, M. (2018). In the eye of the beholder? An eye-tracking experiment on emergent leadership in team interactions. *The Leadership Quarterly*, 29(4), 523–532. DOI: 10.1016/j.leaqua.2017.11.003

Gerpott, F. H., & Van Quaquebeke, N. (2022). Kiss-Up-Kick-Down to get ahead: A resource perspective on how, when, why, and with whom middle managers use ingratiatory and exploitative behaviours to advance their careers. *Journal of Management Studies*. Advance online publication. DOI: 10.1111/joms.12855

Ghobakhloo, M. (2020). Industry 4.0, digitization, and opportunities for sustainability. *Journal of Cleaner Production*, 252, 1–21. DOI: 10.1016/j.jclepro.2019.119869

Ghosh, S. (2022). Challenges in AI Adoption: The Indian Context. *Tech Policy Review*, 15(2), 21–36.

Giubilei, A. (2021). *Business opportunities for Italian companies on Alibaba's e-commerce platforms.*

Global Partnership on Artificial Intelligence (GPAI). (2023). *Ethical AI and Data Privacy: International Standards*. Retrieved from GPAI.

Gomez-Uribe, C. A., & Hunt, P. (2016). The Netflix Recommender System: Algorithms, Business Value, and Innovation. *ACM Transactions on Management Information Systems*, 6(4), 1–19. DOI: 10.1145/2843948

Google. (2020). AI in Enhancing Innovation and Collaboration. Retrieved from https://www.google.com

Google. (2023). *AI for Multilingual Support: Innovations and Applications*. Retrieved from Google AI.

Google. (2023). AI in Enhancing Innovation and Collaboration. Retrieved from https://www.google.com

Google, A. I. (2023). *AI Principles: Building Responsible AI Systems*. Retrieved from Google AI.

Gour, A., Aggarwal, S., & Kumar, S. (2022). Lending ears to unheard voices: An empirical analysis of user-generated content on social media. *Production and Operations Management*, 31(6), 2457–2476. DOI: 10.1111/poms.13732

Government of India. (2023). *Smart Cities Mission: Harnessing Predictive Analytics for Urban Development*. Retrieved from Smart Cities Mission.

Green, E. (2023). AI and the Future of Contract Management. *Business Law Journal*, 20(2), 112–124.

Greenfield, R. (2018). How IBM's Watson Is Revolutionizing Employee Training. Retrieved from https://www.ibm.com

Greenfield, R. (2023). The Role of AI in Employee Training. Retrieved from https://www.ibm.com

Gubbi, J., Buyya, R., Marusic, S., & Palaniswami, M. (2013). Internet of Things (IoT): A vision, architectural elements, and future directions. *Future Generation Computer Systems*, 29(7), 1645–1660. DOI: 10.1016/j.future.2013.01.010

Guerrero, M., Liñán, F., & Cáceres-Carrasco, F. R. (2021). The influence of ecosystems on the entrepreneurship process: A comparison across developed and developing economies. *Small Business Economics*, 57(4), 1733–1759. DOI: 10.1007/s11187-020-00392-2

Gujarat Skill Development Department. (2023). *Annual Report on Skill Development and AI Integration*. Retrieved from Gujarat Skill Development.

Guler, N., Kirshner, S., & Vidgen, R. (2023). Artificial Intelligence Research in Business and Management:A Literature Review Leveraging Machine Learning and Large Language Models. SSRN Electronic Journal. DOI: 10.2139/ssrn.4540834

Gupta, A. (2023). Personalized Learning Paths: How Wipro Uses Machine Learning to Enhance Employee Training. *Business Today (Norwich)*.

Gupta, I., & Nagpal, G. (2020). *Artificial intelligence and expert systems*. Mercury Learning and Information. DOI: 10.1515/9781683925057

Gupta, R. (2022). AI for Legal Access in India: Current Developments. *Indian Journal of Law and Technology*, 13(2), 67–80.

Gupta, R., & Kumar, V. (2022). AI in Recruitment: A Case Study of Indian Corporates. *Journal of Applied AI*, 9(1), 44–58.

Gupta, R., & Patel, M. (2022). Data-Driven Approaches to Talent Acquisition in India: Trends and Challenges. *Journal of Talent Strategy*, 16(2), 77–92.

Gupta, R., & Rao, K. (2023). Personalizing Food Recommendations with AI: Zomato's Approach. *Indian Journal of Food Technology*, 15(2), 102–115.

Gupta, R., & Singh, S. (2023). Enhancing IT Services with AI: HCL Technologies' Approach to Process Automation. *Indian Journal of IT Services*, 11(2), 65–80.

Gupta, R., & Singh, S. (2023). Predictive Analytics in Healthcare: Zebra Medical Vision's AI Approach. *Indian Journal of Health Technology*, 14(2), 90–105.

Gupta, S. (2023). Data Management and Quality Issues in Machine Learning Implementations. *Journal of Data Science : JDS*, 19(3), 34–50.

Gupta, S., & Chen, H. (2018). AI-Based Trading Systems and Their Impact on Market Performance. *Journal of Financial Markets*, 42, 123–135.

Guszcza, J., Kumar, R., & Lai, A. (2020). *How AI is transforming the HR function*. Deloitte Insights.

H5. (2022). AI in Diplomacy: Enhancing Negotiations with H5 Analytics. *H5 Analytics Report*.

Haefner, N., Wincent, J., Parida, V., & Gassmann, O. (2021). Artificial intelligence and innovation management: A review, framework, and research agenda . *Technological Forecasting and Social Change*, 162, 1–10. DOI: 10.1016/j.techfore.2020.120392

Haenlein, M., Anadol, E., Farnsworth, T., Hugo, H., Hunichen, J., & Welte, D. (2020). Navigating the new era of influencer marketing: How to be successful on Instagram, TikTok, & Co. *California Management Review*, 63(1), 5–25. DOI: 10.1177/0008125620958166

Haenlein, M., & Kaplan, A. (2021). Artificial intelligence and robotics: Shaking up the business world and society at large. *Journal of Business Research*, 124(C), 405–407. DOI: 10.1016/j.jbusres.2020.10.042

Haesevoets, T., De Cremer, D., Dierckx, K., & Van Hiel, A. (2021). Human-machine collaboration in managerial decision making. *Computers in Human Behavior*, 119, 106730. DOI: 10.1016/j.chb.2021.106730

Haggerty, J. D. (n.d.). *Influencers are Ordinary People: Why the World and Business is Run by Influencers.*

Hämäläinen, R., Nissinen, K., Mannonen, J., Lämsä, J., Leino, K., & Taajamo, M. (2021). Understanding teaching professionals' digital competence: What do PIAAC and TALIS reveal about technology-related skills, attitudes, and knowledge? *Computers in Human Behavior*, 117, 1–15. DOI: 10.1016/j.chb.2020.106672

Hameed, M. A., Hassaballah, M., Hosney, M. E., & Alqahtani, A. (2022). An AI-Enabled Internet of Things Based Autism Care System for Improving Cognitive Ability of Children with Autism Spectrum Disorders. *Computational Intelligence and Neuroscience,* 2022, 1–12. https.// DOI: 10.1155/2022/2247675

Hamet, P., & Tremblay, J. (2017). Artificial intelligence in medicine. *metabolism, 69*, 36-40.

Hanna, D. M. (2023). The use of artificial intelligence art generator "midjourney" in artistic and advertising creativity. *Journal of design sciences and applied arts, 4*(2), 42-58. https.//DOI: 10.21608/jdsaa.2023.169144.1231

Haque, M., & Ahmed, N. (2023). AI-Powered Personalization in Indian Financial Services: A Study of HDFC Bank. *Indian Financial Review*, 16(2), 92–107.

Haque, S. M. S. (2023). The impact of remote work on hr practices: Navigating challenges, embracing opportunities. *European Journal of Human Resource Management Studies*, 7(1). Advance online publication. DOI: 10.46827/ejhrms.v7i1.1549

Harris, C., & Zhang, J. (2023). Machine Learning for Employee Retention: Insights and Strategies. *Journal of HR Analytics*, 11(2), 112–128.

Harvard Business Review (HBR). (2024). *AI and Personalized Career Development: A Transformative Approach.* Retrieved from HBR Study.

Harvard Business Review (HBR). (2024). *AI and the Evolution of Employee Engagement.* Retrieved from HBR Study.

Harvard Business Review (HBR). (2024). *AI and the Future of Diversity: Innovations and Best Practices.* Retrieved from HBR Study.

Harvard Business Review (HBR). (2024). *AI and the Future of Diversity: Innovations and Challenges.* Retrieved from HBR Study.

Harvard Business Review (HBR). (2024). *AI and the New Era of Decision-Making.* Retrieved from HBR Study.

Harvard Business Review (HBR). (2024). *Mitigating Bias with AI: A New Approach to Recruitment and Promotion*. Retrieved from HBR Study.

Harvard Business Review (HBR). (2024). *Transforming Employee Development with AI: A New Paradigm*. Retrieved from HBR Study.

Harvard Business Review. (2022). The AI-Powered Workplace. Retrieved from https://hbr.org

Harvard Business Review. (2023). How AI is Changing Talent Management. Retrieved from https://hbr.org

Harvard Law Review. (2022). *Regulating Artificial Intelligence: Global Challenges and Perspectives*. Retrieved from Harvard Law Review

Haryana Employment Department. (2022). Career Guidance Portal and Employment Statistics. Retrieved from Haryana Employment.

Haslam, S. A., Steffens, N. K., Reicher, S. D., & Bentley, S. V. (2021). Identity leadership in a crisis: A 5R framework for learning from responses to COVID-19. *Social Issues and Policy Review*, 15(1), 35–83. DOI: 10.1111/sipr.12075 PMID: 33821168

Hassan, A., Anwar, I., Saleem, I., Islam, K. B., & Hussain, S. A. (2021). Individual entrepreneurial orientation, entrepreneurship education and entrepreneurial intention: The mediating role of entrepreneurial motivations. *Industry and Higher Education*, 35(4), 403–418. DOI: 10.1177/09504222211007051

HDFC Bank. (2019). HDFC Bank's AI Chatbot: Enhancing Customer Experience. Retrieved from https://www.hdfcbank.com

HealthifyMe. (2022). *AI-Powered Health and Wellness Solutions*. Retrieved from HealthifyMe.

HealthifyMe. (2022). *Personalized Health and Wellness: An AI Perspective*. Retrieved from HealthifyMe.

He, H., Gray, J., Cangelosi, A., Meng, Q., McGinnity, T. M., & Mehnen, J. (2021). The challenges and opportunities of human-centered AI for trustworthy robots and autonomous systems. *IEEE Transactions on Cognitive and Developmental Systems*, 14(4), 1398–1412. DOI: 10.1109/TCDS.2021.3132282

Hemshorn de Sanchez, C. S., Gerpott, F. H., & Lehmann-Willenbrock, N. (2022). A review and future agenda for behavioral research on leader–follower interactions at different temporal scopes. *Journal of Organizational Behavior*, 43(2), 342–368. DOI: 10.1002/job.2583

Hernández-Méndez, J., & Baute-Díaz, N. (2024). Influencer marketing in the promotion of tourist destinations: Mega, macro, and micro-influencers. *Current Issues in Tourism*, 27(8), 1332–1342. DOI: 10.1080/13683500.2023.2214354

Heuel, L., Otto, A. K., & Wollesen, B. (2024). Physical exercise and ergonomic workplace interventions for nursing personnel—Effects on physical and mental health: A systematic review. *German Journal of Exercise and Sport Research*, 54(2), 291–324. DOI: 10.1007/s12662-023-00922-6

He, Z. (2023). Blockchain and Legal Tech Innovations. *Blockchain Journal*, 14(1), 101–115.

HireVue. (2021). *AI in Recruitment: Reducing Bias through Technology*. Retrieved from HireVue.

Hodge, V. J., & Austin, J. (2004). A survey of outlier detection methodologies. *Artificial Intelligence Review*, 22(2), 85–126. DOI: 10.1023/B:AIRE.0000045502.10941.a9

Hoffmann, C. H. (2023). A philosophical view on singularity and strong AI. *AI & Society*, 38(4), 1697–1714. DOI: 10.1007/s00146-021-01327-5

Hooi, L. W. (2021). Leveraging human assets for MNCs performance: The role of managementdevelopment, human resource system and employee engagement. *International Journal of Human Resource Management*, 32(13), 2729–2758. DOI: 10.1080/09585192.2019.1590443

HR Research Institute (HRRI). (2020). The Impact of AI on Recruitment: Efficiency and Quality. Retrieved from https://www.hrri.org

HR Research Institute (HRRI). (2023). The Role of AI in Enhancing Employee Productivity. Retrieved from https://www.hrri.org

Hua, H., Li, Y., Wang, T., Dong, N., Li, W., & Cao, J. (2023). Edge computing with artificial intelligence: A machine learning perspective. *ACM Computing Surveys*, 55(9), 1–35. DOI: 10.1145/3555802

Huang, B., Kechadi, M. T., & Buckley, B. (2012, January). Customer churn prediction in telecommunications. *Expert Systems with Applications*, 39(1), 1414–1425. DOI: 10.1016/j.eswa.2011.08.024

Huang, C., & Guo, R. (2021). The effect of a green brand story on perceived brand authenticity and brand trust: The role of narrative rhetoric. *Journal of Brand Management, 28*, 60–76.nly Pursuit. *J. Bus. & Tech. L.*, 18, 289. DOI: 10.1057/s41262-020-00213-7

Huang, M. H., & Rust, R. T. (2018). Artificial Intelligence in Service. *Journal of Service Research*, 21(2), 155–172. DOI: 10.1177/1094670517752459

Huang, M. H., Rust, R., & Maksimovic, V. (2019). The feeling economy: Managing in the next generation of artificial intelligence (AI). *California Management Review*, 61(4), 43–65. DOI: 10.1177/0008125619863436

Huang, Y., & Kechadi, T. (2013, October). An effective hybrid learning system for telecommunication churn prediction. *Expert Systems with Applications*, 40(14), 5635–5647. DOI: 10.1016/j.eswa.2013.04.020

Huberman, A. (2014). Qualitative data analysis a methods sourcebook.

Hueso, J. A., Jaén, I., & Liñán, F. (2021). From personal values to entrepreneurial intention: A systematic literature review. *International Journal of Entrepreneurial Behaviour & Research*, 27(1), 205–230. DOI: 10.1108/IJEBR-06-2020-0383

Hughes, C., Robert, L., Frady, K., & Arroyos, A. (2019). Artificial intelligence, employee engagement, fairness, and job outcomes. In *Managing technology and middle-and low-skilled employees* (pp. 61–68). Emerald Publishing Limited. DOI: 10.1108/978-1-78973-077-720191005

Hult, G. T. M., Hurley, R. F., & Knight, G. A. (2004). Innovativeness: Its antecedents and impact on business performance. *Industrial Marketing Management*, 33(5), 429–438. DOI: 10.1016/j.indmarman.2003.08.015

Hülür, G., & Macdonald, B. (2020). Rethinking social relationships in old age: Digitalization and the social lives of older adults. *The American Psychologist*, 75(4), 554–566. DOI: 10.1037/amp0000604 PMID: 32378949

Humble, K. P., & Altun, D. (2020). Artificial Intelligence and the threat to human rights. *Journal of Internet Law*, 24(3), 1–19.

Hwang, G. J., & Yang, S. J. (2021). AI in Education: A Review and Future Directions. *Educational Technology Research and Development*, 69(3), 435–454.

Hyppönen, M. (2022). *If it's smart, it's vulnerable*. John Wiley & Sons.

IBM. (2020). *Diversity and inclusion: Using data and AI to improve workplace equity*. IBM Corporation.

IBM. (2020). Watson AI for Employee Engagement. Retrieved from https://www.ibm.com

IBM. (2022). *AI and Business Strategy: IBM Watson's Impact*. IBM Research Report.

IBM. (2022). *AI Fairness 360: A Toolkit for Fairness in AI*. Retrieved from IBM.

IBM. (2022). *AI-Driven Insights for Strategic Decision-Making*. Retrieved from IBM Website.

IBM. (2022). The Role of AI in Strategic Decision-Making: IBM Watson's Impact. *IBM Research Report.*

IBM. (2023). AI and the Future of Work: Employee Engagement. Retrieved from https://www.ibm.com

IBM. (2023). Watson AI for Employee Engagement. Retrieved from https://www .ibm.com

IEEE. (2022). *Ethically Aligned Design: A Vision for Prioritizing Human Well-being with Artificial Intelligence and Autonomous Systems*. Retrieved from IEEE.

ILIEVA., G. (n.d.). The role of the influencers for the development of cultural and heritage tourism. *Proceedings of an International Conference*, 17.

Imai, S., Patterson, S., & Varela, C. A. (2018). Uncertainty-aware elastic virtual machine scheduling for stream processing systems. 2018 18th IEEE/ACM CCGRID, pp. 62 – 71.

Inaba, M., Katoh, N., & Imai, H. (1994, June). Applications of weighted Voronoi diagrams and randomization to variance-based k-clustering. In *Proceedings of the tenth annual symposium on Computational geometry* (pp. 332-339).

Incerti, F. (2020). *Preservice Teachers? Perceptions of Artificial Intelligence Tutors for Learning*. A dissertation presented to the faculty of The Gladys W. and David H. Patton College of Education In partial fulfillment of the requirements for the degree Doctor of Philosophy, Ohio University.

Indian Institute of Management Ahmedabad (IIMA). (2024). *AI and Diversity: Reducing Bias in Recruitment and Promotion*. Retrieved from IIMA Research.

Indian Institute of Management Ahmedabad (IIMA). (2024). *AI and Organizational Transformation: Focus on Diversity*. Retrieved from IIMA Research.

Indian Institute of Management Ahmedabad (IIMA). (2024). *AI in Employee Development: Trends and Innovations*. Retrieved from IIMA Research.

Indian Institute of Management Bangalore (IIMB). (2024). *AI and Organizational Culture: Trends and Insights*. Retrieved from IIMB Research.

Indian Institute of Management Bangalore (IIMB). (2024). *AI Tools in Recruitment: Enhancing Diversity and Reducing Bias*. Retrieved from IIMB Research.

Indian Institute of Management Bangalore (IIMB). (2024). *AI-Driven Personalized Employee Development: Case Studies from Indian Firms*. Retrieved from IIMB Research.

Indian Institute of Management Calcutta (IIMC). (2024). *AI-Driven Diversity and Inclusion: Indian Perspectives*. Retrieved from IIMC Research.

Indian Institute of Technology Delhi (IIT Delhi). (2022). *Study on Bias in Facial Recognition Systems*. Retrieved from IIT Delhi.

Indian Parliament. (2024). *Personal Data Protection Bill*. Retrieved from Indian Parliament.

Indonesia Ministry of Industry. (2020). AI in Workforce Planning. Retrieved from https://www.kemenperin.go.id

Infosys. (2020). Leveraging AI for Employee Engagement and Performance Management. Retrieved from https://www.infosys.com

Infosys. (2023). AI in Workforce Planning. Retrieved from https://www.infosys.com

Infosys. (2023). Leveraging AI for Employee Engagement and Performance Management. Retrieved from https://www.infosys.com

Infosys. (2024). *AI Ethics Manifesto*. Retrieved from Infosys

Infosys. (2024). *AI-Powered Employee Engagement: Transforming Learning and Development*. Retrieved from Infosys Report.

Ingrassia, M., Bellia, C., Giurdanella, C., Columba, P., & Chironi, S. (2022). Digital influencers, food, and tourism—A new model of open innovation for businesses in the Ho. Re. Ca. sector. *Journal of Open Innovation*, 8(1), 50. DOI: 10.3390/joitmc8010050

International Association for Privacy Professionals (IAPP). (2023). *Privacy and AI: Challenges and Solutions*. Retrieved from IAPP.

International Journal of Human Resource Management (IJHRM). (2019). AI-Driven Performance Management. *Impact and Benefits. IJHRM*, 30(5), 645–658.

International Telecommunication Union (ITU). (2022). *AI and Data Protection: Global Standards and Guidelines*. Retrieved from ITU.

Ireland, R. D., Hitt, M. A., & Sirmon, D. G. (2003). A model of strategic entrepreneurship: The construct and its dimensions. *Journal of Management*, 29(6), 963–989. DOI: 10.1016/S0149-2063(03)00086-2

Isizoh, A. N., Alagbu, E. E., Nwosu, F. C., Nwoye, C. G., & Ogbogu, E. N. (2021). Applications and analyses of expert systems in decision management. *Journal of inventive engineering and technology (jiet), 1*(5), 78-85.

Ismail, M., Binti Mustaffa, S. N., & Abed, M. (2023). AI-Enabled Deep Learning Model for COVID-19 Identification Leveraging Internet of Things. *Wasit Journal of Computer and Mathematics Science*, 2(2), 33–39. DOI: 10.31185/wjcms.146

iSON. (2019). AI-Driven Innovation in South Africa's Service Sector. Retrieved from https://www.isongroup.com

Iyer, R., & Singh, V. (2022). Predictive Analytics for Business Strategy: Insights from Indian Firms. *Journal of Strategy and Management*, 15(1), 28–41.

Jain, A. (2023). The Impact of AI on Legal Transparency in India. *Journal of Indian Legal Studies*, 12(4), 77–90.

Jain, A., & Choudhury, A. (2023). AI and Autonomous Systems: Transforming Business Operations. *Journal of Business and Technology*, 14(2), 89–104.

Jain, A., Murty, M. N., & Flynn, P. J. (1999). Data Clustering. A Review. *ACM Computing Surveys*, 31(3), 264–323. DOI: 10.1145/331499.331504

Jain, P., & Kumar, A. (2023). Machine Learning for Employee Retention: A Comprehensive Study. *Journal of Employee Engagement*, 13(3), 34–48.

Jarrahi, M. H. (2018). Artificial intelligence and the future of work: Human-AI symbiosis in organizational decision making. *Business Horizons*, 61(4), 577–586. DOI: 10.1016/j.bushor.2018.03.007

Jarrahi, M. H., Askay, D., Eshraghi, A., & Smith, P. (2023). Artificial intelligence and knowledge management: A partnership between human and AI. *Business Horizons*, 66(1), 87–99. DOI: 10.1016/j.bushor.2022.03.002

Jaya, I. P. G. I. T., & Prianthara, I. B. T. (2020). Role of social media influencers in tourism destination image: How does digital marketing affect purchase intention? *3rd International Conference on Vocational Higher Education (ICVHE 2018)*, 9–20. DOI: 10.2991/assehr.k.200331.114

JayantTikmani. (2015). *SudhanshuTiwari, SujataKhedkar "Telecom customer segmentation based on cluster analysisAn Approach to Customer Classification using k-means"*. IJIRCCE,Year.

Jean, N., Burke, M., Xie, M., Davis, W. M., Lobell, D. B., & Ermon, S. (2016). Combining satellite imagery and machine learning to predict poverty. *Science*, 353(6301), 790–794. DOI: 10.1126/science.aaf7894 PMID: 27540167

Jennings, N. R., Faratin, P., Lomuscio, A. R., Parsons, S., Sierra, C., & Wooldridge, M. (2001). Automated negotiation: Prospects, methods and challenges. *Group Decision and Negotiation*, 10(2), 199–215. DOI: 10.1023/A:1008746126376

Jha, R., & Gupta, N. (2022). AI in Strategic Planning: Insights from General Electric and Other Global Leaders. *Journal of Strategic Innovation*, 20(1), 74–89.

Jha, S., & Patel, V. (2022). ML and HR: Analyzing the Impact on Employee Productivity. *Journal of Business Research*, 16(4), 76–90.

Jin, S. V., Muqaddam, A., & Ryu, E. (2019). Instafamous and social media influencer marketing. *Marketing Intelligence & Planning*, 37(5), 567–579. DOI: 10.1108/MIP-09-2018-0375

Jobin, A., Ienca, M., & Vayena, E. (2019). The global landscape of AI ethics guidelines. *Nature Machine Intelligence*, 1(9), 389–399. DOI: 10.1038/s42256-019-0088-2

Johan, S. (2021). Enhanced Financial Business Competitiveness by Leveraging Technology and Innovation. CommIT (Communication and Information Technology). *Journal*, 15(2), 79–89. DOI: 10.21512/commit.v15i2.6968

Jöhnk, J., Weißert, M., & Wyrtki, K. (2021). Ready or not, AI comes—An interview study of organizational AI readiness factors. *Business & Information Systems Engineering*, 63(1), 5–20. DOI: 10.1007/s12599-020-00676-7

Johnson, J. (2019). Unilever's Use of AI in Recruitment. Retrieved from https://www.unilever.com

Johnson, J., Whittington, R., Regnér, P., Angwin, D., Johnson, G., & Scholes, K. (2020). *Exploring strategy*.

Johnson, R. B., & Onwuegbuzie, A. J. (2004). Mixed methods research: A research paradigm whose time has come. *Educational Researcher*, 33(7), 14–26. DOI: 10.3102/0013189X033007014

Jordan, A. (2023). *How to identify the right collaboration partner?: A qualitative study of Finnish Instagram micro-influencers*.

Jordan, M. I., & Mitchell, T. M. (2015). Machine learning: Trends, perspectives, and prospects. *Science*, 349(6245), 255–260. DOI: 10.1126/science.aaa8415 PMID: 26185243

Joshi, P. R. (2024) Model for work-life balance: Integrating theory and research. Available at SSRN 4807438. *SP Swag: Sudur Pashchim Wisdom of Academic Gentry Journal*, 1, 11–26. DOI: DOI: 10.69476/sdpr.2024.v01i01.002

Joshi, S., & Kapoor, R. (2023). Challenges in Implementing ML for Talent Management in Indian Enterprises. *Indian Business Review*, 14(2), 102–115.

Jun, S., & Yi, J. (2020). What makes followers loyal? The role of influencer interactivity in building influencer brand equity. *Journal of Product and Brand Management*, 29(6), 803–814. DOI: 10.1108/JPBM-02-2019-2280

Jurafsky, D., & Martin, J. H. (2021). *Speech and Language Processing*. Pearson.

Justianto, M., & Morley, C. (2020). *The influencer effect on tourism: shifting adventure travel behavior towards more sustainability through Instagram influencers.*

Kadwa, I., & Barnard, B. (2019). The impact of leadership on entrepreneurship and innovation: Perceptions of entrepreneurs. *IUP Journal of Entrepreneurship Development*, 16(4), 7–43.

Kaggwa, S., Eleogu, T. F., Okonkwo, F., Farayola, O. A., Uwaoma, P. U., & Akinoso, A. (2024). AI in decision making: Transforming business strategies. *International Journal of Innovation and Scientific Research*, 10(12), 423–444. DOI: 10.51244/IJRSI.2023.1012032

Kalkan, A. (2011). Kişisel tutum, öznel norm ve algilanan davraniş kontrolünün girişimcilik niyeti üzerindeki etkisi: Üniversite öğrencileri üzerine bir uygulama. *Süleyman Demirel Üniversitesi Sosyal Bilimler Enstitüsü Dergisi*, (14), 189–206.

Kansiime, M. (2020). AI in Agriculture: The Kenyan Experience. *Journal of Agricultural Science.*

Kanungo, T., Mount, D. M., Netanyahu, N. S., Piatko, C. D., Silverman, R., & Wu, A. Y. (2002). An efficient K-means clustering algorithm. *IEEE Transactions on Pattern Analysis and Machine Intelligence*, 24(7), 881–892. DOI: 10.1109/TPAMI.2002.1017616

Kapoor, R., & Choudhury, R. (2022). Ethical Considerations in the Use of Machine Learning for HR Management. *Journal of Ethical AI*, 9(2), 19–32.

Kapoor, S. (2022). Future Trends in AI-Driven Legal Services. *Global Legal Tech Review*, 11(3), 89–103.

Karahanna, E., Straub, D. W., & Chervany, N. L. (1999). Information technology adoption across time: A cross-sectional comparison of pre-adoption and post-adoption beliefs. *Management Information Systems Quarterly*, 23(2), 183–213. DOI: 10.2307/249751

Karami, M., Ojala, A., & Saarenketo, S. (2023). Entrepreneurial orientation and international opportunity development by SMEs: The mediating role of decision-making logic. *Journal of Small Business Management*, 61(2), 994–1022. DOI: 10.1080/00472778.2020.1824529

Karantza, P. (2017). *The impact of economic crises on the development of innovation and entrepreneurship* (Doctoral dissertation, Business Administration Programm, School of Economic Sciences and Business, Neapolis University Pafos).

Karnataka Government. (2023). *Karnataka AI Policy 2023*. Retrieved from Karnataka Government.

Kar, S., Kar, A. K., & Gupta, M. P. (2021). Modeling drivers and barriers of artificial intelligence adoption: Insights from a strategic management perspective. *International Journal of Intelligent Systems in Accounting Finance & Management*, 28(4), 217–238. DOI: 10.1002/isaf.1503

Kashwan, K. R., & Velu, C. M. (2013). Customer segmentation using clustering and data mining techniques. *International Journal of Computer Theory and Engineering*, 5(6), 856.

Katsh, E., & Wing, L. (2006). Ten years of online dispute resolution (ODR): Looking at the past and constructing the future. *U. Tol. L. Rev.*, 38, 19.

Kaur Kapoor, K., & Dwivedi, K., Y., & D. Williams, M. (. (2014). Innovation adoption attributes: A review and synthesis of research findings. *European Journal of Innovation Management*, 17(3), 327–348. DOI: 10.1108/EJIM-08-2012-0083

Kaur, M., & Bhatia, R. (2023). The Role of AI in Enhancing Customer Experience in Indian Retail. *Indian Journal of Retail and Customer Research*, 19(4), 120–135.

Kaur, S., & Kapil, R. (2023). Measuring Customer Engagement in Digital Marketing. *Journal for ReAttach Therapy and Developmental Diversities*, 6(6s), 984–992. DOI: 10.53555/jrtdd.v6i6s.2951

Kayser, K., Telukdarie, A., & Philbin, S. P. (2023). Digital Start-Up Ecosystems: A Systematic Literature Review and Model Development for South Africa. *Sustainability (Basel)*, 15(16), 1–24. DOI: 10.3390/su151612513

Keding, C. (2021). Understanding the interplay of artificial intelligence and strategic management: Four decades of research in review. *Management Review Quarterly*, 71(1), 91–134. DOI: 10.1007/s11301-020-00181-x

Kennedy, P. S. J., Tobing, S. J. L., & Toruan, R. L. (2022). Marketing strategy with marketing mix for Lake Toba tourism destination. [JoSTE]. *Journal of Sustainable Tourism and Entrepreneurship*, 3(3), 157–174.

Kenyan Government. (2019). *Data Protection Act*. Retrieved from Kenyan Government.

Kerala Education Statistics. (2023). *Digital Learning Integration in Schools*. Retrieved from Kerala Education.

Kersten, G. E., & Lo, G. (2003). Aspire: An integrated negotiation support system and software agents for e-business negotiation. *International Journal of Internet and Enterprise Management*, 1(3), 293–315. DOI: 10.1504/IJIEM.2003.003822

Khallaf, A. N.Ayman Naji Khallaf. (2024). Using Ai to Help Reduce the Effect of Global Warming. *Power System Technology*, 48(1), 1927–1947. DOI: 10.52783/pst.464

Khan Academy. (2022). *Personalized Learning with AI: Bridging Educational Gaps*. Retrieved from Khan Academy.

Khan, A. A., Jamwal, S., & Sepehri, M. (2010, November 10). Applying Data Mining to Customer Churn Prediction in an Internet Service Provider. *International Journal of Computer Applications*, 9(7), 8–14. DOI: 10.5120/1400-1889

Khan, I., & Ahmed, R. (2022). AI and Autonomous Systems: Strategic Implications for Indian Industries. *Journal of Indian Industrial Research*, 13(3), 54–67.

Khan, M., & Rathi, R. (2022). ML-Based Talent Acquisition Strategies: Innovations and Impacts. *Journal of Human Capital*, 12(3), 50–67.

Kietzmann, J., Paschen, J., & Treen, E. (2018). Artificial intelligence in advertising. How marketers can leverage artificial intelligence along the consumer journey. *Journal of Advertising Research, 58*(3), 263-267. https.//DOI: 10.2501/JAR-2018-035

Kilipiri, E., Papaioannou, E., & Kotzaivazoglou, I. (2023). Social media and influencer marketing for promoting sustainable tourism destinations: The Instagram case. *Sustainability (Basel)*, 15(8), 6374. DOI: 10.3390/su15086374

Kim, J. W. (2022). *How speciesism affects artificial intelligence (AI) adoption intent* (Doctoral dissertation, Queensland University of Technology).

Kira Systems. (2021). *AI for Contract Analysis and Dispute Resolution*. Kira Systems.

Kira Systems. (2023). *Advancements in AI for Contract Analysis and Risk Assessment*. Kira Systems.

Kira Systems. (2023). *AI-Powered Contract Review and Transparency*. Kira Systems.

Kira Systems. (2023). *AI-Powered Contract Review and Transparency. Kira Systems*. Retrieved from Kira Systems.

Kittur, P., & Chatterjee, S. (2023). Role of B2B reliance and brand image in reducing risk perceptions: A serial mediation model. *European Journal of Marketing*, 57(4), 1068–1098. DOI: 10.1108/EJM-05-2022-0362

Kiyabo, K., & Isaga, N. (2020). Entrepreneurial orientation, competitive advantage, and SMEs' performance: Application of firm growth and personal wealth measures. *Journal of Innovation and Entrepreneurship*, 9(1), 1–15. DOI: 10.1186/s13731-020-00123-7

Kleros. (2023). Blockchain-Based Arbitration and Transparency. *Kleros Platform*.

Kleros. (2023). Blockchain-Based Arbitration and Transparency. *Kleros Platform*. Retrieved from Kleros

Kniffin, K. M., Detert, J. R., & Leroy, H. L. (2019). On leading and managing: Synonyms or separate (and unequal)? *Academy of Management Discoveries*, 6(4), 544–571. DOI: 10.5465/amd.2018.0227

Köbis, N., Bonnefon, J. F., & Rahwan, I. (2021). Bad machines corrupt good morals. *Nature Human Behaviour*, 5(6), 679–685. DOI: 10.1038/s41562-021-01128-2 PMID: 34083752

Koivusalo, S. (2023). Digital entrepreneurship: challenges faced by Finnish professional service business owners during venture launch in online business environments. Master's Thesis, School of Business and Economics, Jyväskylä University.

Kolodinsky, J., Hogarth, J. M., & Hilgert, A. (2001). The adoption of electronic banking technologies by American consumers. *Consumer Interests Annual*, 47(3), 1–9.

Koroglu, Ş., & Ozmen, O. (2022). The mediating effect of work engagement on innovative work behavior and the role of psychological well-being in the job demands–resources (JD-R) model. *Asia-Pacific Journal of Business Administration*, 14(1), 124–144. DOI: 10.1108/APJBA-09-2020-0326

Kotler, P., Pfoertsch, W., & Sponholz, U. (2021). H2h marketing: Putting trust and brand in strategic management focus. *Academy of Strategic Management Journal*, 20(2).

KPMG. (2022). AI and Talent Management: Strategies for Success. Retrieved from https://home.kpmg

KPMG. (2023). The Role of AI in Workforce Planning. Retrieved from https://home.kpmg

Kraus, N., Kraus, K., & Manzhura, O. (2021). Digitalization of business processes of enterprises of the ecosystem of Industry 4.0: Virtual-real aspect of economic growth reserves. *WSEAS Transactions on Business and Economics*, 18, 569–580. DOI: 10.37394/23207.2021.18.57

Kreiser, P. M., & Davis, J. (2010). Entrepreneurial orientation and firm performance: The unique impact of innovativeness, proactiveness, and risk-taking. *Journal of Small Business and Entrepreneurship*, 23(1), 39–51. DOI: 10.1080/08276331.2010.10593472

Krey, N., Tom Dieck, M. C., Wu, S., & Fountoulaki, P. (2023). Exploring the influence of touch points on tourist experiences at crisis-impacted destinations. *Journal of Travel Research*, 62(1), 39–54. DOI: 10.1177/00472875211053657

Krueger, N. F., Jr. (1993). Growing Up Entrepreneurial?": Developmental Consequences Of Early Exposure To Entrepreneurship. In *Academy of Management Proceedings* (Vol. 1993, No. 1, pp. 80-84). Briarcliff Manor, NY 10510: Academy of Management.

Kruger, J. B. (2022). *Rising From The Ashes: An Analysis of How One Infamous Promotional Event Caused a Company's Ruin and a Concept on the Future of Influencer Experiences.*

Kulshrestha, N., Kamra, V., & Aggarwal, S. (2023). Leveraging technical analysis and artificialintelligence—Optimisation of global portfolio management through world indices. *International Journalof Public Sector Performance Management*, 12(3), 445–461. DOI: 10.1504/IJPSPM.2023.133588

Kumar, A., & Gupta, R. (2021). The Digital Divide in India: An Analysis of Technology Access and Usage. *Journal of Information Technology & Politics*, 12(2), 45–61.

Kumar, A., & Patel, N. (2023). Virtual Try-Ons and Personalized Eyewear Recommendations: Lenskart's AI Approach. *Indian Journal of Retail Technology*, 11(3), 45–60.

Kumar, A., & Sharma, N. (2023). Data-Driven Decision Making at Reliance Industries. *Journal of Indian Business Strategy*, 20(1), 55–70.

Kumar, N. (2023). Smart Contracts and Blockchain in Indian Legal Systems. *Legal Innovation Journal*, 9(2), 45–59.

Kumar, P. (2021). Challenges in AI Language Translation in India: A Review. *Journal of Language Technology*, 15(2), 45–60.

Kumar, P., & Aggarwal, R. (2023). Future of Machine Learning in Talent Management. *HR Innovations Journal*, 15(1), 34–46.

Kumar, P., Singh, R., & Yadav, P. (2020). Predictive Analytics in Banking: A Case Study of State Bank of India. *Indian Journal of Finance and Banking*, 12(3), 45–60.

Kumar, R. (2023). Revolutionizing Recruitment: Machine Learning in Talent Acquisition. *HRMagazine*.

Kumar, R., & Verma, A. (2022). Data Privacy and Security in ML-Driven HR Systems. *Journal of Information Security*, 21(2), 22–39.

Kumar, V., & Kaushik, A. K. (2022). Engaging customers through brand authenticity perceptions: The moderating role of self-congruence. *Journal of Business Research*, 138, 26–37. DOI: 10.1016/j.jbusres.2021.08.065

Kumar, V., Rajan, B., Venkatesan, R., & Lecinski, J. (2019). Understanding the role of artificial intelligence in personalized engagement marketing. *California Management Review*, 61(4), 135–155. DOI: 10.1177/0008125619859317

Kumar, V., & Singh, K. (2023). Predictive Analytics for Strategic Decision-Making: A Study of Indian Corporations. *Journal of Indian Business Studies*, 15(2), 100–115.

Kumar, V., & Sinha, A. (2023). Optimizing Talent Management with Machine Learning: A Strategic Perspective. *International Journal of Talent Management*, 14(1), 63–79.

Kumar, Y., Koul, A., Singla, R., & Ijaz, M. F. (2023). Artificial intelligence in disease diagnosis: A systematic literature review, synthesizing framework and future research agenda. *Journal of Ambient Intelligence and Humanized Computing*, 14(7), 8459–8486. DOI: 10.1007/s12652-021-03612-z PMID: 35039756

Kumpulainen, S., & Terziyan, V. (2022). Artificial general intelligence vs. industry 4.0: Do they need each other? *Procedia Computer Science*, 200, 140–150. DOI: 10.1016/j.procs.2022.01.213

Kvale, S. (2009). Interviews: Learning the craft of qualitative research interviewing. *Sage (Atlanta, Ga.)*.

Kwapisz, A., Schell, W. J., Aytes, K., & Bryant, S. (2022). Entrepreneurial action and intention: The role of entrepreneurial mindset, emotional intelligence, and grit. *Entrepreneurship Education and Pedagogy*, 5(3), 375–405. DOI: 10.1177/2515127421992521

Labanauskaitė, D., Župerkienė, E., Kumpf, A., Šimanskienė, L., & Koller, S. M. (2021). Development of digital and entrepreneurial competences for the future labour market needs. *Entrepreneurship and sustainability issues., 8*(3), 565-581.

Lakshman, C. (2014). Leveraging human capital through performance management process: The role of leadership in the USA, France and India†. *International Journal of Human Resource Management*, 25(10), 1351–1372. DOI: 10.1080/09585192.2013.870310

Lanz, L., Briker, R., & Gerpott, F. H. (2023). Employees adhere more to unethical instructions from human than AI supervisors: Complementing experimental evidence with machine learning. *Journal of Business Ethics*. Advance online publication. DOI: 10.1007/s10551-023-05393-1

LawGeex. (2023). *AI for Efficient Contract Review*. LawGeex Insights.

Lee, H., & Choi, S. (2023). AI-Driven Personalization in Retail: A Case Study of Sephora. *International Journal of Retail & Distribution Management*, 51(3), 189–204.

Legal Aid India. (2023). *AI-Driven Legal Assistance for Marginalized Communities*. Legal Aid India Publications.

Legal Aid India. (2023). *AI-Driven Legal Assistance for Marginalized Communities. Legal Aid India Publications*. Retrieved from Legal Aid India.

Legal Aid India. (2023). *AI-Driven Legal Assistance for Underserved Communities*. Legal Aid India Publications.

LegalSift. (2022). *AI-driven Contract Review and Dispute Resolution*. LegalSift Technologies.

LegalSift. (2023). *New Features in AI-Driven Due Diligence and Compliance*. LegalSift Technologies.

Legris, P., Ingham, J., & Collerette, P. (2003). Why do people use information technology? A critical review of the technology acceptance model. *Information & Management*, 40(3), 191–204. DOI: 10.1016/S0378-7206(01)00143-4

Lewis, G. (2023). Explainable AI: Enhancing Trust in Technology. *Tech and Society Journal*, 14(2), 112–125.

LexisNexis. (2023). *AI-Enhanced Legal Research Tools: Latest Innovations*. LexisNexis India Publications.

Li, H. (2019). Special section introduction. Artificial intelligence and advertising. *Journal of advertising, 48*(4), 333-337. https.//DOI: 10.1080/00913367.2019.1654947

Liao, H. L., & Lu, H. P. (2008). The role of experience and innovation characteristics in the adoption and continued use of e-learning websites. *Computers & Education*, 51(4), 1405–1416. DOI: 10.1016/j.compedu.2007.11.006

Liberatore, M. J., & Wagner, W. P. (2021). Virtual, mixed, and augmented reality: A systematic review for immersive systems research. *Virtual Reality (Waltham Cross)*, 25(3), 773–799. DOI: 10.1007/s10055-020-00492-0

Lichtenthaler, U. (2020). Extremes of acceptance: Employee attitudes toward artificial intelligence. *The Journal of Business Strategy*, 41(5), 39–45. DOI: 10.1108/JBS-12-2018-0204

Liebowitz, J. (2001). Knowledge management and its link to artificial intelligence. *Expert Systems with Applications*, 20(1), 1–6. DOI: 10.1016/S0957-4174(00)00044-0

Li, H., & Zhang, Y. (2023). Leveraging ML for Effective Talent Retention: Best Practices and Trends. *Journal of Employee Relations*, 19(3), 85–100.

Limanta, A. L., Prihanto, Y. J. N., & Situmorang, R. (2023). Analysis of the influence of work-life balance, work stress, and job satisfaction when working from home on the implementation of permanent telework culture in legal business. [Review]. *Journal of Business and Management Review*, 4(1), 1–16. DOI: 10.47153/jbmr41.5922023

Lin, S., Shi, M., Arora, A., Bassily, R., Bertino, E., Caramanis, C., Chowdhury, K., Ekici, E., Eryilmaz, A., Ioannidis, S., Jiang, N., Joshi, G., Kurose, J., Liang, Y., Lin, Z., Liu, J., Liu, M., Melodia, T., Mokhtari, A., & Ying, L. (2022). Leveraging Synergies Between AI and Networking to Build Next Generation Edge Networks. 2022 IEEE 8th International Conference on Collaboration and Internet Computing(CIC), 16–25.DOI: 10.1109/CIC56439.2022.00013

Liu, H., & Gu, X. (2023). Leveraging AI, big data and educational technology to promote collaborative learning and improve cyberlearning courses: Synopsis and linked presentations of the workshop at Orlando, Florida, 4-6 June 2019, and the online workshop, 13-14 August 2020. *International Journal of Smart Technology and Learning*, 3(2), 118. DOI: 10.1504/IJSMARTTL.2023.129609

Liu, H., & Li, X. (2021). How travel earns us bragging rights: A qualitative inquiry and conceptualization of travel bragging rights. *Journal of Travel Research*, 60(8), 1635–1653. DOI: 10.1177/0047287520964599

Liu, R. (2023). Innovative research on synergistic development of digital integrated media and visual design based on kruskal algorithm. *Applied Mathematics and Nonlinear Sciences*, 9(1), 1–13.

Liu, Y., & Zhang, Y. (2023). The Role of AI in Strategic Decision-Making: A Global Perspective. *Journal of Global Business*, 31(2), 134–145.

Livingston, S., & Risse, M. (2019). The future impact of artificial intelligence on humans and human rights. *Ethics & International Affairs*, 33(2), 141–158. DOI: 10.1017/S089267941900011X

Li, X., Li, J., Yuan, C., Guo, S., & Wang, Z. (2022). Digital infrastructure. In *Development practice of digital business environment in China* (pp. 39–55). Springer Nature Singapore. DOI: 10.1007/978-981-16-8527-9_3

Li, X., Liu, Y., & Zhang, Q. (2021). The Impact of AI-Driven Recommendations on E-Commerce: A Case Study of Amazon. *Journal of Business Research*, 129, 543–553.

Lombardi, F., Aniello, L., Bonomi, S., & Querzoni, L. (2018). Elastic symbiotic scaling of operators and resources in stream processing systems. *IEEE Transactions on Parallel and Distributed Systems*, 29(3), 572–585. DOI: 10.1109/TPDS.2017.2762683

Lou, C., & Xie, Q. (2021). Something social, something entertaining? How digital content marketing augments consumer experience and brand loyalty. *International Journal of Advertising*, 40(3), 376–402. DOI: 10.1080/02650487.2020.1788311

Luan, L., & Shu, H. (2016, June). Integration of data mining techniques to evaluate promotion for mobile customers' data traffic in data plan. In *2016 13th International Conference on Service Systems and Service Management (ICSSSM)* (pp. 1-6). IEEE.

Lu, H., Li, Y., Chen, M., Kim, H., & Serikawa, S. (2018). Brain intelligence: Go beyond artificial intelligence. *Mobile Networks and Applications*, 23(2), 368–375. DOI: 10.1007/s11036-017-0932-8

Luminance. (2023). Enhancing Document Review with AI for Transparency. *Luminance Technologies.*

Luminance. (2023). Enhancing Document Review with AI for Transparency. *Luminance Technologies.* Retrieved from Luminance

Luminance. (2023). Enhancing Document Review with AI. *Luminance Technologies.*

Lumpkin, G. T., & Dess, G. G. (1996). Clarifying the entrepreneurial orientation construct and linking it to performance. *Academy of Management Review*, 21(1), 135–172. DOI: 10.2307/258632

Lumpkin, G. T., & Dess, G. G. (2001). Linking two dimensions of entrepreneurial orientation to firm performance: The moderating role of environment and industry life cycle. *Journal of Business Venturing*, 16(5), 429–451. DOI: 10.1016/S0883-9026(00)00048-3

MacKay and David, "An Example Inference Task. Clustering,"Information Theory, Inference and Learning Algorithms. (2003). (pp. 284–292). Cambridge University Press.

MacKenzie, I.S. (2024). *Human–Computer Interaction: An Empirical Research Perspective.*

MacQueen, J. B. (1967). Some methods for classification and analysis of multivariate observations. *Proceedings of the fifth Berkeley symposium on mathematical statistics and probability*, 1(14), 281-297.

Mahadev Madgule, N. (2023). Vinayaka, Yeshwant M. Sonkhaskar, Dhiren Ramanbhai Patel, R. Karthikeyan, P. Selvakumar,(2023). Mechanical properties and microstructure of activated TIG welded similar joints of Inconel alloys by desirability approaches. *Materials Today: Proceedings*, 77, 528–533. DOI: 10.1016/j.matpr.2022.12.250

Mahajan, M., Nimbhorkar, P., & Varadarajan, K. (2009). The Planar K-Means Problem is NP-Hard. *LNCS, Springer*, 5431, 274–285.

Mahajan, R. (2022). Regulatory Compliance and AI: Global Perspectives. *Journal of Regulatory Affairs*, 7(4), 78–92.

Maharashtra Government. (2023). *Maharashtra State Data Protection Bill.* Retrieved from Maharashtra Government.

Maharashtra Health Services. (2023). *AI in Healthcare: The Impact of Arogya Setu.* Retrieved from Maharashtra Health.

Mahindra. (2020). AI in Workforce Planning at Mahindra & Mahindra. Retrieved from https://www.mahindra.com

Makhloufi, L., Laghouag, A. A., Ali Sahli, A., & Belaid, F. (2021). Impact of entrepreneurial orientation on innovation capability: The mediating role of absorptive capability and organizational learning capabilities. *Sustainability (Basel)*, 13(10), 1–20. DOI: 10.3390/su13105399

Makian, S. (2022). Online tourism communication in destination image formation. In *Handbook on Tourism and Social Media* (pp. 68–80). Edward Elgar Publishing. DOI: 10.4337/9781800371415.00012

Makridakis, S. (2017). The forthcoming Artificial Intelligence (AI) revolution: Its impact on society and firms. *Futures*, 90, 46–60. DOI: 10.1016/j.futures.2017.03.006

Malik, S., Chadhar, M., Vatanasakdakul, S., & Chetty, M. (2021). Factors affecting the organizational adoption of blockchain technology: Extending the technology–organization–environment (TOE) framework in the Australian context. *Sustainability (Basel)*, 13(16), 1–31. DOI: 10.3390/su13169404

Malodia, S., Islam, N., Kaur, P., & Dhir, A. (2021). Why do people use Artificial Intelligence (AI)-enabled voice assistants? *IEEE Transactions on Engineering Management*, 71, 491–505. DOI: 10.1109/TEM.2021.3117884

Malthouse, E. C., Hessary, Y. K., Vakeel, K. A., Burke, R., & Fudurić, M. (2019). An Algorithm for Allocating Sponsored Recommendations and Content. Unifying Programmatic Advertising and Recommender Systems. *Journal of Advertising*, 48(4), 366–379. https.//DOI: 10.1080/00913367.2019.1652123

Mao, E., & Palvia, P. (2006). Testing an extended model of IT acceptance in the Chinese cultural context. *The Data Base for Advances in Information Systems*, 37(2-3), 20–32. DOI: 10.1145/1161345.1161351

Mariotti, S., & Marzano, R. (2021). The effects of competition policy, regulatory quality and trust on inward FDI in host countries. *International Business Review*, 30(6), 1–16. DOI: 10.1016/j.ibusrev.2021.101887

Martinez, J. (2023). AI for Effective Mediation and Negotiation. *Journal of Conflict Resolution Technology*, 18(1), 25–40.

Martins, I., & Perez, J. P. (2020). Testing mediating effects of individual entrepreneurial orientation on the relation between close environmental factors and entrepreneurial intention. *International Journal of Entrepreneurial Behaviour & Research*, 26(4), 771–791. DOI: 10.1108/IJEBR-08-2019-0505

Masriadi, D., Ekaningrum, N. E., Hidayat, M. S., & Yuliaty, F. (2023). Exploring the future of work: Impact of automation and artificial intelligence on employment. *Endless International Journal of Future Studies*, 6(1), 125–136. DOI: 10.54783/endlessjournal.v6i1.131

Matalamäki, M. J., & Joensuu-Salo, S. (2022). Digitalization and strategic flexibility–a recipe for business growth. *Journal of Small Business and Enterprise Development*, 29(3), 380–401. DOI: 10.1108/JSBED-10-2020-0384

Matos, F., Vairinhos, V., Salavisa, I., Edvinsson, L., & Massaro, M. (2020). *Knowledge, people, and digital transformation*. Springer. DOI: 10.1007/978-3-030-40390-4

Matthews, J., Fastnedge, D., & Nairn, A. (2023). The future of advertising campaigns. The role of AI-generated images in advertising creative. *Journal of Pervasive Media, 8*(1), 29-49. https.//DOI: 10.1386/jpm_00003_1

Mauz, E., Walther, L., Junker, S., Kersjes, C., Damerow, S., Eicher, S., Hölling, H., Müters, S., Peitz, D., Schnitzer, S., & Thom, J. (2023). Time trends in mental health indicators in Germany's adult population before and during the COVID-19 pandemic. *Frontiers in Public Health*, 11, 1065938. DOI: 10.3389/fpubh.2023.1065938 PMID: 36908429

Mayer, B. (2012). *The Dynamics of Conflict Resolution: A Practitioner's Guide*. Jossey-Bass.

McKinsey & Company. (2022). *AI in Emerging Markets: Trends and Challenges*. Retrieved from McKinsey.

McKinsey & Company. (2022). How AI is Reshaping Workplaces. Retrieved from https://www.mckinsey.com

McKinsey & Company. (2022). The Impact of Predictive Analytics on Revenue Growth. *The McKinsey Quarterly*, 31(1), 90–105.

McKinsey & Company. (2023). The Future of Work: AI and Automation. Retrieved from https://www.mckinsey.com

McKinsey & Company. (2024). *AI and Decision-Making: Insights from Global Organizations*. Retrieved from McKinsey Report.

McKinsey & Company. (2024). *AI and Decision-Making: The Future of Organizational Strategy*. Retrieved from McKinsey Report.

McKinsey & Company. (2024). *AI and Diversity: Advancing Inclusive Workplaces*. Retrieved from McKinsey Report.

McKinsey & Company. (2024). *AI and Diversity: Bridging the Gap*. Retrieved from McKinsey Report.

McKinsey & Company. (2024). *AI and Employee Experience: Trends in Personalized Engagement*. Retrieved from McKinsey Report.

McKinsey & Company. (2024). *AI and Personalized Career Development: Enhancing Employee Growth*. Retrieved from McKinsey Report.

McKinsey & Company. (2024). *AI-Driven Learning and Development: Improving Employee Outcomes*. Retrieved from McKinsey Report.

McKinsey & Company. (2024). *AI-Driven Personalization in Employee Development: Best Practices*. Retrieved from McKinsey Report.

Mehta, A., & Singh, R. (2022). AI in Talent Management: Innovations and Future Directions. *Journal of HR Innovations*, 12(3), 90–104.

Mehta, S. (2023). Compliance and Data Privacy in Machine Learning. *Indiana Law Review*, 10(2), 15–29.

Mehta, S. (2023). *Predicting Employee Turnover with Machine Learning: Infosys' Approach*. Economic Times.

Merhi, M. I., & Harfouche, A. (2024). Enablers of artificial intelligence adoption and implementation in production systems. *International Journal of Production Research*, 62(15), 5457–5471. DOI: 10.1080/00207543.2023.2167014

Metawa, N., Hassan, M. K., & Metawa, S. (2022). *Artificial Intelligence and Big Data for Financial Risk Management*. Routledge. DOI: 10.4324/9781003144410

Mexican Government. (2023). *Federal Law on Protection of Personal Data Held by Private Parties*. Retrieved from Mexican Government.

Mickiewicz, T., Sauka, A., & Stephan, U. (2016). On the compatibility of benevolence and self-interest: Philanthropy and entrepreneurial orientation. *International Small Business Journal*, 34(3), 303–328. DOI: 10.1177/0266242614555245

Microsoft. (2020). AI in Employee Wellbeing. Retrieved from https://www.microsoft.com

Microsoft. (2022). *Accelerating Decision-Making with Azure AI: Insights and Benefits*. Microsoft Industry Report.

Microsoft. (2022). *AI for Indian Languages: Innovations and Developments*. Retrieved from Microsoft AI.

Microsoft. (2023). *AI Ethics and Compliance: Policies and Practices*. Retrieved from Microsoft.

Miikkulainen, R., Iscoe, N., Shagrin, A., Rapp, R., Nazari, S., McGrath, P., & Lamba, G. (2018, April). Sentient ascend: AI-based massively multivariate conversion rate optimization. In *Proceedings of the AAAI Conference on Artificial Intelligence* (Vol. 32, No. 1), 7696-7703. DOI: 10.1609/aaai.v32i1.11387

Miller, D. (1983). The correlates of entrepreneurship in three types of firms. *Management Science*, 29(7), 770–791. DOI: 10.1287/mnsc.29.7.770

Miller, D., & Friesen, P. H. (1982). Innovation in conservative and entrepreneurial firms: Two models of strategic momentum. *Strategic Management Journal*, 3(1), 1–25. DOI: 10.1002/smj.4250030102

Miller, J., & Turner, J. (2022). Harnessing AI for Hyper-Personalization in Retail. *International Journal of Retail & Distribution Management*, 50(7), 1085–1101.

Ministry of Electronics and Information Technology (MeitY). (2023). *Guidelines for Artificial Intelligence*. Retrieved from MeitY.

Ministry of Electronics and IT. (2022). *BharatNet Project Overview*. Retrieved from Ministry of Electronics and IT.

Ministry of Housing and Urban Affairs. (2023). *Smart Cities Mission: Progress and Future Plans*. Retrieved from Ministry of Housing and Urban Affairs.

Mintzberg, H. (1973). Strategy-making in three modes. *California Management Review*, 16(2), 44–53. DOI: 10.2307/41164491

Misaros, M., Stan, O. P., Donca, I. C., & Miclea, L. C. (2023). Autonomous Robots for Services—State of the Art, Challenges, and Research Areas. *Sensors (Basel)*, 23(10), 1–31. DOI: 10.3390/s23104962 PMID: 37430875

Mishra, A., & Bhardwaj, S. (2022). Machine Learning for Enhancing Employee Engagement: A Review. *HR and Development Journal*, 13(4), 77–92.

Mistry, P., & Shah, D. (2023). AI and ML in Talent Management: Challenges and Opportunities. *Journal of Strategic HRM*, 14(1), 63–78.

MIT Sloan Management Review. (2022). How AI is Changing Work. Retrieved from https://sloanreview.mit.edu

MIT Sloan Management Review. (2023). Leveraging AI for Better HR Practices. Retrieved from https://sloanreview.mit.edu

Mittelstadt, B. D., Allo, P., Taddeo, M., Wachter, S., & Floridi, L. (2016). The ethics of algorithms: Mapping the debate. *Big Data & Society*, 3(2), 2053951716679679. DOI: 10.1177/2053951716679679

Modayil, J., & Kuipers, B. (2008). The initial development of object knowledge by a learning robot. *Robotics and Autonomous Systems*, 56(11), 879–890. DOI: 10.1016/j.robot.2008.08.004 PMID: 19953188

Mohammad Badruddoza Talukder. Sanjeev Kumar, I. R. Das. (2024a). Implications of Blockchain Technology- Based Cryptocurrency in the cloud for the Hospitality Industry. In *Emerging Trends in Cloud Computing Analytics, Scalability, and Service Models* (p. 19). DOI: 10.4018/979-8-3693-0900-1.ch018

Mohammad Badruddoza Talukder. Sanjeev Kumar, I. R. Das. (2024b). Perspectives of Digital Marketing for the Restaurant Industry. In *Advancements in Socialized and Digital Media Communications* (p. 17). DOI: 10.4018/979-8-3693-0855-4.ch009

Mohammed, I. B., & Isa, S. M. (2021). The role of internet of things (IoT) in the containment and spread of the novel COVID-19 pandemic. *Computational intelligence methods in COVID-19: surveillance, prevention, prediction and diagnosis*, 109-119.

Moinuddin, M., Usman, M., & Khan, R. (2024). Decoding Consumer Behavior: The Role of Marketing Analytics in Driving Campaign Success. *International Journal of Advanced Engineering Technologies and Innovations*, 1(4), 118–141.

Møller, M. F. (1993). A scaled conjugate gradient algorithm for fast supervised learning. *Neural Networks*, 6(4), 525–533. DOI: 10.1016/S0893-6080(05)80056-5

Mondejar, M. E., Avtar, R., Diaz, H. L. B., Dubey, R. K., Esteban, J., Gómez-Morales, A., Hallam, B., Mbungu, N. T., Okolo, C. C., Prasad, K. A., She, Q., & Garcia-Segura, S. (2021). Digitalization to achieve sustainable development goals: Steps towards a Smart Green Planet. *The Science of the Total Environment*, 794, 1–20. DOI: 10.1016/j.scitotenv.2021.148539 PMID: 34323742

Moore, G. C., & Benbasat, I. (1996). Integrating diffusion of innovations and theory of reasoned action models to predict utilization of information technology by end-users. In *Diffusion and Adoption of Information Technology: Proceedings of the first IFIP WG 8.6 working conference on the diffusion and adoption of information technology, Oslo, Norway, October 1995* (pp. 132-146). Springer US. DOI: 10.1007/978-0-387-34982-4_10

Moore, T. (2022). AI and Blockchain: Transforming Legal Processes. *International Law Review*, 19(3), 134–146.

Mostafiz, M. I., Hughes, M., & Sambasivan, M. (2022). Entrepreneurial orientation, competitive advantage and strategic knowledge management capability in Malaysian family firms. *Journal of Knowledge Management*, 26(2), 423–458. DOI: 10.1108/JKM-09-2020-0693

Mourtzis, D. (2024). Industry 4.0 and smart manufacturing. In *Manufacturing from Industry 4.0 to Industry 5.0* (pp. 13-61). Elsevier.

Moussawi, S., Koufaris, M., & Benbunan-Fich, R. (2021). How perceptions of intelligence and anthro-pomorphism affect adoption of personal intelligent agents. *Electronic Markets*, 31(2), 343–364. DOI: 10.1007/s12525-020-00411-w

Muralidharan, K., Singh, A., & Suryanarayan, P. (2019). Educational Disparities in India: An Assessment of Access and Quality. *Education Economics*, 27(4), 357–374.

Murphy, L. (2023). AI in Document Review: Efficiency and Accuracy. *Legal Practice Journal*, 21(2), 76–89.

MyAdvo. (2023). *AI-Powered Document Generation Services*. MyAdvo Insights.

MyAdvo. (2023). *AI-Powered Document Generation Services. MyAdvo Insights*. Retrieved from MyAdvo.

MyAdvo. (2023). *Automated Legal Document Generation with AI*. MyAdvo Insights.

Nair, S. (2018). How Sephora Uses AI to Enhance Customer Experience. Retrieved from https://www.sephora.com

Nair, S., & Thomas, J. (2023). AI in Autonomous Decision-Making: Insights from Indian and Global Perspectives. *Journal of AI and Automation*, 12(3), 78–92.

Nambisan, S., Wright, M., & Feldman, M. (2019). The digital transformation of innovation and entrepreneurship: Progress, challenges and key themes. *Research Policy*, 48(8), 1–9. DOI: 10.1016/j.respol.2019.03.018

Naqvi, R., Soomro, T. R., Alzoubi, H. M., Ghazal, T. M., & Alshurideh, M. T. (2021). The nexus between big data and decision-making: A study of big data techniques and technologies. In *The international conference on artificial intelligence and computer vision* (pp. 838–853). Springer International Publishing. DOI: 10.1007/978-3-030-76346-6_73

NASSCOM. (2021). *Artificial Intelligence: Current Trends and Future Projections*. Retrieved from NASSCOM.

NASSCOM. (2024). *AI in HR: Transforming Employee Engagement and Development in India*. Retrieved from NASSCOM Report.

Nazir, F. (2023). Destination branding through social media: Juxtaposition of foreign influencer's narratives and state's presentation on the event of Pakistan Tourism Summit 2019. *Qualitative Market Research*, 26(4), 428–448. DOI: 10.1108/QMR-03-2022-0048

Ndagi, A., & Salihu, A. A. (2019). Technology Entrepreneurship and Fourth Industrial Revolution Era. *LAPAI International Journal of Management and Social Sciences*, 11(1), 142–153.

Nesbit, P. L. (2012). The role of self-reflection, emotional management of feedback, and self-regulation processes in self-directed leadership development. *Human Resource Development Review*, 11(2), 203–226. DOI: 10.1177/1534484312439196

Neumann, T. (2021). The impact of entrepreneurship on economic, social and environmental welfare and its determinants: A systematic review. *Management Review Quarterly*, 71(3), 553–584. DOI: 10.1007/s11301-020-00193-7

Nie, Y., Tian, Y., Wan, X., Song, Y., & Dai, B. (2020). Named entity recognition for social media texts with semantic augmentation. arXiv preprint arXiv:2010.15458. DOI: 10.18653/v1/2020.emnlp-main.107

Nigerian Government. (2019). *National Data Protection Regulation (NDPR)*. Retrieved from Nigerian Government.

Niramai. (2021). *Innovations in Breast Cancer Screening: The Niramai Approach.* Retrieved from Niramai.

Nissen, M. E., & Sengupta, K. (2006). Incorporating software agents into supply chains: Experimental investigation with a procurement task. *Management Information Systems Quarterly*, 30(1), 145–166. DOI: 10.2307/25148721

Nørskov, S., Chrysochou, P., & Milenkova, M. (2015). The impact of product innovation attributes on brand equity. *Journal of Consumer Marketing*, 32(4), 245–254. DOI: 10.1108/JCM-10-2014-1198

O'Kane, C., Zhang, J. A., Haar, J., & Cunningham, J. A. (2023). How scientists interpret and address funding criteria: Value creation and undesirable side effects. *Small Business Economics*, 61(2), 799–826. DOI: 10.1007/s11187-022-00697-4 PMID: 38625286

O'Neil, C. (2016). *Weapons of Math Destruction: How Big Data Increases Inequality and Threatens Democracy*. Crown Publishing Group.

O'Neil, C. (2016). *Weapons of math destruction: How Big Data increases inequality and threatens democracy*. Crown.

Okoli, I. E. N., Nwosu, K. C., & Okechukwu, M. E. (2021). Entrepreneurial orientation and performance of selected SMEs in Southeast, Nigeria. *European Journal of Business and Management Research*, 6(4), 108–115. DOI: 10.24018/ejbmr.2021.6.4.946

Okonkwo, I., & Namkoisse, E. (2023). The Role of Influencer Marketing in Building Authentic Brand Relationships Online. *Journal of Digital Marketing and Communication*, 3(2), 81–90. DOI: 10.53623/jdmc.v3i2.350

Omeish, F., Sharabati, A., Abuhashesh, M., Al-Haddad, S., Nasereddin, A., Alghizzawi, M., & Badran, O. (2024). The role of social media influencers in shaping destination image and intention to visit Jordan: The moderatinImpact of social media usage intensity. *International Journal of Data and Network Science*, 8(3), 1701–1714. DOI: 10.5267/j.ijdns.2024.2.017

OpenAI. (2023). *Ethical Considerations in AI Development*. Retrieved from OpenAI

OpenAi. (n.d.). https.//openai.com. Retrieved February 1, 2023, from https.//openai.com

OpenLaw. (2023). *Blockchain and Smart Contracts in Arbitration*. OpenLaw Innovations.

OpenLaw. (2023). *Blockchain and Smart Contracts in Arbitration. OpenLaw Innovations*. Retrieved from OpenLaw.

Otero-Neira, C., Arias, M. J. F., & Lindman, M. T. (2013). Market orientation and entrepreneurial proclivity: Antecedents of innovation. *Global Business Review*, 14(3), 385–395. DOI: 10.1177/0972150913496719

Ouvrein, G., Pabian, S., Giles, D., Hudders, L., & De Backer, C. (2021). The web of influencers. A marketing-audience classification of (potential) social media influencers. *Journal of Marketing Management*, 37(13–14), 1313–1342. DOI: 10.1080/0267257X.2021.1912142

Owen, J. (2024). *AI and ML in Financial Knowledge Management and Predictive Analytics*.

Oxford University. (2022). *AI and Data Privacy: Policy Recommendations*. Retrieved from Oxford University.

Pallathadka, H., Ramirez-Asis, E. H., Loli-Poma, T. P., Kaliyaperumal, K., Ventayen, R. J. M., & Naved, M. (2023). Applications of artificial intelligence in business management, e-commerce and finance. *Materials Today: Proceedings*, 80, 1–4. DOI: 10.1016/j.matpr.2021.06.419

Panicacci, S., Donati, M., Fanucci, L., Bellin, I., Profili, F., & Francesconi, P. (2018, June). Population health management exploiting machine learning algorithms to identify high-risk patients. In *2018 IEEE 31st International Symposium on Computer-Based Medical Systems (CBMS)* (pp. 298-303). IEEE. DOI: 10.1109/CBMS.2018.00059

Paramita, W., Nhu, H. B. C., Ngo, L. V., Tran, Q. H. M., & Gregory, G. (2021). Brand experience and consumers' social interactive engagement with the brand page: An integrated-marketing perspective. *Journal of Retailing and Consumer Services*, 62, 102611. DOI: 10.1016/j.jretconser.2021.102611

Parent-Rocheleau, X., & Parker, S. K. (2021). Algorithms as work designers: How algorithmic management influences the design of jobs. *Human Resource Management Review*, 32(3), 100828. DOI: 10.1016/j.hrmr.2021.100838

Parviainen, P., Tihinen, M., Kääriäinen, J., & Teppola, S. (2017). Tackling the digitalization challenge: how to benefit from digitalization in practice. *International journal of information systems and project management, 5*(1), 63-77.

Paśko, Ł., Mądziel, M., Stadnicka, D., Dec, G., Carreras-Coch, A., Solé-Beteta, X., Pappa, L., Stylios, C., Mazzei, D., & Atzeni, D. (2022). Plan and develop advanced knowledge and skills for future industrial employees in the field of artificial intelligence, internet of things and edge computing. *Sustainability (Basel)*, 14(6), 1–43. DOI: 10.3390/su14063312

Patel, N., & Jain, S. (2023). AI-Driven Strategic Planning: A Case Study of HCL Technologies. *Indian Journal of Information Technology*, 16(3), 45–60.

Patel, N., & Sharma, A. (2023). Leveraging AI for Personalized Banking: A Study of HDFC Bank. *Indian Journal of Banking and Finance*, 14(2), 78–92.

Patel, R. (2022). *Tailored Career Development at Mahindra & Mahindra: A Machine Learning Perspective*. Financial Express.

Patel, R. (2023). Infrastructure Challenges for Machine Learning Adoption in Indian Corporates. *IT Insights*, 22(1), 45–59.

Patel, R., & Mehta, S. (2023). Hyper-Personalization in Indian E-Commerce: Strategies and Results. *Journal of Indian E-Commerce Studies*, 22(2), 67–81.

Patel, V. (2023). Blockchain and Smart Contracts: Innovations in Indian Law. *Indiana Law Review*, 15(1), 90–103.

Patwardhan, N., Marrone, S., & Sansone, C. (2023). Transformers in the real world: A survey on nlp applications. *Information (Basel)*, 14(4), 242. DOI: 10.3390/info14040242

Pedro, I. L. M. (2023). *The role of micro-influencers for luxury fashion brands.*

Pereira, C., & Rodrigues, J. (2021). Leveraging AI for Demand Forecasting: A Case Study of Amazon. *Journal of Retail Analytics*, 18(2), 45–58.

Pereira, R., Lima, C., Reis, A., Pinto, T., & Barroso, J. (2024) Review of platforms and frameworks for building Virtual Assistants. In: *World Conference on Information Systems and Technologies*. Springer: Cham, Germany, pp. 105–114. DOI: 10.1007/978-3-031-45648-0_11

Pereira, R., & Rodrigues, J. (2021). AI in Inventory Management: Lessons from Amazon. *Supply Chain Management Review*, 25(4), 40–55.

Perez-Vega, R., Kaartemo, V., Lages, C. R., Razavi, N. B., & Männistö, J. (2021). Reshaping the contexts of online customer engagement behavior via artificial intelligence: A conceptual framework. *Journal of Business Research*, 129, 902–910. DOI: 10.1016/j.jbusres.2020.11.002

Perifanis, N. A., & Kitsios, F. (2023). Investigating the influence of artificial intelligence on business value in the digital era of strategy: A literature review. *Information (Basel)*, 14(2), 1–42. DOI: 10.3390/info14020085

Perry, W. L., McInnis, B., Price, C., & Smith, S. (2013). *Predictive Policing: The Role of Crime Forecasting in Law Enforcement Operations*. RAND Corporation. DOI: 10.7249/RR233

Pertusa-Ortega, E. M., Zaragoza-Sáez, P., & Claver-Cortés, E. (2010). Can formalization, complexity, and centralization influence knowledge performance? *Journal of Business Research*, 63(3), 310–320. DOI: 10.1016/j.jbusres.2009.03.015

Peters, R. (2022). AI for Legal Compliance: Current Applications. *Journal of Compliance Studies*, 16(3), 56–70.

Petriglieri, G., & Petriglieri, J. L. (2015). Can business schools humanize leadership? *Academy of Management Learning & Education*, 14(4), 625–647. DOI: 10.5465/amle.2014.0201

Petrova, M., Popova, P., Popov, V., Shishmanov, K., & Marinova, K. (2021, October). Digital ecosystem: Nature, types and opportunities for value creation. In *International Scientific Conference on Innovations in Digital Economy* (pp. 71-85). Cham: Springer International Publishing.

Philippine Government. (2023). *AI and Data Privacy Initiatives*. Retrieved from Philippine Government.

Philips, G.R., Huang, M., Bodine, C., Kuhn, K., Kersken, V., Reuter, B., … & Zimmermann, G. (2023) Accessible computing. *ACM Transactions on*, 16.

Pillai, R., & Sivathanu, B. (2020). Adoption of artificial intelligence (AI) for talent acquisition in IT/ITeS organizations. *Benchmarking*, 27(9), 2599–2629. DOI: 10.1108/BIJ-04-2020-0186

Pinto Borges, A., Lopes, J. M., Carvalho, C., Vieira, B. M., & Lopes, J. (2021). Education as a key to provide the growth of entrepreneurial intentions. *Education + Training*, 63(6), 809–832. DOI: 10.1108/ET-03-2020-0052

Platon, O.-E. (2023). Using instagram for destination marketing: creating the perception of a tourism destination experience and influencing the travel decision-making process. *Challenges of the Knowledge Society*, 669–676.

Pollitzer, E. (2018). Creating a better future. *Journal of International Affairs*, 72(1), 75–90.

Pop, R.-A., Săplăcan, Z., Dabija, D.-C., & Alt, M.-A. (2022). ThImpact of social media influencers on travel decisions: The role of trust in consumer decision journey. *Current Issues in Tourism*, 25(5), 823–843. DOI: 10.1080/13683500.2021.1895729

Pournader, M., Ghaderi, H., Hassanzadegan, A., & Fahimnia, B. (2021). Artificial intelligence applications in supply chain management. *International Journal of Production Economics*, 241, 1–16. DOI: 10.1016/j.ijpe.2021.108250

Prasad, K. D. V., & Satyaprasad, V. K. (2023). The relationship between remote working and work-life balance with mediating and moderating effects of social support: An empirical study of information technology employees. *International Journal of Organizational Leadership*, 12(0), 235–253. DOI: 10.33844/ijol.2023.60366

Punjab Rural Development. (2022). *Smart Village Initiative: Enhancing Rural Infrastructure*. Retrieved from Punjab Rural Development.

Putniņš, T. J., & Sauka, A. (2020). Why does entrepreneurial orientation affect company performance? *Strategic Entrepreneurship Journal*, 14(4), 711–735. DOI: 10.1002/sej.1325

Puwanenthiren, P., & Udurawana, Y. M. W. G. P. K. (2015). Market segmentation and its impact on customer satisfaction with especial reference to commercial bank of Ceylon Plc. *Marketing Information & Strategies: Core for Development, Scitech Publications (India) Pvt Ltd (January 1, 2014).*

PwC. (2020). Using AI to Promote Diversity and Inclusion. Retrieved from https://www.pwc.com

PwC. (2022). The Role of AI in Performance Management. Retrieved from https://www.pwc.com

PwC. (2023). *Responsible AI: Governance and Risk Management.* Retrieved from PwC.

PwC. (2023). Using AI to Promote Diversity and Inclusion. Retrieved from https://www.pwc.com

Qin, X., & Jiang, Z. (2019). The impact of AI on the advertising process. The Chinese experience. *Journal of Advertising, 48*(4), 338-346. https.//DOI: 10.1080/00913367.2019.1652122

Raghupathi, W., & Raghupathi, V. (2014). Big Data Analytics in Healthcare: A Survey. *Journal of Big Data*, 1(1), 3–20.

Rahman, M. S. (2016). The advantages and disadvantages of using qualitative and quantitative approaches and methods in language "testing and assessment" research: A literature review. Journal of education and learning, 6(1).

Raisch, S., & Krakowski, S. (2021). Artificial intelligence and management: The automation–augmentation paradox. *Academy of Management Review*, 46(1), 192–210. DOI: 10.5465/amr.2018.0072

Rajest, S. S., Singh, B., Obaid, A. J., Regin, R., & Chinnusamy, K. (Eds.). (2023). *Advances in artificial and human intelligence in the modern era*. IGI Global. DOI: 10.4018/979-8-3693-1301-5

Ramachandran, K. K., Mary, A. A. S., Hawladar, S., Asokk, D., Bhaskar, B., & Pitroda, J. R. (2022). Machine learning and role of artificial intelligence in optimizing work performance and employee behavior. *Materials Today: Proceedings*, 51, 2327–2331. DOI: 10.1016/j.matpr.2021.11.544

Ramachandran, K. K., Suma, S., Banerjee, D., Mathew, B., Cheepurupalli, N. R., & Mohan, C. R. (2024). The Effectiveness of Influencer Marketing in the Age of AI. *Journal of Informatics Education and Research*, 4(2).

Ramachandran, S. (2023). The Role of AI in Enhancing Transparency in India. *Indian Journal of Technology and Law*, 14(2), 45–58.

Ramakrishnan, T., Mohan Gift, M. D., Chitradevi, S., Jegan, R., & Subha Hency Jose, P. Nagaraja, Rajneesh Sharma H.N., Selvakumar P., Sintayehu Mekuria Hailegiorgis, (2022). "Study of Numerous Resins Used in Polymer Matrix Composite Materials", Advances in Materials Science and Engineering, vol. 2022, Article ID 1088926, 8 pages, 2022. https://doi.org/DOI: 10.1155/2022/1088926

RAND Corporation. (2022). *Ethics and AI: Policy and Implementation*. Retrieved from RAND Corporation.

Rane, N. L., Achari, A., & Choudhary, S. P. (2023). Enhancing customer loyalty through quality of service: Effective strategies to improve customer satisfaction, experience, relationship, and engagement. *International Research Journal of Modernization in Engineering Technology and Science*, 5(5), 427–452.

Ranjan, J., & Foropon, C. (2021). Big data analytics in building the competitive intelligence of organizations. *International Journal of Information Management*, 56, 1–15. DOI: 10.1016/j.ijinfomgt.2020.102231

Rao, K. S., Bhat, R., & Sen, A. (2021). Healthcare Access and Inequality in India: A Regional Analysis. *International Journal of Health Services*, 51(2), 134–152.

Rao, K., & Kumar, S. (2023). Machine Learning for Workforce Optimization: Benefits and Challenges. *Journal of Organizational Development*, 19(4), 45–60.

Rao, K., & Verma, S. (2023). Enhancing Business Outcomes with AI: TCS's Approach. *Journal of Strategy and Management*, 19(2), 78–92.

Rao, M., Patil, A., & Sharma, S. (2020). Deep Learning for Real-Time Text-to-Speech for Visually Impaired Individuals. *IEEE Transactions on Neural Networks and Learning Systems*, 31(12), 5002–5011.

Rao, P., & Kumar, A. (2023). Predictive Maintenance in Manufacturing: Tata Motors' AI-Driven Approach. *Indian Journal of Manufacturing Engineering*, 17(1), 34–50.

Rao, R., & Srinivasan, A. (2022). AI-Driven Recruitment Processes: Case Studies from Indian Industry. *Journal of Talent Acquisition*, 17(3), 102–119.

Rathi, M. (2021). Policy Challenges in Addressing Diversity and Inclusion in India. *Public Policy Research*, 19(1), 65–80.

Rauch, A., Wiklund, J., Lumpkin, G. T., & Frese, M. (2009). Entrepreneurial orientation and business performance: An assessment of past research and suggestions for the future. *Entrepreneurship Theory and Practice*, 33(3), 761–787. DOI: 10.1111/j.1540-6520.2009.00308.x

Raveendhran, R., & Fast, N. J. (2021). Humans judge, algorithms nudge: The psychology of behavior tracking acceptance. *Organizational Behavior and Human Decision Processes*, 164, 11–26. DOI: 10.1016/j.obhdp.2021.01.001

Ravikumar, B., Gupta, S., & Reddy, A. (2020). Algorithmic Bias in Credit Scoring Systems: Evidence from India. *Data Ethics Journal*, 8(1), 88–104.

Razak, R. A., & Mansor, N. A. (2021). Instagram influencers in social media-induced tourism: Rethinking tourist trust towards tourism destination. In*impact of new media in tourism* (pp. 135–144). IGI Global.

Reamer, F. G. (2023). Artificial intelligence in social work: Emerging ethical issues. *International Journal of Social Work Values and Ethics*, 20(2), 52–71. DOI: 10.55521/10-020-205

Reddy, S. (2023). Addressing Data Quality and Security Issues in Machine Learning. *Data Science Journal*, 12(1), 33–47.

Reeves, M., & Ueda, D. (2016). Designing the machines that will design strategy. Harvard Business Review Digital Articles, 2–6. https://hbr.org/2016/04/welcoming-the-chief-strategy-robot

Relativity Trace. (2023). *AI for Compliance and Audit Transparency*. Relativity Trace Solutions.

Relativity Trace. (2023). *AI for Compliance and Audit Transparency. Relativity Trace Solutions*. Retrieved from Relativity.

Reliance Industries. (2020). AI-Driven Employee Training Programs at Reliance. Retrieved from https://www.ril.com

Reliance Industries. (2020). AI-Driven Performance Management at Reliance. Retrieved from https://www.ril.com

Reliance Industries. (2020). AI-Driven Workforce Planning at Reliance. Retrieved from https://www.ril.com

Reuter, K., Wilson, M. L., Moran, M., Le, N., Angyan, P., Majmundar, A., Kaiser, E. M., & Unger, J. B. (2021). General audience engagement with antismoking public health messages across multiple social media sites: Comparative analysis. *JMIR Public Health and Surveillance*, 7(2), e24429. DOI: 10.2196/24429 PMID: 33605890

Riahi, Y., & Riahi, S. (2018). Big data and big data analytics: Concepts, types and technologies. *International Journal of Research and Engineering*, 5(9), 524–528. DOI: 10.21276/ijre.2018.5.9.5

Richards, D. (2023). Blockchain for Legal Integrity and Transparency. *Journal of Digital Law*, 12(1), 89–102.

RiiDL. (2023). *AI-Driven Educational Diagnostics and Support*. Retrieved from RiiDL.

Rijsdijk, S. A., Hultink, E. J., & Diamantopoulos, A. (2007). Product intelligence: Its conceptualization, measurement and impact on consumer satisfaction. *Journal of the Academy of Marketing Science*, 35(3), 340–356. DOI: 10.1007/s11747-007-0040-6

Robinson, M. F. (2019). *Artificial intelligence in hiring: Understanding attitudes and perspectives of HR practitioners*. A dissertation submitted to the faculty of Wilmington University in partial fulfillment of the requirements for the degree of Doctor of Business Administration, Wilmington University (Delaware).

Robinson, C. V., Ahmad, F., & Simmons, J. E. (2021). Consolidation and fragmentation in environmental scanning: A review and research agenda. *Long Range Planning*, 54(3), 1–18. DOI: 10.1016/j.lrp.2020.101997

Robinson, S. C. (2020). Trust, transparency, and openness: How inclusion of cultural values shapes Nordic national public policy strategies for artificial intelligence (AI). *Technology in Society*, 63, 101421. DOI: 10.1016/j.techsoc.2020.101421

Rodgers, S. (2021). Themed issue introduction. Promises and perils of artificial intelligence and advertising. *Journal of Advertising, 50*(1), 1-10. https.//DOI: 10.1080/00913367.2020.1868233

Rogers, S. (2018). How AI is Transforming GE's Predictive Maintenance Strategy. Retrieved from https://www.ge.com

Rogers, E. (2003). *Diffusion of innovations* (5th ed.). Free Press.

Rogers, E. M. (1995). *Diffusion of Innovations* (4th ed.). Free Press.

Rosário, A. T., & Dias, J. C. (2022). Sustainability and the digital transition: A literature review. *Sustainability*, 14(7), 1–18. DOI: 10.3390/su14074072 PMID: 36090804

Ross, M. H. (2000). Creating the conditions for peacemaking: Theories of practice in ethnic conflict resolution. *Ethnic and Racial Studies*, 23(6), 1002–1034. DOI: 10.1080/014198700750018397

Round, C. (2024). Digitizing Responsibility: Emerging Technologies and Power in Environmental and Informational Governance (Doctoral dissertation, George Mason University).

Roy, S., & Sinha, S. (2022). Future of ML in Employee Retention: Trends and Innovations. *Journal of HR Research*, 11(4), 22–39.

Runsewe, O., & Samaan, N. (2017). Cloud resource scaling for big data streaming applications using a Layered Multi-dimensional Hidden Markov Model. Proceedings of IEEE/ACM CCGRID '17, pp. 848 – 857. DOI: 10.1109/CCGRID.2017.147

Russell, S., & Norvig, P. (2020). *Artificial Intelligence: A Modern Approach*. Pearson.

Russo, D. (2024). Navigating the complexity of generative ai adoption in software engineering. *ACM Transactions on Software Engineering and Methodology*, 33(5), 1–50. DOI: 10.1145/3652154

Ruzgas, T., Jakubeliene, K., & Buivyte, A. (2016). Big Data Mining and Knowledge Discovery. *Journal of Communications Technology. Electronics and Computer Science*, 9, 5–9.

Saatçi, E. Y. (2017). Girişimcilik 4.0: Tarihten Sanayi 4.0'a Doğru Girişimciler. *Maliye Finans Yazıları*, 118, 95–112.

Sabuncu, R. G. (2017). *Anadolu Üniversitesi İşletme Fakültesi Öğrencilerinin Girişimcilik Niyetleri ve Çevresel Tutumlarını Ölçmeye Yönelik Bir Araştırma, (Yayın Numarası,463513)* [Yüksek Lisans Tezi, Anadolu Üniversitesi]. Ulusal Tez Merkezi.

Safak, C., & Farrar, J. (2021). Managed by bots. Data-driven exploitation in the gig economy. Worker Info Exchange Report. https://www.workerinfoexchange.org/wie-report-managed-by-bots

Saha, R., & Gupta, S. (2022). AI-Driven Innovation: Case Studies from India and Around the World. *Journal of Technology & Innovation*, 17(1), 45–60.

Sakhi. (2022). *Empowering Women Entrepreneurs: The Sakhi AI Project*. Retrieved from Sakhi.

Santiago, J. K., Magueta, D., & Dias, C. (2020). Consumer Attitudes Towards Fashion Influencers on Instagram: Impact of Perceptions and Online Trust on Purchase Intention. *Issues in Information Systems*, 21(1).

Santoniccolo, F., Trombetta, T., Paradiso, M. N., & Rollè, L. (2023). Gender and media representations: A review of the literature on gender stereotypes, objectification and sexualization. *International Journal of Environmental Research and Public Health*, 20(10), 5770. DOI: 10.3390/ijerph20105770 PMID: 37239498

Sarel, D., & Marmorstein, H. (2003). Marketing online banking services: The voice of the customer. *Journal of Financial Services Marketing*, 8(2), 106–118. DOI: 10.1057/palgrave.fsm.4770111

Saunders, K. T., & Locke, L. G. (2020). Casting lots, gambling, and artificial intelligence. *Journal of Biblical Integration in Business*, 23(1), 58–69. DOI: 10.69492/jbib.v23i1.557

Saxena, P., Priyadarshini, I., Sharma, S., & Jora, R. B. (2022, March). Role of Emotional and Artificial Intelligence on Employee Performance in Service Industry: A Review of Literature. In *2022 8th International Conference on Advanced Computing and Communication Systems (ICACCS)* (Vol. 1, pp. 1564-1567). IEEE. DOI: 10.1109/ICACCS54159.2022.9784989

Schumpeter, J. A. (1934). *The theory of economic development. An inquiry into profits, capital, credit, interest, and the business cycle*. Harvard University Press.

Scuola Holden (2022, March 16). Scuola Holden - School of Writing - Master in Storytelling. Scuola Holden. https.//scuolaholden.it/en/

Sedkaoui, S. (Ed.). (2018). *Big data analytics for entrepreneurial success*. IGI Global.

Selvakumar, P. (2023). Biomedical applications of polymers in biosensors, cancer vaccines and drug delivery systems. *Biopolimery i Kletka*, 39(4), 245–256. DOI: 10.7124/bc.000AA0

Selvakumar, P., Mariappan, P., Shunmugam, S., Paul, R., & Jabez, S. (2024). Removal of chemicals from effluent using photobioreactor technology to improve environmental and health impacts. *Zeitschrift für Physikalische Chemie*, 2024(7), 1295–1302. Advance online publication. DOI: 10.1515/zpch-2023-0450

Selvakumar, P., Palanisamy, S. K., Cinthaikinian, S., Palanisamy, V., Mariappan, R., & Selvakumar, P. K. (2024). Biosensors and its diverse applications in healthcare systems. *Zeitschrift für Physikalische Chemie*, 2024. Advance online publication. DOI: 10.1515/zpch-2023-0406

Semenov, V. P., Chernokulsky, V. V., & Razmochaeva, N. V. (2017, October). Research of artificial intelligence in the retail management problems. In *2017 IEEE II international conference on control in technical systems (CTS)* (pp. 333-336). IEEE. DOI: 10.1109/CTSYS.2017.8109560

Şenyapar, H. N. D. (2024). A comprehensive analysis of influencer types in digital marketing. *International Journal of Management and Administration*, 8(15), 75–100. DOI: 10.29064/ijma.1417291

Serbanescu, A. (2022). Millennials and Gen Z in the Era of Social Media. *Social Media, Technology, and New Generations. Digital Millennial Generation and Generation Z*, 61-78.

Sethi, S., & Mehta, A. (2020). Employment Discrimination and Economic Opportunities in India. *Journal of Labor Economics*, 38(3), 451–472.

Shahriari, B., Swersky, K., Wang, Z., Adams, R. P., & de Freitas, N. (2015). Taking the human out of the loop: A review of Bayesian optimization. *Proceedings of the IEEE*, 104(1), 148–175. DOI: 10.1109/JPROC.2015.2494218

Shahzad, M. F., Khan, K. I., Saleem, S., & Rashid, T. (2021). What factors affect the entrepreneurial intention to start-ups? The role of entrepreneurial skills, propensity to take risks, and innovativeness in open business models. *Journal of Open Innovation*, 7(3), 1–23. DOI: 10.3390/joitmc7030173

Shane, S. A. (Ed.). (2007). *Economic development through entrepreneurship: Government, university and business linkages*. Edward Elgar Publishing.

Shapero, A., & Sokol, L. (1982). *The social dimensions of entrepreneurship, Encyclopedia of Entrepreneurship*. Prentice-Hall.

Sharma, D., & Chanda, K. (2023). Destination marketing in the digital world. *management metamorphosis: navigating the changing landscape*, 128.

Sharma, A., & Singh, A. (2022). Enhancing Supply Chain Efficiency with AI: A Case Study of Reliance Industries. *Indian Journal of Supply Chain Management*, 8(1), 56–70.

Sharma, B. K., Bhatt, V. K., & Arora, L. (2021). Influencer marketing-an instrument to proliferation of the digital occurrence. *International Journal of Enterprise Network Management*, 12(4), 340–357. DOI: 10.1504/IJENM.2021.119662

Sharma, K. (2023). AI and Mediation: Bridging Gaps in Legal Services. *Journal of Mediation Studies*, 20(2), 101–115.

Sharma, L. (2022). *Engagement and Retention: HCL Technologies' Machine Learning Strategy*. Forbes India.

Sharma, L. (2022). Overcoming Resistance to Machine Learning: Strategies for Effective Change Management. *HR Tech Review*, 16(2), 54–68.

Sharma, M., & Jain, K. (2023). ML-Based Talent Management: Enhancing Efficiency and Effectiveness. *Journal of Organizational Behavior*, 19(1), 90–105.

Sharma, R., Lopes de Sousa Jabbour, A. B., Jain, V., & Shishodia, A. (2022). The role of digital technologies to unleash a green recovery: Pathways and pitfalls to achieve the European Green Deal. *Journal of Enterprise Information Management*, 35(1), 266–294. DOI: 10.1108/JEIM-07-2021-0293

Sharma, S., & Gupta, P. (2023). The Future of AI in Strategic Decision-Making: Predictions and Realities. *Journal of Strategic Forecasting*, 14(2), 85–99.

Siddiqui, M. K., & Goyal, K. K. (2023). A Study the Use of E-Payment Systems Based on Artifical Intelligence. *Computing & Intellegent Systems (SCTS)*, 1063-1076.

Sigurðardóttir, G. R. (2019). *Using social proof techniques and attributes of social media influencers to promote fresh fish products.*

Sihombing, L., & Dinus, H. (2024). Analysis of Business Development Strategies in Increasing Customer Trust. *Journal on Economics. Management and Business Technology*, 2(2), 84–92.

Silva, A., Schrum, M., Hedlund-Botti, E., Gopalan, N., & Gombolay, M. (2023). Explainable artificial intelligence: Evaluating the objective and subjective impacts of xai on human-agent interaction. *International Journal of Human-Computer Interaction*, 39(7), 1390–1404. DOI: 10.1080/10447318.2022.2101698

Silver, D., Huang, A., Maddison, C. J., Guez, A., Sifre, L., Van Den Driessche, G., ... & Hassabis, D. (2016). Mastering the game of Go with deep neural networks and tree search. *nature, 529*(7587), 484-489.

Singh, A., & Reddy, S. (2023). AI in Business Strategy: Case Studies from Indian Firms. *The Journal of Business Strategy*, 18(1), 21–35.

Singh, P. (2022). Cost and Scalability of Machine Learning Solutions. *Mint*, 27(3), 45–59.

Singh, P. (2022). *Streamlining Recruitment with Machine Learning: TCS' Success Story*. Mint. Recent Developments in Machine Learning for Talent Management Global Developments.

Singh, P. (2023). AI-Powered Legal Services in India: Opportunities and Challenges. *Indian Journal of Legal Innovation*, 11(3), 56–72.

Sinha, A., & Verma, P. (2023). AI and Hyper-Personalization in Indian Retail: Trends and Insights. *Indian Retail Review*, 20(4), 90–105.

Sinha, P. (2023). Community Mediation and AI: The MediAI Project. *Indian Journal of Science and Technology*, 9(1), 45–60.

Sinha, P., & Patel, S. (2023). Machine Learning in Employee Development: A Strategic Approach. *Journal of Career Development*, 14(2), 76–92.

Sinha, R. (2023). Leveraging Predictive Analytics for Personalization: Flipkart's Strategy. *Indian E-Commerce Review*, 22(1), 56–63.

Si, S., Hall, J., Suddaby, R., Ahlstrom, D., & Wei, J. (2023). Technology, entrepreneurship, innovation and social change in digital economics. *Technovation*, 119, 102484. DOI: 10.1016/j.technovation.2022.102484

Smith, A. (2018). How AI Personalization Increases Amazon's Sales. Retrieved from https://www.amazon.com

Smith, J. (2023). Explainable AI and Legal Decision-Making. *AI Ethics Review*, 13(2), 67–80.

Smith, J., & Lee, K. (2022). Personalized Music Recommendations and User Engagement: A Study of Spotify. *Journal of Digital Media & Policy*, 13(1), 47–60.

Smith, J., & Lee, K. (2023). AI-Driven Resource Allocation and Production Optimization: General Electric's Approach. *Journal of Industrial Engineering and Management*, 16(4), 289–305.

Smith, M. (2023). AI and Blockchain: The Future of Legal Dispute Resolution. *Global Legal Innovations Journal*, 19(4), 123–136.

Smith, S. P. (2021). Landscapes for "likes": Capitalizing on travel with Instagram. *Social Semiotics*, 31(4), 604–624. DOI: 10.1080/10350330.2019.1664579

Society for Human Resource Management (SHRM). (2023). AI in HR: Benefits and Challenges. Retrieved from https://www.shrm.org

Sohn, K., & Kwon, O. (2020). Technology acceptance theories and factors influencing artificial Intelligence-based intelligent products. *Telematics and Informatics*, 47, 1–14. DOI: 10.1016/j.tele.2019.101324

Soni, N., Sharma, E. K., Singh, N., & Kapoor, A. (2020). Artificial intelligence in business: From research and innovation to market deployment. *Procedia Computer Science*, 167, 2200–2210. DOI: 10.1016/j.procs.2020.03.272

Soto-Vásquez, A. D. (2022). YouTube and TikTok as platforms for learning about others: The case of Non-Chinese travel videos in Shanghai Disneyland. *Online Media and Global Communication*, 1(2), 315–338. DOI: 10.1515/omgc-2022-0012

South African Government. (2021). *Protection of Personal Information Act (POPIA)*. Retrieved from South African Government.

Srinivasan, A. (2023). Technological Infrastructure and Machine Learning Challenges. *European Journal of Business*, 12(4), 102–117.

Srivastava, M. (2021). Mapping the influence of influencer marketing: A bibliometric analysis. *Marketing Intelligence & Planning*, 39(7), 979–1003. DOI: 10.1108/MIP-03-2021-0085

Stahl, B. C. (2021). *Artificial intelligence for a better future: an ecosystem perspective on the ethics of AI and emerging digital technologies*. Springer Nature. DOI: 10.1007/978-3-030-69978-9

Stanford University. (2022). AI and the Future of Work. Retrieved from https://ai.stanford.edu

Stanford University. (2023). *AI Ethics and Society: A Research Overview*. Retrieved from Stanford University.

Stanford University. (2023). The Impact of AI on Organizational Behavior. Retrieved from https://ai.stanford.edu

Stefanova, V., Farrell, L., & Latu, I. (2023). Gender and the pandemic: Associations between caregiving, working from home, personal and career outcomes for women and men. *Current Psychology (New Brunswick, N.J.)*, 42(20), 17395–17411. DOI: 10.1007/s12144-021-02630-6 PMID: 35002182

Steils, N., Martin, A., & Toti, J.-F. (2022). Managing the transparency paradox of social-media influencer disclosures: How to improve authenticity and engagement when disclosing influencer–sponsor relationships. *Journal of Advertising Research*, 62(2), 148–166. DOI: 10.2501/JAR-2022-008

Stevens, P. M., Williams, K. P., & Smith, M. C. (2000). Organizational communication and information processes in an internet-enabled environment. *Psychology and Marketing*, 17(7), 607–632. DOI: 10.1002/(SICI)1520-6793(200007)17:7<607::AID-MAR3>3.0.CO;2-5

Stevens, W. E. (2022). *Black Influencers: Interrogating the Racialization and Commodification of Digital Labor*. Temple University.

Streimikiene, D., Svagzdiene, B., Jasinskas, E., & Simanavicius, A. (2021). Sustainable tourism development and competitiveness: The systematic literature review. *Sustainable Development (Bradford)*, 29(1), 259–271. DOI: 10.1002/sd.2133

Strohmeier, S., & Piazza, F. (2013). Domain driven data mining in human resource management: A review of current research. *Expert Systems with Applications*, 40(7), 2410–2420. DOI: 10.1016/j.eswa.2012.10.059

Strzelecki, A., & Rutecka, P. (2020). Direct answers in Google search results. *IEEE Access : Practical Innovations, Open Solutions*, 8, 103642–103654. DOI: 10.1109/ACCESS.2020.2999160

Sturgeon, T. J. (2021). Upgrading strategies for the digital economy. *Global Strategy Journal*, 11(1), 34–57. DOI: 10.1002/gsj.1364

Sugumaran, K. M. D., Pandiyarajan V., Y. B S, Selvakumar P. and M. S, (2024). "Analysis of Electromyography Signals for Control of Mechanical Prosthesis using Machine Learning Techniques," 2024 2nd International Conference on Intelligent Data Communication Technologies and Internet of Things (IDCIoT), Bengaluru, India, 2024, pp. 1059-1067, DOI: 10.1109/IDCIoT59759.2024.10467707

SulekhaGoyat. (2011). *The basis of market segmentation. a critical review of literature*. EJBM,Year.

Sun, X., & Zhou, H. (2023). Autonomous Systems in Finance: A Predictive Approach. *Financial Analysts Journal*, 12(2), 88–99.

Suominen, A., Toivanen, H., & Seppänen, M. (2017). Firms' knowledge profiles: Mapping patent data with unsupervised learning. *Technological Forecasting and Social Change*, 115, 131–142. DOI: 10.1016/j.techfore.2016.09.028

Suoranta, M. (2003). *Adoption of mobile banking in Finland*, Academic dissertation to be publicly discussed, School of Business and Economics of the University of Jyväskylä.

Suresh, A., & Reddy, M. (2022). Machine Learning for Performance Management: Insights and Applications. *Journal of Performance Management*, 10(3), 35–50.

Syam, N., & Sharma, A. (2018). Waiting for a sales renaissance in the fourth industrial revolution: Machine learning and artificial intelligence in sales research and practice. *Industrial Marketing Management*, 69, 135–146. DOI: 10.1016/j.indmarman.2017.12.019

Sycara, K. P. (1991). Problem restructuring in negotiation. *Management Science*, 37(10), 1248–1268. DOI: 10.1287/mnsc.37.10.1248

Sycara, K. P. (1993). Machine learning for intelligent support of conflict resolution. *Decision Support Systems*, 10(2), 121–136. DOI: 10.1016/0167-9236(93)90034-Z

Syed, R., Suriadi, S., Adams, M., Bandara, W., Leemans, S. J., Ouyang, C., ter Hofstede, A. H. M., van de Weerd, I., Wynn, M. T., & Reijers, H. A. (2020). Robotic process automation: Contemporary themes and challenges. *Computers in Industry*, 115, 1–15. DOI: 10.1016/j.compind.2019.103162

Tahar, A., Riyadh, H. A., Sofyani, H., & Purnomo, W. E. (2020). Perceived ease of use, perceived usefulness, perceived security and intention to use e-filing: The role of technology readiness. *The Journal of Asian Finance. Economics and Business*, 7(9), 537–547.

Talukder, M. B., & DAS, I. V. A. R. (2024). *Review papers the technology impacts and ai solutions in hospitality*.

Talukder, M. B., Kumar, S., & Das, I. R. (2024a). Food Wastage on the Economic Outcome: Evidence From the Hotel Industry. *IGI Global, USA*.https://doi.org/https://doi.org/ 10.4018/979-8-3693-2181-2.ch005

Talukder, M. B., Kumar, S., & Das, I. R. (2024c). Mindfulness of Digital Detoxification: Healthy Lifestyle in Tourism. *IGI Global, USA*.https://doi.org/https://doi.org/ 10.4018/979-8-3693-1273-5.ch004 DOI: DOI: 10.4018/979-8-3693-1273-5.ch004

Talukder, M. B., & Das, I. R. (2024). The Technology Impacts and AI Solutions in Hospitality. . . *I-Manager's Journal on Artificial Intelligence &. Machine Learning*, 2(1), 56–72. https://doi.org/https://doi.org/10.26634/jaim.2.1.20291

Talukder, M. B., & Das, I. V. A. R. (2024). The technology impacts and ai solutions in hospitality. [JAIM]. *I-Manager's Journal on Artificial Intelligence & Machine Learning*, 2(1), 56. Advance online publication. DOI: 10.26634/jaim.2.1.20291

Talukder, M. B., Kumar, S., & Das, I. R. (2024b). Mindful Consumers and New Marketing Strategies for the Restaurant Business: Evidence of Bangladesh. In Ramos, C., Costa, T., Severino, F., & Calisto, M. (Eds.), *Social Media Strategies for Tourism Interactivity* (pp. 240–260). IGI Global., https://doi.org/https://doi.org/10 .4018/979-8-3693-0960-5.ch010 DOI: 10.4018/979-8-3693-0960-5.ch010

Talview. (2022). *AI in Talent Acquisition: Enhancing Recruitment Practices*. Retrieved from Talview.

Tambe, P., Cappelli, P., & Yakubovich, V. (2019). Artificial intelligence in human resources management: Challenges and a path forward. *California Management Review*, 61(4), 15–42. DOI: 10.1177/0008125619867910

Tambe, P., & Hitt, L. M. (2022). The Impact of AI on Strategic Decision Making: Evidence from the Tech Industry. *Management Science*, 68(4), 2223–2242.

Tamil Nadu Government. (2023). *Tamil Nadu AI Ethics Council*. Retrieved from Tamil Nadu Government.

Tamil Nadu Health Department. (2023). *e-Sanjeevani Telemedicine Statistics*. Retrieved from Tamil Nadu Health.

Tan, M., & Teo, T. S. (2000). Factors influencing the adoption of Internet banking. *Journal of the Association for Information Systems*, 1(5), 1–42. DOI: 10.17705/1jais.00005

Tanoğlu, Ş. (2019). *Resim İş Eğitimi Öğrencilerinin Dijital Vatandaşlık Düzeyleri İle Dijital Teknolojiye Yönelik Tutumları Arasındaki İlişkinin İncelenmesi, (Yayın Numarası, 588605)* [Yüksek Lisans Tezi, T.C. Erzincan Binali Yıldırım Üniversitesi]. Ulusal Tez Merkezi.

Tan, P. N., Steinbach, M., & Kumar, V. (2006). *Introduction to Data Mining*. Addison-Wesley.

Tashakkori, A., & Teddlie, C. (2003). *Handbook of mixed methods in social and behavioral research*. SAGE Publications.

Tata Consultancy Services (TCS). (2023). AI and Workforce Management. Retrieved from https://www.tcs.com

Tata Consultancy Services (TCS). (2023). *Annual Report*. Retrieved from TCS Annual Report.

Tata Consultancy Services (TCS). (2024). *AI and Employee Engagement: Insights and Outcomes*. Retrieved from TCS Report.

Tata Consultancy Services (TCS). (2024). *AI and Transparency: A New Approach to Decision-Making*. Retrieved from TCS Report.

Tata Consultancy Services (TCS). (2024). AI Ethics Framework. Retrieved from TCS.

Tata Consultancy Services (TCS). (2024). *Diversity and Inclusion Initiatives: AI Tools in Practice*. Retrieved from TCS Report.

TCS. (2021). AI and Innovation at Tata Consultancy Services. Retrieved from https://www.tcs.com

Tech Mahindra. (2020). AI in Employee Wellbeing at Tech Mahindra. Retrieved from https://www.techmahindra.com

Tech Mahindra. (2023). AI for Employee Engagement. Retrieved from https://www.techmahindra.com

Technologies, H. C. L. (2020). Predictive Analytics in Workforce Planning. Retrieved from https://www.hcltech.com

Technologies, H. C. L. (2023). Enhancing Employee Training with AI. Retrieved from https://www.hcltech.com

Technologies, H. C. L. (2024). *AI and Employee Development: Tailoring Learning Opportunities*. Retrieved from HCL Technologies.

Technologies, H. C. L. (2024). *Diversity and Inclusion Report*. Retrieved from HCL Technologies.

Technologies, H. C. L. (2024). *Leveraging AI for Personalizing Employee Development*. Retrieved from HCL Technologies.

Technologies, H. C. L. (2024). *Personalized Development Programs Using AI: Case Studies*. Retrieved from HCL Technologies.

Teixeira, S., Teixeira, S., Oliveira, Z., & Souza, E. (2023). *Using Influencer Marketing as a Digital Business Strategy*. IGI Global. DOI: 10.4018/979-8-3693-0551-5

Tekeoglu, N. (2020). Dijital Teknolojiye Yönelik Tutum ile Sinemaya Gitme Motivasyonlarının Yapısal Eşitlik Modellemesi ile İncelenmesi. *Econder International Academic Journal*, 4(1), 26–46. DOI: 10.35342/econder.678149

Tekin, İ. Ç., & Küsbeci, P. (2021). Dijital dönüşüm sürecinde yükselen bir değer: Dijital girişimcilik. *Stratejik Yönetim Araştırmaları Dergisi*, 4(1), 81–102.

Telemedicine India. (2022). *Telemedicine and AI: Addressing Healthcare Access Challenges*. Retrieved from Telemedicine India.

Thailand Board of Investment. (2022). *AI Policies and Corporate Practices*. Retrieved from Thailand Board of Investment.

Thakur, P., & Sharma, V. (2022). Autonomous Systems in Indian Manufacturing: A Predictive Approach. *Journal of Indian Manufacturing Research*, 12(3), 56–72.

The Brookings Institution. (2022). *AI Governance and Public Policy: A Review*. Retrieved from Brookings.

Thomas, A. (2022). Regulatory AI Tools and Their Impact. *Compliance Technology Journal*, 10(1), 34–48.

Thorpe, R. (2016). *Gower handbook of leadership and management development*. CRC Press. DOI: 10.4324/9781315585703

Tian, Z., Dew, R., & Iyengar, R. (2024). Mega or micro? Influencer selection using follower elasticity. *JMR, Journal of Marketing Research*, 61(3), 472–495. DOI: 10.1177/00222437231210267

Tien, J. M. (2017). Internet of things, real-time decision making, and artificial intelligence. *Annals of Data Science*, 4(2), 149–178. DOI: 10.1007/s40745-017-0112-5

Tigre, F. B., Curado, C., & Henriques, P. L. (2022). Digital leadership: A bibliometric analysis. *Journal of Leadership & Organizational Studies*, 30(1), 40–70. DOI: 10.1177/15480518221123132

Timuroğlu, M. K., & ÇAKIR, S. (2014). Girişimcilerin yeni bir girişim yapma niyetlerinin risk alma eğilimi ile ilişkisi. *Afyon Kocatepe Üniversitesi İktisadi ve İdari Bilimler Fakültesi Dergisi*, 16(2), 119–136.

Tirrell, C. (2023). *Labor control and the experience of work in the platform economy*. Northeastern University. DOI: 10.17760/D20487636

Tiwari, P., & Kumar, R. (2023). AI and Predictive Analytics in Indian Healthcare. *Journal of Healthcare Management*, 30(1), 75–90.

Tiwari, R., & Mishra, P. (2023). Leveraging AI for Talent Acquisition: Current Practices and Future Trends. *Journal of HR Technology*, 18(1), 63–78.

Tjandrawibawa, P. (2020). The effect of using Instagram influencers in building Conseva's brand awareness. *The Winners*, 21(1), 67–73. DOI: 10.21512/tw.v21i1.6497

Todaro, M. P., & Smith, S. C. (2020). *Economic development*.

Toksoy, B. (2019). *Girişimci Kişilik Özelliklerinin Girişimcilik Niyetine Etkisinde Stratejik Güven ve Ortak Değerlerin Moderatör Rolü Üzerine Bir Araştırma, (Yayın Numarası,582619)* [Doktora Tezi, İstanbul Okan Üniversitesi]. Ulusal Tez Merkezi.

Tong, S., Jia, N., Luo, X., & Fang, Z. (2021). The Janus face of artificial intelligence feedback: Deployment versus disclosure effects on employee performance. *Strategic Management Journal*, 42(9), 1600–1631. DOI: 10.1002/smj.3322

Topol, E. (2019). *Deep medicine: How artificial intelligence can make healthcare human again*. Basic Books.

Topol, E. (2019). *Deep Medicine: How Artificial Intelligence Can Make Healthcare Human Again*. Basic Books.

Tornatzky, L. G., & Fleischer, M. (1990). *The processes of technological innovation*. Lexington Books.

Torrado, R. R., Bontrager, P., Togelius, J., Liu, J., & Perez-Liebana, D. (2018, August). Deep reinforcement learning for general video game ai. In *2018 IEEE Conference on Computational Intelligence and Games (CIG)* (pp. 1-8). IEEE. DOI: 10.1109/CIG.2018.8490422

Toshniwal, A., Taneja, S., & Shukla, A.. (2014). Storm@Twitter. *Proceedings of ACM SIGMOD* '14, ACM, pp. 147 – 156.

Tourish, D. (2020). The triumph of nonsense in management studies. *Academy of Management Learning & Education*, 19(1), 99–109. DOI: 10.5465/amle.2019.0255

Tripathi, R., & Joshi, N. (2023). The Role of AI in Strategic Planning and Decision-Making: Evidence from Indian Enterprises. *Indian Journal of Strategic Management*, 17(1), 88–103.

Truby, J. (2020). Governing artificial intelligence to benefit the UN sustainable development goals. *Sustainable Development (Bradford)*, 28(4), 946–959. DOI: 10.1002/sd.2048

Truong, Y., & Papagiannidis, S. (2022). Artificial intelligence as an enabler for innovation: A review and future research agenda. *Technological Forecasting and Social Change*, 183, 1–6. DOI: 10.1016/j.techfore.2022.121852

Tsou, H. T., & Chen, J. S. (2023). How does digital technology usage benefit firm performance? Digital transformation strategy and organisational innovation as mediators. *Technology Analysis and Strategic Management*, 35(9), 1114–1127. DOI: 10.1080/09537325.2021.1991575

Tully, M. (2015). Investigating the role of innovation attributes in the adoption, rejection, and discontinued use of open source software for development. *Information Technologies and International Development*, 11(3), 55–69.

Turienzo, J., Cabanelas, P., & Lampón, J. F. (2023). Business models in times of disruption: The connected and autonomous vehicles (uncertain) domino effect. *Journal of Business Research*, 156, 1–12. DOI: 10.1016/j.jbusres.2022.113481

Turner, C. (2022). Augmented reality, augmented epistemology, and the real-world web. *Philosophy & Technology*, 35(1), 19. DOI: 10.1007/s13347-022-00496-5

Tyagi, A. K., & Chahal, P. (2020). Artificial intelligence and machine learning algorithms. In *Challenges and applications for implementing machine learning in computer vision* (pp. 188–219). IGI Global. DOI: 10.4018/978-1-7998-0182-5.ch008

UNHCR. (2020). *AI for Social Good: Managing Disputes in Refugee Camps*. UNHCR Reports.

United Nations. (2022). *Ethics of Artificial Intelligence: A Global Perspective*. Retrieved from United Nations.

University of Cambridge. (2023). *The Future of AI Ethics: Challenges and Opportunities*. Retrieved from University of Cambridge.

UpGrad. (2023). *AI-Powered Skill Development and Career Enhancement*. Retrieved from UpGrad.

Usman, F. O., Kess-Momoh, A. J., Ibeh, C. V., Elufioye, A. E., Ilojianya, V. I., & Oyeyemi, O. P.Favour Oluwadamilare UsmanAzeez Jason Kess-MomohChidera Victoria IbehAkinola Elumakin ElufioyeValentine Ikenna IlojianyaOluwaseun Peter Oyeyemi. (2024). Entrepreneurial innovations and trends: A global review: Examining emerging trends, challenges, and opportunities in the field of entrepreneurship, with a focus on how technology and globalization are shaping new business ventures. *International Journal of Science and Research Archive*, 11(1), 552–569. DOI: 10.30574/ijsra.2024.11.1.0079

Usman, H., Mulia, D., Chairy, C., & Widowati, N. (2022). Integrating trust, religiosity and image into technology acceptance model: The case of the Islamic philanthropy in Indonesia. *Journal of Islamic Marketing*, 13(2), 381–409. DOI: 10.1108/JIMA-01-2020-0020

Uttar Pradesh Government. (2022). *E-Pathshala and Educational Advancements*. Retrieved from Uttar Pradesh Government.

Vaidya, R., & Karnawat, T. (2023). Conceptualizing influencer marketing: A literature review on the strategic use of social media influencers. *International Journal of Management. Public Policy Research*, 2(Special Issue), 81–86. DOI: 10.55829/ijmpr.v2iSpecialIssue.140

Vaishali, R. (2011). *Patel and Rupa G. Mehta "Impact of Outlier Removal and Normalization Approach in Modified k-Means Clustering Algorithm"*. IJCSI,Year.

Vakilsearch. (2023). Affordable AI-Powered Legal Services. *Vakilsearch Updates*.

Vakilsearch. (2023). Affordable AI-Powered Legal Services. *Vakilsearch Updates*. Retrieved from Vakilsearch

Vakilsearch. (2023). AI-Powered Legal Services: Bridging the Accessibility Gap. *Vakilsearch Updates*.

Vakratsas, D., & Wang, X. (2020). Artificial intelligence in advertising creativity. *Journal of Advertising, 50*(1), 39-51. https.//DOI: 10.1080/00913367.2020.1843090

Van Deursen, A. J., & Van Dijk, J. A. (2014). *Digital skills: Unlocking the information society*. Springer.

Van Doorn, S., Heyden, M., Tröster, C., & Volberda, H. (2015). Entrepreneurial orientation and performance: Investigating local requirements for entrepreneurial decision-making. In *Cognition and strategy* (Vol. 32, pp. 211–239). Emerald Group Publishing Limited. DOI: 10.1108/S0742-332220150000032007

Van Praag, C. M., & Versloot, P. H. (2007). What is the value of entrepreneurship? A review of recent research. *Small Business Economics*, 29(4), 351–382. DOI: 10.1007/s11187-007-9074-x

Vance, A. (2015). *Elon Musk: Tesla, SpaceX, and the Quest for a Fantastic Future*. Ecco.

Vardar, A. (2018). *Girişimcilik Niyetine Etki Eden Değişkenlerin Planlanmış Davranış Teorisi Çerçevesinde Analizi, Açık Öğretim Öğrencileri Üzerinde Bir Araştırma (Yayın Numarası509466)* [Doktora Tezi, Anadolu Üniversitesi]. Ulusal Tez Merkezi.

Varma, N., & Sharma, P. (2022). Social Cohesion and Inter-Group Conflicts in Diverse Societies: The Indian Experience. *Sociology Compass*, 16(1), 23–39.

Vasudevan, K., & Bandyopadhyay, D. (2023). AI-Driven Business Strategies: A Study of Indian Corporations. *Indian Journal of Business Research*, 17(2), 125–139.

Vattani, A. (2011). K-means exponential iterations even in the plane. *Discrete & Computational Geometry*, 45(4), 596–616. DOI: 10.1007/s00454-011-9340-1

Verma, S. (2023). Enhancing Fashion Retail with AI: Myntra's Personalized Recommendations. *Indian Journal of Fashion and Retail*, 16(2), 89–104.

Verma, S., & Patel, N. (2022). Ethical Challenges in ML Applications for Talent Management. *Journal of Business Ethics*, 17(2), 22–39.

Verplanken, B., & Orbell, S. (2022). Attitudes, habits, and behavior change. *Annual Review of Psychology*, 73(1), 327–352. DOI: 10.1146/annurev-psych-020821-011744 PMID: 34587780

Vijayakumar, G., Rajkumar, M., Rajiv Chandar, N., Selvakumar, P., & Duraisamy, R. (2024). Muniyandi Rajkumar, Rajiv Chandar N, Selvakumar P and Ramesh Duraisamy, (2024). Environmentally friendly TDS removal from waste water by electrochemical ion exchange batch-type recirculation (EIR) technique. *Environmental Science. Water Research & Technology*, 10(4), 826–835. DOI: 10.1039/D3EW00793F

Vishwakarma, P., & Sharma, A. (2023). Predictive Analytics in Talent Retention: Case Studies from India. *Journal of Human Resource Analytics*, 15(1), 90–105.

Vlahov, M. M., & Vlahov, A. (2021). Travel influencers as a new strategic partners in tourism. *Proceedings of FEB Zagreb International Odyssey Conference on Economics and Business, 3*(1), 1249–1265.

Von Krogh, G., Ben-Menahem, S. M., & Shrestha, Y. R. (2021). Artificial intelligence in strategizing: Prospects and challenges. *Future of strategic management*, 625-646.

Votto, A. M., Valecha, R., Najafirad, P., & Rao, H. R. (2021). Artificial intelligence in tactical human resource management: A systematic literature review. *International Journal of Information Management Data Insights*, 1(2), 1–15. DOI: 10.1016/j.jjimei.2021.100047

Vrontis, D., Makrides, A., Christofi, M., & Thrassou, A. (2021). Social media influencer marketing: A systematic review, integrative framework and future research agenda. *International Journal of Consumer Studies*, 45(4), 617–644. DOI: 10.1111/ijcs.12647

Waarts, E., van Everdingen, Y. M., & Van Hillegersberg, J. (2002). The dynamics of factors affecting the adoption of innovations. *Journal of Product Innovation Management*, 19(6), 412–423. DOI: 10.1111/1540-5885.1960412

Walia, S., & Kapoor, P. (2022). Predictive Analytics and AI: Shaping the Future of Business Strategy. *Business Analytics Review*, 16(2), 32–47.

Wamba-Taguimdje, S. L., Wamba, S. F., Kamdjoug, J. R. K., & Wanko, C. E. T. (2020). Influence of artificial intelligence (AI) on firm performance: The business value of AI-based transformation projects. *Business Process Management Journal*, 26(7), 1893–1924. DOI: 10.1108/BPMJ-10-2019-0411

Wang, B., Rau, P. L. P., & Yuan, T. (2022). Measuring user competence in using artificial intelligence: Validity and reliability of artificial intelligence literacy scale. *Behaviour & Information Technology*, •••, 1–14. DOI: 10.1080/0144929X.2022.2072768

Wang, L. (2023). AI in Legal Document Analysis: Emerging Trends. *The Journal of Legal Analysis*, 14(1), 89–102.

Wang, Q., & Liu, J. (2022). AI in Strategic Planning: Real-World Applications and Future Directions. *Strategic Management Journal*, 43(5), 789–805.

Watson, I. B. M. (2023). *Explainable AI for Transparent Decision Making*. IBM Watson Insights.

Watson, I. B. M. (2023). *Explainable AI for Transparent Decision Making. IBM Watson Insights*. Retrieved from IBM Watson.

West Bengal Government. (2023). *Sakhi Project: Empowering Women Entrepreneurs*. Retrieved from West Bengal Government.

Wiklund, J., & Shepherd, D. (2005). Entrepreneurial orientation and small business performance: A configurational approach. *Journal of Business Venturing*, 20(1), 71–91. DOI: 10.1016/j.jbusvent.2004.01.001

Williams, C. (2022). Blockchain and Transparency in Legal Processes. *Journal of Legal Technology*, 13(3), 112–126.

Wilson, H. J., & Daugherty, P. R. (2018). Collaborative intelligence: Humans and AI are joining forces. *Harvard Business Review*, 96(4), 114–123.

Wipro. (2020). AI in Talent Management at Wipro. Retrieved from https://www.wipro.com

Wipro. (2023). AI in Talent Management at Wipro. Retrieved from https://www.wipro.com

Wipro. (2023). AI-Driven Talent Management. Retrieved from https://www.wipro.com

Woodgate, D. (2022). *The Augmented Learner: The pivotal role of multimedia enhanced learning within a foresight-based learning model designed to accelerate the delivery of higher levels of learner creat* Yang, J., Chuenterawong, P., Lee, H., & Chock, T. M. (2023). Anthropomorphism in CSR endorsement: A comparative study on humanlike vs. cartoonlike virtual influencers' climate change messaging. *Journal of Promotion Management*, 29(5), 705–734.

World Bank. (2023). *AI and Development: Opportunities and Risks*. Retrieved from World Bank.

World Economic Forum. (2021). *AI Governance: A Holistic Approach*. Retrieved from World Economic Forum

World Economic Forum. (2022). AI and the Future of Jobs. Retrieved from https://www.weforum.org

World Economic Forum. (2023). The Future of Jobs Report. Retrieved from https://www.weforum.org

Wright, C., & Lee, J. (2022). Predictive Analytics and Strategic Decision-Making: Lessons from IBM and Microsoft. *Business Analytics Journal*, 14(1), 21–37.

Wu, L., Dodoo, N. A., & Wen, T. J. (2024). Disclosing AI's Involvement in Advertising to Consumers. A Task-Dependent Perspective. *Journal of Advertising*, 1-19. https.//DOI: 10.1080/00913367.2024.2309929

Wujarso, R. (2023). *Effect of digital transformation on company operational efficiency*. Asadel Publisher.

Wu, W. T., Li, Y. J., Feng, A. Z., Li, L., Huang, T., Xu, A. D., & Lyu, J. (2021). Data mining in clinical big data: The frequently used databases, steps, and methodological models. *Military Medical Research*, 8(1), 1–12. DOI: 10.1186/s40779-021-00338-z PMID: 34380547

Xia, Z. (2023). Addressing the tasks and opportunities of agency using AI-based Chatbots. *International Journal of Communication Networks and Information Security*, 15, 25–42.

Xiong, D., Khaddage-Soboh, N., Umar, M., Safi, A., & Norena-Chavez, D. (2024). Redefining entrepreneurship in the digital age: Exploring the impact of technology and collaboration on ventures. *The International Entrepreneurship and Management Journal*, 20(4), 1–27. DOI: 10.1007/s11365-024-00996-0

Xu, B., Gutierrez, B., Mekaru, S., Sewalk, K., Goodwin, L., Loskill, A., Cohn, E. L., Hswen, Y., Hill, S. C., Cobo, M. M., Zarebski, A. E., Li, S., Wu, C. H., Hulland, E., Morgan, J. D., Wang, L., O'Brien, K., Scarpino, S. V., Brownstein, J. S., & Kraemer, M. U. G. (2020). Epidemiological data from the COVID-19 outbreak, real-time case information. *Scientific Data*, 7(1), 106. DOI: 10.1038/s41597-020-0448-0 PMID: 32210236

Xu, J., Tang, J., Xu, Z., Yin, C., Kwiat, K., & Kamhoua, C. (2019). A deep recurrent neural network based predictive control framework for reliable distributed stream data processing. *Proceedings of IEEE IPDPS*, 19, 262–272. DOI: 10.1109/IPDPS.2019.00036

Xu, K., Wang, X., Wei, W., Song, H., & Mao, B. (2016). Toward software defined smart home. *IEEE Communications Magazine*, 54(5), 116–122. DOI: 10.1109/MCOM.2016.7470945

Xu, R., & Wunsch, D. (2005). Clustering in Data Mining. A Survey. *IEEE Transactions on Knowledge and Data Engineering*, 16(3), 303–316. DOI: 10.1109/TKDE.2004.68

Xu, W., Dainoff, M. J., Ge, L., & Gao, Z. (2023). Transitioning to human interaction with AI systems: New challenges and opportunities for HCI professionals to enable human-centered AI. *International Journal of Human-Computer Interaction*, 39(3), 494–518. DOI: 10.1080/10447318.2022.2041900

Yadav, R. (2023). AI for Transparency and Accountability in Indian Legal Systems. *Indian Journal of Legal Studies*, 16(2), 78–91.

Yadav, R., & Kumar, S. (2023). AI in Strategic Decision-Making: The Indian Perspective. *Journal of Indian Business Research*, 14(2), 45–59.

Yadav, R., & Singh, M. (2023). Challenges and Opportunities in Implementing ML for HR Functions. *The Journal of Business Strategy*, 14(3), 78–93.

Yadav, S., & Gupta, A. (2022). The Role of ML in Enhancing Employee Engagement and Satisfaction. *Journal of Organizational Psychology*, 12(4), 45–60.

Yadav, S., & Sharma, P. (2023). AI in Indian Retail: Personalization Strategies and Outcomes. *Indian Journal of Retail and Distribution*, 21(3), 99–114.

Yadwadkar, N. J., & Choi, W. (2012). Proactive straggler avoidance using machine learning. White paper, University of Berkeley

Yalcin, G., Lim, S., Puntoni, S., & van Osselaer, S. M. (2022). Thumbs up or down: Consumer reactions to decisions by algorithms versus humans. *JMR, Journal of Marketing Research*, 59(4), 696–717. DOI: 10.1177/00222437211070016

Yang, X., He, X., Zhao, J., Zhang, Y., Zhang, S., & Xie, P. (2020). *Covid-ct-dataset: A ct Scan Dataset About Covid-19.arXiv Preprint ArXiv:2003.13865.*

Ye, G., Hudders, L., De Jans, S., & De Veirman, M. (2021). The value of influencer marketing for business: A bibliometric analysis and managerial implications. *Journal of Advertising*, 50(2), 160–178. DOI: 10.1080/00913367.2020.1857888

Yeomans, M., Shah, A., Mullainathan, S., & Kleinberg, J. (2019). Making sense of recommendations. *Journal of Behavioral Decision Making*, 32(4), 403–414. DOI: 10.1002/bdm.2118

Yetimoğlu, S., & Uğurlu, K. (2020). Influencer marketing for tourism and hospitality. In *The Emerald Handbook of ICT in tourism and hospitality* (pp. 131–148). Emerald Publishing Limited. DOI: 10.1108/978-1-83982-688-720201009

Yigitbasi, N., Willke, T. L., Liao, G., & Epema, D. (2013). Towards machine learning-based auto-tuning of MapReduce. Proceedings of IEEE MASCOTS '13, IEEE, pp. 11 – 20.

Yin, R. K. (2018). Case study research and applications.

Yousfi-Monod, M., Farzindar, A., & Lapalme, G. (2010). Supervised machine learning for summarizing legal documents. In *Advances in Artificial Intelligence: 23rd Canadian Conference on Artificial Intelligence, Canadian AI 2010, Ottawa, Canada, May 31–June 2, 2010.* [Springer Berlin Heidelberg.]. *Proceedings*, 23, 51–62.

Yuan, Y., Ma, M., Han, S., Zhang, D., Miao, F., Stankovic, J., & Lin, S. (2021, May). DeResolver: a decentralized negotiation and conflict resolution framework for smart city services. In *Proceedings of the ACM/IEEE 12th International Conference on Cyber-Physical Systems* (pp. 98-109). DOI: 10.1145/3450267.3450538

Yuen, K. F., Wong, Y. D., Ma, F., & Wang, X. (2020). The determinants of public acceptance of autonomous vehicles: An innovation diffusion perspective. *Journal of Cleaner Production*, 270, 1–13. DOI: 10.1016/j.jclepro.2020.121904

Zacheilas, N., Kalogeraki, V., & Zygouras, N.. (2015). Elastic complex event processing exploiting prediction. *Proceedings of IEEE Big Data*, 15, 213–222.

Zafarani, R. (2014). *Social Media Mining: An Introduction*. Cambridge University Press. DOI: 10.1017/CBO9781139088510

Zahra, S. A. (1991). Predictors and financial outcomes of corporate entrepreneurship: An exploratory study. *Journal of Business Venturing*, 6(4), 259–285. DOI: 10.1016/0883-9026(91)90019-A

Zha, H., Ding, C., Gu, M., He, X., & Simon, H. D. (2001). Spectral Relaxation for K-means Clustering. *Neural Information Processing Systems, Vancouver, Canada*, 14, 1057–1064.

Zhang, C., Nahrgang, J. D., Ashford, S. J., & DeRue, D. (2020). Why capable people are reluctant to lead. Harvard Business Review. https://hbr.org/2020/12/why-capable-people-are-reluctant-to-lead

Zhang, W. (2022). *The Engagement Between Social Media Influencers and Their Followers on Instagram: A Case Study of# StopAsianHate*.

Zhang, C., & Lu, Y. (2021). Study on artificial intelligence: The state of the art and future prospects. *Journal of Industrial Information Integration*, 23, 1–9. DOI: 10.1016/j.jii.2021.100224

Zhang, G. P. (2000). Neural networks for classification: A survey. *IEEE Transactions on Systems, Man, and Cybernetics. Part C, Applications and Reviews*, 30(4), 451–462. DOI: 10.1109/5326.897072

Zhang, H., Song, M., & He, H. (2020). Achieving the success of sustainability development projects through big data analytics and artificial intelligence capability. *Sustainability (Basel)*, 12(3), 1–23. DOI: 10.3390/su12030949

Zhang, J., van Gorp, D., & Kievit, H. (2023). Digital technology and national entrepreneurship: An ecosystem perspective. *The Journal of Technology Transfer*, 48(3), 1077–1105. DOI: 10.1007/s10961-022-09934-0 PMID: 35602312

Zhang, J., & Yang, Y. (2022). AI in Talent Management: A Review. *Human Resource Management Review*, 32(4), 100803.

Zhang, J., & Yang, Y. (2023). Advances in AI for HR. *Human Resource Management Review*, 33(1), 100823.

Zhang, L., & Huang, Y. (2022). AI and the Future of Strategic Decision-Making: A Global Overview. *Journal of AI and Strategy*, 9(1), 100–115.

Zhang, L., & Lee, J. (2022). AI-Driven Talent Management: Opportunities and Risks. *Journal of Strategy and Management*, 13(1), 56–71.

Zhang, X., & Zhou, M. (2023). AI and Autonomous Systems: Future Trends in Strategic Decision-Making. *Journal of Future Technology*, 10(4), 145–160.

Zhang, Y. (2023). Innovations in AI and Blockchain for Legal Services. *International Journal of Technology and Law*, 15(3), 56–70.

Zhang, Y., Wang, S., & Xie, L. (2022). Advancements in AI for Accessibility: A Review. *Journal of Artificial Intelligence Research.*

Zhang, Y., Zhang, M., & Yang, J. (2020). Machine Learning Models for Sales Forecasting: A Comparative Study. *Journal of Business Analytics*, 9(4), 197–210.

Zhang, Y., Zhang, M., & Yang, J. (2022). AI Applications in E-Commerce: A Case Study of Alibaba. *International Journal of Retail & Distribution Management*, 50(4), 380–395.

Zhang, Y., Zhang, M., & Yang, J. (2022). AI Applications in Logistics: A Case Study of Alibaba. *International Journal of Logistics Management*, 33(2), 167–182.

Zhao, G., Li, Y., & Xu, Q. (2022). From Emotion AI to Cognitive AI. *International Journal of Network Dynamics and Intelligence*, 65–72. https.//DOI: 10.53941/ijndi0101006

Zhao, Q. (2009). A survey on virtual reality. *Science in China Series F: Information Sciences*, 52(3), 348–400.

Zhao, X., & Li, Q. (2023). Machine Learning and Talent Management: An Overview of Current Applications. *International Journal of HR Tech*, 19(2), 22–37.

Zheng, X. (2022). Explainable AI in Legal Technology: A Comprehensive Review. *AI and Law Review*, 11(2), 45–58.

Zhou, Q. (2023). Blockchain in Arbitration and Dispute Resolution. *Journal of Blockchain and Legal Studies*, 8(4), 89–102.

Zhou, S., Blazquez, M., McCormick, H., & Barnes, L. (2021). How social media influencers' narrative strategies benefit cultivating influencer marketing: Tackling issues of cultural barriers, commercialised content, and sponsorship disclosure. *Journal of Business Research*, 134, 122–142. DOI: 10.1016/j.jbusres.2021.05.011

Zhu, J. (2017). Can Artificial Intelligence Make You a Better Networker? PCMA. https://www.pcma.org/apps-aid-event-networking/

Zolait, A. H. S., & Sulaiman, A. (2008). Incorporating the Innovation Attributes Introduced by Rogers' Theory into Theory of Reasoned Action: An Examination of Internet Banking Adoption in Yemen. *Computer and Information Science*, 1(1), 36–51.

Zuloaga-Rotta, L., Borja-Rosales, R., Rodríguez Mallma, M. J., Mauricio, D., & Maculan, N. (2024). Method to Forecast the Presidential Election Results Based on Simulation and Machine Learning. *Computation (Basel, Switzerland)*, 12(3), 1–16. DOI: 10.3390/computation12030038

About the Contributors

Zafer Adiguzel graduated from Kocaeli University, Faculty of Economics and Administrative Sciences in 2006. After completing his Bachelor's degree in 2010, he graduated from Cardiff Metropolitan University with an MBA in Finance. In 2016, he is a PhD degree graduated from Gebze Technical University, Department of Management. He started his academic career as a faculty member at Istanbul Medipol University, Medipol Business School, and after working for eight years, he continues his academic life as a faculty member at Sakarya University of Applied Sciences with the title of Associate Professor.

Renuka Devi D currently serves as an Assistant Professor in the Department of Computer Science at Stella Maris College(Autonomous) in Chennai, India. With over 15 years of extensive teaching experience, she holds a Ph.D. from the University of Madras. Her academic expertise spans areas such as Data Mining, Machine Learning, Big Data, and Artificial Intelligence. She has authored a book titled "Research Practitioner's Handbook on Big Data Analytics," published by Apple Academic Press, CRC Press, USA, and has contributed articles to various publications, including IEEE, Springer, Scopus, and Web of Science. In addition, she holds patents in the fields of virtual network security and AI. She presented papers at international conferences, earning accolades such as the Best Paper Award and the Best Researcher Award. She is associated with various international societies. She is also an editorial member of the Journal of Advances in Management Sciences & Information Systems and has represented India as a panelist in the "Global Perspectives on Artificial Intelligence in Higher Education - A virtual roundtable on AI" in 2023 organized by Alamo Colleges District, San Antonio, USA.

Sanchita Ghosh is a highly driven worker who holds a Master of Computer Applications degree. Her current position as a Technical Assistant at Brainware University allows her to specialize on IoT,NLP, AI, networking, cybersecurity, and cloud computing. Sanchita is passionate about using technology to solve complicated challenges, and she actively participates in projects and activities that promote innovation and progress the digital transformation. Her diversified skill set and dedication to continual learning make her an invaluable asset in the ever-changing field of information technology.

Muniraju Hullurappa, a Senior Data Engineer and AI/ML Solutions Architect, brings over 13 years of expertise in financial services. At Santander USA, he leads advanced data engineering and AI/ML solutions development, significantly enhancing analytics capabilities and data quality. Technical skills span cloud platforms and AI/ML frameworks. He excels in developing AI models for credit risk assessment and real-time fraud detection systems. His proficiency extends to ETL processes, data warehousing, and financial data management. A certified Data Engineer and Python Programmer, Muniraju is also an IEEE Senior Member and IETE Fellowship, recognizing his significant professional achievements. He actively contributes to the data science community through publications in reputable journals like IGI Global and IEEE, and presentations at international conferences. His participation in faculty development programs at recognized universities and role as a peer reviewer for academic publications demonstrate his commitment to advancing the field. Muniraju's unique blend of industry experience and academic engagement positions him at the forefront of data engineering and AI/ML innovation. His work continues to drive significant advancements in financial services and the broader data science community.

Vigneshwari K is an accomplished professional with a diverse background in academia, research, and industry, specializing in Cyber and Network Security, Image Processing Computer Networks, IoT, Big Data, and Artificial Intelligence.

Swetha Margaret T A is an accomplished professional with a diverse background in academia, research, and industry, specializing in Cyber and Network Security, Cloud Computing, Computer Networks, IoT, IIoT, Big Data, and Artificial Intelligence. With 12 years of experience, she currently serves as an Assistant Professor in the Department of Computer Science at Stella Maris College, bringing seven years of dedicated teaching expertise. Dr. Margaret holds a Ph.D., earned during her three-year tenure as a full-time Doctoral Research Scholar at Quaid E Millath College, Chennai. Prior to her academic pursuits, she gained valuable industry experience with IBM and Citrix, focusing on IBM mainframe backend support, task management, and load creation. Her commitment to professional development is evident through various international certifications, including those from IBM, Big Data University, and Udemy, covering Cloud Computing, Data Science Methodology, and more. As the Chief Information Security Officer

(CISO) at Stella Maris College since 2023, she has demonstrated leadership in securing information assets. Dr. Margaret's research contributions extend to over 20 publications in international journals, including Scopus, IEEE, and Springer. Her expertise has been recognized through accolades such as the "Best Researcher Award" from D K International Research Foundation and the 'Young Faculty in Science' Award during the Contemporary Academic Meet-CAM by Venus International Foundation, both in 2018-2019. Her commitment to innovation is evident through patents, including Innovation patent for "Un Nanban," an AI-based interactive web and voice application, and a Design patent for a "Smart Walking Stick" for visually impaired individuals in 2023. Represented India as a panellist in the "Global Perspectives on Artificial Intelligence in Higher Education - A virtual roundtable on AI" in 2023 organised by Alamo Colleges District, San Antonio, USA

Lakshmi Narasimha Raju Mudunuri is a seasoned Functional Solution Architect with a proven track record of 17 years in the Oil & Gas and Manufacturing industries. He holds a Bachelor of Technology and has a deep understanding of SAP Processes, Architecture, and Implementation. Mudunuri specializes in designing and implementing innovative functional solutions that enhance efficiency, scalability, and security. His expertise lies in creating robust SAP architectures that align with business objectives and drive digital transformation. With a focus on performance and best practices, he ensures organizations leverage SAP technology to its full potential. Beyond his technical skills, Mudunuri excels at translating complex IT concepts into actionable business strategies. This ability makes him a valuable asset in driving organizational growth and maximizing return on SAP investments. His contributions have been recognized through publications in renowned conferences and journals, solidifying his position as a thought leader in the field.

P. Selvakumar is currently an Associate Professor in the Department of Science and Humanities at Nehru Institute of Technology, Coimbatore, Tamil Nadu, India. Since 2023, he has served as the Department IQAC Coordinator at the institute. Prior to joining Nehru Institute of Technology, he held positions as an Assistant Professor in the Department of Science and Humanities various engineering colleges in Coimbatore, Tamil Nadu, India, spanning from 2011 to 2023. Dr.P. Selvakumar's academic and research interests lie primarily in the field of phytochemistry. He has made significant contributions to his field, with an impressive record that includes 30 journal publications, 12 patents, and 20 conference papers. Additionally, he has organized 5 seminars and conferences, further demonstrating his commitment to academic and scientific exchange. Throughout his career, Dr. P.Selvakumar has been recognized for his dedication and excellence in teaching, having been honored with several awards, including the Best Teacher Awards. He holds a prominent position in the academic community, contributing actively to research.

Bitan Roy is a highly driven worker who holds a Master of Computer Applications degree. His current position as a Technical Assistant at Brainware University allows his to specialize on IoT, AI, networking, cybersecurity. Bitan is passionate about using technology to solve complicated challenges, and he actively participates in projects and activities that promote innovation and progress the digital transformation. His diversified skill set and dedication to continual learning make him an invaluable asset in the ever-changing field of information technology.

Piyal Roy is an accomplished academician in the field of Computer Science & Engineering. He has completed his BSc in Computer Science, MSc in Computer Science and MTech in Computer Science & Engineering. Currently, he is working as an Assistant Professor at Computer Science & Engineering department at Brainware University, India.

Mohammad Badruddoza Talukder is an Associate Professor, College of Tourism and Hospitality Management, IUBAT - International University of Business Agriculture and Technology, Dhaka-1230, Bangladesh. He holds PhD in Hotel Management from Lovely Professional University, India. He has been teaching various courses in the Department of Tourism and Hospitality at various universities in Bangladesh since 2008. His research areas include tourism management, hotel management, hospitality management, food & beverage management, and accommodation management, where he has published research papers in well-known journals in Bangladesh and abroad. Mr. Talukder is one of the executive members of the Tourism Educators Association of Bangladesh. He has led training and consulting for a wide range of hospitality organizations in Bangladesh. He just became an honorary facilitator at the Bangladesh Tourism Board's Bangabandhu international tourism and hospitality training institution.

Arunkumar Thirunagalingam is an experienced data professional with deep expertise in Data Engineering, Data Governance, and Data Quality, with a focus on leveraging AI/ML technologies. He has extensive experience across various industries, specializing in building scalable data pipelines and architectures that ensure data accuracy, compliance, and quality. Arunkumar has made significant contributions through publications covering AI/ML advancements, data governance frameworks, and cloud-native solutions. His thought leadership is recognized across the industry, and he is regularly invited to present at conferences, where he shares insights on best practices for data management and integrating AI/ML into data ecosystems. With hands-on experience in cloud platforms such as AWS and Azure,

Arunkumar has successfully delivered complex, scalable data solutions that address real-world business challenges. His expertise in integrating AI/ML techniques has driven improved decision-making and innovation across the organizations he has collaborated with. Arunkumar is an IEEE Senior Member and actively participates in several professional organizations, keeping him at the forefront of emerging trends in data governance and AI/ML integration. He serves as a reviewer for various chapters and journals, ensuring high academic standards, and has judged industry awards recognizing innovation in data management. His passion for cutting-edge technology and his commitment to excellence in data management make him a sought-after expert and a valuable asset to any data-driven organization.

Vamshidhar Reddy Vemula is a highly respected cloud solutions architect and cybersecurity expert, known for his expertise in cloud computing cybersecurity frameworks, and AI applications. With a background in software development and cloud architecture, Vamshidhar has developed scalable, secure solutions for global enterprises, ensuring business continuity and data protection in complex multi-cloud environments. Vamshidhar's hands-on experience with leading platforms such as AWS, Microsoft Azure, and Google Cloud has enabled him to lead high-impact projects, focused on migrating critical workloads to the cloud while maintaining the highest standards of security and data integrity. He is also highly skilled in developing AI-driven security measures to protect businesses from emerging cyber threats. With a Master's degree in Computer Science from Texas A&M University, Vamshidhar has contributed significantly to the academic community through research papers on cloud security and machine learning. His work has been presented at top industry conferences, and he continues to be a thought leader and mentor in the cybersecurity field.

Index

A

B

C

D

E

F

G

H

I

K

M

N

O

P

R

S

T

U

W

www.ingramcontent.com/pod-product-compliance
Lightning Source LLC
LaVergne TN
LVHW080615300926
849162LV00005B/1170